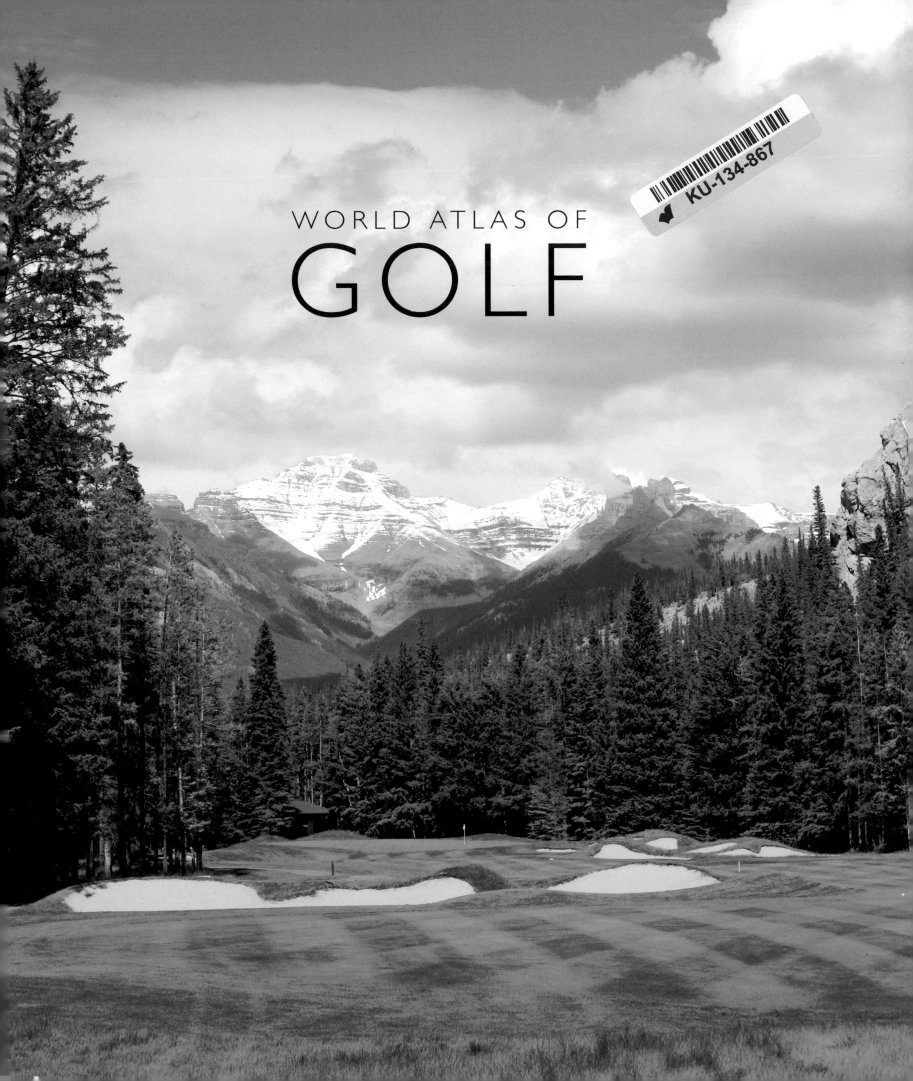

# WORLD ATLAS OF
# GOLF

hamlyn

# WORLD ATLAS OF
# GOLF

THE GREATEST COURSES AND HOW THEY ARE PLAYED

# CONTRIBUTORS

An Hachette UK Company
www.hachette.co.uk

First published in Great Britain in 2008 by
Hamlyn, a division of Octopus Publishing Group Ltd
Endeavour House, 189 Shaftesbury Avenue
London WC2H 8JY
www.octopusbooks.co.uk

First published in paperback in 2010

Distributed in the U.S. and Canada by
Octopus Books USA:
c/o Hachette Book Group
237 Park Avenue
New York, NY 10017

ISBN 978-0-600-62190-4

A CIP catalogue record for this book is available from
the British Library

Printed and bound in China

10 9 8 7 6 5 4 3 2 1

Every effort has been made to ensure that the course
cards, illustrations and text in this book are as accurate
as possible. However, golf courses are frequently being
adjusted and redesigned. The publishers would be
grateful for any information which will assist them in
updating future editions.

*Previous pages: Banff Springs Golf Course, Canada
(page 1); Lahinch Golf Club, Ireland (pages 2–3)*

*Opposite: Nirwana Bali Golf Club, Bali*

*Following pages: The Mountain Course at Spring City
Golf and Lake Resort, China (pages 6–7)*

This book features the greatest golf courses in the
world that display architectural brilliance or are
simply important in the history of the game. These
golf courses were selected by an international panel
of course designers, ex-Tour pros and leading golf
journalists in America, Australia and Europe.

## GENERAL EDITOR

**Mark Rowlinson** (UK) has been associated with
*The World Atlas of Golf* since 1990, both editorially
and as a contributor. He has also written *A Place to
Golf* and *The Times Guide to the Golf Courses of
Great Britain and Ireland*.

## THE PANEL

**Tom Doak** (US) is widely recognized as one of
the world's finest golf-course architects, he has
designed four courses currently ranked among *Golf
Magazine*'s international top 100. Tom's unique
body of historical and design knowledge has also
been showcased in the classic *The Anatomy of a Golf
Course* and the *The Confidential Guide* and *The Life
and Work of Dr Alister MacKenzie*.

**Mike Clayton** (Australia) is one of modern golf's
true renaissance men. He first made his name as
a player, winning the 1978 Australian Amateur
before claiming eight titles on the European and
Australasian Tours. Today Mike enjoys the rare
status of being recognized among the southern
hemisphere's best golf writers (for the *Melbourne
Age* and *Australian Golfing* magazine) and among
its very finest course designers, giving him a unique
insight into great courses worldwide.

**Ran Morrissett** (US) runs the world's premier golf
architecture-related website, GolfClubAtlas.com. He
is also a *Golf Magazine* ratings panelist who has
resided in both the United States and Australia. A
widely respected golf journalist, Ran's extensive
travel and unique eye for great architecture give him
an unsurpassed knowledge of the world's great
courses and the intricacies of their design.

**Daniel Wexler** (US) is a California-based writer
and former golf professional. He is one of America's
leading golf historians, with a particular knowledge
of classic course design. Daniel is the author of four

books including *The Missing Links: America's Greatest Lost Golf Courses and Holes* and *The Book of Golfers: A Biographical History of the Royal & Ancient Game*.

**Iain Carter** (UK) is a golf correspondent for BBC Radio. He has been to every corner of the globe covering the game. As a junior golfer he won a copy of the original *World Atlas of Golf*!

**Richard Goodale** (UK) lives in Fife, Scotland, and is the author of the successful 'Experience' series of golf books, as well as several essays on golf-course architecture. An American, with degrees in literature (Stanford) and strategy (Harvard), he has played competitive golf all over the UK and Ireland for the past 30 years.

**Martin Hawtree** (UK) is a professional course designer who has worked on many leading courses around the world including Royal Birkdale, Sunningdale, Lahinch, Toronto GC, Tarandowah, Vilamoura Millennium Course and the amusingly named 'The Tat' in Turkey.

**Eric Franzén** (Sweden) is a renowned golf writer based near Stockholm.

**Ulrich Mayring** (Germany) is a prolific writer with a passion for golf. He is based in Frankfurt.

**Noel Freeman** (US) works in the financial industry in New York City. He has travelled the globe in study of the greatest golf courses and the allure of finding a hidden gem.

**Ben Cowan-Dewar** (Canada) is the Chairman of GOLFTI, an internationally renowned tour operator. As well as sitting on the *Golf Magazine* panel that is the authoritative rating of the world's finest courses, Ben is a partner of the acclaimed golf architecture-related website GolfClubAtlas.com. He currently resides with his wife and son in Nova Scotia, Canada, where he is overseeing development of Cabot Links.

# CONTENTS

# FOREWORD

During the past 30 years or so the game of golf has undergone a revolution, forced on it by the application of new materials and technology that have made it possible for the golf ball to be hit ever increasing and previously unthinkable distances. Almost every golf course throughout the world has been lengthened, many have been redesigned in more substantial ways and some have been completely rebuilt, simply to avoid being overwhelmed by today's power play. In fact, more changes have been made to golf courses in this period than in the rest of the 20th century.

Coincidentally, it is also just over 30 years since the *World Atlas of Golf* was first published. When it appeared in 1976 it was groundbreaking. The book opened the eyes of millions of golfers – and many a non-golfer – to the subtleties of golf-course design, revealing just why the likes of Cypress Point, the Old Course at St Andrews, The Jockey Club and Royal Melbourne were – and still are – such great courses. As it happens, these particular courses remain virtually unaltered, apart from a little lengthening, but most of the other courses in the first edition have had more serious surgery.

This new *World Atlas of Golf* builds on the great heritage of that first edition and, just like golf, it takes advantage of the latest materials and technology, with state-of-the-art computer-generated course maps at the heart of the book.

The opportunity was taken for a complete reassessment of which courses should be featured. An international panel of writers who have particular knowledge of golf-course architecture was assembled (see pages 4–5) and between them they thrashed out which of the hundreds of potentially eligible courses should be chosen. Those courses that forced their way into the book did so because of the unquestionable distinction of their architecture. Some well-known names have not made the cut, while others that have been included have never held a significant tournament, professional or amateur. Golfing history and the deeds of the great players are important, but this is a book about the courses themselves.

Regrettably, many fine courses had to be omitted because of space. So, new to this *World Atlas of Golf* are substantial regional introductions that allow the authors to share with the reader other courses of significant architectural importance, to chronicle the design history of the region and to single out the most interesting of contemporary developments.

Something that has become apparent during the compilation of this book is that those great old courses of Colt, Macdonald, MacKenzie, Flynn, Tillinghast and their contemporaries (where they have not been ruined by

'improvement') are no less significant in our affections today. They continue to influence the thoughts and work of many of today's top designers. It is heartening to see that, particularly in the United States, there is nowadays sufficient understanding of and appreciation for these inspired designs that efforts are being made to restore them where possible or at least to restore the spirit of the original.

Golf courses, however, are not museum pieces and must be suited to whatever form of the game is currently played. For that reason it seems imperative that golf's governing bodies do something to prevent the continuing quest for greater and greater length before we are no longer able to appreciate these magnificent courses.

While much new golf-course construction is concerned with golf tourism, real-estate development or the hosting of professional tournaments, course design has also taken a giant step in the opposite direction. A number of contemporary golf architects, despite having access to all sorts of earthmoving equipment, have returned to following nature's lead. The results are timeless designs that feel as if they were created during the Golden Age of golf architecture (*c.* 1900–39). It reflects an art of restraint, of having man's hand laid only lightly on the land. Without feeling a connection with nature, golf would undoubtedly decline. Today's architects are, thankfully, once again helping golfers to reconnect with nature. And it is this connection with nature – of making the most of the natural resources of a given site – that has informed the process of selecting the courses for inclusion in this book.

When you play a course for the first time your opinion of that course will be governed not only by how you play but also by something less obvious, the skill with which the designer has laid out the course. You may not notice how it has been done, but the key to a pleasing course is intelligent routing. Each course in this book, however challenging to play, would undoubtedly raise your spirits and put a smile on your face. This new *World Atlas of Golf*, then, is a tribute to those talented golf-course designers who have put a smile on the faces of golfers throughout the world.

*Nothing quite fires the architect's imagination like a piece of genuine linksland. This is the outstanding 13th hole at Paraparaumu Beach in New Zealand designed by Alex Russell in 1949.*

# INTRODUCTION

# ORIGINS OF THE GAME

At its heart, golf is a natural game. Although there is some question whether or not it derived from the Dutch game of *kolven*, which was played on the open ice to a target but not a hole, the game of golf evolved to its present form on the coastal links of Scotland.

Open land near the coast, too sandy for farming, supported the growth of fine-bladed grasses, providing pastures that were loosely maintained by herds of grazing sheep, horses and cows. The high northern latitudes provided long summer days, so that the Scots could venture out for an evening of sport after a full day of work, and the Gulf Stream currents provided weather mild enough to play nearly all year round. On the links a makeshift ball could be hit great distances and still found at the other end to be played on. Thus the game of golf was born.

## THE EARLIEST COURSES

The original courses and clubs were formed in coastal towns by local players. There were no accepted standards for golf courses, so each was adapted to the size and shape of its setting. Leith Links, on the outskirts of Edinburgh, had just five holes, while St Andrews's long strip of undulating turf (see page 40) provided room for 11 holes out and 11 back on the same route, and the Old Musselburgh Links (inside a horseracing track) is the oldest nine in the world, unchanged since 1870. None of these holes was long by today's standards, since the best players could achieve drives of only 160–180 yards (146–165 metres) with feather-stuffed balls and the rudimentary clubs.

On the courses, the hazards were natural ones. Scrapes of sand formed by the combination of

*Top right: Westward Ho! is laid out over common land, where local residents have the right to graze their sheep, cows and horses. It provides an excellent example of how hazards are born and develop, and why the Rules of Golf distinguish about what types of animal scrapes deserve relief.*

*Right: The West Links at North Berwick is distinguished by an old stone wall running through the course. The wall is utilized to great effect as a hazard on two or three holes, giving the course a character all its own.*

# PRESTWICK GOLF LINKS
## The original 1851 layout

The original routing of Prestwick Golf Club by Old Tom Morris was a compact affair, with holes crisscrossing one another and one green played twice in the 12-hole loop. As golf became more popular, such efficient routings had to be scrapped for safety reasons, but this was the course played for the early Open championships.

Of Prestwick's original layout, seven of the greens still survive. The old 1st (Back of Cardinal Hole) and 2nd (The Alps) have become the current 16th and 17th respectively. The shared 3rd and 6th green is now the 2nd. The 4th (The Wall Hole) is now the 3rd green and the 5th (Sea Headrig) and 10th (Lunch House) are the modern-day 13th and 15th greens.

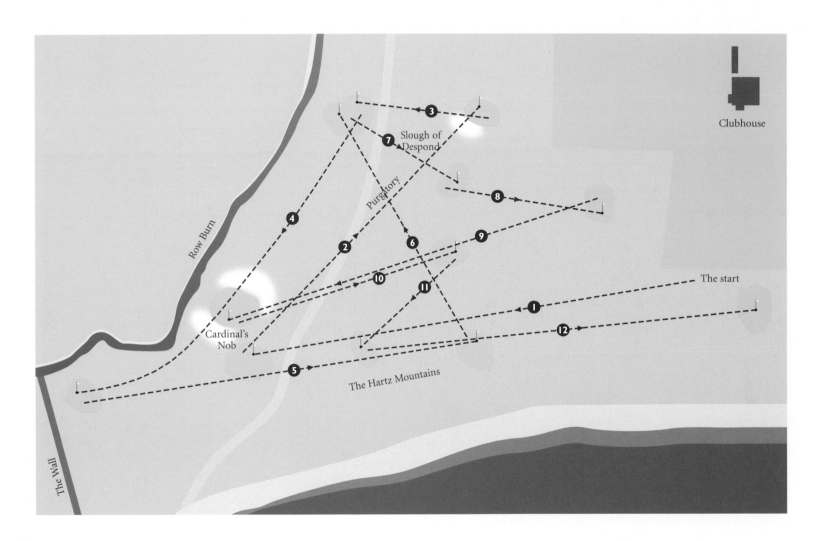

animal activity and wind erosion were eventually formalized into bunkers, while larger sand dunes at the edge of the course provided formidable hazards to be carried. Narrow water courses that snaked their way across to the sea were the first water hazards, and at North Berwick (see left) even the ancient stone walls were incorporated into the local golf course. By the 1840s the wealthier golf clubs had begun to pay someone to maintain their

courses, and soon afterwards revetted bunker faces or wooden bulkheads were introduced to fight ongoing bunker erosion.

## CONSISTENCY OF CHALLENGE

There are several variations on how 18 holes came to be the standard. It is probable, however, that a decision by the Society of St Andrews Golfers to consolidate to 18 holes was followed by a resolu-

tion to hold the first Open Championship, in 1860, over 36 holes. This meant playing three times around the 12 holes of Prestwick (see above), laid out by Old Tom Morris, but conveniently only twice round St Andrews, or four times round Musselburgh. Thus 18 holes was cemented as the standard, just before the game was exported to the rest of the world by two generations of immigrant Scots professionals.

# THE GOLDEN AGE

The early part of the 20th century saw a great economic boom that made possible a similar one in the construction of golf courses, and a new generation of golf-course architects rushed to meet the demand.

Some Golden Age architects, such as James Braid and Donald Ross, were professional golfers who crossed over to design, but the majority were men who loved golf as a recreation, whether they were wealthy amateurs developing their own clubs (such as Charles Blair Macdonald, George Crump and Henry C. Fownes) or professional golf architects (Harry Colt, Dr Alister MacKenzie, Charles Alison, A.W. Tillinghast and William Flynn). These were well-educated men, and they brought a new sophistication to the subject of design; many wrote books on their own design philosophies.

## GREATER VARIETY

The rising tide of wealth in America and in Europe in the years either side of the First World War meant that golf courses were now economically viable even on poor soils or poor sites that would require a great deal of construction, including tree clearing and rock removal. Greens were sculpted from the terrain and bunkers started to be used as prominent visual features, with each designer developing his own particular style.

New business models for golf courses were also developed in this same period. The American 'country club', for example, positioned golf as a central component in the leisure time of wealthy families, while the first 'destination' golf resorts were developed by railway companies and property developers, from Pebble Beach (see page 244) to Gleneagles (see page 66) to Banff Springs (see page 258).

However, this golfing boom suddenly stopped at the start of the Great Depression from 1929, when funds to support new courses became unavailable. Many more courses closed in the 1930s than new courses opened. The only work was provided by publicly funded jobs programmes that developed municipal courses, and in isolated prosperous corners of the world such as South America and Japan. When boom times returned after the Second World War, most of the Golden Age designers had retired or died.

## GREAT ARCHITECTS OF THE GOLDEN AGE

The following golf-course designers were some of the greatest of the Golden Age.

### Charles Blair Macdonald (1855–1939)

A stockbroker from Chicago, Charles Blair Macdonald became a top-notch golfer at St Andrews while at university there in the 1870s, and missed the game terribly when he returned to America. In 1892 he founded the Chicago Golf Club, and in 1895 was its representative at the founding of the United States Golf Association (USGA), as well as the organization's first US Amateur champion. After 1900, Macdonald became fascinated by the idea of creating an American course founded on the principles of the

*George Crump was the founder and designer of Pine Valley (see page 186), with some help from Harry Colt and advice from friends including A.W. Tillinghast and George Thomas.*

best British links, and he found the ideal property on Long Island, where he built the National Golf Links of America (NGLA). Thereafter, he was in great demand to create courses all over the USA, but in fact he participated in only a few, leaving the rest of the design work to surveyor Seth Raynor who had assisted him at NGLA.

*Most influential courses:* NGLA (see page 166), Chicago (see page 222), Mid Ocean (see page 272), Yale, The Creek Club.

## William Herbert Fowler (1856–1941)

Although W.H. Fowler did not take up golf until his mid 30s, he was soon a scratch player. His first design, Walton Heath, received great critical acclaim and further commissions soon followed. He spent some time working in the USA. Some of his designs, such as The Berkshire, were co-designed with Tom Simpson.

*Most influential courses:* Walton Heath (36 holes), Saunton (36 holes), Beau Desert, Lake Merced, Eastward Ho!, Westward Ho!.

## Willie Park Jnr (1864–1925)

This pioneer in the field of golf architecture was Open champion in 1887 and 1889. He started designing courses in the 1890s, but made a strong impact only when he designed the first top-class inland courses in England – Sunningdale (Old) and Huntercombe – just after 1900. Huntercombe was the first golf course to be integrated into a housing development, and notably included a man-made, two-tiered green, apparently a first. Willie Park Jnr also became the first British architect to work extensively in continental Europe. In 1916, he emigrated to North America and pursued a very busy practice until he fell ill in 1923, whereupon he returned to Scotland and died there two years later.

*Most influential courses:* Gullane (Nos. 2 and 3), Western Gailes, Silloth-on-Solway, Sunningdale (see page 100), Huntercombe, Notts., Royal Antwerp, Mount Bruno, Olympia Fields (North), Maidstone (see page 182).

*Willie Park Jnr was not only a two-time Open champion, his professional's duties also included greenkeeping, which was of immense value when it came to the construction of new courses abroad.*

*Harry Colt's success at golf-course architecture caused some professional golfers to suggest that only professionals should lay out courses and led briefly to a controversy over the rules of amateur status.*

## Harry S. Colt (1869–1951)

Harry Colt was a fine golfer for the Cambridge team and a regular competitor in the Amateur Championship. In 1901 he took the job as club secretary at Sunningdale GC, and from that base started to design other courses in the heathlands. After the First World War he formed the partnership of Colt, Alison & MacKenzie (Alister MacKenzie later being replaced by John Morrison), with the younger partners taking the international work.

*Most influential courses:* Rye, Sunningdale (New), Swinley Forest, St George's Hill, Royal Portrush (36 holes; see page 114), Falkenstein (see page 148), St Germain (see page 136), De Pan, Muirfield (see page 60), Toronto Golf Club, Hamilton (see page 260), Kennemer (see page 126), Royal Zoute (see page 130).

## Dr Alister MacKenzie (1870–1934)

Alister MacKenzie trained in medicine at Cambridge, and as an army doctor in the Boer War became fascinated by the art of camouflage, which he brought to golf-course construction. In 1907 he was involved in the formation of Alwoodley GC near his home in Leeds, and thereafter abandoned medicine to pursue golf architecture full-time. After a brief partnership with Harry Colt, he travelled the world, settling in America while also working in Australia and South America.

*Most influential courses:* Alwoodley (see page 92), Lahinch, Royal Melbourne (West; see page 286), Royal Adelaide (see page 290), Cypress Point (see page 248), The Valley Club, Pasatiempo, Crystal Downs, Augusta (see page 206), The Jockey Club (36 holes; see page 278), Kingston Heath (see page 292), New South Wales.

## Donald Ross (1872–1948)

Brought up in Dornoch, Scotland, Donald Ross apprenticed as a club maker to Old Tom Morris in St Andrews. At the suggestion of Royal Dornoch club secretary John Sutherland, Ross emigrated to Boston, where like all Scottish professionals he helped lay out the course where he served as professional, Oakley Country Club. He gained recognition as a designer with his layout at Pinehurst, North Carolina, for Oakley member Leonard Tufts, and for 40 years thereafter was the game's prolific architect, with 400 courses to his credit.

*Most influential courses:* Pinehurst (90 holes), Oakland Hills, Oak Hill (36 holes), Inverness, Scioto, Seminole (see page 212), Plainfield, Holston Hills, Wannamoisett, Teugega CC.

## Albert Warren Tillinghast (1874–1942)

'Tillie' was born in Philadelphia, the son of a successful businessman. He played in a number of US Amateur championships and visited Scotland, where he met Old Tom Morris. After his first course design, which was for a private course that subsequently became Shawnee, his career as an architect took off. Despite his great designs, A.W. Tillinghast was an unsuccessful businessman and eventually lost interest in golf.

*Most influential courses:* Shawnee on the Delaware, San Francisco, Somerset Hills, Winged Foot (36 holes; see page 172), Quaker Ridge, Baltimore (Five Farms), Baltusrol (36 holes), Breckinridge Park, Bethpage State Park (90 holes; see page 176).

## Tom Simpson (1877–1964)

A talented golfer from a wealthy family, Tom Simpson was in the Cambridge University golf team and played much of his early golf at Woking, witnessing for himself the influential design changes of Stuart Paton and John Low. He eventually abandoned his legal career and became a business partner of W.H. Fowler. The flamboyant Simpson looked after most of the firm's work in continental Europe. His designs show originality and flair.

*Most influential courses:* Cruden Bay (see page 64), New Zealand, Fontainebleau, Morfontaine (see page 134), Royal Antwerp (new course), Royal Golf Club des Fagnes.

## Charles Hugh Alison (1882–1952)

Alison was one of the finest players in the Oxford & Cambridge Golfing Society and was mentored by Harry Colt, with whom he remained a partner for his entire career. Since Colt did not like to travel far, Alison was put in charge of most of the firm's projects on other continents, working in America, South Africa and even Australia. He is remembered most of all for his seminal designs in Japan, where he mentored the early Japanese designers Kenya Fujita and Seiichi Inoue.

*Most influential courses:* Hirono (see page 306), Kawana (Fuji), Kasumigaseki (East), Bryanston (South Africa), Milwaukee Country Club, Bob O'Link, Royal Hague (see page 128).

## William S. Flynn (1890–1945)

As the first golf course superintendent at Merion in Philadelphia, William Flynn assisted Hugh Wilson in the construction of the championship East Course,

*Bobby Jones hits practice tee shots to test the position of a fairway bunker on the 8th hole at Augusta National Golf Club in 1932, as Dr Alister MacKenzie (second from left) stands by the tee stake to watch.*

and he also played a significant role in the development of the West Course. The notoriety of Merion as a championship site made Wilson a popular designer, but his health limited his ability to pursue any work. Flynn therefore assumed Wilson's position as an architect and built a considerable number of great courses around Philadelphia and also in the south-eastern USA and as far west as Denver. Flynn and engineer Howard Toomey formed a partnership in a construction company, which built most of Flynn's designs as well as a design for Walter Travis (Westchester) and one for Charles Alison (Burning Tree).

*Most influential courses:* Merion (see page 190), Lancaster, Lehigh, Huntingdon Valley (27 holes), Kittansett, Cherry Hills, Indian Creek, Cascades (see page 200), The Country Club (see page 184), Shinnecock Hills (see page 178), Pocantico Hills (a reversible golf course for the Rockefeller family).

## Stanley Thompson (1894–1952)

Most influential of all Canadian golf architects, Stanley Thompson formed his own company after military service in the First World War, and designed Jasper Park and Banff Springs for the two Canadian railway companies in 1925 and 1927, respectively. This cemented Thompson's fame in Canada; few American designers of the era woked in Canada because he was so dominant. He earned large amounts of money and enjoyed spending it just as quickly. He was a mentor to several later architects, most notably a young Robert Trent Jones, who became a partner of Thompson after finishing his studies at Cornell.

*Most influential courses:* Jasper Park, Banff Springs (see page 258), St George's, Highlands Links (see page 264), Capilano, Gávea Golf and Country Club.

# THE MODERN ERA

After the end of the Second World War, the business of golf-course architecture was essentially reinvented from scratch. A postwar housing boom and the growth of leisure time among the middle classes triggered demand for large numbers of new courses, for which there were only a handful of designers trained to meet the need.

Chief among the designers was Robert Trent Jones Snr, the Cornell-educated golf architect who had trained under Stanley Thompson. Jones capitalized on the opportunity to dominate the business on a large scale, eventually designing projects in 35 countries by leaving construction plans that could be followed by local contractors. His main competitor, Dick Wilson, a former project manager for William Flynn, preferred to build one or two courses at a time and confined his work to the eastern United States. Both men's designs featured grand sweeping contours instead of small detail in the contouring of greens and bunkers, but this was synonymous with this epoch of mass-produced homes and streamlined cars.

## CHANGE IN CLIENT NEEDS

In the modern era, a designer's clients were no longer groups of men wanting to establish a golf club, but instead were corporations seeking to create a resort, or housing developers or wealthy individuals attempting to do the same. Trent Jones's clients included the Rockefellers, the king of Morocco and the Aga Khan. Modern courses are businesses that compete with one another, trying to be more photogenic and better-conditioned than their competitors – and capital costs have spiralled in the process.

Trent Jones was also the first designer to market his own name commercially and thus heralded the era of 'signature designs'. For 20 years the trend towards bigger and bolder designs continued unchecked, fuelled by the advent of motorized golf carts in the USA, until the opening in 1969 of Harbour Town Golf Links, designed by Pete Dye and Jack Nicklaus, provided a prominent counter-example. Since then, the surging golf economy has allowed the business of golf architecture to splinter into many different camps, with each architect developing a personal style in a market big enough to allow for a wide variety of choices. Some designers, including Pete Dye, Jack Nicklaus and Greg Norman, attracted clients who wanted championship-calibre courses and the tournaments they might attract. Others, like the team of Bill Coore and Ben Crenshaw, found a niche as 'minimalist' designers best suited to work with attractive property. And other designers developed their own individual styles, from the rock-and-roll aesthetic of Mike Strantz or Jim Engh to the immaculate order of Tom Fazio's designs. Indeed, as marketing has become centred on the architect's name, demand for new faces has increased to distinguish new courses from their neighbours.

*The downhill approach to the 9th at Mauna Kea Golf Course, Hawaii. Robert Trent Jones saved the cost of importing thousands of cubic feet of topsoil by crushing down the indigenous lava rock to produce a fine soil.*

## WORLDWIDE BOOM

The development of golf architecture in new over-seas markets has been rapid in the past 30 years, and the biggest names in design are now global in scope. Construction in Japan flourished through-out the 1980s and collapsed abruptly in the 1990s, once it was realized that many private member-ships had been bought for their investment value, without enough golfers to back them up. However, today there is great growth of new facilities in China and in South Korea, driven by their interest in attracting international business, and by the success of several Korean players on the US LPGA tour, which has helped to popularize the game.

The growth of the game in continental Europe has been steady since the successes of the European Ryder Cup team made golf a prominent sport in Spain, Germany and Italy, instead of just a diversion for visiting foreigners; and the emerging market countries are now starting to pursue golf as their economies permit. Interestingly, many of these new courses have been designed by Americans or have been built in the 'American' parkland mould; yet, in contrast, the trend in American courses has been to revert to treeless courses modelled after the links, with minimal earthmoving.

There is also a lot of new growth in exotic locales from the Caribbean to the Emirates, as the viability of desalinated water for irrigation starts to remove an important hurdle to development.

*The success of this Jack Nicklaus design at Cabo del Sol at the tip of Baja California set off an incredible boom of development in a once sleepy fishing retreat, including a dozen new courses charging US $250 green fees.*

# DESIGN THEORY

The key to good golf architecture is to solve a paradox – to create a hole that is challenging to the good player while remaining both interesting and playable for the golfer of lesser skill.

Good players are generally seen as the experts on the subject of what makes a golf hole a good one, yet a course will not be successful unless it proves popular with a wide range of players.

Early golf courses were designed by the best players and were largely a test of golfing prowess. Hazards were placed on the fairways to require a good carry off the tee and flanking the fairway as well. A straight drive was rewarded by punishing the wayward shots of others, with little concern for whether those others would play again.

## A NEW CONCEPT

One of the first true design theorists was John Low, from St Andrews, who drew the line between playability and sympathy for the weaker player. Low bemoaned the tendency of early architects to tilt the green towards the player to help them stop their approach shot. Instead he insisted that all players should learn the game and that greens tilted away from the line of play offered an incentive to improve without unduly penalizing the majority. He also answered those who were perplexed by the idea that a hazard could be found within the fairway, by writing that: 'No hazard is unfair no matter where it is placed, as it is the duty of the player to avoid it.' Low's modifications to Woking, near London, at the dawn of the 20th century inspired a generation of designers who looked up to him, including Harry Colt, Charles Alison and Tom Simpson.

## LATER STRATEGIES

Many designers of the Golden Age were amateur enthusiasts who had an intellectual interest in the game and who sought to reward skill over strength.

## COLT'S BUNKER
### Examples of proper bunkering

*Harry Colt provided these examples of proper bunkering in his book,* Some Essays on Golf Course Architecture, *one of the first to express concern about the weaker golfer's enjoyment of the course. Colt wrote that 'Player B, who is rather more cautious from the tee, can get somewhere near the green with his second, if he dares to go close enough to [the bunker just short of the green]. Player C cannot get anywhere near the green with his second except by a miracle, and will have to play accurately to get a 5.'*

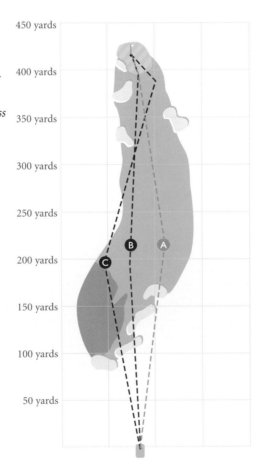

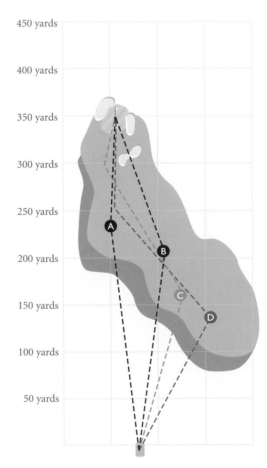

They therefore placed fairway bunkers so these defended an ideal landing area in the fairway. Once designers realized that many poor drives were punished simply because the next shot was much longer and more difficult as a result, the number of bunkers declined. Thus the 'strategic' school of golf-course design was born.

Bobby Jones wrote of Augusta (see page 206) in the 1930s that a tee shot might present one of four different rewards to the player: 'a better view of the green, an easier angle from which to attack a slope, an open approach past guarding hazards, or even a better run to the tee shot itself'.

The upper echelon of courses reward not just long and straight hitting but also the player who can control the trajectory and distance. Challenges that good players appreciate are: to fade or draw the ball to better hold a tilting green; to play with control off an uneven stance; to stop an approach quickly over a bunker; or to run the ball through an opening between hazards. Likewise, the great courses offer the opportunity for recovery play both simple and spectacular.

## VARYING EXPECTATIONS

Ultimately, though, golf architecture is a subjective art, and each golfer enjoys the game on their own terms. Many players are out to revel in the beauty of Nature, and these players are captivated when the features of the course highlight the features of the property, placing tees on prime viewing spots or bringing a natural stream into play. Others are out to enjoy the camaraderie of the game, so they do not want to have to play on separate tees according to their differing abilities. Golfers who play friendly matches will have a very different perspective on the propriety of a severe bunker than they would in a medal competition, where a single wayward approach might cost them three strokes to par. A poor shot for a good player would still be a career shot for the beginner, so it cannot be punished uniformly.

*The 14th hole at Gleneagles (King's Course), a James Braid design. This very short par-four hole can be driven by low-handicap players, but deep bunkers before the green extract severe penalties for a wild attempt. Shorter hitters have several different areas to place their tee shot, depending on their ability and on how aggressive they choose to be.*

# ROUTING THE COURSE

After more than a hundred years, during which 25,000 golf courses have been constructed worldwide, a golfer's idea of what a course ought to be has become more standardized, yet the placement of the 18 holes still gives each course its unique quality.

E arly courses were as different as the linksland on which they were built, because golfers in those days would never have thought to change the landscape to fit the game. Such limitations are no longer accepted by today's architects.

## IMPORTANT DESIGN AIMS

Among an architect's real goals in routing the course is to make the best use of natural features on the property, as Donald Ross did in bringing one of two ridges at Seminole (see page 212) into play on 14 of the 18 holes. It is also important to explore the various aspects of a beautiful property, as Alister MacKenzie did by routing Cypress Point (see page 248) from links to forest to high dunes to forest to links to rocky coastline.

A golf course should ideally be as easy to walk on as possible, and green sites should be positioned so the subsequent tee can be close by. A variety of uphill, downhill and sidehill lies should be provided along the route: for example, at Merion (see page 190), players are asked at the 5th to play a left-to-right shot with the ball well above their feet, and at the 18th they must hit a high iron shot off a downhill lie, as Ben Hogan famously did to secure his spot in the 1950 US Open play-off.

*Modern development courses such as Weston Hills in Florida are designed completely from scratch. Every bit of natural vegetation has to be scrapped in favour of earthmoving to get such flat sites to drain and then the areas surrounding the course are relandscaped with the addition of houses.*

# ROUTING
## Evolving principles

An interestingly routed course will also include frequent changes of directions in windy places – such as William Flynn's routing for Shinnecock Hills (see page 178), which forms a series of small triangles attacking the wind at every angle. Finally, it is essential to provide as much variety as possible within the 18 holes in terms of hole lengths and configurations.

## DIFFERENT PRIORITIES

Sadly, many modern courses are routed with factors other than golf in mind. On many modern projects the siting of housing takes precedent over the position of the golf holes, which are forced to the lower parts of the site so that the houses can look down on them.

Marketability also plays an increasing role in design. In some cultures it is considered essential for a course to have a par of 72 balanced evenly between the two nines, even though iconic courses such as Pine Valley (see page 186), Shinnecock and Muirfield (see page 60) do not. Likewise, in America it is essential for modern courses to exceed 7,000 yards from the back tees, even if few of their members would ever play from there, because the perception that a course is tourna-ment-tough commands greater respect – and higher prices.

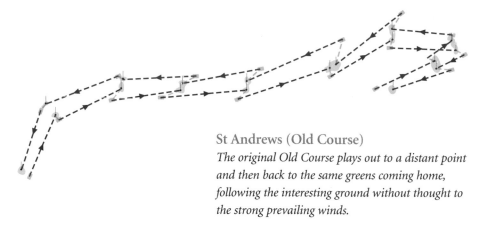

**St Andrews (Old Course)**
*The original Old Course plays out to a distant point and then back to the same greens coming home, following the interesting ground without thought to the strong prevailing winds.*

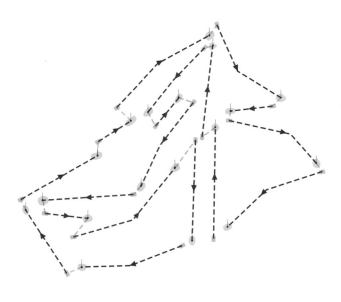

**Muirfield**
*Harry Colt's 1920 redesign formalized the routing into an outer and then an inner loop, with the ninth hole returning to the clubhouse and no more than three holes in the same direction.*

**Shinnecock Hills**
*William Flynn's 1931 redesign of Shinnecock Hills routed the course as a series of triangles, so that the wind was encountered from all quarters during the round.*

# GREENS AND BUNKERS

Design strategy for a golf course is enforced by details such as its greens and bunkers. These are also sculptural elements that separate the true craftsmen of the profession from the rest.

### DESIGNING PUTTING GREENS

No feature is more important to play than the putting green. It is the venue not only for holing out – allowing an average of two putts per hole – but also for receiving the approach shot, or a recovery shot if the green has been missed. Of the several general types of green, one that is tilted towards the player allows the approach to stop more easily, but if the tilt is more than 3 per cent the player must try to stay below the hole or face a fast putt that may run well past. A green with less tilt makes it harder to stop the approach, but putting is less severe.

A green tilted away from the line of play requires the golfer to account for a bit of run after the approach shot lands, while a putting surface tilted from left to right holds more easily an approach shot that comes from the right side of the fairway (or vice versa), rewarding the golfer who can place the drive at will.

The size of the putting surface is also important. A large green makes a bigger target for the approach shot, yet may be divided into several levels or sections to assist good putting, while a small green requires a more accurate approach shot and the player who succeeds will be faced with a relatively easy putt.

*Top right: The 2nd green at St Andrews as seen from the left. The deep bunker in the foreground is actually more in play directly behind the flag on the 16th hole; the moguls and contours in the right of the photo guard hole locations sufficiently while playing the long approach at the 2nd.*

*Right: The 3rd green at The Hideout Golf Club in Utah is set on a promontory offering views across the course and thus requires few bunkers or other hazards to defend it.*

## BUNKER STYLES

These also vary tremendously, both in their appearance and in how they affect play. The early links bunkers were mostly quite small, reflecting their hand-dug nature and also the need to minimize wind erosion. However, their abrupt contours imposed a steep penalty when golfers found them and they came into play often because golf was played more along the ground in those early days. As the game moved inland, where erosion was less of an issue, bigger bunkers were built to reflect the scale of the property, and architects took more freedom to express themselves in the sizes and shapes and edging of their bunkers. Yet, over time, some of the origin of bunkers as rugged hazards has been lost to obsessive grooming and notions of fairness.

*Above: The home green at Royal West Norfolk Golf Club is defended by a wide cross-bunker. Railway sleepers were used to shore up the face of the bunker to keep it from being enlarged by wind erosion and eventually swallowing up the green.*

*Top right: The par-3 5th at Royal Melbourne (West) illustrates the 'flashed' modern bunkers popularized by Alister MacKenzie and by other designers of the Golden Age. In the sandbelt of Melbourne, these bunkers are dug straight into the native sandy soil; the fine sand binds tightly, giving rise to the sharp vertical lips that make these bunkers unique.*

*Right: Ernie Els extricates himself from a stacked-sod pot bunker at Muirfield during the Open Championship. Most of these bunkers are quite small but quite severe; they play much larger because the contours of the surrounding tightly mown ground gathers balls into the hollows.*

# THE BUSINESS OF COURSE DESIGN

Modern golf architects must have an understanding of many disciplines, from design to land planning, from agronomy to civil engineering, from business to construction. Most of all, they must understand golf and the psychology of the game, or as George Thomas, the architect of Riviera (see page 254), wrote: 'He must play golf and love it.'

Because the profession of golf architect is so specialized, and too small to demand the support of university programmes, nearly everyone in the business starts out as an apprentice to an established firm. This mentorship usually explains much about the designer's approach to the business: whether they hope to achieve quality control through meticulous planning or hands-on construction; whether their practice will be regional or international in scope; and whether they will attract clients with aspirations to host championships or ones who simply want to commission affordable and playable courses.

## ROLE OF THE CLIENT

In the early days the players themselves were both the clients and the end-users, and even in the Golden Age most courses were built strictly for golf, so the architect could make the most of the 150 acres he was given.. Today, many courses are the centre-piece of large-scale housing or resort developments and all too often these other uses override the golf architect's ideas. If the course is threaded through houses, all of its natural setting may be stripped away for homes.

Because the value of waterfront real estate is measured by the linear metre, many 'coastal' projects have just a single par 3 playing along

## USGA PUTTING GREEN CONSTRUCTION
### A cross-section

*This diagram illustrates how modern greens are built with layers of sand mix, coarse sand, gravel and drainage pipe to provide a perfect growing medium.*

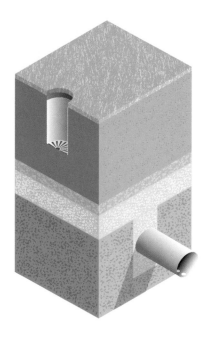

*The 5th hole at Beau Desert is an excellent example of the guile of architect Herbert Fowler, with a drive to a low fairway, angled across the line, followed by an uphill pitch to a three-level green, highest in the middle!*

the water or else a hole that lies towards a green on the coast with the next hole playing back inland. One of Jack Nicklaus's finest designs at El Dorado in Mexico originally had four holes along the Sea of Cortés, but three of these were moved so they could be replaced with housing by a subsequent owner, and the fairways were divided into housing lots that sold for more than US$100 million.

## TEAMWORK

Golf courses are now so elaborate in their construction that no architect works alone. Each project requires an enthusiastic team of engineers, earthmovers, shapers, irrigation contractors and a golf-course superintendent to make the vision a reality. The success of any new course depends on how well this team works together.

*Harry Colt's design for St George's Hill, in England, was one of the very first projects to combine golf with a real-estate development. In contrast with the photograph on page 22, the homes are buffered from the course by woods and are set much further back from the fairways, creating one of the most desirable residential communities around London.*

# THE LIFE OF A GOLF COURSE

A golf course is not a static piece of architecture but a living entity composed of grass, trees and shrubs. It must be actively looked after in order to preserve its playing character. If maintenance is not entirely in harmony with the intent of the design, the character of the course will eventually alter.

Change happens more quickly than most golfers imagine. Trees grow upwards and outwards, blocking recovery shots from wayward drives, while the shapes of the greens and the dimensions of the fairways adjust imperceptibly each day with another pass of the mower. Such modifications were particularly felt in the 1930s and 1940s, when the Great Depression and Second World War forced most private clubs to cut back sharply on maintenance costs. Even when those clubs recovered financially, many had forgotten the nuances of the original design.

In addition to these natural physical changes, the perspective of golfers is constantly shifting as well. New equipment allows players to hit the ball farther, so fairway bunkers may be carried more easily, and golfer safety has become much more of an issue now that the game has become more popular. Our modern culture has inexorably changed golf-course design and golfers now demand holes that are 'fair' from a medal-play standpoint, refusing to accept the rub of the green as a natural component of the game.

## MEETING DEMAND

Higher expectations of maintenance are presented weekly via colour television and the reality of the greenkeeper working within the constraints of the weather has been assaulted by demands for uniform conditions throughout the playing season. The advent of fairway irrigation in the 1950s caused many American clubs to narrow their fairways and then to plant trees to cover up the unirrigated rough areas that were once part of the fairway.

*These fairway bunkers on the 12th hole at St George's Golf and Country Club, Toronto, were restored by architect Ian Andrew based on photographs of Stanley Thompson's original work, complete with steep lips and islands of turf in the sand.*

*When Golden Age fairways of 50–60 yards (45–55 metres) were first irrigated in the 1950s, fairway widths were reduced to about 30 yards corresponding to the effective radius of a single row of irrigation, taking alternate strategies out of play.*

*This plan-view aerial photograph of the 18th green of the West Course at Winged Foot (right), from the 1929 US Open, shows the green's irregular shape. Note how close the edge of the green came to the left-hand bunkers. By the time of the 1949 Walker Cup (above), the green's shape had become more rounded, so that there was enough ground for spectators to stand between green and bunker. In the process, hole locations closest to the bunkers were lost, to be restored by Tom Fazio in 2003.*

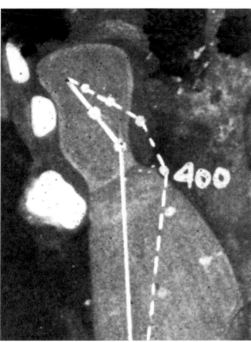

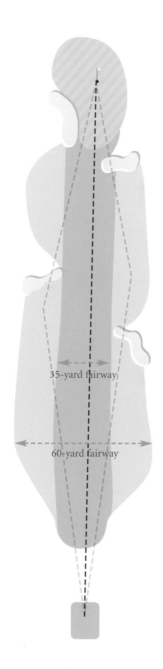

35-yard fairway

60-yard fairway

Green speeds increased as maintenance technology became more advanced and clubs competed to keep their greens better than the club next door. Eventually the speed of the greens dictated that putts could not stop in certain portions of the green because of the tilt that had been designed to create interest – causing many clubs to recontour their greens.

## SEARCH FOR PERFECTION

Last but not least, it is human nature that members, green chairmen and architects propose changes even to the best courses in an effort to make them better still, and to gain the satisfaction from doing so. In years past, these efforts were aimed at renovating older courses; more recently,

some clubs have recognized the merit of restoring lost features of the original design.

Yet restoration, too, is open to interpretation. Should the restorer put the course back exactly as it was, or lengthen a hole to re-establish the shot values of the original design, when the green required a long-iron approach? Was the course really its best on opening day in 1911, as set up for an historic championship in 1930, or as its members recall it set up for an event in 1971? And could not even great courses have evolved for the better in certain areas?

Such questions can never be answered definitively, for in the end golf architecture is a subjective art and the perspective of each golfer is biased by their own abilities.

# GOLF AND THE COMMUNITY

The original golf courses were an integral part of their coastal Scottish communities. They occupied the land that was unfit for other use – too sandy to farm and too close to the coast to provide a stable place for buildings – and they doubled as parkland right on the edge of town.

The same golf courses are now the centre-piece of tourism in those communities, providing the locals with a means of support as well and a source of pride, while continuing their recreational purpose of years past.

Less than 10 per cent of the population plays golf, however, so the non-golfing majority has a right to know that a golf course will be a good neighbour. This is a particular concern in those countries where golf is available only to the wealthy and well-connected, such as in Asia, Africa and increasingly in America, because the majority are likely to fight the development of a golf course if they gain no benefit from its existence. For this reason, new golf-course construction is being pushed to more remote regions where opposition is limited. By contrast, where golf is seen as inclusive and affordable, including in the UK, Australia and New Zealand, and for that matter in the mid-western USA, opposition to new construction is rare.

The supply of fresh water and the preservation of water quality are of primary concern to any community. Chemical and fertilizer use on golf courses must be limited and carefully monitored to minimize the risk of groundwater contamination and surface runoff, but fortunately the leaves and roots of fine turf provide excellent environmental buffers around water sources. Golf-course irrigation systems are also increasingly becoming one of the preferred users for the reclaimed water generated by neighbouring communities.

In America, and now on other continents as well, the majority of new golf courses are built as the centrepiece of 'golf communities', in which even non-golfing residents aspire to have a golf course as an extension of their back yards. While this has been a boon to the demand for new course construction, it remains to be seen whether it will be a long-term plus for the game itself. Many courses are handicapped because the golf takes second priority to the housing in the overall plan; others are built for their short-term marketing value, without a long-term case for golf supply and demand.

*Some of the best modern courses have been the remedy for community eyesores. At Black Diamond Ranch, Tom Fazio used the remains of a limestone quarry to create five holes unlike anything else in Florida.*

*St Andrews is home to the oldest university in Scotland, yet the Old Course has arguably had an even greater impact on the town's economy and on the world at large. Even without Open championships, the course attracts tourists and has driven the development of six other courses owned by the town, as well as the nearby Kingsbarns course.*

# EUROPE

Whatever claims other continents may make about having invented some sort of stick-and-stone pursuit, the Scots and the Dutch have been playing something that would be recognized as a form of golf since the 15th century. Thus Europe was the cauldron of golf.

It was Scotsmen who evangelized for golf, exporting it to other parts of the world: first to England, then America, India, South Africa, Australia and other countries in which Scottish soldiers or engineers found themselves with sufficient leisure time to indulge in their favourite pastime.

Strangely enough, the Scots were slower to take the game to countries closer to home, and so golf was introduced by British émigrés to France only in 1856 at Pau Golf Club, to Belgium in 1888 at Antwerp and to Portugal in 1890 at Oporto.

## PASTIME FOR THE RICH

Although courses were relatively easy to lay out – they involved none of the huge-scale earthmoving required today – golf was nevertheless an expensive sport. Feathery balls could not be made cheaply. The arrival of the gutta percha ball in the mid-19th century and, at the turn of the 20th century, the wound, rubber-core Haskell ball might have made the game cheaper, but by then golf was viewed as an upper-class activity in most European countries. It was inevitable, then, that golf courses were constructed where the wealthy could be found, that is, close to the great cities and in the fashionable watering holes and luxurious resorts of Europe.

Unfortunately, European history has been littered with wars, not least during the 20th century the particularly destructive First and Second World Wars. Country boundaries were formed and revised, political leanings and alignments changed. The emergence of the powerful Communist bloc in eastern Europe after the Second World War effectively redrew Europe's golfing map. Golf was decadent and had no place in the socialist way of life.

## POSTWAR EUROPEAN GOLF

So it was that in western Europe golf continued quietly during the remainder of the 1940s until the mid-1960s, when cheaper, jet air travel began to make overseas holidays more affordable for most people. At the same time social boundaries were being dismantled,

and golf, especially holiday golf, was no longer the preserve of members at the more traditional (and exclusive) golf clubs. The Algarve and Andalucia beckoned, and an explosion in golf course and real-estate construction followed.

Throughout Europe, landowners were encouraged to get out of agriculture and to find other uses for their land. European Union grants aided this to no small extent, and there is now hardly a place in Europe (apart, obviously, from the highest mountain peaks and frozen tundra) without some sort of golfing provision. After the dismantling of the so-called Iron Curtain in the early 1990s, the former Communist countries were soon brimming with golf-course construction projects, most of them aimed at attracting golfing visitors rather than establishing the game at grassroots level in the country itself.

## GOLF IN THE 21ST CENTURY

Eastern European countries such as Bulgaria now seek to woo those who might previously have built a second home in Spain or Portugal, and in this they have been aided by champion golfer Gary Player and English Golf Design in courses overlooking the Black Sea and near Varna, respectively. Meanwhile Jack Nicklaus has been involved in the development called Porto Mariccio in Croatia. Indeed, the Croatian government has established a policy to attract golfing investment to the tune of some 30 courses, with Howard Swan and Jeremy Pern among the architects involved.

Howard Swan has also worked on restoring two courses at Bled, in Slovenia. The Irish golfer, Christy O'Connor, and his company constructed Budapest Gate, again aimed at the high-end golf/residential market. It is one of a number of recent Hungarian enterprises. Poland, on the other hand, has an encouraging number of basic nine-hole courses – just what are required to get the local population out playing. That is not to say that there are not full-length, 18-hole courses to attract the established golfer, and among several are Krakow Valley Golf & Country Club

(architect Ronald Fream), Toya (Jeremy Pern) and Amber Baltic on the island of Wolin. Somehow golf also survived in the former Czechoslovakia with Karlovy Vary GC (opened 1904) and Royal Golf Club Mariánské Lázně (1905) reminding of its early establishment in that country.

Something of a diplomatic coup was achieved in 1988 when work began on the Moscow Country Club,

*Although the Real Club de Golf de Las Palmas dates back to 1891, its present course dates from 1957, when it was laid out by Mackenzie Ross.*

*The nine-hole course of Vestmannaeyjar, on Iceland's only inhabited island, Heimaey, was founded in 1938. Golf here is at one with nature, very similar to early golf in Scotland.*

deep in the Russian forest outside the city. It was designed by Robert Trent Jones Jnr, and the course has been promoted to the extent that it now annually hosts the Russian Open on the European Tour.

Until recently the Ukraine could claim to be the largest country in the world without any golf facilities at all. That, too, changed in 2008, with a project at Kiev overseen by architect Peter Chamberlain and the Swedish company Tema. Undoubtedly the biggest developments of this kind have been in the former German Democratic Republic, led by the remarkable Sporting Club Berlin at Scharmützelsee, Bad Saarow, which runs to three fine courses: one by Arnold Palmer, another by Stan Eby and a gem from Nick Faldo. And there are other important courses at Potsdam, Semlin and Schloss Wilkendorf.

In western Europe, the much longer-established and more widespread development of the game is described in considerable detail in section openers elsewhere in the *New World Atlas of Golf.* Such key golfing areas include the United Kingdom, Republic of Ireland, the Low Countries, France, Italy, Spain, Portugal, Switzerland and Sweden.

## GOLF IN EUROPE'S ISLANDS

Nor should we forget the islands. Golf is immensely popular in Iceland, for instance, with courses dating back to the 1930s at Akureyri, Reykjavik and Vestmannaeyjar, plus a number of newer courses offering 24-hour golf all summer, in incomparable surroundings.

At the other end of Europe is Greece, which only has four courses, two of them on islands – Rhodes and Corfu. But in the Greek part of Cyprus courses have been built in the Paphos region, Donald Steel's one at Tsada being the earliest of them (opened 1994). Across the water and political divide is Turkey (hardly Europe, it is true, but convenient

for golfing purposes) where golf tourism is making great strides with Kemer and Klassis near Istanbul and the intriguingly named Gloria and Tat rubbing shoulders with the National GC and Robinson near Antalya.

Portugal's boundaries extend as far as the Azores and Madeira, and Spain's to the Canaries, far out in the Atlantic. Golf is no novelty on these islands with Real Club de Golf de Las Palmas dating from 1891 and Furnas from 1939.

Finally to Britain's own off-shore courses, of which there are a number, with Castletown Golf Links (Isle of Man) and Machrie Golf Links (Islay) standing out. And nearer to France, just off the Normandy coast, lie the Channel Islands with their three delightful links courses: Royal Jersey, La Moye and Royal Guernsey. Europe stretches far – as does its professional golf tour: in fact, as far as the Far East and South Africa!

# SCOTLAND

It is unlikely that the Scots invented the concept of hitting a ball with a stick to a fixed point – this is an atavistic activity that many cultures developed into a sport of some kind. However, it seems undeniable that they perfected this concept into what we know today as the game of golf.

In many ways the Scots are the natural custodians of golf. It is mentioned in Scottish historical documents going back well over 500 years, but these citations are sparse and often limited to references to the purchase of golf equipment in the financial accounts of wealthy gentlemen. Early references are also often contradictory. For example, Sir Robert Maule (1493–1560) is often cited as the first 'commoner' to play golf, and yet King James's edict of 1457 decrying the playing of golf in lieu of archery practice seems to imply that the game was popular with the working classes much earlier.

## USE OF PUBLIC GROUND

What is known is that the game began to be formalized in Scotland in the early to mid-18th century, at a small number of venues, mostly on the east coast of the country. During that century, golf also became more expensive and exclusive, partly through technology (the feathery ball) and partly through social forces (the entrenchment of Calvinism).

In the early days, the game was largely played over common ground (most of which was linksland, although notable exceptions were Glasgow Green[1] and Bruntsfield[2] in Edinburgh) with players affiliated to clubs rather than to a specific piece of land. As the game increased in popularity, some early clubs moved their venues away from city centres to suburbs, and eventually acquired their own land, for their exclusive play. Among the most notable of these were Aberdeen[3], Burgess Golf Club[4] and The Honourable Company of Edinburgh Golfers who moved to Muirfield (see page 60). Other golf clubs, such as those at St Andrews (see page 40), Montrose[5], North Berwick (see page 46), Carnoustie (see page 50) and Royal Dornoch (see page 54), remained where they were established and played over their land by agreement with local authorities.

From the mid-19th century, rising prosperity, technology (introduction of the gutta percha ball) and improved transport links (particularly rail) brought

25

20
34  Royal Dornoch
    *page 54*

6

16

33
Inverness

Cruden Bay
*page 64*

19

Aberdeen  3

S C O T L A N D

17

Dundee  22    Carnoustie
                *page 50*

29   Perth  35    St Andrews
Gleneagles        8   7   *page 40*
*page 66*        13   31
Loch Lomond       30
*page 70*              10
                        14   Muirfield
9     Edinburgh  27   15   *page 60*
Glasgow       1   18   North Berwick
              2         *page 46*
              4                      5

24                                11

       12
       32
26   Royal Troon
Prestwick  *page 58*
*page 44*

23

Turnberry
*page 68*

21

the game to the masses, both as a spectator sport and as a pastime. This popularity strained the existing resources and so a wave of building new golf courses and remodelling old ones began. Many of these were laid out by the doyen of golf Old Tom Morris, as well as other well-known golfers of the age such as Willie Park Jnr and Archie Simpson. Some of these new courses were built on available linksland: for example, at Lossiemouth[6], the New Course at St Andrews, Royal Dornoch, Royal Troon (see page 58), Prestwick (see page 44), Crail[7] and Muirfield. Other courses were created at inland sites, such as Ladybank[8], Killermont[9], Burntisland[10] and Lanark[11].

Most were designed for the technology of the day, with total course length rarely exceeding 6,000 yards (5,486 metres).

## SEISMIC CHANGES

Around 1900, the invention of the rubber-core Haskell ball revolutionized the game of golf in Scotland, and the rest of the golfing world. Suddenly 250-yard (230-metre), par-four holes became easily drivable by competent players. Not only that, but the new combination of club and ball allowed highly increased rates of spin. Donald Grant of Dornoch recalled watching J.H. Taylor in 1904 hitting a mashie

(equivalent to a 5-iron) to the (then) 165-yard (151-metre) Witch hole and seeing it 'bite into the turf and then spin back for a yard'.

These changes led to additional significant renovations at almost all the great courses. Therefore just about every golf course in Scotland that a visitor looks at today and marvels about its 'timelessness' is in effect less than 100 years old. In addition, following the success of Cruden Bay (see page 64), there arose resort courses built around railway junctions and luxury hotels, particularly at Turnberry (see page 68) and Gleneagles (see page 66) – in the latter case bringing golf more spectacularly into the Scottish heartland.

*Nairn's opening holes run beside the Moray Firth, but the golfer's attention must be firmly on the course for there is much movement in the land and the bunkers are testing.*

# THE LURE OF SCOTTISH COURSES

Scotland's golf courses are different from those that most people play in other parts of the world. Part of this is due to its climate, part its geology and part its culture. Where else in the world might a golfer be able to play some sly holes of golf at ten o'clock at night, over a deserted but sunlit linksland, and then go back to a family hotel where partying at the all-night ceilidh is just starting?

In addition a visitor is largely welcome in Scotland, rather than just tolerated. Such an attitude reflects the historical development of the game, as a pursuit for and of the people. Playing just about any Scottish course, a visitor will be treated as an equal, as a golfer. They will never be just a 'guest'. They will be a temporary 'member', and what they do with this privilege is their choice.

The places where golfers can do some or all of these things are legion. For instance, take Western Gailes[12], one of the jewels of the Ayrshire coast, in no way overshadowed by its near neighbours, Royal Troon and Prestwick. A wonderful stretch of holes from the 5th to the 13th skirts the shore with the short 7th, its green cradled in the dunes and cunningly bunkered, among the most memorable holes. At Elie[13], where the great James Braid developed his golfing skills, a periscope from an old submarine is used to determine when it is safe to drive blind over a hill to the first fairway, but it is the par-four 13th, sweeping in a curve beside the beach, which was credited by Braid as being 'the finest hole in all the country'. Ladybank, a heathland beauty in Fife, has been a final qualifying venue when the Open Championship is played at St Andrews. It demands accurate driving, especially on the doglegged 3rd, 9th, 15th and 16th holes. Gullane[14], which boasts some of the finest turf in Scotland, is unusual in being a links course set on a hill. Over many centuries sand was blown from Aberlady Bay onto Gullane Hill in sufficient quantity to make an admirable base for marrams, bents and fescues. The view from the 7th tee at the top of the hill is one of the finest in all golf. Luffness New[15], Gullane's neighbour, may be flatter but is no easier. Its greens were reckoned by that great putter, Bobby Locke, to be the best he had ever played. Nairn[16], on which it is possible to slice the

*One of the marvels of the construction of Kingsbarns is the way in which the eye is constantly drawn to the sea, emphasising the links nature of the course only recently created out of farmland.*

ball onto the beach on six of the first seven holes, played host to the 1999 Walker Cup. It is a links course for the most part, although it is more heathland in quality for part of the back nine, particularly the demanding 13th with a testing approach to a hill-top green. One of Scotland's finest inland clubs is Blairgowrie[17], with two 18-hole courses and a nine-hole. Its tranquil Rosemount Course weaves a charming path through swathes of heather.

Golf has been played at Dunbar[18] since the early 17th century. Its compact course is squeezed into a narrow strip of land with a stone wall coming into play on several holes. The toughest hole is the 12th, a sturdy par four played to a green on a headland. Lanark is the 25th oldest club in the world with an Old Tom Morris and James Braid moorland course that plays much like a seaside links. Particularly testing are the long par-four 4th and 15th, both of which play into the prevailing wind. Pretty as a picture with the Cairngorms as an imposing backdrop is Boat of Garten[19] in the heart of the Scottish Highlands. At just under 5,900 yards its challenge lies not in its length. Rather the golfer is tested by undulating fairways that are woven through pine and birch woods and outcrops of heather with charm at a premium throughout the round. In the far north is Brora[20], its links hardly changed since James Braid revised the course in the 1920s. It is an object lesson in designing a course to make the most of the natural features of the ground, with the minimum of artificiality.

One of the finest of the more modern – by Scottish standards – courses is Southerness[21], a challenging links overlooking the Solway Firth laid out at minimal cost in the late 1940s by Mackenzie Ross. Although par is only 69 there are no fewer than eight par fours over 400 yards in length, with the dogleg 12th, played towards a green almost on the beach, being particularly memorable. Downfield[22] in Dundee was described by Peter Thomson as, 'One of the finest inland courses I have played anywhere in the world.' For the most part it is a course of the 1960s, but five holes remain from a James Braid course of 1932.

It is a long journey down the mull of Kintyre to reach the remote Machrihanish[23], on which the dramatic opening drive is played across as much beach as you dare. Going out, the 7th involves a long second shot played over a high sand hill, and coming in the second of consecutive par threes, the 15th, is a real bruiser at 232 yards, often into the wind. Even more remote is Machrie[24] on the island of Islay, laid out in 1891 by Willie Campbell and once boasting consecutive holes of 750 and 620 yards. Today's course may be less eccentric but there is no denying the wonderful

natural feel of the links. And it takes a journey to the far north-west of Scotland to find the 20-year-old, community-built, nine-holer at Durness[25], with its par-three finishing hole played across the waves of the Atlantic Ocean.

In fact there are golf courses of great character and originality all over the country, such as the twelve-hole course of the Shiskine Golf and Tennis Club[26] on the west coast of the Isle of Arran, the historic Musselburgh Old[27], near Edinburgh, on which six Open championships were contested between 1874 and 1889, rock-strewn Barra[28], the most westerly of Scottish courses on which the fairways are shared with grazing cattle, the course of the King James VI club in Perth[29], which is entirely located on its own island in the middle of the river Tay, or Auchterderran[30] – an obscure nine-holer more than 100 years old, which sits at the edge of an old mining village in Fife. Some of the holes cross in the old-fashioned way, but most of them have distinct and intriguing character and are fully capable of raising the spirit of the visiting golfer.

The golfing landscape is changing – literally so in the case of Kingsbarns[31].

## KINGSBARNS

Like many British seaside courses, Kingsbarns's venerable nine-hole course had been requisitioned by the military in the Second World War. When peace returned it was left to grow into pasture, and then proper farmland. In 1998 that changed, as two Californian developers, Mark Parsinen and Art Dunkley, teamed up with architect Kyle Phillips for the purpose of creating a new Kingsbarns Golf Links. It was and is a wonder of modern golf-course engineering and design.

The wonderment comes from the fact that, after 50–60 years of arable use, the soil was no longer true links. Effectively, the developers had to recreate links conditions over land that was flat and fertile, rather than lumpy and poor. The skill with which they did so is evident by the fact that it is extremely difficult to identify the hand of man in the creation of what is a superb golf course by any reckoning. Its interest to the golfer starts at the first hole and continues to the very end.

Kingsbarns is arguably the finest of the several world-class courses that have sprung up all over Scotland, such as Loch Lomond (see page 70), its links sibling Dundonald[32] (Kyle Phillips) on the Ayrshire coast, Castle Stuart[33] (Mark Parsinen and Gil Hanse) near Inverness, the Carnegie Club[34] (Donald Steel) near Dornoch and the Castle Course[35] (David McLay Kidd) at St Andrews, the seventh course at the 'home of golf'.

# ST ANDREWS
## St Andrews, Fife

The Old Course at St Andrews may or may not have been the place that some form of the game of golf was first played, but it surely was the place where it was perfected.

First written mention of golf in St Andrews was in 1552, and while there are several further references over the next 150–200 years (mostly in financial accounts and court records) it was not really until the mid-18th century that the game became at all formalized. During that period, the Royal Burgess Society (the Burgess), then the Honourable Company of Edinburgh Golfers (HCEG) and then (in 1754) the Society of St Andrews Golfers were formed.

### DEFINING MOMENTS IN GOLF

While the Burgess was the first organized club, and the HCEG codified the first rules, the St Andrews Golfers (who in time became the Royal & Ancient Golf

that they acquired their own grounds, at Barnton and Muirfield, respectively. Secondly, unlike the Edinburgh clubs, St Andrews was blessed with lots of open land and far fewer competing attractions. While the other early clubs made golf one of their diversions, St Andrews Golfers effectively made it their business, and slowly and eventually took over both the administrative and spiritual aspects of the game. By the time that golf began to take off, St Andrews was poised and able to lead its development into the 20th century and beyond.

Course is in the eye of the beholder and subject to change over time.

### LIVING THE DREAM

The only time that the Old Course looks at all similar to different golfers is the first time they stand on the 1st tee. Leaving the fine old town behind, the player moves onto a green sward that has hosted golf for many lifetimes and more. They probably know the look and the feel of the 376-yard 1st, because they have seen it so many times on television. And, of course,

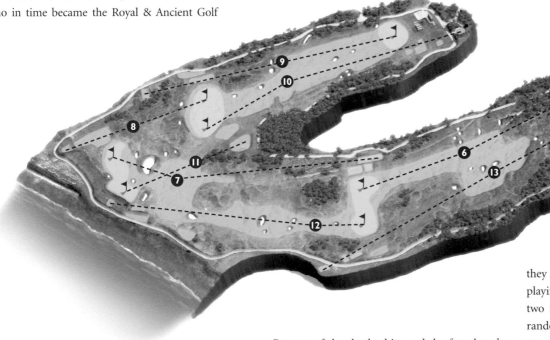

Club of St Andrews, or the R&A) grew to eventually control the game. This situation developed for a number of reasons, which must be speculative, as the historical record is very spotty. Firstly, the Burgess and HCEG played over very cramped venues in and around Edinburgh – at Leith and then at Musselburgh. It was not until the late 19th century

Because of that leadership, and the fact that the Old Course was clearly the most demanding test of all The Open venues, it became the gold standard for golf. Once the course had been reduced from 22 to 18 holes, that became normal, and the practices of its keeper of the green, Old Tom Morris, also became touchstones. Even today, if there were such a thing as a dictionary of golf-course architecture, just about every entry would conclude with the parenthetical remark 'see the Old Course'. And yet the meaning of the Old

they are also very aware of being seen, by friends and playing partners, the starter and maybe a grandee or two from the R&A in the clubhouse behind or by random tourists walking behind the tee. It can all seem so peaceful and easy. There is just the player, the ball, the land, the hole and the prospect of the round to come. It simply and elegantly defines golf.

On the 2nd tee, however, the language becomes more complex. From the teeing ground the land is crumpled and full of humps and bushes, some of which obscure the view to the hole. Whereas on the previous hole the task was clear, on the 453-yard 2nd it is mysterious and obscure. With the help of a caddie or just the player's own sense of adventure

# ST ANDREWS (OLD COURSE) – St Andrews, Fife

Hugh Playfair and Alan Robertson, 1857 and Old Tom Morris, 1870
Major events: Open Championship 1873, 1876, 1879, 1882, 1885, 1888, 1891, 1895, 1900, 1905, 1910, 1921, 1927, 1933, 1939, 1946, 1955, 1957, 1960, 1964, 1970, 1978, 1984, 1990, 1995, 2000, 2005; Amateur Championship 1886, 1889, 1891, 1895, 1901, 1907, 1913, 1924, 1930, 1936, 1950, 1958, 1963, 1976, 1981, 2004; British Ladies' Open Amateur 1908, 1929, 1965, 1975; Walker Cup 1923, 1926, 1934, 1938, 1947, 1955, 1971, 1975; Women's Open Championship 2007; Curtis Cup 2008

CARD OF THE COURSE

| HOLE | NAME | YARDS | PAR | HOLE | NAME | YARDS | PAR |
|---|---|---|---|---|---|---|---|
| 1. | Burn | 376 | 4 | 10. | Bobby Jones | 380 | 4 |
| 2. | Dyke | 453 | 4 | 11. | High (In) | 174 | 3 |
| 3. | Cartgate (Out) | 397 | 4 | 12. | Heathery (In) | 348 | 4 |
| 4. | Ginger Beer | 480 | 4 | 13. | Hole O'Cross (In) | 465 | 4 |
| 5. | Hole O'Cross (Out) | 568 | 5 | 14. | Long | 618 | 5 |
| 6. | Heathery (Out) | 412 | 4 | 15. | Cartgate (In) | 456 | 4 |
| 7. | High (Out) | 390 | 4 | 16. | Corner of the Dyke | 423 | 4 |
| 8. | Short | 175 | 3 | 17. | Road | 455 | 4 |
| 9. | End | 352 | 4 | 18. | Tom Morris | 357 | 4 |
| **OUT** | | **3,603** | **36** | **IN** | | **3,676** | **36** |
| | | | | **TOTAL** | | **7,279** | **72** |

the golfer must pick a line from a cloud or a flower on a piece of gorse. Uncertainty and discipline are added to a golfer's lexicon.

As the humps are climbed over, the player can see a golf hole in front but the land heaves and moves in seemingly random directions. A few bunkers on the right are so small as to seem an afterthought. To the left is Cheape's bunker – not a place that a golfer would want to be. The ball may have ended up far from the expected position, so the player might just think about the humps and hollows in the fairway, and how they can divert the ball seriously due to gravity. While pondering the effects of blindness and gravity, a golfer also learns about the phenomenon of chance.

Looking farther forward, there seems to be a set of waves of land of higher frequency and increased randomness that make the path to the hole anything but obvious, and yet at the green the player is likely to have a pleasant surprise. It is relatively calm and flat, presuming the pin is set to the mid right, as it normally

*Shell bunker, in the foreground, ingeniously protects both the 7th and 11th holes beyond, each perched on its own half of the long sloping green hard by the Eden estuary.*

is for casual play. Getting down in two for a par is very possible for the player of any ability who gets the length right on the second shot. Great golf courses, no matter how hard they may seem, always have some definable and uplifting quality of mercy.

## SOLITARY GOLF

A long time has been spent on the 2nd, not because it is one of the best holes on the Old Course (it is not) but because it is so instructive. The next five holes continue the lessons learned – uncertainty, discipline, gravity, mercy, thought – adding a fillip or two to these concepts and introducing a few of their own.

The 397-yard 3rd ratchets up the uncertainty and the mental challenge. Small pot bunkers to the right that are out of play on the previous hole are now more numerous and more in play, as the best line to the green is from that side. There is masses of room to the left, but from there the second shot must often flirt with the fearsome Cartgate bunker.

On the 480-yard 4th, the player begins to understand the concept of strategy. In order to play this hole successfully a golfer must think of the risks and rewards of various options, as both are heightened due to the vagaries of the terrain. Many of the humps before the greens are angled, complicating plans, and often foiling the execution of these plans.

First of two long holes on the Old Course is the 568-yard 5th. It is very reachable in the prevailing wind by the better players, but requires the negotiation of a deep, wide and lengthy dip before the green. The 412-yard 6th epitomizes its predecessors: a blind tee shot over gorse, a landing area pockmarked with bunkers, a second shot guarded by a hollow and a few humps, and a putting surface fairly gentle but large.

First-time players then seem to confront the same challenge on the 7th tee, but after climbing that hump to the fairway, vive la différence! Suddenly there is visibility – of the hole, of other holes and of other players. Where the round was largely solitary for the past five holes, now it is communal. The 390-yard 7th brings two other words into play – vision and camaraderie. While deception in golf-course architecture can be intriguing, like all good things it can be overdone

and needs an antidote from time to time. This little stretch of the Old Course, called the Loop, provides just that. The second to the 7th is an inviting, cut shot over bunkers to a green nestled into a dune abutting the Eden estuary.

## COMMUNAL GOLF

Next is the first of the two short holes, the 175-yard 8th, which brings back a bit of blindness from the tee, but requires only a confident swing with a mid-iron to reach the green. From there a par should be taken, unless the hole is at the back-right 'Open' position on a tiny knob.

The 352-yard 9th is the least impressive hole on the course, if not in all of championship golf. Nevertheless, those who have watched Open championships at St Andrews know that valuable strokes can be won or lost on this hole, and for all its mundanity it does teach golfers that no course is perfect, nor can they nor should they expect perfection in golf. The 10th comes back parallel to the 9th and looks as simple, but is not. Angled ridges before the green and

# CHAMPIONSHIP TEES
Finding room to keep the Old Course fresh and challenging

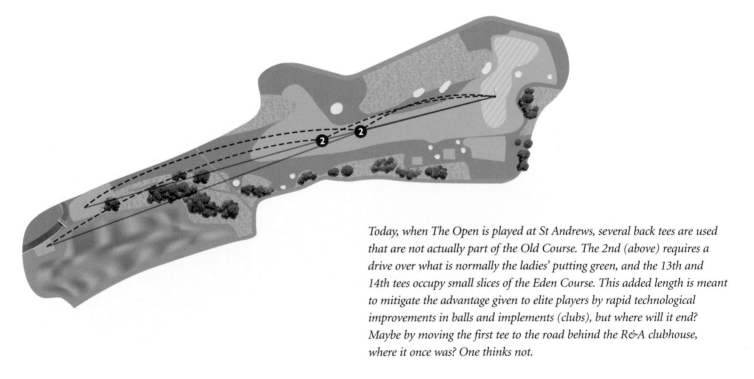

*Today, when The Open is played at St Andrews, several back tees are used that are not actually part of the Old Course. The 2nd (above) requires a drive over what is normally the ladies' putting green, and the 13th and 14th tees occupy small slices of the Eden Course. This added length is meant to mitigate the advantage given to elite players by rapid technological improvements in balls and implements (clubs), but where will it end? Maybe by moving the first tee to the road behind the R&A clubhouse, where it once was? One thinks not.*

on it make it as hard a 380-yard hole to birdie as could be possible. Until 1972, the 10th was nameless. Now it proudly carries the name of Bobby Jones.

As the Irish would say, the 174-yard 11th is itself. Despite the combined efforts of Charles Macdonald, Seth Raynor and countless other Golden Age and modern architects, nobody has come close to recreating this golf hole. A big part of this is the topography – where is it possible to find a ridge in front of a sand dune big enough to accommodate two greens (it is shared with the 7th), looking out over a pristine estuary and enough back-to-front slope to make a downhill putt terrifying? The lesson from this hole is that while interpretation is possible imitation often is not.

## MORE GOLFING LESSONS

Although seemingly open and inviting, the 348-yard 12th has backwards-facing bunkers and an evil, two-tiered green. Highly underrated is the 465-yard 13th, which has an open tee shot but a blind second to a much more complex green than seen before. These two holes are in fact the start of the best part of the original course, which played mostly to today's incoming greens. The lessons learned on the outgoing holes are repeated here, in depth and with greater complexity – the golfing equivalent of the difference between a high school and a university education.

Such complexity is epitomized at the 618-yard 14th. While Dr Alister MacKenzie's famous sketch of the hole, showing alternative strategies, is obsolete for the elite modern player, it still has serious value for the average golfer. Of the numerous route choices and possible outcomes available, far too many are inhospitable. A slight respite occurs at the 456-yard 15th, but only in the context of its adjacent holes. Famous mostly for its centre-line Principal's Nose bunker complex is the 423-yard 16th. However, it (and the 14th) should be just as famous for the angles and slopes that encompass the approach to the green. This hole is a masterclass in both strategy and gravity.

Who in their right mind would build a hole, which requires a blind drive over railway sheds (today a hotel), and then a second shot to a green guarded by a metalled road and wall to the right and a deep pot bunker in the centre? The hole screams not only terror but imagination. This is the iconic Road hole – the 455-yard 17th

Reflecting the opening hole, the 357-yard 18th is both simple and inviting. Against par it is the easiest, but this assumes that players can completely ignore the context. They are returning to the town, which embraces the opening and closing holes, and finishing a round on the most famous course in the world. A good player will want a three but accept a four, while the hacker might expect a five but have a chance of a three. The simplest things are often the most complex. This is the final lesson, and it should inspire the golfer to want to go right then and there back onto the 1st tee. Such a feeling is in itself one of the most reliable definitions of great golf.

*When the pin is at the front of the 17th green, the Road hole bunker hardly comes into play. When it is placed just behind the hazard, however, it can strike fear into even the greatest golfers in the world.*

# PRESTWICK
## Prestwick, Ayrshire

Prestwick was probably the first professionally designed course in the world. Founded in 1851, the club had the great foresight to hire Old Tom Morris (although, aged 29, he was not then particularly 'Old') as its first keeper of the green, ball and club maker. One of his first tasks, naturally, was to build a proper golf course, and this he did brilliantly.

Old Tom Morris stayed at Prestwick for 14 years, during which time the first five Open championships were held on the course (Old Tom winning three of those). His son, Young Tom, was born in Prestwick and learned how to play the game of golf there as well as any man or woman before or since.After moving back to St Andrews, Old Tom Morris often returned to Prestwick, notably to win his fourth (and last) Open in 1867, and to extend the course from 12 to 18 holes in 1883. Even though a number of changes have been made to the course since then, roughly half of the holes played today were designed by him, including some of the very best. One of these is the opening hole.

### A DIFFICULT START

Being only 346 yards long, the 1st seems a gentle opener on the card, but on the tee the player can be unsettled by the Ayr–Glasgow railway line hard down the right, just where the average golfer would expect to hit their gentle fade. Sand dunes that encroach from the left make the only safety play a mid-iron down the middle, but this leaves a longer shot to a green hidden behind a large cross-bunker. It is possibly the most intimidating opening hole in the world of golf.

Having survived the 1st, the golfer then moves to the pleasant and charming, 167-yard 2nd. It is a classic short links hole that asks just for line and length, and for hope if either of the above parameters is breached. The 482-yard 3rd is the famous Cardinal hole, with a drive to a seemingly open field that is abruptly terminated by a huge and eponymous bunker. This requires the good player to lay up off the tee, yet it still strikes fear into the

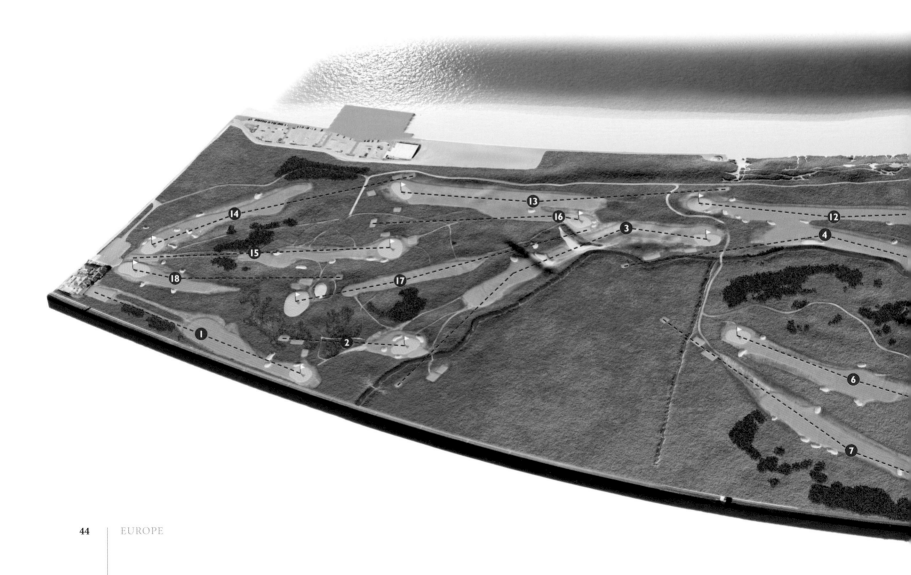

# PRESTWICK GOLF CLUB – Prestwick, Ayrshire

Old Tom Morris, 1851; Old Tom Morris and Charles Hunter, 1883; James Braid, 1918;
and James Braid and J.R. Stutt, 1930
Major events: Open Championship 1860–1870, 1872, 1875, 1878, 1881, 1884, 1887,
1890, 1893, 1898, 1903, 1908, 1914, 1925; Amateur Championship 1888, 1893, 1899,
1905, 1911, 1922, 1928, 1934, 1952, 1987, 2001

CARD OF THE COURSE

| HOLE | NAME | YARDS | PAR | HOLE | NAME | YARDS | PAR |
|------|------|-------|-----|------|------|-------|-----|
| 1. | Railway | 346 | 4 | 10. | Arran | 454 | 4 |
| 2. | Tunnel | 167 | 3 | 11. | Carrick | 195 | 3 |
| 3. | Cardinal | 482 | 5 | 12. | Wall | 513 | 5 |
| 4. | Bridge | 382 | 4 | 13. | Sea Headrig | 460 | 4 |
| 5. | Himalayas | 206 | 3 | 14. | Goosedubs | 362 | 4 |
| 6. | Elysian Fields | 362 | 4 | 15. | Narrows | 347 | 4 |
| 7. | Monkton Miln | 430 | 4 | 16. | Cardinals Back | 288 | 4 |
| 8. | End | 431 | 4 | 17. | Alps | 391 | 4 |
| 9. | Eglinton | 444 | 4 | 18. | Clock | 284 | 4 |
| | **OUT** | **3,250** | **35** | | **IN** | **3,294** | **36** |
| | | | | | **TOTAL** | **6,544** | **71** |

*Sea Headrig heads back towards town and the crumpled land in between reminds you of what much of the Ayrshire coast must have looked like before 'civilization' arrived.*

heart of the average golfer. A caddie or the vision of a world-class architect is needed for the second shot, because the obvious green – straight ahead – is the 16th. Instead, the 3rd green is far to the right, up against the Pow Burn, and it takes the player towards the outer regions of the course. Meandering along the left bank of the Pow is the 382-yard 4th, which requires guile rather than power to be tamed. At the 206-yard 5th, the player stands on a tee box that seems to point straight at a hill. This is the famous Himalayas, a completely blind par three. As with many blind shots (of which this was surely one of the very first), scaling the hill and finding the ball on the green is one of the very special thrills in golf.

## CHANGE OF MOOD

Beyond Himalayas is where much of the expansion of Prestwick has taken place, starting with Old Tom Morris who added two new holes in 1883. Called the 'Elysian Fields' by the members, this land has a kinder, gentler and different feel from the older bits, but the holes on it are no less challenging. Both the 362-yard 6th and 430-yard 7th have uphill greens, and the 444-yard 9th is a testing finish to the outward half.

A long shot off the tee is required on the 454-yard 10th, and then a second straight uphill to a green nestled in the dunes protecting the course from the Irish Sea. It is followed by the 195-yard 11th, an attractive short hole downhill along the spine of the dunes, which begins to bring the player back to the centre of the course. The 513-yard 12th is a reachable par five, although the second shot must be threaded past bunkers, humps and hollows to find the green.

Sea Headrig – the 460-yard 13th – slants from right to left and features one of the wildest greens in golf. Hitting the green is no guarantee of par, and, depending on the pin location, missing it in a place where the player can chip up to the hole can be the preferred option. Two short two-shotters follow: the 362-yard 14th is towards the car park and features a small wetland – a rarity on a Scottish links course – and the 347-yard 15th, which requires an arrow-straight drive along a ridge and then a sure pitch to a small green cut on top of heaving hillocks. The green on the charming 288-yard 16th was once the green site of a fearsome 578-yard 1st hole, which Young Tom Morris holed in three at the 1870 Open.

## INFLUENCE OF PRESTWICK

The 391-yard 17th, with its blind second to a green protected by a huge fronting bunker, is a hole often copied by designers fascinated by quirk; however, the Alps is rarely equalled. Finally, the 18th, a 284-yard par four hit from an elevated tee to a flat green in front of the clubhouse, is not difficult – unless the state of the game demands a birdie.

Like Dr Who's Tardis, Prestwick is a portal to times ahead, as well as to the past. So many features of the course continue to fascinate golf-course architects that the influence of Prestwick's character on future courses will never wane. And, by demonstrating that a course of modest length can still challenge the elite golfer and bring a song to the heart of anyone who plays it, it may yet point to another path to the future.

At North Berwick, fairways stop at the bases of hills, greens sit behind walls and ramblers amble across a player's path with impunity. Just when a player feels at one with the routing, it veers away from the line of instinct. Welcome to golf in Scotland!

## EARLY IMPORTANCE

The West Links at North Berwick is one of the most venerable golfing venues in the world. While the first recorded playing of the game over the land (*c.*1800) was well after historical references at other places such as Royal Dornoch (see page 54), Leith, Aberdeen and even Glasgow Green, it is only the Old Course at St Andrews (see page 40) that has more continuously documented history.

In the 19th century, North Berwick was at the centre of golf development in Scotland, that is, the world. When Muirfield (see page 60) was just a gleam in the eyes of the grandchildren of the gentlemen golfers at Leith, when Turnberry (see page 68) and Gleneagles (see page 66) were remote places on primitive maps, and when Southampton was a scrub-ridden wasteland in the native American reservations east of the potato fields of Long Island, the West Links developed and hosted the greatest players of the game. Its architectural history is murky (as it is with many, if not most, of the older courses in Scotland and Ireland).

The original course (designer and date unknown) was six holes, and three more were added in 1869 (architect again unknown). Reputedly, the first children's course was created in 1893 at North Berwick, and the West Links also played host to the final game of the most significant 'child' the game had or ever has created. Young Tom Morris was playing a match over the West Links with his father, Old Tom Morris, against Willie Park Snr and his son, Willie Park Jnr, of Musselburgh in September 1875 when Young Tom's wife died in childbirth. In the throes of grief, he did not survive the year.

The course that those two great golfing families would have played in 1875 was the nine-holer, only going out as far as what is now the 14th tee. In 1877 it was extended westwards out to the Eil Burn, under the current 7th, to make 18 holes, and then in 1891 land was purchased from the Archerfield estate to make the course one of 'proper' length (in those days, greater than 6,000 yards). This version is pretty much the course played today, even though numerous minor changes were made over the next 50 years, mostly, yet again, by the committee. In 1932, the present 9th and 10th were designed by C.K. Hutchinson on newly added land. However, since the land was commandeered by the Royal Air Force in 1940 and used as a bombing range, the holes had to be completely reconstructed after the war, and included a lengthening of today's 11th to a par five.

## UNUSUAL CHALLENGES

The course at North Berwick starts at a curious place. After a walk of a few hundred metres behind the 18th green, with more obvious linksland to the right, and then past a bunker that proclaims itself a pro shop, the player reaches a modern starter's hut next to a flat tee that seems to point towards an insurmountable pinnacle of rock. If the golfer looks hard enough, however, they can see the top of a very tall flagpole, and as they know the 1st is a very short 'four', only a comfortable mid-long iron shot short of the rise and a pitch are required to get to the green. The green, however, while a bit of a 'punchbowl', slopes sharply to the right and the sea, yet is much slower than it looks. Locals surely know how to play this hole, but visitors must rely on chance to get a birdie or easy par. Complicating things are the distractions of non-golfers walking along a path to the beach at about the length of even the most conservative tee shot. Such an opener is bizarre, in both its zaniness and its ability to stimulate the brain and test concentration.

Then, jarringly but softly, at the 2nd tee the player is confronted with a very conventional golf hole, over glorious linksland. A drive is required as far right as feasible to a fairway curving that way over the beach and on to an inviting green in a small hollow. The 464-yard 3rd is straight, over a wall not far from the tee, and towards a longer short wall, which will interfere with a player's mind on the second shot if inclined to lift the head. The golfer may seem settled but the

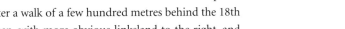

# NORTH BERWICK
## North Berwick, East Lothian

On paper, North Berwick seems like any other ancient links course – out along the water for 2 miles (3 kilometres) or so and then back again to the clubhouse. Once a golfer gets on the ground, however, all preconceptions become misconceptions, and all certainties become ambiguities.

course confuses again by directing players across the line of play to a multiple tee. Ahead is the 175-yard 4th, a lovely short hole into the dunes, and to the left, if a golfer is paying attention, is the famous Redan.

Even though holes 5–9 all have their merits, to the connoisseur they are just appetizers for what is to come. The 510-yard 9th gives a hint of this in that it traverses flat ground littered with recently built bunkers and then rises provocatively to a lovely green in the dunes. A long and well-placed drive will provide the chance of a birdie, but only if the player is skilled at the 230-yard (210-metre) straight shot.

## A RARE TREAT

A daunting one-shotter downhill from a tee in the dunes – the 176-yard 10th – starts a straight run back to the clubhouse that is unparalleled in its quality and variety. The next hole is a right–left, reachable par five

## THE NORTH BERWICK GOLF CLUB (WEST LINKS) – North Berwick, East Lothian

Anon., 1869, 1877 and 1891
Major events: Ladies' British Open Amateur 2008

CARD OF THE COURSE

| HOLE | NAME | YARDS | PAR | HOLE | NAME | YARDS | PAR |
|---|---|---|---|---|---|---|---|
| 1. | Point Garry (Out) | 328 | 4 | 10. | Eastwood Ho! | 176 | 3 |
| 2. | Sea | 431 | 4 | 11. | Bo'ns Locker | 550 | 5 |
| 3. | Trap | 464 | 4 | 12. | Bass | 389 | 4 |
| 4. | Carlekemp | 175 | 3 | 13. | Pit | 365 | 4 |
| 5. | Bunkershill | 373 | 4 | 14. | Perfection | 376 | 4 |
| 6. | Quarry | 162 | 3 | 15. | Redan | 192 | 3 |
| 7. | Eil Burn | 354 | 4 | 16. | Gate | 381 | 4 |
| 8. | Linkhouse | 495 | 5 | 17. | Point Garry (In) | 425 | 4 |
| 9. | Mizzentop | 510 | 5 | 18. | Home | 274 | 4 |
| **OUT** | | **3,292** | **36** | **IN** | | **3,128** | **35** |
| | | | | **TOTAL** | | **6,420** | **71** |

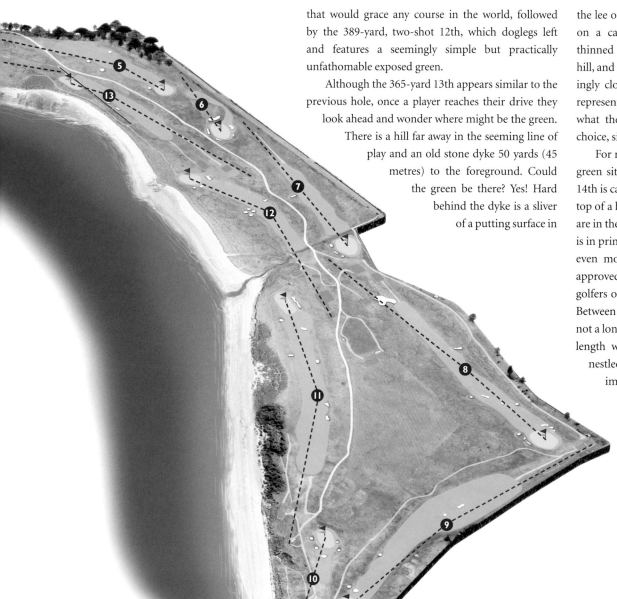

that would grace any course in the world, followed by the 389-yard, two-shot 12th, which doglegs left and features a seemingly simple but practically unfathomable exposed green.

Although the 365-yard 13th appears similar to the previous hole, once a player reaches their drive they look ahead and wonder where might be the green. There is a hill far away in the seeming line of play and an old stone dyke 50 yards (45 metres) to the foreground. Could the green be there? Yes! Hard behind the dyke is a sliver of a putting surface in the lee of the hill. It is eminently hittable, particularly on a calm day. Even then, however, the slightest thinned shot will send the ball careering towards the hill, and a weak shot can drop short and nestle annoyingly close to the wall. Known as the Pit, this hole represents all the core values that make the West Links what they are: natural beauty, deception, freedom, choice, simple complexity and, above all, fun.

For reasons that relate more to the views from the green site than the quality of the hole, the 376-yard 14th is called Perfection. On it, the drive is blind to the top of a hill, and, while the rushes by the sea to the left are in the mind of the golfer, the fact that the 4th green is in prime distance for the slightly cut tee shot weighs even more heavily. Such a routing could never be approved in this litigious age, but the club and the golfers of North Berwick seem to get on with it well. Between the hazards, the ground is heaving but it is not a long hole, and any drive with reasonable line and length will lead to a semiblind pitch to the green nestled down by the edge of the sea. There are many imperfect aspects to Perfection, but any course or hole without faults is doomed to be anodyne. North Berwick is anything but.

*This view from the right of the hole shows the right–left, front–back slope of the green towards the sea and the bastions of Craigleith and Bass Rock. The phalanx of bunkers to the right severely penalizes the pushed shot. Who said golf was meant to be fair?*

## WORLD RENOWNED

The Redan hole, the 192-yard 15th, is one of the most famous golf holes in the world. It is reached by walking up a hill and through a stile to the same confluence of holes that was first encountered when playing the 4th. Again the line of play is crossed, and again the player is confronted by a unique golf hole that tests the imagination. There was a time in the 19th century when the 15th was played from near today's 14th green, making it a two-shotter, both of which would have been blind, but that was too much, even for the experimentalists who were in charge of the West Links.

It is followed by a seemingly simple hole, the 381-yard 16th, which requires at first glance a drive over a stone dyke and a stream. However, the closer the player gets to the green the more they wonder what awaits their next shot. They can see a small plateau to the right, but there also seems to be one to the left and farther back, with a grassy chasm between them. Both knobs and the chasm are in fact part of one of the most intriguing green complexes in the world. The pin will inevitably be on one of the sides and will be an extremely hard target to find, even if a good drive has been hit and only a short-iron is needed. A perfectly judged and executed stroke may not be able to hold either of the two plateaus, but a sensible strategy is to punch a low shot and hope that it runs up the slope.

By the time the 17th tee is reached, the golfer will be both exhilarated and exhausted. In front of them will be one last challenge, a long par four with a fairway full of humps and hollows and then a green up on the same hill as the 1st, but guarded by a slit-trench bunker and usually requiring a mid- to long-iron to reach the green. If maintained at tournament speeds (that is, 11 plus on the stimpmeter), the heaving 17th green would be nigh unplayable. At normal speeds, it is just fun, and as it is somewhat of a punchbowl a second shot of proper length will give a chance of par. Although the longest of the final seven holes, the 17th is possibly the least penal, in that for the bogey golfer anything more than a five can be achieved only with at least one serious mistake.

## RETURN TO THE TOWN

Standing at the back of the penultimate green, much of the West Links and the beach and the dunes that frame it can be seen, and if it is a clear day the views across the Firth of Forth to the East Neuk of Fife can be spectacular. Then, when the player turns round and climbs onto the 18th tee, they are welcomed back into the town. Much as at St Andrews, the 1st and 18th holes at the West Links offer a gateway away from and back into the 'real' world. In front of the player is the 18th green, sitting on a plateau, and beyond the green the common links extend towards the small port and will be full of families with small children at weekends and summer days. The town itself wraps around the right-hand side of the view, ending at the North Berwick Golf Club. From that modest but warming structure, a road extends back towards the tee, with cars parked along the way.

While the 18th is a simple one on the card, being only 274 yards and drivable by most reasonably good players, the cars on the right are always in mind, and more than a few golfers will play safely to the left to protect either their score or their own vehicle. It is an easy par four – a hole that the skilled player should take three strokes more often than five. Regardless of what you score, however, it is nearly impossible to finish the round without a smile.

The West Links at North Berwick is that kind of course. There are harder courses even in its immediate vicinity, such as Muirfield (see page 60), and others that are at least as charming, in their own way, such as Kilspindie. None, however, can be compared to North Berwick, for it is a unique slice of golfing history and design. The best clubs, such as North Berwick, give you pleasure from the time you lace on your shoes to the time you wrenchingly depart.

# THE REDAN – WHAT'S IN A NAME?
One of the most famous golf holes in the world

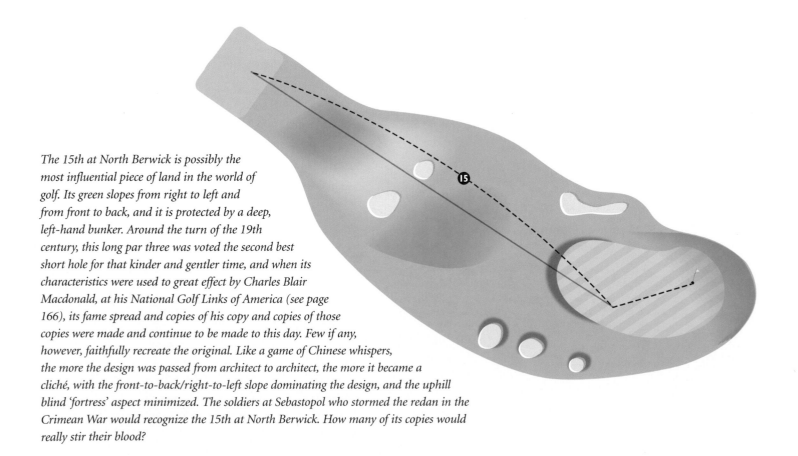

*The 15th at North Berwick is possibly the most influential piece of land in the world of golf. Its green slopes from right to left and from front to back, and it is protected by a deep, left-hand bunker. Around the turn of the 19th century, this long par three was voted the second best short hole for that kinder and gentler time, and when its characteristics were used to great effect by Charles Blair Macdonald, at his National Golf Links of America (see page 166), its fame spread and copies of his copy and copies of those copies were made and continue to be made to this day. Few if any, however, faithfully recreate the original. Like a game of Chinese whispers, the more the design was passed from architect to architect, the more it became a cliché, with the front-to-back/right-to-left slope dominating the design, and the uphill blind 'fortress' aspect minimized. The soldiers at Sebastopol who stormed the redan in the Crimean War would recognize the 15th at North Berwick. How many of its copies would really stir their blood?*

# CARNOUSTIE
## Carnoustie, Angus

Like St Andrews (see page 40), Carnoustie's golf courses lie on public land and are managed by a trust overseen by both the local council and the local golf clubs. At Carnoustie, however, there is no dominant club, and the trust has been involved in a number of changing and intricate relationships.

Over the past 75 years the best golfers in the world have periodically come to Carnoustie. None has dominated the course, although the American golfing hero Ben Hogan came close in 1953 when a nearly flawless final round in The Open gave him victory by four shots. There has not been a player, however, professional or amateur, who has said that they were not tested by the challenge, and there are many who have failed the test.

### EARLY HISTORY

It is not easy to say how this situation came about, because the genesis of the course was modest. In fact, some accounts say that the first 'commoner' to play golf at Carnoustie was the local grandee Sir Robert Maule in the mid-17th century. Until the mid-19th century, golf was very informal, but as with other seaside venues Carnoustie began to prosper around

that time with the advent in 1838 of rail links and a general economic boom, which fuelled the love of the people for the new concept of leisure time.

To meet the burgeoning demand for golf, a local worthy, Robert Chambers, built the first proper course at Carnoustie and then Alan Robertson was brought from St Andrews to improve these early efforts in 1840. This he did, laying out ten holes, many of whose features (for example, the 18th green) can be seen today. Robertson came back to revise the course in 1855, and over the next 40 years extensions and mprovements were made by numerous professionals. First there was George Morris (Old Tom's younger brother and the green-keeper at Carnoustie), and then Old Tom himself, and then Bob Simpson, the golfer and skilled club-maker who had moved to Angus from Fife, and then

Old Tom with Archie Simpson (Bob's brother). Golf-course architecture was very much a family affair in those early days. By 1897, these changes had resulted in a course that extended to 6,082 yards – a long one in those days before the rubber-core Haskell ball.

## CARNOUSTIE GOLF LINKS (CHAMPIONSHIP COURSE) –
### Carnoustie, Angus

Alan Roberton, 1848; Old Tom Morris, 1873; Bob Simpson, 1888; James Braid, 1926; James Braid and James Wright, 1931
Major events: Open Championship 1931, 1937, 1953, 1968, 1975, 1999, 2007; Amateur Championship 1947, 1966, 1971, 1992; Ladies' British Open Amateur 1961, 1973; Scottish Open 1995, 1996.

### CARD OF THE COURSE

| HOLE | NAME | YARDS | PAR | HOLE | NAME | YARDS | PAR |
|---|---|---|---|---|---|---|---|
| 1. | Cup | 406 | 4 | 10. | South America | 466 | 4 |
| 2. | Gulley | 463 | 4 | 11. | Dyke | 383 | 4 |
| 3. | Jockie's Burn | 358 | 4 | 12. | Southward Ho | 499 | 4 |
| 4. | Hillocks | 412 | 4 | 13. | Whins | 176 | 3 |
| 5. | Brae | 415 | 4 | 14. | Spectacles | 514 | 5 |
| 6. | Hogan's Alley | 578 | 5 | 15. | Lucky Slap | 472 | 4 |
| 7. | Plantation | 410 | 4 | 16. | Barry Burn | 248 | 3 |
| 8. | Short | 183 | 3 | 17. | Island | 461 | 4 |
| 9. | Railway | 478 | 4 | 18. | Home | 499 | 4 |
| **OUT** | | **3,703** | **36** | **IN** | | **3,718** | **35** |
| | | | | **TOTAL** | | **7,421** | **71** |

### BID FOR THE OPEN

In 1926 the Carnoustie trust consulted five-times Open champion James Braid on ways to strengthen the course with an eye towards joining the rota of venues for The Open. Braid's work, which was completed in 1927, essentially kept the existing routing but added both length and bunkers, and very much tightened up the entrances to the greens. The results were looked on favourably by the Royal & Ancient Golf Club of St Andrews, who granted Carnoustie the 1930 Scottish Amateur and 1931 Open.

While the Amateur Championship was successful, there was some criticism of the finishing holes, which consisted of three short par fours and a par three.

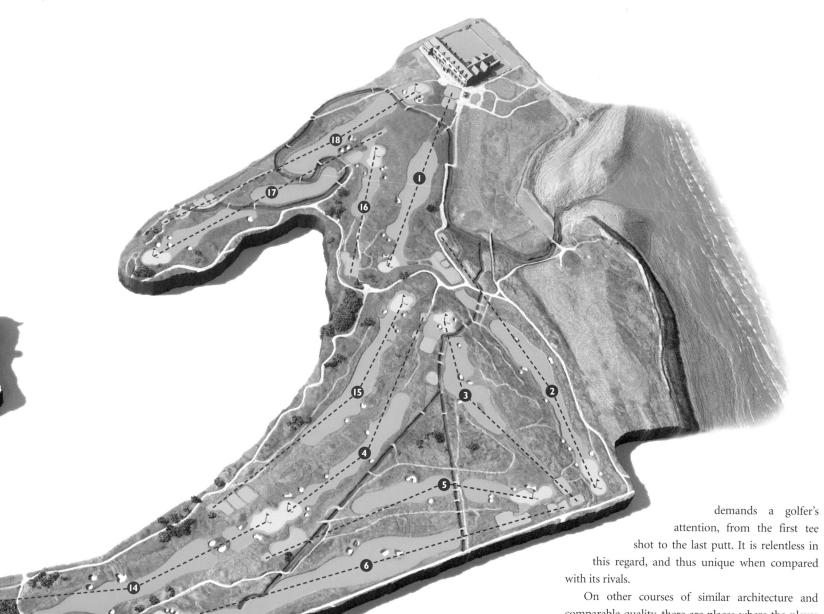

Therefore between that event and the 1931 Open, significant changes were made based on some of Braid's unaccepted recommendations; they were carried out under the supervision of James Wright, captain of the Dalhousie Club. This revision added today's 13th hole and created three great ones (today's 16th, 17th and 18th). The result was pretty much the course now played, yet Carnoustie still continues to evaluate and revise the course regularly.

## UNDERSTANDING THE CHALLENGE

So what is this course, and why do so many players – from the finest in the world to the bogey golfer – seem

to find it so tough? There are two burns that affect the drive on one hole, the approach shots on three others and wayward shots in a few more cases. Yes, the course is long and can play longer when the wind howls, but this is the case for just about any links golf course. There are no brutally long holes or any significant forced carries. The bunkers are well placed, but there are ways to avoid them, and in most cases those ways are obvious or intuitive to the golfer who is paying attention. Attention...now maybe that is the key.

Arnold Haultain wrote in 1910 that attention was the most important element of the stroke. Without it, he postulated, all the good work that goes into a golf swing can be negated. An obvious corollary is that the more a golf shot demands attention, the harder it is to keep the other elements of the swing (for example, sensation, imagination and action) under control. Well, more than any other golf course, Carnoustie

demands a golfer's attention, from the first tee shot to the last putt. It is relentless in this regard, and thus unique when compared with its rivals.

On other courses of similar architecture and comparable quality, there are places where the player can relax, even if just a little bit, and swing freely. The 18th at the Old Course at St Andrews, the 12th at Royal Dornoch (see page 54), the 12th and 13th at Muirfield (see page 60) and the first three holes at Royal Troon (see page 58) come to mind. At Carnoustie, however, golfers can never drop their guard and this continuous mental pressure is what makes the course such a test.

## AN EXACTING EXAMINATION

Only those whose nerves are fragile to begin with are intimidated by the 406-yard 1st with its burn front and left of the tee. While the drive is semiblind and there is a big bunker to the right, a solid poke down the middle will leave a short-iron approach to a hole sitting in a small valley. Paying attention is the primary requirement on this hole and if the player does do so a par should be their reward.

A much sterner test is the 463-yard 2nd, with its annoying pot bunker right in the middle of the fair-

*A skilfully executed drive over the diagonal hazards to the right will leave this seemingly benign shot to the 3rd green. However, if the pitch is too short or hit with too much spin, Jockie's Burn awaits.*

way, at a distance calculated to catch the drives of most mortals. This invention of James Braid's is one of the most iconic of the centre-line hazards beloved of many Golden Age architects. From the tee there are four options: try to carry the bunker, to lay up short, or to play left or right of it. Each has its own risks and rewards. However, even after the player has planned their strategy, it can be very hard to execute, particularly since the bunker is very prominent during the pre-shot routine. Unless the bunker has been carried, the second shot will be a long one, to a narrow, two-tiered green. A five is a good score here for most golfers, but a golfer can require many more strokes if they lose concentration.

The 358-yard 3rd was revamped for the 2007 Open. It requires careful thought not only on the second shot to a green perched above Jockie's Burn but also off the tee, because a series of hillocks and bunkers have defined and added a number of options. Carnoustie provides a little respite at the 412-yard 4th, but if the player opens their shoulders too much on the tee they are liable to end up hitting out of the right rough with a semiblind shot to a well-bunkered green.

Confusion prevails at the 415-yard 5th not only off the tee but also on possibly the best green complex on the course. The second shot requires the proper line and length, and once these and the appropriate club

have been chosen it is still important to keep focused because all sorts of bad things can and will happen here. By now the golfer will hopefully have realized that they are playing over all points of the compass, but in a non-predictable way. Keep that, too, in the back of the mind.

Hogan's Alley, the 578-yard 6th, is rightly famous and perhaps the epitome of the theme used here to describe the course. While there are more than a few ways to play this hole, if a player wants to maximize their chances for birdie they must do as Ben Hogan did and hit two shots down the left-hand side, flirting with the out-of-bounds in both cases. Hogan did it flawlessly four times in a row on his way to winning the 1953 Open, but he was a man whom nobody could ever fault for losing attention.

The 410-yard 7th has the same look and feel as the 6th, but is shorter and requires a full iron rather than a pitch to the similarly narrow and left-to-right, canted green. First of the par threes, the 183-yard 8th demands a smooth swing with the right club to avoid the numerous hazards around the green. To achieve this, a player's powers of concentration and attention must still be intact. A diagonal ridge in the green then complicates the second shot on the 478-yard 9th. Famed more for its name (South America) than for its quality is the 466-yard 10th, where two solid hits will

In this view from behind the 15th, the subtle linkages
between the sinuous fairway and fall-away green can be
seen. A pin behind the right-hand front bunker as per
the picture is particularly challenging.

## CARNOUSTIE'S MOST SIGNIFICANT EXPORT
### Golf professionals, golf teachers and golf clubmakers

*Many Scottish cities have been influential
worldwide culturally and economically:
for example, Dundee imported jute and
exported jam and perfected popular
journalism; Edinburgh imported claret
and exported the Enlightenment and
perfected town planning; and St Andrews
imported clerics and exported scholars
and perfected the game of golf. While
Carnoustie never really imported much,
and other than its own golf course has
never really even perfected much, it has
exported great golf professionals, golf
teachers and golf clubmakers to the rest
of the world.*

*Among these travellers were the Smith
brothers (Alex and Willie), George Low,
the Simpson brothers (Jack Simpson won
The Open in 1884, and Archie and Bob
were regular contenders as well as golf
architects), the clubmaker, architect and
teacher to royalty Cuthbert Butchart
and well over 100 others, mostly in the
1890–1920 period when golf was just
beginning to get established in the New
World. First among equals must be Stewart
Maiden, who learned the Carnoustie swing
by copying Archie Simpson and then passed
the principles of that swing to a young
American, Bobby Jones, who went
on to become one of the most successful
golfers of all times.*

reach a green that sits much farther away from the fronting burn than it seems from the fairway.

While the 383-yard 11th is relatively short but requires precision, the 499-yard 12th can be either a possible eagle if played as a par five or a far too easy double-bogey if played as a par four. Like the 8th, the 176-yard 13th rewards concentration and the true shot and punishes the smallest of errors. It is the last truly short hole.

### THE CLOSING HOLES

Even if a golfer has played reasonably well to now, getting a good score at Carnoustie requires complete mental discipline over the final five holes. The 514-yard 14th should be relatively easy for the good player seeking a five, although it is important to keep the head down to hit the ball over the centre-line hazard of the Spectacles bunkers carved into a hillside. Otherwise the player might hope that on the day the committee has not decided to reduce this hole to a par four.

As hard or harder than the previous hole is the 472-yard 15th, with its reverse camber in the fairway and the protected hidden green. And then the golfer reaches the 16th – 248 yards to a narrow plateau green. In five tries, Tom Watson never did better than four on this hole when he won the 1975 Open here. If you can

afford a four, take it. If you must get a three or better, well, just pay very close attention to your game.

Provided golfers knows their distances, are comfortable with their swings and can block out the view of the seeming ribbons of intersecting water that confront them on the tee, the drive on the 461-yard 17th is simple. If a bad shot is hit, just find it and hit it again, safely. Andres Romero forgot this simple lesson in 2007 and lost his chance to become Open champion.

In the last two Opens at Carnoustie, there has been more excitement on the 499-yard 18th than at any other championship venue's finisher, even though it is not an overly complicated hole. What is needed is a solid tee shot to a reasonably wide fairway and then a lay-up short of the Barry Burn or just over it, depending on circumstances. In the 1999 Open this closing hole witnessed Justin Leonard's careless bogey, the opera buffo of Jean van de Velde's adventures in and around the Barry Burn and the two superb long-irons by Paul Lawrie to get into and then win the play-off. In the 2007 Open, both Sergio Garcia and Padraig Harrington seemed determined to give the hole away, but in the end Harrington's greater attention eventually won the day.

When John Sutherland was appointed secretary of Dornoch in 1883 he was just 19 years old and the club he inherited was even younger, although some form of golf had been played on the links for many centuries before. The course he and his fellow members were playing over was a primitive one, by all accounts, and so in 1886 Sutherland took it on himself to bring in the greatest golf architect of the day, Old Tom Morris, who added nine holes to an existing nine-hole layout. Sutherland confirmed in 1892 that, while the lack of funds did not allow the club to complete all of his plans, Morris 'left minute instructions as to its ultimate extension'. This extension can be seen in maps dated 1892, which show many features of the course that exists today. However, as good as the course then was, Sutherland was still not satisfied.

## SUTHERLAND'S CHANGES

Inordinate effort was put into improving the nature of the course. Since Morris had moved green sites from hollows to plateaus, golfers could not rely on gravity to get their ball towards the hole. Chipping and putting skills became more crucial and there was a need for finer grasses and more tender loving care to allow that skill to be effected. Much as Old Tom had done at the Old Course at St Andrews (see page 40), Sutherland worked over the greens relentlessly, over many seasons, most notably by bringing in fishwives from nearby Embo to pluck weeds off the gradually improving putting surfaces every year.

Gradually and increasingly, the condition of the course improved to match its excellent design and incredible natural beauty. With increased prosperity and improved rail links, and the patronage of the Duchess of Sutherland, who facilitated the awarding of 'Royal' status to the club, Dornoch became a destination resort for some of the great and good of the English golfing world. The five-times Open champion J.H. Taylor was an early visitor, and he worked with Sutherland to extend the course to more than 6,000 yards (5,500 metres) in 1906, to make it both more interesting and more adaptable in the new era of the rubber-core Haskell ball.

Other changes were made, and by the time of the Second World War the course was a hidden gem, as glorious as golf-course architecture could be, but paradoxically both isolated from its natural market and increasingly drawn into the realities of the greater world. The starkest of these realities – the Second World War – led to the military confiscating six holes for an airfield. When John Sutherland died, aged 77, in 1941, the course he had so carefully nurtured had been emasculated by events beyond his control.

This emasculation, however, turned out to be a stroke of luck, because it forced the club to consider an alternative routing, which would extend the course outwards and make use of some fine golfing land close to the sea. In the end, a very good 6,000-yard (5,500-metre) course was replaced by a great 6,500-yard (6,000-metre) one, which can and will be seamlessly stretched to nearly 7,000 yards (6,400 metres) in the future.

## NON-GOLFING DISTRACTIONS

More than any true championship course, Royal Dornoch gives the initial impression of a holiday course used by all types of player, while golfers and non-golfers watch from the clubhouse or wander down the road to and from the glorious beach. Standing on the 1st tee, a player cannot help but wonder, is this really a great golf course? It all seems so simple: hit the ball down the fairway and put it on the green. But maybe they miss their drive, or the second shot, or both, have a missable putt for a par and end up

# ROYAL DORNOCH
## Dornoch, Sutherland

Some great golf courses are exquisitely challenging. Others bring a smile to your face that takes hours, if not a lifetime, to erase. Of all the courses in the world, however, Royal Dornoch combines these two characteristics most seamlessly. In that sense, it is the perfect golf course.

with a five. The 184-yard 2nd seems inviting, just a medium-length shot to an apparently receptive green. If a player happens to hit the green and make par, they trundle to the 3rd wondering what all the fuss is about, but if the 2nd green is missed they may end up with a score in double figures, as many great players have done in competition.

After the 2nd, a player may wonder where the golf course is going. Well, if it is the springtime, they will walk though a corridor of gorse and broom and then come on a vista of spectacular beauty. More than 50 per cent of the course is in their purview, and all they can see is golf holes and golfers, framed by the sea to the right and by the hills straight ahead and to the left.

The 413-yard 3rd is a hole that is seemingly simple, yet complicated off the tee because of bunkers to the right and a sharp left-to-right cant at the green end of the fairway. On this green, a golfer begins to appreciate the time and effort put in by John Sutherland and his Embo fishwives. The 3rd is as true as a green can be, and as subtle as a player would ever want it to be.

The 422-yard 4th at Dornoch is one of the finest golf holes in the world. For the accomplished player, it requires a long and precise drive, a second shot of great imagination and two skilful putts. The green and its approaches are wildly undulating and even for the less-skilled golfer, the hole will never fail to amuse. The 353-yard 5th, with its magnificent view from the tee, is a favourite of honorary member and five-time Open champion, Tom Watson. It seems like a possible birdie, but with its long deceptively angled green and subtly canting fairway, par here is a good score.

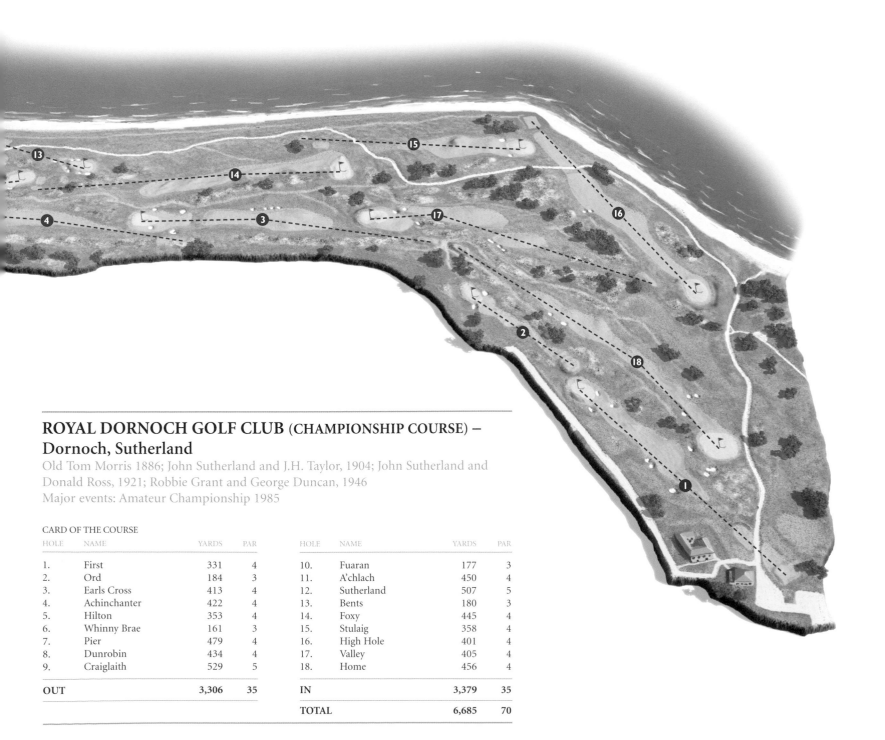

# ROYAL DORNOCH GOLF CLUB (CHAMPIONSHIP COURSE) – Dornoch, Sutherland
Old Tom Morris 1886; John Sutherland and J.H. Taylor, 1904; John Sutherland and Donald Ross, 1921; Robbie Grant and George Duncan, 1946
Major events: Amateur Championship 1985

CARD OF THE COURSE

| HOLE | NAME | YARDS | PAR | HOLE | NAME | YARDS | PAR |
|------|------|-------|-----|------|------|-------|-----|
| 1. | First | 331 | 4 | 10. | Fuaran | 177 | 3 |
| 2. | Ord | 184 | 3 | 11. | A'chlach | 450 | 4 |
| 3. | Earls Cross | 413 | 4 | 12. | Sutherland | 507 | 5 |
| 4. | Achinchanter | 422 | 4 | 13. | Bents | 180 | 3 |
| 5. | Hilton | 353 | 4 | 14. | Foxy | 445 | 4 |
| 6. | Whinny Brae | 161 | 3 | 15. | Stulaig | 358 | 4 |
| 7. | Pier | 479 | 4 | 16. | High Hole | 401 | 4 |
| 8. | Dunrobin | 434 | 4 | 17. | Valley | 405 | 4 |
| 9. | Craiglaith | 529 | 5 | 18. | Home | 456 | 4 |
| **OUT** | | **3,306** | **35** | IN | | 3,379 | 35 |
| | | | | TOTAL | | 6,685 | 70 |

## EXCEPTIONALLY TRICKY FOXY
### 14th hole

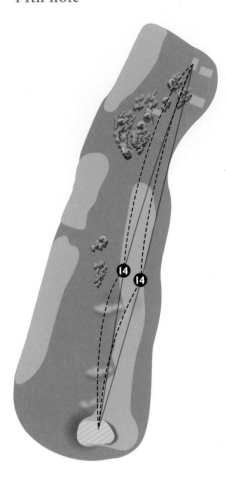

*The 14th at Royal Dornoch has it all. There is ample room on the tee shot, but the closer a player hits the ball towards the left rough the more likely they are to be able to go for the green. The fairway is beautifully crumpled, and also bottlenecked at a distance of 290 yards (265 metres), which can require the big hitter with little nerve to lay up. Regardless of how close a golfer is to the green, the approach is never easy and can always be played high or low and with or without spin. The plateau green complex is just that – complex – heaving and rolling over the land like a microcosm of its fairway. All that is missing are bunkers. Who needs them?*

## SOME OF THE POSTWAR HOLES

The immensely attractive 6th hole has fooled many experts into believing that it has been there forever, but it is the first of the magnificent postwar holes. Cut into a hillside of whins, it begs to be hit, but far too rarely is, and recovering par from the hollow to the right is a task beyond most golfers.

From there the golfer climbs a narrow path through the gorse to the 479-yard 7th, which is a long, hard slog, but more subtle than it seems. The back tee gives glorious views as to where the player has been and where they are going. On the 434-yard 8th a blind drive plunges over a hill to the most crumpled and bumpy fairway a golfer will ever see. The green is a punchbowl, which falls away from front to back. Front pin positions can be treacherous, particularly when the course is playing fast and firm.

At the 529-yard 9th the player turns back towards home, and it becomes immediately apparent why the course had to be routed up the hill to the 7th and 8th. There is barely room for one hole on the land between the sea and the hill of gorse. This is the first par five at Royal Dornoch, and to the right are humps and hollows that will only impede the progress of a drive and complicate the second shot. To the left, near the edge of the beach, past 220 yards (200 metres) or so, is a gradual downslope that propels the accurately and solidly hit drive to a place where a mid-iron can be hit at the pin. This is only the most obvious of the 'fast lanes' at Dornoch. (There are others down the centre of the 3rd, the left of the 4th, the middle of the 11th, the centre of the 12th, the left of the 14th and the centre of the 18th.) On each occasion, a shot with the proper line and length will reap a great reward, often 50 yards (45 metres) and more, but, most importantly, hitting the line without the length will get a player nowhere, and hitting the length without the line can be disastrous.

On the 9th, if a golfer tries for the fast lane and pulls the ball, it will stop abruptly in heavy rough, at least 280 yards (255 metres) from the green. Suddenly, a possible birdie-four becomes a possible bogey-six. Such are the ineffable vagaries of links golf.

## THE NEED FOR ACCURACY

The back nine at Royal Dornoch begins with a seemingly innocuous par three. The double-plateau green seems inviting, framed by the gorse and the sea and most of the rest of the course. From the medal tee, all a player has to do is hit a short-iron, have a putt or two and be gone. Or so it seems. While hitting the green may seem easy, not hitting it can be disastrous, and the more the hole is played the more intimidating the tee shot becomes. A three on this hole is a very good score.

Another great hole is the 450-yard 11th, which snakes through the gorse past the sea, and requires two or three good shots to get on the green. This green was at one time played from the 6th tee, and the remnants of this orientation can be seen in the back half. On the 507-yard 12th, a lovely short par five, a golfer can at last open their shoulders and try to hit the ball right-to-left towards a shallow valley and then use either a low hook or a high cut onto the green. This green was redesigned by John Sutherland from Old Tom Morris's punchbowl to the left; the hump that was added to protect the left side makes it one of the most interesting green sites in the world. The 180-yard 13th is a punchbowl par three that has gone in and out of the routing several times, and is more picturesque than difficult.

Then comes the world-famous Foxy hole – the 445-yard 14th (see feature). The 358-yard 15th is a highly underrated short par four, which is drivable by the best players today in fast and firm conditions, but whose Redan-like green (see  page 169) makes it a great test of the short game. Many consider the 16th to be the weakest hole on the course, due to its flat skyline green, but Peter Allis considers it one of his favourites. The tee is hard by the beach and an old quarry cuts into the fairway on the left, which make the hole one of the strictest tests of driving on the course. Judging distance for the second shot is always difficult, and a par is well earned on this hole. The 405-yard 17th turns back to the north, and is similar to the 8th with a drive either to a guarded left corner or straight over a hill. It too has a punchbowl green, which is among the largest and most complex on a course known for its expansive greens. The 456-yard 18th is relentlessly challenging, requiring two solid shots to reach a large obscured green. With whins to the right and left off the tee, if a four is required it can be a tense slog, relieved only by the stunning views of Struie Hill across the Dornoch Firth if the golfer has the vision (or misfortune) to look up.

## THE PERFECT COURSE?

All in all, the perfection that Sutherland strove to create at Royal Dornoch is largely there. The green sites and surfaces are magnificent. The playing angles and micro-undulations in the fairways are exquisite. The course flows beautifully from tee to green to tee. Most importantly, what imperfections the course does have only serve to highlight its overall quality and mystery. Complete perfection would ruin some of the fun.

*From behind the 14th green looking north the golfer can see how the back nine flows along the seaside looked down upon by some of the finest mountains in Sutherland.*

# ROYAL TROON
## Troon, Ayrshire

Much like the Old Course at St Andrews (see page 40), the more a player experiences Royal Troon the more they relish it and rise to its challenge. And then, the more they think about the course, the more attractive it becomes.

At first glance, Royal Troon appeals least of The Open venues. The first holes are too straightforward, the middle ones too complicated and the last ones just too hard. It is difficult to find a rhythm there, but underneath Royal Troon's awkwardness – and within the shingle beach, the main road, the airport and the caravan park that frame it – is a gem-like beauty that has to be experienced to be appreciated.

According to conventional wisdom concerning the three championship courses on the west coast of Scotland, Prestwick (see page 44) has more history and the quirkiness loved by many, Turnberry (see page 68) appeals more immediately to the eye and is larger, while Royal Troon lies somewhere between the two. It is more respected than loved. However, a closer examination of Royal Troon will reveal that it is larger and possesses more obviously great holes than Prestwick and has more quirk and history than does Turnberry.

### GRADUAL EVOLUTION
While Royal Troon was founded in 1878, it took ten years to get 18 proper golf holes, which were designed over time by George Strath and Willie Fernie. In the the next 35 years, changes were made to improve the course by the committee of the club, but, when they were asked to prepare for their first Open Championship, they hired James Braid to bring the course up to (then) modern standards. Other than 'tiger' back tees added to many holes to lengthen the course and a new green built for the 9th, Royal Troon looks today very much as Braid left it in 1923.

One hole that could not be lengthened is the 1st, because the championship tee sits perched on a mound

at the extreme northern end of the property, in full view of the passing cars. It is a 361-yard hole that was driven regularly by the professionals in the 1982 Open when the wind was strong from behind and the turf was firm, and can be reached even by lesser mortals in the 21st century. It is a simple hole, but a drive into the often-thick Troon rough can lead to trouble. The next two holes are also short par fours, while the 558-yard 4th, the 210-yard 5th and the 599-yard 6th complete the march along the shore, with a strong short hole sandwiched between two very good three-shotters. The latter are very reminiscent of Turnberry to the south, with fairways laid along a winding valley, leading to tiered greens resting in the dunes. An air of peacefulness prevails in these six opening holes – due partly to their gentleness and partly to their proximity to the sea. Perhaps this peacefulness and relative similarity is why Royal Troon does not get the respect it deserves. Well, if a player does not like tranquillity, the final 12 holes will suit them.

### INCREASING THE CHALLENGE
The 403-yard 7th is a fine hole from an elevated tee into a well-defended fairway, requiring both strategy and precise execution.

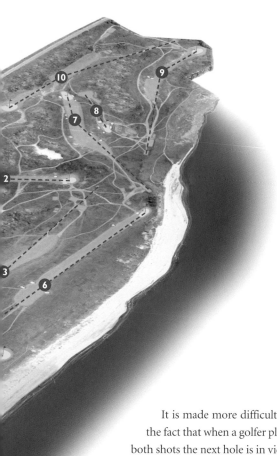

# ROYAL TROON GOLF CLUB (OLD COURSE) –
## Troon, Ayrshire

George Strath and Willie Fernie, 1888 and James Braid, 1923
Major events: Ladies' British Open Amateur 1904, 1925, 1952, 1984; Open
Championship 1923, 1950, 1962, 1973, 1982, 1989, 1997, 2004; Amateur
Championship 1956, 1968, 1978, 2003

CARD OF THE COURSE

| HOLE | NAME | YARDS | PAR | HOLE | NAME | YARDS | PAR |
|---|---|---|---|---|---|---|---|
| 1. | Seal | 361 | 4 | 10. | Sandhills | 438 | 4 |
| 2. | Black Rock | 391 | 4 | 11. | The Railway | 488 | 4 |
| 3. | Gyaws | 379 | 4 | 12. | The Fox | 431 | 4 |
| 4. | Dunure | 558 | 5 | 13. | Burmah | 470 | 4 |
| 5. | Greenan | 210 | 3 | 14. | Alton | 178 | 3 |
| 6. | Turnberry | 599 | 5 | 15. | Crosbie | 481 | 4 |
| 7. | Tel-el-Kebir | 403 | 4 | 16. | Well | 542 | 5 |
| 8. | Postage Stamp | 123 | 3 | 17. | Rabbit | 222 | 3 |
| 9. | The Monk | 423 | 4 | 18. | Craigend | 453 | 4 |
| **OUT** | | **3,447** | **36** | **IN** | | **3,703** | **35** |
| | | | | **TOTAL** | | **7,150** | **71** |

It is made more difficult by the fact that when a golfer plays both shots the next hole is in view, and that one is the (in)famous Postage Stamp – the shortest hole in championship golf and one of the most unusual. From a tee high above the 7th green, the 123-yard 8th is just a drop kick onto a green that is bigger than it may seem when the wind is blowing – or even when it is calm. No championships are won at this hole, but some can be said to have been lost here – particularly Tiger Woods in 1997. Playing the Postage Stamp is one of the hundred things golfers should do before they die.

From there, the 423-yard 9th is a bit of a respite, but the 438-yard 10th has a blind drive over a huge sand hill onto a narrow fairway and then uphill again to an elusive green. The first 200 yards (183 metres) of the 488-yard, par-four 11th is a sea of gorse, and it played as one of the hardest 'par' fives in the 1962 Open, won by Arnold Palmer. Brutally hard two-shotters with blind shots, crumpled fairways and well-guarded greens are to be found on the 431-yard 12th, the 470-yard 13th and the 481-yard 15th. If Mark Calcavecchia had not improbably holed a 60-yard (55-metre) wedge shot on the 12th in the 1989 Open, his name would not be on the Claret Jug. While the 178-yard 14th and the 542-yard 16th are manageable, the 222-yard 17th is a long-iron to a green falling off on all sides. Fortunately, the 453-yard 18th is relatively easier – but only in this very tough company.

*Joyce Wethered once sank a putt on the 11th green just as a train passed by. Someone asked her if it had not bothered her. 'What train?' was her reply.*

As well as a course, Muirfield is a club – the Honourable Company of Edinburgh Golfers (HCEG), to be precise – and while the club preceded the course by a century and a half, its character and its values are embedded in its links, so the name Muirfield will be used hereafter to refer to both club and course. The first codified rules of golf were published in 1744 by the HCEG (when they were playing on Leith Links), and the principles underlying those 13 Rules still largely define the conduct of the game. To this day, Muirfield includes many important members of the Scottish judiciary, and underlying both the club and the course is a sense of justice.

## MIXED OPINIONS

Critics of the course use terms from the practice of law to damn Muirfield with faint phrase. Some call it too 'penal' – thinking particularly of the unforgiving rough, which can cause multiple lost shots, even on a calm day. Others, paradoxically, call it too 'fair', in that the course has relatively few blind shots and seems to have less of the element of chance built into the results obtained on other courses, such as Prestwick (see page 44) and the Old Course at St Andrews (see page 40). There is less mystery to the links of Muirfield than the more primordial courses, but there is also less uncertainty. In general, a well-planned and well-executed shot is rewarded, and one that goes awry is not. To connoisseurs of the vagaries of the game and the quirk of some of its courses, this is at least a venial sin.

The aficionados of Muirfield, on the other hand, see the course as a sea of relative tranquillity in a largely stormy world. While it has repeatedly proven its ability to test the finest players in the world, it can still be enjoyed by the club golfer of indifferent form, particularly if they are playing matchplay rather than strokeplay. It can be peaceful walking round Muirfield, and when the sun is shining the views over the course and across to Fife can be mesmerizing. It is hard to play Muirfield and not come off the 18th green with a quiet smile.

That the HCEG differs from clubs attached to most of the other great Scottish courses is first seen in the approach to it, which involves turning at a nearly imperceptible sign, then driving along a suburban road, to a small gate, through which the course can be seen in all its splendour. While this sort of set-up is common at courses in both England and America, it is fairly unusual in Scotland. Carnoustie (see page 50), the Old Course, Prestwick (see page 44) and North Berwick (see page 46) all sit within and are an integral part of their town or village. Muirfield is somehow set apart.

Once on the course itself, the player can marvel at the genius of the routing by Harry Colt in 1925. Building on the bones of the pre-Haskell-ball course designed by Old Tom Morris in 1892, Colt weaved his nines in an outward and an inward loop, both starting and ending at the same place, and offering constant changes in direction. While this was not the first great circular routing – Portmarnock (see page 118) and Royal County Down (see page 116) being earlier – it is arguably the most elegant, particularly in Colt's creative use of the ridge that bisects the course from the 5th tee to the 6th fairway, crossing the 4th, 12th, 13th and 11th holes in the process.

## FIRST IMPRESSIONS

While standing on the 1st tee, several other unique impressions emerge. For one thing, the course just does not look like any other links course. Muirfield grass seems to be of a lighter colour and the rough moves in the wind like grain. The course is also spread out over a vast area. Individual holes are evident, but they are not obviously linked together. Even when playing the course a golfer is

often not sure as to where the next hole might be until they exit the green. Muirfield will probably seem to be empty, even if it is a visitor day. There is little of the enforced intimacies that derive from the narrow routings of many of the older courses. If a bad or a good shot is hit, it will be seen only by playing companions and caddies. The player may also note that the holes they can clearly see from the clubhouse – 1, 18, 10 and 9 – intimate the double loop routing, unique among the current rota of Open courses.

From the 1st tee, a seeming ribbon of fairway surrounded by long grass gently curves to the right to a partially hidden green. Because it is slightly downhill, the hole is not as long as it appears, yet the demand of hitting a relatively solid and straight drive can be unnerving, and first-time visitors would be wise to hit a club within their capabilities. The second shot, even if with a mid- to long-iron, is less demanding than

# MUIRFIELD
## Gullane, East Lothian

Although the 'new' Muirfield was dismissed in 1892 as just an 'auld water meadie' (old water meadow), the land chosen is in fact superb for golf. The turf is ideal, and the holes flow through the links grasses like notes in a great symphony or phrases from a favourite novel. There is seduction rather than flash, and the golfer who is bored with Muirfield can only be tired with life itself.

it appears. While a nest of bunkers to the short-right looks menacing, par can be achieved by a player who can chip and putt.

The 1st green then flows seamlessly onto the 2nd tee, which is a lovely short par four tight up against the stone dyke boundary to the left. It seems wide, but as the fairway slopes sharply left it really is not, and a slightly pushed drive can leave the golfer either in a fairway bunker or perched on a slope trying to hit over green-side bunkers from an often dodgy lie. Once a route has been identified off the tee to the preferred position on the left, the long and narrow green makes proper club

selection key to conquering the 2nd. Even though the player will probably be hitting some sort of wedge, this is not the easiest of tasks so early in the round, particularly when there has not yet been time to judge the firmness and the pace of the greens.

On the 378-yard 3rd, the golfer can just see the flag through a gap in the ridge that bisects the fairway at the normal driving range. Going right or far left will leave a blind second shot to a green hidden on all but the entry side (left) to a clearing in the dunes.

## FALSE SENSE OF SECURITY

Up until now, canny club members might be level par, the touring professional one or two under and the straight-hitting visitor left wondering what all the fuss is about. The greens have all been relatively flat, if immaculate, and the views mostly limited and parochial. Two of the holes have been a drive and a pitch, and the fairways roll more gently than most

# THE HONOURABLE COMPANY OF EDINBURGH GOLFERS – Muirfield, Gullane, East Lothian

Harry Colt, 1925
Major events: Open Championship 1892, 1896, 1901, 1906, 1912, 1929, 1935, 1948, 1959, 1966, 1972, 1980, 1987, 1992, 2002; Amateur Championship 1897, 1903, 1909, 1920, 1926, 1932, 1954, 1974, 1990, 1998; Curtis Cup 1952, 1984; Walker Cup 1959, 1979; Ryder Cup 1973

## CARD OF THE COURSE

| HOLE | YARDS | PAR | HOLE | YARDS | PAR |
|------|-------|-----|------|-------|-----|
| 1. | 448 | 4 | 10. | 475 | 4 |
| 2. | 351 | 4 | 11. | 389 | 4 |
| 3. | 378 | 4 | 12. | 381 | 4 |
| 4. | 213 | 3 | 13. | 191 | 3 |
| 5. | 560 | 5 | 14. | 448 | 4 |
| 6. | 468 | 4 | 15. | 415 | 4 |
| 7. | 185 | 3 | 16. | 186 | 3 |
| 8. | 443 | 4 | 17. | 546 | 5 |
| 9. | 508 | 5 | 18. | 449 | 4 |
| OUT | 3,554 | 36 | IN | 3,480 | 35 |
| | | | TOTAL | 7,034 | 71 |

'proper' links courses. There have been no hidden bunkers and no heather and no gorse, and there are even trees to the left of each hole.

However, after emerging from the hollow of the 3rd green, the player walks left and upwards to the 4th tee and suddenly the land becomes more 'links-like'. The lower part of the course has been left behind and ahead is a classic par three, uphill to an exposed plateau green surrounded by bunkers. To the left are now not trees but unfettered views over the Firth of Forth; ahead is the long climbing 5th fairway and a lovely downhill green (the 12th). Whatever breeze there is will be heightened and the demands on shot-making intensified. At the 4th tee players must hit a

solid mid-iron to avoid the trouble, and at the 560-yard 5th they must avoid the hidden bunkers behind the apparently safe carry to the right and then hit two more solid shots to reach the green – if they are mortal. Suddenly, the concept that Muirfield is a penal course does not seem too unlikely at all.

At the very top and farthest part of the course are the 5th green and 6th tee, and the next four holes taking the player back to the clubhouse for the first time are as fine and varied a set of challenges as can be found in the world of golf. The 468-yard 6th is a blind dogleg left over a cliff that starts at the length of a modest drive. Bunkers left and a rough ridge to the right force the drive through a narrow channel, but if a

*At the top of the course, the views across the 11th and 5th greens over to Fife can be spectacular. The waves on the Forth testify to the fact that the wind is never far away from Muirfield.*

# PERFORMANCE INDICATOR
## A mirror into the golfer's soul

*The 17th at Muirfield is a protean hole, constantly changing its character as its environment shifts with the seasons. Downwind in a dry summer it can be two steady shots to the green. On a dreary winter day, into a north-east wind, the hole never seems to end. Its personality also reflects the mind of the beholder. To one on their game, regardless of handicap, a way to the hole can be navigated, yet to any golfer in poor form the myriad hazards can seem unavoidable. Such a hole is as fascinating in matchplay as strokeplay, and if it can be conquered, like Proteus, it might reveal the future of a player's game.*

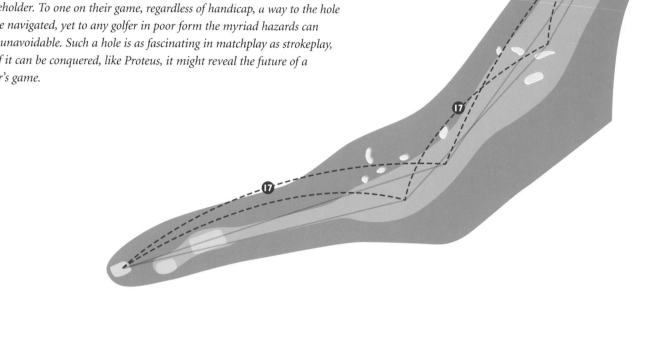

golfer manages to avoid the trouble an Elysian field awaits at the bottom of the hill, and a lovely, two-tiered green can be seen in the distance. The 185-yard 7th has one of the most interesting green complexes on the course – highly sloped with a varied range of hazards, while the 443-yard 8th, a downhill dogleg to the right with a nest of bunkers in the driving area, is often cited as one of the best holes in the world. The final hole on the outward half – the 508-yard 9th – is a classic 'par' four and a half, which still holds its own against modern technologies.

## THE SECOND NINE

The inward and inner loop of the course starts with a long but pedestrian two-shotter and then throws in a marvellous bit of quirk with a drive over a seemingly insurmountable hill at the 389-yard 11th. Once over the ridge, the 11th has a demanding shot to a well-guarded, skyline green. From this point near the top of the course, there then starts a series of lovely, downhill two-shotters, exposed to the wind, with views down to Fife and subtle hazards abounding on the fairways and around the greens. Punctuating this flow is the 191-

yard 13th, which climbs back up to a green heavily sloped from front to back. Ernie Els, who made a spectacular recovery from an impossible lie in a left-hand bunker there on the final round of his 2002 Open win, will probably never forget this hole.

The last of the short holes is the 186-yard 16th, with yet another false front. It is a hole on which to think par rather than birdie, especially for contenders in an Open Championship.

A possible opportunity for a birdie, or even eagle, occurs at the 546-yard 17th, yet this hole is as well known for its exposure of weaknesses as it is of strengths (see above). Several modern Opens have been won and lost here, often simultaneously. The most famous of these occasions was in the 1972 Open, when Lee Trevino improbably chipped in for a five while the leader, Tony Jacklin, three-putted for a six. In the 1987 and 1992 Opens, Paul Azinger and John Cook, respectively, faltered there while in the lead, giving Nick Faldo two of his three Open wins. In 2002, Gary Evans got into the play-off largely by making an improbable five after losing his second shot in the rough to the right of the green.

A superb finisher and the epitome of Muirfield, the 449-yard 18th has a narrow fairway with hazards at both sides, followed by a nerve-wracking second shot to a green sublimely poised in front of the members' lounge. In the 2007 British Senior Open, Tom Watson needed only a bogey to win and he just made that number after several errors along the way. It was Watson's second win at Muirfield – the first coming at the 1980 Open. The quality of the course is self-evident when a review is made of the winners from the Golden Age and modern era including Walter Hagen, Henry Cotton, Gary Player and Jack Nicklaus (in addition to those already mentioned). Even in the 19th century when Muirfield may have been a 'water meadow' the roll call reads Harold Hilton, Harry Vardon, James Braid and Ted Ray – all outstanding golfers of those earlier days.

All in all, playing Muirfield is one of the most special experiences in the world of golf – and do not forget to partake of the timeless lunch.

The mystery of Cruden Bay golf course is compounded for the first-time visitor by the fact that the links appear so benign. They roll gently on the lower land between the clubhouse and the dunes protecting the sea. But, of course, all links look more benign when viewed from a height, rather than at human eye-level. What seems gentle may in fact be rough, and what seems rough (such as a distant hill) may actually be brutal. A player has to get on the ground, with a club in hand, to understand any golf course, particularly Cruden Bay.

## PLAYING THE COURSE

Golfers walk down a steep hill to get to the 1st tee, standing hard by a pavilion that looks as if it has not changed since Victorian days. It has not, except it now just serves as a shelter from the elements. This opening hole of 415 yards is a challenging one, with a pinched driving area and a large, interesting green, built into a little dip in the flowing terrain: nothing special, but an easy bogey. The 331-yard 2nd raises the stakes a bit, as it were. It is possible to see the table-top green from the tee and this forces a lay-up shot and then a simple, but severe, test of the wedge game.

Then, at the 3rd, begins one of the most glorious stretches of links golf in the world. It is a tee shot seemingly into nothing. Although the hole is a mere 274 yards, only the fairway is visible, not the green. There is an opening in the dunes to the right, and the question is, does a golfer go for the gap or hit another lay-up iron as on the last hole? Going for the gap, hitting the ball straight and true, and then finding it on the green is as good as it gets in golf. Well, maybe not, for next is the 195-yard 4th that, with its view out over the Port Erroll estuary, and the green sitting naturally in the dunes fronting the sea, is a thrilling mid- to long-iron shot, depending on the wind.

The 5th and 6th are typically good links golf. The 455-yard 5th is one of those long par fours with a drive between dunes to a sheltered green – reminiscent of Turnberry (see page 68) or Birkdale (see page 86) – while the 525-yard 6th is a sinuous, reachable par five with one of the finest green complexes in golf. It is called Bluidy Burn to commemorate a battle in 1012 in which the Scots defeated the invading Danes, whose blood coloured the burn that runs in front of the green. Tom Simpson (who made significant changes to the course with W.H. Fowler in 1926) called this one of his favourite holes in the British Isles, rather ironically, as he had only re-routed the hole and kept the

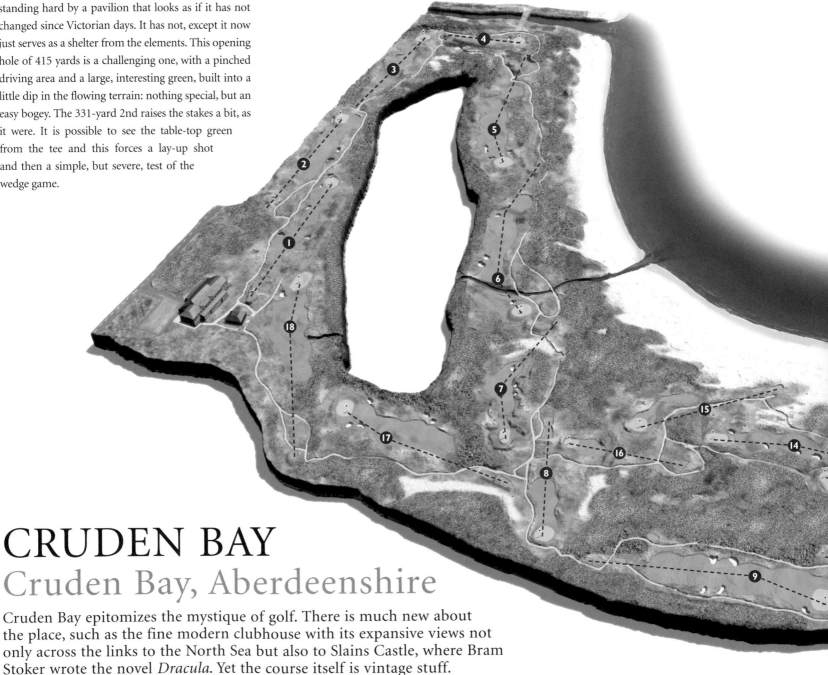

# CRUDEN BAY
## Cruden Bay, Aberdeenshire

Cruden Bay epitomizes the mystique of golf. There is much new about the place, such as the fine modern clubhouse with its expansive views not only across the links to the North Sea but also to Slains Castle, where Bram Stoker wrote the novel *Dracula*. Yet the course itself is vintage stuff.

original green site, designed by Old Tom Morris and Archie Simpson. The 380-yard 7th is a dogleg left to a skyline green hidden between sand hills.

## FURTHER MYSTERIES

At the 8th tee the mystery begins again, with the course suddenly moving away from the links. A driver is needed to reach the green cut into the hill of a head-land. There are all sorts of problems right and left, and the player can also see the gravelled path winding behind the green to a seemingly inordinate height. All things considered, a four at this 257-yard hole is a good score. Then, at the top of the headland, is a magnificent vista of golf holes, sand and sea. The 452-yard 9th, however, is unfortunately just a meadowland slog.

Not much better is the 380-yard 10th, with a drive from an elevated tee to what Andrew Kirkcaldy, a famous 19th-century professional, would have called a 'water meadie' (water meadow). The green, however, is linksy, fostering some hope, and that hope is fulfilled by the 147-yard 11th, 311-yard 12th and 575-yard 13th; all are back on the links and great holes, architec-turally in the league of the 3rd to 7th.

It is at the 389-yard 14th that the player reaches the 'House of Quirk'. A bit like the 3rd, the drive over

*Looking over the 17th green you can see the mound that dominates its fairway. Could it have once been a green or is it just a burial mound for fallen soldiers, or maybe both?*

crumpled land is obvious, even though the green is not. Once a player hits the approach to the marker post and walks over the hill, they realize what the term 'bathtub' green means. If links soil did not drain so well, it would be possible to hold a swimming gala on that landform after a heavy rainstorm.

And then the 15th is reached. There are many blind par threes in the world, but very few of them measure 200 yards (183 metres) over the side of a hill to a fall-away green. Needless to say, there is contro-versy in the golf world, and even at Cruden Bay, over the merits of Blin' Dunt. The 16th seems to be a simple, 180-yard par three, but when the course is fast and firm (that is, most of the summer), the only way to

get the ball to stay on the blind fall-away green is to have it land well short on the fronting plateau and hope that it will trickle gently down the hill. The 424-yard 17th is distinguished by a fortress-like landform in the middle of the fairway that some think is a burial ground for the Danes slain in 1012 and others suggest was the original Old Tom Morris/Archie Simpson green. Either way, the hole is creepy. Much more meadow than links, the 397-yard 18th is merely an adequate finishing hole.

Then, sitting in the clubhouse looking at those uniquely mysterious vistas, many a golfer wants to go out and play again. That in itself is the measure of a world-class golf course.

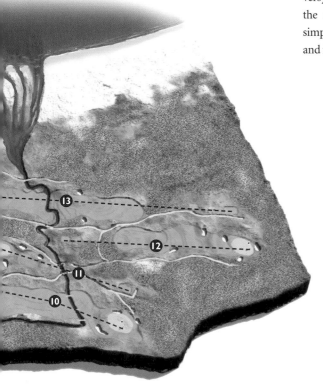

## CRUDEN BAY GOLF CLUB – Cruden Bay, Aberdeenshire

Old Tom Morris and Archie Simpson, 1899; and Tom Simpson and W.H. Fowler, 1926
Major events: Ladies' British Open Amateur 1997

### CARD OF THE COURSE

| HOLE | NAME | YARDS | PAR | HOLE | NAME | YARDS | PAR |
|---|---|---|---|---|---|---|---|
| 1. | Slains | 415 | 4 | 10. | Scaurs | 380 | 4 |
| 2. | Crochdane | 331 | 4 | 11. | Mishanter | 147 | 3 |
| 3. | Claypits | 274 | 4 | 12. | Finnyfal | 311 | 4 |
| 4. | Port Erroll | 195 | 3 | 13. | Bents | 575 | 5 |
| 5. | The Buck | 455 | 4 | 14. | Whins | 389 | 4 |
| 6. | Bluidy Burn | 525 | 5 | 15. | Blin' Dunt | 200 | 3 |
| 7. | Whaupshank | 380 | 4 | 16. | Coffins | 180 | 3 |
| 8. | Ardendraught | 257 | 4 | 17. | Bilin' Wallie | 424 | 4 |
| 9. | Hawklaw | 452 | 4 | 18. | Hame | 397 | 4 |
| **OUT** | | **3,284** | **36** | **IN** | | **3,003** | **34** |
| | | | | **TOTAL** | | **6,287** | **70** |

# GLENEAGLES
## Auchterarder, Perthshire

Although Gleneagles has never held a Major, its King's Course is not a minor one. Not being particularly long, the course no longer interests the European tour, and not being a links it is shunned by many overseas visitors to Scotland, who relate quality to proximity with the sea. The latter are sadly misinformed.

King's is not a links, but neither are the great heathland courses of England – or virtually all of the great courses in other parts of the world. What it does share with most of these others is its sandy soil, timeless architecture and turf that springs under the feet – and even crackles on the greens if a player is wearing metal spikes and the course is particularly fast and firm. The course was built to a James Braid design in 1919, five years before the magnificent Gleneagles Hotel opened its doors in the middle of the Roaring Twenties. It (and its sister course, the Queen's) were intended to act as a draw for hotel customers, and its elegance and beauty served this purpose very well. Still today the King's perfectly reflects and contributes to the grandeur of the Gleneagles experience.

### PLAYING THE COURSE

The 362-yard 1st is surprisingly prosaic, with a southerly drive to a largely featureless fairway towards a visible green cut into a far hill. The key to playing it well is taking a club or two more than normal on the second shot, because the green is long

## THE GLENEAGLES HOTEL (KING'S COURSE) – Auchterarder, Perthshire

James Braid, 1919
Major events: Ladies' British Open Amateur 1933, 1957; Curtis Cup 1936; Scottish Open 1987–94

CARD OF THE COURSE

| HOLE | NAME | YARDS | PAR | HOLE | NAME | YARDS | PAR |
|------|------|-------|-----|------|------|-------|-----|
| 1. | Dun Whinny | 362 | 4 | 10. | Canty Lye | 499 | 5 |
| 2. | East Neuk | 436 | 4 | 11. | Deil's Creel | 230 | 3 |
| 3. | Silver Tassie | 374 | 4 | 12. | Tappit Hen | 442 | 4 |
| 4. | Broomy Law | 466 | 4 | 13. | Braid's Brawest | 464 | 4 |
| 5. | Het Girdle | 178 | 3 | 14. | Denty Den | 309 | 4 |
| 6. | Blink Bonnie | 480 | 5 | 15. | Howe o' Hope | 459 | 4 |
| 7. | Kittle Kink | 444 | 4 | 16. | Wee Bogle | 158 | 3 |
| 8. | Whaup's Nest | 178 | 3 | 17. | Warslin' Lea | 377 | 4 |
| 9. | Heich o' Fash | 409 | 4 | 18. | King's Hame | 525 | 5 |
| | **OUT** | **3,327** | **35** | | **IN** | **3,463** | **36** |
| | | | | | **TOTAL** | **6,790** | **71** |

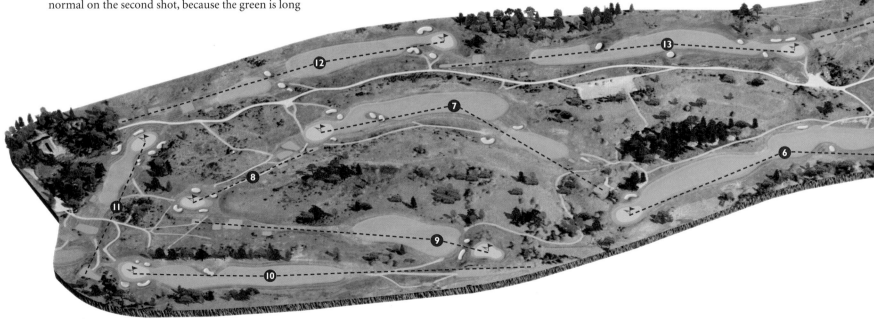

and the elevation more severe than might be thought. On the other hand, the 436-yard 2nd is a spectacular golf hole from a high tee down to a right–left sloping valley. The approach shot is downhill and provides a stunning view over the Perthshire countryside to a green set in the gorse and surrounded by bunkers. A highly enjoyable folly, the 374-yard 3rd needs a drive over heaving ground with no ultimate target in sight. Its green is hidden behind a high ridge and, if the player remembered to note the pin position indicated on the tee, a well-executed pitch will get them near the hole.

Meandering along the southern boundary of the property in a steady climb is the 4th, which at 466 yards makes it a difficult par four, even though the green is

Inspiration is needed, because the next several holes are challenging, starting with the 444-yard 7th, a superb dogleg through a valley to a green sitting well below the fairway. This is followed by the fine-looking but relatively tame, 178-yard 8th (again, those views...). The 409-yard 9th is not long for the current era of ever more powerful clubs, yet it defends itself well with a number of devices, including a stand of trees off the tee and two cavernous bunkers short of the elevated green. Then comes the 10th, a three-shot hole of nearly 500 yards, through the trees. If a player pars it they can reward themselves with a beverage from the half-way house behind the green.

### STERN TEST

On this upland section, in the middle of the course, the views are less expansive yet the golf is more intense, starting with the 230-yard 11th, a par three with a nest of bunkers short of the green – just where players not on their game are likely to end up. Rolling nicely through the trees is the 442-yard 12th, with its

*The downhill view to the 2nd green is one of the most pleasing in golf. You are now fully away from civilization and have only to play your shots and enjoy the tranquillity.*

par. What must it have been like when it was built? Next is the 309-yard 14th – one of the most entertaining, short par fours in the world. It is eminently drivable, but the shot needs to have the perfect line and length, because bunkers in the left fairway and behind the green punish the slightly imperfect shot. In the 1992 Scottish Open, Peter O'Malley eagled this to start a remarkable run of seven under for the last five holes, to win the championship over Colin Montgomerie.

The 459-yard 15th is a long par four, but downhill, with another back-to-front sloping green and beautiful views from the tee. It is followed by the lovely, 158-yard 16th, with its tee in the trees to a small green between two hillocks and surrounded by pot bunkers. This hole was built *c.*1980, replacing a more prosaic one to a valley on the left. At 377 yards, the 17th is not long for a hole in the final stretch, but it is a dogleg left with a reverse-camber fairway, which complicates the tee shot. The second shot, to a high plateau green, might be hit off a sidehill lie, making the judgement of line and length difficult. By taking the player uphill again, the King's Course offers another lovely view from the 18th tee.

For the mid-handicap player, the par-five 18th is two modest shots and then a pitch to a huge green, with a ridge running through its heart. A stronger player, however, can take on the gap between two hillocks and be rewarded with an iron to the green if the drive is hit straight; otherwise, they will be in the gorse, which is not a place to be – just ask Seve Ballesteros. The King's has never held a Major, but it is not a minor course.

relatively gentle. Fortunately, the 178-yard 5th allows a pause in the climb with a volcano short hole, which looks harder than it actually plays. The 480-yard 6th resumes the trek upwards and would be an easy three-shotter if not for the terrain and the sharply contoured green. As a player climbs, the views along this journey get better and better, and from the green they can be spectacular – looking west towards the Trossachs across fertile countryside. Although the colours of the view change according to the season, the scenery itself never fails to be inspirational.

wide fairway bisected by a gentle ridge that must be carried to see the pin. Its green is one of the best on the course, with pot bunkers on a hill to the left protecting the ideal angle of approach to the right–left, back–front sloping putting surface. After holing out, there is a short calming walk through a spinney of trees – one of a number of similar tee-to-green transitions on the course.

Such rest is needed, because the 464-yard 13th is the No. 1 handicap known as Braid's Brawest. Because of its length, the drive over a hill that must avoid a deep bunker on the preferred, left-side line of play, and a front-to-back, sloping green, the 13th is a very hard

# TURNBERRY
## Turnberry, Ayrshire

That the setting for the course, between the grand Turnberry hotel and the grander sea, is spectacular is agreed. What is not, however, is the greatness of the Ailsa Course. It is the latest of the courses on The Open rota, and as the new boy it is not always treated with the same deference as its older brethren.

The Ailsa Course at Turnberry peacefully occupies ideal linksland on the south Ayrshire coast. Three times this peace has been shattered. Firstly, the First World War intervened, and the hotel and golf course were taken over for military training. Secondly, at the start of the Second World War the Royal Air Force built an airfield mostly on the old Arran Course, but taking the Ailsa out of play too. Thirdly, under threat of bombers of the golfing kind, the course has been lengthened and strengthened. Through all of this, its worthiness has survived, thanks in no small part to the excellent architectural work of Philip Mackenzie Ross in 1951.

He laid his design over earlier routings of Willie Fernie (1901) and Major C.K. Hutchinson (1938), each of which had been disfigured by wartime activities. Ross used those routings, however, as a palimpsest rather than a template, and what is seen and played today is very much his course.

Some golfers argue that the routing at Turnberry is too pedestrian, going between the high dunes rather than across or astride them, while others wonder about lack of 'quirk', and some people consider that it is largely a resort rather than a club; yet these are mere quibbles. As a whole, Turnberry is as good as any but the very greatest courses, and its quality has been reflected in the names of its Open champions – Tom Watson, Greg Norman and Nick Price.

## BENIGN START

The opening hole can be a hard one for the average golfer, with its flanking fairway bunkers, heavy rough and well-guarded green, but for the elite players it is a drive and a flip – if they can hit the tee shot straight. It is also the last short two-shot hole that they will see. Although the 430-yard 2nd and 489-yard 3rd do not immediately stir the blood, they are solid and difficult par fours running parallel – the 2nd uphill and the 3rd downhill to a green overlooking Ailsa Craig. The 165-yard 4th is as close as the course gets to the sea, and it features an elevated and contoured green in the dunes.

While walking to the 5th tee, the player might wonder about all the fuss until they arrive there and see the heroic curve of the fairway between two ridges,

leading to a green to the left perched in the sand hills. It is the start of a magnificent run, and was even hospitable to the golfer when it was considered to be a par five. Now, as one of many long fours, it challenges even the best of players.

## MEMORABLE HOLES

The glorious stretch continues with the 231-yard 6th over a valley to an elusive green and then the 538-yard 7th, the first of the two long holes on the course – comparable to the 5th, but a true par five that has a sharper angle and a slightly more accessible green. A similar path is followed by the 454-yard 8th. Its similarity with the 5th and 7th could be a technical criticism of the routing, but each is so thrilling that the golfer never tires of playing these three holes.

After the 8th green, a short climb leads to a tee heading slightly inland, the reason for which is visible as the climb is finished – the famous lighthouse, which identifies Turnberry from both land and sea, stands in the way of another coast-hugging hole, so the 454-yard 9th heads inland. Its championship tee sits on a rocky promontory above the sea and its fairway is convex – unlike the concave holes up to this point. A straight drive over the small cairn in the middle of the fairway will allow for a view of the green and enough length will enable the golfer to hit the second shot with confidence. However, anything offline will be punished. Bruce's Castle, as the 9th is known, refers to the ruins where Robert I of Scotland spent his formative years and to which in 1306 he lay siege, in the first engagement of the war with England, which would lead to Scottish independence and his coronation.

First of the inward nine is the 458-yard 10th. It rolls gently downhill to a green with a fronting doughnut-shaped bunker, which obscures yards of dead ground in front of the green. The 174-yard 11th heads back inland and has a relatively trouble-free green.

*The 10th hole flows along the coast from Bruce's Castle and always plays longer than it looks. This is the last seaside hole at the Ailsa Course and perhaps its finest.*

# THE WESTIN TURNBERRY RESORT (AILSA COURSE) –
## Turnberry, Ayrshire
Willie Fernie, 1901; Major C.K. Hutchinson, 1938; and Philip Mackenzie Ross, 1951
Major events: Ladies' British Open Amateur 1912, 1921, 1937, 2002; Amateur Championship 1961, 1983, 1996, 2008; Walker Cup 1963; Open Championship 1977, 1986, 1994; Women's British Open 2002

CARD OF THE COURSE

| HOLE | NAME | YARDS | PAR | HOLE | NAME | YARDS | PAR |
|---|---|---|---|---|---|---|---|
| 1. | Ailsa Craig | 358 | 4 | 10. | Dinna Fouter | 458 | 4 |
| 2. | Mak Siccar | 430 | 4 | 11. | Maidens | 174 | 3 |
| 3. | Blaw Wearie | 489 | 4 | 12. | Monument | 446 | 4 |
| 4. | Woe-be-Tide | 165 | 3 | 13. | Tickly Tap | 412 | 4 |
| 5. | Fin' Me Oot | 476 | 4 | 14. | Risk-an-Hope | 449 | 4 |
| 6. | Tappie Tourie | 231 | 3 | 15. | Ca Canny | 209 | 3 |
| 7. | Roon the Ben | 538 | 5 | 16. | Wee Burn | 458 | 4 |
| 8. | Goat Fell | 454 | 4 | 17. | Lang Whang | 558 | 5 |
| 9. | Bruce's Castle | 454 | 4 | 18. | Ailsa Hame | 465 | 4 |
| **OUT** | | **3,595** | **35** | **IN** | | **3,629** | **35** |
| | | | | **TOTAL** | | **7,224** | **70** |

Starting the homeward trek is the straightforward, 446-yard 12th. From the tee a player can begin to see the remnants of the Second World War airstrip to the left, which comes into full view when they reach the plateau green of the 412-yard 13th, after which holes become progressively harder. Two long shots heading back to the sea are needed to the raised and well-bunkered green of the 449-yard 14th, while, on the 209-yard 15th, the long- to mid-iron shot from hillock to hillock will be fully exposed to the wind. In the 1977 Open, it was here that Tom Watson pulled level with Jack Nicklaus by holing a huge putt from off the green.

## TOUGH FINISH

In order to force the best players to hit long- to mid-irons for their second shot across the stream, the famed 458-yard 16th has been altered. The tee has been lengthened and moved well to the right, increas-ing the challenge while restoring the shot values of the approach to the burn-defended green. The change in direction has also freed up ground to add length to the 17th, which makes it now a truly long hole and brings the dunes that frame the approach to the green much more in play for second shots.

The 465-yard 18th is on fairly flat ground and a number of attempts have been made to add to its interest by modifying the green complex; however, any hole with history such as this has needs no such altera-tion. On the first occasion that Turnberry hosted the Open Championship, Tom Watson matched Jack Nicklaus's characteristically improbable birdie on the 18th during the final round and so clinched the title. It had been a battle between the two greatest competitors of their era, in which the whole golfing world was a winner. What a magnificent finish to such a superb debut on the highest stage of the golfing world.

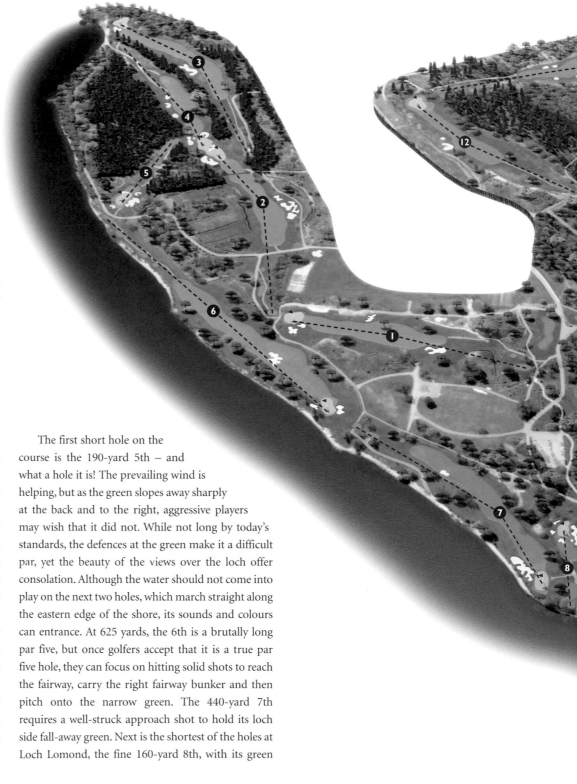

Of the Scottish courses profiled in this book, Loch Lomond is special in two ways. Firstly, it is the only true parkland course. Secondly, it is still very much a work in progress. The architect, the owner, the members and the staff all continue to strive to improve the experience of the course and the club.

The opening nine holes are set within mostly open ground, to the east side of the property, with the loch never far away and the hills ever-present in the distance. The stunning scenery never overwhelms the course, but it does distract the less than assiduous golfer. Distraction is a theme that runs throughout the course: from bunkers that guide rather than hinder a golfer; to trees that do not really affect strategy but do play games with the mind; to fairways that are wider than they seem and greens made smaller by hidden slopes; and, most of all, to the beauty of the natural environment, which cannot and should not be ignored. Loch Lomond is three-dimensional camouflage of the most effective kind.

## THE NEED FOR CLEAR THINKING

Fortunately, the 425-yard 1st is straightforward, with the first distraction on the tee – an ancient oak tree on the right-hand side of the fairway, which seems more troublesome than it really is. If the player aims just to its left, they are rewarded with a good angle to the gentle green. It is followed by a longer par four, the 455-yard 2nd, which can be hard to reach in the prevailing southerly winds. Its green is shared with the 4th, but this is more for fun than for function. The tee shot from the 510-yard 3rd needs to be hit between two thick rows of modern pines. Once they are avoided, a well-judged and executed shot to a green close to the shore can set up a two-putt birdie. The 390-yard 4th doubles back alongside the 3rd, and while it is not long, the green slopes off sharply to the left and at the front, requiring guile to get to many pin positions. In addition, Ben Lomond looms in the distance, competing for your attention on every shot.

The first short hole on the course is the 190-yard 5th – and what a hole it is! The prevailing wind is helping, but as the green slopes away sharply at the back and to the right, aggressive players may wish that it did not. While not long by today's standards, the defences at the green make it a difficult par, yet the beauty of the views over the loch offer consolation. Although the water should not come into play on the next two holes, which march straight along the eastern edge of the shore, its sounds and colours can entrance. At 625 yards, the 6th is a brutally long par five, but once golfers accept that it is a true par five hole, they can focus on hitting solid shots to reach the fairway, carry the right fairway bunker and then pitch onto the narrow green. The 440-yard 7th requires a well-struck approach shot to hold its loch side fall-away green. Next is the shortest of the holes at Loch Lomond, the fine 160-yard 8th, with its green

# LOCH LOMOND
## Luss by Alexandria, Dunbartonshire

People tend to fall in love with Loch Lomond. Tom Weiskopf chose to live on site for two summers while he and Jay Morrish designed the course. Five years later, Lyle Anderson decided to rescue the project from bankruptcy after just one visit, in 1994. Today, a large international membership enjoys and supports the club and the course.

# LOCH LOMOND GOLF CLUB –
## Luss by Alexandria, Dunbartonshire
Tom Weiskopf and Jay Morrish, 1993
Major events: Solheim Cup 2000; Scottish Open 2001–2008

CARD OF THE COURSE

| HOLE | NAME | YARDS | PAR | HOLE | NAME | YARDS | PAR |
|---|---|---|---|---|---|---|---|
| 1. | Scots Pine | 425 | 4 | 10. | Arn Burn | 455 | 4 |
| 2. | Deer Park | 455 | 4 | 11. | Sherrif's Mount | 235 | 3 |
| 3. | Garden Cottage | 510 | 5 | 12. | Court Hill | 415 | 4 |
| 4. | Ben Lomond | 390 | 4 | 13. | Gallow's Hill | 560 | 5 |
| 5. | Creinch | 190 | 3 | 14. | Tom and Jay's Chance | 345 | 4 |
| 6. | Long Loch Lomond | 625 | 5 | 15. | Glen Fruin | 415 | 4 |
| 7. | Yon Bonnie Banks | 440 | 4 | 16. | Dun Na Bruich | 495 | 5 |
| 8. | Inchmoan | 160 | 3 | 17. | The Bay | 205 | 3 |
| 9. | Shi G'Arten | 345 | 4 | 18. | Rossdhu Castle | 435 | 4 |
| | **OUT** | **3,540** | **36** | | **IN** | **3,560** | **36** |
| | | | | | **TOTAL** | **7,100** | **72** |

exposed not only to the wind but also to the gazes of members enjoying their après-golf in the clubhouse. With its green impregnably protected by bunkers, the task at hand at the 345-yard 9th is deciding how far down the fairway to hit and, particularly, whether or not to take on the centre-line bunker.

## DIFFERENT CHARACTERISTICS
The back nine brings the player into the western half of the course, where the distractions are more likely to be the wildlife, bogs and abandoned out-buildings. It is a marvellous change of pace and scenery, and provides the opportunity for great golf. On the superb, 455-yard 10th, a slightly downhill drive is needed towards a distant stream and then an approach shot with a mid- to long-iron to a green perched at the edge of a small inland loch. The 235-yard 11th is a long, uphill 'short' hole requiring judgement as well as brute strength, and complicated by a green bisected by a

deep hollow. There is ample width off the 12th tee (where the local family used to hang its enemies), but its green falls off sharply front–right and back–left. Following it is the 560-yard 13th, which, although downhill from the tee, is achievable in two only by the longest hitters.

Sitting in full view of the next tee is the 14th green, which can be reached with a long carry over a primordial bog. Branches of oaks by the tee catch the eye, although they should never threaten the ball. It is a moment for calm resolve, but if this is not possible a player can escape to a fairway on the left. This is the Weiskopf–Morrish, 'signature', death-or-glory, short par four, and, ironically, where Tom Weiskopf got trapped in the peat for several hours during construction.

At the 415-yard 15th the golfer begins again to get a more expansive view of the surrounding hills, before settling down to tackle the horizontally tiered green, sloping right to left. A great hole for this stage of the game is the 495-yard 16th, a reachable par five with a fronting burn to the green. The 205-yard 17th brings the player back near the loch and its peaceful Rossdhu Bay, and it needs a final mid- to long-iron to the lochside green. Not only is the multitiered 18th green one of the most interesting on the course, but a golfer's nerve is also well tested on a drive with bunkers on the right and water down the left. In the 2007 Scottish Open, Phil Mickelson found the bunkers on his 72nd hole and then the water in losing a play-off to Gregory Havret. Afterwards, Mickelson gave interviews with a resigned but warm smile on his face. Loch Lomond is that kind of place.

*Looking over the double green shared by the 2nd and 4th holes to the loch and Ben Lomond, it is not hard to see why so many golfers succumb to the charm of this course.*

# ENGLAND AND WALES

Unlikely as it may seem, it was the death of Queen Elizabeth I in 1603 that brought golf to England. She was succeeded by King James VI of Scotland who became King James I of England. Travelling south to London, he brought with him a sizeable entourage of courtiers and servants. The king took up residence at Greenwich Palace, and it was not long before his courtiers sought out a place to play their golf.

T hey found a suitable spot close by, on Blackheath, overlooking the palace. Indeed the king's son, Henry Frederick, Prince of Wales, is recorded as having played there in 1606. It is generally assumed that the 'The Golf Club' at the Chocolate House at Blackheath was instituted in 1608, although the club's earliest records, which might have verified this, were lost in a fire towards the end of the 18th century. Theirs was a course of five holes, expanding in 1843 to one of seven. By playing the course three times, a round of 21 holes became the norm. The course remained in use until increasing motor traffic on the roads crossing the fairways caused the club to relocate to nearby Eltham, where the Royal Blackheath Golf Club[1] flourishes to this day. It boasts one of the most magnificent clubhouses of all (a 1664 mansion) and a fabulous collection of early golfing memorabilia.

Another Scot – Alexander Carlisle from Edinburgh – introduced golf to another royal palace, Hampton Court, in the mid-18th century, greatly impressing those who saw him drive a golf ball a considerable distance into the River Thames, thereby inspiring them to take up the game. A club was formed in Manchester in 1818 – it still exists but no longer has a course of its own.

## ROYAL NORTH DEVON

The club that is able to consider itself the cradle of English golf is Royal North Devon[2], often referred to as Westward Ho! or RND, founded in 1864. The current course barely resembles the one originally laid out by Old Tom Morris, while W.H. Fowler came up with the test that is played today. A figure that looms very large in Westward Ho's history, though, is J.H. Taylor. Born in neigh-

15
16
17
89
14
18 19
13
Ganton
page 94
20
77
Alwoodley
page 92
Leeds
12
Royal Lytham
page 88
10
Royal Birkdale
page 86
11
8
9
75
4
Hoylake
page 82
Liverpool
6 7
Sheffield
21
5
22
Woodhall Spa
page 98
27
74
23
24
82
25
Nottingham
28 31
26
88
76
Birmingham
92
73
86
72
91
30
ENGLAND
WALES
33
32 34
78
81
36
87 43
Royal North Devon
42
44
70
85
Sunningdale
page 100
47
London
71
69
79
1 39
Royal Porthcawl
page 108
68
Cardiff
38
35
83
53 41
50
48
45
37
Royal St George's
52
page 104
65
49
46
90
40
80
54
2
51
55
64
58
59 Portsmouth
56
67
60
57
63
61
66
84
62

bouring Northam in 1871, he grew up caddying on the links, learning the game to such an extent that he went on to become part of the great triumvirate with Harry Vardon and James Braid. J.H. Taylor won five Opens and his portrait sits proudly in the clubhouse museum.

Royal North Devon is by no means an outdated test of golfing ability. Just as it has always done, it provides a thorough examination – yet it is golf in the raw. Play here and a golfer will have a very good idea of what links courses looked and played like a hundred years ago. Furthermore, while using modern technology in the form of graphite and titanium clubs to play the course, the golfer will be wondering in awe as to how it could possibly have been negotiated with the kind of equipment exhibited in the excellent museum. The 170-yard (155-metre) carry over the sleeper-faced Cape bunker on the 4th must have been a formidable undertaking in those days.

The course sits on common land, roaming sheep are encountered, and the greens are roped off to shield the putting surfaces, so the course can never be presented in the pristine fashion sought by modern greenkeepers. For this reason it is easy to see why Westward Ho! polarizes opinion. There are those who feel it is scruffy, untidy and unfair, but for players who like their golf rough and ready and who realize that this game was never intended to be 'fair' Westward Ho! is the place. If the Old Course at St Andrews (see page 40) had not undergone so many Open-funded makeovers it would not be far removed from what is on offer at Westward Ho!. Let nature do its best (or worst!) and tackle it head on – that was the essence of golf and so it remains at Westward Ho!.

## EQUALLY OLD

At around the same time that Royal North Devon came into being members of the London Scottish Rifle Volunteers met to form the London Scottish GC[3], although it is very likely they had been playing golf on Wimbledon Common for some time before that. They are still there today, wearing their distinctive red golfing shirts. With the foundation of the Royal Liverpool Golf Club (see page 82) in 1869 golf was slowly but surely becoming established in different parts of the country.

And Liverpool is as good a place as any to start when considering other English and Welsh courses of architectural merit. On the Wirral coast, Wallasey[4] has a fine links with imposing dunes and majestic seascapes, and inland in Cheshire there is the handsome Delamere Forest[5] (architect W.H. Fowler) and inspiring Prestbury[6] (Harry Colt), while just into the

*The imposing, sleeper-faced Cape bunker on the 4th hole at Royal North Devon must be carried from the tee, a terrifying prospect in the days of gutta balls and hickory shafts.*

hills of the Derbyshire Peak District is Alister MacKenzie's Cavendish[7], one of his last British courses before emigrating to America.

In the northern outskirts of Liverpool begins a marvellous stretch of duneland running all the way to Southport, giving distinction to the links courses of West Lancashire[8], Formby[9], Southport and Ainsdale[10] and Hillside[11], as well as Royal Birkdale (see page 86). Beyond Royal Lytham (see page 88), whose neighbour St Annes Old Links[12] is a serious test, are two marvellous seaside outposts on the Cumbrian coast: Seascale[13] and Silloth-on-Solway[14], both full of the best kind of old-fashioned links qualities.

Crossing over the backbone of England along Hadrian's Wall brings the golfer to England's North Sea coast and the quaint charms of Bamburgh Castle[15] and the remote links of Berwick on Tweed[16] at Goswick. Farther south, The Northumberland[17] boasts a strong Harry Colt and James Braid course. County Durham is well stocked with interesting courses, with the honours shared between Harry Colt's Brancepeth Castle[18], with its imposing and unusual, back-to-back par threes in mid-round, and the

admirable links at Seaton Carew[19], in which the great Dr Alister MacKenzie had a hand.

England's largest county, Yorkshire, has a long coastline, but its golfing treasures are mostly inland, with Alwoodley (see page 92) and its Leeds neighbour Moortown[20] heading a long list of MacKenzie courses. Lindrick[21], near Sheffield, saw a (then) rare home win in the 1957 Ryder Cup, and these three clubs plus Ganton (see page 94) form a powerful Yorkshire quartet.

## CENTRAL ENGLAND

In Nottinghamshire there is good golf to be had at Coxmoor[22] and Sherwood Forest[23], the latter with one of the toughest back nines in England. However, it is the Notts Golf Club[24], affectionately known as Hollinwell, which stands out here.

## NOTTS GOLF CLUB

Notts GC was founded in 1887 at the council-owned Bulwell Common. Non-golfers using the area made life inconvenient, and it was decided by the club that a 'suitable tract of land that could be acquired on practicable terms and devoted exclusively to the game' should be found. The potential of land in Kirkby Forest was spotted in 1889, and Notts GC moved there a year later.

Willie Park Jnr laid out the course on the undulating land, which was seemingly made for golf as it headed through wooded hillsides with gorse, heather and fern in abundance; it opened for play in 1901. Five-time Open champion J.H. Taylor was later paid five guineas (£5 5s.) to make modifications. These were primarily to the bunkering. It is not as fearsomely bunkered as Ganton (see page 94) or Woodhall Spa (see page 98), but their positioning is spot on.

Almost from the start the golfer becomes aware that they are facing a special test. The 2nd, for example, climbs uphill and doglegs right to left. Architecturally it is a fine hole. Positioned by the 8th tee is the 'holy well' from which Hollinwell takes its nickname. Golfers are able to sample the water at an ideal time in their round, before having to make an intimidating drive over water between trees. There is no room for conjecture on the famous, 228-yard 13th – a gorgeous, downhill par three. Many regard this hole as their favourite at Hollinwell. If it has a rival then it is probably the 439-yard 15th. This is where a golfer even gets a whiff of links golf with a narrow green surrounded by gorse.

## THE MIDLANDS AND EAST ANGLIA

Moving on to the industrial west Midlands, Little Aston[25] (architect Harry Vardon) is the aristocrat, but no lover of golf architecture should miss Beau Desert[26] on Cannock Chase, a W.H. Fowler design full of intrigue.

Before heading eastwards for East Anglia a detour should be made to Woodhall Spa (see page 98), arguably England's finest inland course. A further detour, to the Lincolnshire coast, repays the effort with the entertaining links of Seacroft[27]. Directly across the Wash on Norfolk's short west coast stands the venerable links of Hunstanton[28], with its run of magnificent holes from the 6th to the end. East Anglia may not have a great density of golf courses, but the average quality is high. Lovers of firm-and-fast conditions should certainly play well-bunkered Aldeburgh[29], and

*The short 4th at Royal West Norfolk is played from the top of one sand dune to the summit of another where a wide but shallow green provides the target.*

those who appreciate subtlety should not miss Royal Worlington and Newmarket[30] – Britain's finest nine-hole course. And then, in a unique – and aristocratic – world of its own, there is Royal West Norfolk[31] at Brancaster.

## ROYAL WEST NORFOLK

If ever proof were needed that God intended humans to play golf it is to be found at Brancaster. It is land fashioned by the elements and perfect for golf in its purest form: the player is not just challenged by the naturally sculpted holes but also by the elements. These include the weather, which given the club's exposed position next to the North Sea can be wild, and the tides, which can have a marked affect on strategy during a round.

The club was first established in 1891, and by 1900 the course was laid out pretty much as it stands today – nature and the elements seeming to dictate the only alterations at Brancaster. Thus the immediate proximity of the sea has forced several changes when defences have been breached. The sea may have even influenced the journey to the course itself. At high tide, the clubhouse – which is surely as exposed as any in the UK – can be cut off and players are forced to walk along a raised bank to access the club.

There is something of a similarity with St Andrews at the start with the 1st and last fairways shared, the 2nd and 17th, too. It is very much an out-and-back layout in the tradition of the Old Course, and there is marvellous golf to be had throughout the round, but it is at the far end of the course that the two most remarkable holes are to be found.

Here the magnificent 8th and 9th holes stand amid the encroaching sea waters. The 494-yard 8th is by modern standards a short par five. But it is a great hole. The tee shot is played over the tidal marshes (the sea becomes casual water at high tide) to an island fairway. Depending on the outcome of the drive a decision must be made on whether or not to risk going for the green, which stands beyond another stretch of water. It is a fabulous hole and is made such solely by the forces of nature. The same applies to the 405-yard 9th, which in many respects is a par-four version of the 8th, with a drive over a marsh and a heavily-sleepered green.

*The 4th hole at Woking with its influential centre-line bunkers, which force the golfer to choose between the left- or right-hand route. The latter gives an easier second shot, but the risks are patently higher.*

## SOUTHERN ENGLAND

London beckons, but not before taking in the delights of Berkhamsted[32] (a rare bunkerless course) in Hertfordshire. Approaching London from the north Harry Colt's grand Moor Park[33] and a Harry Vardon gem, Sandy Lodge[34], should be visited.

The finest London golf is to be found in that great swathe of heathland (based on sandy, acidic soil with brilliant drainage, capable of sustaining the growth of heather, that most traditional of Scottish golfing flora) flowing to the south-west of London from close to Heathrow Airport and Windsor Castle in the north-west, more or less following the M25 London orbital motorway, as far as the A3, the main London–Portsmouth road, in the south. Much of this lies in the county of Surrey, but it extends also into parts of Hampshire and Sussex. Sunningdale (see page 100) has been chosen to represent the best of these heathland courses, but the earliest of them was Woking[35].

## WOKING

Many golf authorities have fallen under the charm of Woking, including eminent writer Bernard Darwin. Indeed, golf architect Tom Simpson and art historian H.N. Wethered wrote in *The Architectural Side of Golf* that they would select Woking as the course they would play for the rest of their lives, if condemned to but one choice.

Woking was the first of the heathland courses to be built. Play commenced in 1893 based on work done by Tom Dunn. All but a few of his playing corridors are still in use. However, Dunn is not known for his bunkering or imaginative green complexes and yet today's Woking is celebrated for just these characteristics. They were largely the work of Woking member Stuart Paton, described by Darwin as the man 'who really made Woking'.

Over nearly 40 years, Paton added and subtracted bunkers, rebuilt all the greens and monitored the growth of the heather as a hazard to avoid. Another Woking member, John Low, was an influential writer and he chronicled the transformation of the course, highlighting the fact that Paton's attention to detail meant that every hole offered something worthy of study.

The 277-yard 1st is made by its cleverly contoured green. Tom Simpson and H.N. Wethered considered the 221-yard 2nd hole 'of really outstanding merit'. A solitary bunker at the front right of the 3rd green epitomizes the thoughtfulness of Paton's work. American architect Tom Doak wrote that this was 'one of the trickiest approaches I've ever seen'. So impressed, he seized on the opportunity five years after seeing Woking to create a similar bowl effect at the 8th green at Pacific Dunes (see page 238).

Next comes a hole whose importance in the development of golf-course architecture cannot be overstated. At the turn of the 20th century, golf courses of a high standard in Great Britain were confined to its coastline. Inland courses were a poor substitute

*Swinley Forest's 12th green has some of the most startling contouring to be encountered on the course, indeed anywhere in the architecture of the first two decades of the 20th century.*

because their architecture was primitive, with man lacking the ability to add features of strategic merit that looked natural. Paton changed that in 1901 when he created central bunkers on the 4th fairway. Though the bunkers garner most of the attention, the green itself is equally cunning as it runs away from the golfer, adding to the dilemma of the hole. Quite the fan of this hole, Tom Simpson featured one or two greens that sloped away from the golfer on his own courses later.

Despite being just over 6,500 yards (6,000 metres), par is a tight 70 and Woking calls for a number of quality, long approach shots. One of the best is at the 455-yard 8th, where the second shot must skirt past a satellite of four heather-clad bunkers to an elevated green with interesting rolls. The back nine then features some of the best interior contours that can be found in greens anywhere, with none more worthy of study than the extraordinary rolling sea 13th green.

If Woking represents the most visionary of early design, then Swinley Forest[36] must be its perfection.

## SWINLEY FOREST

The balance between grass, pine, heather and sand, set within the time capsule of one man's style, produces a golfing landscape that is a true icon of early British golf architecture. Harry Colt's 'least worst course' (his own modest epitaph) is to all others quite simply a jewel.

If a golf club's name alone can call forth images of serenity, solitude and beauty, then Swinley Forest's is quite the equal of those of Pine Valley (see page 186), Sunningdale (see page 100) or Woodhall Spa (see page 98). It was indeed an early masterpiece of Harry Colt, laid out in 1907 when Colt was secretary at the nearby Sunningdale. The site was magnificent heath and forest land, leased from the Crown Estates.

Colt's preference for this course over many of his others can be attributed to an outstanding site with which he had to work, the time which his own proximity allowed him to spend at Swinley Forest searching for the right combination and setting of holes, and his ability to attend to details during the construction of the course. He is said to have spent many days roaming

the forest to find the best land in which to arrange the holes. The process of tree clearance was a further act of discovery.

Yet with the finished course a par-68, with a playing length of 6,045 yards (5,528 metres), it is reasonable to ask why it is held in special regard within the golf design world, especially as it has never hosted a major tournament. One reason for this – and indeed for its particular charm – is that the course is much as Colt left it in 1908: there has been no perennial search for a back tee here or a new drive bunker there. It is there to be thoroughly enjoyed and savoured as a vintage, just as the clubhouse and the atmosphere of the club are too.

The course has the typical Colt feel of a very simple loop arrangement of holes with a smaller counter-loop at 12, 13 and 14. Yet during play, the holes always seem to be striking out in new directions, exploring new territory. The large internal masses of forest give many holes a peaceful, almost isolated feeling, but the forest itself binds the whole layout together in a most unified, coherent manner. Three signal Colt features mark Swinley Forest's greatness.

First there was Colt's imaginative development of the short holes as a series of climaxes through the round. He searched out drama, beauty and challenge for them, and found five wonderful sites here. Their various positions in the round, their diversity of length, interest and penalty, their natural beauty and sense that they could only be short holes, belong to the hand of a master. It would be hard to find a finer set of par threes.

The second great feature of Swinley Forest is the variety contained within the longer holes, the changes in their direction and the interplay of their length and topography. This is especially so on the front nine.

And the third delight that Colt delivers is a cornucopia of beautiful greens. He was one of the first and most ardent advocates of greens developing their topography from the form and surrounds of the green site. At Swinley Forest there is a multitude of putting surfaces of great variety and interest created through skilful introduction of borrows, ridges, levels, tiers and cambers – some subtle, some fierce. But all feel natural and entirely appropriate to their setting.

Swinley Forest's quietly confident reserve is in total contrast to the impact made by Walton Heath[37] from the moment it opened in 1904.

## WALTON HEATH

Since the very beginning the greatest names in golf have been playing Walton Heath, while kings, prime ministers, captains of industry and the newspaper barons who owned it have held court in the clubhouse. The Prince of Wales was the club's first captain in 1935–36, and during this period became King Edward VIII.

Businessman Sir Cosmo Bonsor acquired the land with golf in mind and commissioned his brother-in-law, W.H. Fowler, to design the Old Course. Fowler, who was a struggling banker with no course design experience but a fine golf player, desperately needed the work to establish his design credentials. On horseback he surveyed the gently rolling, elevated sea of heather and came up with a golfing paradise. It was the making of him, and he went on to join Tom Simpson in a hugely successful partnership.

It seems probable that Fowler followed the blueprint of St Andrews as he scythed the route of the Old Course. It heads out from the clubhouse, loops around the turn and then heads back, though not in a straight line. It is intertwined with the New, which was nine holes laid out in 1907 extended to 18 by 1913.

On the Old Course, the fairways are wide but play narrower in typical fast-running conditions. Bunkers are deep with heather faces, and the heather invariably runs down the back of fairway traps some yards beyond to significantly extend the carry to safety. Heather also borders the fairways. It seems to offer a decent lie and a chance to advance the ball, but its tangled structure means this is rarely the case. With the possible exception of Hankley Common[38], there is no greater profusion of heather in English golf than at Walton Heath.

Heading east from Walton Heath into the leafy suburbs of Croydon leads to what was one of the best-known Surrey clubs of the 1920s and 30s, The Addington[39]. It then suffered years of comparative neglect, but that has ensured that little or nothing has been done to damage the architecture in the intervening years.

## THE ADDINGTON

In the modern age there are few better courses than The Addington for testing a player's ability to produce accurate golf. For the first-time visitor, its reputation as a difficult masterpiece might come as a surprise. The views from many tees suggest wide, inviting fairways and a pleasant but relatively straightforward route to the green. Do not be fooled! The task from the tee is for the player to find the correct part of the fairway on this course designed by a great master, John Frederick Abercromby.

In many ways Abercromby's genius was to come up with a design that has stood the test of time. In 1912, when he was laying out the course along with Harry Colt in a consultant role, he produced for the time a 6,200-yard (5,670-metre) monster. Today it is only 150 yards (137 metres) longer, yet it remains relevant, testing and thoroughly enjoyable to the modern player. The Addington will reward a well and accurately struck shot, but heathery ravines, sparingly placed bunkers and the birch, oaks and chestnuts that nowadays create holes of splendid isolation are there to trap players incapable of finding the correct line.

The Addington was a favourite of P.G. Wodehouse. The comic writer once scribbled: 'Anyone wishing to write to the author should address all correspondence to: P.G. Wodehouse, c/o the sixth bunker, The Addington Golf Club, Croydon, Surrey.' This hazard is where the course steps up a gear. A ravine, which must be carried with the second shot, sits just short right of the green, and a long, narrow wooden bridge helps the golfer traverse the heathery depression. Sitting at the bottom is that bunker where P.G. Wodehouse set up home.

There are many uplifting holes, but two in particular deserve mention, the 12th and 13th. With a half-decent score to protect, the driver should stay in the bag at the 12th because it would bring into play a mixture of heather and fairway as the hole heads steeply downhill on what amounts to a giant's staircase. Abercromby wanted the player to hit a 200-yard (183-metre) drive to the brow of the hill. From there it is a mammoth second to the green, which sits high at the other side of the valley, or a lay-up of the utmost precision. The fairway shrinks to a narrow ribbon running up the right side of the hole. Ideally a player should leave a 100-yard (90-metre) third shot to the elevated green, and the challenge is to find the correct tier to get a crack at what would be a hard and sensibly earned birdie.

Renowned golf writer Henry Longhurst said of the 230-yard 13th: 'With the possible exception of the 5th at Pine Valley, the greatest one-shot hole in inland golf.' It is stunningly beautiful and again precision is the watchword. Behind the green in the foreground to

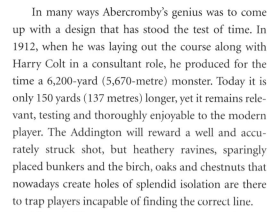

*The 16th hole on Walton Heath's Old Course is a short par five for the members, but a very demanding par four for competitors in the professional tournaments played there.*

denser woodland stand two trees. To the left is a silver birch. A golfer might want to fade the ball off that one, or take direct aim at the maple that stands to its right. That is the correct line, because anything left will roll off the green, potentially gobbled by two bunkers. But, then again, there is no room to miss on the right. A nasty, heather-rimmed bunker is cut out of the ridge that runs along the edge of the green.

## WEST SUSSEX

You could hardly describe Pulborough as being a London suburb, for it is deep in the Sussex country-side, but here is to be found the very last and farthest south-east outcrop of 'Surrey' heathland in England. It is the home of the West Sussex Golf Club[40].

For those who love their golf to be conducted in absolute peace and quiet and in over-rewardingly challenging terrain, a debt of gratitude is owed to the wandering eye of Commander George Hillyard. These were precisely the qualities that turned a routine early morning shave into something far more significant.

From the bathroom window of his rather grand home Commander Hillyard recognized that the land-scape before him was the natural setting for a golf course. Tennis was Hillyard's game – he was a

Wimbledon doubles finalist in 1891 and secretary of the All England Lawn Tennis & Croquet Club (1907–21) – but he also clearly had a more than capable eye for golfing terrain.

Soon after spotting the potential of this tract of sandy heathland, it was bought and leased to West Sussex. The course was designed by Major C.K. Hutchinson, who, with James Braid had been responsible architecturally for Gleneagles (see page 66) and with Guy Campbell for Prince's GC[41] at Sandwich. Colonel Stafford Vere Hotchkin, the man behind Woodhall Spa (see page 98), was also involved. Between them they created a course that has more than retained its youth, and to this day provides glorious golf in the most tranquil of locations. Situated 12 miles (19 kilometres) inland from England's south coast, West Sussex, also referred to as Pulborough, is the epitome of traditional golf set amid pine, birch, oak and heather.

Although too short for championship golf, leading women's amateur events are staged at West Sussex. It provides challenges, risks and rewards for golfers of pretty much any standard. Where one player might dare to carry a bunker, there will invariably be an alternative for the golfer who wants or needs to take a safer route.

*As many as six short holes punctuate the round at The Addington, and pride of place must be given to the long and demanding 13th.*

Fairways tend to be generous, though some land-ing areas are tight and often bordered by penal heather, sometimes with no first-cut of rough to slow down an offline hit. Bunkers are large and filled with sand excavated from the course. It is fine and white but over time takes on more of an emulsion colour, help-ing to give the course a unique feel. Unusually for a heathland course, water is a hazard on two holes, adding to the difficulties of the tough par-three 6th.

Little bar the pushing back of tees and the addition of the odd bunker by Donald Steel in 2000 has been done to modernize West Sussex since it was opened by the former Ladies' British Open Amateur champion Joyce Wethered in 1931. Renovation has not been and still is not required, and it might be suspected that Commander Hillyard could have predicted as much when he gazed from his bathroom window all those years ago. He was a man of vision and he made golf in southern England all the richer for it.

## FURTHER HEATHLAND GEMS

Before leaving the heathlands it would be rude not to mention some of the other fine courses that could so easily have made it into this book, had it been three times the length. Plausible cases could readily have been made also to include both courses at The Berkshire[42], St George's Hill GC[43], the East and West courses at the Wentworth Club[44], Worplesdon[45], West Hill[46], New Zealand[47], Camberley Heath[48], Hankley Common, North Hants[49], Liphook[50] and the superb (and famously bunkerless) Royal Ashdown Forest[51].

## THE SOUTH COAST

The knowledgeable golfer will want to continue the journey to that part of the English mainland closest to continental Europe, the Kent coast. Here are to be found three Open Championship courses, although only one of them is currently on the roster, Royal St George's (see page 104) at Sandwich. Host back in 1932 was Prince's[52], which shares a boundary with Royal St George's, but that course was flattened during the Second World War, and today's 27-hole layout is very different. The other great Kent links is Royal Cinque Ports[53], a few miles away at Deal.

## ROYAL CINQUE PORTS

In 54 BC, Julius Caesar's Roman legions landed at Deal and marched inland over crumpled sand dunes that two millennia later became the Royal Cinque Ports Golf Club (commonly referred to as Deal). Mighty Caesar's troops demanded full submission, and the links built here has a similar ethos.

Deal's evolution dates from 1892 when Tom Dunn or Ramsey Hunter completed a nine-hole design. Harry Hunter (Ramsey's brother) then constructed the course that subsequently has seen amendments by James Braid, Charles Alison, John Morrison, Sir Guy Campbell, Henry Cotton, Donald Steel and, currently, Martin Ebert. Many of the changes have been necessitated by flooding from the North Sea and army occupation during the First and Second World Wars. In 1979 a sea wall built to protect the links from future sea encroachment resulted in further design amendments and consequent loss of sea views. Deal was an early mainstay on the Open roster, holding the 1909 and 1920 Open championships as well as the 1923 and 1982 Amateur championships. High tides caused the 1939 and 1949 Open championships to be moved to other venues.

In design, Deal unquestionably resembles the Old Course at St Andrews (see page 40). Like most early links, the holes run out along the seashore and return snugly inland. Deal's major asset is a long sand-dune ridge, beginning at the 2nd tee, contorting until reaching its zenith at the 6th green and then dwindling thereafter to the 11th hole. Play is over and through the landform giving the golfer a series of hanging lies and challenging putts. Bunkers are sod-faced, revetted monsters whose size is multiplied because the surrounding terrain often directs balls into them. They are severely penal and should be avoided at all costs.

With the prevailing south-westerly the final seven holes play straight into the wind. Deal's finish with its long par fours and relative narrowness may be the most testing and severe of all championship links venues.

## RYE

Then it is on past the White Cliffs of Dover towards other-worldly Romney Marsh. On the Kent side of it is the enjoyable links course at Littlestone[54], while on the far, Sussex side of it stands one of England's great old golfing institutions, Rye Golf Club[55].

On the wall next to the secretary's desk at Rye, graphs illustrate the speed of the club's greens. It is invaluable information for a course renowned for the pace of its putting surfaces, but unusually these charts show that the greens are at their slickest in winter.

Rye has provided fabulous golf, whatever the time of year, throughout an illustrious history. When the days are at their shortest, the Old Course really comes into its own: *Poa bulbosa*, a twin-leaf grass that sits in its own tiny bulb, flourishes and is responsible for a smooth fast surface, making it possible to putt accurately from well off the greens. This is ideal because Rye is a traditional links where it is usually profitable to play a low running game.

The club was formed in 1893, and golf first started to be played a year later, when the clubhouse was built. Although intended to be a temporary structure, the much-altered building is still in use today, offering magnificent views of the course, the town of Rye and the English Channel.

When the course was first properly laid out in 1895 it signalled the beginning of one of the most influential careers in golf-course architecture. Harry Colt was a solicitor and Rye's first captain. He became secretary and then went on to fulfil that role at Sunningdale (see page 100) while developing his career as a leading architect. Colt was the first course designer who had not first been a professional golfer, and he was involved in design work on many of the game's leading courses. However, only two holes remain at Rye from his original 1895 design: the 5th and 16th.

The club and course come particularly alive during the famous President's Putter, played in the first week of January. The scratch knockout tournament is for members of the Oxford & Cambridge Golfing Society. A champion will have to play and win up to eight matches in four days.

A great strength of the present-day course at Rye is its roster of five first-rate par-three holes, each subtly defended, the world-class par-four 4th, the gloriously old-fashioned, blind 13th and an 18th that Donald Steel describes as 'in the world's top ten of finishing holes'.

*The hardest shots at Rye are said to be the second shots on the short holes, an understated way of referring to the brilliant defences of these holes. This is the 7th.*

## THE SOUTH-WEST

There is little else of interest, heading westwards along the south coast, until the links course Hayling[56], near Portsmouth, and a fine Willie Park inland course at Stoneham[57] outside Southampton. Then a cluster of heathy courses around Bournemouth calls: Broadstone[58], Ferndown[59], Parkstone[60] and Isle of Purbeck[61]. On the tip of Cornwall is humpy-bumpy West Cornwall[62], where Jim Barnes, winner of the 1921 US Open and 1925 Open Championship, learned his golf. Moving northwards mention should be made of the Harry Colt links at Trevose Golf and Country Club[63], the two strong links courses at Saunton[64] (one by W.H. Fowler) and the outstanding Burnham and Berrow[65], perhaps deviating to take in Fowler's Yelverton[66] on Dartmoor. One course certainly not to be missed is St Enodoc[67].

## ST ENODOC

Despite any aching legs, clambering up to the final tee at St Enodoc is a most worthwhile experience. The 360-degree panorama provides a perfect vista of the extraordinary setting for this magnificent course. It also offers confirmation as to why a player's limbs are sore, with dramatic views of the rugged terrain negotiated to reach this point in the round.

An architectural delight, St Enodoc provides a very special kind of golf, and has to be among the toughest par-69 tests. Golf has been played here in a remote spot above the Camel estuary since the club was officially founded in 1890. Huge sand dunes dominate the ever-changing terrain, particularly on the holes closest to the estuary, while farther inland the less severe topography still provides opportunity for the art of golf-course design to shine.

How inspired James Braid must have been in 1907 as he plotted the first 18-hole layout. Yes the land is made for golf, but to conjure a workable routing could not have been easy. Indeed the layout was altered significantly by Herbert Fowler, and then Tom Simpson, before Braid returned to complete the job with alterations to the 17th and 18th. It was further enhanced in

2004 by the former Amateur champion and Walker Cup captain Peter McEvoy, who has made a series of subtle changes and extensions to bolster the course's defences against the distance flown by the modern ball.

The routing is first class and only on the 6th hole will a golfer have played two holes in the same direction, and for its sheer visual impact it is perhaps the most memorable on the course. A colossal, yawning bunker carved out of a huge sand dune blocks the view of the punchbowl green. It is the scale of hazard found on the 4th at Royal St George's (see page 104), but this one has no railway sleepers and is there to inconvenience the second shot. The hardest hole is the 457-yard 10th. Sand dunes run all the way down the right side while a water hazard borders the left. The fairway swings downhill, right-to-left and a little church, the burial place of the poet Sir John Betjeman, sits just to the back right of the green. Peter McEvoy's lengthening of the par-five 16th has made a telling contribution to a stern finishing trio.

## AND SO TO WALES

After Royal Porthcawl (see page 108), the must-plays in the south include delightful, upland Southerndown[68], the rugged links at Pyle and Kenfig[69], the old-world charms of Tenby[70] (Wales's oldest established club) and fabulously idiosyncratic Pennard[71]. Travelling north via the west coast enables golf writer Bernard Darwin's favourite Aberdovey[72] and stern Royal St David's[73] to be played, while on the north Wales coast the serious championship test is Conwy[74]. There is also huge fun (and great views) to be had at Bull Bay[75] and Nefyn[76].

## MORE MODERN COURSES

Almost every one of the courses above is old (pre-Second World War). But what of the modern era? Most of the big names since the mid-20th century have worked in England and Wales: Robert Trent Jones Snr (at Moor Allerton[77], Stockley Park[78] and Celtic Manor[79]), Robert Trent Jones Jnr (Celtic Manor and Wisley[80]), Rees Jones (The Oxfordshire[81]), Jack Nicklaus (Carden Park[82], The London GC[83] and St Mellion[84]), Gary Nicklaus (Machynys Peninsula[85]), Jack Nicklaus II (Hanbury Manor[86]), Kyle Phillips (The Grove[87]), Dave Thomas (The Belfry[88], with Peter Alliss, and Slaley Hall[89]), Nick Faldo (Chart Hills[90]), Johnny Miller (Collingtree Park[91]) and Donald Steel (Forest of Arden[92]). While many of these ventures are undoubtedly successful – as they have to be, considering the cost of building them – they are, for the most part, in what has to be considered an international style. Courses of a similar nature can be found throughout the rest of Europe. Few give more than a casual glance to the heritage of the Golden Age. To experience and understand English and Welsh golf at its finest it is to the great links and heathland courses that the student should go.

*Left: This enormous sand dune and cavernous bunker must be cleared with the second shot on the par-four 6th at St Enodoc.*

*Right: Constant change has been the order of the day since the first holes were opened at Celtic Manor in 1995. Driving this has been the desire to create a new, spectator-friendly course to host the 2010 Ryder Cup.*

# HOYLAKE
## Wirral, England

Royal Liverpool's credentials as possessing one of the greatest championship courses have been known throughout the history of golf. It staged its first Open Championship in 1897, 12 years after becoming the inaugural venue for the Amateur Championship – the oldest event of its kind in the world.

For aficionados of England's second oldest course, watching the 2006 Open Championship at Hoylake, as Royal Liverpool is affectionately known, was a somewhat confusing experience. The order of the famous links was altered to accommodate the return of the championship for the first time in 39 years. Iconic holes that have figured prominently in the history of British golf were to be found in unfamiliar places on the card: the famous dogleg 1st had become the 3rd and the round concluded with the par five that normally serves as the 16th. Regardless, the course stood up to the test and did what all great layouts are supposed to do. It identified the best player in the world – Tiger Woods, who became the first player since Tom Watson in 1983 to win back-to-back Opens.

Woods's victory was awash with emotion coming as it did in the wake of the death of his father, Earl. He executed a tactical plan with clinical precision to finish 18 under par and two clear of the field. It was a win dedicated to his father, and Woods would say afterwards: 'He was always on my case about thinking my way around the golf course, and not letting emotions get the better of you.'

Hoylake is a course to stir the soul of anyone playing it and the prophetic words of Earl Woods to his son are worth remembering whenever taking on this challenge, whatever the circumstances.

## STEEPED IN HISTORY

Hoylake is situated at the mouth of the Dee estuary to the south of Liverpool. The course was built in 1869 on the racecourse of the Liverpool Hunt Club. Robert Chambers and George Morris laid out the original course, which was extended to 18 holes in 1871. In the same year the club was accorded 'Royal' status through the patronage of Queen Victoria's younger son, the Duke of Connaught. For the first seven years of its existence the golf and racecourse lived together – hence the names of the 1st and 18th holes 'Course' and 'Stand'.

Royal Liverpool is notable for its number of firsts. In addition to the events mentioned above, it staged the first international match between England and Scotland in 1892, and the inaugural clash between Great Britain and the United States was held there in 1921, which proved a forerunner to the Walker Cup.

The rules of the amateur game were laid down at Hoylake and ironically the club's most famous son nearly fell foul of them. John Ball received £1 for finishing tied fourth as a 16-year-old in the 1878 Open. Seven years later, this modest recompense threatened his entry to the Amateur Championship. Perhaps the fact that he was a Hoylake member helped his cause. Famously he went on to win eight Amateurs and was runner-up twice. Ball was one of only three amateurs to win The Open, and the other two can also boast strong Hoylake links.

Harold Hilton was a Hoylake player and he won the Open Championship on his home course in 1897. It was his second Open title – having five years earlier, at Muirfield, won the first to be staged over 72 holes. Hilton was Ball's great rival and won four Amateur championships and the 1911 US Amateur. Bobby Jones is the only other player from the unpaid ranks to

have won The Open, and his success in 1930 came at Hoylake en route to his unique grand slam.

Sandy Herd, persuaded to use a rubber-core Haskell ball rather than his faithful gutta percha one, triumphed by a single stroke over his great rivals Harry Vardon and James Braid in the 1902 Open. The 'guttie' was finished as a result. Five years later French golfer Arnaud Massy became Open champion and in celebration named his newborn daughter Hoylake.

J.H. Taylor, Walter Hagen, Fred Daly and Peter Thomson were all great and worthy Open winners at Hoylake, as was Roberto Di Vicenzo, who proved an exceptionally popular winner when he triumphed in 1967. It seemed thereafter that The Open had outgrown the course. Fortunately the acquisition of an adjacent disused school field meant that a site could be found for the necessary infrastructure to allow the championship to return.

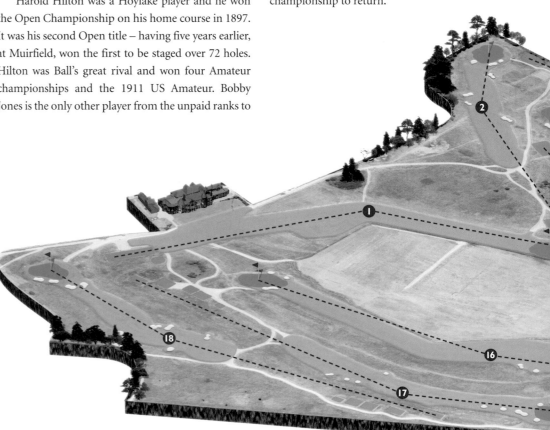

# ROYAL LIVERPOOL GOLF CLUB – Hoylake, Wirral, England

Robert Chambers and George Morris, 1869 and 1871; Cameron Sinclair, 1993 and 1998; and Donald Steel, 2001

Major events: Amateur Championship 1885, 1887, 1890, 1894, 1898, 1902, 1906, 1910, 1927, 1933, 1939, 1953, 1962, 1969, 1975, 1995, 2000; Ladies' British Open Amateur 1896, 1989, 1996; Open Championship 1897, 1902, 1907, 1914, 1924, 1947, 1956, 1967, 2006; Walker Cup 1983; Curtis Cup 1992

## CARD OF THE COURSE

| HOLE | NAME | YARDS | PAR | HOLE | NAME | YARDS | PAR |
|------|------|-------|-----|------|------|-------|-----|
| 1. | Course | 427 | 4 | 10. | Dee | 446 | 4 |
| 2. | Road | 371 | 4 | 11. | Alps | 193 | 3 |
| 3. | Long | 528 | 5 | 12. | Hilbre | 454 | 4 |
| 4. | New | 200 | 3 | 13. | Rushes | 158 | 3 |
| 5. | Telegraph | 451 | 4 | 14. | Field | 552 | 5 |
| 6. | Briars | 421 | 4 | 15. | Lake | 457 | 4 |
| 7. | Dowie | 196 | 3 | 16. | Dun | 558 | 5 |
| 8. | Far | 533 | 5 | 17. | Royal | 449 | 4 |
| 9. | Punch Bowl | 390 | 4 | 18. | Stand | 434 | 4 |
| **OUT** | | **3,517** | **36** | **IN** | | **3,701** | **36** |
| | | | | **TOTAL** | | **7,218** | **72** |

*The approach to the new 17th green located away from the bordering Stanley Road. This served as the opening hole at the 2006 Open Championship staged at Royal Liverpool.*

## THE TRADITIONAL COURSE

Although the course can appear relatively benign and flat, looks are deceptive. By the time the most spectacular part of the course is reached – the undulating string of holes that run down the side of the shoreline – pretty much every facet of a player's game will have been tested. The winds that frequently sweep in from the Irish Sea will determine to what extent. This description of the Hoylake course will stick to the routing that has generally served throughout the club's history, rather than the one used for the 2006 Open.

The 427-yard 1st is framed by the most controversial aspect of the course. Running all the way down the right side of this left-to-right, sharp dogleg is out-of-bounds. To the other side of the small ridge border (a legacy of the days when the course shared its existence with the racecourse) lies the practice ground. Many golfers have an instant aversion to the concept of internal out-of-bounds. They argue that no such thing should exist and that it is artificial. Such a point of view could be applied to Hoylake's opening hole and, indeed the 16th, which also borders the practice

ground. However, such a feature does mean that the 1st proves a test of nerve as well as shot-making. The tee shot needs to be well positioned to open up the approach on this bunkerless hole. All the time the out-of-bounds is preying on a player's mind, with next to no room to the right of the flat green.

A 371-yard par four follows, heading gently downhill to the only green that remains from Hoylake's original layout. It is heavily protected and for the best approach the 2nd tee shot needs to go down the left side, where two fairway bunkers are ready to catch anything slightly mishit, while a diagonal run of mounds bisects the fairway.

In 2001 three new greens, designed by Donald Steel, were built. The first of these comes at the 528-yard 3rd, while the other two are on the closing holes. They provide challenging putting surfaces, and because of their relatively severe undulations they are somewhat out of keeping with the rest of the course. To reach the green at the 3rd, it is first necessary to thread the drive past the gorse on the left and the strategically placed bunkers on the right. The hole swings from right to left and more fierce bunkering

protects the landing area for the approach, while three greenside bunkers guard the left side of the green.

Driving prowess is the prerequisite for the 451-yard 5th and 421-yard 6th, where it is important to miss strategically placed bunkers at driving distance. Then comes another controversial Hoylake hole – the 196-yard 7th – though it is less so nowadays. Until alterations were made in the early 1990s to this downhill par three, out-of-bounds lay no more than 1 yard (1 metre) from the left of the green. Now bunkers guard the front corners of the putting surface with clever hollows left and right ready to collect anything that errs from the straight and narrow. These collection areas provide a stern test of the short game.

## COASTAL HOLES

From there the route goes uphill to the farthest point of the course – the excellent 533-yard 8th. Mounds run down the right side of the fairway while the out-of-bounds down the left will only be a factor for the wildest of right-handed hooks. There is only one bunker, the deepest trap on the course, and it sits just short right of what effectively is a plateau green. It was in this bunker that Bobby Jones jeopardized his 1930 grand slam, running up a damaging seven on a hole that most regard as a decent birdie chance.

In this stretch of the course are to be found four holes all running along the shoreline, providing spectacular views of the estuary and north Wales beyond. In the dry, firm conditions that usually prevail underfoot, the ball can advance vast distances if a player catches the downhill portions of the many humps and hollows that mark the terrain in this part of the course. The 390-yard 9th is called Punch Bowl for good reason with a collecting green the target. But three pot bunkers mean the utmost concentration is required for the approach shot.

From the 10th tee the course heads inland before angling back to the coast in a right-to-left dogleg that has four bunkers waiting to greet any drive that is pushed too far right on a fairway that slopes towards the hazards. There are no more bunkers to be negotiated on this 446-yard hole, just a raised green that puts a premium on distance control.

In 1993, a new tee was introduced for the 193-yard 11th, a delectable downhill par three that is probably Hoylake's most photographed hole. Three large sand dunes stand to the right of the green, and a lone deep bunker guards the front right of a putting surface subtly angled diagonally from the tee. Like the 10th, the 454-yard 12th is a right-to-left dogleg to a raised green.

## RETREAT INLAND

The shortest hole on the course with the smallest green – the 158-yard 13th – is the start of the journey back inland, with the 552-yard 14th being the first of two par fives in three holes. Four bunkers at landing range down the left exert a seemingly magnetic pull on the drive, but if they can be avoided the green should be in range in two for the bigger hitters.

Next comes the robust, straight 457-yard 15th, where the internal out-of-bounds can be of mild concern (especially with a left-to-right wind). Of greater significance are more wonderfully placed bunkers that encourage thoughts of a lay-up, which in turn would leave a mammoth second shot to a two-tier green with a narrow entrance. Add into the mix the four greenside bunkers and it is easy to see how par can be difficult to achieve on this hole.

The contentious out-of-bounds runs down the right of the 558-yard 16th and, provided that is avoided, the other main concern is a steep-faced bunker guarding the front left of the green. It is a fine hole and was the final one in the 2006 Open because the next two holes did not have the room for the

# THE 17TH – OLD AND NEW
A change that helped bring back
The Open to Hoylake

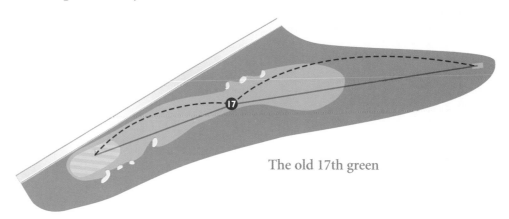

The old 17th green

*The old green sat between a cluster of bunkers on the left-hand side and a slender fence through which a ball could easily trickle onto Stanley Road and out-of-bounds on the right. It was a target that demanded courage and skill, so it was with reluctance that designer Donald Steel moved the green, in changes he described as, 'rearranging the furniture'. By moving the green to the left and away from the roadside, room was made for safer spectator movement. The new, heavily contoured green puts a premium on an accurate approach with three greenside bunkers ready to gobble any that fall foul of its undulations. For the 2006 Open it proved a stout first hole – the champion, Tiger Woods, dropped a shot on his first round.*

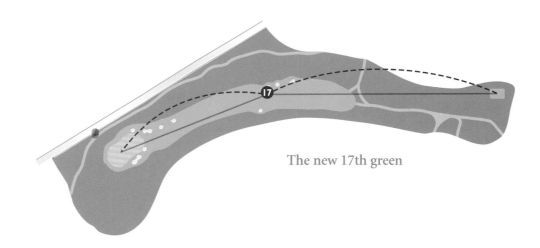

The new 17th green

infrastructure that goes with closing holes at a modern-day Open.

Undulating Donald Steel greens provide the test on both final holes. On the 449-yard 17th the putting surface was originally near Stanley Road, but in its current position it still presents an awkward test

before the player moves almost in the opposite direction for the 434-yard 18th. Any one of five bunkers lies in wait for the drive, and four more guard the green. Chasing challenging pin positions is fraught with danger, given the rapid roll-offs that will gather anything slightly off target.

# ROYAL BIRKDALE
## Southport, Lancashire, England

To turn into the drive of Royal Birkdale is to be confronted with one of the most extraordinary views in the world of golf – a vast surf of dunes rolling in from the distant horizon of the real sea and scarcely a golf hole to be seen.

First impressions at Royal Birkdale are much as they would have been in 1896 to the early pioneers of the Birkdale GC, when they sought out a new and altogether grander site to the south of the nine-hole course that had been founded in 1889. Forward thinking and a perennial search for new standards of excellence, all concealed within the massive bulwarks of the Birkdale dunes, have been constant themes ever since. By 1909 there were 18 holes, 'very sporting' according to the *Golfing Annual* when the course was chosen for the Ladies' British Open Amateur Championship.

At the start of the 1930s, the 18-hole course was more than 6,000 yards (5,500 metres). Yet the Ladies' British Open Amateur had not returned. Something needed to be done. In 1931 the Southport Corporation bought the land from the Weld-Blundell estate and offered the club a 99-year lease.

### MULTIGENERATIONAL CONNECTION

Royal Birkdale then appointed the firm of Hawtree and J.H. Taylor to design and build a championship course. A large tract of additional land to the south was on offer, but the designers chose to keep the development within the confines of the original course. Drainage problems within the low-lying areas between the dunes, known as 'slacks', were the reasons for not extending further south. Frederick Hawtree's son, Fred Hawtree, was to make use of the land many years later in the extension of neighbouring Hillside.

Birkdale is rather different from some Open Championship venues. It has a robustly architectural layout, as does Muirfield (see page 60). Nearly all holes change the previous hole's direction of play. There is no interweaving of the two nine-hole loops, which both return to the clubhouse. The short holes play into different winds, and there is a general absence of blindness in the holes, although many holes have doglegs. The sheer breadth of this part of the Lancashire sand-dune system allowed it to exploit these features. This same breadth and development of dune ridges gave rise to the laying out of holes within the low, intervening slacks. Sometimes these slacks were wide enough to allow holes to play transversely from one ridge to another. So a naturally galleried golf links was born.

The course did not hold a tournament until 1946, when the Amateur Championship came. Its first Open Championship was in 1954 and subsequently in 1961, when wind and rain washed out the second day's play.

Partly arising from crowded and rather wretched conditions during this second day, Fred Hawtree was invited back to make changes. The old 17th short hole disappeared, because it was arguably a hindrance to a strong championship finish, and was replaced by the present 12th. The new hole rebutted the old reproach of four 'high to low' short holes and became a favourite of many when The Open returned in 1965.

Change and development have continued through the hands of the third generation of the family to be involved with Birkdale – Martin Hawtree. He supervised the reconstruction of the greens in the 1990s, when agronomic problems emerged to disturb the 1991 Open. At the same time he took the opportunity to integrate the greens more strongly into their dune

*The 12th green is typical of many at Royal Birkdale, being wholly integrated into the dunes, which are kept rough enough to prevent a stray ball being given a kindly bounce back onto the putting surface.*

settings, producing bolder but often subtle contouring. More recently Martin Hawtree tightened up some of the fairways, with dune featuring and bunkering. He has also repositioned five of the championship tees to improve line and frame rather than simply add length, and has remodelled the 17th hole.

## SUPERB SEASIDE CHALLENGE

It is the scale of the dunes that produces the most memorable quality of Birkdale. Its Olympian tees, which play so spectacularly into fairways, sometimes far below, are framed by dunes on both sides. Greens are self-contained targets that ask to be attacked. They are frequently surrounded by high dunes that need to be kept rough if they are not to shed balls towards the green. Therefore the cardinal virtue of Birkdale – straightness – is enshrined in nearly every green site. The perennial fascination of the course is the way in which high drama is so tightly kept in control of the emotions by the need for accurate and thoughtful play.

The 450-yard 1st typifies much of Birkdale. There is a fine frame of dunes down both sides, a moderately wide fairway and a deep drive bunker. The long second shot is to a green cradled behind and between hillocks and hollows. It is, however, the only green with a fall-away from the player, and when running fast it requires great accuracy and judgement. Then the following four holes twist and turn through many directions before the player reaches a monster of a hole at the 509-yard 6th, a par five for members but a formidable par four for an Open Championship. A substantial dune on the right of the drive needs to be boldly carried to shorten the length of a second shot hoping to reach the green. The safer route to the left must negotiate fairway bunkers on the left and an approach bunker set into the steep rise in front of this elevated green.

The 412-yard 10th is a dogleg left with a second shot played into a sublimely uplifting green site, nestled into dunes. The fairway is dramatically more undulating than elsewhere on the course, and the green is engagingly contoured to match. A delightful calm before the storm is the 201-yard 14th, although its deep hollow beyond slides insidiously into the back of the green.

The drive at the 572-yard 17th is bunkered on the right beyond the turn in the fairway. The second leg of the fairway zigzags past a peninsula of cross-dunes emerging from the right side of the hole, 100 yards (90 metres) back from the green. The green is contoured at times wildly and exoticly, yet it only continues in the line of strong contouring found on the 11th and 15th greens.

## PROTECTED AREA

Birkdale lies within a Site of Special Scientific Interest, and the club take their ecological responsibilities as seriously as any, by for example clearing invasive trees such as birch and white poplar. The open, rolling landscape that confronted the visitor in the drive is now yet more open but nothing has diminished this giant of a course, sleeping peacefully among the dunes, ready to spring up and engage with the next championship to be held there.

## ROYAL BIRKDALE GOLF CLUB – Southport, Lancashire, England

George Low, 1909; F.G. Hawtree and J.H. Taylor, 1930s; Fred (W.) Hawtree 1961–65; Martin Hawtree 1993–95 and 2004–07 Major events: Ladies' British Open Amateur 1909, 1962, 1999; Amateur Championship 1946, 1989, 2005; Walker Cup 1951; Open Championship 1954, 1961, 1965, 1971, 1976, 1983, 1991, 1998, 2008; Ryder Cup 1965, 1969; Women's British Open 1986, 2000, 2005; Curtis Cup 1948

CARD OF THE COURSE

| HOLE | YARDS | PAR | HOLE | YARDS | PAR |
|------|-------|-----|------|-------|-----|
| 1. | 450 | 4 | 10. | 412 | 4 |
| 2. | 421 | 4 | 11. | 434 | 4 |
| 3. | 450 | 4 | 12. | 183 | 3 |
| 4. | 203 | 3 | 13. | 498 | 4 |
| 5. | 346 | 4 | 14. | 201 | 3 |
| 6. | 509 | 5 | 15. | 544 | 5 |
| 7. | 177 | 3 | 16. | 439 | 4 |
| 8. | 458 | 4 | 17. | 572 | 5 |
| 9. | 411 | 4 | 18. | 472 | 4 |
| **OUT** | **3,425** | **35** | **IN** | **3,755** | **36** |
| | | | **TOTAL** | **7,180** | **71** |

# ROYAL LYTHAM
## Lytham St Annes, Lancashire, England

If golf courses were rated on looks alone Royal Lytham would struggle for recognition. It is a links course that offers no view of the sea; instead the vista is filled with housing and a railway line. Yet this is one of the greatest in the world.

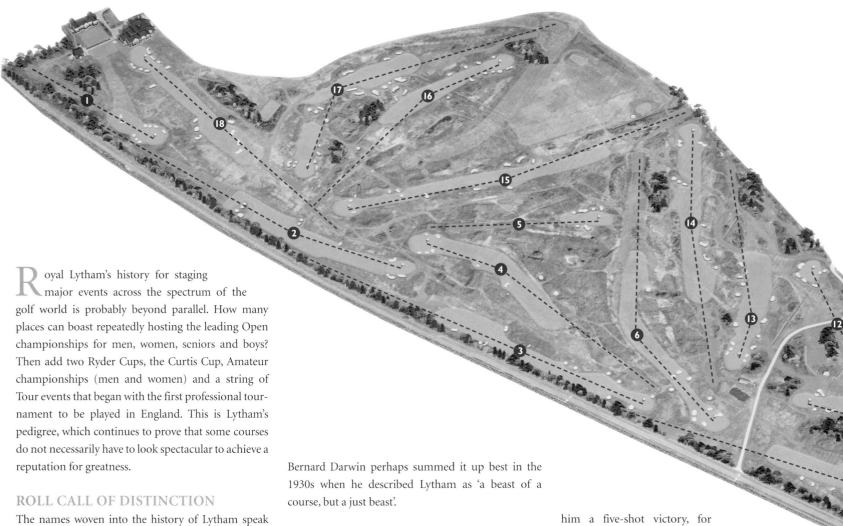

Royal Lytham's history for staging major events across the spectrum of the golf world is probably beyond parallel. How many places can boast repeatedly hosting the leading Open championships for men, women, seniors and boys? Then add two Ryder Cups, the Curtis Cup, Amateur championships (men and women) and a string of Tour events that began with the first professional tournament to be played in England. This is Lytham's pedigree, which continues to prove that some courses do not necessarily have to look spectacular to achieve a reputation for greatness.

## ROLL CALL OF DISTINCTION

The names woven into the history of Lytham speak volumes. Bobby Jones, Severiano Ballesteros, Gary Player, Peter Thomson, Tony Jacklin and Annika Sorenstam have all departed from this portion of north-west England clutching hard-earned major trophies. It is little wonder that the club invites the golfer to 'walk the path of legends' in its promotional literature.

Characterized by strategic, penal bunkering that often eats into small greens, Lytham's other strength is its routing. A player needs to make their score on the way out, and then preserve it as they tack back into the prevailing wind – Lytham having one of the toughest finishing stretches in all of golf. Legendary golf writer Bernard Darwin perhaps summed it up best in the 1930s when he described Lytham as 'a beast of a course, but a just beast'.

## EARLY HISTORY

The origins of the club date back to an 1886 meeting at the St Annes Hotel. Quickly a course was created close to the local railway station, and the layout was accessed via the platform and a level crossing. Within four years the course was staging English golf's inaugural professional tournament.

Ten top players, including Old Tom Morris, took part to allow members the chance to see 'the Royal & Ancient game as it was played by the leading exponents'. A special train from Manchester was laid on to bring spectators to the course. Played over two rounds it was won by Willie Fernie. Rounds of 77 and 78 gave him a five-shot victory, for which he received a share of the £53 prize fund.

Although the greens on the original course were excellent there was no security of tenure so the club was moved a little farther down the railway line. The professional George Lowe, who had finished fourth in that exhibition tournament, laid out the new course. This design provided the blueprint for the course as it stands today. Many changes have since been made: for example, in 1911 Harry Colt was invited to suggest how the course might be improved. Numerous bunkers were added, greens and tees repositioned and the course lengthened.

## A SHORT START

Lytham is unique among the Open venues in that it begins with a par three. On the 206-yard 1st the championship tee is tucked away in a corner behind the pro's shop. The player is likely to be downwind, but judging its strength is not easy from such a sheltered starting point. No fewer than seven bunkers guard the green, making tucked-away pins difficult to access. Therefore the first shot of the round should land on the front edge, carrying two more bunkers that sit short of the green.

As with the 1st, the railway line with tall trees alongside runs down the right of the next two holes. The ideal line from the 2nd tee is over the centre of a bunker complex located around 200 yards (180 metres) from the tee on the right side of the fairway. The concern downwind on a fast links is likely to be running into one of two more bunkers guarding the left side 275 yards (250 metres) from the tee. Again the green offers a small target. Three awkward bunkers surround the green along with two tricky humps to the left, ensuring that any approach lacking in accuracy will lead to an early short-game test.

Bunkers created down the right side of the fairway in 2006 and another located on the left at landing range call for a demanding drive on the 457-yard 3rd. The raised green is gently undulating and there are damaging drop-aways to be avoided.

There is an abrupt about-turn for the 391-yard 4th. It is the only hole played into the prevailing wind on the front nine. A dogleg swings to the left for the final third of its

distance and the bunkering provides definition that forces the drive into the correct position down the right side of the fairway. Provided the ball has been hit far enough the player will have a clear view of the green. This is the reward for risking a driver; those who lay up short of the trouble down the left are left with a semiblind approach.

## TACKLING THE LONG HOLES

After the 210-yard 5th come consecutive par fives. At 494 yards, the 6th could soon be downgraded. The issue is whether the narrow green with savage pot bunkers eating into it is suitable for a par four requiring a long approach. It is a target originally designed to test short shots, whether they were floated pitches or, more likely, a canny bump-and-run through the gap at the front. Although the 555-yard 7th is the longest hole on the course, Tiger Woods, playing his first Open as a professional in 1996, found the green with a driver and a 9-iron. Heavily bunkered for almost its entire length, there are ten traps running down the right side of the fairway and another five down the left. Three more guard the left side of the green.

Out-of-bounds threatens on the 417-yard 8th, with the railway still on the right, but the main feature is the dramatic raised green beyond three deep, sunken bunkers. The nature of the putting surface puts a premium on distance control. A lovely little hole, the downhill, 164-yard 9th sits amid the characterful, red-brick housing that surrounds the far end of the course. Eight bunkers and an undulating green lie in wait. If the ball is over-hit, a golfer will be playing three off the tee.

## ROYAL LYTHAM & ST ANNES GOLF CLUB – Lytham St Annes, Lancashire, England

George Lowe, 1897 and Harry Colt, 1911
Major events: Ladies' British Open Amateur 1893, 1913, 1948, 1993; Open Championship 1926, 1952, 1958, 1963, 1969, 1974, 1979, 1988, 1996, 2001; Amateur Championship 1935, 1955, 1986, 2006; Ryder Cup 1961, 1977; Curtis Cup 1976; Women's British Open 1998, 2003, 2006

### CARD OF THE COURSE

| HOLE | YARDS | PAR | HOLE | YARDS | PAR |
|------|-------|-----|------|-------|-----|
| 1. | 206 | 3 | 10. | 334 | 4 |
| 2. | 436 | 4 | 11. | 540 | 5 |
| 3. | 457 | 4 | 12. | 196 | 3 |
| 4. | 391 | 4 | 13. | 340 | 4 |
| 5. | 210 | 3 | 14. | 443 | 4 |
| 6. | 494 | 5 | 15. | 464 | 4 |
| 7. | 555 | 5 | 16. | 358 | 4 |
| 8. | 417 | 4 | 17. | 467 | 4 |
| 9. | 164 | 3 | 18. | 410 | 4 |
| **OUT** | **3,330** | **35** | **IN** | **3552** | **36** |
| | | | **TOTAL** | **6,882** | **71** |

## INTO THE WIND

The homeward journey begins with the 334-yard 10th, where the target is a raised green guarded by five bunkers, and the entrance is narrow. But this short par four gives little indication of Lytham's tough finish. Likewise, the 540-yard 11th is another birdie chance. A large mound with two bunkers beneath has to be carried to find the ideal position for the approach. The area to the right of the fairway is featureless and offers disproportionate room, while bunkers guarding the green are there to punish those who go for it in two and fail. Laying up ensures an easy pitch.

Now Lytham starts to bear its teeth. The 196-yard 12th is as good a par three as there is on the Open rota. From the tee shot, the player needs to shape the flight of the ball left to right to access the gap at the front of the diagonally positioned green. But beware the false front; if the ball comes up short, it will kick into deep traps. The three bunkers guarding the left penalize those failing to account for the green's shape.

After the 340-yard 13th, which should offer some respite, the golfer is into the famous Lytham finishing stretch. It starts with the 443-yard 14th, which is a tough driving hole into the wind. Any one of four bunkers awaits the tee shot that is pushed too far right, while the green is full of subtle breaks. On the 464-yard 15th a saddle-back fairway can kick drives

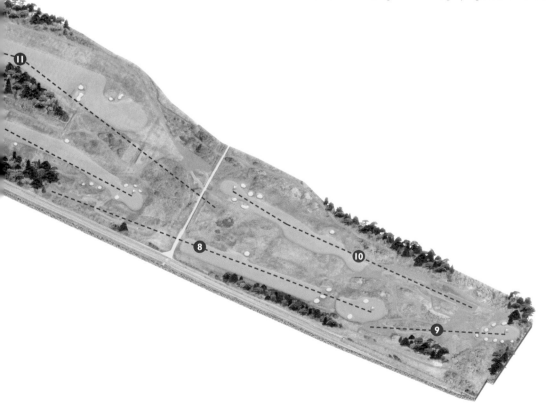

# MIRACLE SHOT FROM THE RUBBISH
## When Bobby Jones became a Lytham legend in 1926

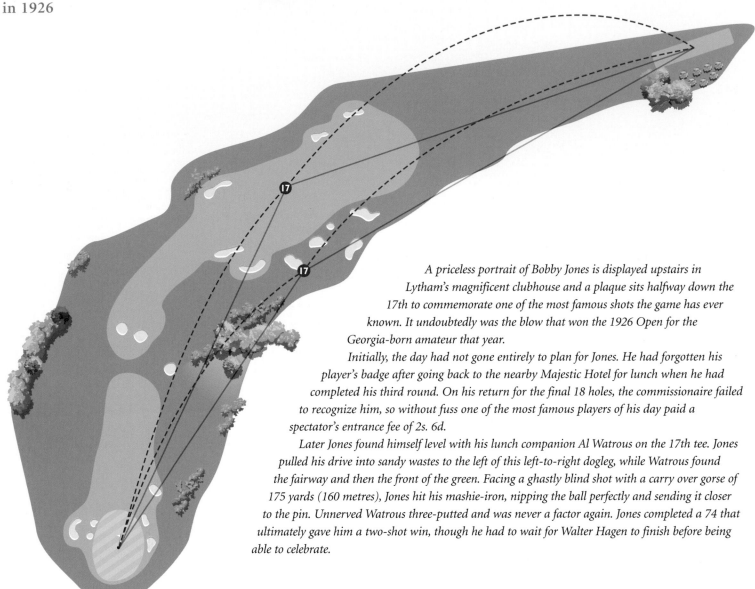

*A priceless portrait of Bobby Jones is displayed upstairs in Lytham's magnificent clubhouse and a plaque sits halfway down the 17th to commemorate one of the most famous shots the game has ever known. It undoubtedly was the blow that won the 1926 Open for the Georgia-born amateur that year.*

*Initially, the day had not gone entirely to plan for Jones. He had forgotten his player's badge after going back to the nearby Majestic Hotel for lunch when he had completed his third round. On his return for the final 18 holes, the commissionaire failed to recognize him, so without fuss one of the most famous players of his day paid a spectator's entrance fee of 2s. 6d.*

*Later Jones found himself level with his lunch companion Al Watrous on the 17th tee. Jones pulled his drive into sandy wastes to the left of this left-to-right dogleg, while Watrous found the fairway and then the front of the green. Facing a ghastly blind shot with a carry over gorse of 175 yards (160 metres), Jones hit his mashie-iron, nipping the ball perfectly and sending it closer to the pin. Unnerved Watrous three-putted and was never a factor again. Jones completed a 74 that ultimately gave him a two-shot win, though he had to wait for Walter Hagen to finish before being able to celebrate.*

into the semirough, making approaches to a heavily guarded green awkward to judge.

## SCENES OF EPIC GOLFING
Seve Ballesteros made famous the 358-yard 16th with his wild driving into an impromptu car park well to the right of the fairway on his way to Open victory in 1979. He was not out-of-bounds; in fact the illegally parked cars were and when the owners could not be found the swashbuckling Spaniard received a free

drop. He hit a sand-wedge to 15 feet (4.5 metres) and holed for birdie.

If the 16th belongs to Ballesteros and the 467-yard 17th to Bobby Jones (see above), then the 410-yard 18th is Tony Jacklin's for satisfying the raging thirst of the home nation for a British winner. In 1969 he did it with wonderfully controlled golf, typified by the composed way he negotiated the sea of bunkers that can be so ruinous on this final hole. Despite almost suffocating levels of expectation, his drive at the last

split the fairway, and on BBC Television Henry Longhurst summed up this tremendous shot in three words: 'What a corker!'

Seve Ballesteros would return to Lytham in the 1988 Open with the same clubs and clothes as nine years earlier to win again, this time in a Monday finish after Saturday's play had been washed out. Poor Hubert Green had played the first eight holes in five under par only for his efforts to be scrubbed from the record as the round was ordered to be replayed a day later.

Ballesteros won with a course-record equalling final round of 65, which he described as the best of his life.

Tom Lehman ended the American jinx at Lytham Opens in 1996, and David Duval ensured the Stars and Stripes were raised again five years later. America also enjoyed success in both Ryder Cups played on the course. The 1977 match featured Jack Nicklaus, Tom Watson, Hale Irwin and Lanny Wadkins. They helped the US to a 12½–7½ win. It was the last clash before the GB and Ireland opposition was expanded to the whole

of Europe. In 1961, some 35,000 spectators saw ten of the 25 matches go to the final green in a 14½–9½ US victory. Henry Longhurst said it was 'the finest exhibition ever put before the public'. And this perhaps helps sum up the magic of Royal Lytham. Whatever the format, playing or watching, the golf is never anything other than utterly compelling. Indeed, even if there were spectacular seaside views to admire, the game would probably be too absorbing for its surroundings to be noticed.

*The 6th green, a fiendishly difficult target to find from distance. The angle of approach has to be spot on to thread a running shot onto the putting surface.*

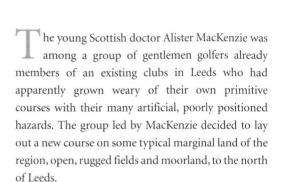

The young Scottish doctor Alister MacKenzie was among a group of gentlemen golfers already members of an existing clubs in Leeds who had apparently grown weary of their own primitive courses with their many artificial, poorly positioned hazards. The group led by MacKenzie decided to lay out a new course on some typical marginal land of the region, open, rugged fields and moorland, to the north of Leeds.

Harry Colt, at that time regarded as an acknowledged expert in the field of golf-course development, was called in to reassure the fledgling club that MacKenzie was not running away with himself. Colt's later description of his first meeting with MacKenzie – and they were to set up a partnership until the early 1920s – gives the overriding impression of MacKenzie as the industrious student and enthusiast. He was teeming with ideas and plans, revelling in a new subject, a real site, grappling with principles and philosophies gathered probably from Colt's own early writings, and also from his own excursions into the art of camouflage in South Africa during the Boer War. The affirmation of the design by a leading expert, a cold winter for construction giving rise to no interference from MacKenzie's committee, and his own rapidly hardening ideas and principles gave MacKenzie free rein to build the course of his dreams.

At his disposition was a long and narrow property, in the form of a fish hook, curiously like that of St

Andrews (see page 40), his favourite course. MacKenzie's layout produced an out-and-back loop of holes with a subsidiary loop in the middle where the site was broadest. But the course is more complicated than this: MacKenzie seems to have worked hard to achieve a figure-of-eight arrangement, striking a balance between holes on the slice side and those on the hook side of the boundaries.

### MACKENZIE'S GREAT SKILL

The course sets off with a gently rising, 404-yard par four, bunkered up the right-hand side, with a wide open green, fully in view from the tee, and set against a lovely hillside. Like most on the course, the green is rather large, which allowed MacKenzie the opportunity to create contours. Through such contours and angling of greens he was able to develop the principle of rewarding certain lines of play.

The 305-yard 2nd is a blind drive over the hill to a tightly guarded, long and narrow green. Across Manor House Lane, the 514-yard 3rd is played to a heather-fringed fairway, which seems to narrow as it advances. The hole has always required a walk across the 16th fairway to find the fairway. It is played on towards a two-level green, split the length of the playing axis, one level being an extension of the fairway, the other falling away into a depression – a fine example

of MacKenzie's ability to blend artifice with the natural surroundings.

MacKenzie skilfully crafted his layout by the use of natural sloping ground to influence play on the 369-yard 5th and the 455-yard 6th. From the 5th tee the fairway slopes strongly left to right all the way to the green, demanding only the strongest and most precise drives from anyone attempting to reach the green. And half the 6th fairway also slopes to the right, while a lone fairway bunker on the flatter left-hand side interrogates the player over whether to gamble and obtain an easier shot to the well-defended green. The safer drive is to the right but leaves a most difficult long shot into the green. The risky drive to the left, defended with bunkers and rough and not as visible from the tee, yields a less stressful approach shot. It is, then, fascinating to see the principles of risk and reward, so

# ALWOODLEY
## Leeds, Yorkshire, England

Although his first course, The Alwoodley was to be very far from an expected 'prentice work' for Dr Alister MacKenzie. He was the honorary secretary of the group sponsoring the course, and he went on to become one of the most enigmatic golf-course architects of the Golden Age.

# THE ALWOODLEY GOLF CLUB –
## Leeds, Yorkshire, England

Dr Alister MacKenzie, 1908

Major events: Ladies' British Open Amateur
1971, 2007

### CARD OF THE COURSE

| HOLE | YARDS | PAR | HOLE | YARDS | PAR |
|------|-------|-----|------|-------|-----|
| 1. | 404 | 4 | 10. | 475 | 5 |
| 2. | 305 | 4 | 11. | 167 | 3 |
| 3. | 514 | 5 | 12. | 365 | 4 |
| 4. | 478 | 4 | 13. | 402 | 4 |
| 5. | 369 | 4 | 14. | 206 | 3 |
| 6. | 455 | 4 | 15. | 409 | 4 |
| 7. | 143 | 3 | 16. | 414 | 4 |
| 8. | 584 | 5 | 17. | 434 | 4 |
| 9. | 191 | 3 | 18. | 470 | 4 |
| **OUT** | **3,443** | **36** | **IN** | **3,342** | **35** |
| | | | **TOTAL** | **6,785** | **71** |

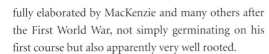

*The putting surface of the 11th green at Alwoodley is the most deceptive on the course, with a big slope from back to front and another pronounced break from left to right. Only a truly struck tee shot holds this green.*

fully elaborated by MacKenzie and many others after the First World War, not simply germinating on his first course but also apparently very well rooted.

The 475-yard 10th and 167-yard 11th depended on the acquisition of further land to build the 10th green where MacKenzie certainly wanted it, as well as the 11th tee, to play back uphill as a par three. The 11th resembles his other great early short hole at nearby Moortown, the present 10th (Gibraltar), one of the many courses in Yorkshire he was to design before travelling overseas.

## COPING WITH THE WIND

With the turn back to the clubhouse after the 11th, there follow six stern par fours that develop a crescendo of lengths to the 18th; they are played generally into the prevailing wind, except for the 414-yard 16th hole where there is a cross-wind. There is a pause for the 206-yard, par-three 14th with a plateau green that is next to and parallel to the similar 7th, a most interesting cross-over in the round. At first sight the layout of the two holes feels strange, surely avoidable, the work of an amateur; but Harry Colt could apparently see no better solution to getting through this narrow neck of land to produce a figure-of-eight arrangement. A late dogleg and a wickedly contoured green give distinction to the 15th, while an understanding of how the cross-wind might be used is advantageous on the 16th.

The final two holes are into the wind, with the 434-yard 17th green being set down a steep hillside. The hole might be the origin of MacKenzie's later declared dislike for blind holes. Perhaps the rather dull, flat piece of ground, together with the road crossing, inclined him against opting for a short blind hole here at the climax of the round, even though a one-shotter was much the most logical if unexciting solution to this difficult piece of ground.

His final hole is as stern a test as any finishing hole. From an elevated tee the 470-yard par four is bunkered the length of the hole. There is reward for risking the left-hand and out-of-bounds side in the form of an open entrance to the green.

## A BEACON OF EXCELLENCE

Alwoodley is one of MacKenzie's best-preserved courses. His style would evolve through confrontations with new countries, sites, new friends and colleagues, and a ripening self-confidence, not entirely rare in his chosen profession. But Alwoodley represents a fine insight into the developing mind of one of the pioneers of golf-course architecture in the Golden Age. It is far more than the seedbed for the development of the fundamental principles of the golf architectural profession, still being practised today, and in its rugged, isolated, moorland beauty it still provides a fine test of golf for, among others, Open Championship qualifiers.

# GANTON
## Ganton, North Yorkshire, England

Circling crows can frequently be spotted overhead at Ganton. Could it be these carrion seekers have developed a taste for recently deceased scorecards? Plenty are surely to be found amid the punishing bunkers and gorse on a course that rightly figures prominently in the history of English golf.

Ganton is a tough but proper and honest test. It is a course that through its early years benefited from the input of some of the great designers. Not one has messed up the masterpiece.

The result is a layout that has proved a worthy host to leading professional and amateur tournaments for men and women. When the Walker Cup came to this corner of North Yorkshire in 2003, it meant Ganton was able to join Muirfield (see page 60) and Royal Birkdale (see page 86) in being able to boast about having staged all three major transatlantic team jousts with the USA: the Ryder, Walker and Curtis cups.

Although 11 miles (18 kilometres) inland from the coastal town of Scarborough, the course has a links feel. The turf is springy and usually plays fast and firm. Thousands of years ago the site was an inlet from the North Sea, leaving a natural sandy subsoil. Even today the odd ancient sea shell can be found on the golf course.

Ganton's bunkers are hazards to be feared, often steep-faced front and back. Doing the job they were intended to do – of punishing errant shots – they most definitely are not the sandpits of most modern designs that have commentators so frequently stating: 'He's better off in the sand rather than just missing it.'

Then there is Ganton's gorse and ever-varying routing that means players constantly need to adjust their shot-making, with the wind very often an important factor. Even though away from the coast, the Vale of Pickering seems to serve as something of a wind tunnel to create breezy conditions. Five holes swing from left to right, while five more dogleg in the opposite direction. The ability to move the ball through the air in both directions is an invaluable asset for a player, as is a delicate but sure putting touch on large, undulating greens.

### GANTON GOLF CLUB –
### Ganton, North Yorkshire, England

Tom Chisholm and Robert Bird, 1891; Harry Vardon, Ted Ray, James Braid and J.H. Taylor, 1905; Harry Colt, 1907, 1911 and 1931; Dr Alister MacKenzie, 1912 and 1920; Tom Simpson, 1934; and C.K. Cotton, 1948 and 1952
Major events: Ryder Cup 1949; Ladies' British Open Amateur 1954, 1985; Amateur Championship 1964, 1977, 1991; Curtis Cup 2000; Walker Cup 2003

### CARD OF THE COURSE

| HOLE | YARDS | PAR | HOLE | YARDS | PAR |
|------|-------|-----|------|-------|-----|
| 1. | 372 | 4 | 10. | 171 | 3 |
| 2. | 448 | 4 | 11. | 428 | 4 |
| 3. | 355 | 4 | 12. | 404 | 4 |
| 4. | 412 | 4 | 13. | 538 | 5 |
| 5. | 160 | 3 | 14. | 281 | 4 |
| 6. | 474 | 4 | 15. | 465 | 4 |
| 7. | 441 | 4 | 16. | 450 | 4 |
| 8. | 416 | 4 | 17. | 251 | 3 |
| 9. | 507 | 5 | 18. | 438 | 4 |
| **OUT** | **3,585** | **36** | **IN** | **3,426** | **35** |
| | | | **TOTAL** | **7,011** | **71** |

### VARDON AND THE DESIGN DREAM TEAM

Like so many of the golf courses built in the late 19th century, Ganton owes its existence to the railway, because it opened up membership possibilities for those living throughout the West Riding of Yorkshire – Ganton Halt being just a quarter of a mile (0.5 kilometres) from the clubhouse. The course formed part of Sir Charles Legard's Ganton Estate and was rough ground covered with a variety of grasses and wild flowers.

Golf was first played there in 1891 on a course laid out by Tom Chisholm of St Andrews, assisted by the club's first professional and greenkeeper Robert Bird. Within five years the great Harry Vardon had been appointed as professional and during his seven-year stay he won three of his six Open championships as well as the 1900 US Open.

Vardon's matches against J.H. Taylor and Willie Park Jnr just before the turn of the 20th century served to put Ganton on the golfing map. More significantly for the club, in 1905 Vardon contributed to a major redesign of the course in conjunction with his successor as Ganton professional, Ted Ray. James Braid and J.H.

Taylor also assisted. Arguably the four most prominent minds in the game had come together to help make the most of the terrain.

Many more architects were to add their influence, including such distinguished people as Harry Colt and Alister MacKenzie. All made significant design contributions. They fashioned a course that requires finesse and accuracy, power and nerve. In the splendour of its heathland setting, Ganton is one of the finest inland courses in the world.

## PLAYING THE COURSE

From the very first tee it is essential to be accurate. The 372-yard 1st moves to the right of the direction of the tee box and a drive that finds the right half of the fairway is ideal, but this means flirting with a network of five bunkers bordered with gorse. At the green the front-right bunker serves notice that severe, revetted faces to hazards are a Ganton trademark. There is also a significant indicator of the varied routing as players turn back on themselves for the next.

Not only does the 448-yard 2nd head in the opposite direction but it also moves the other way, encouraging the right-hander to hit a gentle draw from the tee. The opening to the green is relatively generous but, almost unseen, a nasty bunker lurks in the back-left corner and becomes a significant factor if the pin is cut anywhere near. With the green sloping from front to back a controlled approach is a must.

At only 355 yards, the 3rd is a short par four but majestic bunkering means it requires the utmost care. A fierce, large diagonal bunker runs down the left side. To reach the widest and safest part of the fairway there is a significant carry, and if a player goes too far another bunker is ready to lure the ball down the right side. The green is large and undulating, the right side gathers towards another hazard so a precise approach is again required.

Harry Colt was responsible for the 412-yard 4th, which runs in roughly the same direction as the opening hole. The second shot is played over a gentle valley to an undulating green that has gorse growing tight to its back fringe. Another steep-faced bunker guards the right side.

### A SEVERE TEST

There is again little margin for error at the 160-yard 5th, the first short hole on the course. Perhaps this is one hole that borders on being unfair – particularly the back-right pot bunker. The thigh-high lip is the same front and back, and it is there to grab an over-hit tee shot. Inevitably this is likely to run to the back of the bunker from where there is no room for a backswing and, indeed, no shot – no matter how skilled the practitioner. Does the punishment fit the crime? Perhaps it is a tad draconian.

Played as a par five by the members, the 474-yard 6th is a fearsome two-shotter for modern-day monster hitters, while the 441-yard 7th is a hole of breathtaking beauty framed in gorse, birch and pine as it swings from left to right. Attractively and thoughtfully bunkered, the hole plunges downhill close to the landing area to reward the accurately struck tee shot before climbing back up towards the green. The putting surface is relatively wide and strategically guarded. It is easy to run through the back and only a fool would take on a pin cut close to the left edge.

Running parallel to the A64 – the main road that links Scarborough to York – is the 507-yard 9th, but the golfer is shielded from the traffic (or should that be the other way round?) by a thick line of tall pines. It is a testing if not long par five. The landing area off the tee is narrow and those tempted to find the green in two will have to contend with two penal bunkers 40 yards (36 metres) short of the putting surface. If a golfer decides to lay up short of those hazards, the ground is undulating and likely to provide a testing and uncomfortable lie for the pitch to a green guarded either side at the front by two more bunkers.

### THE BACK NINE

The 171-yard 10th moves in the same direction and, as on the previous hole, it is played to a narrow green. At its widest it is a mere 16 yards (15 metres) across and at its narrowest 12 yards (11 metres). This green is more heavily bunkered, the hazards eating enthusiastically into the area of safety. At the back is a sneakily placed one hidden from view from the tee, while on a sunny morning the shadows cast by the pines can play havoc with the lining-up process.

Risk and reward is a recurring theme at Ganton and it applies at the 428-yard 11th, where moving the ball from left to right is what is required from the tee. A

## THE GANTON GREATS
### Players of outstanding quality

*That was certainly the entitlement of Michael Bonallack in the 1968 English Amateur, when Britain's finest amateur of his era – future secretary of the Royal and Ancient Golf Course – thrashed David Kelley in the final. Bonallack came home in 29 for an approximate 61 in probably the best display of golf ever played on the course.*

*Ganton is the only inland course to have staged The Amateur Championship and justifies its selection by identifying winners of the highest calibre. The great Peter McEvoy was the champion in 1977, and Gary Wolstenholme, a member of the victorious 2003 Walker Cup team at Ganton, was the winner in 1991.*

*Fewer professional events have been staged on the course, but those that have can also boast champions of outstanding quality. Six times a Major winner, Nick Faldo was the champion in the 1981 PGA Championship, and former European Ryder Cup captain Bernard Gallacher was the 1975 Dunlop Masters winner. The legendary Ben Hogan led the American team that won 1949 Ryder Cup at Ganton. Max Faulkner was the star of the Great Britain team, while the US line-up included Sam Snead. The visitors won a close contest by claiming the last four singles for a 7–5 win.*

*The 2003 Walker Cup was another closely fought affair, but this time Great Britain and Ireland won the trophy for a record third match running. Victory was achieved by the narrowest of margins 12½–11½ . It was the kind of golf that is synonymous with Ganton. It was exciting, challenging and richly rewarding. It is a course steeped in history that should forever be capable of staging elite events as well as providing great entertainment for the humble handicapper and the abundant birdlife watching overhead.*

*The 3rd is one of the easier par fours but remains a demanding test. The large green provides an inviting target, but tough, clever bunkering ensures challenging pin positions are plentiful.*

*The true difficulty of the majestic 4th is only realized when you arrive at the green. Full of subtle change it tests the full putting skills, including reading lines and judgement of pace over a large undulating surface.*

player will probably take aim on the bunker 270 yards (247 metres) down the left side of the hole and move the ball into the fairway from there. The landing area is tight, but to lay up short leaves a long, blind approach. If a golfer goes for a big drive they risk bringing into play the bunkers that guard either side of the fairway, yet they stand a good chance of being rewarded with a relatively straightforward route to the green.

It is a similar story on the 404-yard 12th, while the 538-yard 13th also puts a premium on good, accurate driving. The 281-yard 14th is a beauty that again is all about dare and gain. Does the golfer take on the phenomenally deep bunker 45 yards (41 metres) short

of the green? If they do, they might get a birdie. Mess it up and the crows may be scenting a ripped-up score-card. A more timid (sensible) mind-set will have a player aiming a lay-up on the distant church spire nestling in the glorious countryside.

## UNFORGETTABLE GOLFING MOMENTS

If the wind is in a player's face on the 15th tee a unique 40-yard (36-metre) long bunker that runs down the left side may be significant. It is a magnificent, 465-yard hole that stretches out before golfers, and the demands on their putting strokes are likely to be at their greatest on an undulating and rolling green that makes judging the pace of a putt very awkward. The cavernous bunker visible from the 16th tee should never be a factor. If it is, the golfer should not be playing from the championship tees; the deep pot bunker that guards the front-right of the green, however, will prey on their mind, especially if their scorecard is still intact.

For the leading players the 251-yard 17th plays as a monster par three. If the green is out of range the uphill landing area in front is generous, and although there are five substantial bunkers it would take a seriously wayward strike to find them.

And so to the 438-yard 18th, which is a fitting closer to a course of such majesty. The tee shot on this right-to-left dogleg is blind, but there is a marker post to assist. Key to it is to be far enough right to ensure tall, ancient pines do not block the approach to the green. The putting surface is a big target, but this presents several demanding hole locations that in turn can bring into play any of the three bunkers that surround the green.

By the time sanctuary and a slice of famous Ganton cake are sought in the traditional old club-house, every facet of a golfer's game and probably every club in the bag will have been tested. If they have come through it, they are entitled to bask in a sense of huge self-satisfaction.

# WOODHALL SPA
## Lincolnshire, England

Investigate the history of the National Golf Centre Woodhall Spa and you will detect the fingerprints of many a famous golfing hand. From Harry Vardon, J.H. Taylor through to Harry Colt, Ben Sayers and on to Donald Steel some of the greatest architectural minds have provided input. But their contributions pale when compared with the towering influence of Colonel Hotchkin.

Colonel Stafford Vere Hotchkin was a single-figure handicapper and local landowner as well as an MP and councillor and before the First World War had served as high sheriff of Rutland. Somehow he also found time for his life's passion – Woodhall Spa.

### EARLY HISTORY

There is little to suggest the flat agricultural land of Lincolnshire could yield good golf, but the game has been played at Woodhall Spa since 1890. In the formative years there were nine holes at two sites. But Woodhall Spa GC had to move for a third time just after the turn of the 20th century and a sandy tract of land was offered at an annual rent of £50 by the Hotchkin family.

In 1903 Harry Vardon, who had by then won four of his six Opens, was invited to lay out an 18-hole course. J.H. Taylor recommended extra bunkering and Colonel Hotchkin, who had financed and monitored the construction, opened the course with a ceremonial first drive. Much of the routing of the front nine today is as it was in 1905, although from the 8th to the 17th there is significant difference. Most of the course is built on sand and gravel, while some of the back nine (and the 7th) are situated on boulder clay. Trees are prolific in this part of Woodhall Spa and the course faces a constant challenge to keep their spread in check.

At the time the Hotchkin Course was being established, the game of golf was undergoing massive change with the advent of rubber-core Haskell balls, which travelled much farther. Leading golf historian Richard Latham estimates the course measured a little less than 5,500 yards before Harry Colt, among others, had by 1914 changed it to its present layout. Five years later Colonel Hotchkin took control of the club from the members. After his death in 1953 his son Neil took over until he sold it to the English Golf Union in 1995. Woodhall Spa is now England's National Golf Centre.

### THE COLONEL'S DESIGN PHILOSOPHY

It was in the period immediately after taking over the club in 1919 that Colonel Hotchkin made the course what it is today. He wanted it to be of penal nature, so the journey to the green was the ultimate test. This meant often narrow entrances to putting surfaces and bunkers that were genuine hazards. They would demand strategic thinking to be avoided and skill to escape. These principles have been followed ever since, leaving deep traps, some of which require a staircase to access.

There is more to the Hotchkin Course than its extraordinary bunkering, but it is for these hazards that it is best known. A popular myth is that there is a bunker for every day of the year. It may feel that way, but this is actually nonsense. There were perhaps as many as 159 but the current count is 111.

Being relatively gentle, the 361-yard 1st gives little indication of the demands that will be put on a player's game. In summer, the springy, dry turf is likely to be parched with fast-running fairways nearly white, and in winter it provides excellent golfing conditions. If on the 2nd tee the drive heads down the right side of the

# THE NATIONAL GOLF CENTRE WOODHALL SPA (HOTCHKIN COURSE) – Woodhall Spa, Lincolnshire, England

Harry Vardon, 1903; Harry Colt, 1911; Ben Sayers and Jack White 1912; and Col. S.V. Hotchkin, 1922

Major events: Ladies' British Open Amateur 1980

CARD OF THE COURSE

| HOLE | YARDS | PAR | HOLE | YARDS | PAR |
|---|---|---|---|---|---|
| 1. | 361 | 4 | 10. | 338 | 4 |
| 2. | 442 | 4 | 11. | 437 | 4 |
| 3. | 415 | 4 | 12. | 172 | 3 |
| 4. | 414 | 4 | 13. | 451 | 4 |
| 5. | 148 | 3 | 14. | 521 | 5 |
| 6. | 526 | 5 | 15. | 321 | 4 |
| 7. | 470 | 4 | 16. | 395 | 4 |
| 8. | 209 | 3 | 17. | 336 | 4 |
| 9. | 584 | 5 | 18. | 540 | 5 |
| OUT | 3,569 | 36 | IN | 3,511 | 37 |
| | | | TOTAL | 7,080 | 73 |

fairway the golfer will receive a rapid introduction as to what golf at Woodhall Spa is all about. The ball will bounce farther right and nestle in one of three deep bunkers located a mid-iron or so short of the green. Forget any notion of finding the putting surface and take the Hotchkin-prescribed medicine. It is worth pointing out that, although his philosophy was penal, he was fair as well. Behind the 3rd green stands the mysterious, ancient tower that is the club's emblem.

The 414-yard 4th has a gentle, right-to-left dogleg on which the strategy is to miss the savage trap that guards the left edge of the fairway on landing distance. Another nasty hazard guards the front left of the green. It is a narrow bunker with steep faces front and back, and it takes a staircase of ten steps to climb down into it. First of three par threes – all of which are protected by heavy bunkering – is the 148-yard 5th.

For the big hitters the 6th green can be in range in two, but they must be mindful of the trap 50 yards (45 metres) short-left of the green, while on the 9th there is a carry over heather from the tee to a generous fairway. Cross-bunkers 350 yards (320 metres) from the tee should be eye- rather than ball-catching, while the staggered bunkering right and left as the fairway narrows to the green is more likely to prey on a golfer's mind.

## LINKS-STYLE LAYOUT

In the mould of a traditional links the design of the Hotchkin Course is essentially out and back. The 338-yard 10th is at the farthest point of the course, before the routing heads into a far more wooded section of the course. A player becomes increasingly aware of the trees through the 437-yard 11th, 172-yard 12th and 451-yard 13th. The most famous of these is the 12th, regarded as the signature hole, where bunkers with faces in excess of 11 feet (3.3 metres) protect a slightly elevated green, which sits ahead of a backdrop of gorse, birch and pine. Not that two members noticed much of the surroundings in 1982. In a singles match L.D. Henshaw holed in one and J.A. Wilson followed him in for the perfect half. By the time the tee is reached on the par-five 14th the woods can feel almost claustrophobic.

Like a piece of fine music, rhythms shift subtly and then dramatically. Suddenly there is a different kind of golf to face, on three consecutive, tight par fours – the 321-yard 15th, the 395-yard 16th and the 336-yard 17th. Then comes the excellent, closing par five, where the course breaks free from the woodland. The right side of this 540-yard hole is shielded by tall, ancient pines, while the left is open to leave clear views of where the round started. Just past the dogleg, the large oak to the right of the fairway 165 yards (151 metres) short of the 18th green should encourage a shot aimed left from the tee. A long second shot or a tight lay-up is needed, with cross-bunkers 135 yards (123 metres) short and more hazards left and right of the fairway closer to home. But it is the oak that makes this hole. It predates golf in this part of the world and perfectly illustrates Hotchkin's principle that a course should remain sympathetic to its natural surroundings.

Woodhall Spa, a course that can boast every hole unique to itself, has been voted in various magazines the finest inland layout in England, and it always features in the upper echelons of any list of the world's best. It is a lasting legacy to Colonel Hotchkin.

*The club's emblem is taken from the ancient tower that stands at the back of the 3rd green, which is guarded at the front by one of Woodhall Spa's more generous bunkers.*

Three great traditions were inaugurated in the realization of the course at Sunningdale: the development of heathland golf; estate development, which saw mutual benefits between the laying out of golf courses and residential properties adjacent to a golf course; and the employment of a professional architect, rather than a local man, to lay out the course.

## INLAND COURSE DEVELOPMENT

When golf first arrived in England in the 1880s the courses were built as much on inland commons as on coastal links; any marginal land could serve the purpose. At the time golf was a sport for the Victorian professional middle classes, to be played over long weekends at quaint seaside towns, where some of the most important links were found, or in nearby commons and parks of London and other cities.

Towards the end of the 1890s two enterprising brothers by the name of T.A. and G.A. Roberts developed the idea of creating an inland golf course accessible by rail from London, with residential development around the golf course forming an integral part of the economics and design of the estate. Their sights were set on Chobham Common, well known for its healthful properties and pretty much waste ground. A new railway line from London came through the area, with a dedicated stop in Sunningdale. With that critical element in place they simply needed a lease and a golf-course architect.

The architect was Willie Park Jnr, son of the first Open champion and himself twice winner of that title. He had come south from Scotland a few years earlier, and a trip to the United States had brought home to him the concepts of integrated development. Within a short time of the start of Sunningdale he was setting up his own enterprise of estate and golf development at Huntercombe in Oxfordshire.

One major obstacle for the new course that Willie Park had to overcome was the perception that a golf course would not thrive on heathland soils – perceived as being too poor to support a fine turf-grass sward. Until then, inland golf had developed mainly on heavy clays (of the London commons and parks), where the particular problem was drainage. But the barren, infertile ground of Sunningdale was another

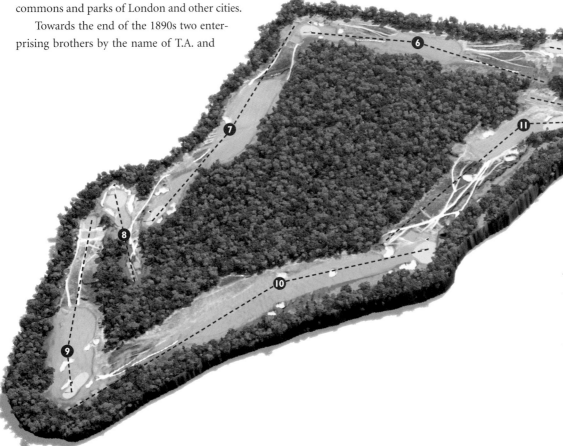

# SUNNINGDALE
## Sunningdale, Berkshire, England

Sunningdale is an inspiration to all golfers with its extraordinary frame of heather and pines, and it possesses a layout as fit to challenge the best golfers now as in the early 1900s.

### SUNNINGDALE GOLF CLUB
### (OLD COURSE) – Sunningdale, Berkshire, England

Willie Park Jnr, 1900 and Harry Colt, early 1900s and 1920s
Major events: Walker Cup 1987; Women's British Open 1997, 2001, 2004; Ladies' British Open Amateur 1956

CARD OF THE COURSE

| HOLE | YARDS | PAR | HOLE | YARDS | PAR |
|------|-------|-----|------|-------|-----|
| 1. | 492 | 5 | 10. | 475 | 4 |
| 2. | 489 | 4 | 11. | 322 | 4 |
| 3. | 318 | 4 | 12. | 442 | 4 |
| 4. | 156 | 3 | 13. | 185 | 3 |
| 5. | 419 | 4 | 14. | 503 | 5 |
| 6. | 433 | 4 | 15. | 239 | 3 |
| 7. | 406 | 4 | 16. | 434 | 4 |
| 8. | 193 | 3 | 17. | 425 | 4 |
| 9. | 273 | 4 | 18. | 423 | 4 |
| OUT | 3,179 | 35 | IN | 3,448 | 35 |
| | | | TOTAL | 6,627 | 70 |

matter, and opinions were not slow to suggest that the whole idea of a golf course on this type of land would end in disaster. This might have been the reason why Park's commission was not simply to lay out the course but also to deliver it to the shareholders ready for play.

## AN ANTICLOCKWISE PERAMBULATION

Willie Park Jnr's routing of the Old Course was a classical out-and-back arrangement that roamed the boundaries of a wonderfully rolling, heath-strewn property,

searching out the most intriguing features of the open, at the time, nearly tree-less terrain. But the boundaries were quite irregular and the frequent change of direction in the holes then became a cardinal principle of golf-course layout.

There is great variety at Sunningdale, with its elevated tees and greens, broad valleys, plateaus and intervening high ground. Park was not afraid to confront the topography head-on, and the number of blind shots must have been a feature of this course, however much a source of lament and future work to the succeeding Sunningdale architect, Harry Colt. Yet each hole is of such individual character and strength that academic criticisms seem small-minded. Until the late 1800s many inland courses were rather rudimentary with not altogether successful experiments in imitating the natural qualities of links golf courses. Park's original 18 holes on the Old Course seem to have been forged in a transitional style with some natural as well as some artificial features.

Much of the original style, however, lies buried beneath the work of the second Sunningdale architect, Harry Colt, who was appointed secretary to the club in 1901 and began modifications as Park's own consultancy broadened worldwide. Some ten of the original greens have disappeared. Over a 20-year period Colt replaced greens – certainly the blind and more primitive ones – and moved holes to make way for the New Course in

the 1920s. Even though he added a good many bunkers, Colt was always fulsome in his praise of Park's work and acknowledged the course as Park's. It is testimony to both men's work that the course today presents a unified, coherent image and is of the highest quality.

## HEATHER-DOMINATED ROUTE

Sunningdale's opening hole sets the scene of boundary holes with a 492-yard, downhill par five but with plenty to go wrong for the over-ambitious. There is room for the bold player to place the drive onto a fairway with a slight cross-slope, so that a second shot to the green is possible. A strange, heather-clad mound in the middle of the fairway, between the landing area and the green that seems to spring from nowhere, is an old boundary corner that Colt left when the hole was moved to the right to make way for the New Course's construction in 1923.

The 489-yard 2nd hole reinforces the Sunningdale stage with a fine heather carry, sharp ridge banks and ditches, and heather and banks down the side of the fairway. It is a very strong par four that has played as a par five for most of its life. The fairway is crested in the landing area and this creates a blind second shot to a green; it is all but hidden except for the most prodigious of drives and falls away from the player alarmingly for anyone trying to reach the green in two.

Following this is the 318-yard 3rd, which tempts the player to drive the green in spite of attendant danger ringed around the green, and a cross-fall over the green from left to right that can menace a short approach as much as a full drive. Directly behind the green are the tees of the 156-yard 4th, a fine uphill hole that has the strongest back-to-front fall on any green on the course. A shot hit pin-high or above the cup will require the utmost putting finesse.

Three cracking two-shot holes follow (see panel, over), with the 7th playing to a new Colt green. The shift in the position of the 7th green required alteration to the 193-yard 8th, originally yet another uphill par three. Colt's hole lies at right angles to the 7th with a green almost precariously situated on a narrow ledge, with steep falls to the right and back and surrounded by sand on three sides.

Another quite drivable par four finds the 273-yard 9th playing across a valley to a modern green doing its best to defend the shortness of the hole with an offset green, formed in two tiers, and not visible from the tee except for the flag. Behind the green the stage is set for the magnificent 475-yard 10th, where the high tee looks down onto a plunging heather and tree-lined fairway below that moves surely onwards and a little

## HARRY COLT'S GEMS
Three majestic par fours

*From the elevated tee of the 419-yard 5th is seen the full vocabulary of Sunningdale in all its heathery splendour. Here is superb elevation, contour, vista and heather carries as well as rough, bunkers, pond and pre-historic-looking mounds. Then the 433-yard 6th has a ridge-and-furrow heather carry, an island fairway and yet more ridge-and-furrow to find an original Park green with its savage bank falling away to the right.*

*A truly old-style, blind tee shot for the 406-yard 7th is the prelude to one of the loveliest parts of the course beyond the crest of the hill. On reaching the top of the hill a formidable sloping fairway steers to the left towards a green that Colt moved back from where Park set it. It is now one of the wonders of Sunningdale – a massive green, veritably fortified with bastions of sand and heather.*

uphill, past bunkers, to a large green in front of the half-way house.

The 322-yard 11th is a classic. From a blind tee shot across a tumbling mass of heather, the fairway bends to the right at the very last moment to a raised upturned saucer of a green. The tee shot must be precise: too long a drive can easily run through the fairway and the green is bunkered on its left to defend any shot coming from that direction. The contouring of the green and a heather-bordered ditch very close to the right of the green provoke the most thoughtful of approach shots.

Colt made changes to the 442-yard 12th, moving the green to a more dramatic setting higher up the slope beyond the old green. A wonderful series of echeloned cross-bunkers running across the axis of the hole, under the second shot, create a split fairway that well justifies the nickname Bottle hole.

## CHARACTERISTIC HOLES
From a perched tee position the 185-yard 13th presents an expansive sea of heather down to a green with a small ridge line that neatly bisects the front from the back of the green. Rough-cut gullies, close to the green, are hardly seen from the Olympian heights of the tee yet are truly horrid to recover from. This hole has gone through more than one transformation since

1900, including a Colt bunker almost within the green, which was soon discarded.

Cross the road to the 14th tee and Sunningdale's personality is shown to perfection. A fine heather carry, a cross-ditch bank, strategic fairway bunkers as well as echelon cross-bunkers farther on, heather and rough bordering the fairway are all spread out majestically before the player as the fairway rises gently uphill to a green provocatively undefended. The stern 239-yard 15th then follows, with its tee shot to a green only just visible above the long heather carry and well guarded either side of the putting surface by bunkers, hollows and heather banks.

## CLOSING HOLES

Turning 180 degrees back into the prevailing wind for the final three holes, the difficult 434-yard 16th demands two well-struck shots to reach the elevated green. A prodigious drive is required to find a point in the fairway that might be flat; anything shorter leaves a long, uphill shot from a downhill lie, psychologically further complicated by a necklace of bunkers fortifying the mid-fairway ground and distorting the distance to the green.

The course finishes with the 17th and 18th bending gracefully together towards the clubhouse. An elevated downhill drive off the 425-yard 17th ends in open heathland with an offset sloping green; the hole demands a strategic drive to avoid trees, bunkers, a large cross-bunker and to keep clear of wing-bunkers and deep fescue, heathery rough around the green for the second.

To close the round the uphill 423-yard 18th turns gently left to right, drive bunkers on both sides, with another fine set of cross-bunkers dividing the last half of the fairway. The green is a model Colt one with a long wing-bunker on the left, two smaller bunkers on the right divided by a thin rib. All this is set within the precincts of a much larger Park green, the outside features still visible, with a contribution from a Second World War bomb thrown in for good measure. The huge emblematic Sunningdale oak tree beyond the green provides the backdrop to the finish of a thrilling yet sublime golfing experience.

## THE NEW COURSE

Sunningdale's New Course was built in 1923, to handle an increasing number of golfers, in the second great boom in golf-course development. Harry Colt was called on to design the course after having by that time left the club to pursue golf-course design on a full-time basis.

The New Course is a stern test, indeed sterner than the Old, being longer and tighter, and is a fine complement to the latter with its classic charm. Like the Old, the New Course weaves itself out and back over varied topography and features, changing directions on nearly every hole, with a strong triangular pattern lying below the surface of the layout. Heather plays a vital role in the defence of this course, too.

*The ridge of heather, the man-made pond (one of the earliest in golf) and the mound to the left-front of the green are typical of the period features surviving at Sunningdale.*

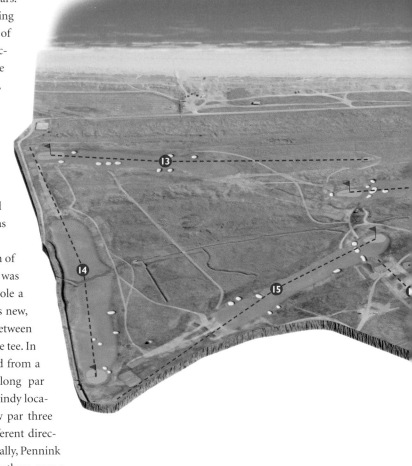

Laidlaw Purves initially laid out the course in 1887 with help from greenkeeper Ramsay Hunter, a Scot. It cost £1,000, a considerable sum in those days. Little was done in terms of modifying the natural dunescape. St George's was to represent seaside golf at its very best, with the game played over and around tumultuous sand dunes. In addition, it enjoyed the advantage of being the closest great links to the ever-growing city of London.

When it opened, St George's was penal in nature, reflective of its blind shots and Purves's love of cross-hazards. Both thrilling and demanding, the course immediately won accolades and was granted the 1894 Open Championship. J.H. Taylor's winning score of 326 spoke as to the course's difficulties.

### TOUGHENING THE COURSE

As a result of the introduction of the rubber-core Haskell ball, the winning score at the 1904 Open was below 300. Changes needed to be made. Though the course already measured more than 6,200 yards (5,670 metres), the back nine was nearly 600 yards (550 metres) longer than the front nine. Significant modifications took place to remedy this disparity in yardage, including transforming the 5th from a one-shot hole of no great merit into a very fine, dogleg-left par four of 400 yards. The extension of the 5th hole led to the demise of the blind par-three 6th – the feared Maiden hole – then played over the top of the massive Maiden sand dune. In addition, the 9th hole was shifted left through a valley and lengthened by 75 yards (68 metres) to become more daunting. On the back nine, a dangerous hole was created when the 10th green was moved to its present position atop a dune as opposed to at its base, and it was made famous in Ian Fleming's *Goldfinger* as one that 'had broken many hearts'. Tom Kite would agree as he went from bunker to bunker in 1985, thus ruining his Open bid.

Royal St George's continued to host the Open Championship regularly until 1949, after which the

event did not return for 32 years. Because of the property's rolling topography, a certain number of blind shots still existed, a characteristic out of vogue after the Second World War. In addition, the 3rd hole known as Sahara, which Bernard Darwin dearly loved, was now viewed as strangely antiquated. This 250-yard hole required a blind tee ball in the general direction of the green. Its unconventional nature that had won it fans was now seen as a shortcoming.

In order to attract the return of the Open, Frank Pennink was brought in. He made the 3rd hole a long, stiff par three. Though his new, two-tiered green was nestled between two dunes, it was visible from the tee. In addition, the 11th was modified from a short par four into another long par three. As important, given the windy location, was the fact that this new par three played towards the sea in a different direction to the other short holes. Finally, Pennink also changed the 8th from a par three over a giant bunker into a stout dogleg-right par four. Its approach shot is a thrilling one, over broken ground to a green nestled in a hollow. The sum of these changes brought the two nines to within 50 yards (45 metres) of each other, a desired attribute for a championship course.

### RETURN OF THE OPEN

The Open Championship was awarded to Royal St George's again in 1981, when the straight-hitting Bill Rogers became champion, proving that despite its changes the course still rewarded accurate driving first

and foremost. Sandy Lyle's Open win in 1985 was a proud moment for British golf, and the stage was set for the epic 1993 Open.

Great courses have a way of producing memorable events, and one of the unforgettable days in Open history occurred during final day's play of the 1993 Open. With the world's best congregated at the top of the leader board, the course was set up in a manner to allow them to display their talent. After a titanic struggle Greg Norman's final round score of 64 was a tribute both to his prodigious talent, which was seen

# ROYAL ST GEORGE'S
## Sandwich, Kent, England

Courses grand enough to host major events frequently must be altered for the sake of continuing to have such events. Handling a course's evolution is tricky, however, as a club struggles to preserve its unique character while accommodating the needs of the modern game. One club that has done particularly well in these respects is Royal St George's.

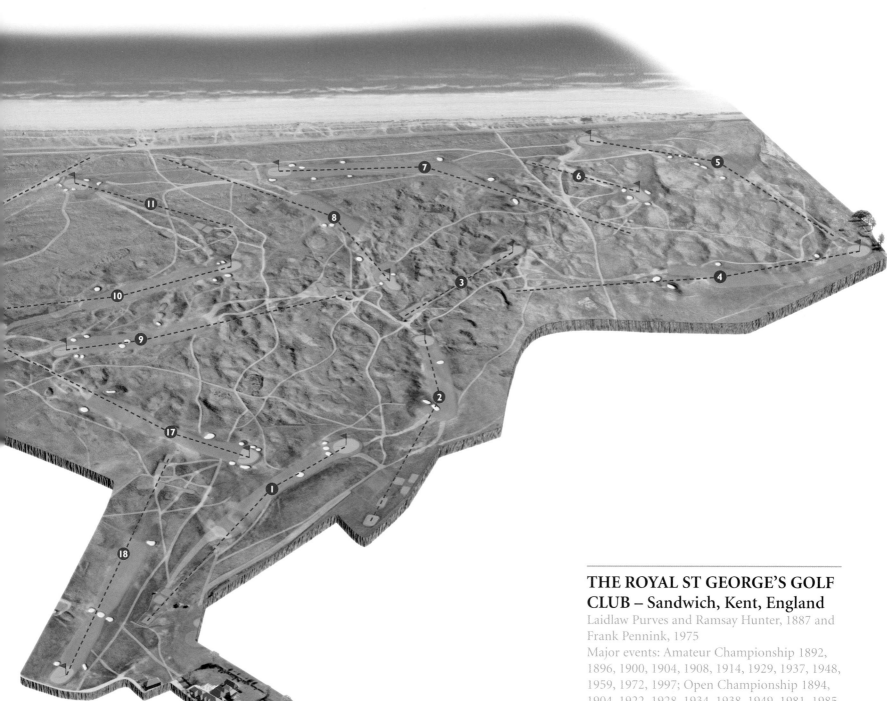

## THE ROYAL ST GEORGE'S GOLF CLUB – Sandwich, Kent, England

Laidlaw Purves and Ramsay Hunter, 1887 and Frank Pennink, 1975

Major events: Amateur Championship 1892, 1896, 1900, 1904, 1908, 1914, 1929, 1937, 1948, 1959, 1972, 1997; Open Championship 1894, 1904, 1922, 1928, 1934, 1938, 1949, 1981, 1985, 1993, 2003; Walker Cup 1930, 1967; Ladies' British Amateur Open 1964; Curtis Cup 1988

in full flight on that glorious day, as well as to Royal St George's. The course shone brilliantly, testing all aspects of the game while encouraging bold positive play.

### UNIQUE CHARACTERISTICS

Throughout its evolution, the constant that has remained is the seclusion enjoyed during a game at Royal St George's. The course occupies a huge tract of land, giving it a rare sense of spaciousness. More often than not, players are in their own valley or playing corridor, blissfully unaware of other games. Apart from the 9th and 10th, no two holes are parallel, and the wind comes from every direction.

The sand hills on the front nine are the largest of any Open course and are used to great effect. With the exception of the Old Course at St Andrews (see page 40), the fairways contain the most interesting landforms on the current rota of Open venues, and thus produce unpredictable bounces. Thankfully, too, the course still retains several blind tee shots. These bounces and blind shots tend to annoy the

### CARD OF THE COURSE

| HOLE | YARDS | PAR | HOLE | YARDS | PAR |
|------|-------|-----|------|-------|-----|
| 1. | 440 | 4 | 10. | 412 | 4 |
| 2. | 416 | 4 | 11. | 240 | 3 |
| 3. | 208 | 3 | 12. | 379 | 4 |
| 4. | 495 | 4 | 13. | 457 | 4 |
| 5. | 418 | 4 | 14. | 548 | 5 |
| 6. | 170 | 3 | 15. | 473 | 4 |
| 7. | 530 | 5 | 16. | 161 | 3 |
| 8. | 453 | 4 | 17. | 426 | 4 |
| 9. | 386 | 4 | 18. | 458 | 4 |
| OUT | 3,516 | 35 | IN | 3,554 | 35 |
| | | | TOTAL | 7,070 | 70 |

# A CASE STUDY IN STAYING RELEVANT
## The 14th hole and the Suez Canal

*Laidlaw Purves was a fan of cross-hazards, and it is interesting to note how the relevance of the Suez Canal at Royal St George's shifted over its 100-plus year existence, from being a threat on the second shot to being one on the first. The championship card in 1896 for the course shows that the 14th measured 505 yards. Getting past the Suez Canal, which crosses the fairway 330 yards (300 metres) from the tee, in two shots was quite an accomplishment pre-1900 because the gutta percha ball was in use. On the arrival of the faster, rubber-core Haskell ball early in the 20th century, the Suez Canal became less fearsome unless a strong wind was dead against the golfer. However, the out-of-bounds down the right of the fairway meant that the hole remained nerve-wracking. Indeed, when the Royal and Ancient Golf Club changed the penalty for going out-of-bounds to both stroke and distance, between the First and Second World Wars, the 14th was as fraught with terror as ever. Almost unheard of for a par five in the modern era, there were 22 sevens or worse scored on this hole during the 1993 Open. And, by the turn of the 21st century, the strongest golfers – with their ever more powerful clubs – had become concerned about driving their tee ball into the Suez Canal.*

*Because the club was keen for the rest of the 14th to continue to require good golf, in 2004 the green complex was moved back 43 yards (39 metres). Craftily, the green was placed beside the out-of-bounds and two central fairway bunkers were added 60 yards (55 metres) in front, in line with the left of the green. In this manner, if a golfer courageously plays down the right, there is unfettered access to the green. If played cautiously to the left, the next shot becomes progressively more difficult, with both the fairway bunkers and out-of-bounds weighing on the thought process. Therefore, once again, the 14th frequently calls for three well-hit shots, in keeping with how it played those many years ago when Purves first built it.*

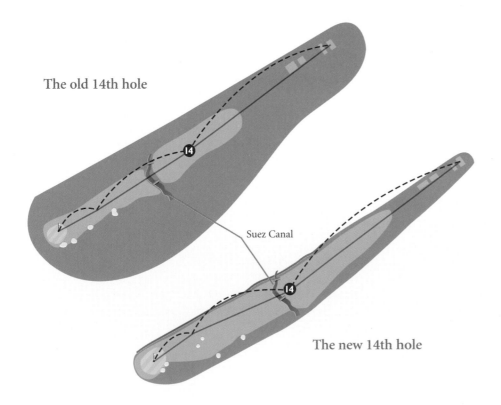

The old 14th hole

Suez Canal

14

The new 14th hole

professional. And yet without the odd bounce or the excitement of scurrying over a dune to see where the ball has finished, where would golf be?

The putting surfaces offer a variety of challenges and have more imaginative contouring than most links. This is evident from the 440-yard 1st. Though its green is hidden behind three bunkers, the front of the green actually slopes away from the player as it feeds off the back of the main bunker. Contrast that with the challenge presented at the 416-yard 2nd, where the elevated green's false front sends balls into the waiting, deep, right-front bunker.

The boldness of the landforms on the front nine yield holes reflective of their surroundings. One of the most noted is the 495-yard 4th, where the drive must clear the shoulder of a dune into which a 30-foot (9-metre) deep bunker is cut. Just as dramatic is its green, perched on a plateau with a wicked 5-foot (1.5-metre) false front. Totally uncompromising, this kind of stirring golf is more commonly found on holiday courses around the United Kingdom than on the more conventional Open courses.

The fairway at the 418-yard 5th is free flowing, barely even hinting that a golf hole falls over the tumbling landscape. A tightly defined, narrow fairway would look artificial and out of place, not to mention doing an injustice to the random undulations. Mercifully, the club appreciates this and the connection with nature that the golfer feels while playing the 5th is strong.

After tackling the 170-yard 6th hole with its green nestled at the base of the giant dune (Laidlaw Purves originally thought to name the hole Jungfrau before settling on the Maiden) and hitting a blind drive over a crest of a dune at the 530-yard 7th, the fairway undulations become slightly less challenging. The 9th green, however, has a pronounced hump front-left that kicks balls across the putting surface and down its tightly mown, right bank.

## GREENS TO REMEMBER
Starting with the skyline, plateau green at the 412-yard 10th, the back nine features a most appealing array of green sites, some of which are extremely difficult. On the exposed green site on the 10th, for example, there were 16 sixes or worse carded here during the 1993 Open. Though some still grumble about the conversion of the 240-yard 11th to a par three, no one doubts that the current green complex functions well as a links hole in accepting a draw that runs up the front of the green. The deep fronting bunker at the drive-and-pitch, 379-yard 12th is followed by two greens that play as extensions of the fairways.

An interior ridge running the length of the 13th green, dividing it into a higher left and lower right section, has long been admired for its influence on the approach shot. Meanwhile the golf architect Tom Simpson was a particular fan of the saucer-shaped 15th green, set beyond a dip with cross-bunkers cut into a ridge. A back-right hole location at the 16th will haunt golf professional Thomas Bjorn for ever because the green's shoulder and contours delivered two consecutive bunker shots tragically back to his feet

in the fourth round of the 2003 Open. The final piece of artistry is Duncan's Hollow, a depression in the left of the 18th green that gathers in approach shots that are steered away from the deep, right-front pot bunker.

From its requirement for long, accurate driving to the finesse shots required around its greens, Royal St George's epitomizes championship links golf. At the same time, a round here contains a sense of adventure – an attribute missing from courses that provide perfect visuals but lack such inspiration.

*One of the most appealing drives at Sandwich is on the 5th, with its crumpled fairway tumbling away to the left. During the 2003 Open, several big hitters drove the distant green!*

# ROYAL PORTHCAWL
## Rest Bay, Mid-Glamorgan, South Wales

In 1899 the big four – Harry Vardon, Sandy Herd, J.H. Taylor and James Braid – played exhibition matches at Porthcawl to celebrate the opening of the clubhouse – a wooden structure bought from the India Exhibition at Crystal Palace in London.

In the Porthcawl clubhouse, half-way through his final at the 1965 Amateur Championship, Michael Bonallack slipped a coin into the fruit machine. The wheels whirred and moments later he was pocketing the jackpot. Such a win capped a fine lunch and an even better afternoon, as the future Royal and Ancient Golf Club secretary went on to complete a 2-and-1 victory over Clive Clark.

But lucrative lines of bells or prestigious titles are not required to feel a sense of good fortune in this rugged corner of south Wales. Just being a golfer on this magnificent links is sufficient because every facet of the game is honestly tested, amid spectacular surroundings. The club was accorded royal status in 1909.

### THE NEED FOR STRATEGIC PLANNING

Ever present is a view of the sea. Rest Bay, surely a misnomer, borders the course. There is no rest, physical or mental, as Royal Porthcawl wends its undulating way in ever-varying directions. A golfer is expected to plot a route round. A keen sense of course management is invaluable. Tiger Woods, winner of many Majors, can attest to that after being famously beaten here by the always wily Gary Wolstenholme in the 1995 Walker Cup.

A golfer will feel exposed to the wind, which usually blows in from the sea. There is no natural shelter, because the course is not terrain based on dunes in the traditional mould of a links course. In fact, when Royal Porthcawl darts inland after the first three holes, the course takes on a heathland feel. The difference between a blowy day and one of rare, flat calm can be as much as ten shots – though locals will reassuringly tell of Royal Porthcawl's microclimate. The worst of the elements tend to divert north or head down the Bristol Channel and miss the course.

### RETAINING CHAMPIONSHIP STATUS

The 384-yard 1st is relatively gentle, though it was extended in 2006 using a tee built on recently acquired land. This brings into play a lone pot bunker to the right of the fairway and three that guard the left side. At the same time a pot bunker to the right was created on the 3rd, which not only prompts concern from the tee but also adds direction, depth and definition on a hole that swings right-to-left to a raised green.

They are typical of alterations that the club have had to make in order to maintain the course's championship status. Such status first became possible when

Porthcawl moved from being nine holes on nearby Locks Common to its present site in 1895. Harry Colt in 1912 and Tom Simpson later updated the course to one capable of staging top amateur events and leading professional tournaments.

After the 3rd, the player heads inland to the 212-yard 4th – a testing par three more often than not with the wind behind. Measuring 611 yards from the back tee is the 5th, where those prepared to cope with a 264-yard (241-metre) carry over heather can take a strategic short cut. The hole then climbs steeply to an elevated green, with a sunken pot bunker short right of the green. Such a hazard needs careful consideration when weighing up how far to hit the second shot.

For the excellent 394-yard 6th the land flattens. It is a hole that has a classic heathland rather than links feel to it and would hardly seem out of place at, say, Walton Heath. The right-to-left dogleg has a narrow entrance to a green rich with devilish pin positions.

The 122-yard 7th, perhaps the most memorable hole, is played from a tee with a low stone wall at its back. How the grazing cattle must be entertained as players try to take on the six pot bunkers and sundry mounds guarding the front half of the narrow green. Only a short-iron – as little as a wedge – is needed, but distance control is essential. If the wrong portion of the putting surface is hit, a player is left with a long putt of many a subtle borrow; if the tee shot is long, erring right or left, the golfer needs a chip of the utmost delicacy.

Flirting with out-of-bounds is the 474-yard 8th. Any player who emerges unscathed can have their sense of wellbeing reinforced on the 9th tee, which offers spectacular views of the entire layout. The movement of the course is completely in tune with the land, as can be seen by the fairway to the 10th green, which sweeps from left to right. Any pin cut at the back brings into play a pot bunker with a face that would require crampons to negotiate. With an abrupt change of direction comes another gem of a par three. A string of pot bunkers will grab anything tugged left, while the front-right of the 11th green is also well guarded to punish a mishit push off the tee.

## RAISING THE CHALLENGE

David Williams is the architect of the major change of 2006 to the 570-yard 12th. While two bunkers remain to catch drives down the right side of a hole that climbs steadily uphill, the fairway has been re-routed leaving the hazards guarding the left side instead. The wind is likely to blow the drive in this direction, so now the bunkers gobble balls that miss to the left. What had become a benign par five is now a monster.

On the 475-yard 13th, the player heads back for a robust par four that moves from right to left into the prevailing wind with a relatively blind, downhill approach shot. The 149-yard 14th offers a degree of respite before a tough finish that requires strategic planning on the 15th and 16th tees to avoid running out of fairway.

Friendliest of the par fives is the 504-yard 17th – the chimneys of a white farmhouse offering directional assistance to an uphill, blind tee shot. Then, in keeping with the course layout, the 445-yard 18th provides a contrast in direction and contouring as it heads downwards to the green. The course remains what it has always been – a supreme test of golf. The wooden clubhouse, though added to, still stands, as does Royal Porthcawl's reputation for providing pure golfing joy.

# ROYAL PORTHCAWL GOLF CLUB – Rest Bay, Mid-Glamorgan, South Wales

Charles Gibson, 1895; Ramsey Hunter, 1897; Harry Colt, 1912; F.G. Hawtree and J.H. Taylor, 1925; Tom Simpson, 1933; and David Williams, 2006
Major events: Ladies' British Open Amateur 1934, 1953, 1974; Curtis Cup 1964; Amateur Championship 1965, 1973, 1980, 1988, 2002; Walker Cup 1995

## CARD OF THE COURSE

| HOLE | YARDS | PAR | HOLE | YARDS | PAR |
|------|-------|-----|------|-------|-----|
| 1. | 384 | 4 | 10. | 336 | 4 |
| 2. | 451 | 4 | 11. | 184 | 3 |
| 3. | 445 | 4 | 12. | 570 | 5 |
| 4. | 212 | 3 | 13. | 475 | 4 |
| 5. | 611 | 5 | 14. | 149 | 3 |
| 6. | 394 | 4 | 15. | 466 | 4 |
| 7. | 122 | 3 | 16. | 430 | 4 |
| 8. | 474 | 5 | 17. | 504 | 5 |
| 9. | 400 | 4 | 18. | 445 | 4 |
| **OUT** | **3,493** | **36** | **IN** | **3,559** | **36** |
| | | | **TOTAL** | **72** | **7052** |

*Rest Bay provides a stunning backdrop to the 2nd green. The first three holes run along the shore before the course heads inland, but the Irish Sea remains visible from every hole.*

# NORTHERN IRELAND AND THE REPUBLIC OF IRELAND

Despite the fact that ball-and-stick games such as hurling have been active in Ireland for more than a millennium and its unique, point-to-point sport of road bowling for more than 300 years, proper golf has been played in Ireland for little more than a hundred years.

While primitive courses may have existed from 1850 or so, the first proper golf courses and clubs in Ireland arose from the Anglo-Scottish stronghold of Belfast, when Ireland and Britain were one state. It was in 1881 that the Belfast Golf Club (later Royal) was organized, and from that club emanated the great links courses at Portrush (see page 114) and County Down (see page 116), both through the efforts of George Baillie, a Scotsman from Musselburgh who was a founding member of Royal Belfast[1]. Soon afterwards, clubs began to spring up in the south, including Royal Dublin[2] in 1885, Lahinch[3] in 1892, Ballybunion (see page 120) in 1893 and Portmarnock (see page 118) in 1894.

## UNIQUE CHARACTERISTICS

Fortunately, the Irish were blessed not only with enthusiasm but also some of the best linksland in the world. In subtle ways it is different land from that in mainland Britain, due to geomorphology and climate. Its combination of relative warmth and precipitation makes the countryside eternally green, although still capable of playing fast and firm when properly maintained.

Even more striking is the fact that, whereas linksland in Britain is largely flat with gentle undulations; in Ireland tends to be bolder and more hilly. As a result, one of the distinctive characteristics of the great Irish courses is the quality and nature of their more inland holes. There are tee shots over the sides of dunes to crumpled fairways and greens sprinkled among these dunes, either hidden behind them or on a plateau created from one of them. More than any courses in the world, it is very difficult to see the hand of man on the great Irish links, although that hand of man was certainly there.

Royal Portrush
*page 114*

NORTHERN IRELAND

Royal County Down
*page 116*

Portmarnock
*page 118*

REPUBLIC OF IRELAND

Ballybunion
*page 120*

Waterville
*page 122*

## EARLY HISTORY

Much as with most new courses to the east of the Irish Sea, the first stabs at taking this magnificent land and turning it into a golf course were generally undertaken by locals usually aided by expatriate or imported Scotsmen. As in Britain, these courses evolved over time as technology changed, as more land became available and as members demanded more and better golf. By the mid-1920s most of today's great courses had pretty much the layouts they have today.

Because of Ireland's special relationship with the rest of the British Isles, the development of the game in the early years was unique. For example, nobody wanted to get on the wrong side of the Royal and Ancient Golf Club, so the earliest Irish amateur competition was called the 'Close' rather than the 'Open'. As a result, many of the long-standing and most important golf tournaments in Ireland are in fact closed to non-Irish players. Because of this and the creation of the Irish Free State in 1922, the growth of the game in the south (today's Republic) was parallel to that in the United Kingdom rather than fully integrated with it. Nevertheless, relationships between the golfing nations remained cordial, and the best British architects of the day, such as Harry Colt, Dr Alister MacKenzie and Tom Simpson, put the finishing touches on some of Ireland's greatest courses, including Royal County Down, Lahinch and Ballybunion.

After the Second World War, Ireland helped the golfing world return to normality by hosting first the Amateur Championship at Portmarnock in 1949 and then The Open at Royal Portrush in 1951. While The Open has never returned, possibly due to the increasing demands on venues for ancillary facilities, as well as to the political unrest, the Amateur returned to Royal Portrush (in 1960 and 1993) and to Royal County Down (in 1970 and 1999). The Canada Cup at Portmarnock in 1960 brought Sam Snead back across the Atlantic for the first time since his Open win at St Andrews in 1946 and Arnold Palmer for the first time ever. Portmarnock hosted the Walker Cup in 1991 and Royal County Down in 2007. In recent years, a number of Senior Opens have been played at Royal Portrush or Royal County Down with Christie O'Connor Jnr providing home wins on both courses.

*There has been a course at Ballyliffin since 1947, but it is only in recent years, furthered by*
*Nick Faldo's interest in it, that Ballyliffin has attained international fame.*

## GAME OF WIDESPREAD APPEAL

There are numerous aspects to golf within Ireland. At the simplest, the country is the king of pitch-and-putt venues. These little courses are dotted all over the land, often in the gardens of country house hotels. It is golf at its most primitive and for all abilities and ages. As in Scotland, and to a lesser extent England, there are also numerous 'small' courses scattered throughout the land (predominantly on or near the seaside) and usually associated with a small village. Such courses,

ranging mostly in length from 5,000 to 6,500 yards are the backbone of golf in Ireland. Their names – such as Ardglass[4], Greencastle[5] and Dooks[6] – evoke a day and age when golf was a kinder, gentler game. Ardglass enjoys a captivating, rocky site overlooking the Irish Sea. Dooks – founded in 1889 – is magically sited between the mountains of County Kerry and the Atlantic coastline. Recent modifications – by Martin Hawtree – have stretched this 'small' course to around 6,500 yards in length.

*What succeeding generations of golf-course architects have each used to maximum strategic effect at Lahinch is the wonderful movement in the ground, producing marvellously natural holes.*

## LAHINCH

Martin Hawtree is also the most recent architect to make alterations to Lahinch, regarded by many as Ireland's St Andrews. Old Tom Morris was 72 when he travelled from St Andrews to lay out the original course in 1894. Even today that road and ferry journey takes most of a day – what must it have been like then!

A third of a century later, a slightly younger Dr Alister MacKenzie did a significant revamp of the Lahinch course at a time when he was working globally. Times had surely changed. For various reasons, however, much of MacKenzie's work was unravelled in less than a decade, particularly his wild greens, and by the end of the 20th century the course's architectural pedigree had been seriously violated. While the course was not at all 'bad', observers believed that it 'could be better'. The club eventually agreed and hired Hawtree, whose effective brief was a golf-course architect's dream: 'What would MacKenzie do?' This five-phased project was completed in 2005.

The mantra of all healers is 'firstly, do no harm', and the club and its architect took this to heart on the 381-yard 1st. It was and is a superb introduction to the course, with a tee intimately linked to the clubhouse heading gently uphill into the heart of the course, and nothing but golf in the eye of the beholder. A few arte-facts of the old Lahinch remain on the new Lahinch, and the 4th and 5th are the most telling. Each is an Old Tom Morris hole and virtually unchanged from a hundred-plus years ago. At 475 yards, the 4th starts with a drive to a narrow valley in the heart of the course but there is no visible flag. The player eventu-ally learns that their second must be hit over a white stone on a distant hill and that the hole crosses the 18th fairway to a green hard against a boundary of the course. It is to the club's great credit that they preserved 'Klondyke' in their restoration. Heading back the other way is the 154-yard 5th, with another stone on another hill as a guide. This is the famous 'Dell' hole, a mere pitch over a high dune to a hidden green, which is as fun as any golf hole can get.

The 424-yard 6th is played towards the shore. A drive over a hill to another bit of plateau leaves the player with a mid- to long-iron over a deep pit to a new green tucked in the marram grass. One of the two MacKenzie holes, which had been lost to coastal erosion many years ago, is faithfully reproduced on the 411-yard 7th. It requires a precise second shot to a small green by the sea. Martin Hawtree designed the 166-yard 8th – one of two short holes by him. It is a clever layout, with a tee that looks past a green flanked by hillocks towards a classic Irish country landscape – a MacKenzie-like distraction. Perched high on one of

the dunes is the 9th tee, from which the fairway heads back towards the centre of the course and eventually to a marvellously long, narrow and tiered original MacKenzie green. By this point the player has experi-enced one of the most thrilling opening nines in golf.

The back nine is no less thrilling and when a player has finished Lahinch, they want to go out and do it again, which is the golfer's ultimate compliment. It has always seemed so at Lahinch, but the fact that the feeling is still there speaks volumes about the sensitivity with which the course has been both reno-vated and restored.

## NEW DEVELOPMENTS

Golf in Ireland is clearly flourishing, particularly at the high end of the market. Traditional courses such as Ballybunion and Ballyliffin[7] have added second 18-holers and others, such as Portsalon[8] and Carne[9], have upgraded their courses from 'small' to 'large'. The Old Links at Ballyliffin has recently been refined by Nick Faldo's design team, while the new Glashedy Links stretches to over 7,200 yards of rough-and-tumble dunes holes. Ballybunion's second course, the Cashen, is much longer-established. It was completed in 1984, the lone Irish design of the prolific American architect Robert Trent Jones Snr. He was given a seriously rugged stretch of sand dunes in which to build the course and he produced one of the most challenging of all his courses, very unforgiving and very hard – some say too hard – but with a very distinctive personality.

Starting with Waterville (see page 122) in the early 1970s, but really taking off two decades later, signifi-cant private money has been invested in new, high-end projects. These include American-style inland courses, mostly located around Dublin, such as the K Club[10] and Mount Juliet[11], as well as such coastal develop-ments as Old Head[12] and Doonbeg[13]. The one common characteristic of these new venues is their relative exclusivity, high maintenance and high cost.

The K Club has been a regular stop on the European Tour for some years and was the venue for the 36th Ryder Cup matches in 2006. For all its length, innumerable water hazards and plethora of bunkers, Ireland's Darren Clarke has shown that the Palmer Course can be tamed, cruising round in a mere 60 shots in the second round of the 1999 European Open. Mount Juliet is also American designed (Jack Nicklaus) and hosted the 2002 and 2004 American Express World Golf championships won by Tiger Woods and Ernie Els respectively. A similarly opulent resort course also seeing European Tour action is Druid's Glen[14], but it was designed in a very un-Irish

style by two Irishmen, Tom Craddock and Pat Ruddy, a far cry from their work on Ballyliffin's Glashedy Links. Two Irish opens have also been played at Carton House[15] in County Kildare, a resort hotel (as also the K Club) able to boast two full 18-hole courses, nominally by Colin Montgomerie and Mark O'Meara.

Old Head is an extraordinary venture, perched on a high, rocky promontory near Kinsale. It is one of the most expensive courses for a visitor to play anywhere in Europe and – in good weather – the ocean views are incomparable, but it is no place for the vertigo sufferer, for a number of fairways are lined right along the edge of the cliffs. Doonbeg, on the other hand, is right down at wave height, although some of the sand dunes through which Greg Norman and his team have routed the course are on the mountainous side. Norman himself rates the par-four 15th as the star hole, played alongside the Atlantic to a raised table green set in a ring of dunes.

Such ventures can be realistically developed in Ireland for two reasons. First, they have successfully promoted the country as a destination resort for golfers, particularly the American market. Secondly, Ireland has become a very wealthy and vibrant coun-try over the past 20 years, with a per capita GDP higher than that of its old colonial master, the United Kingdom, and some of this money is being redirected into the golf business. Such investment and the expec-tations for a return on that investment are making golf an expensive sport for visitors and locals alike.

## LOCAL TALENT

Grassroots development of golf has also continued, with local architects such as the legendary Eddie Hackett, often working to minimal budgets, and Pat Ruddy. The cost and popularity of Irish golf will always be constrained by the weather and the logistics of getting from point A to point B. As long as a car is the preferred form of transport, golf in Ireland will always have a homely feel to it. For the traveller who takes their time and is inclined to stop along the way, to smell the flowers, drink a pint of Guinness or just play a local pitch and putt, simply getting there can be as much fun as playing good and great golf courses, no matter how superb they are.

# ROYAL PORTRUSH
## Portrush, County Antrim, Northern Ireland

The only occasion that The Open was held outside Britain was at Royal Portrush, in 1951. Why that event has not returned to Ireland is understood only by the inner circles of the Royal and Ancient Golf Club.

What is known more widely is that the reputation of its Dunluce links has only grown since then, as the boom in golf travel has allowed more and more people to experience its charms. Even though the club is venerable, having been founded in 1888, most of the Dunluce course is relatively new. Unlike other remodelling projects of the Golden Age, Royal Portrush was almost a completely new build, to a Harry Colt design, of an original design by George Baillie and others. Colt kept one of the old holes (the current 18th), one other green (the 11th), created new ones over some of the land (mostly in the area now occupied by holes 1–2 and 10–12) and then added some spectacular new holes using 80 acres (32 hectares) of new land leased by the club. Colt first discussed this project with the committee in 1923, saw his proposed budget of £10,000 reduced by two-thirds, and ended up receiving a fee of £212 on completion in 1932, only 19 years before it was chosen for The Open. For the club, it was the bargain of the century.

### UNDULATING TERRAIN

The quality of the bargain is evident at the 392-yard 1st, even though it is a straightforward hole over rolling land that would be considered quite good for most courses, yet for Portrush is benign. What makes the hole is the green Colt found at the top of a small rise, which puts just enough pressure on the golfer for an opening hole. A par five follows, which is reachable with a good drive and a brave heart, but requires a lay-up second if a nest of bunkers short of the 2nd green cannot be carried. The first hole on the 'new' land – the

155-yard 3rd – is a fine short one to a slightly elevated green that falls off on all sides. A long drive threaded between bunkers left and out-of-bounds right is needed on the very testing, 457-yard 4th if a player is to reach the green. After this, the long march eastwards ends, and the player heads northwards, towards the sea.

Nestled behind the previous green is the 5th tee, from where the view downhill to the water is spectacular. Although the green can be identified from the tee, it is far to the right and the first question

asked of the golfer is how far dare they cut the corner? As the hole is of modest length the answer could be 'not much', but a sensible poke to the left could leave a much more difficult shot to a very elusive green, partially obscured by a knob in the fairway. Its putting surface slopes sharply uphill, while out-of-bounds behind the upper shelf makes going for a back pin problematical. The 5th green melds neatly into the 6th tee, which stands on the edge of the dunes, heading back to the middle of the course. These dunes were severely eroded in the early 1980s and saved only through a worldwide fund appeal. On most courses in the world, the 189-yard 6th would be the best short hole, but this is Royal Portrush and, with 'Calamity' still to come, just being great must suffice for the 6th.

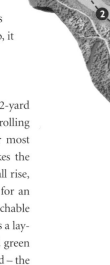

Its green is long, narrow and canted from left to right. Hitting it with the necessary mid-iron is an act of skill. Like the 5th, the 6th relies entirely on contours and angles for defence – there is not a sand bunker between them. What design skill does that suggest!

## HARRY COLT'S LEGACY

Colt's routing genius is displayed to the full in this part of the course: on a cramped piece of land he manages to fit six holes of great variety. There are doglegs left and right and long, short and medium holes. Hardest of all is the 431-yard 7th, while the 384-yard 8th charms the most, with its long and narrow green nestled in the dunes. Fortuitously, the 475-yard 9th and 478-yard 10th, as shortish par fives, may improve a player's card, if the ball is kept straight. A lovely drop-shot hole – the 170-yard 11th – uses an ancient green, while the 392-yard 12th, with fall-aways to three sides, only needs one greenside bunker. Most impressively, the greens of the odd-numbered holes in this sequence and the tees of the evens fit into an area no bigger than a rugby pitch, without losing their sense of intimacy.

## THE FINISHING STRETCH

This starts with two cracking holes. The 386-yard 13th is a dogleg left with a drive to an unseen fairway. Right is safest off the tee, but gives the player a longer shot and a bad angle at the left–right canted green. If the drive is long and accurate enough, the golfer will be rewarded with another fine view of the sea. Calamity, the 201-yard 14th, is world famous and requires a shot from dune to dune with ball-eating scrub all the way to the green with an even more fearsome wasteland to the right. South African golfer Bobby Locke tamed this hole in the 1951 Open Championship by hitting left into a small hollow and then chipping and putting for par each day.

# ROYAL PORTRUSH GOLF CLUB (DUNLUCE LINKS) – Portrush, County Antrim, Northern Ireland

Harry Colt, 1932

Major events: Ladies' British Open Amateur 1895, 1903, 1911, 1924, 1939, 1955, 1969, 1995; Irish Open 1930, 1937, 1947; Open Championship 1951; Amateur Championship 1960, 1993

CARD OF THE COURSE

| HOLE | NAME | YARDS | PAR | HOLE | NAME | YARDS | PAR |
|---|---|---|---|---|---|---|---|
| 1. | Hughie's | 392 | 4 | 10. | Dhu Varren | 478 | 5 |
| 2. | Giant's Grave | 505 | 5 | 11. | Feather Bed | 170 | 3 |
| 3. | Islay | 155 | 3 | 12. | Causeway | 392 | 4 |
| 4. | Fred Daly's | 457 | 4 | 13. | Skerries | 386 | 4 |
| 5. | White Rocks | 384 | 4 | 14. | Calamity | 201 | 3 |
| 6. | Harry Colt's | 189 | 3 | 15. | Purgatory | 365 | 4 |
| 7. | P.G. Stevenson's | 431 | 4 | 16. | Babington's | 428 | 4 |
| 8. | Himalayas | 384 | 4 | 17. | Glenarm | 548 | 5 |
| 9. | Tavern | 475 | 5 | 18. | Greenaway | 469 | 4 |
| OUT | | 3,372 | 36 | IN | | 3,437 | 36 |
| | | | | TOTAL | | 6,809 | 72 |

A tricky green tests players on the 365-yard 15th, while the final three holes demand length and accuracy over the flatter upper ground. Colt added bunkers to this land, and committees have narrowed the fairways to make the finish challenging. The 18th, which was an average par five, has been made a strong two-shotter by reducing its length to 469 yards.

Another Open Championship is probably not likely in the near future at Royal Portrush – at least as long as protecting 'par' is of concern to the R&A. As marvellous as it is, Dunluce links could thwart most professionals only by narrowing the fairways to widths that would make it unplayable, and not really fun, for less expert golfers. What a pity that would be.

*The 14th green is eaten into by a severe drop-off to the right. As most golfers tend to hit in that direction, particularly when under pressure, 'Calamity' is a very apt name.*

# ROYAL COUNTY DOWN
## Newcastle, County Down, Northern Ireland

When golfing cognoscenti gather to contemplate which course might just be the best in the world, Royal County Down is one of the 5–10 golf courses whose name invariably crosses their lips.

Few people who have played Royal County Down have come away with anything but great love and respect. The stunning beauty of the land in the shadows of the Mourne Mountains would make any course built over it memorable, but this is not just any course. No, this is simply one of the finest examples of golfing architecture in the world that any lover of golf should try to play before they die.

Founded at the end of the 19th century, Royal County Down was graced by the availability of superb golfing land, hillier and less predictable than most of the great links of Scotland. In its development it was also blessed with the services of some great golfing minds, including those of Old Tom Morris, Harry Colt and, most importantly, George Coombe, whose 1907 layout bears a striking resemblance to the course known today.

### INCREASING DIFFICULTY
As with many great courses, the 539-yard 1st allows for a gently entry into the fray, weaving through a valley, much as do many of the holes at Royal Birkdale (see page 86). The intensity ratchets up quickly, however, and it becomes clear at the 444-yard 2nd that the player must not stray much from the intended line, with its semiblind tee shot and upturned saucer of a green. These plateau greens, shaved around the edges to allow mishit or misjudged shots to roll into secret and often fearsome hollows, are one of the great strengths of the course. Similar but harder is the 477-yard 3rd, yet playing to handicap is not impossible for even the average golfer on these opening holes beside the sea.

To reach the 213-yard 4th involves a climb to a hill and then a turn back towards the clubhouse; here all changes, utterly. In front lies much of the course, but it is largely hidden behind a warren of dunes. The Mountains of Mourne are now in front, and, if the player is lucky enough to be there on a fine spring day when the gorse is in bloom, there are fewer more pleasing vistas in the world of golf. This hole was one of the discoveries of Harry Colt, when he made a small

number of inspired changes to the course in 1926, turning a very good course into the great one known today.

### BEST OF THEIR KIND
That discovery also led to the transformation of the 440-yard 5th, which was a long and straight three-shotter, but is now a sharp dogleg-right par four with a blind drive over an angled ridge. The perfect tee ball is the power fade, but how many can conjure up that shot under pressure?

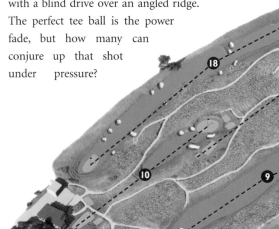

Five fairway bunkers add to the challenge and as the view of the green is partially hidden behind a dune, the player needs depth perception too. Although the 398-yard 6th may seem like a respite on the card, the drive is blind and the crowned green will accept only the well-struck and judged pitch. That it was once played in one in an Irish Amateur testifies to its marvellous elasticity and not to its ease.

Next is the delightful short hole, the 145-yard 7th, with its green partially obscured from the tee. There is always a mixture of anticipation and apprehension

when hitting a solid shot to such a green and then walking forward to see the final result. On the 7th, if the pitch is straight a player will be fine, but, if it has drifted left, a deep hidden bunker lies in wait. Yet another difficult hole is the 430-yard 8th, to an inspired table-top green high in the dunes added after Colt's work. The change was a magnificent decision, turning a good hole into a great one. At nearly 500 yards, the 9th looks like a long par four on the card, but the fairway lies well below the tee. The drive must be straight, however, and the heaving green is hard to hold as well as to putt.

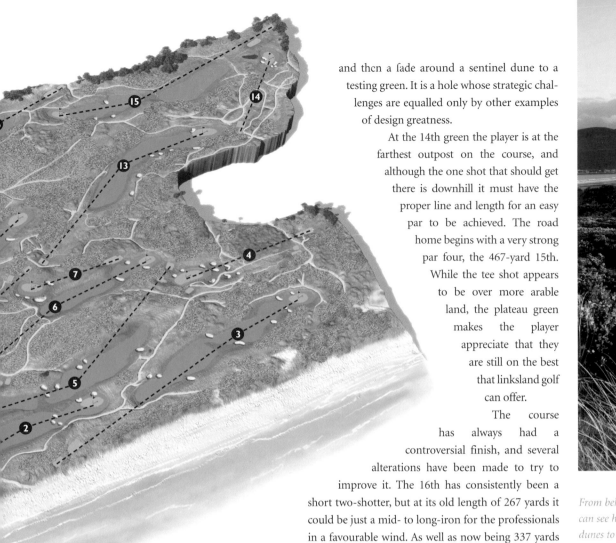

and then a fade around a sentinel dune to a testing green. It is a hole whose strategic challenges are equalled only by other examples of design greatness.

At the 14th green the player is at the farthest outpost on the course, and although the one shot that should get there is downhill it must have the proper line and length for an easy par to be achieved. The road home begins with a very strong par four, the 467-yard 15th. While the tee shot appears to be over more arable land, the plateau green makes the player appreciate that they are still on the best that linksland golf can offer.

The course has always had a controversial finish, and several alterations have been made to try to improve it. The 16th has consistently been a short two-shotter, but at its old length of 267 yards it could be just a mid- to long-iron for the professionals in a favourable wind. As well as now being 337 yards long, the newer version of the 16th is narrower at the green entrance; however, the thrill of possibly driving the green has been taken away. Even though an incongruous pond sits in the middle of the fairway, the 435-yard 17th is a fine hole with an excellent green complex.

Over the years the 550-yard 18th has been tightened and while relatively flat, is a very good finishing hole. Its quality was demonstrated in the 2007 Walker Cup when the competition went down to the very last match and was settled by Jonathan Moore's exquisite 4-iron shot, which flew straight and low and then along the ground for seeming ages until nestling by the hole to set up the winning eagle for the American team.

That competition was a magnificent one and showed how well Royal County Down could challenge some of the best amateur players in the world. Why, then, has it never held an Open Championship? Perhaps the topography of the course is too lumpy to accommodate 40,000 spectators a day, or perhaps Newcastle is just too small for the Royal and Ancient Golf Club to imagine holding their premiere event there. Who knows? All those who have played there, however, realize what a fine and exhilarating Open Royal County Down would provide.

## GLORIOUS GOLF

After this, the player quickly heads out again from a tee hard by the clubhouse. The 10th itself is an attractive, 197-yard one-shotter, and at the green end represents the best-preserved remnant of Old Tom Morris's original design. On the 440-yard 11th, the drive must scale an enormous hill that lies near where Morris had designed a short hole called Matterhorn, but once over it the fairway wends softly over lower ground. George Coombe designed the hole, and its front-to-back, canted green is yet another example of the club improving the quality of their course.

Elite players should reach in two shots on the 527-yard 12th, which offers numerous challenges for all golfers, particularly on the second shot, which must find its way over a deep hollow and between two sets of bunkers flanking the last third of the fairway. Continuing northwards, the 444-yard 13th is a wonderful double dogleg, requiring a draw off the tee

*From behind the 3rd green at Royal County Down, one can see how the fairway snakes narrowly between the dunes to a hidden green.*

## ROYAL COUNTY DOWN GOLF CLUB – Newcastle, County Down, Northern Ireland

George Coombe, 1907 and Harry Colt, 1926
Major events: Ladies' British Open Amateur 1899, 1907, 1920, 1927, 1935, 1950, 1963, 2006; Irish Open 1928, 1935, 1939; Curtis Cup 1968; Amateur Championship 1970, 1999; Walker Cup 2007

CARD OF THE COURSE

| HOLE | YARDS | PAR | HOLE | YARDS | PAR |
|------|-------|-----|------|-------|-----|
| 1. | 539 | 5 | 10. | 197 | 3 |
| 2. | 444 | 4 | 11. | 440 | 4 |
| 3. | 477 | 4 | 12. | 527 | 5 |
| 4. | 213 | 3 | 13. | 444 | 4 |
| 5. | 440 | 4 | 14. | 212 | 3 |
| 6. | 398 | 4 | 15. | 467 | 4 |
| 7. | 145 | 3 | 16. | 337 | 4 |
| 8. | 430 | 4 | 17. | 435 | 4 |
| 9. | 486 | 4 | 18. | 550 | 5 |
| **OUT** | **3,572** | **35** | **IN** | **3,609** | **36** |
| | | | **TOTAL** | **7,181** | **71** |

The club was founded by an Irishman and a Scotsman – George Ross and W.C. Pickeman – who rowed from Sutton to Portmarnock on Christmas Eve 1893, looking for a golfing venue. What a venue they found – a peninsula of pure linksland, contained by broad beaches and shifting dunes, with enough undulations in the middle to create interest, but not so much that golf holes had to be compromised, constructed or contrived.

Delighted with what they saw, Pickeman and Ross did a deal with the owners (the Jameson family, of whiskey fame), and hired Mungo Park as head professional and greenkeeper. Mungo was a former Open champion who had worked with his brother (Willie Park Snr) and his nephew (Willie Park Jnr) – each Open champions in their own right – on course design in Great Britain and Ireland in the 1880s and 1890s. Along with Old Tom Morris, the Park family were at the forefront of the nascent practice of golf-course architecture at that time. The collaboration of these three men created nine holes of golf in just over a year – Portmarnock opened for play on St Stephen's Day 1894. Two years later the course was extended to 18 holes by Pickeman and Park.

Over time other changes have been made to the course. While only a few holes (2nd, 16th and 17th) retain the site of an original green, most follow pretty similar paths through the dunes as their predecessors – perhaps at different angles and to different greens, but the overall flow of play would not be completely unfamiliar to a time-traveller from the late 19th century. Two things such a visitor would notice, however, are the prosperity of the club and the growth of the land it sits on, because the peninsula is accreting, rather than eroding, as other links are.

## SEPARATE ROUTES

The championship course today consists of two returning loops as at Muirfield (see page 60), but they are separate rather than embedded within each other. As a result there are more changes of direction as the

holes of each nine weave among themselves. More than anything, the routing of Portmarnock reminds a golfer of the intertwined braids of the head of a Celtic cross – each thread separate in theory, but linked together as a whole.

Whereas Muirfield takes a clockwise route, Portmarnock goes the other way. Maybe it is one of those contrary Irish things. Golfers can hit the controlled slice to their heart's content in East Lothian, but in the shadow of the Hill of Howth they had better bring a controlled draw to the 1st tee. The first four holes roll with the flow of the land from right to left around the bay while flirting with the gnarlier linksland at the centre of the property. Much as at Royal Troon (see page 58), the first three holes are testing rather than taxing, fairly flat but with subtle and well-bunkered greens.

# PORTMARNOCK
## Portmarnock, County Dublin, Republic of Ireland

Portmarnock's routing of circles within circles mirror the style of writing and exposition of James Joyce. When that great Irish writer was alive, a player had to take a boat across the river Liffey from Howth to the 1st tee of a course initially imagined by a gentleman farmer.

## PORTMARNOCK GOLF CLUB – Portmarnock, County Dublin, Republic of Ireland

W.C. Pickeman and Mungo Park, 1896; and H.M. Cairnes, Harry Colt, Eddie Hackett, Fred Hawtree and others, 1897–2007
Major events: Irish Open 1927, 1929, 1934, 1938, 1946, 1948, 1976, 1977, 1978, 1979, 1980, 1981, 1982, 1986, 1987, 1988, 1989, 1990, 2003, 2004; Ladies' British Open Amateur 1931; Amateur Championship 1949; Walker Cup 1991

### CARD OF THE COURSE

| HOLE | YARDS | PAR | HOLE | YARDS | PAR |
|------|-------|-----|------|-------|-----|
| 1. | 388 | 4 | 10. | 373 | 4 |
| 2. | 378 | 4 | 11. | 429 | 4 |
| 3. | 384 | 4 | 12. | 152 | 3 |
| 4. | 441 | 4 | 13. | 564 | 5 |
| 5. | 398 | 4 | 14. | 383 | 4 |
| 6. | 601 | 5 | 15. | 189 | 3 |
| 7. | 184 | 3 | 16. | 525 | 5 |
| 8. | 398 | 4 | 17. | 469 | 4 |
| 9. | 437 | 4 | 18. | 412 | 4 |
| **OUT** | **3,609** | **36** | **IN** | **3,496** | **36** |
| | | | **TOTAL** | **7,105** | **72** |

*The finishing hole at Portmarnock is not long by today's standards, but its rolling green surrounded by gorse and bunkers and hollows timelessly challenges all calibres of golfer.*

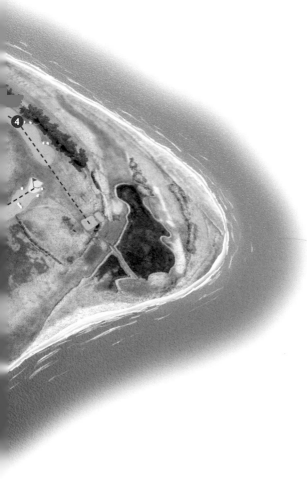

The 4th raises the ante with 441 well-protected yards along the shore, in a direction that is nearly 180 degrees from that which the golfer was playing on the 1st. The 398-yard 5th reverses into the dunes, and then the 6th goes back towards the shore. This hole, at 601 yards from the championship tee, can be reached in two when the course is playing fast and firm in the summer by the big hitters, but if the wind is from the east and the course is at all soft it can take three good hits to reach the green by even moderately good players.

The 184-yard 7th is the first of the three short holes on the course and is a lovely mid-iron to a green settled into the bayside dunes. In the 1991 Walker Cup, Phil Mickelson famously hit the middle of the green and disdainfully flipped his club to his caddy, causing not a little bit of ruction with his playing partner. The 398-yard 8th and 437-yard 9th angle back towards the clubhouse at the other side of the peninsula. Then there is a marvellous confluence of golf holes at the 9th tee, as the previous green and the 10th green and 11th tee are all in close proximity.

### WIND-DOMINATED TEST

That 429-yard 11th takes the player to the northern part of the course, the heart of the second nine built in 1896. Second of the short holes is the 152-yard 12th, which was originally played to a semiblind punchbowl of a green, but now sits up by the edge of the dunes. While the 383-yard 14th is a simple-looking hole, this is deceptive. The green sits on a plateau near the sea and can be baked hard by the sun and wind in the summer. Often the best play can be to the left of the green, where a pitch back to the hole is far easier than trying to putt down the slope.

Undoubtedly, the 189-yard 15th is the most memorable hole at Portmarnock, and a fine one it is – a mid-iron played along the shore to a narrow elevated green, beautiful to the eye but jangling to the nerves. Holes 16, 17 and 18 are all solid, requiring strength and good judgement of line and length. For the competitive golfer trying to maintain a score, this finish can be hard as nails.

The last five holes will have covered the whole compass, giving a variety of challenges, particularly when the wind blows, which it rarely does not. There will have been no respite for the golfers with a card in hand. However, if they are out not only to test their skill but also to enjoy the fresh air and the scenic beauty, and the great architecture and the camaraderie, then the finish at Portmarnock can be the game of golf at its finest.

# BALLYBUNION
## Ballybunion, County Kerry, Republic of Ireland

Sustaining a great golf course far from the centres of 'civilization' can be daunting.
Ballybunion, faced with coastal erosion and the need to build new facilities,
reached out in the 1980s to overseas visitors for funds, created a significant and
loyal international membership, and secured the future of the course and the club.

Ballybunion was not always so prosperous. Founded in 1893, the club ran out of money five years later, started up again in 1906 and did not have 18 holes until 1927. Continuous work by the locals turned it into a very fine course, and its greatness was revealed after Tom Simpson tweaked a few holes in 1936.

The clubhouse is the third built on the present site since the Second World War. In one sense it seems anomalous, in that its modernity is in such stark contrast to the ancient feel of the course. However, it is both testimony to the love that visitors – members and guests alike – have for the course, and an example of the incredible economic progress of Ireland since its accession in 1973 to what is now the European Union.

### EXPERIENCING THE COURSE
Like many of the other top links courses, the quality of Ballybunion can be felt, rather than seen, on the 1st tee. It is a 403-yard hole, down to the left off the tee, with an apposite graveyard awaiting the hacker's bungling shots to the right. Only a hint is given of the topography that follows. The 439-yard 2nd heads off to the middle of the course and raises the golfing test with fine examples of two of Ballybunion's most defining characteristics: rolling fairways, which heave like waves between random dunes; and small greens guarded by slopes as much as by bunkers.

Looking backwards after the climb to the 3rd tee reveals much of the course, and even in those holes hidden by the dunes it is possible to imagine what golfing challenges are to come. Turning back to the task at hand, the long downhill iron shot to the lovely, narrow 3rd green concentrates the mind and blocks out the more mundane views of the caravans and the village.

The 529-yard 4th, 552-yard 5th and 382-yard 6th take the player in a sweeping leftward curve towards the sea. Heavily bunkered fairways and relatively benign greens characterize the relatively flat par fives that used to be the closing holes of the course when the clubhouse was located at the edge of town. By an overwhelming consensus, the Old Course is believed to have been improved when these holes were made less prominent in the routing. One notable exception was the European PGA, which reverted to the previous layout when the 2000 Irish Open was held at Ballybunion.

While the fairways narrow in the driving range at the 6th, it is not long, so no more than a short-iron is then required to reach the bunkerless, highly contoured green. Tom Watson (a long-time member), however, considered this the hardest second shot at Ballybunion. As a bonus, the player finally can see and smell and feel that they are nearing the Atlantic.

### COASTAL STRETCH
Facing them is the 420-yard 7th – a hole that has as much quality and history as any on the course. Quality is evident from its tee, where the golfer stands 70 feet (21 metres) above the shore and finally can see, smell and feel that they are nearing the ocean. The best visibility of the green from the fairway is from the left, but the best angle from the right. Regardless of which line is chosen (or achieved), the second shot will test all of a player's mid-iron skills, because the green is long and very narrow. Again this hole is bunkerless, proving that slopes can protect a hole at least as well as sand. The hole is one of Simpson's contributions, and a fine one. An alternative green, set in the left-hand dunes, was built and played on at the height of a coastal erosion crisis in the 1980s.

A solid short hole, the 154-yard 8th, brings the player back inland for a brief stretch, while the 456-yard 9th is a brutish two-shotter with a drive between sand hills and a green with a large false front. Starting with a drive and a pitch, the inward nine brings the player back to the sea.

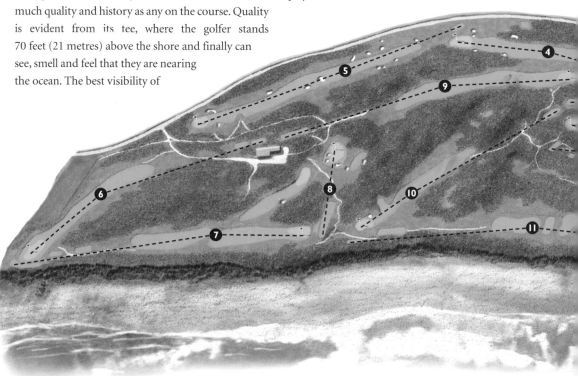

## BALLYBUNION GOLF CLUB
### (OLD COURSE) – Ballybunion, County Kerry, Republic of Ireland

Lionel Hewson, 1906; Mr Smyth, 1926;
Anon., 1927; Tom Simpson, 1936; Eddie
Hackett, 1964; and Tom Watson, 1995
Major events: Irish Open 2000

CARD OF THE COURSE

| HOLE | YARDS | PAR | HOLE | YARDS | PAR |
|---|---|---|---|---|---|
| 1. | 403 | 4 | 10. | 361 | 4 |
| 2. | 439 | 4 | 11. | 451 | 4 |
| 3. | 220 | 3 | 12. | 200 | 3 |
| 4. | 529 | 5 | 13. | 486 | 5 |
| 5. | 552 | 5 | 14. | 135 | 3 |
| 6. | 382 | 4 | 15. | 212 | 3 |
| 7. | 420 | 4 | 16. | 499 | 5 |
| 8. | 154 | 3 | 17. | 376 | 4 |
| 9. | 456 | 4 | 18. | 379 | 4 |
| **OUT** | **3,555** | **36** | **IN** | **3,099** | **35** |
| | | | **TOTAL** | **6,654** | **71** |

*The short 10th flows lovingly and attractively through a narrow valley towards a green hard by the sea. In the background can be seen the incomparable 11th.*

The 10th (see above) is a charming wee hole but the 451-yard 11th is rightly world famous for both its view and its challenge. Its fairway twists and rolls downhill beside the sea to a fairly flat bit, from which a precise shot is needed to find a very small green nestled in the dunes.

## HIGH-QUALITY HOLES

The next five holes have an interesting routing through the inland dunes with no par fours among them. They start with the 200-yard, 'short' 12th to a fortress green on the top of a high hill. Next is a reachable par five, but requiring a precise, long shot to reach the canted green in two. Both the 135-yard 14th and 212-yard 15th are short holes, but very different – the 14th being a beautiful short-iron over rough ground to yet another bunkerless green on a plateau in the hills, while on the 15th a long-iron or a wood is needed downhill to a narrow green, protected this time by sand. The 499-yard 16th is a par five away from the cliff tops, which is reachable, at least theoretically. Unfortunately, the need for a long draw along the dogleg followed by a solid wood through a narrow defile to a skyline green is beyond the capability of most golfers. It is majestic.

There are two final turns to be made: the 17th back towards the ocean, which is a shorter mirror image of the 16th and just as good, requiring a drive out of the hills towards the sea and then a second along the cliffs to a green in a small hollow. Finally, the 379-yard 18th goes back uphill to the clubhouse, and has resisted all efforts to make it anything more than a pleasant hole, though it is made more acceptable by its proximity to the bar and to the company within it.

Like all the finest things in Ireland and golf, Ballybunion is 'itself'.

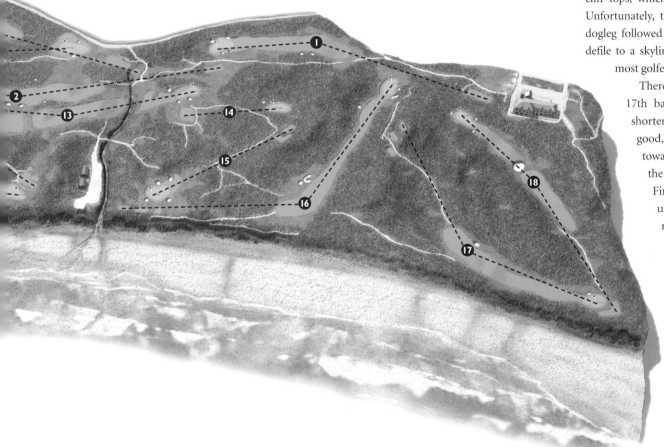

# WATERVILLE
## Waterville, County Kerry, Republic of Ireland

In the 1970s, the dreams and vision of a member of the Irish diaspora transformed an abandoned and primitive golf links into one of the finest in Ireland, and the fading company town of Waterville into a thriving golf destination.

Near the end of the 19th century Waterville was just a point on a map, when an American company chose it to be the initial eastern landfall for a transatlantic telephone cable. It built today's town and provided recreational facilities for its employees, including a rudimentary nine-hole golf course to the north. The company and the course had long closed down when an Irish-American expatriate, John Mulcahy, visited the site in the 1970s and decided it was here that he would build the golfing venue of his dreams. Mulcahy's goals were lofty, and he invested heavily in the course and other facilities, using Eddie Hackett to design an 18-hole course over the links – providing him with some spectacular dunesland to the north, as well as the flat land of the original nine-holer.

Investment continues to be poured in by the current owners, most significantly in the form of a 2006 renovation by Tom Fazio. The result has been a tougher and more mannered design, with two of the holes completely changed and another 13 significantly remodelled. Waterville now plays within the footprint given to it by Hackett, with many of the finishing touches being pure Fazio.

## UPGRADE CHANGES

Why this major renovation was needed can be seen on the opening hole. As originally built it was a basically featureless hole that got the player out into the course, but not much more. Now, mounding down the left gives the hole more texture and a hint of the landscape to come. The 464-yard 2nd has lower mounding on the left, and the green was shifted to the right to bring the Inny estuary more into play. Like the 1st, it is now a better hole, but by no means a great one.

A more difficult early test is posed by the 417-yard 3rd, a classic Cape hole with the green perched out on the estuary to the right. It is important to avoid blocking the tee shot, while an echelon of bunkers to the left makes a straight drive essential. On the 179-yard 4th, a framing dune on the left leads up to the first short hole on the course – a mid-iron to a green in a hollow between dunes. The old centre-line bunker has been replaced by flanking ones to allow a run-up shot to the green. In this area, the dunes are natural, and the 5th tee sits up in them and then heads downhill to the lowlands in a long and graceful sweep. For most players this is a true three-shot hole.

Tom Fazio's most radical changes were to the 6th and 7th, and were by far his most successful. Gone is the old, bland, uphill, two-shot 6th, to be replaced by a stunning, downhill, 194-yard hole with a view over the river. The slight walk to the tee is well worth the change.

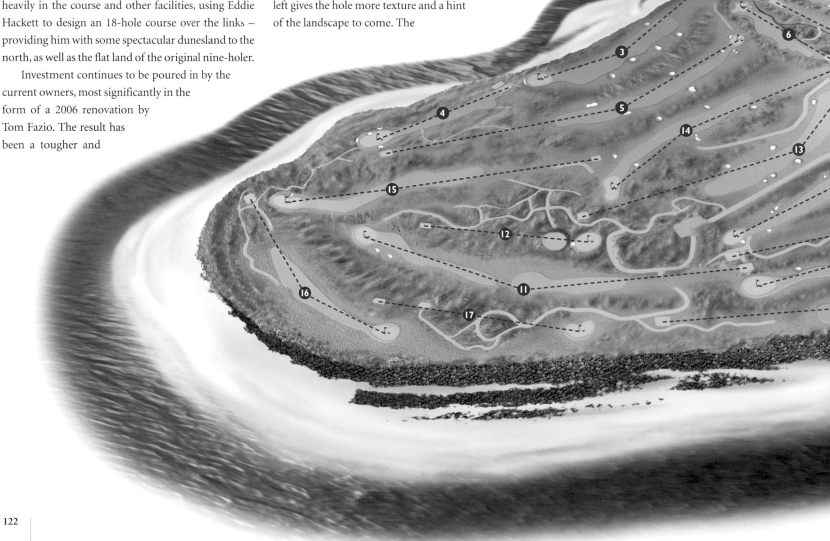

Then the 424-yard 7th, which used to be a one-shot hole to a flat green over an incongruous pond, is now a solid par four, bending gently right to an elevated green. Sand hills hiding the driving range protect the left side of the fairway. After this, the golfer plays to the north on the 432-yard 8th, whose fairway lies between low hillocks to a green tucked in the higher dunes and canted against the right–left line of play. The 445-yard 9th goes back the other way, finishing near the clubhouse.

The distances of the 7th through the 9th have increased gradually, and a player can wonder if they will ever get another manageable hole. No such luck will await them on the 10th, which is 475 yards out to the edge of the dunes. There can be respite, however, on late summer days when a quick nine is all that was needed, and the round can move directly to the beguiling and tranquil 19th hole.

## AN ARCHITECT'S DELIGHT

One can only imagine the look in Eddie Hackett's eyes when he saw the land that became the 506-yard 11th. After climbing a sand hill a gorgeous, long valley unfolds in front, rolling far into the north-west to a shallow green. Hackett boasted that he did not move one stone in building Waterville, and the naturalness of this

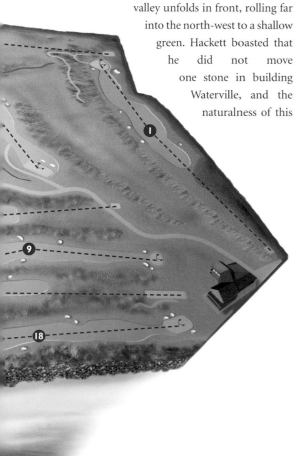

*Only the most humble architect will have the restraint to find paths that follow the contours of dunesland naturally, as if the golfer were just a gust of wind.*

hole exemplifies his respect for the land. He was very religious, too, and in designing the bedevilling, 200-yard 12th he skirted a hollow where Catholics used to meet secretly to pray during the Cromwell era.

Although the 13th is a 488-yard par five, a player must be able to draw the drive to avoid two flanking rows of bunkers, if they want to be in reach of the green for the second shot. A few yards shorter and wider than the previous hole, the 14th plays as a par four and can be longer if the wind is from the north. Its bunkerless green cants from right to left, leaving a small, effective target for a mid- to long-iron second shot. On the 428-yard 15th there is a bunkerless fairway, while the tee shot must be to the left to get the best angle for the green nestled in the right-hand dunes.

The 386-yard 16th is a sharp dogleg left at the northern tip of the property, and it is famous for having once been aced by the local professional Liam

Higgins. To do this he would have had to hit a high draw with a huge carry and have enjoyed more than a touch of the Irish luck. Most other players will play to the right and hope for a birdie at best.

Up to now the golf and the terrain at Waterville have increasingly stimulated the player, and the course peaks, literally and figuratively, on the citadel tee of the 196-yard 17th, its highest point. It is no wonder that John Mulcahy chose to be buried on this spot where there is such an inspiring view. Today's players are lucky to share that bliss as they try to find the putting surface that Eddie Hackett found at the top of another dune.

A strong par five along the ocean completes the course. Even though the 594-yard 18th has been lengthened and toughened by Tom Fazio moving the green back to the left, it is a bit of an anticlimax after the 17th. What hole would not be?

## WATERVILLE GOLF LINKS –
## Waterville, County Kerry, Republic of Ireland
Eddie Hackett, 1973 and Tom Fazio, 2006

CARD OF THE COURSE

| HOLE | NAME | YARDS | PAR | HOLE | NAME | YARDS | PAR |
|------|------|-------|-----|------|------|-------|-----|
| 1. | Last Easy | 430 | 4 | 10. | Red Breast | 475 | 4 |
| 2. | Christy's Choice | 464 | 4 | 11. | Tranquility | 506 | 5 |
| 3. | Sanctuary | 417 | 4 | 12. | Mass Hole | 200 | 3 |
| 4. | Dunes | 179 | 3 | 13. | Meadow Lark | 488 | 5 |
| 5. | Tipperary | 595 | 5 | 14. | Judge | 458 | 4 |
| 6. | Inny Valley | 194 | 3 | 15. | Vale | 428 | 4 |
| 7. | Teacher | 424 | 4 | 16. | Liam's Ace | 386 | 4 |
| 8. | Hare | 432 | 4 | 17. | Mulcahy's Peak | 196 | 3 |
| 9. | Prodigal | 445 | 4 | 18. | O Grady's Beach | 594 | 5 |
| **OUT** | | **3,580** | **35** | **IN** | | **3,731** | **37** |
| | | | | **TOTAL** | | **7,311** | **72** |

# THE LOW COUNTRIES

By their name, the Low Countries should be flat. Wrong! In golfing terms, at least, they are anything but flat, so both Belgium and The Netherlands offer some of the finer golf courses and golf-course design in Europe.

Belgium and The Netherlands both enjoy expansive North Sea beaches. But what keeps the sea from invading their precious farmland? Great engineering for sure, but also some of the most valuable sand dunes in the world – and that gives the possibility of links golf. While it is true that The Netherlands do not change level by more than a few feet, that does not preclude contour alterations, and it only takes a few feet of height difference to produce blind shots – visit Hilversumsche Golf Club[1] and you will experience this. Belgium is hardly mountainous but get into the hills above Spa and it is possible to play bracing upland golf at the Royal Golf Club des Fagnes[2]. Even the former hunting grounds of the Royal Donation at Tervuren, home to the engagingly handsome Royal Golf Club de Belgique[3], have sufficient hills and vales to work up at least a gentle puff in the walking golfer.

## BELGIAN COURSES

Belgium established its earliest golf club and course at Antwerp, just before The Netherlands founded a club. As so often in Europe, they were British golfers who set up what became the Royal Antwerp[4]: in March 1888 W.J.R. Watson invited to his house a number of Englishmen who had already been displaying their golfing prowess on a sandy heath at Wilryck. They adopted the rules of the Royal Wimbledon GC for their own, and laid their first course out on an army training ground. Some years later they moved to a woodland site at Kapellen, north of Antwerp, and engaged Willie Park Jnr to create the course. In the 1920s Tom Simpson expanded the course to what it is today – a masterly design given that the land does not change level by more than a foot or two, being hardly that much above the water table. Yet this is a wonderfully strategic course, cleverly bunkered and with brilliant moundwork that looks entirely natural, yet cannot possibly be.

The claim to have the second earliest Belgian course and club lies between Royal Zoute (1899) (see

Kennemer
*page 126*

Royal Hague
*page 128*

Royal Zoute
*page 130*

page 130) and a course near Dinant for the Royal Golf Club Château Royal d'Ardenne[5] built in the former royal park there (1900). And it was royal support that changed the face of Belgian golf in the opening years of the 20th century.

King Leopold II was not a golfer, but he understood the potential of golf to further his young country's ambitions in the diplomatic and business world. He made land available for the purpose (fortuitously good land), and he gave Belgian golf royal blessing and patronage, which it enjoys to this day. The earliest beneficiary of this initiative was a links course at Royal Ostend[6] in 1903. It is still there, although it has been much changed and some of its links qualities lost.

Then, in 1906, came Belgium's ravishing beauty, the Royal Golf Club de Belgique. Perhaps it is too short for today's big hitters, but it is a gem for other golfers. Debate rages about who first designed the course, possibly Seymour Dunn. Tom Simpson is certainly credited with the major surviving work. No matter who may have designed it, this is a course to delight the reveller in classic golf-course architecture, the arboriculturist (the course is lined by specimen trees from the royal arboretum) and the architect (with a clubhouse dating from 1748, a former royal hunting lodge).

There are other good royal courses in Royal Golf Club du Sart-Tilman[7] (completed just before the Second World War) near Liège and Royal Golf Club du Hainault[8] near Mons. Royal Latem[9] has charm but is undeniably flat, while Royal Waterloo's[10] two courses are relatively modern and so not those at which the great Henry Cotton was once professional. There were no further significant courses built until 1967, when Golf du Bercuit[11] (designed by Robert Trent Jones Snr) and Golf and County Club Limburg[12] (F.W. Hawtree) opened. In the 1980s and '90s something of a golf explosion took place with 44 new clubs added to the meagre stock of 16, which were all that had been created in the previous hundred years.

## GOLF IN THE NETHERLANDS

It is quite possible that the Dutch invented golf. They were certainly playing *kolf* in the 13th century, and *kolf* and *kolfers* feature in Dutch painting by *c.*1625, suggesting that it was a popular recreation. But golf as we now know it arrived in The Netherlands in 1889 with a three-hole course in The Hague, followed by the establishment of clubs in Utrecht and Arnhem (Rosendaelsche[13]) in the 1890s. By the time of the First World War the important Kennemer (see page 126) and Hilversumsche Golf Club had also been founded. But they did not yet possess great courses.

That transformation was largely due to the work of the company of Colt, Alison and Morrison during the 1920s and '30s. Their catalogue of first-rate courses in Holland is important with new courses, rebuilds, upgrades and extensions, including Royal Hague (see page 128), Kennemer, Hilversumsche,

Utrechtse Golf Club de Pan[14], De Dommel[15], Eindhovensche[16], Amsterdam Old Course[17] and Golfclub Toxandria[18]. From the early 1990s to 2007, the Dutch architect Frank Pont did sensitive restoration work on some of these courses.

Another landmark course (for an old club – de Noordwijkse[19]) was designed by the Dutch-born architect Frank Pennink in 1969. It has been a frequent host to the Dutch Open and has produced such winners as Payne Stewart, Bernhard Langer and Colin Montgomerie. Although it features a couple of excursions into the woods, it is a course that could almost have been lifted from the Lancashire coast, with dunes reminiscent of Royal Birkdale (see page 86) and Hillside GC. For that matter, Utrechtse Golf Club de Pan and Hilversumsche GC, with their swathes of heather and undulating fairways, bear more than a passing resemblance to Swinley Forest and The Berkshire GC.

It is unlikely that there will be further courses built in Holland's sand dunes or heathland. Instead new developments will almost certainly be on polder – land reclaimed from the sea. Such land imposes considerable restrictions on the course designer, with a high water table, few natural features and plentiful ditches and dykes. More interesting recent courses include De Lage Vuursche[20] (designed by Kyle Phillips and Robert Trent Jones Jnr) and Goye[21] (Bruno Steensels), on polder, both from 1999.

*The 420-yard 4th hole at Royal Golf Club du Sart-Tilman is typical of the heavily wooded nature of this attractive course. The bunkering is more sparing here than on most of Simpson's other Belgian courses.*

# KENNEMER
## Zandvoort, The Netherlands

Several of the finest golfing countries were markedly influenced by one man. Examples include Dr Alister MacKenzie in Australia and Charles Alison in Japan. The Netherlands too benefited from its relationship with Harry Colt, which began at Kennemer and lasted for 11 years.

After the 18-hole Kennemer course opened in 1928, Colt and his firm built nine more courses in this relatively small country. Eight of the ten courses are still in play today, many closer to their original form than found in other countries.

Kennemer's appreciation of Colt and his work proved crucial after the Second World War. Even more so than most clubs in Europe, the German occupation had a devastating effect. At one point 120 German bunkers were built on the club's property in addition to anti-tank walls. After the horrors of the war had concluded, the detailed correspondence between Colt and the club during the design and course build proved invaluable in guiding the course's restoration. To this day, Kennemer's archives serve as the basis for sound decision-making.

### KENNEMER GOLF & COUNTRY CLUB – Zandvoort, The Netherlands

Harry Colt, 1928
Major events: KLM Open (formerly Dutch Open) 1920, 1931, 1933, 1935, 1939, 1951, 1955, 1958, 1961, 1966, 1971, 1976, 1977, 1983, 1989, 1990, 2006, 2007, 2008

CARD OF THE COURSE

| HOLE | YARDS | PAR | HOLE | YARDS | PAR |
|---|---|---|---|---|---|
| 1. | 450 | 4 | 10. | 355 | 4 |
| 2. | 158 | 3 | 11. | 471 | 4 |
| 3. | 528 | 5 | 12. | 551 | 5 |
| 4. | 328 | 4 | 13. | 376 | 4 |
| 5. | 348 | 4 | 14. | 386 | 4 |
| 6. | 479 | 5 | 15. | 164 | 3 |
| 7. | 370 | 4 | 16. | 483 | 5 |
| 8. | 185 | 3 | 17. | 171 | 3 |
| 9. | 424 | 4 | 18. | 400 | 4 |
| OUT | 3,270 | 36 | IN | 3,357 | 36 |
| | | | TOTAL | 6,627 | 72 |

### COLT AT HIS BEST

This course is a grand example of Harry Colt's dunesland work on the country's west coast. Though set slightly away from the North Sea, the breadth of the dunesland in The Netherlands is wider than in the United Kingdom and Colt made the most of the linksland at Kennemer. Standing on the 1st tee in front of the imposing, thatched-roof clubhouse with the fairway below, the golfer draws similarities with the sensation of teeing off at Shinnecock Hills (see page 178). With the closely related game of *kolven* having been depicted in paintings since the 1500s, the visitor is very aware of the strong Dutch ties to the roots of golf. With the club's knowledgeable members gazing from the nearby clubhouse, the first tee shot becomes particularly nervy. Up ahead, Colt made the most of the land's random movements, with the 1st green in a hollow and the 2nd green majestically high on a plateau.

After the attractive 528-yard 3rd, the next several holes follow the perimeter of the property in a general westerly/south-westerly direction. These holes are frequently into the wind, adding to their challenge. Highlights include the imaginative 5th green, as it swoops low and to the right behind a deep bunker, and the 370-yard 7th, which epitomizes the worth of cross-hazards. Long famous, the tee shot at the 7th is blind over a dune with the approach calling for a low-flighted ball under the prevailing wind that must clear a fearsome 7-feet (2.1-metre) deep cross-hazard. Though Colt was at the lead of strategic bunkering, he recognized the worth of confrontational fronting hazards when utilized on a limited basis. In this case, the hazard is 15 paces shy of the green, so golfers of all ability still enjoy the hole.

Colt next delivered another fine one-shotter – the 185-yard 8th – which he described as 'a long-iron shot, with excellent places for bunkers and hazards all round the green'. Standing on the 9th tee, the player appreciates that Colt's anticlockwise loop of the front brought them here for a reason. In the distance, the most recognized clubhouse in The Netherlands stands. Below is a classic links hole that unfolds across rippling dunes-

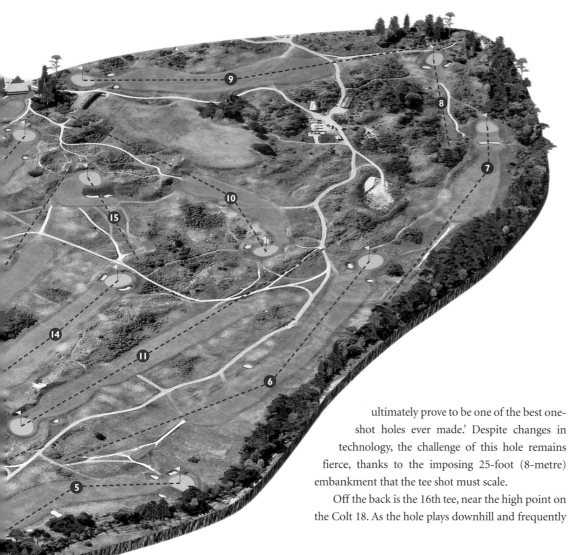

downwind, getting away a booming drive is tremendously satisfying as the ball tumbles down the fairway, ideally ending up left of centre. Otherwise, to the right, a ridge that protrudes into the fairway obscures the view of the green, attractively set at the base of a dune. The final two holes play towards the clubhouse, which remains in clear view.

## LATER COLT ADDITION

After playing Harry Colt's original 18, a fascinating rendering is found in the clubhouse's foyer, showing the routing that Colt devised for a third nine. This nine was built in 1985, nearly 50 years after Colt first drew it. Frank Pennink was the logical choice for building the holes. He had succeeded Henry Cotton, who in turn had followed Harry Colt at Kennemer. Colt's routing took advantage of the rolling topography, highlighted by the 5th, 7th and 9th holes, none of which requires any bunkers because the ground is so well suited to golf. At 3,555 yards, it is the longest of the three nines.

When Kennemer hosts the Dutch Open, this nine is used as the front. Contestants then play the first three holes followed by the last six holes of Colt's original 18. This sequencing makes for a very fine test indeed, though regretfully holes such as the 7th, 9th and 10th do not get their just attention.

ultimately prove to be one of the best one-shot holes ever made.' Despite changes in technology, the challenge of this hole remains fierce, thanks to the imposing 25-foot (8-metre) embankment that the tee shot must scale.

Off the back is the 16th tee, near the high point on the Colt 18. As the hole plays downhill and frequently

land. In the finest of links traditions, level stances are rare in this fairway, forcing players constantly to fiddle with their stance and set-up.

## HOMEWARD INNER ROUTE

Playing inside the loop created from the front nine holes, the back nine starts with a clever par four that swings to the right. From the elevated tee, the golfer is wooed along the line of charm towards the flag flapping in the breeze. In fact, the golfer needs to resist the short way home because the best line into the small angled green is from the fairway's left side.

Two holes follow where success depends on how well the approach is judged or controlled; it is often played along the ground because the holes play downwind. Turning home, the elevated 13th green complex calls for a precise approach and the beautiful rolls within the 14th green making it quite a test.

Fond of first locating the par threes when routing a course, Colt designed the 164-yard 15th early on. In his letter to the club in April 1926 he wrote: 'This will be a most spectacular one-shot hole...[it] should

*The short 15th calls for a precise shot up to the plateau-top green. The steep slope ensures that a ball played even the least bit short will roll all the way down to the bunkers below.*

# ROYAL HAGUE
## Wassenaar, The Netherlands

Koninklijke Haagsche (Royal Hague in English) is the oldest club in The Netherlands, with golf being played over a three-hole course in 1889. J.D. Dunn expanded the course to nine, and in 1920 J.F. Abercromby turned it into the first 18-hole course in that country.

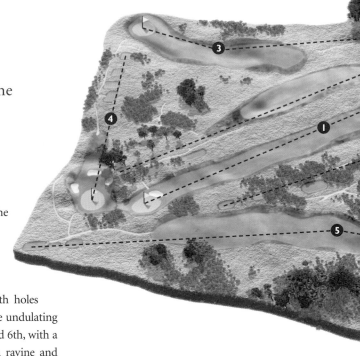

Set on relatively flat land, the Abercromby design at Royal Hague had merit but, as was so common throughout Europe, German occupation during the Second World War ravaged the course and clubhouse.

Meanwhile, in 1936, Stuart Wolf, a wealthy merchant, had commissioned the firm of Colt, Alison & Morrison to build an 18-hole course over some of the most dramatic dunes in Europe, which were lying on his estate and were 2 miles (3 kilometres) from the Abercromby course. After the war, Wolf then sold his course to the homeless Royal Hague, who brought in Guy Campbell to prepare it for play again. Ever since, its members have enjoyed golf in one of the game's most inspired settings.

### CHARLES ALISON'S LEGACY

The credit for today's course belongs to Charles Alison. At the time of Stuart Wolf's commission, Harry Colt's travelling days were near an end, so the work fell to Alison. Given the scale of the dunes, Alison's routing is a marvel. Only twice in the round does the golfer face markedly uphill tee shots – those coming at the 2nd and 9th. However, a majority of approach shots are uphill to greens attractively placed either on knolls, hollows or saddles. As a result, the course plays longer and is more challenging than the scorecard might indicate. Jimmy Adams won the Dutch Open here in 1949 and promptly called it the toughest course he had ever seen. Fortunately for Alison, steel shafts and rubber-core Haskell balls were already in use when he built the course. Thus, the occasional heroic forced carry was entirely reasonable.

Playing the course is akin to a thrilling roller-coaster ride: the 1st fairway tumbles downhill, the 2nd brings the player back uphill crossing a gully before heading to the excellent skyline green created in 2006. At the 369-yard 3rd, Alison captured a big depression within the left side of the fairway; if the tee shot does not stay to the right and on higher ground, the approach is blind from within this bowl. With its tees set into the shoulder of a dune and the green

60 feet (18 metres) below in the valley, the 222-yard 4th is exhilarating, with its difficulty being in maintaining control of the tee shot from the high tee on a windy day.

This thrilling pace never lets up, with holes continuing to reflect the uniqueness of the undulating property. One such treasure is the 484-yard 6th, with a long and true tee ball needed to carry a ravine and somehow find the fairway as it swings to the right between two dunes. Its green complex is merciless, falling away on all sides with its left false side of no help as it feeds the ball into a 11-foot (3.3-metre) deep green-side bunker. Even if somewhat dazed standing on the 7th tee, the golfer should not be fooled by this 379-yard par four: although requiring as little as a mid-iron off the tee, a sloppy short-iron approach missed right or long potentially leaves the ball 30 feet (9 metres) below the green. Miss short and the ball is tangled up in dunes.

Flighting the ball through the wind from a sloping stance is at the essence of links golf, with this requirement highlighted around the turn. Ceaselessly undulating, the topography provides plenty of the challenge. For instance, at the 361-yard 9th, it is important to control the approach through the wind from one hill top to the green on another while avoiding the green's dramatic false front and single greenside bunker, characteristically quite deep.

### AMEN CORNER

Indeed, blessed with such terrain, Charles Alison's design is free of artificiality. There are only 23 green-side bunkers, and the sole fairway bunker on the course comes at the 430-yard 13th – the start of what members at Royal Hague refer to as their own Amen Corner. In 2007, Frank Pont moved the green centre 15 yards (14 metres) back and 5 yards (4.5 metres) to the right, cleverly tucking it into a little pocket around the shoulder of a hill.

Confronting the golfer next is the most intimidating tee shot on the course, where only a ribbon of the

## KONINKLIJKE HAAGSCHE GOLF & COUNTRY CLUB – Wassenaar, The Netherlands
Charles Alison, 1936 and Frank Pont, 2007
Major events: Dutch Open (later KLM Open) 1919, 1924–28, 1930, 1932, 1938, 1949, 1954, 1959, 1967, 1972, 1973, 1981

CARD OF THE COURSE

| HOLE | YARDS | PAR | HOLE | YARDS | PAR |
|---|---|---|---|---|---|
| 1. | 506 | 5 | 10. | 483 | 5 |
| 2. | 390 | 4 | 11. | 416 | 4 |
| 3. | 369 | 4 | 12. | 168 | 3 |
| 4. | 222 | 3 | 13. | 430 | 4 |
| 5. | 485 | 5 | 14. | 422 | 4 |
| 6. | 484 | 5 | 15. | 415 | 4 |
| 7. | 379 | 4 | 16. | 385 | 4 |
| 8. | 230 | 3 | 17. | 160 | 3 |
| 9. | 361 | 4 | 18. | 510 | 5 |
| OUT | 3,426 | 37 | IN | 3,389 | 36 |
| | | | TOTAL | 6,815 | 73 |

14th fairway is visible. The player's eyes unfortunately tend to focus more on the wild, rolling dunes covered with bracken and the out-of-bounds left. A bold, positive swing is crucial. Past the shoulder of a hill 150 yards (137 metres) from the tee, the fairway fans to the right and is much wider than perceived from the tee. In this manner, Alison fulfilled a design principle embraced in the Golden Age, namely giving the golfer an apparently

fearsome task while in actuality providing plenty of room for them to accomplish it. The sense of satisfaction that sweeps over the golfer from properly executing such a nervy shot is its own rich reward. Not letting up though, Alison has the player bear down again with an exacting uphill approach to a green nestled in a saddle. Its false front returns under-hit balls as far back as 30 yards (27 metres) into the fairway.

Its sister hole, the 415-yard 15th, plays parallel in the opposite direction. Though set over the same rambunctious portion of the property, the challenges are different because the elevated tee gives a better perspective of the task at hand. In fact, the fairway is wide and plays wider, courtesy of Alison incorporating a hill on the left into the fairway. Golfers use its slope to work the ball into the middle right of the fairway from where there is a clear look at the green; approaches played from elsewhere are blind with the green obscured behind a dune. The green's tantalizing location in the dunes is better appreciated following tree clearing, with wonderful long views restored beyond it.

## CLOSING HOLES

In a refreshing change from most modern designs, the final three holes call for precision and thought as opposed to brute length. The 385-yard 16th has what every good links course needs, namely a tilted fairway that asks the golfer to shape the shot. In this case, its left-to-right slope insists on a draw in the summer months to hold the browned-out fairway. The rub is that a ravine tracks down the right of the fairway on a diagonal. Though modest in length, the conundrum posed on the tee is a fine one.

Improved in 2007, the large 17th green gives this 160-yard par three great variety with vexing hole locations right near a steep drop-off and back-left where

the green runs away. Returning along an avenue of trees, the 510-yard 18th is noted for its grand view of the clubhouse, the only view that the golfer has of it during the round. Being Stuart Wolf's private home, he wanted the golf course over the dune and out of view. The course benefited immeasurably from this unusual stipulation because it freed up a few hectares of prime terrain for golf. Under most scenarios, the broad area around today's 1st and 10th tees would have been lost – that high point naturally suggesting itself for a clubhouse. Without being so confined, Charles Alison was able to build the stirring sequence of holes that he did.

# ROYAL ZOUTE
## Knokke-Heist, Belgium

At the turn of the 20th century, British residents played golf in the dunes that were owned by the Compagnie Immobiliére du Zoute near the well-to-do Belgium resort town of Knocke (now Knokke). Its chairman, Count Maurice Lippens, realized the attraction of the sport and formed in 1908 what is now called Royal Zoute Golf Club.

To build the golf courses, Count Lippens brought in Harry Colt from England, who at the time was considered among the top of his profession, along with such architects as Willie Park Jnr and W.H. Fowler. Being keen to get established on the Continent, Colt busily set about laying out two courses between 1910 and 1913, chronologically well before his work in the nearby Netherlands. Colt's two courses were such a success that he eventually needed to build a third course 9 miles (15 kilometres) away. Sadly, all three courses were destroyed in the Second World War. Thanks in part to work carried out by Lieutenant Colonel Allen, golf resumed at Royal Zoute in 1947.

Colt's initial two courses comprise Royal Zoute of today. The championship course plays along the perimeter of the club's property, whereas the par-64 competition course is within the loop created by

the big course. He had a propensity for creating loops within loops, be it 18-hole loops like here or nine holes within another nine-hole loop as at Kennemer (see page 126) and Muirfield (see page 60). One reason that Colt did so is that as the holes tack around the perimeter, generally no more than two play consecutively in the same direction. Thus, the golfer always needs to make allowances for shifts in wind direction.

### RISING EXPECTATIONS

There is room to play on the first two holes, but the challenge becomes exacting at the 148-yard 3rd. Interestingly, this hole does not show up on a 1928 course routing that appeared in a European golf guide entitled *Guides Plumon – Les Golfs du Continent*, so it is an example of a hole that may have emerged after the Second World War. Its long, pushed-up green is bedevilling to hit, only 13 paces wide at the back and even narrower in the front. Sloping away on all sides, care needs to be taken not to hit the recovery shots from side to side.

Signifying the start of promising golf country, the 4th tee ball is blind over a ridge. The excitement starting to build is fully realized at the 479-yard 5th, where Harry Colt placed the fairway in the valley between two rows of dunes. As the valley and fairway twist to the left, a pair of bunkers pinch the fairway in 100 yards (90 metres) from the

*Although houses overlook the course and trees are plentiful, Royal Zoute is, nevertheless, a true links with plenty of movement in the ground, exemplified on the par-three 8th hole.*

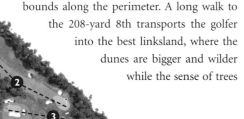

green. Decisions abound. Can these bunkers be carried, as well as the deep cross-bunker 40 yards (36 metres) from the green? Or is it best to lay back and, if so, to where? Such decisions make this a great half-par hole.

As opposed to the 5th through the valley, the 6th and 7th fairways bob up and down over interesting undulations. Indeed, at this stage in the round, comparisons with Royal Lytham (see page 88) are fairly drawn as the land is ideally suited for golf without being tumbling, and the player is vaguely aware of the red-brick houses periodically seen out-of-bounds along the perimeter. A long walk to the 208-yard 8th transports the golfer into the best linksland, where the dunes are bigger and wilder while the sense of trees bordering the holes dissipates. The golfer is now within 1 mile (2 kilometres) of the English Channel, so calm playing conditions are rare.

## COPING WITH COASTAL BREEZES

The 405-yard 9th and 386-yard 10th are parallel so the wind affects these par fours markedly differently. Particularly well conceived is the 10th, with its fairway swinging left around a 10-foot (3-metre) high landform with two bunkers cut into it. Carrying this feature is the bold line, leaving a shortish iron into a green that sets up for shots from the left. Unfortunately, most golfers have neither the nerve nor the ability to try such a drive and so play cautiously to the right. From there, the approach is over bunkers to an angled green with its right-to-left tilt exacerbating the difficulty. Rarely does a golfer find a sub-400 yard (365-metre) hole so frustrating – a compliment to those who built it.

Such clever uses of angles are again seen at the 535-yard 12th, where a dune line diagonally crosses the fairway 240 yards (220 metres) from the tee. Its crumpled fairway swings right, then back left over this ridge line, and right again past two bunkers. Originally, this hole was played as two fairly straight holes of no great merit, and the club deserves credit for being a good steward in allowing the transformation to occur into such a fine, S-shaped hole.

Bunkerless, the 449-yard 13th fairway disappears over the crest of a ridge before swinging left and up to the green. The approach shot can be played in a number of ways, from hitting a low scooter that feeds in from the right to flying the ball all the way. Admiring both its effortless challenge as well as how it accommodates all ranges in skill level, the player ruefully wishes other courses had more uncluttered holes like this.

As has been seen, a game at Royal Zoute is not about brute force; it is better than that, relying on subtle angles instead. Another example is at the 362-yard 14th, the shortest par four on the course, where the ideal tee ball rubs past a steep hillside 220 yards (200 metres) from the tee, at the base of which is a penal bunker. As a player shies away from that bunker off the tee, the approach to the green becomes progressively more difficult, bringing directly into play its greenside bunkers and wicked false front.

## PICKING UP LOST STROKES

Of the four holes left to play, two are par fives, giving the good golfer hope of reclaiming a stroke or two that has invariably bled away during the round. Such high ambitions, however, should not be extended to the 184-yard 16th, an exacting par three to a green set into the hillside with its 9-foot (2.7-metre) deep, right greenside bunker to be avoided at all costs. Trees have grown in, giving the hole a friendlier look than in days gone by, when the green complex was more exposed. Regardless, playing the hole, the golfer soon finds that it retains the same bite.

After escaping the 16th and not doing any harm to the scorecard at the 549-yard 17th, the round concludes most satisfactorily on the 18th green, which features the best random interior contours of any hole at Royal Zoute. The Lippens of today, and Belgium in general, are left with a wonderful monument to what Count Lippens originally envisaged a hundred years ago.

# ROYAL ZOUTE GOLF CLUB –
# Knokke-Heist, Belgium
Harry Colt, 1910 and Lieutenant Colonel Allen, 1947
Major events: Belgian Open 1912, 1950, 1998, 1999, 2000

CARD OF THE COURSE

| HOLE | YARDS | PAR | HOLE | YARDS | PAR |
|---|---|---|---|---|---|
| 1. | 422 | 4 | 10. | 386 | 4 |
| 2. | 397 | 4 | 11. | 210 | 3 |
| 3. | 148 | 3 | 12. | 535 | 5 |
| 4. | 381 | 4 | 13. | 449 | 4 |
| 5. | 479 | 5 | 14. | 362 | 4 |
| 6. | 418 | 4 | 15. | 484 | 5 |
| 7. | 388 | 4 | 16. | 184 | 3 |
| 8. | 208 | 3 | 17. | 549 | 5 |
| 9. | 405 | 4 | 18. | 385 | 4 |
| OUT | 3,246 | 35 | IN | 3,544 | 37 |
| | | | TOTAL | 6,790 | 72 |

# FRANCE, LUXEMBOURG AND ITALY

*Jeu de mail* – a game similar to golf – had been popular in France from the 16th century, and there is a theory that Scottish soldiers fighting with the French against the English in the 14th century may have taught their French comrades the rudiments of early golf.

Napoleon and his European military excursions at the turn of the 19th century caused golf as it is known today to be introduced into France, albeit very indirectly. The French had taken possession of Portugal in 1807 and Napoleon's brother Joseph had become king of Spain in 1808. British troops under the command of the Duke of Wellington regained control of the Iberian Peninsula in 1813 and then entered France, forcing Napoleon's abdication in 1814. Among Wellington's officers were some Scots, a few of whom had taken their golf clubs with them. While stationed in Pau, birthplace of Henri of Navarre (later Henri IV of France), they discovered the plain of Billère, which, with its views of the Pyrénées and its 'wee burn' (small stream), reminded them of home. More importantly, it had a permeable, rocky subsoil, which made it mud-free even in winter.

## EARLY FRENCH GOLF COURSES

Pau, with its agreeable winter climate, appealed to the British officers in general, and a colony of retired military families was established there by the mid-19th century. They introduced steeplechasing and foxhunting, and, in 1856, they founded the Pau Golf Club[1], which still flourishes. It was not until the 1880s that further French clubs emerged. Among these was Dinard GC[2] (1887) founded by Britons living in the area (who also set up France's first tennis club). At Dinard, records indicate that it was quite possible to see the grand duke of Russia playing golf on the same course as local tradesmen. Grand Duke Michael of Russia was also responsible for the introduction of golf to the Riviera in 1891, at Golf Club de Cannes-Mandelieu[3].

Dinard was laid out by Tom Dunn, son of Old Willie Dunn of Musselburgh. Although Tom had been born in England he was familiar with traditional Scottish links, and Dinard as first built was very

Scottish in feel. Some of those traits remain today – and a little of Tom's original work. His much younger brother, Young Willie Dunn, helped Tom with the early redesign of the 1888 course at Société des Golfs de Biarritz[4], and soon after Young Willie became the first of the Dunns to emigrate to the United States, where the family became pioneer golf-course designers. Sadly, that part of the Biarritz course known as the Chambre d'Amour was badly damaged during the Second World War and was later sold. Biarritz gave its name to a style of three-level green, higher at the front and back, lower in the middle, and Biarritz holes

survive at North Berwick (see page 46) and Yale among other period courses.

Further courses followed on the Channel coast, such as Dieppe-Pourville[5] and Wimereux[6], and at such fashionable resorts as Aix-les-Bains. A number of these early courses no longer exist, including those at Argelès-Gazost, Sainte Barbe, St Malo, Hyères and Le Mesnil-le-Roi. Golf de Compiègne[7] (1896) holds the distinction of being the first course to have hosted Olympic Games golf, which it did in 1900, being at that time the nearest course to Paris, where the games were being held. It was not long before further golf courses were built around Paris, with Morfontaine (see page 134), Fontainebleau[8] and of Chantilly[9] appearing in the first decade of the 20th century. British architects such as Tom Simpson and Harry Colt were in demand, contributing such classics as St Germain (see page 136), Granville[10], Deauville Saint-Gatien[11], Golf Club du Lys[12], Hardelot (Les Pins course)[13], Chantaco[14] and Golf du Touquet (La Mer course)[15].

prestigious Trophée Lancôme. But the status quo was about to change.

A number of factors contributed to this situation, not least the advent of the European Community, a worldwide explosion of interest in golf, the downturn in agricultural prosperity, the realization of the tourism potential of golf and the possibility of grant-aid for those seeking a new use for their farmland. Golf courses sprang up all over France particularly during the 1980s and '90s. Native designers were responsible for the majority of the architecture, but the big international names were attracted to France, too. Leading the invasion from overseas were Robert Trent Jones Snr (Moliets[17], Sperone[18], La Grande Motte[19]), Robert Trent Jones Jnr (Saint Donat[20], Joyenval[21]), Pete Dye (Barbaroux[22] with his son P.B. Dye), Bill Coore (Golf du Médoc[23]), Jack Nicklaus (Paris International[24]), Gary Player (Le Chateau de Taulane[25]), Ronald Fream (Golf Disneyland[26]) and particularly Robert von Hagge (Le Kempferhof[27], Les Bordes[28], Royal Mougins[29], Seignosse[30] and Le Golf National[31]).

## GOLF IN LUXEMBOURG

The first official golf club constructed in Luxembourg was Golf Club Grand Ducal[32], which was constituted in 1934 and opened for play in 1936. It was the only course for more than 50 years, until the arrival of Golf Gaichel[33], a nine-hole course on the Belgian border, designed and built by the club's founding members. Since then 18-hole golf courses have followed at Belenhaff[34], Clervaux[35], Japanese-designed Kikuoka Country Club[36] and the diminutive Christnach[37].

## ITALIAN COURSES

It was in 1889 that golf came to Italy with the foundation (by Britons living in the city) of the Florence GC[38], which went on to host Italy's first national championship in 1905. By then Acquasanta (see page 138) had been opened (1903) and in 1907 a nine-hole course, Menaggio & Cadenabbia[39], overlooking Lake Como, was built, once again founded by Britons. And it was a few years later at Menaggio that one of the most influential designers in Italian golf became honorary secretary, the Irishman Peter

*The Ugolino Course of the Florence Golf Club enjoys a beautiful setting amid the vine-covered hills of Chianti. The 7th hole is a short par four to a green protected at the front by a tree.*

Gannon. He had already revamped the Old Course at Karlovy Vary, in what is now the Czech Republic, and done alterations for the Engadine GC in Switzerland. These experiences prepared Gannon for construction of his masterpiece in 1926, the immensely beautiful Circolo Golf Villa d'Este[40] near Lake Como. Further top-class Italian courses followed, such as Milano[41] (1928), which Gannon built in collaboration with his friend Cecil Blandford, and the Florence course at Ugolino[42] (1933), in the Chianti hills. In all 30 Italian Opens have been played on seven different Gannon courses.

A couple of Englishmen made some impact on Italian course design in the 1950s and '60s: Ken Cotton (Olgiata[43]) and John Morrison (Biella Le Betulle[44]). More recently the limelight has been taken by well-known architects such as Robert Trent Jones Snr (Pevero[45], Castelconturbia[46], Castelgandolfo[47], I Roveri[48]), Pete Dye (Franciacorta[49]), Jack Nicklaus (Le Robinie[50]), Bernhard Langer (Modena[51]) and Jim Fazio (Monticello[52]).

*Map labels:*
ITALY
39
50
40
Lake Como
46
52
49
41
Milan
44
48
51
38
Florence
42
Rome
43
47
Acquasanta
*page 138*
SICILY

## POSTWAR FRANCE

Golf in and around Paris was very much socially elite, and it remained so after the Second World War. With membership restricted to the favoured few it was largely unnecessary to build new courses. When one of the few new ones, Saint-Nom-la-Bretèche[16], with its two F.W. Hawtree courses, opened in 1959 it immediately joined the cadre of highly exclusive clubs. It was quite the place to be seen, particularly during its years hosting the

*There is more fairway beyond these bunkers on the 8th hole than appearances might suggest, making the second shot one of the most satisfying on the course.*

## THE INITIAL TEST

The 453-yard 1st has a spacious dogleg to the right that promotes a bold, positive opening drive. Nonetheless, reaching the green in two requires a pair of solid shots. Set across the only level piece of property on the front nine, Tom Simpson's bunkering gives the long par-three 2nd its character. At 197 yards, another solid long-iron or utility club is called for.

The next six holes highlight Simpson's use of the rolling topography with the 7th and 8th – both 430 yards – being especially well regarded in France and beyond. A high draw off the tee on these holes shortens the approach considerably, as the drive may also get a favourable kick towards the green from the far side of the hill's shoulder. Unfortunately, the fairway at the 7th also slopes from left to right, so holding the fairway is the challenge. Ahead at the green, a bunker left and false front right make this an elusive target to hold in regulation.

Similar problems confront the player off the 8th tee with the need for a high tee ball to at least reach the crest of the far hill. From there, the fairway cascades towards the green with two giant bunkers eating into the fairway off a hillside 40 yards (36 metres) short of the green. Approach shots that just carry these bunkers are propelled forwards and often find the large putting surface, making this long approach shot a thrilling one to watch unfold.

## HEATHLAND GOLF

The golfer is in the midst of playing six par fours in a row. Starting at the 152-yard 11th, the golfer now plays three holes without one.

Unlike its British counterparts, which can struggle with maintaining heather, Morfontaine's sandy soil is ideal for heather, which grows here in abundance. Combined with the wide playing corridors cut through pine and birch trees, the setting is one of seclusion and charm, even though Paris is less than an hour's drive south.

Tom Simpson was commissioned to build the original nine holes for the Duc de Gramont in 1910, making it one of his earliest works. As a person Simpson was strong in character, and his passion for golf-course architecture is poured in an unbridled manner into these nine holes (the Vallière Course). A day at Morfontaine is incomplete without playing this course because it captures in an inland setting the exuberance that golfers have long appreciated at Simpson's designs at Cruden Bay (see page 64) and Ballybunion (see page 120). Though short in length at 2,805 yards, the nine is rich with character, featuring greens with 2-foot (0.6-metre) and 3-foot (1-metre) interior contours and striking bunkering. Yes, the golfer may well hit short-irons into the first five greens, but what greens they are! To sniff at this nine's lack of length is to miss the point that golf is meant to be fun. The half-par 473-yard 5th and the 451-yard 8th are as good as any holes on the property with the former featuring a green sunk in its own dell while the latter has an enormous cross-hazard.

In 1927, Simpson then created a new 18-hole course beside the Vallière Course. Unusual for many heathland courses, the main course at Morfontaine possesses five par fours greater than 430 yards (390 metres) and one true three-shotter that stretches well past 600 yards (550 metres). For those lucky enough to play it, for this is a very private club, Morfontaine strikes the perfect balance of golf in an idyllic environment while possessing sufficient challenge to hold the attention of the best. The golfer senses this standing on the 1st tee.

# MORFONTAINE
## Senlis, France

After a winding drive through a forest of pines and birch with glimpses of heather and green fairways, the golfer might expect to find a quintessential British clubhouse but instead a French château greets them. This is the only true sign that this is somewhere other than one of the famous heathland courses surrounding London.

Sandwiched between the 11th and 147-yard 13th is the 620-yard 12th, a brute of a three-shotter. This hole was not nearly that long in 1927 during the days of hickory-shafted clubs when Simpson designed the course. However, it did play as a three-shotter, and the club successfully restored that requirement when Kyle Phillips relocated the green 60 yards (55 metres) past where Simpson originally placed it.

The most controversial feature on the course is not this new green but a 15-metre (50-foot) pine tree directly between the tee and the green on the 13th. Disconcerting at first, the golfer comes to realize that the tree is well back from the tee and that it only interferes with a badly thinned shot. Given its prominence, the shame of the tree is that it masks one of Simpson's great greens, 52 paces long with a tier in its middle and a devilish back-right hole location. A four-club variation – from a pitching wedge to a 6-iron – between front and rear hole locations provide the 13th with great flexibility, unusual for a hole of 147 yards.

Tough, back-to-back par fours act as the anchor on the back nine. Standing on the elevated 15th tee, a player appreciates that a high draw is a useful tee shot to possess here. If successfully executed, the golfer enjoys a level stance in the fairway well below, from where the approach shot crosses a band of heather to reach the bunkerless green. In contrast to the 15th, the 16th plays uphill. Another swathe of heather bisects this fairway, making this one of the most handsome holes on the course. In some ways, the 16th summarizes the entire course: the golfer delights in the challenge while appreciating that a game played in solitude in such lovely environs is always time well spent.

The best of the holes are now done, but the slick, back-to-front green at the 170-yard 17th causes its own problems. After that, big hitters look for a birdie on the 493-yard final hole.

## MORFONTAINE GOLF CLUB –
## Senlis, France
Tom Simpson, 1927

### CARD OF THE COURSE

| HOLE | YARDS | PAR | HOLE | YARDS | PAR |
|------|-------|-----|------|-------|-----|
| 1. | 453 | 4 | 10. | 418 | 4 |
| 2. | 197 | 3 | 11. | 152 | 3 |
| 3. | 500 | 5 | 12. | 620 | 5 |
| 4. | 179 | 3 | 13. | 147 | 3 |
| 5. | 350 | 4 | 14. | 373 | 4 |
| 6. | 392 | 4 | 15. | 450 | 4 |
| 7. | 430 | 4 | 16. | 456 | 4 |
| 8. | 430 | 4 | 17. | 170 | 3 |
| 9. | 371 | 4 | 18. | 493 | 5 |
| **OUT** | **3,302** | **35** | **IN** | **3,279** | **35** |
| | | | **TOTAL** | **6,581** | **70** |

The terrain at St Germain had modest movement save at the end of the course where Harry Colt put an abandoned quarry to great use on the final two holes as well as numerous bunkers. At Portrush, the rumpled links landscape coupled with the wind meant that far fewer bunkers were required.

## THE RAILWAY LINE

To compound Colt's challenge, a railway line bisected the estate. Where some architects might have seen this as a curse, Colt used the massive mounds of soil cast aside during the construction of the line to create arresting green complexes, especially at the 7th, 10th and 11th on the clubhouse side of the tracks. The intimacy of these three holes to one another and the skilful way in which Colt spread the dirt make it appear that this section of the property was blessed with natural movement. Such was not the case, though no one would guess so today. On the south/forest side of the line, the most pronounced green complex, the long two-tiered 14th green, is also close to the railway.

Apart from such imaginative greens, the principal challenge in playing St Germain lies in avoiding its bunkers. Considered among Colt's most heavily bunkered courses – with 116 – some are used as cross-hazards to break up the line of sight. For example, at the long, par-five 6th, cross-bunkers are found a mere 110 yards (100 metres) from the back markers, masking what might otherwise be an uninspired view of a level field. The more important benefit of the bunkering schemes is to provide the strategic challenge to a site that had few natural features.

## AVOIDING THE BUNKERS

Out-of-bounds tight down the right, as opposed to bunkers, is the primary threat at the 428-yard 1st. Fairway bunkers begin to make their presence felt at the 498-yard 2nd, with three bunkers down the right of this par five.

The 459-yard 4th swings to the left with two pairs of bunkers guarding the inside of the dogleg. The closer the golfer drives to these bunkers the better, because a 6-foot (1.8-metre) deep bunker dominates the right front of the green. Colt cleverly created this greenside bunker's height by extending it off the back of the built-up 5th tee. Only in this way was he able to create vertical challenge on a flat site while still ensuring that the hazard remained natural in appearance. This inside-outside bunkering scheme is a timeless classic.

After the tough 4th, the golfer faces one of the great par threes in Europe – the 189-yard 5th. The cross-bunkers are not even half-way to the green, which is long and none too wide. What is not immediately evident is the deep grassy hollow along the back half of the green. Hole locations on the higher back tier are particularly testing.

With its dramatic false front of 7 feet (2.1 metres) in height, the 178-yard 7th is another classic Colt par three. It should always be played to the centre back of the green, regardless of the day's hole location. Otherwise, recovery shots are played from well below the putting surface on this built-up green.

The 8th and 10th are superlative holes in the 360-yard (330-metre) range, an endangered class of hole in the modern game. Impressively, the two holes feel and play quite differently. At the 8th, Colt created mounds on either side of the fairway 60 yards (55 metres) from the green, narrowing the focus towards the green. The short-iron approach to this green, which is handsomely framed by trees, is one of pleasurable difficulty. The 10th green is pushed up more than 8 feet (2.4 metres) from its surrounds. With the green bunkered across its front, golfers feel as if they are storming a fortress. No matter how far the ball is driven, the resulting wedge shot is a nervy one with the temptation to look up on the shot very real.

# ST GERMAIN
## St Germain-en-Laye, France

How a golf-course architect works with varying sites makes for interesting study. In 1921, well before his links course at Royal Portrush (see page 114), Harry Colt tackled a very different site with equal aplomb. It was comparatively featureless inland ground set in the beautiful, leafy suburb of St Germain west of Paris.

At 40 yards (36 metres) in depth, it is one of the longest greens on the course and a par is a wonderful score.

The 527-yard 15th is notable for how Colt dug out two deep hollows, the first one 220–270 yards (201–247 metres) on the right from the tee and the second one 150 yards (137 metres) from the green on the left. A way down the hole must be woven without getting into the hollows, with their depths of 6–12 feet (1.8–3.6 metres), because any shot from them is blind.

### THE COURSE AT ITS BEST

The finishing stretch highlights the variety of holes that make St Germain an outstanding course. As the 320-yard 16th is nearly drivable, it creates all sorts of greedy and poor decisions on the tee. Played over a sand quarry, the 155-yard 17th was a natural at the corner of the property with the wild and woolly characteristics of the quarry at Colt's disposal. As good as this hole is, the best may have been saved for last with the drive at the 444-yard 18th over the edge of the same quarry to the widest fairway on the course. Thanks to the firm playing conditions presented by the green staff, the long approach is ideally fed off the down-slope in the fairway past a nest of bunkers and onto the green. Colt subtly shaped this green approach, and the intelligent chasing shot is well rewarded.

When finished, the golfer can look back on a well-played round with deep satisfaction, knowing a great range of challenges has been conquered. Just as he did at Portrush, Harry Colt maximized the opportunities here, though for entirely different reasons.

Play on finesse continues on the 153-yard 11th, where seven bunkers ring the none-too-big putting surface. The 'coffin' bunker at the right of the green is so dubbed because of its very slender nature, which leaves awkward recovery attempts.

On a course noted for its bunkers, the 341-yard 13th is unusual for its lack of them, especially just to the right front of the green where bunkers are generally expected. Their relative absence makes the hole look benign from the tee, but ultimately many golfers find themselves in the grassy swale right of the green, 3 feet (1 metre) below the putting surface, from where an up-and-down is a rarity. Only after carding a five or worse does a golfer begin to appreciate how deftly Colt used a lack of defined hazards as a crafty tool!

Standing on the 14th tee is a different sensation because the hole's merit is immediately evident. Rugged bunkers protect the inside of this dogleg left. After a good drive with a slight draw, the golfer peers past bunkers that pinch in the fairway from both sides 100 yards (90 metres) from the green. A long-iron or utility wood is required to reach this bunkerless green in two.

## GOLF DE SAINT GERMAIN –
## St Germain-en-Laye, France
Harry Colt, 1921
Major events: French Open 1927, 1936, 1949, 1952, 1958, 1962, 1967, 1981, 1985

CARD OF THE COURSE

| HOLE | YARDS | PAR | HOLE | YARDS | PAR |
|---|---|---|---|---|---|
| 1. | 428 | 4 | 10. | 365 | 4 |
| 2. | 498 | 5 | 11. | 153 | 3 |
| 3. | 380 | 4 | 12. | 439 | 4 |
| 4. | 459 | 4 | 13. | 341 | 4 |
| 5. | 189 | 3 | 14. | 446 | 4 |
| 6. | 574 | 5 | 15. | 527 | 5 |
| 7. | 178 | 3 | 16. | 320 | 4 |
| 8. | 359 | 4 | 17. | 155 | 3 |
| 9. | 491 | 5 | 18. | 444 | 4 |
| **OUT** | **3,556** | **37** | **IN** | **3,190** | **35** |
| | | | **TOTAL** | **6,746** | **72** |

# ACQUASANTA
## Rome, Italy

Something akin to golf was played by the Romans – they stood side-on in order to strike a leather ball with a club. Their game was called *paganica*. It was to be a further two millennia before golf as we know it was established in modern Rome.

The Circolo del Golf di Roma Acquasanta is not only the oldest surviving golf course in Rome but also in Italy. British diplomats founded the club in 1903, following the establishment of a British Embassy in Rome after the unification of Italy in 1870. A suitable property was acquired 2 miles (3 kilometres) from the Porta Maggiore where, according to ancient Roman tradition, the *aqua santa* (holy water) flowed. Here it was, in the Almone stream, that the cultish items associated with the worship of Cybele, the so-called *Magna Mater Deorum* (Great Mother of the Gods), were ritually cleansed. Today's visiting golfer is provided with ample opportunities to negotiate the water.

When it was founded, the course was on the outskirts of Rome. It has since been engulfed by the sprawling Eternal City and is perhaps the only world-class course that sits right in the middle of a seriously busy metropolitan area. Nevertheless it is characterized by a very special ancient and noble atmosphere, aided by its being situated within a parkland of old stone pines, elms and poplars, divided by the meandering Almone, and surrounded by the ruins of the Via Appia Antica and the Claudius aqueduct.

### EARLY HISTORY

Like most golf clubs in Italy, Acquasanta started out as a decidedly non-Italian affair. All the club's documents, the articles of association and the minutes of the meetings were drafted in English. The transformation into an Italian golf club took place in 1930 when Alfredo di Carpegna became president. In the Fascist era, Benito Mussolini's son-in-law and later foreign secretary Galeazzo Ciano all but took over the club. Besides unpopular extensions to the clubhouse and the inevitable Italianization of golf terms, he is primarily remembered as a bad golfer, forever causing trouble for his caddies who were required to ensure that his ball always found a good lie. In 1944 the German *Wehrmacht* occupied the course, but treated it fairly well – as did the Allied British and US armed forces. They were among the first to tee off when the course reopened in June 1945. At that time it was still the only 18-hole course in Italy south of Florence.

### A PARKLAND COURSE

A round at Acquasanta today is a journey back to the Golden Age with a little twist. It combines the old English parkland style with stunning Mediterranean vegetation. The wide and rolling fairways facilitate strategic play and no rough to speak of contrains

Obviously, at 6,563 yards, Acquasanta cannot be confused with a modern championship venue. While there is still the occasional top amateur tournament being hosted, the Italian Open has not been played here since 1980, when Massimo Mannelli scored his only European Tour win. Incidentally, he is still on site, working as club professional and perhaps testifying to the club's considerable old-time flair.

## PEACE AMONG THE MAYHEM

Despite one or two noisy corners, where traffic *alla Romana* buzzes the course, Acquasanta proudly exhibits the enchanting beauty of a classic layout. The club has resisted the temptation to bring in a big-name architect and 'modernize' the course, so the plentiful diversity and strategic merit of the old routing is retained. After a picturesque downhill drive, the holy water is introduced: two side-arms of the Almone defend the 1st green, while the main arm, lined with poplars, lurks in the back waiting to come into play on the 154-yard 2nd, a par three across it to a green surrounded by typical Roman pines.

With the tee shot on the 347-yard 3rd blind to an elevated, right-to-left sloping fairway, it soon becomes apparent that nobody has tried to redesign the course to remove its period-piece architecture. The course was, after all, laid out by its early members, not a well-known architect, and has since been modified several times.

As you make your way over the rolling terrain of the next few holes, taking in views of the Claudius aqueduct and crossing the Almone again from the 6th tee, a golfer encounters another eccentric feature in the sneaky false front of the 8th green, barely visible to the unsuspecting. It conceals a gaping chasm that catches even the best-intentioned run-up shot and leaves a puzzling chip up the plateau. A semiblind, long drive is

the player. All aspects of classic golf architecture contribute to the balanced variety of the course, with large and undulated greens, elevated and blind tees, ditches, ponds, hedges, solitary trees on the fairway, intimate green sites, a drop-shot par three over water and fairly restrained bunkering.

# CIRCOLO GOLF ROMA ACQUASANTA – Rome, Italy

Dr Flach, Vanni, de Castro and Young, 1913
Major events: Italian Open 1950, 1973, 1980

CARD OF THE COURSE

| HOLE | YARDS | PAR | HOLE | YARDS | PAR |
|------|-------|-----|------|-------|-----|
| 1. | 334 | 4 | 10. | 486 | 5 |
| 2. | 154 | 3 | 11. | 131 | 3 |
| 3. | 347 | 4 | 12. | 446 | 4 |
| 4. | 393 | 4 | 13. | 381 | 4 |
| 5. | 215 | 3 | 14. | 362 | 4 |
| 6. | 384 | 4 | 15. | 360 | 4 |
| 7. | 551 | 5 | 16. | 349 | 4 |
| 8. | 402 | 4 | 17. | 428 | 4 |
| 9. | 435 | 4 | 18. | 405 | 4 |
| OUT | 3,215 | 35 | IN | 3,348 | 36 |
| | | | TOTAL | 6,563 | 71 |

needed on the 427-yard 9th, in order to secure a workable angle for the second shot on this curling fairway.

Ancient and modern are rarely far apart, with the Claudius aqueduct and mad Roman traffic both visible from the 10th green. The 12th is the only really long hole at 446 yards and well protected, but some of the two-shotters that follow will tempt the long hitters.

Acquasanta finishes with a pair of classic holes, the 428-yard 17th, on which many players will have to lay up short of the Almone with their second shots, hoping for a single pitch and putt. However, it remains a dangerous pitch to pin positions on the left, where the green nestles up against the holy water. The 405-yard 18th is an uphill struggle all the way back to the clubhouse. A drive up the left side of the fairway and over the hump will open up the green, which hides behind a line of trees on the right.

# SPAIN AND PORTUGAL

With their temperate winter climates, Spain and Portugal – or, rather, certain parts of Spain and Portugal – have become popular destinations for visitors from northern Europe, where for months on end the light is gloomy and the weather can make a round of golf a wet and cold experience.

PORTUGAL

SPAIN

BALEARIC ISLANDS

‡13
● Santander    11 ‡

12
‡ 15
● Barcelona

‡3
● Oporto

10
‡ 14
● Madrid

‡ 24

● Valencia
‡ El Saler
*page 142*

4 ● Sintra
9 ‡ ● Lisbon
● Setubal
‡ 8

2 5
‡ 7 ‡ 6 ‡
San Lorenzo
*Algarve    page 144*

● Seville
‡ 25

16
*Andalucia* 17
18
‡ 22          ‡ 19 ● Malaga
● Cadiz        ‡ Marbella
‡ 23    21 ‡ ‡ 1
20    *Costa del Sol*

---

**G**olf is a major feature of the Iberian Peninsula's lucrative tourist industry. It is also a significant lure in the property market with many people buying second, or even permanent, homes on vast complexes centred on golf courses. Along the coast of southern Spain, the Costa del Sol has become the Costa del Golf. Unfortunately developments on such a grand scale come at an environmental cost. The rainfall in southern Spain is sparse, and the demands of golf courses, real estate and intensive farming are such that the World Wildlife Fund has declared Spain to be 'the country at greatest risk of desertification in the whole of Europe'.

The great majority of Spanish and Portuguese golf courses have been built since the mid-20th century, with Robert Trent Jones Snr's Sotogrande[1] leading the way in Spain in 1964 and Henry Cotton's course at Penina[2] of 1966 opening the eyes of golfers and property developers to the potential of the Algarve in Portugal.

## SLOW START IN PORTUGAL

British merchants in the port wine trade established a course at Oporto[3] in 1890, but none followed until 1922 when a course was constructed for the Lisbon Sporting Club[4]. By 1945 there were three courses on the mainland. The Portuguese themselves did not play golf, and that is largely true today with only about 12,000 native Portuguese playing the game actively.

In addition to Penina, Henry Cotton was also responsible for the original course at Vale de Lobo[5] and made plans for several other courses locally. The Dutch-born, English-educated Frank Pennink was next with the charming Vilamoura[6] Old Course (1969), one of the jewels of the Algarve, returning a few years later to build Palmares[7]. Oddly enough, it was not Robert Trent Jones Snr who became the first American to build a course in Portugal. That honour fell to William Mitchell who, in the early 1970s, designed the first course on the vast Quinta do Lago estate, on which Joe Lee's San Lorenzo course of 1988 stands out (see page 144). Only in 1980 did Robert Trent Jones Snr venture into Portugal, designing the links-like Tróia[8] course near Setubal, while his son, Robert Trent Jones Jnr, built the handsome Atlantic[9] course at Penha Longa near Sintra in 1992.

By the turn of the 21st century there were more than 50 courses, with Americans Cabell Robinson and Rocky Roquemore and Britons Martin Hawtree and Donald Steel adding to the list of courses at the higher end of the market. However, it has to be admitted that the developers have taken full advantage of the marketing potential of golf courses, cramming vast numbers of houses and hotels as close together as possible to the fairways, spoiling the delights of what should be ravishing countryside with forests of overwhelming concrete.

## SPANISH EXCLUSIVITY

Initially in Spain golf was played only by the wealthy. Early courses were set up around Madrid (Real Club de la Puerta de Hierro[10], 1896), on the Canary Islands (Real Club de Golf de Las Palmas, 1891), in the north (San Sebastian[11], 1910) and Barcelona (Sant Cugat[12], 1914). Golf around Madrid remains an exclusive pastime, with very few courses, old or new, allowing visitors on the fairways other than as members' guests.

Fortunately, the first great professional Spanish golfer, Severiano Ballesteros, came from a family with golfing connections. His three brothers and an uncle were professionals, and the young Ballesteros was able to gain access to courses, although much of his earliest play was with a single club on the beach. With his dashing looks, dogged determination, cavalier style and amazing skill in manufacturing the most unlikely shots under the direst circumstances, Ballesteros was a marvellous ambassador for Spanish golf, and the subsequent success of José María Olazábal, Sergio García, Miguel Angel Jiménez and others has emphasized the strength in depth of Spanish players on the world stage.

Unfortunately, very few Spanish courses remain intact from the Golden Age. Happily one that still exists to some extent is Real Golf de Pedreña[13], on the north coast near Santander, and this was where Ballesteros grew up. He was able to refine his technique on a course laid out by the great English designer Harry Colt, in the late 1920s. The course has been lengthened since Colt's day, but his trademark skills in siting greens and using the topography in the most strategic way have ensured that the charm and character of the course have endured. The other survivor is Puerta de Hierro, a spacious course designed by Tom Simpson and Commander John Harris in the hilly suburbs of north-west Madrid, giving splendid views over the city. Another club,

Campo Villa de Madrid, had a golf course from 1932, but it did not survive the Spanish Civil War a few years later. During the 1950s a new course was constructed in the beautiful grounds of the Patrimonio Nacional, designed by Javier Arana.

## JAVIER ARANA

Javier Arana's name is little known outside Spain – he did not work in any other country – which is somewhat surprising given the large number of important tournaments played over the Club de Campo[14] course, including the Canada (World) Cup, nine Spanish Opens and nine Madrid Opens. Arana's masterpiece is undoubtedly El Saler (see page 142), and there was much anguish when his original 18 holes at El Prat[15] beside Barcelona Airport were ploughed up.

Andalucía was a very different place when Arana ventured south to lay out the first course at Guadalmina[16] in 1959. His last course, Aloha[17] (1975), just outside Marbella, was in many ways the forerunner of the new wave of Spanish resort courses, but Arana died before he could enjoy its success. By this time, the honour of foremost architect in southern Spain had fallen to the prolific American Robert Trent Jones Snr.

## THE AMERICAN INFLUENCE

Jones had budgets to work with that Javier Arana could only have dreamed of. Sotogrande brought the flavour of America to Spain and to Europe for the first time. Tees were monstrously long, greens were expansive, the bunkering was eye-catching and the fairways were turfed in Bermuda grass.

Las Brisas[18] and Los Naranjos[19] followed, and there was a second course at Sotogrande, known then as the New Course. In time it was bought by a Bolivian tin magnate, Jaime Patino, who brought Robert Trent Jones Snr back to rebuild the course. Patino's aim was to turn it into an examination for the world's best golfers. They were truly tested in the 1997 Ryder Cup, the American Express championships of 1999 and 2000 and a string of Volvo Masters. The course, now known as Valderrama[20], is not liked by all, and changes made by Ballesteros for the 1997 Ryder Cup were not popular with many participants, but it has definitely realized its owner's aims.

For better or for worse Robert Trent Jones Snr's influence in Spain is great. Almost every new course could be said to imitate the style of American tournament golf (target golf). Dave Thomas (San Roque[21]), Jack Nicklaus (Montecastillo[22]), Severiano Ballesteros (Novo Sancti Petri[23]), Bernhard Langer (Panoramica[24]) and José María Olazábal (Real Club de Golf de Sevilla[25]) have each made contributions to the list of glamorous courses designed to attract well-heeled visitors and big tournaments. Yet it is the subtlety and restraint of Arana's designs that are legacies of a more elegant Spain, in an era before the explosion of golf tourism.

*Large, beautifully contoured greens are the hallmark of the prolific Robert Trent Jones Snr. Sotogrande was his first Spanish course and heralded a boom in Iberian course construction.*

# EL SALER
## Valencia, Spain

For as long as the golfing press has been ranking golf courses, listing top tens, 50s, 100s or 200s, El Saler has found a regular spot in the European upper echelon. Yet it is probably the least known of the big names.

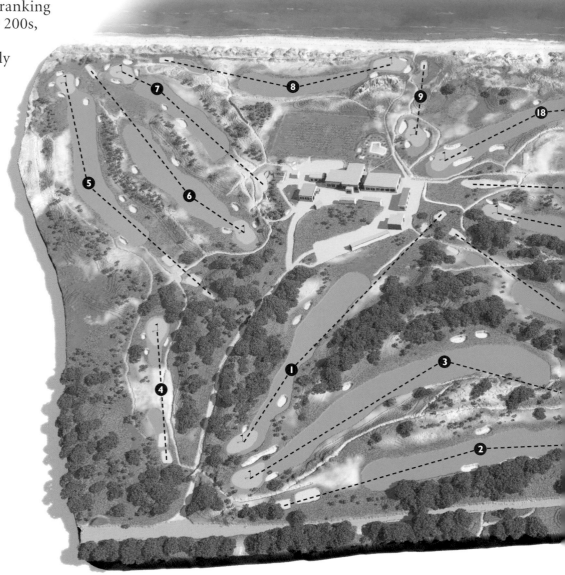

El Saler stands on its own, a few miles south of Valencia, which is a fine, vibrant city and the true home of paella. Because few of the surrounding golf courses are special, only the aficionado is going to make the effort to visit Valencia to play golf. It is one of the facilities of the luxury Parador Luis Vives, but there is also a thriving members' club, so this is a busy course. Occasionally such events as the Spanish Open, Turespaña Masters and Seve Trophy have been held here.

The divergent requirements of the world-class professional, the scratch club player and the hotel visitor are well catered for at El Saler, with wide fairways and big greens. Many of those fairways rise to a crest, curving one way or the other exactly where the good player expects his tee shot to finish. Often these critical spots are further strengthened by bunkers staggered on either side. The expansive greens are mostly constructed in a way that allows forward pin positions to be accessed easily for everyday play, but with much more demanding positions available towards the back of the green or to the sides with a number of stepped greens, contradictory borrows, diagonal or longitudinal spines, fall-aways, tight bunkering and, from time to time, a pine or palm tree abutting the putting surface, presenting a solid obstacle should the ball finish behind it. Most of the bunkers are enormous, but their style is conservative, generally having flat floors allowing easy escape for the competent player. Those bunkers with steep faces (some of them exceptionally so) can be fiendish should the golfer finish tight against or on the face.

## LINKS WITH A DIFFERENCE

Seven holes – five on the front nine, two on the back – occupy a stretch of coastal sand dunes that give a linksland feel to these parts of the course, although the grass strains and maintenance practices preclude the traditional ground game. For the rest, the course roams a pine forest. Importantly, the trees are not so tight to the fairways that they interfere with the good player's strategy, except where a tree or trees are used as a specific design feature, and the ground continues to undulate as it does on the links-like holes, producing fairways that give a wide variety of stances, calling, therefore, for a variety of shot-making options – a hallmark of good golf-course architecture. The credit for all this goes to Javier Arana, the visionary Spanish designer who never built a course outside his native country.

El Saler lies on the edge of the extensive Albufera National Park, with its thousands of acres of wetlands, from which many species of waterfowl and waders find their way onto the course. Migratory birds on their annual pilgrimages from Africa to northern Europe and vice versa frequently drop in on their way through, and the course's extensive pine forests give shelter to many songbirds and their predators. Golf here is always accompanied by twitterings and tweetings, and the delicious scent of pine, and it is amid the pine trees that the course begins with a relatively straightforward par four. The 2nd introduces that characteristic semiblind drive over a ridge, the fairway leading to a typically multifaceted green, open at the low apron, but sloping steeply up to a rolling rear section, with a treacherous bunker through the back left of the putting surface. Another semiblind drive

CARD OF THE COURSE

| HOLE | YARDS | PAR | HOLE | YARDS | PAR |
|---|---|---|---|---|---|
| 1. | 428 | 4 | 10. | 399 | 4 |
| 2. | 376 | 4 | 11. | 568 | 5 |
| 3. | 532 | 5 | 12. | 198 | 3 |
| 4. | 189 | 3 | 13. | 348 | 4 |
| 5. | 515 | 5 | 14. | 414 | 4 |
| 6. | 442 | 4 | 15. | 564 | 5 |
| 7. | 358 | 4 | 16. | 427 | 4 |
| 8. | 359 | 4 | 17. | 213 | 3 |
| 9. | 156 | 3 | 18. | 466 | 4 |
| **OUT** | **3,355** | **36** | **IN** | **3,597** | **36** |
| | | | **TOTAL** | **6,952** | **72** |

significantly from right to left, the former route is much preferable. The front nine ends with a much-photographed but fairly innocuous short hole.

## THE BACK NINE

Returning to the pine woods, the 10th is a pretty hole, with a deceptive green, and the 11th features another drive to a semiblind, curving fairway on the longest hole on the course. While the 12th is memorable only for its dull runway tee and hugely long putting surface, the 13th is rather a charming drive-and-pitch to a beautifully sited green raised up in a grove of trees. The course now goes back and forth in parallel, and, while the fairways of the 14th and 15th undulate admirably, the 16th is prosaic, with a flat fairway and only a fence separating it from the main practice ground.

The course returns to the dunes in a big way at the 17th, the longest of the par threes played to a raised green gathered in the dunes and generously bunkered. Again, there are wicked bunkers through the green awaiting the over-adventurous (or over-confident) approach shot. And then it is up onto the dunes for a stirring view, overlooking the Mediterranean and the beach all the way to Valencia, and a fitting closing hole. The 18th fairway slopes and curves to the left and there is some seriously rough country if the drive stays out right. Although the green front is open, the big putting surface features another ridge, adding complexity the farther back the pin is set. There have been few professional tournaments here, but Bernhard Langer's 62, which he set in winning the 1984 Spanish Open here, is still held in awe by his fellow competitors, so highly did they rate El Saler.

adds to the complications of the par-five 3rd, with precise location of the tee shot the key to future success. Through a gap in the trees, the 4th green is presented as a sloping target, the putting surface angled away to the left, too.

## THE FIRST OF THE DUNES HOLES

The 5th is visually appealing with a drive to a skyline fairway and the eager anticipation of walking up the hill to find out what is on the other side. A view of the green, nestled into the dunes, with the Mediterranean sparkling in the background is fair reward. This is one of the greens featuring a spine, which runs through the

green in such a way as to leave the smaller and higher portion on the right much harder to attain.

Another strong hole follows, the drive at the 6th being played back across a valley to a fairway climbing to the top of a ridge, before plunging down the far side towards a cunningly domed green with a steep false front and a very inaccessible area falling away behind the giant bunker, attendant on the right. The 7th offers a breather, taking play back to the sea, cleverly using another two-level green with a big bunker visible on the right and another, beyond it, quite invisible until the player finds themself in it. Running parallel to the beach, the 8th is a curious hole, involving a long carry over hummocks of sandy waste from the tee or a potential skirmish with a mighty sand hill if a more conservative line is taken; with the green sloping

A 5,500-yard, par-64 layout is unlikely to please someone looking to attract the Ryder Cup, nor is a 7,500-yard, all-or-nothing course likely to bring repeat visits from recreational golfers if they get a mauling first time out. They need to feel that they have gone round something special, the course immediately showing up their technical shortcomings, but they also want to feel that they have achieved something special themselves when that lifetime-best shot happens to come off. The golfing world is full of courses that appear to achieve this goal – and remember that most of those playing these courses are doing so with handicaps in double figures, the vast majority at the worse end of that particular scale. This is the world of resort golf.

But what is there on such courses to challenge the very good player? Bobby Jones and Alister MacKenzie found the answer to that dilemma when they built Augusta National (see page 206). There are other examples of such successful solutions at Pinehurst No 2 (see page 202), Pebble Beach (see page 244) and the Cascades Course at The Homestead (see page 200). But the high-handicap resort golfer does not play these courses set up as they might be for the US Open or US Amateur. Equally, when a professional tour event is played over many a resort course (the above excepted), that course is often immediately revealed to be one-dimensional and shallow. A degree of compromise, then, seems inevitable, and is perhaps best exemplified by Joe Lee's 1988 course at San Lorenzo, where such an approach might be seen more as a strength than a weakness.

### AN EXERCISE IN COMPROMISE

San Lorenzo is the jewel in the crown on the vast Quinta do Lago estate, a veritable rabbit warren of golf courses secreted away amid a concrete jungle of villas big, huge and gigantic, some of which serve to remind that the dividing line can be very thin between opulence and vulgarity. Lee's course is opulent, but never vulgar. In fact, the course has never been violated by the professional circus, so it must remain a matter of conjecture exactly how tournament professionals might respond to the challenges Lee sets. However, in examining how the architect copes with compromise it can be seen how Lee has set relatively easy challenges for resort play, yet retained a capacity to turn the screw were the course ever subjected to a serious test.

The first compromise comes with the bunkering. Visitors should not need ten shots to get out of a fairway bunker – as might happen with the Coffin bunkers on the 13th at St Andrews (see page 40) – yet if the bunkers are placed at the right length from the back tee they will challenge the professional. This is especially so on the par-five 8th and 15th, which might be considered compulsory birdie chances

to the Tour star; however, carries of 280–300 yards (255–275 metres) from the tee are not guaranteed even for them. Yet with the bunkers featuring low lips and flat floors, most professionals would fancy a long-iron shot from them. This is when the green-front defences kick in if the shot is good but not quite good enough.

Another area of compromise is with the greens themselves. Lee has defended many putting surfaces with green-front bunkers, but he has always provided room for relatively easy everyday pin positions, quite often to one side or the other. To do this he has left a number of generous green-front openings, such as on the short holes. Look more critically at these holes: three of them (2nd, 14th and 16th) are particularly shallow with the potential for some truly wicked pin positions, were they ever needed. On longer holes Lee

# SAN LORENZO
## Almancil, Algarve, Portugal

Successful architecture is about designing exactly the right product – at the right price. If the client requires a bus shelter there is no point in coming up with a cathedral, nor is a swimming pool likely to satisfy a client seeking a hospital. It is no different in golf.

# SÃO LOURENÇO GOLF COURSE
## – Almancil, Algarve, Portugal

Joe Lee, 1988

### CARD OF THE COURSE

| HOLE | YARDS | PAR | HOLE | YARDS | PAR |
|------|-------|-----|------|-------|-----|
| 1. | 540 | 5 | 10. | 568 | 5 |
| 2. | 177 | 3 | 11. | 383 | 4 |
| 3. | 365 | 4 | 12. | 432 | 4 |
| 4. | 372 | 4 | 13. | 393 | 4 |
| 5. | 143 | 3 | 14. | 172 | 3 |
| 6. | 422 | 4 | 15. | 517 | 5 |
| 7. | 377 | 4 | 16. | 208 | 3 |
| 8. | 574 | 5 | 17. | 376 | 4 |
| 9. | 400 | 4 | 18. | 406 | 4 |
| **OUT** | **3,370** | **36** | **IN** | **3,455** | **36** |
| | | | **TOTAL** | **6,825** | **72** |

*The Ria Formosa brings a maritime charm to the 6th and 7th holes at San Lorenzo, allowing the golfer to forget (albeit briefly) the proximity of housing on the front nine.*

has often opened the putting surface out behind the approach bunkers and, on more than one occasion, he has hidden a deceptive drop-away beyond a bunker. While of little consequence as the course is normally set up, these drop-aways could be quite mischievous with the closer-shaved green surrounds and imaginative pin locations associated with serious tournament play.

## GAMBLER'S DELIGHT

What is it that sets San Lorenzo apart from its myriad neighbouring Algarve courses as set up for normal play? Simply, if there are the natural resources to create holes such as the 6th, 7th, 8th, 17th and 18th the architect is onto a winner. Each of them is a good gambler's hole, and a challenge to a golfer's vanity is irresistible.

One such challenge is the drive at the 6th, from an elevated tee that is angled suggestively towards a tree-clad hill on the left. With the waters of the Ria Formosa Nature Reserve plainly visible on the right, it is tempting to try to bite off too much of the hill in preference to a close encounter with a little egret. It is similar on the 7th, except that this time the green is set behind an incursion of beach, and it is hardly a deep green. While it may be a disappointment to turn away from the beach at this point, the golfing challenge of the 8th is not to be shirked. The obvious risk comes from the lagoon running the entire length of the hole on the right, but for the good player the challenge manifests itself in the bunker-clad shoulders of land interrupting matters, the former taunting the good drive, the latter a lay-up after a conservative tee shot. Everyone is

concerned about approaching the shallow green over water, whatever the length of shot, for the putting surface is only 20 yards (18 metres) deep.

## WATER HAZARD

Following this, the early part of the back nine is more straightforward, no different from a hundred other holes within a few kilometres' radius, but Lee has retained two trump cards to finish. He returns play to the lagoon with its egrets and gallinules, ducks and waders. By utilizing a lozenge-shaped tee on the 17th, he has offered the course manager a wide choice of teeing positions, with those on the left bringing the water more dangerously into play. The fairway is wide and flat where the handicap player might finish, but it narrows increasingly the longer the tee shot. There is also a wide variety of potential pin locations, with many sucker positions around the edges.

Water is again the chief visual element of the 18th, but it ought not to be a factor when playing. A competent tee shot of 250–260 yards (230–240 metres) in the general direction of the lone fairway bunker leaves only a short- to mid-iron to the target green surrounded on three sides by water. The mighty hitter's eye will likely be drawn to a spit of land far over the water on the direct line to the green. It demands a no-compromise carry of almost 270 yards (247 metres). Watch play on that tee for long enough for five or six matches to pass through, and some golfer is bound to have a go at it. Almost certainly it will end in failure, but Lee has, once again, successfully appealed to the gambler's instinct.

# CENTRAL EUROPE

'It seems odd that Germany should be behind every other civilized country in Europe in her appreciation of golf. The game ought to suit the placid temperament of the German, and his love of long walks with refreshments to follow,' commented Kenneth Brown in *Golf Illustrated* (May 1914).

Although initially golf was slow to make an impact in Germany, the situation has greatly improved. Germany today has the second largest number of golf courses in Europe – its almost 700 layouts trailing only England's 1,900. Countries such as Sweden, France, Spain and even Scotland are clearly distanced, so in many ways Germany can consider herself to be at the forefront of the European golf scene. There is just one minor problem, however. According to Cabell Robinson in *Golf Course News* (November 1997): 'Germany with all its money has turned out the fewest first-rate courses of all the western European countries.'

An exaggeration? Conventional wisdom has it that great courses breed great players. Looking at the exploits of German Tour professionals paints a fairly one-sided picture: there is only Bernhard Langer for Germany, while in the rest of Europe there is an armada of great Scandinavian players, several Spanish stars and even the French have managed to come up with more than just Arnaud Massy. Switzerland and Austria, Germany's smaller neighbours to the south, rarely produce golfers of international standard either.

## GERMANY

So where did it all go wrong? Certainly not in the beginning, when 17-year-old Philipp Heineken and a bunch of friends decided to bring the English idea of lawn-based sports to Germany. Starting in 1890 they played everything from rugby, football, cricket and tennis to golf on the Cannstatt parade grounds, besides the river Neckar. Heineken translated the Royal & Ancient Golf Club rules, produced a permanent, if makeshift, course and published the first golf book in German. However, the Cannstatt gymnastics establishment frowned on these free-wheeling and decidedly unpolitical efforts. The Cannstatt pioneers were accused of *Ausländerei* (a nationalist term decrying the adoption of foreign habits) and were soon forgotten. Thus the opportunity of a true grassroots development was missed for golf – although football did catch on admirably.

The German spa of Bad Homburg[1] had had its first glimpse of golf about 1880, when British guests were beating balls around the public gardens. In 1889 the Prince of Wales (later Edward VII) oversaw the building of a permanent course, of which six short holes survive. They are not fenced off, so a golfer might still feel like the British pioneers playing there amid the general, golf-agnostic crowd. Clubs followed in other spa towns such as Wiesbadener Golf-Club[2] (1893) and Baden-Baden[3] (1905), as well as at Berlin-Wannsee[4] (1895), which has become one of the leading clubs in Germany.

By the 1920s the heyday of German golf was in full swing. Harry Colt and John Morrison designed courses at, for example, Frankfurt[5] (1928), Aachen[6] (1928) and Falkenstein (1930) (see page 148). Many more spa courses emerged, with Mittelrheinischer Golf-club Bad Ems[7] leading the charge. Bernhard von Limburger's initial courses were for Feldafing[8] (1926), Bad Saarow and Föhr (both lost).

*Formerly known as Plan-Bramois, the Severiano Ballesteros course at Crans-sur-Sierre has been the home of the European Masters and before it, the Swiss Open, since 1939.*

After the war he designed notable ones for Köln[9] and Hubbelrath[10] as well as his masterpiece Club zur Vahr's Garlstedter Heide[11] course near Bremen. Until the 1990s the German Open was almost exclusively played on a course that von Limburger either created or remodelled.

Inevitably, a number of Tour courses have been built since, such as St Leon-Rot[12], Gut Kaden[13], München Eichenried[14] and Gut Lärchenhof[15]. However, two other modern projects are more interesting: Sporting Club Berlin[16] has a rough-and-tough, Nick Faldo layout and Marine GC[17] is a true links, 18-hole course, which in 2006 opened on the North Sea island of Sylt. Downright quirky tracks or at least unconventional designs are very rare, though Bad Münstereifel[18] may be one and Altenhof[19] possibly another.

In Germany the best among the resort courses are Jakobsberg Hotel[20] near the Loreley (a very sound routing, and great fun to play), Balmer See[21] on the island of Usedom (36 holes in a most delightful and very remote setting) and St Wendel[22] (a 27-hole, spectacular rollercoaster ride, American style). The Bad Griesbach[23] area with its six full-length courses and three nine-holers and Fleesensee[24] with its 72 holes are the leaders in Germany when it comes to amenities.

## GOLF IN SWITZERLAND AND AUSTRIA

In the end golf spread throughout central Europe as it did to most other regions in the world: British tourists, diplomats, military officers or businessmen abroad introduced the game or at any rate suggested that a links might be profitable for the locals.

In the Swiss resort of St Moritz the hoteliers commissioned a short track in St Moritz Bad[25] (1890), followed by a full 18-holer for Engadine Golf Samedan[26] (1893). Equally shrewd entrepreneurs were soon opening courses at Montreux[27] (1900), Lucerne[28] (1903), Bad Ragaz[29] (1905), Crans-sur-Sierre[30] (1907) in Crans Montana and at the Parc des Sports[31] in Geneva (1899), which enjoyed considerable American patronage by 1901.

Austrian golf waited until 1901, but then got off to a good start by bringing Willie Park Jnr over to lay out a course in the famous Prater park in Vienna, which unfortunately was destroyed in the Second World War. The second and therefore oldest existing course came 25 years later, at Semmering[32] (1926), although it must be admitted that Bohemia belonged to the Habsburg monarchy before the First World War and Austrian royalty played golf at Marienbad and Karlsbad (today Mariánské Lázně and Karlovy Vary of the Czech Republic).

Switzerland and Austria, by way of the Alps, have an edge over Germany because of their mountain courses, where the quirk factor is practically built into the land. Altitudes of up to 5,900 feet (1,800 metres) and views reminiscent of the best Canadian sites are provided at places such as Arosa, Davos, Lenzerheide, Samedan, Sedrun and Verbier (all in Switzerland) and Brand, Seefeld-Wildmoos and Tiroler Zugspitz (in Austria). The latter country also features perhaps the most varied topography in Europe: in some regions (for example, Zell am See) it is possible to play golf and ski on the same day.

The annual Austrian Tour event is staged at the high-rolling Fontana[33], a Doug Carrick design near Vienna. Popular Tour venues in Switzerland are Crans-sur-Sierre and Bad Ragaz, while Limpachtal[34] boasts Europe's longest hole, a par six at 728 yards.

## ADVANTAGES OF THE REGION

It can therefore be seen that, although the first-rate courses are still the classic designs by Harry Colt, John Morrison and Bernhard von Limburger, there is plenty of other interesting and scenic golf to be found in central Europe, where courses are considerably less crowded and green fees lower than at many premium international ones. Furthermore, the spectacular views on alpine golf courses are unrivalled in Europe.

# FALKENSTEIN
## Hamburg, Germany

An important and influential club in German golfing circles, the Hamburger Golf Club celebrated its centenary in 2006, having started life with a nine-hole course in Grossflottbek.

As time went on it became apparent that the Hamburger Golf Club required a full 18-hole course if it was to retain its pre-eminence. So, in 1928 work began on a completely new course in the suburb of Falkenstein, close to the river Elbe to the west of the city centre.

For the design the club chose the company of Colt, Alison & Morrison, and the firm of Frank Harris to build the course. What is more, they had selected a superb piece of land for Harry Colt to work with. It was hilly ground – not too hilly – and Colt was able to exploit it ingeniously to create many brilliant green sites and teeing grounds. The sandy subsoil provided heathland conditions, and the vast expanses of heather enthused Colt.

### INGENIOUS USE OF SPACE

A glance at a map of the property shows that Colt managed to use every available inch of ground that was suitable for golf. Yet the course never feels forced or contrived. During play the golfer cannot help marvelling at the way the round unfolds naturally, that

there is an excellent balance to the holes and that the challenges are constantly varying. It is a masterpiece of routing, and it is hardly coincidental that Colt also contrived to start and finish each nine close to the clubhouse. Most of his original course survives, although a few modifications were made by Bernard von Limburger in the 1960s.

For the most part the fairways are wide, encouraging the golfer to strike confidently from the tee, despite the woods that encase almost every hole. Occasionally, however, the trees are an important part of the strategy.

### PLAYING THE COURSE

After a gentle opener, the 549-yard 2nd is a very strong par five, the trees gradually closing in on the fairway, first from the right and then from the left. But good length from the tee is vital, for there is a deceptive depression about 100 yards (90 metres) in front of the

green, the fairway then rising significantly to the front of the putting surface, and there is a very narrow entrance between a bunker on the left and falling ground on the right. As originally designed by Colt this was a much shorter hole.

A short climb up the hill on the right gives access to the 3rd tee, and what a sight awaits! There, on the far side of a deep valley, is the 3rd green, angled from right to left and almost hidden behind two bunkers. They are on the higher left side and only a controlled draw or almighty, high iron shot could avoid them to reach the putting surface. Yet the right side of the entrance to the green is open, allowing the less-confident golfer the chance of driving there, raising the possibility of a decent chip and single putt. Originally this hole was played from a different angle and was much shorter.

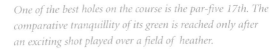

deliciously bunkered green. Heather features in abundance on the short 8th, while the 421-yard 9th is all about engineering the right line in to the green.

## TREES AND HEATHER

Another par three to an angled green begins the back nine, followed by the stern two-shot 11th, semiblind and narrow through the trees. Heather makes a reappearance on the 400-yard 12th, a delightful hole played to a promontory green set out above a bunker and with something of an abyss beyond. High tees provide enticing starts to the next two holes, both eminently strategic despite their modest length, and both involve a drive over a heathery bank. Taking golfers to the edge of the property once more, the 155-yard 15th is almost as far down as it is long! It seems quite out of character with the rest, as does the 329-yard 16th, a short par four that involves a drive that must pierce the narrow gap between two tall trees. Neither is a Colt original.

The hole played as the 478-yard 17th is certainly by Harry Colt, once again driving to a distant ridge before bearing left and downhill towards a vast expanse of heather interrupting the fairway. Who can drive far enough on this testing tee shot to be able to clear the heather with the second shot? And a lay-up is not easily judged, either. A great indecision hole!

*One of the best holes on the course is the par-five 17th. The comparative tranquillity of its green is reached only after an exciting shot played over a field of heather.*

On the 474-yard 4th the golfer encounters the first example of a recurring theme, driving towards a distant crest with little idea of what might await beyond – in this case a downhill run into a mischievously contoured green. The crest is much higher on the 399-yard 5th, which then swings sharply down to the right. To make up for this the 410-yard 6th climbs steeply to a skyline green, while the 354-yard 7th plunges from a high tee to a low fairway that ends in a

# HAMBURGER GOLF CLUB –
## Hamburg, Germany

Colt, Alison & Morrison, 1930
Major events: German Open 1951, 1952, 1955, 1959, 1962, 1964, 1965, 1981

### CARD OF THE COURSE

| HOLE | YARDS | PAR | HOLE | YARDS | PAR |
|------|-------|-----|------|-------|-----|
| 1. | 321 | 4 | 10. | 171 | 3 |
| 2. | 549 | 5 | 11. | 438 | 4 |
| 3. | 233 | 3 | 12. | 400 | 4 |
| 4. | 474 | 5 | 13. | 363 | 4 |
| 5. | 399 | 4 | 14. | 349 | 4 |
| 6. | 410 | 4 | 15. | 155 | 3 |
| 7. | 354 | 4 | 16. | 329 | 4 |
| 8. | 177 | 3 | 17. | 478 | 5 |
| 9. | 421 | 4 | 18. | 366 | 4 |
| **OUT** | **3,338** | **36** | **IN** | **3,049** | **35** |
| | | | **TOTAL** | **6,387** | **71** |

And from a hillside tee the player strikes out towards yet another ridge on the 366-yard 18th. What lies beyond cannot be seen, but the line of the trees indicates that the hole swings sharply to the left. The fairway descends to lower ground across an angled ridge before green-front bunkers demand the aerial route, with the ball stopping dead in its tracks – a further departure from Colt's philosophy of letting the ball run utilizing the contours.

The loss of a small part of Harry Colt's work might be lamented, but the creation of today's 2nd and 3rd holes have strengthened a superbly strategic course.

# NORDIC COUNTRIES

Golfing here can be traced back to 1888, when the Sager family built a six-hole course at the scenic Swedish Ryfors estates. Now, some 120 years after Ida Sager opened the course by hitting the first shot, the game is thriving in the countries of the Nordic region.

Nordic golfers have achieved numerous victories on the worldwide professional circuits, and more than 900 clubs cater for the roughly 900,000 active players in Denmark, Finland, Sweden and Norway, where golf is a very public and accessible game. With the exception of one private club in Sweden, a golfer can easily arrange a tee time just by getting in touch with any club.

Varied terrain and the rich natural environment within the Nordic region have resulted in a wide range of different architectural styles – from raw seaside links to modern parkland golf. A brief timeline on the evolution of golf-course architecture in this area would start with the early notable designs by British architects and club professionals. These were followed by the first wave of local golf-course architects, who spread interest in the game by working on numerous projects with minimal budgets. By the second half of the 20th century a more diversified output was evident, with established local architects seeking inspiration from the classic British links courses or from modern target golf. So far in the 21st century there has been a steady flow of notable courses from American architects, who have been hired mainly for the next generation of the region's high-profile projects.

### DANISH COURSES

A historical odyssey of Nordic golf might begin with the ferry ride from Esbjerg to Denmark's oldest golf course, Fanø Golf Links[1]. The diminutive course by Robert Dunlop (a professional at Prestwick) was opened in 1901, and it still comprises 18 holes set among majestic sand dunes and challenging wind. Also near Copenhagen is Rungsted Golfklub[2], where in 1936 C.A. MacKenzie (brother of Dr Alister MacKenzie) laid out a course in this romantic parkland surrounded by mature trees. Another alternative golfing venue for those visiting the capital of Denmark is the Robert Trent Jones Jnr course at Skjoldenaesholm[3], which opened in 2007. This challenging layout lies in a beautiful country setting with rolling topography and numerous man-made ponds.

### GOLF IN SWEDEN

Two of the most reputable clubs in the history of Swedish golf are easily reached by car from Copenhagen over the Øresund bridge. At Barsebäck[4], the Masters Course is internationally recognized since it hosted the 2003 Solheim Cup and several events on the men's and ladies' European tours. The course is characterized by an intriguing routing that blends rugged seaside holes with more traditional parkland golf. Scene of the 2007 Solheim Cup was Halmstad[5], which is set in glorious dense woodland in which architects Rafael Sundblom and Frank Pennink successfully created 18 holes in the spirit of Harry Colt's work at Wentworth in England. Further holes were constructed by Nils Sköld, giving Halmstad two full-length courses.

page 152

Falsterbo (see page 152) is Sweden's third oldest golf club and the country's only links course. Beautifully situated on a peninsula, Falsterbo impresses with a rustic and genuine golf experience that is enhanced by the remodelled green complexes.

One of Sweden's most-acclaimed modern designs is by the North American architects Arthur Hills and Steve Forrest, who in 2006 moved massive amounts of soil during construction at Sand GC[6], which is situated outside Jönköping. The end result is an artificially shaped course that utilizes the same futuristic, inland-links character that Pete Dye unveiled at Whistling Straits (see page 224). Another course on which the Hills and Forrest duo were hired was Hills GC[7], outside Gothenburg. Opened in 2005, its more typical modern forest course was laid out on a tree-lined site sweeping across rolling hills.

For the Stadium Course at Bro Hof Slott[8], the firm of Robert Trent Jones Jnr worked with the biggest budget in the history of Nordic golf. Their demanding and strategic, target-golf course, which opened in 2007, is beautifully laid out in front of Lake Mälaren on the outskirts of Stockholm.

## NORWAY AND FINLAND

Robert Trent Jones Jnr also made a contribution to Norwegian golf in 2002 with his work at Miklagard Golf[9], which lies just outside Oslo. Golfers appreciate the way that the natural topography of the site blends well with the architect's characteristically elevated and well-bunkered green complexes. American influence can also be seen at Oslo GC[10], where the country's oldest course opened in 1925. In 2007, all 18 holes were redesigned by Hills and Forrest, providing a new routing in order to enhance the strategic values of the parkland setting. Golfers also relish a round at Larvik GC[11], where Swedish architect Jan Cederholm designed his course on a picturesque piece of land close to Larvik fjord. The wind from the sea keeps the player alert with several testing approaches to small greens.

Despite its rough winter climate, Finland now boasts more than a hundred courses. Ruuhikoski Golf[12] opened in 1992 outside Seinäjoki in northern Finland and marked Robert Trent Jones Jnr's debut on Scandinavian soil. The course wanders over rolling terrain, where woods and water accompany generous fairways. After an hour-long drive from Helsinki, Tim Lobb, from European Golf Design, encountered challenging terrain beside the ancient Castle Hotel Vanajan Linna. With its pine and birch forest, natural lakes and rocky outcrops, Linna Golf[13] has one of the most interesting modern forest courses in northern Europe; it provides wonderful golf in a marvellous setting.

*The 153-yard 3rd hole at Larvik GC in Norway. The course benefits from the microclimate of the Skjomenfjorden, bringing admirable playing conditions north of the Arctic Circle.*

# FALSTERBO
## Falsterbo, Sweden

Falsterbo, located at the very southern tip of Sweden, attracts the attention of connoisseurs from all over the world as one of the few true links courses in continental Europe. The club is a typical product of the British-influenced roots of Swedish golf.

During the early years of the 20th century, a number of distinguished professionals and architects from England worked in Sweden, such as Falsterbo's first head professional and greenkeeper, William Hester. The club had been founded in 1909 by mainly wealthy families with holiday homes in the area, who had started to play on a primitive course east of Falsterbo. In 1911 Robert Turnbull, professional at Copenhagen GC, laid out the first nine holes on the club's present site, and then in 1930 the course was extended to 18 holes by a local doctor, Gunnar Bauer. With the exception of the present 16th and 17th, which were added in 1934, the routing has not changed since then. Between 1995 and 2001, major renovation work on the greens and immediate surroundings was carried out by Peter Chamberlain (former head professional at Falsterbo) and Peter Nordwall. They enhanced the links character of the course with new and more challenging green complexes yet retained the original atmosphere of the course.

### PLAYING THE COURSE

Among Swedish golfers, Falsterbo is renowned for its picturesque position on a peninsula dominated by its lighthouse and for its excellent firm and fast condition. First-time visitors may believe that the course looks gentle and straightforward from the tees. Although there is the occasional blind shot, Falsterbo generally uses subtle ways to test the player's imagination and mental strength. Wind, grass and bunkering are the main factors to be reckoned with, although there are some natural architectural features such as delicate bumps and hollows on the fairways.

A few steps to the right of the dark brown, wooden clubhouse, built in 1914, take the golfer to the 449-yard 1st – a somewhat tough and long par four. This tree-lined hole, with out-of-bounds to the right, provides a fair share of excitement with demanding tee and approach shots. The green complex on the 191-yard 2nd is semiblind from the tee and is surrounded by bunkers, as well as thick native grass to the right.

Next on the course is the first par five – the 558-yard 3rd – where the tee shot must avoid the white marker posts placed very close to the right side of the fairway. A small pond interferes with the second shot and underlines the architect's initial aim of creating a long hole that demands three well-thought-out and executed shots.

### TOUGH LINKS GOLF

One of Falsterbo's most difficult challenges is the 443-yard 4th. It has a testing tee shot, straight into the wind, with water to the right and rough with fescue and stripes of heather to the left, all of which leave little room for error. The approach is played towards a green situated at a 45-degree angle from the fairway and protected by water on the front right and a fierce bunker on the left. There is no time to catch breath because another excellent and difficult par four follows.

While the 5th may have a slightly less dramatic tee shot than the 4th, it still possesses one of the best green complexes that Swedish golf has to offer. The first bunker in front of the green is a useful visual guide as to the required distance, while the other traps and the well-defined run-off areas effectively guard against the imprecise aerial shot. Still, the player is allowed a narrow opening at the front for a running ground shot, which might be handy when the wind picks up.

After the 170-yard 6th, which requires a carry over a pond, the player is encouraged to hit out on the

317-yard 7th, a wide and inviting par four. The screws are tightened again at the second shot, which has to trickle to the pin through a heavily bunkered green complex. A long par three, the 197-yard 8th features a blind Sahara bunker to the right. It is followed by two par fours, which take the player northwards again.

Most golfers are thrilled by the short 159-yard 11th, where the generously sized green, partly surrounded by water, calls for a precise shot. The final and longest of the one-shot holes is the 230-yard 14th. Played with the old lighthouse as a scenic backdrop to the blind green, the golfer still has to maintain concentration to avoid the bunkers placed in front of the flag on this typical hit-and-hope hole.

*The Baltic Sea runs the length of the 18th hole. Prevailing winds, encroaching dunes and subtle fairway bunkering test a golfer's accuracy off the tee on this short par-five dogleg.*

## CLOSING HOLES

Falsterbo's epic finish begins with the 514-yard 15th, an entertaining par five that tempts the player to go for the slightly lofted green, which is protected by a small pond, with the second shot. Moving farther out to the tip of the peninsula, the 388-yard 16th is reached, the first of two solid back-to-back par fours.

Having finished admiring the breathtaking views of Denmark in the distance, the big hitter then needs to plan carefully the shot from the 17th tee. Here, a driver might not be appropriate because the fairway abruptly narrows, with a small pond to the right, after 250 yards (230 metres). The route is towards the clubhouse along the impressive line of rugged dunes.

It was at the 481-yard 18th – a classic par five in the history of Swedish golf – that the outcome of the European Team championships was decided in 1963. The hole's slight dogleg right calls for a tee shot aimed as much as possible over the right clusters of heather. As the sun sets while putting out on the final green and the scents of the Baltic Sea invade the senses, a golfer will find it hard not to admire the elegant simplicity of Falsterbo; its intricate design and unique setting will continue to stand the test of time.

## FALSTERBO GOLFKLUBB – Falsterbo, Sweden

Robert Turnbull, 1911; Gunnar Bauer, 1930 and 1934; and Peter Chamberlain and Peter Nordwall, 1995–2001

### CARD OF THE COURSE

| HOLE | YARDS | PAR | HOLE | YARDS | PAR |
|------|-------|-----|------|-------|-----|
| 1. | 449 | 4 | 10. | 383 | 4 |
| 2. | 191 | 3 | 11. | 159 | 3 |
| 3. | 558 | 5 | 12. | 406 | 4 |
| 4. | 443 | 4 | 13. | 563 | 5 |
| 5. | 405 | 4 | 14. | 230 | 3 |
| 6. | 170 | 3 | 15. | 514 | 5 |
| 7. | 317 | 4 | 16. | 388 | 4 |
| 8. | 197 | 3 | 17. | 377 | 4 |
| 9. | 421 | 4 | 18. | 481 | 5 |
| **OUT** | **3,151** | **34** | **IN** | **3,501** | **37** |
| | | | **TOTAL** | **6,652** | **71** |

# NORTH AMERICA

# UNITED STATES AND CANADA

Unlike in Scotland, where the game has long been accessible to the masses, golf in North America began largely as a province of the wealthy, played almost exclusively at private clubs and resorts that, by virtue of catering solely to the affluent, were themselves essentially private.

Early resorts occasionally lay in remote locales, while private club development came almost entirely in the major population centres, where fortunes were made. The continent's first golf club (Royal Montreal) was established in 1873 in Canada's second largest city, and the majority of America's prominent early entries were situated in cities such as New York, Chicago, Boston, Philadelphia and San Francisco.

Early course design was generally rudimentary, performed in what today would seem a remarkable hurry by all manner of Scottish émigrés who, to an audience of neophytes, surely appeared accomplished experts. Men such as Alex Findlay, Robert and James Foulis, and the prolific Tom Bendelow (who claimed to have completed more than 600 projects) were among the first to make golf architecture a primary source of income, often simply walking a property once, marking the locations of prospective tees and greens, then moving on in a design style pejoratively referred to by historians as 'eighteen stakes on a Sunday afternoon'.

## THE GOLDEN AGE

Though courses such as Myopia Hunt Club and Garden City signalled the dawn of a more strategically interesting approach, it was Charles Blair Macdonald's 1911 National Golf Links of America (see page 166) that jump-started the process, literally lifting the continent's perception of what a golf course could be, and kicking off the glorious two-decade era known as North American golf design's Golden Age.

The Golden Age is primarily recalled for its famous architects, which included visiting Britons (Willie Park Jnr, Harry Colt and Charles Alison), transplanted Britons (Donald Ross and Dr Alister MacKenzie) and North American natives (Charles Blair Macdonald, A.W. Tillinghast, Stanley Thompson, William Flynn and George Thomas). But far beyond these names, this was an era that saw North American design take a quantum leap forward in terms of both quantity and quality. Regarding the former, in the United States alone the total number of courses rocketed from fewer than 750 in 1916 to nearly 6,000 in 1930, as advanced earthmoving equipment allowed the reshaping of less-advantageous terrain and as modernized agronomical techniques opened up previously ill-suited hot-weather climates to sustainable turf growth. But it was the leap in quality that was most significant. Working in an era when more first-class sites remained available, and before myriad environmental issues limited their ability to reshape the land to their every whim, the designers of the Golden Age succeeded in producing a generation of strategic, aesthetically inviting facilities so fine that they have continued to dominate pretty well every prominent course ranking in the past 75 years.

Though a handful of significant courses were completed during the 1930s, in broad terms the Golden Age ended with the October 1929 crash of the American stock market. The economic ravages of the ensuing Depression, combined with the austerity of the Second World War, added up to a nearly two-decade hiatus in golf-course construction, an extended stagnancy that outlived the careers (and lives) of most Golden Age designers. When the industry's postwar recovery started during the 1950s, a new generation of architects was led by Robert Trent Jones Snr, former apprentice to the great Canadian designer Stanley Thompson and a man whose self-proclaimed 'heroic' design style did much to transform the industry. Robert Trent Jones's primary national competition

*Island greens, surrounded by water, are apparently obligatory features of the resort courses of the Carolinas and Florida. These are the 7th and 9th holes at Island Green Country Club, Myrtle Beach.*

came from a William Flynn protégé, Dick Wilson, as well as Wilson's one-time partner Joe Lee, while men such as Geoffrey Cornish, Robert von Hagge, George Cobb, Clinton 'Robbie' Robinson and William Mitchell headed a long list who found great success on a more regional level.

## THE MOVE TO SUBURBIA

With major urban areas no longer regularly offering sufficient developable land, golf construction moved out to the suburbs, as well as into the far wider destination resort market. Largely at the impetus of Robert Trent Jones, courses became longer, and featured larger greens and the copious use of sand and water. It was, unfortunately, a design style that bequeathed little in the way of long-term greatness, with relatively few of that era's top new courses rating among the continent's best today.

A welcome turn back to more strategically interesting courses began in the late 1960s and early '70s, led primarily by Pete Dye, an ex-insurance salesman who, after a 1963 visit to Scotland, began to incorporate into his designs such Old World features as railway sleepers, unmanicured rough and pot bunkers. Even more importantly, Dye's most famous period courses typically measured under 6,800 yards and thus placed only the occasional emphasis on power – a significant shift from the Jones-inspired norm.

## THE RISE OF RESORT COURSES

As travel became ever easier, post-1970s course development ranged even farther afield, frequently centring around resort areas such as Palm Springs or Myrtle Beach, or late-developing cities or regions of Atlanta, Orlando and the American desert south-west. Pete Dye was joined by prominent competitors – Tom Fazio, Arthur Hills and Robert Trent Jones's sons Rees and Robert Jnr – but a major new factor in the marketplace was the 'player–architect', a big-name group of superb players led by Jack Nicklaus, with Arnold Palmer, Gary Player, Tom Weiskopf and, more recently, Greg Norman all following suit. In this era where an architect's name became a key marketing tool for developers, and where the frequent use of less-than-ideal sites mandated major earthmoving, overall project expenses rocketed – occasionally costing as much as US$20 million.

The new millennium has seen at least a partial rejection of such profligacy, with most of the continent's top new courses representing classically natural designs, built relatively inexpensively by men such as Bill Coore and Ben Crenshaw, Tom Doak and Gil Hanse. It has been a welcome trend both stylistically and economically, but with unchecked advances in playing equipment fuelling the demand for larger sites, located increasingly farther from major metropolitan markets, can the future of North American golf-course development remain a rosy one?

*Gator Hole Course in North Myrtle Beach, South Carolina, is a 6,000-yard public course designed in 1980 by Rees Jones. These are the 7th and 12th holes.*

# NORTH-EASTERN STATES

The north-eastern states were the first in America to embrace golf on a large scale, so the game has enjoyed a particularly long history there; indeed, four of the five founding clubs of the United States Golf Association (USGA) were located in this region, and the organization's 1995 list of the 124 oldest clubs in America included 88 north-eastern representatives.

The early golfing crowd was largely an affluent one, generally residing in population centres such as New York, Philadelphia and Boston, and building courses both in their home neighbourhoods and at summer resort retreats such as Southampton and Newport. Given the prosperity of these golfers, the great majority of these courses were private. These Golden Age designs have also come to represent an especially high percentage of the north-east's total course inventory, because huge postwar suburban growth left little land for modern golf development. In fact, nowhere else in the United States does the balance, both in quality and quantity, so favour the old over the new.

## GOLF AROUND NEW YORK

The New York metropolitan area was the north-east's first hotbed of golf, with well over 200 pre-Second World War courses springing up between northern Westchester County and the eastern tip of Long Island, most built (or rebuilt) by the great architects of the day. Westchester itself remains one of the nation's best provided golfing counties, led by a cluster of A.W. Tillinghast-designed parkland courses, which include one of the world's great 36-hole facilities at Winged Foot (see page 172), its comparably ranked next-door neighbour Quaker Ridge[1], and, just 2 miles (3 kilometres) to the north, a recently restored gem, Fenway[2]. Westchester also features two regular professional tournament sites, the 36-hole Walter Travis-designed Westchester Country Club[3], whose West Course annually hosts the PGA Tour, and Wykagyl[4], a perennial stop for the LPGA. It also has historically prominent venues: Apawamis[5], site of Harold Hilton's landmark 1911 US Amateur victory; Siwanoy[6], the home of 1916's inaugural PGA Championship; Sleepy Hollow[7]; Knollwood[8]; and, though rebuilt by Jack Nicklaus in 1985, St Andrew's[9].

Within New York City proper, golf is largely confined to under-maintained but occasionally interesting public courses. A prominent exception is Inwood[10], which lies across the marshes from Kennedy

International Airport and was the site of Bobby Jones's first Major title, the 1923 US Open.

Long Island golf is generally associated with the links-like terrain of the ever-trendy Hamptons, where the National Golf Links of America (see page 166), Shinnecock Hills (see page 178) and Maidstone (see page 182) perennially lead the way. Elsewhere, the public 90-hole megacomplex at Bethpage State Park (see page 176) stands out, but Long Island is also noteworthy for its remarkable number of good-quality Golden Age layouts. Charles Blair Macdonald/Seth Raynor designs at The Creek[11] and Piping Rock[12] are

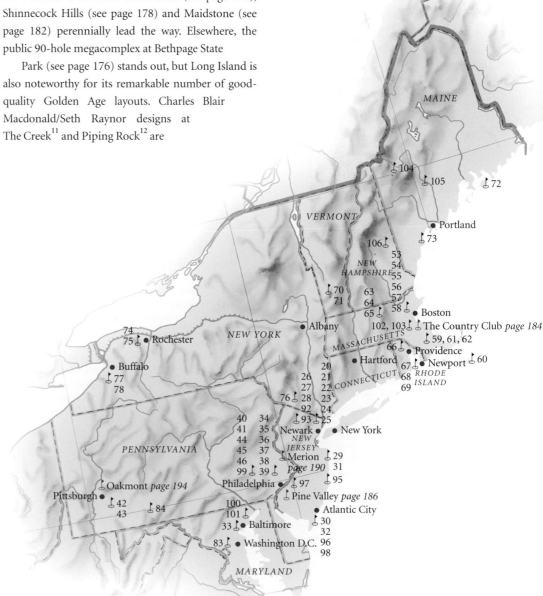

especially significant, as is a long list of charmingly quirky facilities such as Engineers[13], Huntington[14], Fresh Meadow[15] and the Rockaway Hunting Club[16], and such ancient, historic venues as Nassau[17] and Cherry Valley[18]. And, though geographically far closer to Connecticut, Fishers Island (see page 170) represents a final blue chip asset on the Long Island ledger. A special place, however, is reserved for Garden City Golf Club[19], arguably America's first truly great course, whose development owes much to the great amateur golfer Walter Travis, an Australian by birth but an immigrant to the United States aged 24.

## GARDEN CITY GOLF CLUB

Unlike such period stars as Willie Anderson, Alex Smith or Alec Ross – all of whom polished their golfing skills in Scotland long before emigrating to the USA – Walter Travis took up the game in America and, despite starting aged 35, quickly found huge success, claiming three US Amateur titles between 1900 and 1903, then famously becoming the first foreigner to win the (British) Amateur Championship in 1904. He joined Garden City in 1899, two years after its foundation.

Garden City had opened as a Devereux Emmet-designed nine-holer known as the Island Links in 1897.

The following year Emmet, a wealthy man of leisure who would go on to build more than 75 courses over a distinguished architectural career, revised and extended this loop to 18 holes. In order to do this, he took a cue from the many Scottish courses he had visited: moving minimal earth, he created greens that were little more than natural extensions of each hole's fairway. This layout – which followed virtually the same routing still in play today – was quickly deemed strong enough to host the 1900 US Amateur (Travis's first national title) and the 1902 US Open (where he tied for second). However, the course remained somewhat limited in terms of strategic interest and artistic flair.

In 1906, Travis, both a highly influential figure and regular critic of the game's rudimentary nature in America, provided Garden City with a list of proposed renovations that were quickly implemented. Central to these changes was his strong dislike of the many cross-bunkers that fronted Emmet's fairways, hazards Travis believed penalized lesser players heavily while scarcely challenging the skilled man. These were thus replaced by more than 50 new bunkers built alongside and at angles to many fairways, enhancing the course's strategic aspect considerably. Travis further added contour to a number of greens as well as the occasional

perimeter mounding, which, though undeniably outlandish in spots, feels delightfully quaint and old-fashioned today. His final renovative touch was the impressively deep bunkers. Travis viewed sand as a hazard from which extrication was a challenge; it was not simply an alternative playing surface from which to attack the pin.

## NEW JERSEY GEMS

With its clubs sharing membership in the Metropolitan Golf Association, northern New Jersey enjoys a similar golfing history and demographic to New York, with classic courses – the vast majority private – dominating the landscape. Best-known among these are A.W. Tillinghast's 36 holes at Baltusrol[20] (the only club to host US Opens on both its courses), Tillinghast's charming Somerset Hills[21], and national tournament venues including Donald Ross's Plainfield[22], 36 holes at Montclair[23] and 27 fine Tillinghast holes at Ridgewood[24], host to the 1935 Ryder Cup. Former Seth Raynor partner Charles Banks's designs at Forsgate[25] and The Knoll[26], 36 much-altered holes at Canoe Brook[27], and Ross's Mountain Ridge[28] top a long list of honourable mentions, most of which would stand out in other regions.

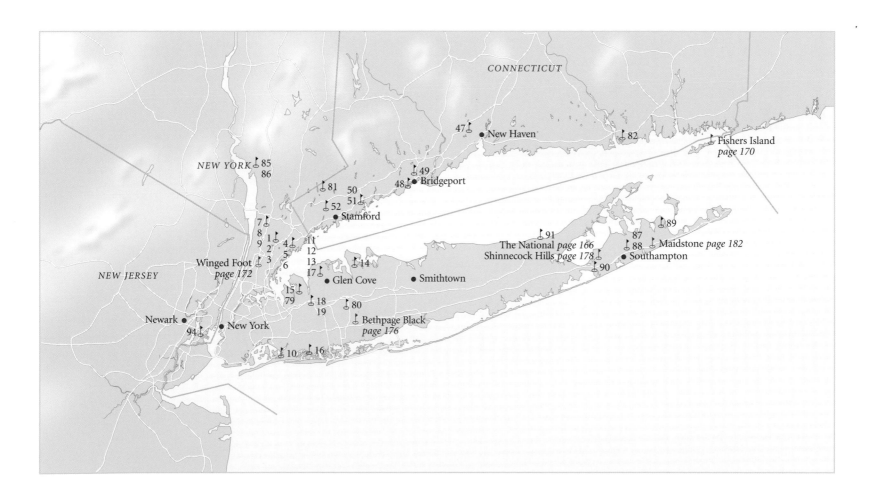

Southern New Jersey is best known for Pine Valley (see page 186), rated in many quarters as the game's finest course. But the region's golf history is most deeply rooted in early resort development along the Atlantic, where ancient courses such as Hollywood[29], the 36-hole Seaview Resort[30], Lakewood[31] and the recently modernized Atlantic City CC[32] have long entertained seasonal visitors. Farther south, Maryland offers a particularly fine entry – A.W. Tillinghast's East Course at the historic Baltimore CC[33].

## PENNSYLVANIA COURSES

Though perhaps somewhat overshadowed by New York, the Philadelphia area features an impressive classic course collection of its own, including the legendary Merion (see page 190) as well as Donald Ross's recently restored work at Aronimink[34], his self-proclaimed masterpiece. Although in total Ross designed or renovated nearly a dozen Philadelphia-area courses, the architect most closely associated with the city is William Flynn, whose stable of first-class suburban courses is led by Huntingdon Valley[35], Manufacturers[36], Rolling Green[37] and the Philadelphia

CC[38]. Like New York, Philadelphia's list of second-rank classics is also a long one, and includes A.W. Tillinghast's Philadelphia Cricket Club[39] and Donald Ross's Gulph Mills[40], as well as Flynn and Willie Park Jnr designs at the 36-hole Philmont CC[41].

Prewar golf throughout the rest of Pennsylvania may not have matched Philadelphia, but Oakmont (see page 194) and Seth Raynor's Fox Chapel[42] have long kept the Pittsburgh area on the golfing map. Elsewhere, Tillinghast's Sunnehanna[43] continues to host its eponymous, nationally prominent amateur event, Herbert Strong's Old Course at Saucon Valley[44] has welcomed a US Amateur and two Senior Opens, and both Lancaster[45] and Lehigh[46] help extend William Flynn's regional dominance beyond Philadelphia proper.

## NEW ENGLAND VARIATIONS

In some circles, classic Connecticut golf has been viewed as Yale University[47] and everything else, but the southern part of the state – whose clubs are also part of the Metropolitan Golf Association – offers several more fine courses. These include a seaside Raynor/Tillinghast

*The 1st hole at Baltimore Country Club's Five Farms Course is played over gently rolling ground to a rectangular period-piece green attended by two bunkers.*

hybrid at the CC of Fairfield[48], its near neighbour Brooklawn[49], Willie Park Jnr's Woodway[50], Devereux Emmet's Wee Burn[51] and Charles Banks's virtually unaltered design at Tamarack[52].

## YALE GOLF COURSE

It is entirely reasonable to single out Yale, for in the often overlooked world of collegiate golf facilities, it can confidently be stated that none has ever approached the challenge, scale and style of the golf course at Yale. Golf has deep roots in Yale University's hometown of New Haven, initially dating to the arrival on campus of John Reid Jnr, the highly talented son of the founder of New York's pioneering St Andrew's Golf Club. Subsequent students of Yale to distinguish themselves in the competitive arena included US Amateur champions Eben Byers (1906), Robert

Gardner (1909 and '15) and the best of them all, Jess Sweetser, who claimed the American title in 1922 and the British Amateur crown four years later. Thus when, in 1924, the widow of former Yale football star Ray Tompkins donated more than 700 acres (283 hectares) of wooded land located just 1 mile (1.6 kilometres) west of the Yale Bowl, plans were quickly made to build a golf course befitting so rich a heritage.

The cost of working on this hilly, rock-filled site was huge, with the eventual US$450,000 tab ranking Yale among the most expensive layouts yet built. To handle so large a project, the school turned to an older man whose place in the game's hierarchy was unassailable, Charles Blair Macdonald – though as with most of Macdonald's later architectural projects the actual creative work ended up being done primarily by his partner Seth Raynor. The result was a masterpiece of brawny, almost over-the-top design, with impressively wide fairways, enormous, wildly contoured greens and bunkers, which, to say the least, were not built with the undergraduate novice golfer in mind. Although there have been some regrettable alterations to the detail design of a few holes, Yale remains one of the most individual courses produced in an era of vision and invention.

## NORTHERN NEW ENGLAND

Very cold winters bring shorter seasons in the northern New England states, where old-money clubs anchor affluent suburbs, and summer resorts have long prospered in coastal and mountain districts. The Boston area ranked closely with New York and Philadelphia for early golfing prominence and offers an impressive number of classic courses, topped by The Country Club (see page 184) but strongly bolstered by the timeless Myopia Hunt Club[53] (a four-time US Open venue in the early days), the short-but-fascinating Brae Burn[54] (another early US Open and Amateur site) and a quartet of important

*Among Macdonald's favourite replica holes was the Biarritz, featuring two raised putting surfaces separated by a valley of lower ground. The 9th at Yale is a fine example.*

*W.H. Fowler used the naturally undulating topography of the Massachusetts coastline to create Eastward Ho!*
*There are no superfluous bunkers or contrived tees or greens, just a naturally beautiful, but challenging, course.*

Donald Ross designs: Salem[55], Charles River[56], Winchester[57] and Essex County[58]. Early Boston resort-seekers often headed south to the coastline of Buzzard's Bay, where the William Flynn/Frederic Hood-designed Kittanset Club [59] occupies the tip of a windblown peninsula. While the links-like Sankaty Head[60] has been a long-time favourite on Nantucket Island on perennially popular Cape Cod, a pair of classics, Ross's Oyster Harbors[61] and Eastward Ho![62] are among the best.

## EASTWARD HO!

Few American courses are as consistently testing of a golfer's ability to play both the wind and the often significant rolls of the terrain as Eastward Ho! It is, very simply, one of the US's most natural and attractive layouts, and a true testimonial to the impressive creative skills of W.H. Fowler, an architect whose courses could never be described as formulaic.

In a golf-architecture world that loves catchy marketing phrases, few have become as popular as that new millennium standard 'minimalism'. For many a modern designer, its use represents little more than lip service to a level of naturalism seldom actually employed; with less than 2 million cubic yards (1.5 million cubic metres) of earth moved and no island greens, the land has been embraced! But in the hands of a skilled practitioner the fundamental concept – a less-is-more approach to reshaping the native terrain – is inherently useful at two levels: it takes maximum advantage of topographical subtleties while also being extremely cost-effective. Indeed, as one of contemporary design's great classicists, Tom Doak, has incisively observed: 'The most noteworthy courses of the past decade have been among the least expensive to build.'

By definition, all early golf design was minimalist, because man's ability to reconfigure hill and dale was comparatively negligible. This was especially true in the

UK, both in the very early years and at the beginning of the 20th century, when a boom in course construction made designers such as Harry Colt, Willie Park Jnr and James Braid undisputed giants of the pre-mechanized approach. Also on this list, however, is a man whose name, though little known in America, carries great sway in the UK – Herbert Fowler.

Fowler did not take up golf until he was 35, but he eventually became both a scratch player and an elite architect. His design philosophy was once memorably summed up as: 'God builds golf links, and the less man meddles the better for all concerned.' His break-through project was the Old Course at Walton Heath.

*A meeting of minds for two of golf's great thinkers, Jack Nicklaus and Tom Doak, Sebonack exploits the natural movement of the land on this prime Long Island site.*

In the early 1920s, with British golf in the post-First World War doldrums, Fowler travelled to America where his work was generally confined to a number of projects in California. The one geographic exception, however, was his enduring seaside creation at Eastward Ho!

Originally called the Chatham Country Club, Eastward Ho! sits near Cape Cod's south-eastern corner on a narrow, elevated spit of land sandwiched between the Atlantic's Pleasant Bay and a wide inlet understatedly known as Crows Pond. Though unlikely ever to host a Major championship at only 6,356 yards, it is one of the most uniquely minimalist courses ever created, its holes flowing with seeming effortlessness over a wildly tumbling, windblown landscape. Simply finding a solidly playable routing was challenging enough here; that Fowler created so many spectacular holes upon which the skilled player can utilize the terrain to gain an appreciable advantage is evidence of a certain kind of genius. And the course has been altered comparatively little since Herbert Fowler's day.

## ELSEWHERE IN NEW ENGLAND
Central and western Massachusetts offer considerably fewer golf courses of excellence, though Ross designs at Longmeadow[63] and Whitinsville[64] (widely considered America's best nine-hole course), and Mount Holyoke College's The Orchards[65] (site of the 2004 US Women's Open) certainly stand out.

Neighbouring Rhode Island is a tiny state, but one blessed with a disproportionately large number of fine early designs, largely because Donald Ross spent his summers there during the 1920s. His layout at Wannamoisett[66] – a veritable clinic on building a world-class course on a tiny piece of land – has long been viewed as the state's best, with his works at Sakonnet[67] and the delightfully quirky Rhode Island CC[68] following close behind. Ross even had a hand in the historic Newport CC[69], though the present layout (which hosted the 1995 US Amateur and 2006 US Women's Open) owes far more to a 1925 A.W. Tillinghast redesign.

While Vermont's Dorset Field Club[70] can lay claim to being the oldest continuously active golf club in America (est. 1886), early Green Mountain golf featured largely player-friendly resort courses, with the Walter Travis/John Dunn-designed Ekwanok CC[71] rather remarkably remaining the state's finest course for more than a hundred years! Neighbouring New Hampshire followed a similar path, its White Mountain region rating as America's leading summer destination at the turn of the 20th century, with the majority of courses being of the shorter, highly scenic

variety. Maine, the nation's easternmost state, differed little from this model, though several courses in its famed coastal region remain engaging period pieces, notably Bar Harbor's Kebo Valley[72] and Kennebunkport's Cape Arundel[73].

Though not a part of New England, upper New York State cannot be overlooked, particularly the Rochester area. Donald Ross dominated this region, where his much-altered East Course at Oak Hill[74] has hosted seven Major championships, and the club's West Course as well as the nearby CC of Rochester[75] and Monroe CC[76] are all worthy Ross tests. Farther west, his underrated CC of Buffalo[77] and its neighbour, Charles Alison's Park CC[78], also set a particularly high prewar standard.

## POSTWAR COURSES
Following the war, the surge in suburban development meant that suitable land was at a premium, but the occasional golf course of note still managed to be built around major north-eastern cities. Throughout the region, designers such as Robert Trent Jones Snr, Dick Wilson, Hal Purdy and William Gordon attracted the lion's share of the work, generally completing bland (though often difficult) projects typical of the day. Rare period exceptions included Wilson's mid-1950s Long Island designs at Deepdale[79] and Meadowbrook[80], Gordon's Stanwich[81] and Jones's Black Hall[82] (both in Connecticut), Jones's rebuild of four-time Major championship venue Congressional[83] (Maryland), and Wilson's Laurel Valley[84] (Pennsylvania), site of the 1965 PGA and 1989 US Senior Open.

## RECENT DEVELOPMENTS
If this seems precious little to show for the first 50 years after the war, the region's golfers are buoyed by the knowledge that the contemporary era has done them considerably better. Modern development has generally been led by large-budget private clubs built in the outermost reaches of suburbia, distant enough to secure sufficient land but close enough to remain economically viable.

In New York's heavily developed Westchester County, where potential golf sites are at a particular premium, Tom Fazio's Hudson National[85] and brother Jim's conversion of the former Briar Hall into Trump National[86] are generally rated the best of a limited crop. The story is considerably more impressive on Long Island. The Hamptons have further benefited from a pair of profusely bunkered Rees Jones layouts (Atlantic[87] and The Bridge[88]), as well as Bill Coore and Ben Crenshaw's considerably more natural East Hampton GC[89]. But the limelight has been taken by a

pair of new millennium additions, Tom Doak and Jack Nicklaus's Sebonack[90], and Bill Coore and Ben Crenshaw's spectacular north-shore creation, Friar's Head[91], both quickly establishing themselves among the nation's best.

## FRIAR'S HEAD
Friar's Head successfully recaptures what the great American golf writer Max Behr once praised as golf-course architecture that is 'uncontaminated by the hand of man'. No greater compliment could be given to its architects, Bill Coore and Ben Crenshaw, who were selected by Ken Bakst in 1997 to build a course that embraced the design principles from the Golden Age of golf-course architecture.

Long Island, thanks in part to its sandy soils, shoreline settings and windswept, interesting land-forms, is home to arguably the best courses ever built by Charles Blair Macdonald, Willie Park Jnr, William Flynn, Herbert Strong, Devereux Emmet and the firm of Harry Colt and Charles Alison. When Bakst found 350 acres (142 hectares) on the North Fork of Long Island with these very same attributes, he felt another architectural masterpiece could be built provided a patient approach was adopted.

The initial construction at Friar's Head took 30 months, nearly triple the usual construction period, after Bill Coore had already taken 16 months to find a routing that would, in his words, 'balance the visuals without overpowering the substance of the golf'. Working with dunes that gave way to 200-foot (60-metre) bluffs overlooking Long Island Sound to the north and farmland with some natural depressions to the south, each nine in Coore and Crenshaw's routing starts and finishes in the dunes by the clubhouse. Crucial to the overall success of the design is the way in which the dune and farmland areas were seamlessly knitted together. Importantly, these transitions occur gradually within the length of the course's four par-five holes rather than between holes, thereby creating a Cypress Point-like routing (see page 248), which ebbs and flows its way around the property.

Thanks to a wide-ranging variety of shapes, sizes and interior contours, the green complexes at Friar's Head are an equal match with those of the most heralded Long Island courses. No matter how severe or undulating the greens may be in spots, a player can somehow almost always navigate from one section to another provided they have the imagination and talent to do so. In so doing, the golfer always relishes a game at Friar's Head, where accomplished players are allowed to display their skills while the less talented still find the course equally enjoyable.

## OTHER MODERN COURSES

Northern New Jersey offers a bit more rural landscape than visitors might expect, resulting in a solid collection of modern courses which includes: Tom Fazio's Ridge at Back Brook[92]; Michael Hurdzan and Dana Fry's impressively bunkered Hamilton Farm[93]; the recent addition to the Trump National family in Bedminster; and the Bayonne GC[94], a stunningly contrived links remarkably situated on the edge of New York harbour.

The economic rebirth of Atlantic City, combined with a surfeit of sandy, occasionally heath-like land, has generated an even larger rush of modern development in the state's southern half, initially led by Robert Trent Jones's Metedeconk National[95], then, more recently by Tom Fazio's Galloway National[96] and his Pine Valley homage, Pine Hill[97], and Bill Coore and

Ben Crenshaw's particularly tasteful Hidden Creek[98]. Pennsylvania, for its part, has seen fewer modern layouts of note, though the Old Course at Stonewall[99], an early Tom Doak effort, can more than hold its own. The region's southernmost state, Maryland, features a pair of high-profile contemporary courses: Caves Valley[100] in Owings Mills and Pete Dye's Bulle Rock[101], located in Havre de Grace.

Outside Boston, Bill Coore and Ben Crenshaw's Olde Sandwich[102] and Gil Hanse's GC of Boston[103] rank as Massachusetts' finest postwar courses, while the more sparsely populated northern New England states still tend to rely mostly on resort development, with Maine's Sugarloaf GC[104] and a pair of Clive Clark designs – Maine's Belgrade Lakes GC[105] and New Hampshire's Lake Winnipesaukee CC[106] – ranking among the best of the new breed.

*The very natural look of the course at Friar's Head is the product of painstaking research before a single scoop of earth was moved, followed by intricately detailed craftsmanship in construction, as exemplified here by the transition from field to dunes at the 14th.*

# THE NATIONAL
## Southampton, New York

Has ever a golf course been saddled with a more presumptuous name? For those familiar with the life of its founder, Charles Blair Macdonald, however, no lesser title would have been appropriate.

Charles Blair Macdonald was one of the game's great figures – arguably the single greatest when the conversation is confined to American golf – and what he accomplished at the National literally changed the face of Stateside course design. Macdonald, ironically, was not even American, being born in Niagara Falls, Ontario in 1855 to a Scottish father and Canadian mother. He did, however, spend most of his life south of the border, growing up in Chicago before being packed off to Scotland to study at St Andrews University in 1872. Of his academic career little is known, but his exposure to golf was entirely another matter.

### THE ST ANDREWS INFLUENCE

Being introduced by his grandfather to a then not-so-Old Tom Morris, Macdonald fell in love with the game, quickly gaining enough proficiency to play regularly with the likes of Old Tom Morris and his son, Young Tom Morris, the Strath brothers and other 19th-century Scottish golf dignitaries. More importantly, with the seed deeply planted, Macdonald returned to America determined to spread the gospel of the Royal & Ancient game in his adopted homeland.

Macdonald's 1892 creation of the Chicago Golf Club (see page 222) did much to kick-start American golf, and his subsequent achievements (and pomposities) as the first official US Amateur champion, USGA guiding light, administrator and general father figure to the game's American development have been well chronicled. But it was only after the turn of the 20th century, when his brokerage career moved him to New York, that Macdonald set out to build the ideal golf course, a facility that would, in his words, 'serve as an incentive to the elevation of the game in America'.

### STUDYING THE CLASSICS

For several years Macdonald laid his plans, revisiting Britain to study the most famous holes, hunting for the perfect site and putting together a list of affluent founder members that included no fewer than five US Amateur champions (Macdonald himself, his son-in-law H.J. Whigham, Herbert Harriman, Findlay Douglas and Eben Byers). After a search that

# NATIONAL GOLF LINKS OF AMERICA –
## Southampton, New York
Charles Blair Macdonald, 1911
Major events: Walker Cup 1922

CARD OF THE COURSE

| HOLE | NAME | YARDS | PAR | HOLE | NAME | YARDS | PAR |
|------|------|-------|-----|------|------|-------|-----|
| 1. | Valley | 322 | 4 | 10. | Shinnecock | 450 | 4 |
| 2. | Sahara | 330 | 4 | 11. | Plateau | 432 | 4 |
| 3. | Alps | 426 | 4 | 12. | Sebonac | 435 | 4 |
| 4. | Redan | 195 | 3 | 13. | Eden | 174 | 3 |
| 5. | Hog's Back | 478 | 5 | 14. | Cape | 365 | 4 |
| 6. | Short | 141 | 3 | 15. | Narrows | 397 | 4 |
| 7. | St Andrews | 478 | 5 | 16. | Punchbowl | 404 | 4 |
| 8. | Bottle | 424 | 4 | 17. | Peconic | 375 | 4 |
| 9. | Long | 540 | 5 | 18. | Home | 502 | 5 |
| **OUT** | | **3,334** | **37** | **IN** | | **3,534** | **36** |
| | | | | **TOTAL** | | **6868** | **73** |

ranged as far north as Cape Cod, and out to the very tip of Long Island, a rough, undulating property immediately adjacent to the well-known Shinnecock Hills Golf Club (see page 178) was procured in spring 1907. Whigham, founder member Devereux Emmet and three-time US Amateur champion Walter Travis were engaged as consultants, and construction began that summer.

To aid in the building process, Macdonald hired a local Princeton-educated surveyor by the name of Seth Raynor. Rather fortuitously, Raynor, a non-golfer, quickly proved himself highly skilled in bringing blueprints to life. In fact, in addition to eventually becoming Macdonald's full-time partner, Raynor went on to be one of the Golden Age's most successful architects, ultimately completing more than 50 solo designs from New York to Hawaii, many of which remain golfing landmarks today.

## DEFINING A PHILOSOPHY
At the National, Raynor executed a Macdonald plan that included replicating several of the finest holes in Great Britain, as selected in a 1901 contest in the UK's popular *Golf Illustrated* magazine. The intent was not to copy these holes precisely but to adapt their general tenets to the available land – an approach that both designers successfully carried on for the duration of

their careers. Other holes were, in Macdonald's words, 'more or less composite', blending various appealing shots from the Old Country, while others were entirely original. Also of interest was the green contouring, for where no basic template was inherent to a particular hole's design, Macdonald often followed the advice of the great British player/writer Horace Hutchinson who, believing that man could never outdo nature in this regard, advocated dropping a handful of pebbles on a map of the proposed green, then sculpting its undulations to match their random pattern.

In studying Macdonald's finished product, it is worth recalling that at the time of its construction the National's out-and-back routing began and ended adjacent to the Shinnecock Inn, a prominent period hotel located near the present 10th tee. Upon the inn's fiery demise in 1909, however, the club selected a high plateau near the property's northern end to build

its famed ocean-view clubhouse, altering the sequence of play dramatically. Thus while the present order has existed nearly from the beginning, Macdonald's initial conception of what today seems the perfectly constituted golf course did, in fact, have its nines playing in reverse.

## REPLICAS OF DISTINCTION
The National opens with a 322-yard drive-and-pitch played to a large, elevated green, a solid starter but one quickly overshadowed by the run of three superb adaptations that immediately follows. The 330-yard 2nd is largely modelled after the late-lamented Sahara hole at Royal St George's, which was a blind par three played over what the eminent golf writer Bernard Darwin once called a 'heaving waste of sand'. At the National the drive is aimed over a high ridge, the face of which is one massive bunker. While the timid can

play safely away to the right (leaving an awkward, downhill/sidehill pitch), the more aggressive can attempt the full carry, with the green potentially within reach of longer hitters.

The 426-yard 3rd is Macdonald's de luxe version of Prestwick's celebrated 377-yard Alps 17th (see page 44). Here, after a drive across a large diagonal bunker to a fairway that grows progressively narrower, the golfer is faced with a long, steeply uphill approach to a blind target – a challenge compounded by the line of cross-bunkers (also hidden from view) that front the large, squarish green. Of a similarly thrilling appeal is the 195-yard 4th, whose deep front-left bunker and sloping green mirror the famed Redan 15th at North Berwick (see page 46). Stopping an approach on the left side of the putting surface is virtually impossible; instead the player must aim short and right, allowing the ball to follow the contour of the land from there. Given that the original is semiblind, there are many who consider Macdonald's version substantially better, and its significance as the first of numerous Redan replicas throughout North America cannot be overstated.

Following the 478-yard par-five 5th comes a classic Macdonald original, the 'Short' one-shot 6th. Like so many renditions of the Short that would appear on subsequent Macdonald/Raynor designs, this slightly downhill 141-yarder requires little muscle. Its challenge instead lies in a bunker-ringed putting surface marked by a pronounced horseshoe-shaped ridge – the Short's unique and quirky trademark.

## THE TURN

The 478-yard 7th is Macdonald's adaptation of St Andrews' legendary Road hole (see page 40), the principal differences being a sea of gnarly right-side sand replacing the original's notorious railway sheds, and a 5-foot (1.5-metre) deep bunker flanking the rear of the putting surface in place of the much-feared road. But it is the hole's central ingredient – the greenside Road bunker itself – that lingers longest in the memory, for it is configured more like a mineshaft than a sand hazard, actually requiring the use of a ladder to descend to its depths. Though somewhat shallower today than in days of yore, it surely remains among the most dangerous golfing hazards in all of

North America. Now approaching the far southern reaches of the property, the golfer encounters the 424-yard split-fairway 8th, where a narrower left-side option affords the best angle of approach, and the 540-yard 9th, a long, gently uphill hole modelled loosely – but only loosely – after the 14th at St Andrews.

From here the long march back to the clubhouse begins with a run of three strong par fours, the longest of which, the 450-yard 10th, runs immediately parallel with the 2nd and 3rd holes at next-door Shinnecock Hills. The 432-yard 11th is of particular architectural significance, for it was here that Macdonald introduced another staple of his repertoire, the double-plateau green. In this case it is the front-left and back-right segments that are elevated, creating numerous interesting pin placements as well as something of a 'slot' for over-struck approaches to run through the putting surface into a single rear bunker.

The 174-yard 13th replicates the 11th at St Andrews, the influential par three known as High In, which owing to its proximity to the eponymous estuary, Macdonald and Raynor colloquially referred to as the Eden. The primary components of the hole – a steeply sloping green fronted by two dangerous bunkers – were easy enough for Macdonald to recreate, but what of the backing estuary? Lacking a comparable water hazard, he instead built a long, narrow bunker beyond the putting surface, a creative substitute perhaps inspired by Walter Travis's 18th at Garden City – the rare American course of architectural significance to actually precede the National.

## THE ORIGINAL CAPE

Though much altered from its initial design, the 365-yard 14th is one of Macdonald's most famous original creations. His initial version measured just over 300 yards (275 metres) and curved along an inlet of Bullhead Bay, its 'Cape' green jutting excitingly out into the water in the area where Sebonac Inlet Road passes today. Wary of equipment advances rendering it drivable, however, Macdonald moved the putting

*The approach to the 397-yard 15th, with the National's famed windmill in the distance and a small pond hidden behind the elevated putting surface.*

# THE REDAN IN AMERICA
## The National's 4th hole – the Nation's 1st

*Chief among Charles Blair Macdonald's replica holes at the National Golf Links of America is the
4th – the Redan – which is modelled after the hole of the same name at Scotland's North Berwick
Golf Club. The word 'redan' is a military one, drawn from a fortified position at Sebastopol,
during the Crimean War. In golfing terms, it has generally translated to a reasonably long
par three played to a green sloping prominently from right to left, and falling away notably
at the back. The signature front-left bunker is invariably a steep and deep one – so much so
that the North Berwick original was buttressed with wooden sleepers a good century before
Pete Dye brought such things into vogue in America.*

*Macdonald's rendition at the National was America's first Redan, and was frequently
imitated, initially by Macdonald himself (and his protégés Seth Raynor and Charles
Banks) but later by all manner of architects in all sorts of locales, ranging from
A.W. Tillinghast's 2nd at Somerset Hills (New Jersey) to Chandler Egan's rebuild
of the 12th at Pebble Beach (see page 244). With classically minded modern
designers still utilizing the template to this day, the Redan ranks, without
question, as the single most-copied hole in the history of golf.*

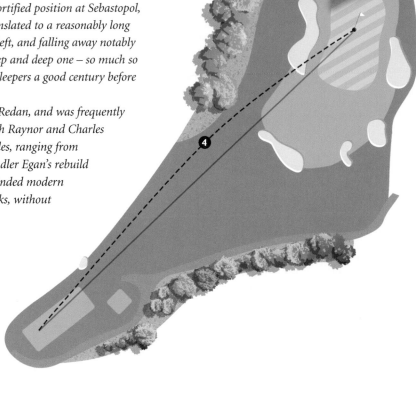

surface to its present site in the mid-1920s, making the
enduring Cape moniker rather a misnomer, but leaving a still-tricky test featuring an elevated, heavily
bunkered green.

The 397-yard 15th and 404-yard 16th (the latter
played blindly to an amphitheatre-like 'punchbowl'
green) continue the trek northward and climb to high
ground, from which begins the world-renowned 17th.
Today measuring 375 yards, this relatively short two-
shotter runs downhill, with the waters of Peconic Bay
providing a wide panoramic backdrop. Like any great
strategic hole it offers multiple options off the tee,
though the fundamental test is to open up the best
angle of approach by hugging the left side of the fairway – where a large, sandy waste area, small pond and
tall native rough await. Predictably, the disadvantages
of playing safely to the right are several, for a pair of
large, sand-topped mounds partially impair the view
of the putting surface and a huge bunker enveloping
its entire right side comes ever more into play.

The National concludes with an uphill par five of
502 yards, which Bernard Darwin once rated the finest
finisher in the world. The key to the 18th is a cluster of
highly invasive, left-side fairway bunkers, the carrying
of which leaves a relatively unimpeded second to a
reachable green. Come up short, or lay up safely right,
however, and three full shots will be in order. Though
bunkered only at its rear, the green lies adjacent to the
Peconic Bluffs, with sliced approaches generally turning threes or fours into sixes – or worse.

## MONUMENT TO MACDONALD

Nearly one hundred years after its inception, the
National retains more of the handiwork of its founder
than virtually any prewar American course, and thus
remains a stirring monument to the driven, princi-
pled, pretentious, but above all talented man that was
Charles Blair Macdonald. Macdonald's ego was epic –
the statue he commissioned of himself still lords over
the National's library – and his rule over the club was

utterly autocratic. Indeed, the story is still told of an
early club member, Daniel Pomeroy, suggesting the
construction of a windmill atop the hill that houses the
17th tee. Macdonald liked the idea and immediately set
about having it built – then, on completion, presented
Pomeroy with a bill for the entire cost of construction.

Perhaps just such a personality was necessary to
conceive of a project as revolutionary as the National,
and to see it through to a brilliant, uncompromising
completion. Likewise, having learned the game at the
feet of Old Tom Morris, then driven its expansion in a
nation of neophytes, perhaps Macdonald was not so
wrong in considering his view as the only one that truly
mattered. Regardless, his thoughts on the National
were summed up nicely in comments he wrote about
the 2nd hole in which, after drawing comparisons to its
English role model at Royal St George's, he acknowledged several important differences, then concluded,
with characteristic bluntness: 'I am confident that it is a
much better hole than the original.'

# FISHERS ISLAND
## Fishers Island, New York

Although not an international household name in golf circles, the Fishers Island Club occupies a lofty perch among golf-design aficionados, its delightfully secluded waterfront layout representing one of the finest and least-altered courses of American architecture's vaunted Golden Age.

Great acclaim for this course has hardly been a constant; indeed, Fishers Island long maintained such quiet anonymity that the most established of American golf publications – a magazine with its headquarters little more than an hour from the club – managed to overlook the course entirely in each of its biannual Top 100 rankings from 1975 to 2000. Thankfully, the Fishers Island membership was atypical in their reaction to the slight, being happy enough with their own splendid links to ignore such trendy options as calling in Robert Trent Jones to 'modernize' things or throwing a lavish party for ratings panellists. Instead the club quietly carried on, unconcerned with what the so-called 'experts' thought, and in the end, inevitably, its greatness was well and fully recognized.

### NEW YORK OR CONNECTICUT?

Fishers Island enjoys one of golf's more idyllic locales, occupying the eastern end of an island that, though situated nearly within shouting distance of the Connecticut shoreline, manages through some ancient geographic quirk, to be a part of New York State. A resort hotbed during the late 19th century, it was redeveloped as a private summer retreat during the mid-1920s, modelled after what would become its long-time seasonal sister club, Mountain Lake in Lake Wales, Florida. Smartly, Fishers Island followed its sibling's successful lead in two important ways: hiring the famed landscape design firm of Frederick Law Olmsted to masterplan the island; and retaining golf-course architect Seth Raynor to design its spectacular oceanfront links.

By the time the Fishers Island Club approached Raynor, he had established rather an envied status within the architecture world because of his partnership with the renowned course designer Charles Blair Macdonald, landing all manner of high-society projects

in Florida, New York and, eventually, the Midwest and Hawaii. Sticking with the established Macdonald formula, Raynor replicated great holes from the Old World, a technique that, combined with the quasi-geometric stylings of his squarish greens and angular bunkers, gives his courses a splendidly old-fashioned appeal today. At Fishers Island, this classic ambience is enhanced by the paucity of housing along the course's perimeter and by the general distinctiveness of the property, for its tumbling, links-like terrain offers ocean views from every hole and all the coastline any designer might wish to employ.

### A FAST GETAWAY

Several of the club's most recognized holes come during an early march along the island's southern shoreline, beginning with the 172-yard 2nd (the rare Redan replica to be played across a pond) and the 335-yard 3rd, a potentially drivable par four that curves

gently right and climbs to a skyline green sited above the beach. A laid-up tee shot will leave only a short pitch here, but with 10-foot (3-metre) deep, grass-faced bunkers flanking the green on three sides danger lies eminently close at hand.

The 397-yard 4th then continues along the coastline and is a palpably exciting affair, with most drives to its plateau fairway facing an approach of the Alps variety – that is, an uphill shot to a green almost completely hidden behind a large, rough-covered hill. A fine strategic element lies in the fact that a glimpse of the green can be had from the fairway's far right side, but the drive must flirt with a brush-filled plunge to the beach in order to gain such an advantage.

### THE BIARRITZ

Fishers Island's definitive hole must surely be the 229-yard 5th, a wonderful rendition of perhaps *the* Macdonald/Raynor standard, the Biarritz. These

## FISHERS ISLAND CLUB –
## Fishers Island, New York
Seth Raynor, 1926

CARD OF THE COURSE

| HOLE | YARDS | PAR | HOLE | YARDS | PAR |
|------|-------|-----|------|-------|-----|
| 1. | 396 | 4 | 10. | 401 | 4 |
| 2. | 172 | 3 | 11. | 164 | 3 |
| 3. | 335 | 4 | 12. | 389 | 4 |
| 4. | 397 | 4 | 13. | 400 | 4 |
| 5. | 229 | 3 | 14. | 425 | 4 |
| 6. | 520 | 5 | 15. | 533 | 5 |
| 7. | 363 | 4 | 16. | 146 | 3 |
| 8. | 465 | 5 | 17. | 415 | 4 |
| 9. | 364 | 4 | 18. | 452 | 5 |
| **OUT** | **3,241** | **36** | **IN** | **3,325** | **36** |
| | | | **TOTAL** | **6,566** | **72** |

demanding par threes were patterned after a long-deceased cliff-top hole in Biarritz, France, and feature a large putting surface fronted by a deep swale, with narrow, symmetrical bunkers along either side. The French original required an initial carry over a deep coastal chasm, something the seaside Fishers Island version uniquely matches among the hole's many 20th-century inland replicas.

Another pre-eminent front-nine hole is the 465-yard 8th, a short, into-the-wind par five roughly modelled after the Road hole at St Andrews (see page 40). Here a stretch of scrub-lined beach substitutes for the original's railway sheds in protecting the optimum right side of the fairway, the area from which the green's deep Road bunker can best be avoided. The 401-yard 10th also challenges the prevailing breeze, and features a crowned, bunkerless putting surface built to repel any ball not played assertively into its heart.

### THE BACK NINE

The finest hole on the back nine may well be the 164-yard 11th, a thrillingly windblown adaptation of the 11th at St Andrews, complete with deep bunkers to mimic the original Hill and Strath, and complemented by the expanse of East Harbor as an Eden estuary-like

*The heroic 229-yard Biarritz 5th, requiring a well-struck long-iron or fairway metal to carry the chasm and reach the deep, symmetrically bunkered green – often in a stiff breeze.*

backdrop. Also noteworthy are the 400-yard 13th and 425-yard 14th, the former played to another seaside green defended by sand and water, the latter a tough dogleg left around a coastal lagoon that, given today's enhanced equipment, just might be drivable under favourable conditions.

A singular criticism of Fishers Island – that too many greens sport perfectly symmetrical, left-and-right greenside bunkering – might be applied to the 533-yard 15th and the 415-yard 17th, though both are amply challenging and situated attractively alongside the harbour. The 146-yard 16th also merits a mention, being a downhill, over-water rendition of Charles Blair

Macdonald's original Short hole, the 6th at the National Golf Links of America (see page 166). It might be observed that the 452-yard 18th, while featuring a superbly contoured green, is not the grandest of finishers. However, this cannot be blamed on Seth Raynor, who originally built both the 18th and the beachside 8th as difficult par fours (measuring 433 and 418 yards respectively), but the membership later opted to lengthen them. In the bigger picture, such alterations are minor and seem trivial at Fishers Island, where panoramic beauty and classic replica-oriented design continue to rank Raynor's golf course high among America's very best.

A dominant figure in regional architectural circles, Tillinghast was one of the Golden Age's great all-rounders, having played the game quite well (finishing 25th in the 1910 US Open and competing in numerous US Amateurs), written about it extensively, edited perhaps its finest-ever American magazine (*Golf Illustrated*) and been a highly successful agronomist, all in addition to building first-class courses quite literally from coast to coast. Tilly, as he was commonly known, was also one of golf's epic characters. Coming from an affluent Philadelphia family, he avoided education almost entirely, yet still possessed the resources necessary to travel extensively, get driven daily to his Manhattan office by chauffeured limousine and, through it all, drink copiously.

Eschewing the drawing of detailed plans, Tillinghast was a man who, flask in hand, developed his design ideas in the field, moulding and shaping as he went. Though certainly capable of building less demanding courses, the backbone of his portfolio – the Winged Foots, Baltusrols and Bethpages (see page 176) – tended to be longer, stronger, heavily bunkered and stocked with smallish, often elevated greens. But beyond their striking challenge and fine strategic sense, Tillinghast's course designs also possess a hard-to-define aesthetic component – the renowned 'Tillinghast polish' – which has long given them an aura of stylish grandeur seldom equalled in the annals of American design.

## DESIGN PHILOSOPHY

At Winged Foot, Tilly found 280 rolling, partially wooded acres (113 hectares) dotted with large formations of ledge rock, some of which were dynamited, with the remainder serving as foundations for many of the club's more elevated putting surfaces. Famously instructed by the founders to 'Give us a man-sized course', Tillinghast responded

## WINGED FOOT GOLF CLUB (WEST COURSE) – Mamaroneck, New York

A.W. Tillinghast, 1923
Major events: US Open 1929, 1959, 1974, 1984, 2006; USPGA 1997; US Amateur 1940, 2004; Walker Cup 1949

CARD OF THE COURSE

| HOLE | NAME | YARDS | PAR | HOLE | NAME | YARDS | PAR |
|------|------|-------|-----|------|------|-------|-----|
| 1. | Genesis | 450 | 4 | 10. | Pulpit | 188 | 3 |
| 2. | Elm | 453 | 4 | 11. | Billows | 396 | 4 |
| 3. | Pinnacle | 216 | 3 | 12. | Cape | 640 | 5 |
| 4. | Sound View | 469 | 4 | 13. | White Mule | 214 | 3 |
| 5. | Long Lane | 515 | 5 | 14. | Shamrock | 458 | 4 |
| 6. | El | 321 | 4 | 15. | Pyramid | 416 | 4 |
| 7. | Babe-in-the-Woods | 162 | 3 | 16. | Hells-Bells | 478 | 4 |
| 8. | Arena | 475 | 4 | 17. | Well-Well | 449 | 4 |
| 9. | Meadow | 514 | 4 | 18. | Revelations | 450 | 4 |
| **OUT** | | **3,575** | **35** | **IN** | | **3,689** | **35** |
| | | | | **TOTAL** | | **7,264** | **70** |

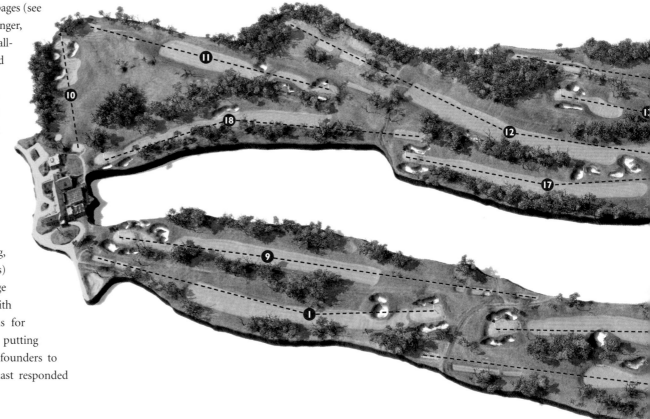

# WINGED FOOT
## Mamaroneck, New York

Named after the popular logo of the New York Athletic Club, from where its founding members came, Winged Foot was intended for big things right from its inception, beginning with the selection of a top designer for its golf courses – Albert Warren ('A.W.') Tillinghast.

with 36 epic holes, virtually all of which amply demonstrated his belief that 'a controlled shot to a closely guarded green is the surest test of a man's golf'. At Winged Foot, however, he outdid himself by building some of the most heavily contoured putting surfaces in his portfolio, and configuring them in ways designed to favour approach shots played from specific fairway angles, thus creating somewhat more driving strategy than might be apparent at first glance.

Within the club membership, opinion has long been closely divided as to which course is better. The West is unquestionably longer and tougher, as its hosting of five US Opens, two US Amateurs and one USPGA has readily attested. It is, quite simply, an utterly relentless course, its unceasing challenge representing perhaps the purest examination of a great golfer's skills as exists in the United States. But the East Course nips closely at its heels, lacking a bit of

distance, certainly, but possessing far more variety and general playing interest.

What both courses share is a marvellous golfing ambience, their richly green, tree-lined fairways timelessly suggesting that perhaps it really was not so very long ago that the legendary Bobby Jones won here, or that Craig Wood manned the pro shop, or that Tommy Armour spent many a summer holding court in the bar before he went on to win the 1927 US Open, the 1930 USPGA and the 1931 Open. And in point of fact, not so much has really changed since those halcyon days; tees have been added certainly, and the odd bunker here or there. But with its stately fairway corridors of oaks, elms, birches and pines trimmed back in recent years, and several greens enlarged to recapture lost pin positions, Winged Foot comfortably ranks among the least-altered of America's great championship venues.

## A FEARSOME START

Should the visiting golfer wonder if the West Course's revered toughness might be somehow overrated, such thoughts are quickly doused by the 450-yard 1st, one of the toughest opening holes in golf. Bending slightly leftward, this par four gives a true foretelling of how accurately a golfer must drive the ball. Assuming the fairway to be hit, however, the fun is just beginning, for the 1st green is a true terror, sloped steeply from back to front, dangerously contoured within, and flanked by long, deep bunkers on both sides – an attention-getter of the very highest order.

The 453-yard 2nd is one of West's more overtly strategic holes, the left side of the fairway offering the optimum line of approach to a larger green angled left-to-right behind another notably deep bunker, and overhung at the back by a massive elm. It is followed by one of America's toughest par threes, the 216-yard 3rd, which plays slightly uphill to a startlingly narrow, bunker-flanked green. So difficult is this target that, during his victory in the 1959 US Open, Billy Casper deliberately laid up short each day, taking his chances – successfully, as it turned out – that he'd do better attempting to get up-and-down four times from the fairway than who-knew-how-many times from the sand.

## A BRIEF RESPITE

The downhill 469-yard 4th, once a marathon in days of old, is today fairly manageable, paving the way for three shorter holes that, as a group, represent the golfer's lone sustained opportunity to pick up strokes. The 515-yard 5th runs back up the long grade but is easily reachable in two by better players. Several deep bunkers guard the small putting surface, but a five here will certainly lose ground to a professional field. The 321-yard 6th then ambles back downhill and is by far the West's shortest par four. Though theoretically drivable, its tiny green turns rightward around a yawning bunker and is rather surreptitiously backed by a brook that will gobble up anything coming in hot. This 'easy' stretch then closes with the 162-yard 7th, just a short-iron but one played to a substantially elevated green guarded right and left by sand. The right bunker is particularly menacing, as defending champion Johnny Miller found out during the opening round of the 1974 US Open when he thrice failed to extricate his ball and scored a seven.

Things return to cruising speed at the 475-yard 8th, though this is the rare hole possibly made

easier by a bit of lengthening. Measuring 442 yards (405 metres) in 1974, the early rightward bend of its fairway once called for a hard, controlled fade to avoid the left rough, whereas today, with 36 yards (30 metres) more to play with, a much freer swing with a fairway metal generally sets the golfer up nicely. The front nine then closes with the 509-yard 9th, a manageable par five for members, but one historically played as a 470-yard par four during the Opens. The hole gained an element of notoriety in 2006, however, when a USGA trying desperately to keep up with unchecked equipment advances stretched it to 514 yards (472 metres) – the longest two-shotter in Major championship history.

## TILLY'S BEST

Tillinghast was a designer known for the richness of his par threes and Winged Foot's 10th is universally rated among his very best. Once described by the great golfer Ben Hogan as a 'three-iron into some guy's bedroom' (in reference to a home that *looks* especially close to the green), it is today more of a five or six played to a steeply sloping putting surface built in the shape of an upside-down pear. On both sides of the green the terrain falls immediately away, left towards a nasty bunker, right into a bunker so deep that 1965 USPGA champion Dave Marr, a one-time Winged Foot assistant, used to joke that he received his mail there. The back of the green, though substantially wider, is also no bargain – though its sharply downhill putt is actually easier now than in Tillinghast's day, the surface having been flattened a bit prior to the 1959 US Open. Tilly himself reportedly called this the best par three he ever built. A golfer would, at any rate, be hard-pressed to find many that surpass it.

## THE FINAL PAR FIVE

There follows a modest respite, for the better player needs only an iron and wedge at the 396-yard 11th, and the 12th – despite being extended to 640 yards (587 metres) for the 2006 US Open – is the tournament layout's final par five. The difficult 214-yard 13th, playing slightly uphill to another notably narrow green, represents the last of the par threes, and then begins a closing run of five two-shotters that, particularly in Major championship conditions, truly separate the serious contenders from those merely cashing cheques.

Ranking among the more striking holes at Winged Foot is the 458-yard (420-metre), dogleg-left 14th, its drive flirting with a single left-side trap, its second travelling uphill to a left-to-right sloping green guarded by sand and several overhanging trees. At 416 yards, the 15th is the shortest of the finishers but plays deceptively

*Looking up the fairway at the 509-yard 9th, a manageable par five for everyday play but a backbreaking par four during Major championships.*

long, as the tiny creek that represents the layout's lone water hazard trickles across its fairway, necessitating a laid-up tee shot. Then the approach is played – often from a downhill lie – to a deep, very narrow green that is among the West's most heavily contoured.

## TURNING FOR HOME

The 478-yard 16th is the second par five converted to two-shot status for Major championship play and, much like the 9th, the switch abruptly transforms it from pleasant to vicious. There is not much subtlety here; just launch a huge tee shot, drawn significantly to stay out of the willows, then a comparably long approach to yet another narrow, deeply bunkered green – this one also guarded front-left by several overhanging sweetgums. A personal favourite of Jack Nicklaus's, the 449-yard 17th may seem short by comparison, but plays only slightly easier, its tee shot requiring a fade past a cluster of bunkers to a left-to-right curving fairway, its second a mid-iron to a crescent-shaped green that is among the West Course's slenderest.

## MEMORABLE FINISH

As arduous as holes 14–17 may be, however, they largely pale in comparison to both the challenge and individuality of the 450-yard 18th, one of America's most historic finishers. A sweeping dogleg left, this demanding, tree-lined test first requires either a straight fairway metal or a drawn driver, lest a modern-era bunker guarding the outside of the dogleg catch the ball. The approach is then played to an elevated, false-fronted green that, notably, is the only one on the West Course where sand is not a primary hazard. The putting surface is steeply pitched, however, with a prominent rise in its front-right section defending a tricky Sunday pin position. The biggest danger to the approach is certainly the false front, for balls coming up even slightly short will invariably roll 25 yards (23 metres) back into the fairway (from where Geoff Ogilvy made a superb four to close out the 2006 US Open). But shots lost right (an uphill chip from deep rough), long (a scary downhill chip or putt) or left (the green's lone relevant sand) often present even greater dilemmas, making the 18th a truly unforgiving hole. Perhaps more importantly, on a course whose sole perceived weakness may be a lack of variety, its nearly bunker-free naturalness makes for rather a different sort of climax to what remains, in its ninth decade, one of the game's great championship tests.

## THE EAST COURSE
The best 'second' course in America

*The East Course's 151-yard 3rd: playing slightly downhill to a narrow green flanked by a deep left-side bunker, typical of the layout's shorter, but often more dangerous, challenge.*

*To course-ratings cognoscenti, Winged Foot's West Course has long ranked among the world elite, but among club membership debate has forever raged as to whether it is even the better course on the property. Despite popular reports to the contrary, Winged Foot's East Course was not originally selected to host the 1929 US Open, but it has enjoyed several moments in the championship sun, hosting the 1957 and 1972 US Women's Opens, and the inaugural US Senior Open in 1980. At 6,816 yards, it is somewhat shorter than the US Open-stretched West, yet with holes such as the 197-yard 6th, 473-yard 7th and 448-yard 16th it features several of the toughest tests on either layout. What the East also offers, however, is far greater variety, with several intriguing shorter par threes and par fours, and green complexes severe enough to prompt the late Dave Marr, the 1965 USPGA champion, to observe that while 'the West is a bogey course, the East is a double-bogey course'.*

*Could the East host a Major championship? With the 502-yard 2nd and 451-yard 8th converted to par fours, absolutely. But with the West being perhaps the prototypical new millennium US Open course, such an event is not likely to happen in the near future.*

The brainchild of a headstrong and controversial New York State parks commissioner named Robert Moses, the Bethpage project involved the acquisition (and subsequent Tillinghast renovation) of the Devereux Emmet-designed Lenox Hills Country Club, the construction of three additional Tillinghast courses and, some two decades later, the addition of a fifth and final course laid out by A.H. Tull. Of the four Tillinghast designs, three started in 1935, but it was the 1936 launch of the fourth, the highly ambitious Black Course, that attracted so much attention to the new megafacility.

## A GENUINE TILLINGHAST?

It must be noted that Tillinghast's status as the primary designer of the Black Course has occasionally been questioned, with some suggesting that credit should actually go to the property's manager, Joseph Burbeck. The preponderance of evidence, however, fails to support such assertions, though Tillinghast did credit Burbeck with initiating the concept of making the Black Course 'something which might compare with Pine Valley as a great test'. Remarkably, in many ways, it actually succeeded in doing just that.

The Black Course is built over sandy, rolling terrain at least somewhat akin to that of Pine Valley (see page 186) and, save for the opening two and closing three holes, is routed through similarly dense woods. Its bunkering and overall length were created on a comparable scale, leaving only its relatively benign greens significantly different. For some, this latter point is suggestive of Joseph Burbeck's alleged design role, though a far more likely

scenario is that Burbeck's inexperienced WPA work crews constructed greens without the benefit of either detailed plans (which Tillinghast seldom employed) or the frequently travelling architect's direct supervision.

For many years the Black existed as something of a local legend, recognized throughout the New York metropolitan area as a layout whose difficulty could match anything in the north-east, yet whose municipal course upkeep rendered it something of an after-thought at the national level. But in an effort to put a more attractive face on municipal golf, the USGA broke with decades of private club tradition by awarding Bethpage the 2002 US Open. To renovate the facility in preparation for this event, it went into partnership with New York State and architect Rees Jones.

CARD OF THE COURSE

| HOLE | YARDS | PAR | HOLE | YARDS | PAR |
|---|---|---|---|---|---|
| 1. | 430 | 4 | 10. | 492 | 4 |
| 2. | 389 | 4 | 11. | 435 | 4 |
| 3. | 205 | 3 | 12. | 499 | 4 |
| 4. | 517 | 5 | 13. | 554 | 5 |
| 5. | 451 | 4 | 14. | 161 | 3 |
| 6. | 408 | 4 | 15. | 478 | 4 |
| 7. | 489 | 4 | 16. | 479 | 4 |
| 8. | 210 | 3 | 17. | 207 | 3 |
| 9. | 418 | 4 | 18. | 411 | 4 |
| OUT | 3,517 | 35 | IN | 3,716 | 35 |
| | | | TOTAL | 7,233 | 70 |

# BETHPAGE BLACK
## Farmingdale, New York

In 1935, near the height of America's Great Depression, legendary architect A.W. Tillinghast received a very prestigious government project: a Works Progress Administration (WPA) undertaking on Long Island that would eventually become the grandest municipal golf facility ever built in the United States. It was for Bethpage State Park.

## THE RE-EMERGENCE OF A CHAMPIONSHIP COURSE

Restored to a championship level of conditioning for the landmark event, the Black is today a bona fide powerhouse, a layout virtually devoid of weak holes and well stocked with many of a world-class nature. Perhaps the best of the bunch is the 517-yard 4th, a prodigious two-shotter that requires the aggressive player to drive across a large left-side bunker if the green is to be reached in two, but also allows those laying up to decide among multiple strategic options on their second.

The 451-yard 5th is another exacting hole, requiring a prodigious carry over sand to reach the optimum right side of the fairway, from which a long, uphill approach remains over two deep bunkers fronting the green. Although played as a 489-yard par four during the 2002 US Open, the dogleg-right, 553-yard 7th is similarly thought-provoking, daring a drive across another huge fairway bunker if the green is to be approached in two. For its part, the 210-yard 8th bears a certain stylistic resemblance to the 14th at Pine Valley, but despite being sharply downhill and having a pond, it is actually a very different hole altogether.

## THE BACK NINE

The inward half is most notable for a series of tremendously long par fours, beginning with the heavily bunkered 492-yard 10th, a real monster requiring a long approach over a valley to an elevated green. The 499-yard 12th turns sharply left around an ultra-invasive corner bunker, while the most engaging hole in the back nine may well be the 161-yard 14th, which plays over a wide depression to a green angled behind a deep front-right bunker. The 478-yard 15th, with its steeply elevated, two-tiered green, is commonly rated the Black's single toughest hole. The run of gruelling two-shotters ends with the 479-yard downhill 16th, setting up to a difficult penultimate test, the 207-yard 17th, whose shallow green is surrounded by five large bunkers.

The 411-yard 18th is a moderate finisher effectively illustrating both the pluses and minuses of Rees Jones's pre-Open modernization work. Jones was able to build nearly 40 more yards (36 metres) of length onto an otherwise short closing hole, which was a substantial improvement for Major championship play. On the downside, his 'restored' bunkering, both fairway and greenside, is manifestly overdone, little resembling Tillinghast's original hazards and giving the hole – and, sadly, a number of others – a sort of Florida-with-fescue feel.

Still, Bethpage remains an inspiringly grand design, conceived and built on a scale that few courses (virtually none of them public) can match, and it acquitted itself notably well during Tiger Woods' three-shot 2002 victory.

*An aerial view of the par-five 4th, where the left-hand bunker must be challenged off the tee if the golfer hopes to reach the distant, tightly bunkered green in two.*

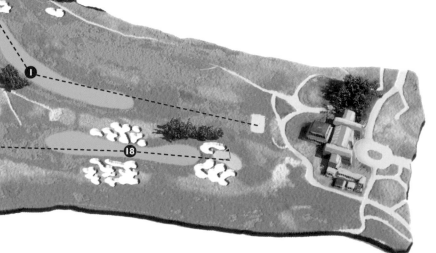

# SHINNECOCK HILLS
## Southampton, New York

Though several more loosely organized American golf clubs certainly played the game sooner, Long Island's Shinnecock Hills can lay claim to being, indisputably, the nation's first incorporated golfing entity. That its incorporation is of relevance is entirely appropriate given that its founders were three prominent New York businessmen.

While on holiday in Biarritz, France during the winter of 1891, New Yorkers William Vanderbilt, Duncan Cryder and Edward Mead saw a demonstration of the game of golf by the Scottish professional Willie Dunn. Enthralled, they returned to America determined to build what they likely believed to be the US's first course. Borrowing professional/architect Willie Davis from North America's oldest golf club, Royal Montreal, they forged ahead during the summer, clearing and reshaping the rough native landscape to make a 12-hole layout that was ready by late August. The official date of incorporation was 21 September 1891.

### DESIGN EVOLUTION

As the game found immediate popularity among the affluent Southampton set, a nine-hole women's course was added two years later, and the men's layout was expanded to 18 holes by Willie Dunn in 1895. Shinnecock hosted the second US Amateur and Open in 1896 (won by H.J. Whigham and James Foulis respectively), then, perhaps due to the relative low scores recorded therein, dropped out of the national tournament limelight immediately thereafter. With the arrival of the livelier rubber-core ball eventually rendering the early course obsolete, Charles Blair Macdonald and Seth Raynor, builders of the neighbouring National Golf Links of America (see page 166), designed a new 6,108-yard layout in 1916, remnants of which still dot the club's practice areas today. Finally, when the 1930 expansion

# SHINNECOCK HILLS GOLF CLUB –
## Southampton, New York
William Flynn and Howard Toomey, 1931
Major events: US Open 1896, 1986, 1995, 2004; US Amateur 1896;
US Women's Amateur 1900; Walker Cup 1977

CARD OF THE COURSE

| HOLE | NAME | YARDS | PAR | HOLE | NAME | YARDS | PAR |
|------|------|-------|-----|------|------|-------|-----|
| 1. | Westward Ho | 393 | 4 | 10. | Eastward Ho | 412 | 4 |
| 2. | Plateau | 226 | 3 | 11. | Hill Head | 158 | 3 |
| 3. | Peconic | 478 | 4 | 12. | Tuckahoe | 468 | 4 |
| 4. | Pump House | 435 | 4 | 13. | Road Side | 370 | 4 |
| 5. | Montauk | 537 | 5 | 14. | Thom's Elbow | 443 | 4 |
| 6. | Pond | 474 | 4 | 15. | Sebonac | 403 | 4 |
| 7. | Redan | 189 | 3 | 16. | Shinnecock | 540 | 5 |
| 8. | Lowlands | 398 | 4 | 17. | Eden | 179 | 3 |
| 9. | Ben Nevis | 443 | 4 | 18. | Home | 450 | 4 |
| **OUT** | | **3,573** | **35** | **IN** | | **3,423** | **35** |
| | | | | **TOTAL** | | **6,996** | **70** |

of state Route 27 directly across the property's mid-section forced yet another change, the club hired William Flynn to create the splendid Shinnecock Hills layout that has now stood among the world's elite for nearly 80 years.

## THE FLYNN LAYOUT
William Flynn was provided with new land to the north on which to build what essentially amounted to a brand new golf course, though several pieces of its Macdonald/Raynor predecessor (most notably the 13th and 14th holes – today's 3rd and 7th) were retained. Flynn worked in partnership with his faithful engineer/business manager Howard Toomey, and a construction crew that included future architects William Gordon and Dick Wilson – an arrangement that would prove a posthumous problem for Flynn when, some 30 years later, Wilson briefly muddied the historical waters by trying (unsuccessfully) to claim primary credit for the course's design.

It is also worth noting that, while the talented Flynn had cut his design teeth primarily around Philadelphia, a links-like landscape such as Shinnecock's was hardly unfamiliar to him; while considerably flatter, his now-defunct courses at Florida's Boca Raton Club and much-altered work at the Atlantic City Country Club were both open, wind-exposed designs routed across sandy, treeless tracts bearing at least a passing similarity to linksland. At Shinnecock, of course, there were hills, but Flynn utilized them to great effect, generally placing tees or greens above them in a way that added to the challenge and excitement, and allowed for the virtual elimination of blind shots.

## AN UNPREDICTABLE WIND
In addition to the distinctiveness of Flynn's design, several additional factors combine to give Shinnecock a playing ambience unlike any other American golf course. The biggest component is the wind, not only because it blows steadily but also because the term 'prevailing' is of limited relevance here. Though the south-west breeze is most likely, alternative conditions are common, their effect heightened by a routing that runs in every direction imaginable, with consecutive holes in the same direction on only three occasions.

Shinnecock is also famously defined by its rough, a sea of knee-high, golden brown native grass whose shaggy styling has become trendy in the modern era, but which has delineated these links since the beginning. And finally there is the layout's spaciousness, for while many holes are, strictly speaking, parallel, there is generally so much room between them that the golfer scarcely seems to notice.

## A GENTLE GETAWAY
Still playing out of America's first golf clubhouse – built in 1892 by celebrated New York society architect Stanford White – Shinnecock begins on high ground,

# DECADES BEFORE HIS TIME
## Shinnecock's John Shippen: an American golfing trailblazer

*The son of a black Presbyterian pastor, John Shippen grew up on the nearby Indian reservation, where his father served as a minister. As a youth he reportedly helped to build the club's original links and learned the game at the feet of its first professional, Willie Dunn. Encouraged by an apparently progressive membership, a 16-year-old Shippen (along with an Indian caddie, Oscar Bunn) elected to participate when the club hosted the 1896 US Open, only narrowly making it into the field after then-USGA President Theodore Havemeyer stood his ground against a threatened boycott from some less-than-tolerant professionals.*

*Remarkably, Shippen's first-round 78 was actually tied for the lead, but the final-round pressure proved too much for so inexperienced a competitor, with a disastrous 11 at the 31st leading to a closing 81 and a tie for 5th. Now established as golf's first competitive African-American player, Shippen played in five more US Opens and made something of a name for himself in regional tournament circles. Even more notably, he was hired, aged 19, to serve as head professional at Philadelphia's prestigious Aronimink Country Club, making him, by at least half a century, America's first minority club pro.*

with the relatively benign 393-yard 1st running downhill and turning gently right, suggesting an uneventful getaway. The challenge picks up immediately, however, at the 226-yard 2nd, a slightly uphill one-shotter with a line of three bunkers to be carried some 25 yards (23 metres) in front of the putting surface. Though reasonably sized, the green itself is tightly bunkered, often making the smartest shot one that carries the cross-bunkers and chases up from there.

The 478-yard 3rd has not been hugely altered since its days as the Macdonald/Raynor layout's 13th, although a bit of added length requires a strong tee shot to reach a level lie on the gently downhill fairway. The 4th then turns 180 degrees to the south and, although 43 yards (39 metres) shorter, often plays harder than its predecessor because of a pair of insidious right-side fairway bunkers, an aggressively contoured green and a prevailing headwind – when, in fact, it chooses to prevail.

Following the 537-yard 5th (where a distinctive Y-shaped bunker formation frames the driving zone) comes a pair of Shinnecock's more illustrious tests, beginning with the 474-yard 6th. Known as the Pond hole, this classic began life as a short three-shotter, complete with sand dunes flanking its right, an alternate left-side fairway and a prominent water hazard crossing some 75 yards (68 metres) from the green. Today the dunes are long gone and the left-side fairway represents little more than a safe area for shorter hitters, yet the remaining 215-yard (196-metre) sand carry to the right fairway is not easy, and the farther a golfer hedges their bets left, the more a tricky front-left greenside bunker presses into play.

## THE REDAN

The 189-yard 7th, on the other hand, is a mid-length Redan, which dates back to Macdonald and Raynor's 14th hole. Flynn chose to retain their original Redan concept here but reshaped the green complex, narrowing the front-right entrance with bunkers, which makes an all-carry approach clearly safer than any type of run-up. With the right-to-left fall of the putting surface demonstrating typical Redan severity, this can truly be a dangerous test – as 2004 US Open competitors discovered when a botched Sunday course set-up made it nearly impossible to stop a ball close to the hole, requiring a halt in play for emergency watering.

To close the outward half comes the difficult 443-yard 9th, a slight dogleg left requiring a drive to a rolling fairway, then a long second to an elevated green pitched into a broad slope below the clubhouse. There is little margin for error here; approaches missed short will find a cluster of four small bunkers or get ensnared in the hillside rough, while anything flying long leaves a nearly impossible chip or putt running straight down the dangerously cambered putting surface.

## AN ELITE NINE

There are many who rate Shinnecock's back nine the best in American golf and the 412-yard 10th certainly kicks it off in impressive style. Decision-making begins on the tee: does a golfer use a fairway metal and safely lay up on a crest some 240 yards (220 metres) out or try to blast a driver down the fairly steep plunge that follows? The former leaves a 160-yard (146-metre) approach over a valley to another starkly elevated green, the latter an uphill pitch – but to be caught in purgatory on the downhill slope in between means trouble. Because the steep run-up to the green is closely mown, it is guaranteed that approaches left even slightly short will generally roll back at least 30–40 yards (27–36 metres). Throw in the wind and Shinnecock's standard firm-and-fast conditioning and the 10th is a straightforward, lay-of-the-land classic.

Entirely different in character but of a comparably select design standard is the 158-yard 11th. Played straight uphill to a small skyline green, it is guarded left by a single long bunker and front-right by three of the deepest hazards on the golf course. Though requiring little more than a short-iron, this green is a particularly wind-exposed target that offers no easy options. The golfer either finds the putting surface or struggles mightily to make three.

The 468-yard 12th, which for many years was played as a three-shotter, and the 370-yard 13th run out-and-back across quiet Tuckahoe Road, setting up a memorable finish that begins with the 443-yard 14th. Playing from an elevated tee located only feet behind the clubhouse, this famous two-shotter begins with a downhill drive to a fairway pinched by sand at the 300-yard (275-metre) mark. The approach is then uphill to a smallish green situated in something of a saddle, with rough- and tree-covered hillsides converging on it from right and left. Compounding the challenge is a putting surface that actually falls away from the player, and which is guarded short by four bunkers carved into the grade.

The downhill 403-yard 15th represents something of a breather – little more than a fairway metal and a wedge to a tightly bunkered green – setting the stage for a final threesome that, taking full advantage of the wind, run in entirely different directions. The 540-yard 16th proceeds directly south and thus faces the greatest likelihood of a stiff headwind, a condition that not only makes it a full three-shotter but also brings a left-side bunker cluster far more into play on the second shot. Like several other Shinnecock greens, this narrow putting surface is guarded by more bunkers (ten) than might seem necessary, though this surely speaks more to the natural texture of the sandy terrain than any design profligacy on the part of William Flynn.

## THE FINISHERS

Turning to the north-west, the 179-yard 17th plays to a green angled right-to-left behind a line of three bunkers. This design template appears frequently on Flynn courses but is particularly tricky at this juncture, for the prevailing wind is blowing left-to-right, demanding a hard draw into the breeze (and towards the bunkers) for any left-side pin to be accessible. The 450-yard 18th then returns to the south-east, the breeze and general flow of the terrain favouring a tee shot played up the right side. From

here the golfer is left with a mid-iron to a sloping but reasonably open green, bunkered right and left but not immediately short. Evidence of its relative playability was provided at the 1995 US Open, when Corey Pavin – a shorter hitter in a shorter era – memorably knocked a 238-yard (218-metre) 4-wood to 6 feet (1.8 metres) to clinch a two-shot victory over Greg Norman.

## THE QUINTESSENTIAL OPEN TEST

Shinnecock Hills remains an ideal national championship venue – enough so, in fact, to make one wonder how the present layout could possibly have been overlooked in this regard for nearly six decades following its inception. Its 6,996 yards will surely rate it among the very shortest of 21st century US Open courses, but its ever-changing winds, elevated, contoured greens and naturally firm-and-fast conditions generally comprise a far stronger test than nearly any 7,400-yard 'Tiger-proofed' layout going. Perhaps even more impressively, being neither back-breakingly long nor stocked with the sort of all-or-nothing shots that afflict so many water-laden modern designs, Shinnecock also remains a fair and fascinating layout for everyday member play as well.

And how many US Open-ready golf courses can genuinely make that claim?

*This clubhouse view of the green at the 443-yard 9th, with the 18th green visible just beyond, provides some sense of Shinnecock's rolling, fescue-lined terrain.*

# MAIDSTONE
## East Hampton, New York

For more than half a century, the Hamptons' three great golfing clubs –
Shinnecock Hills, the National and Maidstone – were always spoken
of together, viewed on a nearly equal status as the Holy Trinity of
Long Island golf.

Though still ranked firmly among America's finest courses, Maidstone today lies somewhat in the shadows of Southampton golf, following the US Open's triumphant return to Shinnecock Hills in 1986 (see page 178) and America's newfound interest in classic course design re-elevating the National Golf Links (see page 166) to pre-eminent status as the place where the Golden Age of architecture all began.

Located some 12 miles (19 kilometres) east of its higher-profile neighbours, Maidstone occupies an enviable, if slightly disjointed, property along Long Island's southern shore, a site that includes not only a

bit of flattish inland terrain but also some splendid oceanside land that, in spots, might pass for genuine links. A low-key, family-oriented place, the club began playing golf over three purely primitive holes in 1894. The present layout did not come into being until 1922, when two-time Open champion Willie Park Jnr utilized the newly acquired seaside tract to create a diminutive but exceedingly interesting 18-hole course.

### WILLIE PARK JNR
Willie Park Jnr (along with his brother Jack) had previously been credited with helping Maidstone member Adrian Larkin build the club's initial 18-hole course back in 1899, but as Willie Park spent all

of that year in Britain his involvement could not have been more than a long-distance consultation. By the early 1920s, however, Willie Park was residing full-time in America and doing much of his best design work – that same year of 1922, for example, also seeing the completion of perhaps his best-known American project, the North Course at Olympia Fields. Alas, because of frequent design-related travel, Willie Park had never managed to see the finished Maidstone course when he suffered a nervous breakdown in summer 1923. He soon returned home to Scotland, where he died, essentially in a state of dementia, two years later.

## PLAYING OUT TO THE DUNES

Following a forthright 380-yard opener, Park's Maidstone design hits its stride at the 537-yard 2nd, a straight hole flanked closely on its left by Dunemere Road (out-of-bounds) and played to an angled green modelled loosely on that of the well-known Road hole at St Andrews (see page 40). The 408-yard 3rd is another solid test – routed dead into the prevailing wind, its green small and heavily bunkered – before the wide expanse of Hook pond is encountered and the challenge picks up in earnest.

With the pond being far too wide to drive across (particularly in 1922), the 171-yard 4th hole was created by building a mid-water tee on a narrow isthmus, which connects to the southern banks via a long bridge. This well-bunkered one-shotter is followed by the tricky 5th, a 325-yard drive-and-pitch played to a two-level green backed flush against the pond. Front-right pins (tucked beyond a small bunker) are tricky, but back placements (perched on the top tier, with water just beyond) will test the nerves of any player. Continuing southwards into the breeze, the 403-yard 6th is a foretaster for a run of holes once referred to by the celebrated golf writer Bernard Darwin as 'the finest stretch I have seen in America'.

The fun begins with the 335-yard 7th, a dogleg right carved

hill was actually built by Willie Park) before climbing to an elevated, windswept green angled left to right around a 10-foot (3-metre) deep bunker. The 382-yard 10th then backtracks westwards through the sand hills, its similarly exposed hill-top green guarded short-left by five smaller bunkers and long by a steep slope.

## RETURNING TO THE SEA

After briefly detouring inland at the 422-yard 11th and 179-yard 12th, play returns to the sea at the 490-yard 13th, an into-the-wind par five whose long, narrow green sits among the dunes, flanked left by a deep, grass-faced bunker. This is just a warm-up, however, for Maidstone's second world-renowned hole, the idyllic 148-yard 14th. For here stands a tricky little one-shotter that would be at home on even the finest British links, a tiny, windblown test that is 100 per cent carry to a green surrounded by a wasteland of rough-hewn hillocks, pot bunkers and the beach itself immediately to the rear.

The ocean has now been visited for the last time, yet a bit of excitement still remains, for the 471-yard 16th is outstanding. It is just barely a par five but one that requires a drive angled across a wide expanse of Hook pond. As this tee shot is generally played straight downwind, the golfer can achieve a huge amount here – but mishit or miscalculate and five quickly becomes the best-case scenario.

Though somewhat less challenging than in Willie Park's day, the 328-yard 17th remains a gem nonetheless. One final carry across the pond is required on the tee shot, and it allows some opportunity to drive on or very close to the green. The rub, however, is a tiny, angled putting surface that actually opens up more readily from the safer right side of the fairway and which is both tightly bunkered and closely flanked by intersecting roads (out-of-bounds) just off its back edge. With relative modesty the 378-yard 18th then closes things out, running straight to an ample, heavily bunkered green.

tightly along the edge of the pond that, despite the long carry into the prevailing headwind, is potentially drivable. Then the 151-yard 8th runs directly into the oceanside dunes, its small, tightly bunkered green somewhat hidden by a huge sand hill cutting in from the right. Recalling the great blind par threes of the UK, it is a throwback in the truest sense.

Impressive as the 8th may be, however, it is the 402-yard 9th that many consider Maidstone's best. Running nearly parallel to the beach, its fairway slithers between large dunes (the massive left-side

## WILLIE PARK'S LEGACY

Though notably short in this era of enhanced equipment, Maidstone relies on the ever-present elements, deep bunkers and thicket-strewn scrub as well as the waters of Hook pond to remain a challenging and distinctively charming course. Olympia Fields has hosted four Major championships, yet Maidstone with its windswept landscape reminiscent of the UK is, for Willie Park Jnr at least, a most appropriate legacy.

# MAIDSTONE GOLF CLUB –
## East Hampton, New York
Willie Park Jnr, 1922

### CARD OF THE COURSE

| HOLE | YARDS | PAR | HOLE | YARDS | PAR |
|------|-------|-----|------|-------|-----|
| 1. | 380 | 4 | 10. | 382 | 4 |
| 2. | 537 | 5 | 11. | 422 | 4 |
| 3. | 408 | 4 | 12. | 179 | 3 |
| 4. | 171 | 3 | 13. | 490 | 5 |
| 5. | 325 | 4 | 14. | 148 | 3 |
| 6. | 403 | 4 | 15. | 493 | 5 |
| 7. | 335 | 4 | 16. | 471 | 5 |
| 8. | 151 | 3 | 17. | 328 | 4 |
| 9. | 402 | 4 | 18. | 378 | 4 |
| OUT | 3,112 | 35 | IN | 3,291 | 37 |
| | | | TOTAL | 6,403 | 72 |

# THE COUNTRY CLUB
## Brookline, Massachusetts

Though The Country Club dates back to 1892, golf was not introduced until the following year, when it was played over a rudimentary six holes. These were extended to nine by newly arrived professional Willie Campbell in 1894. That December, the club made history as one of the five founding members of the United States Golf Association (USGA).

The concept of the modern country club – the full-service, family-oriented facility featuring recreational aspects beyond golf – is largely an American one, its standing as a mark of suburban affluence wielding more impact in the USA than anywhere else. As such, nearly 6,000 American courses use the phrase 'Country Club' within their names. This is a large enough number to give the notion of any single one calling itself *The* Country Club an apparent touch of arrogance nonpareil. The club in question happens to be The Country Club, situated in the prosperous Boston suburb of Brookline and, not coincidentally, the very first of its type in the entire US – a circumstance under which, admittedly, the name rings more original than haughty.

By the turn of the 20th century, The Country Club golf course had 18 holes (mostly Willie Campbell's), and these ranked among the best of a rather primitive American crop. The club then hosted local hero Francis Ouimet's seminal play-off victory over England's Harry Vardon and Ted Ray at the 1913 US Open, before undergoing a substantial renovation (including the addition of a third nine) by another area native, William Flynn, in 1927.

It is essentially this 1927 configuration (with a dash of contemporary paint from Rees Jones) that the members still play today. When US Opens and Ryder Cups come to The Country Club, the par-four 11th is actually a composite hole, cobbled together in a temporary manner from a pair of shorter holes on the club's third nine. Indeed, this entire tournament course is itself a composite, mixing holes from all three nines to create an otherwise-nonexistent championship 18.

### A TIMELESS CHAMPIONSHIP TEST

To suggest that a course that retains several 19th-century holes is old-fashioned hardly passes for insight, but The Country Club serves as a particularly illuminating example of early New England architecture, its tiny greens, rock outcroppings and frequent blind shots beautifully illustrating the natural design style of a less mechanized time. Occupying land where the club's ancient racetrack once sat, the opening two holes are reasonably flat before the topography asserts itself at the 451-yard 3rd, where drives positioned close to a left-side fairway bunker leave an open approach while those played from the right will be blind – unless the shot is long enough to carry an impeding clump of ledge rock, after which only a simple wedge shot remains. The 335-yard 4th is drivable, but its miniscule putting surface is flanked by six bunkers, while the 7th, a 197-yarder to an elevated, wonderfully contoured green, is the only surviving hole from Willie Campbell's 1894 nine.

In the eyes of many, the composite course's best hole is the 513-yard 9th, known colloquially as the Himalayas for its rough-and-tumble terrain. From an

elevated tee, the drive is played to a twisting fairway pinched on the right by another encroaching rock formation. To have a chance to reach the green in two, a player must either hit the ball between the rocks and thick left-side woods or attempt to carry the rocks entirely. Either method, if brought off successfully, leaves the golfer with an uphill long-iron to a notably small green behind a series of five bunkers stepped into the hillside.

## TESTING PAR FOURS

The composite course's back nine begins with a run of four consecutive long and difficult two-shotters. Most notable is the 11th, a 450-yarder requiring a drawn tee shot to a tightly wooded fairway, then a long approach over a pond to a green small enough to serve normally as the putting surface of a 108-yard par three. If possible, the 12th (which regularly plays as the Primrose Course's par-five 8th) is even more difficult, stretching to 486 yards, the latter third of which is elevated. Here the green is tucked away to the left, leaving any tee ball not placed down the right side of the fairway with an approach at least partially obscured by trees. The 436-yard 13th is also not easy, with a right-side lake and the possibility of an awkward downhill lie leading many to lay up with an iron or fairway metal off the tee.

The horseshoe-shaped mounding that guards the left side of the fairway at the 534-yard 14th is vintage throwback material, and the hole itself – reachable in two, but featuring an elevated, steeply pitched green – is another of admirable quality. From here on, however, The Country Club's final holes are more functionally solid than truly excellent. The 15th, at 432 yards, is a road-crossed two-shotter squeezed between the clubhouse complex and the northern property boundary, the 186-yard 16th a fairly basic par three.

The 17th, though only 370 yards, has influenced three US Opens. It was here that Harry Vardon famously drove into a left-side fairway bunker, ending his hopes of capturing the 1913 US Open play-off, and where Justin Leonard's clinching 45-foot (14-metre) putt sparked the over-the-top celebration that marked America's remarkable come-from-behind victory in the 1999 Ryder Cup.

The 436-yard 18th has also seen its share of drama, such as Curtis Strange's fine up-and-down from the front bunker to force a Monday play-off with Nick Faldo at the 1988 US Open, a contest Strange ultimately won by four shots. This particular bunker seems a perfect way to finish, too, for its wall-to-wall, essentially penal nature represents one final engaging reminder of the architecture of a bygone day, an era from which The Country Club remains a shining, and still highly challenging, standard-bearer.

# THE COUNTRY CLUB –
## Brookline, Massachusetts

Willie Campbell, 1894 and William Flynn, 1927
Major events: US Open 1913, 1963, 1988; US Amateur 1910, 1922, 1934, 1935, 1957, 1982; US Women's Amateur 1902, 1941, 1995; Ryder Cup 1999; Walker Cup 1932, 1973

*The 513-yard 9th, where the successful tee shot avoids woods on the left and rock outcropping on the right, setting up a long approach to an elevated, sand-fronted green.*

### CARD OF THE COURSE

| HOLE | YARDS | PAR | HOLE | YARDS | PAR |
|------|-------|-----|------|-------|-----|
| 1. | 450 | 4 | 10. | 447 | 4 |
| 2. | 190 | 3 | 11. | 450 | 4 |
| 3. | 451 | 4 | 12. | 486 | 4 |
| 4. | 335 | 4 | 13. | 436 | 4 |
| 5. | 432 | 4 | 14. | 534 | 5 |
| 6. | 310 | 4 | 15. | 432 | 4 |
| 7. | 197 | 3 | 16. | 186 | 3 |
| 8. | 378 | 4 | 17. | 370 | 4 |
| 9. | 513 | 5 | 18. | 436 | 4 |
| **OUT** | **3,256** | **35** | **IN** | **3,777** | **36** |
| | | | **TOTAL** | **7,033** | **71** |

# PINE VALLEY
## Clementon, New Jersey

Widely ranked the finest course in the world for as long as such ratings have been in vogue, Pine Valley was the brainchild of one man, a Philadelphia hotel owner and fine amateur golfer named George Crump.

**PINE VALLEY GOLF CLUB –**
**Clementon, New Jersey**
George Crump, 1915
Major events: Walker Cup 1936, 1985

CARD OF THE COURSE

| HOLE | YARDS | PAR | HOLE | YARDS | PAR |
|---|---|---|---|---|---|
| 1. | 421 | 4 | 10. | 161 | 3 |
| 2. | 368 | 4 | 11. | 397 | 4 |
| 3. | 198 | 3 | 12. | 337 | 4 |
| 4. | 451 | 4 | 13. | 486 | 4 |
| 5. | 235 | 3 | 14. | 220 | 3 |
| 6. | 387 | 4 | 15. | 615 | 5 |
| 7. | 636 | 5 | 16. | 475 | 4 |
| 8. | 326 | 4 | 17. | 345 | 4 |
| 9. | 459 | 4 | 18. | 483 | 4 |
| **OUT** | **3,481** | **35** | **IN** | **3,519** | **35** |
| | | | **TOTAL** | **7,000** | **70** |

Yet while Crump located this matchless site among the southern New Jersey pine trees, and bore primary responsibility for its design, he also called upon the services of a number of distinguished Golden Age architects to aid in its planning.

### AN ARCHITECTURAL DREAM TEAM

Initially there was Walter Travis, America's first genuinely great player (and later a prolific course designer) from whom Crump solicited suggestions. Far more involved was the eminent British architect Harry Colt, who, according to four-time US Amateur champion and Crump friend Jerome Travers, was engaged 'to come to this country to plan a course of surpassing merit and extraordinary beauty'. Colt, Travers explained, 'pitched his tent in the woods and camped there for a week or more. He emerged from his hibernation enthralled.' This enthralment led to the production of an 18-hole plan, aspects of which – but only aspects – appeared in Crump's eventual finished product.

When it was time to build, George Crump himself directed Pine Valley's construction in a painstak-

ing, hole-by-hole process. For five years he lived as a semirecluse, residing in the woods with only his hunting dogs, and on his untimely death in 1918 four holes (today's 12th–15th) remained unfinished. In duc course Crump's plans for this final quartet were brought to life by Merion-designer Hugh Wilson and his brother Alan, apparently with suggestions from Colt's esteemed partner Charles Alison. Alison also provided additional renovative ideas to the finished course, while other noted designers to offer their services included William Flynn (early construction work and minor 1929 renovations), George Thomas (in support of William Flynn), Perry Maxwell (several green rebuilds/alterations) and A.W. Tillinghast (sundry thoughts, little documented).

## A PRIVATE RETREAT

Pine Valley is situated on land described by Jerome Travers as 'neither flat nor hilly', and resembling 'a desert into which have been dropped clusters of beautiful trees'. But over the decades those 'clusters' have certainly grown, for today's layout features none of the open vistas of yesteryear, with each hole now hemmed in almost entirely by woods. Still, the spaciousness of the property is impressive. Crump's initial plans utilized less than 200 acres (81 hectares) in total, while subsequent land purchases have given the club more than 600 acres (250 hectares), effectively creating a vast wooded sanctuary, delightfully immune to whatever growth takes place beyond it.

The course itself has long been viewed as an unbeatable monster, the world's hardest inland layout, and stories of astonishingly high scores (such as Bobby Jones's 88 on his first visit) abound. But while it certainly is difficult – as a USGA slope of 155 on a 7,000-yard layout conclusively attests – assertions that it is a purely penal house of horrors miss the mark widely. True, its fairways must be hit, because there is no rough in the accepted sense, just trees, scrub and huge stretches of wild, unmaintained sand.

Most of Pine Valley's fairways are generously wide, its greens usually present ample targets, and with six par fours under 400 yards (365 metres), it is hardly backbreaking. There are, perhaps, more death-or-glory shots here than on any other golf course, and with little in the way of breathers the examination is relentless from first drive to final putt. But Pine Valley also presents numerous strategic challenges within its rigours; indeed, the 6th, 7th, 13th and 16th are highly thought-provoking tests, with several additional holes being of nearly a comparable standard.

The 421-yard 1st, a sharp dogleg right, is a fairly stout opener, but the challenge really picks up at the 368-yard 2nd – one of golf's epic drive-and-pitches. Here the golfer must carry 150 yards (137 metres) of sandy scrub just to reach a fairway that, though only 30 yards (27 metres) wide, really should not be missed with a long-iron or fairway metal. What remains, however, is frightening: little more than a wedge shot, but one to be played sharply uphill to a massive green behind a steep wall of sand and deep grass.

## MEMORABLE PAR THREES

Like most elite courses, Pine Valley features an exceptional set of par threes, beginning with the downhill 198-yard 3rd, whose heavily contoured, sand-ringed putting surface offers several very demanding pin placements, particularly back-left and front-right. Following the 451-yard 4th (a long but not overly difficult two-shotter) comes the epic 5th, a 235-yarder of worldwide renown. George Crump's initial intent was to make this a relatively short hole played to a waterside green, but this plan was scrapped when Harry Colt suggested shelving the putting surface upon a distant hillside. The result was an uphill hole of almost singular difficulty, with a long carry required to reach a narrow ribbon of fairway or, ideally, the smallish, back-to-front sloping green. Balls pulled left find sand or trees, but this is the preferred side to miss on, for the banking immediately right of the green plunges into a dangerous wilderness from which Gene Littler memorably made an eight during the inaugural Shell's Wonderful World of Golf match with Byron Nelson in 1962.

Where the 5th is unquestionably penal, the 387-yard 6th is the polar opposite. Doglegging sharply right around a scrub-filled valley, it dares the player to make the 230-yard (210-metre) carry across the corner, because this leaves but a short, unimpeded pitch straight up the body of the green. The farther the drive moves leftwards, however, the more a large greenside bunker begins to impede play.

### 'HELL'S HALF ACRE'
The recently lengthened 636-yard 7th has long been known as 'Hell's half acre' in celebration of the 100-yard (90-metre) long sandy waste area that crosses the fairway some 330 yards (300 metres) off the tee. A.W. Tillinghast would later claim credit for this hazard, and he utilized its fundamental strategy – that a drive off the fairway might require the second shot to be laid up short of the sand – at such classic facilities as Baltusrol, the Baltimore Country Club and Ridgewood. Tillinghast's holes, however, did not replicate the greenside terrors of Crump's legendary original, for here the hole culminates in a putting surface that is nearly an island within even more sandy waste.

Things get shorter, but in no way easier, at the 326-yard 8th – a remarkably dangerous hole that legendary British golf writer Bernard Darwin once observed places 'no limit on the player's liabilities'. Indeed, a tougher drive-and-pitch would be difficult to imagine, though the nature of the challenge is simple and clearly defined. Following a relatively unobscured tee ball, the golfer is expected to float a wedge softly onto an exceedingly narrow green, the edges of which fall sharply away into some of Pine Valley's deepest bunkers. Suffice to say that many a player (including Bernard Darwin), perhaps salivating at what appears on the scorecard to be a breather, have seen their rounds irreparably damaged here.

The 459-yard 9th offers dual greens – one higher, one lower – while the 161-yard 10th is virtually surrounded by sand, though its primary hazard, a tiny, especially nasty pot bunker with an unprintable nickname, actually evolved naturally and was not a part of George Crump's original design. Two shortish two-shotters follow – the 11th and 12th (the latter made interesting by an extremely late 90-degree turn to the left) – and then it is on to a finishing run that fully lives up to the visitor's grandest expectations.

### A MODERN EXPANSION
One of the game's celebrated par fours, the 486-yard 13th, has as its central feature a green angled off to the left, behind a large patch of scrub and slightly encroaching trees. The challenge has long been to hit the uphill tee shot far enough to make attempting this hazardous crossing viable, the alternative being a safe lay-up to the right with hopes of getting up and down for four. Modern equipment had for several years affected that

# THE PENAL SHORT PAR FOUR
## 8th hole

*The strategic short par four is in many ways golf's most captivating hole. The abbreviated nature of the approach allows designers to build smaller putting surfaces and provide the sort of dangerous hazarding that triggers a player's adrenaline – the entire package being further amplified by the prospect of the longer hitter perhaps attempting to drive the green.*

*At Pine Valley the 8th can slightly alter a golfer's course game plan, because driving to what amounts to an island green requires immense luck while there are few strategic risks in hitting the generous fairway. The challenge, very definitely of the make-or-break variety, is to hit the purest pitch the golfer can muster – and not to miss! Particularly with the speed and firmness of greens achieved through modern agronomical practices, this must be among the scariest wedge shots in golf, for it leaves wide open the prospect of finding the gravely deep bunkering on either side and then having severe problems in extricating the ball. The great Bernard Darwin met just such a fate on his first visit, in 1922, later memorably concluding that: 'It is all very well to punish a bad stroke, but the right of eternal punishment should be reserved for a higher tribunal than a green committee.'*

*The 483-yard 18th, a mammoth finisher that requires an intimidating carry over typical Pine Valley terrain off the tee, then a long approach over both a pond and fronting bunkers.*

balance substantially, but with the recent addition of 40 extra yards (36 metres) the hole's fundamental shot values have been restored to a considerable extent.

Also newly lengthened is the 220-yard 14th – a hole of real beauty played downhill and across a lake to a flattish, sand-ringed green. This was one place where considerable earth was moved during construction, for the green site actually began life as an island, which Crump expanded (to house the 15th tee) and connected to land. More visually intimidating during those early treeless days, the 14th green is today no less difficult but considerably more attractive.

The 615-yard 15th is an obvious brute, beginning with a 115-yard (105-metre) forced carry over the lake, then sweeping uphill to a distant green. Central to this hole's challenge is the fact that it narrows progressively as it goes, calling into question the value of blasting a second close when the lay-up area some 125 yards (114 metres) short is infinitely safer.

Even greater thought is required on the 475-yard 16th, its 85-yard (78-metre) wide fairway angling left-to-right beyond a vast expanse of sand. Up ahead, the

huge green has water on its right side, with trees and sand creeping in from the left. What this all adds up to is a wonderfully strategic hole. Those golfers capable of the longest sand carry are left with a straight-on approach shot to an open green, while those opting for the shorter left-side route face an ever more difficult approach angle, with water looming progressively larger in the background the farther left the golfer has driven.

The 345-yard drive-and-pitch 17th is today seldom rated among Pine Valley's best, though in its early years, when an elevated alternate fairway offered a better view of the tiny green, it was surely among the more strategic. Rather less so is the 483-yard 18th, a punishing par four where the recent addition of 60 yards (55 metres) has reintroduced much of the challenge that once defined this impressive finisher. Following a drive to a fairway guarded left by woods and right by sandy waste, the real highlight is the approach shot, a mid- to long-iron played over a pond and a cluster of hillside bunkers to a huge, slightly elevated final green. It is a suitably brawny close to perhaps golf's grandest round.

## INTIMIDATING AND REVERED

Though Pine Valley has expanded more than 550 yards (500 metres) since the early years, and narrowed by extensive tree growth, it has always been intimidating. Indeed, typical is the story of seven-time Philadelphia Amateur champion Woody Platt who, playing a friendly round during the 1940s, birdied the 1st, holed out a 7-iron to eagle the 2nd, made a hole-in-one at the 3rd, and curled home a long putt for birdie at the 4th. Standing an inconceivable six under par after four holes, Platt adjourned to the adjacent clubhouse for some liquid reinforcement before facing the fabled par-three 5th – and he never re-emerged.

Ultimately, Pine Valley was perhaps best described by the driving force behind the first *World Atlas of Golf*, Pat Ward-Thomas, who observed that: 'No course presents more vividly and more severely the basic challenge of golf – the balance between fear and courage. Nowhere is the brave and beautiful shot rewarded so splendidly in comparison to the weak and faltering; nowhere is there such a terrible contrast between reward and punishment, and yet, withal, the examination is just.'

# MERION
## Ardmore, Pennsylvania

There has long been a certain cachet associated with golf's true amateur course designers, men who, with little prior background, ventured into the field to build just a handful of courses – in some cases, perhaps even just one – such as Hugh Wilson at Merion.

Theoretically, with a limited body of work, the concepts of amateur course designers are fresh, their efforts focused exclusively on the legacy-building task at hand. There are no issues of being spread too thinly or, when stuck for an idea, discreetly recycling a previous entry from some grand catalogue of past work. Evidence in support of this theory is plentiful: George Crump exemplified it at Pine Valley (see page 186), as did Henry and William Fownes at Oakmont (see page 194) and, to a large extent, Bobby Jones at Augusta National (see page 206) and Jack Neville and Douglas Grant at Pebble Beach (see page 244). And to this stellar list must be added perhaps the pre-eminent example of first-time golf design greatness: Hugh Wilson at Merion.

### STUDYING ABROAD

Strictly speaking, the evidence suggests that had he not died tragically young, Hugh Wilson at least intended to pursue a full-fledged architectural career, but he is only known to have worked on four courses, and his entrance into the field was more a matter of being drafted than a studied career choice. Indeed, as a former Princeton golf team captain and a good (but not great) Philadelphia-area amateur, he was appointed in 1910 to lead the then Merion Cricket Club's committee in charge of building a new golf course. To prepare, the committee sent Wilson on an extended trip to the British Isles to study the world's great layouts, stopping en route in Southampton, New York to meet America's course design pioneer, Charles Blair Macdonald. Wilson ultimately returned to Philadelphia armed with piles of notes and sketches of the UK's finest holes and, with apparent continuing advice from Macdonald, went to work.

The site of Merion's East Course was a none-too-spacious L-shaped tract that held the remains of two farms, as well as an abandoned rock quarry. Working with a construction crew that included future Golden Age designer William Flynn, Flynn's eventual partner Howard Toomey and future long-serving Merion greenkeeper Joe Valentine, Wilson formulated a 6,235-yard layout that essentially laid the foundation for that in play today. Significant change would first come in 1922 when the 10th, 11th and 12th holes were reconfigured to avoid

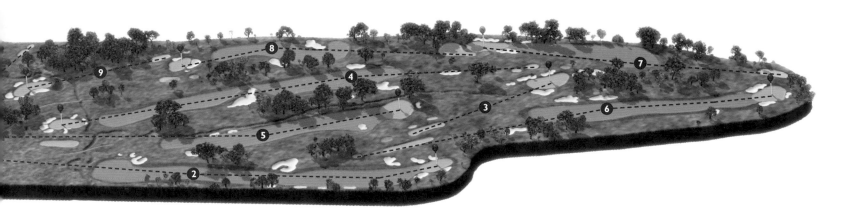

# MERION GOLF CLUB
## (EAST COURSE) –
## Ardmore, Pennsylvania

Hugh Wilson, 1912
Major events: US Open 1934, 1950, 1971,
1981; US Amateur 1916, 1924, 1930, 1966,
1989, 2005; US Women's Amateur 1904, 1909,
1926, 1949; Curtis Cup 1954

CARD OF THE COURSE

| HOLE | YARDS | PAR | HOLE | YARDS | PAR |
|------|-------|-----|------|-------|-----|
| 1. | 350 | 4 | 10. | 325 | 4 |
| 2 | 556 | 5 | 11. | 367 | 4 |
| 3. | 219 | 3 | 12. | 403 | 4 |
| 4. | 597 | 5 | 13. | 120 | 3 |
| 5. | 504 | 4 | 14. | 438 | 4 |
| 6. | 487 | 4 | 15. | 411 | 4 |
| 7. | 345 | 4 | 16. | 430 | 4 |
| 8. | 359 | 4 | 17. | 246 | 3 |
| 9. | 206 | 3 | 18. | 505 | 4 |
| **OUT** | **3,623** | **36** | **IN** | **3,245** | **34** |
| | | | **TOTAL** | **6,868** | **70** |

crossing Ardmore Avenue, a quiet country road at the time of the course's inception but fast becoming a popular thoroughfare in the postwar era. Wilson planned to upgrade things further by performing a 1925 overhaul of the course's bunkering, but died of pneumonia before its completion.

The project was carried on by William Flynn, Howard Toomey and Joe Valentine, who famously spread bedsheets in the locations of proposed hazards so as to gauge their visual impact before building them, a technique that resulted in bunkers widely rated among the game's most strategic and attractive. Finally, in 1929, the 1st fairway was moved farther away from the adjacent Golf House Road and that, except for some minor nips and tucks and a bit of recent lengthening, finalized the Merion layout, which for more than three-quarters of a century has remained universally hailed among the world's elite.

## RICH CHAMPIONSHIP HISTORY

Following Charles Blair Macdonald's National Golf Links (see page 166), which opened in 1911, Merion was widely considered America's second truly modern course and it quickly established itself among the nation's finest tournament venues, eventually hosting two of the defining events in golf history. In 1930, the club witnessed Bobby Jones's peerless victory at the US Amateur. Exactly 20 years later it was Ben Hogan's turn to achieve immortality, returning from his near-fatal car accident to capture his second US Open, in an 18-hole play-off with Lloyd Mangrum and George Fazio. And if these epic events did not for ever secure Merion's competitive legacy, other landmark moments among the club's 14 national championships have included Chick Evans becoming the first man to claim both the US Open and Amateur in the same season on winning the latter here in 1916, Bobby Jones winning his first Amateur title in 1924, and Lee Trevino memorably tossing a rubber snake at Jack Nicklaus before defeating him in a play-off for the 1971 US Open.

## A FAST GETAWAY

The course itself begins in measured but eminently stylish fashion, for the 350-yard 1st doglegs gently right, its shortish boundaries flanked by no fewer than 13 bunkers. With the fairway slightly elevated and the green of fairly good size, three is definitely a possibility here.

With the entire right side of its narrow fairway flanked by the out-of-bounds of Ardmore Avenue the 556-yard 2nd is somewhat stiffer, while the 219-yard 3rd plays slightly uphill and across a swale, its elevated, left-to-right sloping green protected by a particularly dangerous bunker short-right. The 597-yard brook-fronted 4th may occasionally be reachable in two nowadays, and certainly provides what amounts to a third birdie opportunity in the first four holes.

## THE HEROIC FIFTH

Strokes gained early may well be repaid at the 5th, Merion's number one handicap hole and one of the finest par fours in America. Featuring a new US Open-friendly tee measuring 504 yards, it is a wonderfully natural test with fairway and green sloping noticeably towards the stream that flanks the hole's entire left side. The challenge here is to aim the driver as close to this lateral hazard as possible, for tee shots bailed out to the right leave a long-iron second from a hook lie to a green running towards the immediately adjacent stream – a tricky shot made even more so by a short-right bunker that visually impedes the line.

Driving at the 487-yard 6th is similarly thought-provoking. The ideal angle of approach lies along the fairway's right side, but to reach it requires a faded tee shot skirting dangerously close to out-of-bounds. The journey back then begins with a pair of short par fours, the 345-yard 7th (where right-side out-of-bounds again guards the ideal driving area) and 359-yard 8th, a straight test made appealing by staggered fairway bunkering and a heavily contoured green.

Ending the front nine – though not quite back at the clubhouse – is the 206-yard 9th, a slightly downhill par three played to a large, right-to-left curving green. While the putting surface is behind a pond and flanked well right by a creek, a greater challenge lies in the five bunkers that guard its sides and rear, leaving little room for misses. There is also a degree of variance in a pair of alternate tees, with the newer left-side option creating a tougher angle, particularly for back-left pins.

## A PROCESSION OF FAMOUS HOLES

Played from an elevated, wooded tee, the 325-yard, dogleg-left 10th ranks among America's better drive-and-pitch par fours, though seldom will anyone attempt to drive its narrow, tightly bunkered green during Major championship play. A long-iron is the preferred option here and it must not be lost left, lest the golfer be stuck with a three-quarter shot from deep rough to what will have become a very shallow target indeed.

Overshadowing the 10th, and nearly everything else at Merion, is the renowned 367-yard 11th, another short two-shotter, this one played to a pear-shaped green wedged into the semicircular curve of Cobb's Creek. With the creek also crossing the fairway at approximately 275 yards (250 metres), the tee shot must be a lay-up – disappointing in a strategic sense, yet also a guarantee that today's players face virtually

*The 219-yard 3rd, one of the game's great short par threes, highlighted by its natural amphitheatre, a tiny green, five surrounding bunkers and, most memorably, the club's trademark dune grass.*

## THE UNIQUELY HISTORIC 11TH
### Where Jones achieved immortality

*The 367-yard 11th has been widely trumpeted as one of America's great par fours, its shortish approach being played to a green whose right half juts dangerously outwards into Cobb's Creek. It is a wonderful hole certainly, requiring great touch and more than a dash of daring, yet its reputation has also been enhanced by its rather fortuitous place in history. For it was here, on 27 September 1930, that Bobby Jones closed out Gene Homans 8-and-7 to win the US Amateur, the final leg of his never-to-be-equalled grand slam.*

*But the 11th is also a place where fortunes have been lost, particularly for the great Gene Sarazen who arrived with a one-shot lead in the final round of the 1934 US Open, attempted to play safe with an iron off the tee and promptly made seven. A different sort of fame was achieved during the third round of that same Open, when a wayward approach by the diminutive Scot Bobby Cruickshank hit a rock, bounded out of the creek and onto the green. Cruickshank playfully tossed his iron into the air in thanks – only to be knocked unconscious when it landed on his head.*

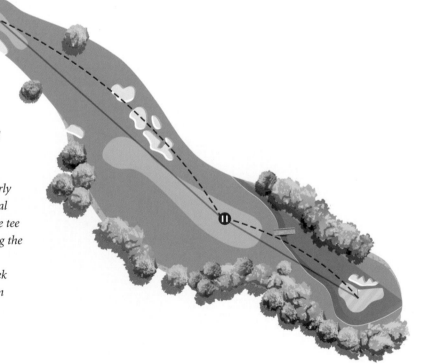

the same death-defying pitch that challenged Bobby Jones, Ben Hogan and Jack Nicklaus.

With the other par threes all measuring at least 200 yards (183 metres), the 120-yard 13th is by far Merion's shortest hole, but its small, bowl-like putting surface is ringed by five bunkers, the largest of which, sitting directly front and centre, is dotted by clumps of dune grass. Situated in a natural amphitheatre beneath the south end of the clubhouse and flanked several feet right by Cobb's Creek, this has long ranked among America's vaunted short par threes.

Though slightly less memorable, the 438-yard 14th and 411 yard 15th – both featuring left-side out-of-bounds in the form of Golf House Road – are eminently solid holes; they simply pale in compasrison with the epic finishers to follow.

## THE QUARRY HOLES

The 430-yard 16th is an impressive two-shotter that begins with a semiblind, downhill tee shot. Today most who find the fairway will be playing their second across the quarry to a two-tiered green sloping heavily from back to front, but shorter hitters may still consider the once-common option of laying up to a patch of right-side fairway, hoping to pitch over sand to save their fours. Notably, the 16th is the only hole among the final five not to be lengthened substantially in the new millennium, because its tee already sits against the club's northern boundary.

Less confined, however, is the par-three 17th, recently stretched into a 246-yard monster playing from an elevated tee back across the quarry. While the carry is significant, better players will be bothered less by the quarry itself and more by the green complex, for the putting surface is narrow and sloping left to right, and is flanked on three sides by sand. The exception is in front, where a hollow that Hugh Wilson patterned after the Valley of Sin on the 18th at St Andrews (see page 40) tends to lure balls coming up even slightly short.

And then there is the 505-yard, par-four 18th, a hole immortalized by perhaps the most recognized image in American golf, Hy Peskin's photograph of

*The golfer's first encounter with the quarry: the approach to the 430-yard 16th. For the faint of heart, a narrow lay-up area exists well out to the right.*

Ben Hogan's 1-iron approach to the 72nd hole of the 1950 US Open. The fun begins here with a 250-yard (230-metre) carry over the quarry – this just to reach a narrowing fairway with trees and out-of-bounds flanking its left side. The second shot, generally played off a downhill lie, then requires a long-iron to a shallow green positioned atop an upslope, and guarded both right and left by sand.

Measuring only 6,482 yards during the 1981 US Open, Merion was for many years viewed as notably short by postwar championship standards. All of that has changed, however, as its recent lengthening has stretched it beyond 6,800 yards (6,220 metres), with holes such as the 3rd, 5th, 6th, 14th and 15th all being extended by at least 40 yards (36 metres). Yet despite its added length, Merion remains one of America's most traditional courses, with numerous world-class holes, the occasional dune-grass-laced bunker and virtually no strategic alterations since the 1930s. Surrounded by stately old homes and nearby Haverford College, and still abutted by the railway line that long ago helped make the site so logistically desirable, it exudes a timeless feel that is further accentuated by the club's long-time trademark: wicker baskets atop the flagsticks.

## THE WEST COURSE

Merion also possesses a second Hugh Wilson-designed course, the 5,989-yard West, situated on a separate site several blocks away. Too short for modern championship play, the West still holds a place in golfing history, for it was here, in qualifying for the 1916 US Amateur, that a 14-year-old Bobby Jones first announced his presence when his surprising 74 actually led after the opening medal round. Despite a subsequent 89 on the East, Jones still qualified, ultimately losing in the quarter finals to defending champion Robert Gardner, but not before marking himself, with an exclamation point, as a young man who would be heard from in the future.

After nearly a century, Merion's East Course still has few equals as a thinking man's layout, giving timeless relevance to the words of golf champion Tommy Armour, who long ago observed: 'You must play [Merion] with two heads – the one on your shoulders and the one on your club. If I had just two weeks to live, I'd want to go to Merion and play there everyday.' And unlike so many heavily altered Golden Age courses, at Merion Tommy Armour would still very much recognize the course he would find there today.

# OAKMONT
## Oakmont, Pennsylvania

It is not entirely certain when it was decided that Oakmont should be the toughest golf course in America, nor whether such a decision was made by the club's founder, Henry Fownes, or the man who played the largest role in shaping its present layout, Henry's son, William.

As generations of golfers, both professional and amateur, can attest, if Oakmont is not *the* toughest American golf course, it surely doesn't miss by much. It was the brainchild of Henry Fownes, a steel industry tycoon in turn-of-the-century Pittsburgh. An avid and capable golfer, Fownes decided in 1903 to build his own club. Purchasing 200 acres (81 hectares) of rolling, mostly open farmland on the south side of the Allegheny river, he staked out his course that autumn, opening it for play in spring 1904. This initial layout was sparsely bunkered and not, by most accounts, epically difficult, but cognizant of the unprecedented liveliness of the new Haskell ball, Fownes stretched the course beyond 6,400 yards (5,850 metres), making this home-made test among the longer courses of the day. Relying primarily on the natural twists and turns of the land for playing interest, this initial track was undeniably successful in at least one regard: with minor exceptions, its fundamental routing has gone nearly unchanged for more than a century.

### FATHER-AND-SON TEAM

Though Henry was no slouch, his son William's status in early 20th-century golf was really quite significant: for he was the 1910 US Amateur champion, twice a Walker Cup participant (serving as a playing captain in 1922) and president of the USGA in 1926 and '27. Such honours obviously added credibility to his inheritance of the Oakmont mantle, and while some question remains as to precisely who was in charge of the course design it is generally believed that William, in his long-term run as the club's second major-domo, was the man most responsible for the golf course's eventual metamorphosis into a man-eating monster.

Engaging the help of the club's long-serving professional/superintendent Emil 'Dutch' Loeffler, systematic revamping by William Fownes began in the early 1920s and included the addition of numerous bunkers, the rebuilding of greens, some inevitable lengthening and the construction of an entirely new 16th hole. It was also during this period that the club enhanced its reputation for being hell-bent on difficulty by beginning a four-decade practice of furrowing its bunkers – that is, utilizing a specially designed rake to create golf-ball-wide grooves in the sand that, when drawn at 90-degree angles to the target line, made anything more than a rudimentary blast virtually impossible. 'You could have combed North Africa with it,' the three-times Masters champion Jimmy Demaret once quipped regarding the slightly gimmicky rake, 'and Rommel wouldn't have gotten past Casablanca.'

### REGULAR HOST TO MAJORS

A course of such renowned difficulty appeals to the USGA and the 2007 US Open represented an unprecedented eighth time that the American championship has visited Oakmont. The club has

### OAKMONT COUNTRY CLUB – Oakmont, Pennsylvania

Henry Fownes and William Fownes, 1904
Major events: US Open 1927, 1935, 1953, 1962, 1973, 1983, 1994, 2007; US Amateur 1919, 1925, 1938, 1969, 2003; USPGA 1922, 1951, 1978; US Women's Open 1992; Curtis Cup 1986

CARD OF THE COURSE

| HOLE | YARDS | PAR | HOLE | YARDS | PAR |
|------|-------|-----|------|-------|-----|
| 1. | 482 | 4 | 10. | 435 | 4 |
| 2. | 341 | 4 | 11. | 379 | 4 |
| 3. | 428 | 4 | 12. | 667 | 5 |
| 4. | 609 | 5 | 13. | 183 | 3 |
| 5. | 382 | 4 | 14. | 358 | 4 |
| 6. | 194 | 3 | 15. | 500 | 4 |
| 7. | 479 | 4 | 16. | 231 | 3 |
| 8. | 288 | 3 | 17. | 313 | 4 |
| 9. | 477 | 4 | 18. | 484 | 4 |
| **OUT** | **3,680** | **35** | **IN** | **3,550** | **35** |
| | | | **TOTAL** | **7,230** | **70** |

further hosted five US Amateurs, three PGA championships and a US Women's Open, but the numbers themselves pale in comparison to the list of players who have triumphed here.

Oakmont's Open winners have included Tommy Armour (who scored a rare birdie at the 72nd to force a play-off with Lighthorse Harry Cooper in 1927), Ben Hogan (who claimed his fourth Open here in 1953), Jack Nicklaus (who assumed Arnold Palmer's position as the world's best golfer in a 1962 play-off) as well as Johnny Miller (1973), Larry Nelson (1983) and Ernie Els (1994). Further, the closing 63 that clinched Johnny Miller's 1973 title may well be the greatest round of tournament golf ever played. Even a local professional, Sam Parks, gained a bit of historical prominence for his 11-over-par 299 in 1935, which remains the highest US Open-winning aggregate of the post-hickory era – that is, since steel shafts replaced wooden ones during the 1930s. Among other tournaments, Bobby Jones claimed his second US Amateur title in 1925, and Gene Sarazen and Sam Snead both won PGA championships, in 1922 and 1951 respectively.

## DISTINCTIVE GREENS

The present Oakmont layout is greatly expanded from Henry Fownes's day, its 7,230-yard US Open set-up representing an especially long test with par reduced to 70. There is, however, much more to consider here than just overall distance. Despite featuring five Open par fours in excess of 460 yards (420 metres), of far greater concern to the professional are the layout's more than 175 bunkers as well as some of the nastiest rough in American golf.

Oakmont's true claim to fame lies in its greens, a set of utterly special putting surfaces unmatched anywhere in the world for their mix of size, firmness, speed and, above all, contour. Indeed, at the 2007 US Open, stimpmeter readings were drawn from only 12 of the 18 putting surfaces, because the other six lacked any areas flat enough for the ball to stop rolling. At Oakmont, then, hitting greens in regulation is not necessarily a predictor even of making pars, never mind birdies.

But much like that other bell-wether of American golfing toughness, Pine Valley (see page 186), Oakmont's reputation for sheer, unadulterated difficulty largely obscures the fact that it also offers a number of strategically excellent holes. This may not be immediately apparent to the golfer facing one of the game's hardest openers – a 482-yard par four played

# NO PUSHOVER UNDER PRESSURE
The 17th hole

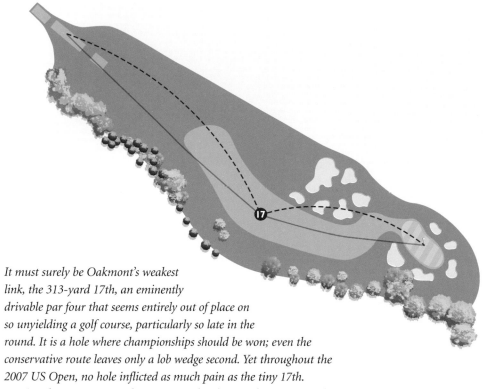

*It must surely be Oakmont's weakest link, the 313-yard 17th, an eminently drivable par four that seems entirely out of place on so unyielding a golf course, particularly so late in the round. It is a hole where championships should be won; even the conservative route leaves only a lob wedge second. Yet throughout the 2007 US Open, no hole inflicted as much pain as the tiny 17th.*

*First there was eventual winner Angel Cabrera, whose apparently comfortable two-shot lead was unexpectedly halved when a 6-foot (1.8-metre) putt for par was missed. Next came local hero Jim Furyk, whose near-miraculous run of three straight back-nine birdies had tied him for the lead until the unthinkable – a bogey at 17 – derailed his chances. And finally there was Tiger Woods, who, able to reach the greenside bunker with only a fairway metal, holed a brave 6-foot (1.8-metre) putt for par – but, alas, it was a birdie that was needed.*

*Of course, such late-tournament flounderings are hardly anything new. Trailing Sam Parks by one in the final round of the 1935 US Open, long-hitting Jimmy Thomson drove mightily to the fringe – then promptly took four to get down, and lost the Open by two.*

downhill to a putting surface that falls dangerously away from front to back – but after crossing the wide ravine that houses the property-bisecting Pennsylvania Turnpike it is quickly visible at the 341-yard 2nd. Though occasionally drivable in today's rocket-powered game, this short two-shotter is more frequently played with a long-iron or fairway metal, followed by a short pitch. The problem is that, with the

green slanting toward ten o'clock, the tee ball must flirt with a cluster of six right-side bunkers, plus a single newer hazard added mid-fairway, in order to gain the optimum angle of approach.

## THE CHURCH PEWS
The 428-yard 3rd is memorable for introducing the famed Church Pews, a 120-yard (110-metre) long

left-side bunker broken by a dozen nearly symmetrical grass ridges reminiscent of rows of wooden benches. One of golf's more original and striking hazards, it frequently requires escapes to be little more than sideways pitches back to safety. But even from the fairway the approach is not easy: the green is perched on a large knob, dictating delicate bump-and-run recoveries for shots missed either short or slightly long.

If Oakmont offers any sustained opportunity to score, it comes on holes 4–6, which include the par-five 4th followed by a pair of shortish tests – at 382 yards and 194 yards respectively – all of which can be approached with a fair degree of aggressiveness. The challenge quickly resumes at the 479-yard 7th, then at the long one-shot 8th, which garnered a great deal of 2007 attention for a new US Open tee measuring 288 yards. With its green curving leftwards around a massive bunker known as the Sahara, this oversized par three was originally designed to be played with a driver, measuring 253 yards for the 1927 US Open.

The 477-yard 9th has long been a sporting par five for club members but is now played as a monstrous two-shotter for the professionals. Central to its challenge is a blind tee shot to a fairway whose left edge is menaced by one of several man-made ditches (staked as lateral water hazards) that appear throughout the property. The approach is then played between multiple bunkers to a nastily rippled putting surface that, at 20,000 square feet (1,858 square metres), actually doubles as the club's practice green. As difficult as the 9th plays, however, the 435-yard 10th is statistically even harder, its downhill approach somewhat resembling that encountered on the 1st hole, complete with sloping putting surface. All told, any golfer achieving par figures from the 7th through the 10th may well pick up more than a single stroke against even a world-class field.

The challenge is reduced once more over the next few holes, with the 379-yard 11th offering a reasonable birdie chance. Then comes the par-five 12th, normally a 602-yard test that the USGA extended to an unprecedented 667 for the 2007 Open. With nearly 20 bunkers and multiple ditches in play, this may not resemble the 13th at Augusta (see page 206) for strategy, but fours are hardly commonplace. It is followed by the 183-yard 13th and 358-yard 14th, which both present noticeably less daunting opportunities for disaster.

## POWERHOUSE FINISHERS
Oakmont's suitably big finish begins with the famous 15th, a long par four now played from a 500-yard tee wedged tightly between the 14th green and 18th fairway. With a second set of Church Pews on the favoured

left side and with sand and multiple ditches to the right, this blind tee shot may be the toughest on the course. If brought off successfully, there is still a long approach to a huge green angled slightly left to right behind a 80-yard (73-metre) long bunker. Amazingly, this green once ran the entire length of the hazard, but given the speed and surface contours inherent at Oakmont, chipping from the fairway is surely easier than the possible 180-foot (165-metre) putts of yesteryear

The 231-yard 16th is another stiff test, in no way deceptive but requiring a very well-struck long-iron to finish anywhere near the pin, particularly when it is cut back-right. On the other hand the 17th is an incongruously short but highly interesting two-shotter played to a narrow green behind a huge, 12-foot (3.6-metre) deep bunker. Despite running steadily uphill, this 313-yarder is readily drivable by the modern professional, provided, that is, that the golfer is first able to carry a set of six left-side fairway bunkers, then manage to run the ball between the aforementioned front bunker and a rough-laden bank that creeps in from the left. All told, a fascinating hole,

and certainly as strategically engaging as any late-round test in the USGA's unofficial US Open rota.

Oakmont closes with a dangerous par four measuring a robust 484 yards, its initial challenge lying not just in avoiding a left-side ditch and five bunkers but also in holding anything but a well-struck draw in its narrow, left-to-right sloping fairway. The approach is then slightly uphill to a green filled with enough pitches and rolls to make even short-iron approaches extremely difficult to stop close to the hole. Tommy Armour did make birdie here to force a play-off in 1927, but given the 18th's special brand of difficulty the golfer senses that, even some eight decades later, history is not likely to repeat itself in the near future.

## RESTORING THE LINKS-LIKE FEEL

Perhaps the highest accolade that can be bestowed on Oakmont as a championship test is the recognition of how little alteration has been required to keep its challenge intact in the modern era. True, under US Open conditions, over-the-top rough and rock-hard greens do their part to boost scores artificially, but beyond

such one-week artifice little more than length has been altered at Oakmont since before the Second World War. Indeed, in recent years the club has attempted to turn the clock back towards its Golden Age roots by removing more than 4,000 trees and restoring knee-deep fescue rough, re-establishing the windswept, links-like feel that Henry Fownes so long ago envisioned.

Oakmont stands, then, as one of American golf's grand old haunts, a course of unparalleled history and fearsome reputation, yet also a place where strategic and shot-making options arise with surprising frequency. It is these latter features that significantly boost the layout's greatness, yet Oakmont's ultimate selling point remains its sheer, unmitigated difficulty and its myriad hazards, combined with the most demanding greens in all golf, allowing it to embody the design philosophy of William Fownes, who so memorably and starkly opined: 'A shot poorly played should be a shot irrevocably lost.'

*Rear view of the dangerous 484-yard 18th. Tommy Armour made birdie here to force a play-off at the 1927 US Open, but even the world's best are generally happy with pars.*

# SOUTH-EASTERN STATES

Although the first recorded golf clubs in America existed, temporarily, in Charleston, South Carolina and Savannah, Georgia during the 1740s, the modern game of golf was slower to take root in the south-east, largely due to pre-1930s difficulties in consistently growing high-calibre turf grass amid the heat and humidity.

A s the game reappeared in the south-eastern states towards the end of the 19th century, it was essentially in a rudimentary, sand-green form, located in areas catering primarily to seasonal resort guests. Agronomical advances have long since replaced the sand greens – and even, to some extent, the nasty grain inherent in their primary replacement, Bermuda grass – while more than a century later resorts remain a leading component of south-eastern golf, with a healthy number of real-estate development courses thrown in.

Traditional private clubs – those not built around the selling of houses – have always existed in the region, and so long as the wealthy desire less crowded, more secluded places to play, they always will. But with land acquisition and course construction costs climbing ever higher, real estate has become a necessary component to many a course development plan – and the idea is hardly a new one. In 1926, Sarasota – Florida's Sara Bay Country Club[1] (then called Whitfield Estates) – began selling plots around its Donald Ross-designed course with no less than Bobby Jones leading a team of 'salesmen' that included Jim Barnes, Johnny Farrell, the Briton Archie Compston and the French star Arnaud Massey. Indeed, while Florida's grandest course, the Seminole Golf Club (see page 212), was built residence-free, even Miami's Indian Creek[2] – an ultra-exclusive Golden Age club situated on a private island in Biscayne Bay – was laid out with a row of expensive plots for houses lining its perimeter, remaining ultra expensive today.

## MOUNTAIN RETREATS

Before the real-estate projects, however, there were resorts, the earliest being located primarily in mountain regions where rich city dwellers travelled to escape

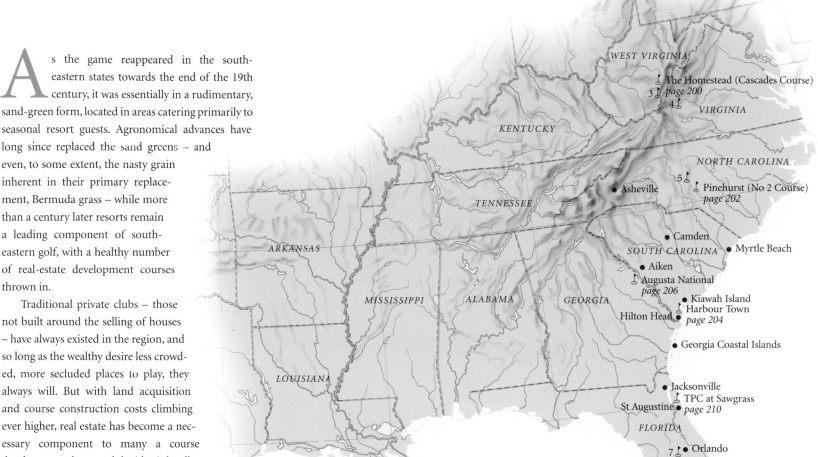

the summer heat. Among the very earliest were The Homestead[3] (1766) and The Greenbrier[4] (1778), a pair of stately 18th-century Blue Ridge establishments straddling the Virginia–West Virginia state line. The Homestead, in particular, was a ground-breaker, with its first six holes of golf opening in 1892, even though the game had been played near The Greenbrier in 1884 at the Oakhurst Links. This short-lived (but later restored) nine remains America's oldest still-active golf club, but the resort itself did not really get involved in golf until the building of C.B. Macdonald's Old White Course in 1914. Today both facilities remain world-class destinations, each featuring 54 holes of golf with The Homestead's Cascades Course (see page 200) being among the nation's very best.

Another early resort centre was Pinehurst, initially a health-oriented retreat in the sand-hills region of south–central North Carolina that, by 1898, was embracing the game of golf. In 1900 the resort hired Donald Ross to be its winter professional and, within a few years, the transplanted Scot's architectural prowess had turned Pinehurst into the self-proclaimed 'St Andrews of America'. Today the resort's eight courses serve as the hub of the sand-hills golf explosion, with well over 30 area layouts catering to public, resort and private golfers alike. Pinehurst's famous No 2 course (see page 202) remains the centre-

*Pete Dye's Ocean Course at Kiawah Island had been awarded the 1991 Ryder Cup matches even before it was completed.*

piece, although its No 4 and No 8 courses, plus nearby Pine Needles[5] (a three-time US Women's Open site) are also worthy of note.

## DOMINANCE BY FLORIDA

Numerous other resorts also drew early golfers to the region, with places such as Camden and Aiken (South Carolina), Asheville (North Carolina), Augusta National (see page 206) and the coastal islands of Georgia, and the Mississippi gulf coast all appearing prominently on any period golfing map. But by the onset of the Depression in the early 1930s, the giant of south-eastern golf was – as it remains today – Florida.

Once upon a time the Sunshine State's golf centres sprang up along pioneering 19th-century railway lines built by men such as Henry Flagler and Henry Plant, with Miami, Palm Beach and St Augustine the first major destinations. In the postwar era, however, agronomical advances, the widespread advent of air conditioning and a more affluent society sparked a second boom, with Doral[6], Disney World[7] and Innisbrook[8] leading the game farther inland, where vast quantities of inexpensive land suitable for golf could still be secured.

Resorts continued to be built right into the new millennium, though by the 1970s the broader body of course construction had moved into residential club development, particularly on the south-eastern coast where large golf-oriented communities began eating up massive chunks of real estate. Today Boca Raton heads a boom that has created a veritable golfing greenbelt from Fort Lauderdale all the way north to ultra-affluent Hobe Sound, with the more inland facilities often encroaching on the everglades – sites that would have been deemed unsuitable for development (based on heat and a lack of verifiable terra firma) until the 1950s. Orlando, the coastal region south of Jacksonville (led by Pete Dye's landmark Tournament Players' Club at Sawgrass (see page 210) and much of outlying Fort Myers have also expanded considerably, but the heavyweight champion of contemporary Florida golf growth is certainly Naples, which since the early 1990s has come to hold its own with any of America's golfing addresses.

All told, Florida today offers more than 70 prominent resorts (many featuring multiple courses) and more than 450 private clubs (the vast majority tied to real-estate developments) – though almost all are hampered by the state's pancake-flat landscape, which makes the over-use of water, sand and palpably unnatural mounding a frequent design issue.

## ECONOMIC SIGNIFICANCE OF GOLF

Such large-scale postwar development has hardly been confined to Florida, for in South Carolina major coastal areas, particularly Hilton Head and Kiawah islands and Myrtle Beach, largely define south-eastern contemporary golf, drawing tourists and seasonal residents from across the nation. Hilton Head offers more than 45 courses on-island or in its immediate environs, highlighted by Pete Dye's seminal Harbour Town Golf Links (see page 204). Kiawah is both newer and smaller, but several of its seven layouts rate highly, chiefly Dye's spectacular Ocean Course, site of the highly competitive 1991 Ryder Cup. Myrtle Beach, on the other hand, represents mass-produced resort golf at its grandest, with more than 120 area courses serving as a clear demonstration of golf's huge importance to the economy of the entire south-eastern region.

Many are the American resorts that predate the Golden Age of golf design or, for that matter, the modern game's 19th-century US birth altogether. Indeed, a small collection of these timeless getaways have actually existed since before the American Civil War (1861–65). But a resort that predates America itself – the actual formation of the country – well, that is another matter entirely. But such is precisely the case at The Homestead in Hot Springs, Virginia, where the discovery of mineral springs led to the construction of the resort's first accommodation fully ten years prior to the Declaration of Independence, in 1766.

## SINCE 1892

The modern conception of The Homestead, however, really came into being under the ownership of legendary financier J.P. Morgan, who masterminded the expansion in the 1890s that created some of the older buildings still in use today. Golf, for its part, arrived in 1892 in the form of a rudimentary six-hole layout. This course was eventually extended to 18 by Donald Ross in 1913, though its original first tee was incorporated into the new design, making it the oldest continually used opening tee in America.

The Cascades Course came a decade later, after golf's booming popularity threatened to overwhelm the Ross layout entirely. But logistically there were problems, because The Homestead, like most of America's great mountain resorts, is situated in a valley, its golf course occupying reasonably flat land along the floor, with the surrounding hills serving mostly as a wonderfully scenic backdrop. By the early 1920s, there was no further usable land close to the hotel, forcing the consideration of an alternative tract in the nearby village of Healing Springs. Initially, no less than Seth Raynor and A.W. Tillinghast pronounced this site too mountainous to develop, verdicts that might have settled the issue. But a young William Flynn begged to differ, and with his more opti-

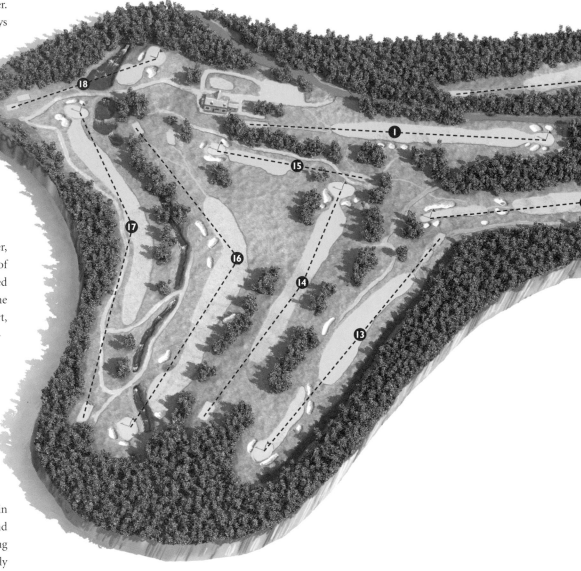

mistic assessment managed to land himself – despite little national reputation – a very high-profile design commission indeed. Not only were trees cleared and unsuitable terrain dynamited, but the waters of the Swift Run, which meaningfully affects play on six holes, were actually re-routed in several places. It was a

monumental task indeed, and though looking remarkably natural given the work performed, there was still more to be done, for Flynn continued tinkering with the Cascades right up until his death in 1945.

In 1934 The Homestead hired an unknown local named Sam Snead to serve as its golf professional.

# CASCADES
## Hot Springs, Virginia

Although it lies mostly along a valley floor, the Cascades has long been known as America's 'best mountain golf course' for a reason, requiring William Flynn to go to extraordinary lengths in building a masterpiece.

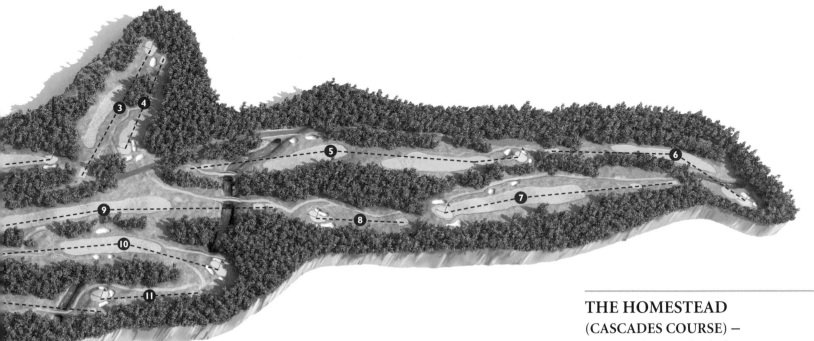

## THE HOMESTEAD
### (CASCADES COURSE) –
### Hot Springs, Virginia
William Flynn, 1923
Major events: US Women's Open 1967; US
Amateur 1988; US Women's Amateur 1928;
Curtis Cup 1966

Within three years, Snead was making his living on the PGA Tour, but he never moved far from his roots, retaining an affiliation with either The Homestead or the nearby Greenbrier right up until his death in 2002.

## OVER HILLY TERRAIN

The layout's front side becomes more hilly and wooded as it extends south-westwards into a narrow section of the valley, while the back opens up somewhat and is flatter. The outward half features a good early run in the form of three holes wedged into tougher land to the east of Route 220, beginning at the 423-yard 2nd. Here, a heavily drawn tee ball is needed to offset the sharp left-to-right slope of the fairway, while the 289-yard 3rd requires careful planning because a rough-filled gully lies in front of the shallow, elevated green. Attempting to drive to the putting surface seems a low percentage play, but then not many golfers find their blood racing at the prospect of laying up with a 3-iron. The demands are much clearer at the 210-yard, downhill 4th, a Redan-like one-shotter with a green angled right-to-left behind a bunker, a steep drop-off to its rear.

The next four holes – the 575-yard, semiblind 5th, the 367-yard 6th, the uphill 417-yard 7th and tiny 153-yard 8th – do an impressively engineered out-and-back over occasionally tumultuous ground, setting the stage for the demanding par-four 9th. Measuring 448 yards from a tee positioned deep in a chute of trees, this brute requires a nearly 260-yard (240-metre) drive to carry first a deep ravine, then the crest of a steep rise in the fairway, leaving a long second (likely at least to be partially blind) to a green bunkered both left and right.

## AN IMPOSING BACK NINE

The back nine has few weak holes and is particularly noteworthy from the 12th through to the 17th. At 476 yards, the 12th is easily the Cascade's longest par four and very likely its toughest, its elevated tee looking down on a fairway pinched right by a thickly wooded hillside and left by the Swift Run. From the fairway, a line of cross-bunkers 80 yards (73 metres) in front of the putting surface shouldn't present a problem, but finding the narrow, tightly bunkered green certainly is. The creek then accompanies the 440-yard 13th northwards, guarding the inside of this downhill dogleg-left two-shotter. If slightly less interesting, the 429-yard 14th and stiff 229-yard 15th are both strong tests, setting the stage for the back-to-back par fives, which are the Cascades's centrepiece.

A genuine classic, the 527-yard 16th doglegs right around a cluster of three bunkers that longer hitters will surely attempt to carry. Then comes the big decision: whether to lay up with a mid-iron or have a go at the putting surface, which is behind a pond and backed by bunkers – a decision made trickier by the green sitting only inches above the waterline, resulting in a not-so-clearly defined target. The 513-yard 17th then bends sharply left, with a small creek catching any drives that skip through the fairway. The approach is then played to another pond-guarded green, though this time a narrow corridor of left-sidefairway allows some possibility of running a well- struck ball onto the putting surface. Following these fine three-shotters, the 203-yard 18th may feel a bit anti-climactic, but some allowance had to be made in order to site its illustrious predecessors in their ideal spots.

CARD OF THE COURSE

| HOLE | YARDS | PAR | HOLE | YARDS | PAR |
|------|-------|-----|------|-------|-----|
| 1. | 398 | 4 | 10. | 381 | 4 |
| 2. | 423 | 4 | 11. | 192 | 3 |
| 3. | 289 | 4 | 12. | 476 | 4 |
| 4. | 210 | 3 | 13. | 440 | 4 |
| 5. | 575 | 5 | 14. | 429 | 4 |
| 6. | 367 | 4 | 15. | 229 | 3 |
| 7. | 417 | 4 | 16. | 527 | 5 |
| 8. | 153 | 3 | 17. | 513 | 5 |
| 9. | 448 | 4 | 18. | 203 | 3 |
| OUT | 3,280 | 35 | IN | 3,390 | 35 |
| | | | TOTAL | 6,670 | 70 |

*The approach to the 527-yard, par-five 16th. From here the golfer faces a pitch over water to a green perched just inches above the hazard line.*

Initially, James Walker Tufts, the resort's owner, hired Donald Ross as the head golf professional, and his duties were club-making and giving lessons. However, within two years, Ross had adjusted to the Bermuda grass and the sand greens and was keen to improve the golf offerings at Pinehurst. Being used to links courses in his native Scotland, Ross was struck by the opportunity that the soil provided in the sand hills of North Carolina. He wrote: 'Only in sandy soil will the drainage problem permit construction of the rolling contours and hollows natural to Scotch seaside courses where golf was born.'

## THE BUILDING OF MORE COURSES

By 1903, golf at Pinehurst consisted of Pinehurst No 1 and a nine-hole course called No 2. To keep up with golf's growing stature in the United States, the Tufts family asked Ross to redesign Nos 1 and 2 and build courses 3 and 4. Despite four courses, the game was so popular by the early 1920s that the resort was turning away almost 20,000 golfers during its seven-month playing season (prior to air conditioning, the town of Pinehurst emptied during the hot summer months). Further high-quality Ross designs followed in the surrounding area, highlighted by Pine Needles. Unfortunately it opened in 1929, the year of the great stock market crash and the start of a deep economic depression in North America.

By the early 1960s, the concept of using golf to sell residential property led to golf courses once again being constructed, both in Pinehurst and in selected areas across the US. This time, heavy duty construction equipment was available to the architects – as opposed to the mules and drag pans with which Donald Ross worked. Yet, none of the courses built in the Pinehurst area since Ross's death in 1948 enjoys the sustained playing interest of his masterpiece, No 2.

## GRADUAL EVOLUTION

Not only did Donald Ross design No 2 but he also oversaw all its significant changes and modifications. Thus it enjoyed the unheard luxury of having its architect lavish his personal attention on it for a 45-year period, and even to this day No 2 has a unified feel quite unlike most championship courses. The slow evolutionary process included numerous changes to its general routing. In 1908 No 2 grew to an 18-hole course, measuring under 6,100 yards (5,580 metres), and today's 3rd and 6th holes were added in 1923. All the current holes were finally in place by 1935, when the 4th and 5th holes were created.

In that same year, thanks to advances in agronomy, Ross converted all 18 greens from sand to grass. While the course was closed, he also added 12 new back tees, partly because of the increasing switch to steel shafts for golf clubs. When it reopened in 1936, No 2 measured more than 6,950 yards (6,355 metres) and featured its now-famous greens, which were shaped like the back of a turtle and shed mishit approach shots off its mown sloping sides. These turtleback greens, especially at the firmness that can be achieved with modern agronomy, provide an extremely exacting target. Though they average 5,500 square feet (510 square metres), more than half of the technical green space does not support a hole location

as such greens gradually slope off on all sides. Thus, the effective hitting area at No 2 is about 2,500 square foot (232 square metres), smaller than Pebble Beach's notoriously tiny greens.

## PINE FOREST SURROUNDINGS

No 2 is in no way visually flashy; the only water is a small pond easily carried off the 16th tee. A game here is played on fairways through wide corridors of pine trees that culminate with sophisticated green

## PINEHURST RESORT
### (NO 2 COURSE) – Pinehurst, North Carolina

Donald Ross, 1908
Major events: USPGA 1936; Ryder Cup 1951; US Amateur 1962, 2008; US Women's Amateur 1989; US Open 1999, 2005

CARD OF THE COURSE

| HOLE | YARDS | PAR | HOLE | YARDS | PAR |
|------|-------|-----|------|-------|-----|
| 1. | 404 | 4 | 10. | 607 | 5 |
| 2. | 469 | 4 | 11. | 476 | 4 |
| 3. | 336 | 4 | 12. | 449 | 4 |
| 4. | 565 | 5 | 13. | 378 | 4 |
| 5. | 472 | 4 | 14. | 468 | 4 |
| 6. | 220 | 3 | 15. | 203 | 3 |
| 7. | 404 | 4 | 16. | 492 | 4 |
| 8. | 467 | 4 | 17. | 190 | 3 |
| 9. | 175 | 3 | 18. | 442 | 4 |
| OUT | 3,512 | 35 | IN | 3,705 | 35 |
| | | | TOTAL | 7,217 | 70 |

# PINEHURST NO 2
## Pinehurst, North Carolina

The arrival in the United States in 1899 of a man who appreciated how the game was played in the United Kingdom helped golf gain a foothold in many places there. For instance, pre-1900 the Pinehurst course was rudimentary and of no strategic interest. However, Donald Ross changed all that, and Pinehurst is now often seen as the home of American golf.

complexes. Cumulatively as challenging as any set in the world, these greens allow Pinehurst to host the biggest events in American golf.

The course flows along with holes that give and take away. The downhill three-shot 4th, where ground can be made up, is followed by as hard a consecutive pair of holes as can be found in American golf. Indeed, Donald Ross considered the approach to the 5th as the hardest shot on the course. Regardless of the difficulty, it is almost impossible to lose a ball while playing No 2. Though the course is thoroughly testing, resort guests delight in finishing their round with the same ball with which they started.

Play concludes under the shadow of the clubhouse where members and resort guests sit in the shade on the porch, mesmerized by the vast range of recovery shots possible around the home green. Symbolic of the options around all the greens, one golfer may elect to putt up the 3-foot (1-metre) bank onto the green while another plays a chip-and-run into the bank. Still others pitch the ball directly onto the putting surface while some use their utility club. Therein lies the joy of No 2: these recovery shots are within the physical abilities of all golfers; whether or not the golfer has the nerve to pull off the shot is what makes the game so fascinating here.

## INFINITE ATTRACTION

Golfing giants from Ben Hogan to Arnold Palmer and Jack Nicklaus to Tiger Woods have expressed their admiration for this style of golf, where short grass replaces water and thick grass as being the principal challenge. Open champion Tommy Armour summed up the allure of No 2 when he wrote: 'The man who doesn't feel emotionally stirred when he golfs at Pinehurst beneath those clear blue skies and with the pine fragrance in his nostrils is one who should be ruled out of golf for life. It's the kind of course that gets into the blood of an old trooper.'

# HARBOUR TOWN
## Hilton Head Island, South Carolina

Period newspaper accounts, as well as shipping records for golf equipment from the port of Leith, in Scotland, clearly indicate that a period version of golf was being played in Charleston, South Carolina as early as the mid-1740s. The South Carolina Golf Club was chartered there in 1786 and staked its claim as America's first organized golfing club.

The South Carolina Golf Club was no longer functioning by the early 19th century, but in a blindingly good public relations move the builders of Hilton Head Island's Harbour Town Links reestablished the club's charter in 1968. They moved its 'headquarters' from Charleston (some 70 miles/112 kilometres distant) and established a small museum of ancient clubs and memorabilia. Such traditionalist trappings would surely burnish any new club's reputation, but this was of particular relevance at Harbour Town, because this was the layout that, quite literally, changed the face of American golf-course design.

### THE DAWN OF A NEW ERA

Opened in 1969, Harbour Town was built by Pete Dye with input from Jack Nicklaus. Though not actually the first course to show Dye's innovative modern-traditionalist style (both Crooked Stick and The Golf Club preceded it), its immediate platform as permanent host of the PGA Tour's Heritage Classic gave it infinitely wider exposure. Dye, a former Ohio insurance salesman, was a fine player himself who began his design career building little-known Midwestern courses in the late 1950s. A 1963 visit to Scotland broadened his horizons, however, and soon Dye was incorporating such Old World touches as pot bunkers, blind shots and hazard-buttressing railway sleepers into his repertoire. Furthermore, with Harbour Town as an example, Dye's accent on shorter, more varied holes, smaller greens and greater strategic interest single-handedly reversed the postwar trend towards huge layouts that were heavy on challenge but light on character. Thus, with an opening day yardage of 6,655 yards (and some astonishingly high scores in the inaugural Heritage), Harbour Town provided an entirely new idea of what thoughtful course design could, and should, be about.

Though inevitably lengthened over the years, Harbour Town still opens benignly, with a pair of moderate par fours surrounding the relatively simple par-five 2nd. The initial chance to experience Dye's

## THE SEA PINES RESORT
(HARBOUR TOWN GOLF LINKS) –
Hilton Head Island,
South Carolina

Pete Dye and Jack Nicklaus, 1969

CARD OF THE COURSE

| HOLE | YARDS | PAR | HOLE | YARDS | PAR |
|------|-------|-----|------|-------|-----|
| 1. | 410 | 4 | 10. | 444 | 4 |
| 2. | 502 | 5 | 11. | 436 | 4 |
| 3. | 437 | 4 | 12. | 430 | 4 |
| 4. | 200 | 3 | 13. | 373 | 4 |
| 5. | 530 | 5 | 14. | 192 | 3 |
| 6. | 419 | 4 | 15. | 571 | 5 |
| 7. | 195 | 3 | 16. | 395 | 4 |
| 8. | 470 | 4 | 17. | 185 | 3 |
| 9. | 332 | 4 | 18. | 452 | 4 |
| OUT | 3,495 | 36 | IN | 3,478 | 35 |
| | | | TOTAL | 6,973 | 71 |

creative style comes at the 200-yard 4th, the first of a quartet of exciting par threes, where the left third of a typically small green is lined with railway sleepers and juts dangerously into a pond. More forgiving is the right side of the putting surface, and a safe area exists still farther right, but the challenge of going for a left-side pin is considerable.

### THE SETH RAYMOR INFLUENCE

Pete Dye has long admitted to being heavily influenced by the work of course designer Seth Raynor, so it is probably not a coincidence that the 195-yard 7th – which was originally only 165 yards (151 metres) – bears a clear resemblance to so many Macdonald/ Raynor short holes, which regularly feature greens almost completely surrounded by sand. Here, their trademark horseshoe-shaped ridge built into the putting surface is absent, and several overhanging trees (which can deflect even slightly wayward approaches) differ markedly from the prototype, but the overall similarities are difficult to ignore.

The front nine then closes with back-to-back par fours of utterly varied character. The 470-yard 8th is perhaps Harbour Town's toughest hole, bending gently leftwards through a narrow, wooded driving zone, then threading through more trees to a small green guarded left by sand and water. The 9th, on the other hand, measures only 332 yards and is, theoretically at least, drivable. But its distinctive Y-shaped green has end-to-end sand in front, and several tiny pot bunkers fill the top of the Y, making it impossible to putt (and difficult to chip) from one spoke to the other.

### THE UNIQUE 13TH

The back nine begins with three consecutive par fours of similar lengths but varying characters before encountering one of the club's best-known holes, the 373-yard 13th. Until this point, railway sleepers have been used to bulkhead only water hazards, but here is found a tight drive-and-pitch whose green is so buttressed, especially a narrow finger of putting surface that extends forwards into the sand. Such a design might feel faintly gimmicky today but was entirely ground-breaking in 1969 – and the concept, Dye has long emphasized, was provided by his wife Alice, a top amateur player with a good bit of course-design knowledge in her own right.

The 192-yard 14th has grown 40 yards (36 metres) since its inception but still features a green guarded tightly by a pond and a nasty back-left pot bunker. The once-untouchable 571-yard 15th and 395-yard 16th (a 90-degree dogleg left where the modern waste bunker came into fashion) then lead to the windblown shores of Calibogue Sound and an extraordinary water-side finish.

### AN EPIC CLOSE

First comes the 185-yard 17th, a true Dye original featuring a narrow, banana-shaped green situated on a peninsula, its left side guarded by a wide expanse of marsh and the ends of an 80-yard (73-metre) long bulkheaded bunker. A single, ideally placed bunker also muscles in on the right side of the putting surface, all of which combines with normally stiff breezes to make this a great one-shotter and a thrilling 71st hole of a championship.

The 18th, for its part, is a sprawling 452-yard par four, which features a peninsula of fairway extending westwards into the marshes. A tee shot successfully finding the peninsula leaves an all-carry mid-iron to a narrow, deep green situated at the water's edge. A drive, however, played safely to the right of this 90-yard (82-metre) wide fairway leaves a much longer approach, raising the prospect of a right-side lay-up. Both strategic and highly dramatic, it is a suitably distinctive finish for one of America's most inventive, and highly important, works of golf-course design.

As perhaps *the* icon of pre-Second World War American sporting life, Bobby Jones was a unique and accomplished sportsman. In addition to claiming 13 Major championships and winning the Amateur and Open titles of both the United States and Great Britain in 1930, Jones was also an educated man of the highest order. With degrees in mechanical engineering (Georgia Tech) and English literature (Harvard), he went on to study law at Emery University, passing the Georgia state bar after only three semesters and becoming, in his post-golf life, a practising attorney.

## THE IMMORTAL BOBBY

Retiring from competitive play at the ripe old age of 28, Jones soon decided to build a world-class golf course intended largely as a secluded playground for him and his friends – an idea really more utilitarian than elitist, given that enormous crowds still invariably turned out anytime the 'Immortal Bobby' played in public. To the surprise of many, Jones chose to locate his course not in his native Atlanta but, rather, 150 miles (240 kilometres) east in Augusta, a then sleepy city that, along with nearby Aiken, South Carolina, was already well established as a winter golfing retreat. For his site, Jones selected a tract that previously housed the South's first commercial nursery, a 365-acre (148-hectare) plot originally developed by a titled Belgian émigré Louis Berckmans. Known as Fruitlands, the property was enviably attractive with its wide array of exotic plantings and handful of natural water hazards, but it was also surprisingly hilly, its highest point sitting nearly 150 feet (45 metres) above its lowest.

Jones left most of the development's business affairs to his close friend Clifford Roberts, an Iowa-born investment banker whose autocratic leadership of the club would eventually become the stuff of legends. Also smart enough not to consider himself wholly qualified as a course designer, Jones further enlisted the help of the game's highest-profile architect, Dr Alister MacKenzie, to help make his conceptual dream a reality.

## AUGUSTA NATIONAL GOLF CLUB – Augusta, Georgia

Bobby Jones and Dr Alister MacKenzie, 1933
Major events: The Masters 1934–present

### CARD OF THE COURSE

| HOLE | NAME | YARDS | PAR | HOLE | NAME | YARDS | PAR |
|------|------|-------|-----|------|------|-------|-----|
| 1. | Tea Olive | 455 | 4 | 10. | Camellia | 495 | 4 |
| 2. | Pink Dogwood | 575 | 5 | 11. | White Dogwood | 505 | 4 |
| 3. | Flowering Peach | 350 | 4 | 12. | Golden Bell | 155 | 3 |
| 4. | Flowering Crab Apple | 240 | 3 | 13. | Azalea | 510 | 5 |
| 5. | Magnolia | 455 | 4 | 14. | Chinese Fir | 440 | 4 |
| 6. | Juniper | 180 | 3 | 15. | Firethorn | 530 | 5 |
| 7. | Pampas | 450 | 4 | 16. | Redbud | 170 | 3 |
| 8. | Yellow Jasmine | 570 | 5 | 17. | Nandina | 440 | 4 |
| 9. | Carolina Cherry | 460 | 4 | 18. | Holly | 465 | 4 |
| **OUT** | | **3,735** | **36** | **IN** | | **3,710** | **36** |
| | | | | **TOTAL** | | **7,445** | **72** |

# AUGUSTA NATIONAL
## Augusta, Georgia

For many, Augusta National represents the epitome of the desirable golf course: an idyllic setting, a stiff challenge and an unrivalled fame that transcends the sport itself.

## THE JONES/MACKENZIE PARTNERSHIP

Expectations for the Jones and MacKenzie collaboration were high, imbuing the project with a sense of anticipation and an aura of glamour rare in Depression-era America. Yet despite this wide level of public interest, little record exists as to the precise who-did-whats, with the ever-modest Jones always citing his own role as essentially that of a consultant. It is generally believed that MacKenzie bears the responsibility for the course's routing, but Jones is known to have hit countless test shots during its construction, and the finished product's restrained use of sand was a marked stylistic departure from most previous MacKenzie designs. Thus it can be reasonably assumed that Jones's overall input, though

not conclusively documented, widely exceeded that of most of today's player–architects.

Conveniently (though surely not coincidentally) Jones and MacKenzie shared a number of beliefs about course design. These included a primary emphasis on strategy over simple power, wider fairways to encourage the use of the driver, heavily contoured putting surfaces, the occasional green complex favouring a judicious use of the ground game and, above all, the absence of annoying, play-slowing rough. Indeed, Jones believed that Augusta might introduce a new sort of design to American golf – a welcoming style giving the less-skilled plenty of room to enjoy themselves while requiring the professionals to find just the right locations amid the huge fairways if they were to aggressively attack the pin on their

approach. In this he and MacKenzie unquestionably succeeded, for their original design provided well-defined strategic options on virtually every shot despite incorporating a stunningly minimal 22 bunkers on opening day.

## REPLICATING THE CLASSICS

While Bobby Jones stated publicly that Augusta National would not repeat any classic holes from Great Britain, Dr MacKenzie's own notes indicate that their influence was, at the very least, strongly felt. On no fewer than nine of Augusta's original holes, MacKenzie drew comparisons to British models, these parallels ranging from 'embodies the most attractive features of' to being 'similar in character'.

Among the most 'similar in character' was the 6th, with its huge front-left bunker. This was MacKenzie's rendition of the Redan (see Redan feature on page 49). Most intriguing perhaps was the 7th, today a long and

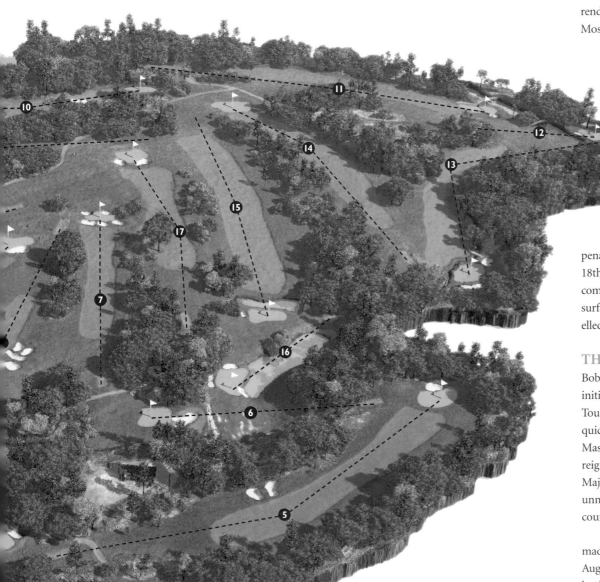

penal test but in its infancy an approximation of the 18th at St Andrews (Old Course) (see page 43), complete with faux Valley of Sin before the putting surface. This green complex was completely remodelled in 1938, leaving no trace of the hole's noble roots.

## THE MASTERS

Bobby Jones and friends inaugurated what was initially called the Augusta National Invitation Tournament in 1934, with the small, but spirited event quickly growing – in both name and stature – into The Masters by decade's end. As a result, Augusta has long reigned as the only permanent site of one of golf's four Major championships, a status that has led to unmatched fame and a remarkably high degree of course alteration.

While many earlier architectural changes were made in efforts to inject more playing strategy, most of Augusta's 21st-century alterations have been triggered by the lack of meaningful regulation of modern equipment. Augusta National, after all, is a layout whose period yardages of 6,700 (1935) and 7,020 (1974) gave

# THE EVER-CHANGING FACE OF AMEN CORNER
## 11th, 12th and 13th holes

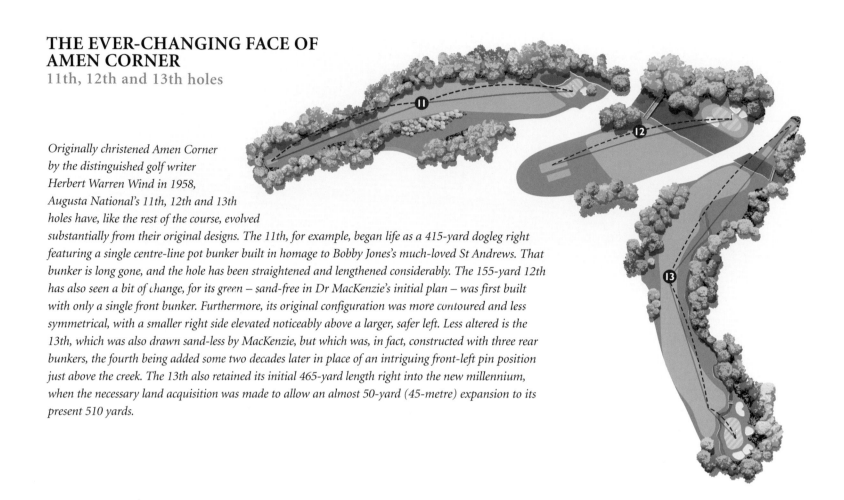

*Originally christened Amen Corner by the distinguished golf writer Herbert Warren Wind in 1958, Augusta National's 11th, 12th and 13th holes have, like the rest of the course, evolved substantially from their original designs. The 11th, for example, began life as a 415-yard dogleg right featuring a single centre-line pot bunker built in homage to Bobby Jones's much-loved St Andrews. That bunker is long gone, and the hole has been straightened and lengthened considerably. The 155-yard 12th has also seen a bit of change, for its green – sand-free in Dr MacKenzie's initial plan – was first built with only a single front bunker. Furthermore, its original configuration was more contoured and less symmetrical, with a smaller right side elevated noticeably above a larger, safer left. Less altered is the 13th, which was also drawn sand-less by MacKenzie, but which was, in fact, constructed with three rear bunkers, the fourth being added some two decades later in place of an intriguing front-left pin position just above the creek. The 13th also retained its initial 465-yard length right into the new millennium, when the necessary land acquisition was made to allow an almost 50-yard (45-metre) expansion to its present 510 yards.*

it a well-deserved reputation as a long hitter's haven, but which, by the new millennium, routinely witnessed Masters competitors hitting short-iron seconds into par fives such as the famed 13th and 15th. Logical it was, then, to extend things to the club's present 7,445-yard standard. Perhaps less so, however, was the wholesale growing of rough and planting of fairway-narrowing trees – additions wholly antithetical to the design philosophies of Bobby Jones and Dr MacKenzie. The results of such changes have been predictable: higher scores certainly, but also a more regimented style of Masters play that, except for the committee's placing of final-day pins in some highly accessible spots, has removed much of the drama that has long made the Masters the most exciting event in golf.

Yet despite this throttling of strategy and tradition, Augusta National still remains a hugely compelling golf course, a majestically scaled test filled with unique and inspiring challenges. In some cases, these trials come in the form of all-or-nothing water hazards; in others they lie more in the spectacular

shape and contouring of the putting surfaces, whose difficulty has only been accentuated in this era of enhanced green speeds.

The green complexes particularly affect play on the water-free front nine, where holes such as the 575-yard 2nd (with its shallow but immensely wide putting surface) and the 350-yard 3rd (which features an elevated, heavily sloped green) have their optimum lines of play vary with specific pin placements. Alternatively, the steep contouring of greens at the 455-yard 5th, the 180-yard 6th and the 450-yard 7th generally require an uncommon amount of precision, lest a reasonably accurate approach find itself some 60 feet (18 metres), and several nasty breaks, from the flagstick.

The 570-yard 8th features a deep, bunkerless green surrounded by distinctive mounding, which was once removed (1956), then later restored (1979), while the 460-yard 9th is renowned for its uphill second shot to a steeply pitched putting surface – an approach that, if missed even the slightly bit short, can trickle agonizingly back a good 30 yards (27 metres).

## SCENE OF EPIC GOLF

But no matter the quality of the outward half, it is inevitably towards Augusta's epic back nine – where eight decades of Masters tournaments have been settled in hallowed emerald splendour – that a golf enthusiast's attention naturally focuses. Things kick off in grand style at the downhill 495-yard 10th, where the tee shot, if properly turned down the left side, will run out to an impressive distance. The approach is then played across a swale to a steeply sloping putting surface that offers few easy options. On the green and below the hole is the ideal result for the second shot. Miss long or left, however, and five suddenly becomes a palatable score.

As the start of Augusta's famous Amen Corner (see above), the 505-yard par-four 11th is keyed by the small left-side pond behind which much of the green is angled, a hazard so well positioned as to weaken the knees of even the world's best as they stand over the long, downhill approach. In the pre-rough days, players chose to aim their drives towards either the

extreme right side of the fairway (attempting to open the most water-free angle of approach) or the extreme left (making the pond more of a frontal, carry hazard), a splendid strategic dichotomy now removed by the long grass that overgrows both areas. For his part, Ben Hogan rendered the question moot by opting to lay up his approach short and right, a safe play equally employable from any part of the fairway – but even with the hole measuring 505 yards, such conservative tactics seldom find favour with today's more aggressive, power-oriented players.

The 155-yard 12th ranks among golf's most treacherous short par threes, its hourglass green angled behind Rae's Creek, with a single bunker front-centre and two more carved into the rear hillside. Two factors dominate play here: the shallowness of the putting surface (particularly the far-right side) and winds that seem constantly to change in strength and direction. The most disciplined players, such as six-time Masters champion Jack Nicklaus, play to the fatter left side of the green regardless of situation, but with only a short-iron in hand the temptation to attack a right-side pin – particularly should the golfer be trailing by two or three strokes on the final day of a tournament – must be maddening.

## TWO SUPERLATIVE EPIC PAR FIVES

Amen Corner ends with perhaps the game's greatest strategic par five – and the site of as many memorable moments as any hole in golf – the 510-yard 13th. Playing from a new championship tee situated on land purchased from the adjoining Augusta Country Club, this gem sweeps majestically leftwards, the inside of its dogleg tightly flanked by a winding tributary of Rae's Creek. Presuming a long, drawn tee ball has found the fairway, the golfer now faces a truly taxing decision, for the heavily contoured green may well lie within reach, but its front and right side are guarded by a particularly deep section of the creek, while back and left are menaced by a grassy swale and

four large bunkers. The game of golf, it can be stated emphatically, possesses few more exhilarating holes.

The 440-yard 14th is memorable primarily for its bunkerless, faintly over-the-top MacKenzie green complex, while the 15th gives the back nine its second terrific go-for-it-or-not par five. Indeed, for those finding the fairway off the tee, the challenge is spine-tingling: a long, downhill second played across a pond to a shallow, steeply sloped putting surface, or, alternatively, a simple short-iron lay-up. But just like the 13th, laying up is no bargain, for the water may well be more unnerving on a delicate three-quarter swing than to the uninhibited rip of a long-iron – a superbly subtle gambit on Dr MacKenzie's part.

Augusta's last true all-or-nothing prospect comes at the 170-yard 16th, a hole added by Robert Trent Jones in 1947 as a dramatic replacement for a much shorter original. With its huge green curving leftwards around the corner of a man-made pond, it has hosted countless memorable Masters moments, mostly on the final day when the traditional back-left pin position allows all manner of shots to funnel towards it. Pins cut on the elevated right tier – both front and back – have long proved dramatically harder, and proportionally less theatrical.

The dual par-four closers offer considerably less flair than their immediate predecessors but quite a measure of toughness. The 440-yard 17th, which was originally sand-free and designed to receive a run-up approach, today requires its drive to dodge the famed Eisenhower tree (named for President Dwight

Eisenhower, whose tee shots regularly challenged its air space) and a high, soft second to carry a fronting bunker. The 465-yard 18th then demands a long, faded drive in order to avoid a pair of left-side fairway bunkers added in 1966, followed by an uphill approach to a two-tiered green behind some particularly deep sand. While perhaps not among the world's truly great finishers, the 18th has certainly provided its share of Masters drama – though 72nd-hole birdies to win the Green Jacket have been relatively few and far between.

## A PROCESSION OF CHANGE

Today's Augusta National is a decidedly different layout from that created by Bobby Jones and Dr MacKenzie, with the perennial need to keep Major championship-ready fuelling its unending procession of change. Yet even in its present rough-and-treed state, Augusta remains one of the game's seminal courses, featuring a wide range of world-class holes that are as impressive in their fame as they are in their frequently superb design. Indeed, a round here offers perhaps the ultimate chance to walk in the footsteps of golfing idols, with every hole providing its own special page of golfing lore. Augusta, then, stands not only as one of golf's most famous places, but also as one of its most sublimely wonderful. Whether this might be enough to sell its modern incarnation to Jones and MacKenzie, however, is another question altogether.

# TPC AT SAWGRASS
## Ponte Vedra Beach, Florida

Deane Beman's goal in building the TPC was to create a high-profile showpiece for the PGA Tour. In that regard he succeeded admirably, because despite being built specifically for tournament golf, the course represents a fascinating, stylish test and is surely among the very best of modern American design.

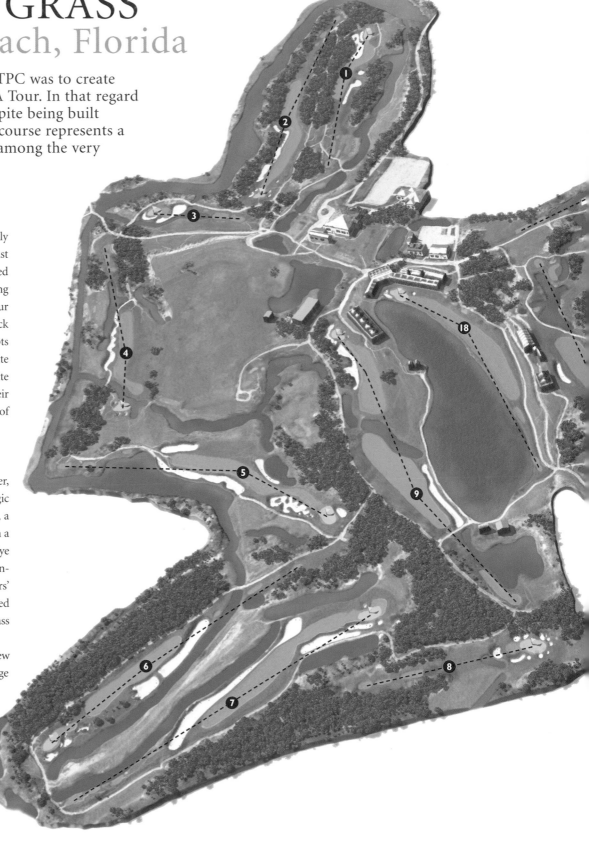

Contrary to popular belief, the fan-friendly notion of stadium golf – which includes not just large spectator mounding but also holes clustered together for more convenient accessibility and viewing – did not originate entirely with then-PGA Tour commissioner Deane Beman. However, while Jack Nicklaus had previously incorporated such concepts into his 1976 design of long-time Canadian Open site Glen Abbey, it was Beman who, in attempting to create a marketable home course for his players and their tournament, set about perfecting them on a piece of snake-infested Florida jungle in 1981.

### COMMISSION FOR PETE DYE

A famously diminutive hitter during his playing career, Beman was a fan of Pete Dye's shorter, more strategic design at Harbour Town Golf Links (see page 204), a layout that, the commissioner observed, was built on a similarly featureless tract. Thus the ever-inventive Dye was hired to create the first course in what would eventually become the PGA Tour's Tournament Players' Club (TPC) network – a mixed bag of fan-oriented layouts, few of which have ever approached Sawgrass for creativity, playing interest or style.

Working off a pre-drawn plan for one of the few times in his career, Dye began by excavating huge amounts of soil with which to create the desired spectator mounding, leaving the dug-out areas to become the vast network of water hazards that today come into play at least tangentially on nearly every hole. Ultimately, Dye's mounding grew beyond all intended proportion, yet aesthetically still somehow managed not to overshadow the golfing landscape too badly.

### FAN AND PLAYER REACTION

From day one, fans took an immense liking to Sawgrass, but the initial response from Tour players

## TPC AT SAWGRASS
## (STADIUM COURSE) –
## Ponte Vedra Beach, Florida

Pete Dye, 1981
Major events: US Amateur 1994

CARD OF THE COURSE

| HOLE | YARDS | PAR | HOLE | YARDS | PAR |
|------|-------|-----|------|-------|-----|
| 1. | 392 | 4 | 10. | 424 | 4 |
| 2. | 532 | 5 | 11. | 535 | 5 |
| 3. | 177 | 3 | 12. | 358 | 4 |
| 4. | 384 | 4 | 13. | 181 | 3 |
| 5. | 466 | 4 | 14. | 467 | 4 |
| 6. | 393 | 4 | 15. | 449 | 4 |
| 7. | 442 | 4 | 16. | 507 | 5 |
| 8. | 219 | 3 | 17. | 137 | 3 |
| 9. | 583 | 5 | 18. | 447 | 4 |
| **OUT** | **3,588** | **36** | **IN** | **3,505** | **36** |
| | | | **TOTAL** | **7,093** | **72** |

was overwhelmingly negative. Most comments centred around the greens, which were considerably contoured and fell away at odd angles. Yet amid all this criticism, Jerry Pate's winning score in the course's first Players Championship was an eight-under-par 280, with his two-stroke margin of victory coming from thrilling birdies at the 71st and 72nd holes. If that was not enough to validate Dye's fan-friendly approach, Pate's affable post-round tossing of the architect and Beman into the lake immediately adjacent to the 18th green quickly became a defining moment in the history of the PGA Tour. Still, this being the players' own course, Beman had little choice but to heed their complaints, and a range of modifications was subsequently made.

Tinkered with from time to time (including a complete greens rebuild in 2006), Sawgrass is today a layout of only modest championship length (7,093 yards), though it regularly employs several longer tees during the Players Championship, extending the course to 7,215 yards.

### PLAYING THE COURSE
Like many of Dye's best designs, Sawgrass begins fairly tamely, with the first real danger arising at the 384-yard 4th, where water presses flush against the angled front of a smallish, steeply sloping green. The 466-yard 5th is the first of Sawgrass's longer par fours and requires a strong tee shot to a fairway turning left to right around an enormous bunker, then a long-iron to a deep, rolling green guarded by sand and grass bunkers alike. The outward half's best two-shotter, however, may well be the 442-yard 7th, where an angled putting surface protected front-right by two huge bunkers clearly favours an approach shot played from the left, daring the golfer to drive aggressively across a 200-yard (183-metre) long bunker that slants up that side of the fairway.

Following the 219-yard 8th (a relatively unexciting Dye par three that can be stretched to 240 yards/220 metres) the front nine closes with a vintage three-shotter – the 583-yard 9th. Occasionally reachable in two by longer hitters, it is the gentlest of double-doglegs, first edging right, then back left, but each with just enough turn to materially affect tactics. A tee shot driven far down the centre of the fairway, for example, leaves the line to the green bothered by left-side trees

*The famed island-green 17th, perhaps the world's most famous – and controversial – golf hole. The golfer either hits the island or reloads – for as many tries as it takes.*

and bunkers, whereas a drive placed close to the creek, which angles across the fairway from right-to-left, allows a more unfettered path.

Another excellent par five is the 535-yard 11th, where a long drive laid close to a large left-side bunker opens up the best angle to attack a push-up green angled left-to-right beyond sand and water. Those electing to lay up, however, must also consider these hazards, for balls placed courageously close to them are left with a fairly open pitch, while those hit safely to the left have to cope with a third shot made tricky by a small, deep bunker near the centre of the putting surface.

### WORLD-FAMOUS FINISHERS
The 467-yard 14th and the 449-yard 15th are strong par fours, yet they are largely overlooked amid the excitement that surrounds the three holes immediately to follow. For as Players Championship viewers can readily attest, the real fun begins at the 507-yard 16th, a sweeping dogleg left that can surely be reached in two by every professional and most skilled amateurs – yet the slightly awkward angle of the green plus the huge danger imposed by the lake curling directly behind the putting surface add a very real dash of risk to the hole.

Then there is the 17th, which, in its quarter-century of existence, has become a genuine golfing icon, its widely photographed (and copied) island green breaking entirely new ground in the realm of all-or-nothing hazards. Annually the site of so much dramatic angst throughout the Players Championship, it is surely the most widely recognized hole – and, very likely, the most controversial – anywhere in tournament golf.

The 447-yard 18th is something of a template hole for Dye, because versions of this curving, waterside two-shotter appear on a number of his courses. This one ranks among the toughest, however, particularly considering the narrowness of the fairway, and the trees that minimize any bailout room to the right.

# SEMINOLE
## Juno Beach, Florida

Seminole Golf Club is said to be the only design job the great Donald Ross ever campaigned for, and while evidence suggests that he may also have lobbied Bobby Jones a little regarding Augusta National (see page 206), his infatuation with Seminole is easy to understand.

(see page 206)

The legendary Donald Ross was perhaps *the* dominant player in Florida's Golden Age golf-design market, building or renovating around 40 courses statewide, nearly all of which occupied the sort of pancake-flat terrain typical of the region. Seminole, however, would be radically different, because its site was a seaside expanse marked on both its beach and inland boundaries by a pair of high, sand-dune-covered ridges utterly incongruous to those parts. The property's mid-section was typically Florida-flat, but also ideal for the digging of drainage ponds, allowing Ross to create multiple water holes to any configuration of his choosing.

### A UNIQUELY SPECIAL ROUTING

But beyond simply being blessed with a superior site, there are several additional aspects of Seminole's design that set the course apart. The most obvious is a routing that manages to bring the ridges into play on 14 holes, with both nines utilizing the inland dunes and four of the final six holes filling those along the Atlantic. Also noteworthy is the bunkering, which in

### SEMINOLE GOLF CLUB –
### Juno Beach, Florida
Donald Ross, 1929

CARD OF THE COURSE

| HOLE | YARDS | PAR | HOLE | YARDS | PAR |
|---|---|---|---|---|---|
| 1. | 370 | 4 | 10. | 382 | 4 |
| 2. | 387 | 4 | 11. | 420 | 4 |
| 3. | 501 | 5 | 12. | 367 | 4 |
| 4. | 450 | 4 | 13. | 168 | 3 |
| 5. | 202 | 3 | 14. | 499 | 5 |
| 6. | 383 | 4 | 15. | 495 | 5 |
| 7. | 432 | 4 | 16. | 410 | 4 |
| 8. | 235 | 3 | 17. | 175 | 3 |
| 9. | 494 | 5 | 18. | 417 | 4 |
| **OUT** | **3,454** | **36** | **IN** | **3,333** | **36** |
| | | | **TOTAL** | **6,787** | **72** |

*Called 'an impressively original hole' by Herbert Warren Wind, the 383-yard 6th requires a left-side tee ball in order to open the optimum angle to a superbly bunkered green.*

its right side – closes out the nine. Another pair of downwind par fours open the back nine, with the 382-yard 10th featuring the layout's sole green directly guarded by water. Often overlooked is the 367-yard 12th (whose odd, L-shaped putting surface features some tight rear pin placements), while the 168-yard 13th, its bunker-ringed green elevated against the oceanfront dunes, is comparably celebrated.

### A RESOUNDING FINISH

Seminole's best run of holes comes at the finish, beginning with one of Ross's most thought-provoking par fives, the 495-yard, split-fairway 15th. Here the golfer faces a clear-cut dilemma: aim the tee ball at a small section of right-side fairway tightly squeezed between a pond and four bunkers (thus opening the ideal angle to a green now comfortably within reach) or play safely to the left, making it a three-shot hole and possibly bringing a small extension of the pond into play on the second shot.

The 410-yard 16th is similarly strategic, its right-to-left angled green challenging the aggressive player to gain a significant advantage by driving over three bunkers filling the corner of its dogleg. Then comes the 175-yard 17th, played entirely among the dunes and into a stiff, quartering breeze that makes the narrow, bunker-ringed green an extremely elusive target.

The 18th is a fine hole running parallel to the coast. At 417 yards, it is not overly long, but its elevated tee tempts the golfer to shortcut the sand-guarded dogleg, setting up the ideal angle of attack to a green hoisted among the beach-front dunes. This green, historians will note, is the design of architect Dick Wilson, who in 1947 moved Ross's original version towards the sand dunes – perhaps only one of a series of rumoured green and bunker modifications about which the club has long remained quiet.

### SEASONAL ATTRACTION

Being solely a winter operation, Seminole is a seasonal bastion of affluent golfers and is thus largely reclusive. It does, however, hold a prominent amateur invitational event and, throughout the 1950s, it hosted an annual March pro-am that saw eminent golfers Lloyd Mangrum, Sam Snead, Cary Middlecoff and Arnold Palmer among its winners. The club's most impressive visitor, however, surely was Ben Hogan, who came for a month of practice each spring in preparation for the Masters. 'Seminole is the only course I could be perfectly happy playing every single day', Hogan famously concluded regarding this magnificent venue. 'If you can play well there, you can play well anywhere.'

addition to being abundant (there are more than 175 man-made hazards quite apart from the natural stretches of sand) shows a much flashier cape-and-bay style than Ross's normally staid shaping. However, Seminole's grandest feature may simply be its ambience, because reasonably intact Golden Age courses are a rarity in South Florida, allowing the club's 1920s stylings – its pink stucco clubhouse, famed locker room and stately old palm trees – to shine brilliantly upon a regional golf landscape that is, for the most part, of a distinctly modern vintage.

### INTO THE DUNES

Seminole begins with a pair of shortish, downwind par-fours, with the 387-yard 2nd especially standing out for its beautifully bunkered green benched into the side of the inland ridge. The 501-yard, dogleg-right 3rd features both tee and green elevated among the dunes before the challenge arrives in earnest at the 450-yard 4th, the layout's longest par four, where a right-side tee shot allows the golfer to minimize the impact of a huge bunker on the left some 40 yards (36 metres) in front of the green. Turning back into a three-quarter prevailing breeze, the 202-yard 5th then plays across a wide expanse of open sand to a raised green surrounded by no fewer than eight bunkers – no simple target for long- or even mid-irons.

Play has now reached the property's inland boundary, yet despite residing far from the ocean the 383-yard 6th is surely Seminole's most celebrated hole, its photograph serving as the primary image that many hold of the club. Continuing southwards into the wind, its key feature is a line of four bunkers that begin nearly 100 yards (90 metres) in front of the putting surface, angling across the fairway from left-to-right all the way to the green. The ideal tee shot keeps to the left side of the fairway (close to several more bunkers) as right-side approaches face an extremely difficult angle, with the pin giving the appearance of actually being *in* the sand.

The 432-yard 7th (its fairway flanked by 11 bunkers, its green affected by water) and the 235-yard 8th continue this strong run before the 494-yard 9th – with a distinctly post-Donald Ross lake now flanking

# MIDWESTERN STATES

Despite a climate cold enough to rule out any hope of playing for at least one-third of the year, the American Midwest remains home to several states boasting long golfing histories and admirable rosters of important courses.

The most golf-mad of these states must surely be Illinois, for Midwestern golf – indeed, all American golf west of Pennsylvania – started there when Charles Blair Macdonald founded the Chicago Golf Club (see page 222) in 1892. By the turn of the 20th century, more than 30 additional courses had sprung up around the Chicago area, leaving it second only to New York among period American cities. And many of these layouts were of significant quality: in addition to the Chicago GC's three US Opens and four US Amateurs, Major championship play visited the Windy City regularly before the First World War, with Glen View[1], Onwentsia[2] and Midlothian[3] all hosting US Opens, and Onwentsia adding the 1899 US Amateur as well.

## A MAJOR GOLFING CENTRE

Beyond simply providing an early alternative to popular Eastern tournament venues, Chicago was also something of a second American golfing capital, with its Western Golf Association (WGA) taking on a major national profile, occasionally butting heads with the USGA on administrative issues and questions of amateur status. The city was also the base of operations for early course designers such as Robert and James Foulis, H.J. Tweedie and the legendary mass-producer of early links Tom Bendelow, in addition to one of the Golden Age's more overlooked design stars, William Langford. Thus by the onset of the Depression in the early 1930s well over a hundred courses populated Chicagoland, none more prominent than five-time Major championship venue Medinah[4], whose much-altered No 3 Course remains one of the toughest parkland tests in American golf. It was the scene of Tiger Woods's first PGA Championship victory in 1999.

A similarly high profile is enjoyed by Olympia Fields, whose Willie Park Jnr-designed North Course has hosted two US Opens and two PGA championships, most recently the US Open of 2003. Today Olympia Fields[5] offers 36 fine holes but in its infancy the club was, quite literally, a town of its own, complete with the world's largest clubhouse, a private railway stop and four 18-hole courses.

Among the area's additional notables are a Donald Ross/William Langford hybrid at Skokie[6] (host of the

1922 US Open won by Gene Sarazen) and Seth Raynor's often-overlooked gem Shoreacres[7], a ravine-laden mix of original holes and Raynor's favoured replicas. Another important Ross course, sensitively restored by Ron Prichard, is to be found at the Beverly Country Club[8], venue for the 1931 US Amateur, won by Francis Ouimet, and several Western Opens, the last being in 1967, when the victor was Jack Nicklaus. It benefits from greater elevation change than most Chicago courses as it was constructed on what were once the shores of prehistoric Chicago Lake complete with dune-like sandy soil.

Chicago has enjoyed a fair amount of contemporary golf expansion, as architects Larry Packard, Ken Killian and Dick Nugent altered many older courses and added several new ones of their own, most prominently Killian and Nugent's Kemper Lakes[9], site of the 1989 PGA Championship. The area's best-known postwar layout, however, must surely be George Fazio's Butler National[10], a famously difficult course in suburban Oak Brook and, for many years, host of the Western Open.

## MICHIGAN COURSES

Michigan is another state bearing a significant golfing pedigree, particularly in the Detroit area, where Donald Ross built several prominent courses and England's Charles Alison maintained a 1920s office on behalf of Harry Colt and himself. The inimitable Oakland Hills (see page 220) has long been the area's Major championship calling card, although clubs such as Colt and Alison's Country Club of Detroit[11], their 1921 course at Plum Hollow CC[12] in Southfield, Donald Ross's North Course at the Detroit GC[13] and Wilfrid Reid's splendidly rustic Old Course at Indianwood[14] stand out in their own right.

Michigan has also enjoyed a boom in contemporary construction on its resort-oriented Northern Peninsula, notably the links-like, daily-fee Arcadia Bluffs[15], set along the shores of Lake Michigan, Tom Doak's Lost Dunes[16], created out of a redundant quarry, and Mike DeVries's Kingsley Club[17], in rugged country outside Traverse City, worthy challengers to the supremacy of venerable Crystal Downs[18], which ranks among America's prewar elite.

*The North Course at Olympia Fields has been much altered over the years to keep it in the forefront of championship play. This is the approach to the 12th green.*

## CRYSTAL DOWNS

If there is one thing that stands out about Crystal Downs, it is the golf course's utter originality. It is stocked with all manner of uniquely innovative holes, and its putting surfaces are among the most distinctive ever created by Alister MacKenzie and Perry Maxwell.

With the possible exception of his one-time partner Charles Alison, it is doubtful if any Golden Age golf-course designer travelled as much of the world as MacKenzie. He managed the impressive feat of leaving a major architectural imprint on four continents, beginning with his considerable early work in the UK, then with a whirlwind 1926 visit to Australia and New Zealand, a permanent late-1920s move to the United States and, finally, a 1930s excursion to South America. Yet even with this legacy of intercontinental wanderings, it is easy to imagine MacKenzie's reported displeasure at being diverted from a 1926 cross-country trip (from Pebble Beach to New York, en route to England) to examine a property just outside the remote northern Michigan town of Frankfort.

Travelling with his friend and partner Perry Maxwell, MacKenzie may indeed have resented this detour initially, but his mood surely changed on seeing the land in question – a rolling stretch of occasionally links-like land with commanding views of Lake Michigan and the smaller Crystal Lake. On agreeing to replace an existing nine holes of little distinction with a new 18, MacKenzie and Maxwell remained on site for several days, during which time Maxwell was once sent into town in search of supplies. Returning several hours later, he found MacKenzie seated on a hillside near the present 1st tee, boasting that he'd completed his routing of the front nine.

Maxwell examined the sketch excitedly and, much to his amazement, found that perhaps the greatest golf architect of all had completed his layout with only eight holes! Clearly not wishing to alter his plans, for the 9th hole MacKenzie quickly appropriated the 175 yards (160 metres) of ridge on which they sat, and so was created one of America's more distinctive par threes.

The front nine at Crystal Downs is essentially an open affair, played over an excitingly undulating stretch of ground with fairways framed by thick native grasses, with the really rich golf coming in the nine's latter half, beginning with the 353-yard 5th. Dog-legged to the right, the 384-yard 6th can be shortened considerably by any golfer capable of hitting over a large tree as well as an imposing bunker cluster, known as the Scabs.

The 335-yard 7th is a typical Crystal Downs hole. It requires either a laid-up iron that remains on high ground or else a drive to a lower fairway, from which the approach is at least partially blind. However, the central attraction here is the green, a huge, crescent-shaped surface whose back third is hidden from view by a broad, sand-filled hillside on the right. Similarly well regarded is the 550-yard 8th, a long dogleg right routed across the sort of rolling terrain that affords few level stances. Second shots positioned on the higher right side of the fairway leave the best angle of approach, but the hilltop green remains a tricky target from any angle. Lastly on the outward nine is MacKenzie's afterthought, the 9th, which also plays to an elevated green. This one is flanked left by a dangerous drop and has a fescue-covered hillside to the right while sand awaits an overlong shot.

Perry Maxwell oversaw construction of Crystal Downs following MacKenzie's departure for England. It is known that he took it on himself to amend Mackenzie's plans for the closing pair, though the 311-yard 17th – widely hailed as one of the game's fascinating short par fours – seems little the worse for it. Playing from an elevated tee, its 25-yard (23-metre) wide fairway emerges from the woods and pitches wildly to and fro before climbing to a tiny, windswept green. Potentially drivable (at least in calmer conditions), the 17th does provide a bit of room on the final uphill slope for straight attempts that come up slightly short; however, deep greenside bunkers, plus the generally stiff breezes, still make the risk of having a go considerable.

With the heavily bunkered par-four 18th playing back across open ground, Crystal Downs completes one of golf's most attractive and varied routings. Its path incorporates spectacular scenery, strategic challenge and provides some classic MacKenzie design quirkiness to match.

## NICKLAUS COUNTRY

In golfing circles, Ohio immediately brings to mind the name of favourite son Jack Nicklaus, but the game was deeply rooted in the Buckeye State long before Nicklaus ever picked up a club. Seven-time Major championship host Inverness[19] – a somewhat-altered Donald Ross classic in Toledo – is perhaps best known, although Cleveland's Canterbury[20] and Columbus's Scioto[21] (where Nicklaus learned the game) also rank highly among the region's older venues. Canterbury hosted the US Opens of 1940 and 1946, both of which had to be decided by a play-off, while Scioto's Open took place in 1926, with Bobby Jones victorious. Once held up as a bell-wether of postwar design, Robert Trent Jones Snr's South Course at Akron's Firestone CC[22] has hosted three PGA championships and an endless number of PGA Tour events, though its difficult, none-too-subtle stylings no longer carry the panache they once did. However, both Nicklaus's Muirfield Village (see page 218) and The Golf Club[23] (Pete Dye's 1967 creation in New Albany) continue to rate among the top modern courses in the United States.

## MINNESOTA AND OTHER STATES

Despite being one of America's very coldest states, Minnesota has embraced the game only since the latter years of the 19th century, with the great majority of its top courses situated in the Minneapolis–St Paul region. A number of Golden Age designs remain central to this golfing landscape, but none more so than Interlachen[24], where Bobby Jones memorably skipped a ball across a lake at the 9th hole en route to claiming the 1930 US Open, the third leg of his legendary Impregnable Quadrilateral. Nearby Minikahda[25] also grabbed a piece of history by hosting Chick Evans's 1916 US Open victory, which formed part of Evans becoming the first man ever to claim both the Open and the US Amateur in a single season. Perhaps best known to contemporary readers, however, is a postwar course: Robert Trent Jones Snr's Hazeltine National[26], which, following blistering player criticism at the 1970 US Open, was redesigned and has since successfully hosted another Open (1991) as well as the 2002 PGA Championship.

While the Milwaukee CC[27] is certainly prominent (having hosted the 1969 Walker Cup), golf in Wisconsin has come to be centred around Kohler's American Club resort, which features 72 Pete Dye-designed holes, highlighted by his career-defining layout Whistling Straits (see page 224). Despite more than 50 earlier courses laid out by native son William Diddell, Indiana too has seen most of its elite constructed in the modern era, led by Pete Dye's 1967 design at Crooked Stick[28] (site of John Daly's memorable triumph at the 1991 PGA), Steve Smyers's difficult-but-engaging layout at Wolf Run[29] and Tom Fazio's spectacular Victoria National[30], a water-dominated course routed through an abandoned coal mine.

*There is no compromising on the 16th hole at Hazeltine National, with a tight tee shot to a narrow fairway bounded by trees and a ditch and an approach shot to an angled green surrounded on three sides by water.*

# MUIRFIELD VILLAGE
## Dublin, Ohio

Having modelled much of his career after that of his boyhood idol Bobby Jones, it was perhaps inevitable that Jack Nicklaus would embrace the idea of building a world-class course to host an important tournament event in his home state – a concept that, perhaps predictably, was hatched during a conversation with friends at the 1966 Masters.

I t took Jack Nicklaus the better part of a decade to bring his dream course to fruition, during which time he gained invaluable architectural experience while partnering/consulting on several projects with a young Pete Dye, most notably at South Carolina's seminal Habour Town Golf Links (see page 204). Dye, in fact, prepared multiple prospective routing plans for the golf course that would eventually become Muirfield Village, but by the time ground was actually broken Nicklaus was working with the eccentric Desmond Muirhead and Dye's early input was forgotten.

### A SHARED DESIGN

Whereas Jack Nicklaus was more of a creative consultant and Pete Dye the primary designer during their time working together, it is less clear who bears the greater responsibility for Muirfield Village. Commonly held belief cites Desmond Muirhead, an experienced planner of real-estate developments, as mainly responsible for the layout's routing, with he and Nicklaus battling over each hole's design specifics thereafter. But several who were on site during the design process have said Nicklaus was overwhelmingly in charge of the entire product. In any event, their short-lived partnership dissolved soon after Muirfield Village's 1974 opening, with Muirhead going on to debase the architectural profession with 'symbolic' holes and bunkers shaped like goldfish, while Nicklaus ventured off into one of the more prolific design careers on record.

### HOME TO THE MEMORIAL TOURNAMENT

Though Muirfield Village is, in fact, the centrepiece of a real-estate development, its conception as the permanent host of the PGA Tour's annual Memorial Tournament meant that it was planned largely with professional-calibre golf in mind. Situated on a piece of rolling, frequently wooded land in suburban Columbus, it begins with the long but largely straight-forward 470-yard 1st. It then grabs the golfer's full attention with a pair of tricky par fours – the 455-yard 2nd, with a creek passing dangerously close to the right

side of the green, and the 401-yard 3rd, where a tee shot played beside a left-side stream opens the best angle of approach to a shallow putting surface behind a pond.

The first truly outstanding hole is the 527-yard 5th, a highly strategic dogleg right. Here, the problem is the creek, which cuts in from the left side just beyond the 300-yard (275-metre) mark, then splits the fairway in two all the way to the putting surface. Angling leftwards beyond the water, the green clearly favours an approach played from the right fairway, a particularly difficult place to reach should the tee ball not be hit long and very straight.

## MUIRFIELD VILLAGE GOLF CLUB – Dublin, Ohio
Jack Nicklaus and Desmond Muirhead, 1974
Major events: US Amateur 1992; Ryder Cup 1987; Solheim Cup 1998

CARD OF THE COURSE

| HOLE | YARDS | PAR | HOLE | YARDS | PAR |
|------|-------|-----|------|-------|-----|
| 1. | 470 | 4 | 10. | 471 | 4 |
| 2. | 455 | 4 | 11. | 567 | 5 |
| 3. | 401 | 4 | 12. | 184 | 3 |
| 4. | 200 | 3 | 13. | 455 | 4 |
| 5. | 527 | 5 | 14. | 363 | 4 |
| 6. | 447 | 4 | 15. | 503 | 5 |
| 7. | 563 | 5 | 16. | 215 | 3 |
| 8. | 182 | 3 | 17. | 478 | 4 |
| 9. | 412 | 4 | 18. | 444 | 4 |
| OUT | 3,653 | 36 | IN | 3,680 | 36 |
| | | | TOTAL | 7,333 | 72 |

*The 363-yard 14th, where sand and a narrow green sloping precipitously towards the water make approaching from the left side a necessity, and a four is a desirable score.*

## MEMORABLE HOLES

The close of the front nine offers a pair of memorable holes, beginning with the 182-yard 8th, which plays across a small valley to a narrow, elevated green very nearly surrounded by two huge grass-faced bunkers. Even more dramatic, however, is the 412-yard 9th, a wooded two-shotter featuring a downhill approach to another narrow green, this one angled left-to-right behind a pond.

The inward half starts with the 471-yard 10th, a slightly uphill hole that, in 1976, was featured among the first *World Atlas of Golf*'s best 18 holes worldwide. Curiously, though a long and difficult par four, it lacks much of the strategic flair apparent throughout Muirfield Village's best holes, two of which follow immediately in its wake.

At the 567-yard 11th an elevated tee encourages a long drive to a fairway flanked left by a small creek. At roughly 325 yards (295 metres), the creek cuts across the fairway to guard the favoured right side of the lay-up area, before curving back in front of the heavily pitched green. A hole long enough to make even the big hitters work to get home in two, it manages to require a bit of thought on every shot – and thus quickly became something of a template hole, reappearing in varied but similar forms on many subsequent Nicklaus designs.

Of even greater note, however, is the 184-yard 12th, an adaptation of one of Nicklaus's favourites, the illustrious one-shot 12th at Augusta National (see page 206). Here Nicklaus borrowed the original's two-tiered putting surface, as well as the front-and-back bunker scheme, but then included a deeper, more elevated green and a longer carry over water. Never was it destined to equal Alister MacKenzie's spectacular original, but as a venue for final-day tournament drama Muirfield's version is certainly a superb alternative.

## SHORTER IS BETTER?

For many years, critics of Nicklaus's work claimed that he created courses slanted heavily towards his own powerful, left-to-right style of play, yet two of Muirfield Village's pivotal holes are of a markedly short variety. The 363-yard 14th is a gem of a two-shotter, its narrow green protected by water and sand, and greatly favouring an approach played from the creek-guarded left side of the fairway. Tumbling over hilly, wooded ground to a sharply elevated green, the 503-yard 15th is similarly engaging, being reachable in two by every player on the PGA Tour, yet routinely causing one or two key Memorial Tournament meltdowns with its creek, trees and deep greenside bunkering.

As the course's raison d'être, the Memorial has led to Nicklaus making countless changes, large and small, to the layout. But if great champions are indeed indicative of a golf course's supremacy, then Muirfield Village must surely qualify. In addition to Nicklaus himself, legendary golfers such as Tom Watson, Hale Irwin, Greg Norman and Tiger Woods have all recorded multiple wins here, while Raymond Floyd, Vijay Singh, Fred Couples and Ernie Els lead a long list of Major championship winners who have captured the Memorial title once.

Originally built in 1917, Oakland Hills' South Course always rated among the personal favourites of its esteemed designer Donald Ross, who noted that: 'Its topographical formation could hardly be surpassed, and the area available is so extensive that I was able to lay out a very open and roomy course.' This verdict was seconded by the USGA, which quickly brought the 1924 US Open here (won by Englishman Cyril Walker) and then returned for a second national championship engagement in 1937. This time Ralph Guldahl stepped to the fore, winning the title with a then-record 72-hole aggregate of 281 – guaranteeing that when the US Open returned for a third time in 1951, massive change would be in order. No matter that Guldahl was, in 1937, the finest golfer in the world, nor that the area's normally steady breezes were largely absent during his record-setting triumph. With a push from that great pioneer of USGA course modification, executive secretary Joe Dey, Robert Trent Jones Snr arrived in 1950 to set things right.

### TRENT JONES'S LEGENDARY CHANGES

Performing one of the most historically significant renovations of all time, Trent Jones smartly retained all of Ross's original routing and all but one of his wonderfully contoured putting surfaces. Instead, his alterations were focused on minimizing lines of play from tee to green, removing roughly 80 obsolete bunkers and adding 66 new ones – at least 40 of which severely pinched tee-shot landing areas. Interestingly, Trent Jones added virtually no overall length to the layout; indeed, with the par-five 8th and 18th holes converted to long par fours for The Open, the 1951 layout actually played 110 yards (100 metres) shorter than in 1937 – but it was infinitely tougher.

The results spoke for themselves. While Ben Hogan's winning score of 287 actually matched his previous year's winning aggregate at Merion (see page 190), the reduced par of 70 placed his championship total at plus-seven, the highest relative-to-par finish since Sam Parks won with a plus-15 total of 299 at Oakmont (see page 194) in 1935. Providing further perspective is the fact that Hogan reached plus-seven only by closing with a remarkable 67. In his estimation, this was the finest round of competitive golf he ever played, and it prompted him to assign the course the 'Monster' nickname that it carries to this day.

Subsequently further altered by Trent Jones, Arthur Hills and, most recently, by Trent Jones's son Rees, Oakland Hills remains among the nation's most relentlessly demanding championship venues. Thanks to its Donald Ross pedigree, however, a number of really fine golf holes manage to survive within its unending rigour.

### AN OVERLOOKED FRONT NINE

While the majority of the best holes are found on the back nine, the outward half does offer the 387-yard 6th, where bunkers and trees pinching the fairway suggest either an all-out drive or laid-up iron, and the 449-yard 7th, where a recently enlarged pond guards the preferred right side of the fairway and redesigned bunkers edge in from the left.

# OAKLAND HILLS
## Bloomfield Hills, Michigan

The more frequently a club hosts Major championships, the more regularly its fundamental design will be altered, with many of the nation's finest courses having been changed permanently just to accommodate four rounds of professional golf once every decade or so. Such has been the fate of Detroit's Oakland Hills.

## OAKLAND HILLS COUNTRY CLUB (SOUTH COURSE) – Bloomfield Hills, Michigan

Donald Ross, 1917 and Robert Trent Jones, 1950
Major events: US Open 1924, 1937, 1951, 1961, 1985, 1996; PGA Championship 1972, 1979; US Amateur 2002; US Women's Amateur 1929; US Senior Open 1981, 1991; Ryder Cup 2004

### CARD OF THE COURSE

| HOLE | YARDS | PAR | HOLE | YARDS | PAR |
|------|-------|-----|------|-------|-----|
| 1. | 453 | 4 | 10. | 462 | 4 |
| 2. | 529 | 5 | 11. | 455 | 4 |
| 3. | 198 | 3 | 12. | 593 | 5 |
| 4. | 446 | 4 | 13. | 191 | 3 |
| 5. | 490 | 4 | 14. | 501 | 4 |
| 6. | 387 | 4 | 15. | 401 | 4 |
| 7. | 449 | 4 | 16. | 406 | 4 |
| 8. | 491 | 4 | 17. | 238 | 3 |
| 9. | 257 | 3 | 18. | 498 | 4 |
| OUT | 3,700 | 35 | IN | 3,745 | 35 |
| | | | TOTAL | 7,445 | 70 |

*Rear view of the green at the famous 406-yard, par-four16th, with the uphill, 238-yard 17th in the background. Many a Major championship contender has floundered here.*

Hopefully reaching the turn relatively unscathed, the golfer begins the much-anticipated inward half with a stiff 462-yard par four before reaching one of the layout's elite holes, the 455-yard 11th. Here the ideal tee shot moves diagonally across a long stretch of rough (where both Ross and Trent Jones bunkers have been removed) to a twisting, sloping fairway guarded right by more carefully positioned sand. Once this has been safely accomplished, there remains an uphill approach shot to a narrow, saucer-like green flanked by four bunkers, rough-covered slopes to either side and a nasty slope beyond.

### A BACKBREAKING FINISH

The hardest hole at Oakland Hills is very probably the 501-yard 14th, a newly enlarged par four so challenging that even Trent Jones saw no need to bunker the fairway. Apart from a relatively narrow driving area, the danger here lies mostly in the green, a large, somewhat elevated surface marked by a depression running vertically through its middle. With the resultant pin placements in its higher corners being of unusual difficulty, the 14th yielded not a single birdie during the 1951 US Open, and at its extravagant modern length it plays little easier today.

The 401-yard 15th, a sweeping dogleg left, represents the rare case of Trent Jones actually enhancing a hole's strategic possibilities. He did this by adding a bunker in the very centre of the fairway, suggesting either a laid-up tee ball or an aggressive drive squeezed between the sand and some thick left-side woods.

Oakland Hills is surely best known for the 406-yard 16th, a dogleg right played to a smallish green set attractively behind a pond. The site of a glorious Gary Player 9-iron to 4 feet (1.2 metres) that clinched the 1972 PGA Championship, this frequently photographed hole actually remains much as Donald Ross first built it. Although Robert Trent Jones Snr rebunkered the green and enhanced the dogleg by moving the fairway farther left, the fundamental challenge – whether to flirt with the water by going for the green or to search for a safe patch of short-left fairway – remains vintage Ross. Finally, the 238-yard, slightly uphill 17th and the converted par-four 18th (played as a par five by members) are notoriously difficult tournament closers.

# CHICAGO
## Wheaton, Illinois

There have been many important clubs in the history of American golf, yet none has played a larger role – or had its name more prominently recalled – than that early Western outpost of the Royal & Ancient game, the Chicago Golf Club.

## CHICAGO GOLF CLUB –
## Wheaton, Illinois
Charles Blair Macdonald, 1895 and
Seth Raynor, 1923
Major events: US Open 1897, 1900, 1911; US
Amateur 1897, 1905, 1909, 1912; US Women's
Amateur 1903; Walker Cup 1928, 2005; Curtis
Cup 1928, 2005

### CARD OF THE COURSE

| HOLE | YARDS | PAR | HOLE | YARDS | PAR |
|---|---|---|---|---|---|
| 1. | 450 | 4 | 10. | 139 | 3 |
| 2. | 440 | 4 | 11. | 410 | 4 |
| 3. | 219 | 3 | 12. | 414 | 4 |
| 4. | 536 | 5 | 13. | 149 | 3 |
| 5. | 320 | 4 | 14. | 351 | 4 |
| 6. | 395 | 4 | 15. | 393 | 4 |
| 7. | 207 | 3 | 16. | 525 | 5 |
| 8. | 413 | 4 | 17. | 382 | 4 |
| 9. | 406 | 4 | 18. | 425 | 4 |
| **OUT** | **3,386** | **35** | **IN** | **3,188** | **35** |
| | | | **TOTAL** | **6,574** | **70** |

The Chicago story was written largely by the legendary Charles Blair Macdonald, who learned the game from Old Tom Morris while studying at St Andrews University in Scotland and then endeavoured to introduce it to Chicago upon his return to America in 1874.

Macdonald's first recorded effort came a year later when he and a visiting St Andrews college friend batted gutta percha balls around the grounds of an abandoned Civil War-era fort. They soon gave up after, as he later wrote: 'The hoodlums in the vicinity tormented us to death.' There followed what Macdonald called the 'Dark Ages', in which he played the game only during visits back to the UK, but by 1892 he had finally gathered enough local support to build the first recorded course in the American heartland.

### AMERICA'S FIRST 18-HOLER
This first Chicago Golf Club was a seven-hole affair erected on the estate of Senator C.B. Farwell, but it was soon replaced by nine holes on a suburban Belmont farm. At this point accounts differ. Macdonald himself claimed to have expanded the Belmont track to 18 holes in 1893, but this story is refuted by several period newspaper articles, which instead cite Chicago's third and final facility – a layout opened in Wheaton in 1895 – as the region's sole complete 18. Whatever the truth, the Chicago GC, in one location or another, enjoys the historical distinction of having possessed the first 18-hole golf course in the United States.

According to legend, Macdonald – a chronic slicer – built the Wheaton course to suit his own style of game. Though his motivation will never be known for certain, it is true that the layout all but ignored the interior of the large rectangular property. Instead, it fanned out in a clockwise manner along the perimeter, with out-of-bounds repeatedly affecting play on the left. Such quirkiness notwithstanding, Macdonald's design quickly became one of America's elite tournament venues, hosting three US Opens and four US Amateurs between 1897 and 1912. Especially notable among these were Harry Vardon's victory in the 1900 US Open (the highlight of his ground-breaking American tour), John McDermott's triumph as the first native-born American to claim The Open in 1911, and both H.J. Whigham and H. Chandler Egan successfully defending their US Amateur Championship titles in 1897 and 1905 respectively.

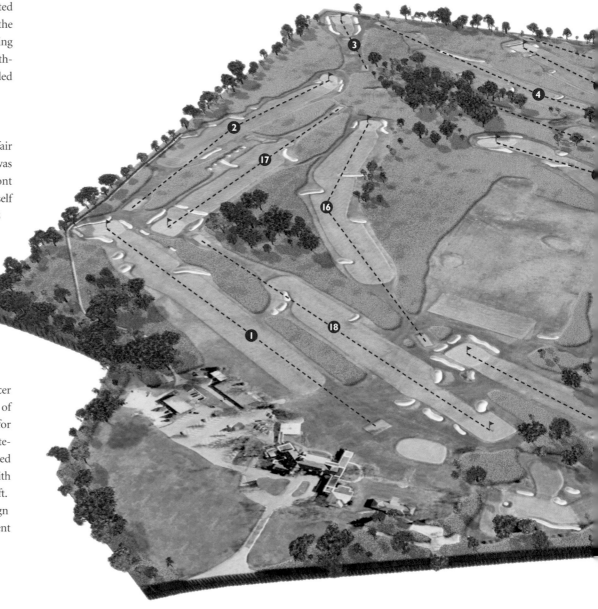

## ENTER SETH RAYNOR

By the early 1920s the old layout was in need of upgrading, a job for which Macdonald – now largely retired from architectural work – designated his protégé Seth Raynor. Raynor's redesign essentially represented the creation of an entirely new golf course: it maintained the corridors of play of several Macdonald holes but otherwise reconfigured things completely. Though not significantly longer, it was a considerably more balanced and refined test, while also introducing a number of the famous Macdonald/Raynor replica holes, none of which had been incorporated previously.

Little has changed from Raynor's day, the present course represents one of America's grand old designs. It is laid out across mostly flat Midwestern farmland, with tall waves of native fescue and large putting surfaces defining most holes. Oak trees dot the landscape but seldom affect play, while water, in the form of a single lake, is encountered only twice. Thus in no way fancy or overbearing, Chicago is a course defined by two overriding charms. Firstly, despite today being surrounded by suburbia, the vast expanse of the land and thickly foliaged boundaries still give the club a wonderfully isolated feel. Secondly, it represents the quintessential demonstration of the Macdonald/Raynor design style, for its squarish greens and bunkers, and man-made contours are obviously at odds with the native terrain, yet somehow manage to feel quite natural just the same.

### A FIRST-CLASS START

Chicago is not an arduous golf course, but its opening three holes can match up to almost any in the USA. It begins with a long, straightaway 450-yard par four, then turns in the prevailing wind at the 440-yard Road hole 2nd. The 219-yard Biarritz 3rd also angles into a quartering breeze, making the swale-fronted, geometrically bunkered green a particularly difficult target. With just a standard wind blowing, even the scratch golfer is pleased to reach the 4th tee at even par.

Another replica of merit is the 207-yard 7th, a longer-than-average Redan playing into the property's south-western corner. With little natural variance to the terrain, the only way to recreate the back-left fall-away and deep front-left bunker of the Redan green was to artificially elevate the entire putting surface that, like many here, is squared off at the edges. In still conditions the hole is challenging. Into the wind, it calls for a low, drawn shot of a highly skilled nature.

The closest thing to a vintage 1895 hole is the 139-yard 10th, which mirrors the forced water carry of Macdonald's old 9th, but with the trappings of the Short hole – two huge bunkers nearly encircling the putting surface, and not one but two horseshoe-shaped ridges – built in. The 425-yard 18th also bears some resemblance to Macdonald's original closer, though that hole was played at 466 yards when, in the final stages of the 1897 US Open, Joe Lloyd made an improbable three to edge the soon-to-be-great Willie Anderson by one.

### A NATIONAL TREASURE

The Chicago Golf Club may not be done hosting US Opens, but with its shimmering native grasses, classic replica holes and a layout so unaltered that it differs by only 5 yards (1.5 metres) from that which hosted the 1928 Walker Cup, it remains among the most interesting and historic golf courses in the United States.

# WHISTLING STRAITS
## Sheboygan, Wisconsin

The brainchild of plumbing-fixtures magnate Herb Kohler, Whistling Straits was built as an amenity for Kohler's popular American Club resort, which already featured 36 well-known Dye holes, an inland complex known as Blackwolf Run.

For his new course at Whistling Straits Herb Kohler wanted a waterfront layout to mirror the great links of Ireland, even though Wisconsin lies some 1,000 miles (1,600 kilometres) from the nearest ocean. Fortunately, however, the American Club was fairly close to the shoreline of Lake Michigan. Thus one complicated land swap later, Kohler had acquired an extensive piece of lakefront, with spectacular waterfront bluffs as high as 70 feet (21 metres). Unfortunately, the property's interior, a long-abandoned army training base, was essentially pancake-flat and pockmarked with roads and other military detritus, leaving a great deal of work to be done before any comparisons with Ballybunion (see page 120) might be even remotely in order.

### A MAN-MADE MASTERPIECE

Never one to shy away from a challenge, Dye brought in enough sand to replicate the Sahara, then apportioned it entirely as he wished. The resulting metamorphosis was astonishing, even by Pete Dye's singularly innovative standard, with massive dunes springing up as needed and literally hundreds of bunkers of every shape and size carved into the landscape. If anything, there were perhaps too many bunkers, occasionally making strategic choices tough to delineate, but overall Dye's creation of an imaginery Irish coastline left before-and-after observers in admiring awe. In order to vary shoreline usage, Dye built each nine like a figure of eight, allowing both outgoing and returning holes to abut the lake, with the nines divided by a large, jungle-like ravine that was the property's only inland feature.

### TO THE LAKEFRONT

Following a straightforward opener and a long par-five 2nd, the first taste of the Lake Michigan shorefront comes at the 183-yard 3rd. This is a downhill, Redan-like hole where balls missed left will tumble to the beach. The 455-yard 4th is a stiff test played to a narrow bluff-top green guarded short-left by a massive, typically rough-edged bunker complex. A 584-yard affair that zigzags between lakes, the 5th is an unfortunate anomaly here, necessitated by the recreation of significant wetlands for environmental permitting reasons.

## THE STRAITS COURSE AT WHISTLING STRAITS –
## Sheboygan, Wisconsin
Pete Dye, 1998
Major events: USPGA Championship 2004

### CARD OF THE COURSE

| HOLE | NAME | YARDS | PAR | HOLE | NAME | YARDS | PAR |
|---|---|---|---|---|---|---|---|
| 1. | Outward Bound | 405 | 4 | 10. | Voyager | 389 | 4 |
| 2. | Cross Country | 592 | 5 | 11. | Sand Box | 619 | 5 |
| 3. | O'Man | 183 | 3 | 12. | Pop Up | 166 | 3 |
| 4. | Glory | 455 | 4 | 13. | Cliff Hanger | 403 | 4 |
| 5. | Snake | 584 | 5 | 14. | Widow's Watch | 372 | 4 |
| 6. | Gremlin's Ear | 391 | 4 | 15. | Grand Strand | 465 | 4 |
| 7. | Shipwreck | 214 | 3 | 16. | Endless Bite | 535 | 5 |
| 8. | On the Rocks | 462 | 4 | 17. | Pinched Nerve | 223 | 3 |
| 9. | Down and Dirty | 415 | 4 | 18. | Dyeabolical | 489 | 4 |
| **OUT** | | **3,701** | **36** | **IN** | | **3,661** | **36** |
| | | | | **TOTAL** | | **7,362** | **72** |

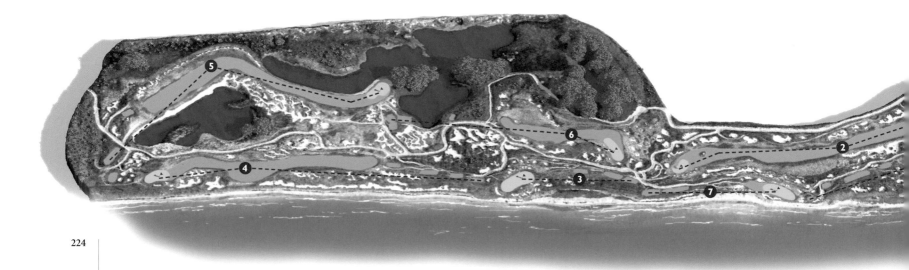

The drive-and-pitch 6th on the Straits Course quickly leads one back to the links-like milieu, however, before the shoreline is revisited with a vengeance on perhaps the club's most photographed hole. This is the low-lying 214-yard 7th, its deep, left-to-right angled green closer to the waves than any other Whistling Straits putting surface. There is no room to miss right here, and a large dune to the left offers comparably little bailout room. A blind tee shot away from the water begins the 462-yard 8th, followed by an approach that returns to it, the large green set into a left-to-right slope framed by a vast Lake Michigan vista.

## THE INWARD HALF

The back nine starts with a pair of typically creative inland holes: the 389-yard 10th, where a single centre-line bunker some 255 yards (230 metres) out provides multiple tee-shot options; and the 619-yard 11th, a strategically engaging test featuring a huge bunker lined with railway sleepers and guarding the left side of the second-shot landing area. Carry this imposing hazard and a simple pitch remains; hit a seemingly easier shot to the right and a nasty front-right green-side bunker looms large.

Back along the lakefront, the 166-yard 12th is the layout's shortest hole and features one of the more interesting greens a golfer may encounter. Its left side is large and welcoming, essentially hittable with any reasonably struck ball. But this putting surface grows progressively narrower as it turns towards the water, culminating in a tiny back-right segment representing little more than a narrow spit of green wedged between dunes and a steep fall-away. With a standard

*A side view of the green at the 214-yard 7th. Like many of Whistling Straits's lakeside holes, there is little room to miss this putting surface in any direction.*

lakefront breeze, this is a pin position that requires real guts to attack.

## THE EPIC 17TH

Following yet another bluff-top green at the 403-yard 13th, and the temptation to shortcut the bunker-guarded dogleg at the 372-yard 14th, come some nicely varied finishing holes. The 465-yard, par-four 15th is difficult as it runs downhill towards the lake, while the 535-yard 16th is a reachable par five. It is the 223-yard 17th, however, that truly dominates the homestretch. Its larger-than-it-looks green is angled right-to-left along a bulkheaded precipice that plunges 20 feet (6 metres) towards the lake. The right side of the putting surface, which is obscured by a somewhat contrived-looking bunker, does provide a bit of bailout room – but hardly enough for comfort.

The 489-yard, two-shot 18th is a quirky and demanding driving hole, and not to every golfer's taste. Its 18,000-square-foot (1,670-square-metre), sham-rock-shaped putting surface feels manifestly over-the-top and is rather at odds with the less-flashy nature of the other 17 greens.

## TRULY A WORLD-CLASS TEST

Whistling Straits successfully hosted Vijay Singh's play-off victory in the 2004 USPGA and Brad Bryant's triumph at the 2007 US Senior Open. Singh's winning total of 280 was the PGA's highest in 14 years and was recorded in only a modest breeze, suggesting that in a strong wind the Straits Course – despite its highly strategic underpinnings – must certainly rank among the very hardest on Earth.

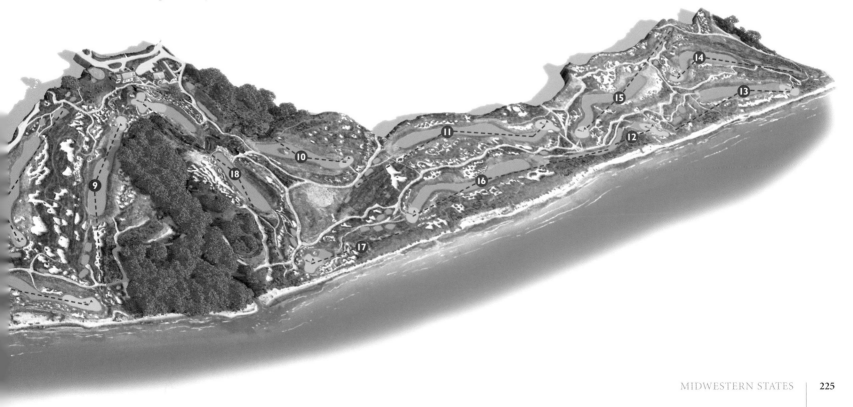

# CENTRAL STATES

With a four-hole course reportedly being played on a Burlington, Iowa farm during the summer of 1883, and Scottish émigré Alex Findlay batting a ball about the Nebraska prairie in 1887, golf laid some very early roots in America's central states.

Much of this region's vast, wide-open countryside is topographically limited, and its central and southern sections regularly bake under scorching summer heat, making the great majority of early courses basic affairs faced with considerable agronomic hurdles. Consequently, this is probably the only region of America where contemporary courses, as a whole, consistently outshine their Golden Age brethren – frequently by a wide margin.

A conspicuous exception lies in Kansas where Prairie Dunes (see page 228), Perry Maxwell's seminal links-style layout, remains one of America's uniquely attractive courses more than 70 years after the opening of its initial nine holes. Most of the state's other top courses are found in the Kansas City area, led by the venerable Kansas City Country Club[1] – an A.W. Tillinghast design that launched Tom Watson on the road to fame – and a pair of far newer tests, Tom Fazio's Flint Hills National[2] and Tom Weiskopf and Jay Morrish's Shadow Glen[3].

## MAINLY MODERN COURSES

In Missouri, the St Louis area was an early centre of play, but only one of its Golden Age courses can truly rank among the region's elite; it is Charles Blair Macdonald and Seth Raynor's St Louis Country Club[4], site of the 1947 US Open and the 1921 and 1960 US Amateurs. On the modern side, Gary Nicklaus's Dalhousie GC[5] (located in Cape Giradeau) is often rated the state's best and features a bit more rustic appearance than most entries in the Nicklaus family portfolio. A pair of Robert Trent Jones Snr standards – Old Warson[6] and three-time Major championship site Bellerive[7] – also deserve a mention, though being built in 1955 and 1960 respectively these layouts can now be chronologically linked far more closely with the Golden Age than the modern.

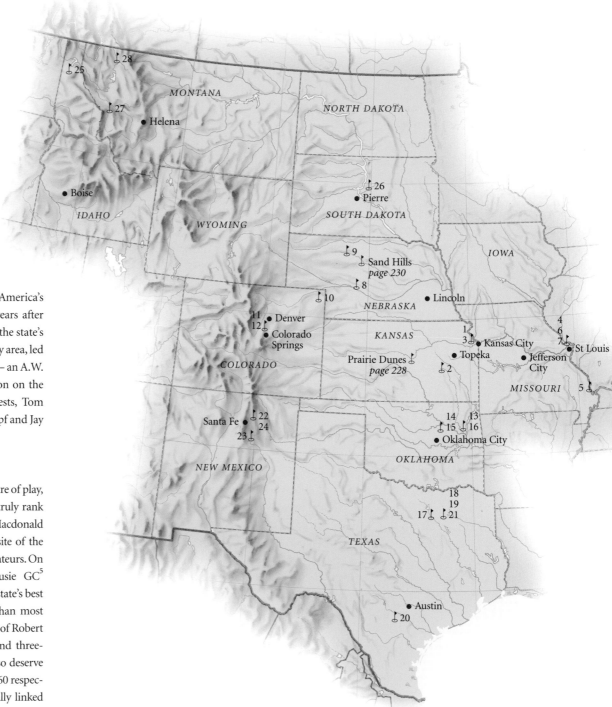

## DUNES AND BIGGER HILLS

Seldom viewed as a golfing centre during the century that followed Alex Findlay's early adventures, Nebraska has become an object of much attention since the arrival of Bill Coore and Ben Crenshaw's spectacular Sand Hills (see page 230) in 1995. Perhaps the finest American course built since the Second World War, its dunes-covered landscape was bound to draw imitators to the state's west–central region, an assemblage led by the public Wild Horse[8] in Gothenburg and, more recently, Jack Nicklaus's stunning design at Dismal River[9]. Geographic inaccessibility and a sparse population are likely to limit large-scale development in this region, yet the links-like nature of the rolling, treeless terrain will surely draw further entries before the financial cup runs dry.

One such example lies in nearby north-eastern Colorado, where comparable terrain allowed Tom Doak to fashion a similarly authentic test at Ballyneal[10], just outside the farming town of Holyoke. However, most Colorado courses of distinction lie in more developed areas, and virtually all of the best older designs are around Denver, where recently restored, six-time Major championship venue Cherry Hills[11] has perennially garnered most of the acclaim. Modern development was for many years centred along the north–south axis of Interstate 25, particularly on the southward run to Colorado Springs, where Jack Nicklaus's design at Castle Pines[12] served as long-time host of the now-defunct International Tournament on the PGA Tour. In recent years, however, new courses have been springing up regularly within the enormously scenic valleys that dot the Rocky Mountains, as the region continues to transform from skier's paradise to a year-round recreational destination.

Despite its stifling summer heat, Oklahoma embraced the game fairly early, helped by the presence of Perry Maxwell who, in addition to partnering with Alister MacKenzie for a spell, lived and built some 18 courses there. Most notable among these is the state's consensus number one layout – seven-time Major championship host Southern Hills[13] – but here again many more of the best are of a modern vintage. Pete Dye's Oak Tree[14] (site of the 1984 US Amateur and 1988 PGA) carries the highest national profile among these newer courses, but Tom Fazio's designs at Oklahoma State University's Karsten Creek[15] and the Golf Club of Oklahoma[16] generally draw comparable acclaim.

## NURSERY TO MANY FAMOUS GOLFERS

Few states offer more golfing history than Texas, which groomed Hall-of-Famers Ben Hogan, Byron Nelson, Jimmy Demaret, Lloyd Mangrum and Ralph Guldahl within a single era, and players such as Jack Burke Jnr, Lee Trevino, Ben Crenshaw and Tom Kite thereafter. Curiously, though, the state has produced precious few nationally prominent courses, particularly prior to the Second World War when difficult agronomic conditions helped limit the elite to 1941 US Open site (and perennial PGA Tour stop) Colonial[17] and nearby Brook Hollow[18], an A.W. Tillinghast design restored by Bill Coore and Ben Crenshaw in 1992. In the modern era, once-prominent tournament venues such as Dallas's Preston Trail[19] and San Antonio's Pecan Valley[20] (site of the 1968 PGA Championship) have been pushed aside by a spate of newcomers, with more than 800 courses now in play state-wide. Yet despite so much new course construction, only Tom Fazio's Dallas National[21], a 2000 design situated south-west of downtown Dallas, draws serious attention for consideration among the nation's best.

The region's remaining five states – New Mexico, Idaho, Montana and the Dakotas – are spread across many kilometres and, for the most part, feature virtually no classic courses of prominence. But, with the growth in modern holiday/retirement homes there, some striking newcomers have appeared. In New Mexico, Jack Nicklaus's 36 holes at Las Campanas[22] is particularly noteworthy, as are Ken Dye's Paa-Ko Ridge[23] and Baxter Spann's Black Mesa[24], while Idaho is led by Jim Engh's slightly over-the-top Club at Black Rock[25]. Sutton Bay[26] – a dune-filled Graham Marsh design in Agar, South Dakota – represents the consensus choice as the Dakotas' best, but it is Montana, an increasingly popular holiday and second-home destination, that has begun producing the most noteworthy courses. Tom Fazio's Stock Farm[27] and Iron Horse[28] set the present state-wide standard, but this high-growth market promises to attract an increasing number of worthy challengers in the years immediately ahead.

# PRAIRIE DUNES
## Hutchinson, Kansas

Prairie Dunes Country Club in Kansas lies almost precisely at the centre of the continental United States, far distant from major oceans. Yet ironically the rolling, dunes-covered terrain to the north-east of Hutchinson are most probably the closest approximation of the game's most hallowed seaside terrain in North America.

Unlike the more recently developed Sand Hills region of Nebraska (see page 230), nobody had to travel great distances to discover the site on which the Prairie Dunes Country Club sits. The club was built by the Carey family, a local salt-mining clan whose love of golf led them to develop a remarkable five courses in this landlocked town with a 1930s population of 25,000. Of this quintet Prairie Dunes is easily the best, due not only to its superior terrain but also to the Careys' selection of Perry Maxwell as their architect.

### FATHER THEN SON

Perry Maxwell, a Kentucky native, turned Oklahoma banker, was a man of means, building his first course (Dornick Hills) on his own land in Ardmore before later partnering with Dr Alister MacKenzie for three years, handling construction on several of MacKenzie's prominent American projects. Widely remembered for the scale and contouring of his putting surfaces, Perry Maxwell took full advantage of the rare opportunity that was Prairie Dunes, producing a course whose genuinely British style was extremely unusual in prewar American golf. The layout in play today is, however, only half Perry Maxwell's work – the economic realities of the Depression having limited its initial construction to nine holes. It was his son J. Press Maxwell who in 1957 seamlessly blended nine entirely new holes to his father's original nine.

To play Prairie Dunes is to encounter a particularly skilful blend of the natural and the man-made. The natural is represented in the setting for beyond the sandy, dunes-covered landscape the property is bathed in a sea of tall native grasses, plum thicket, yucca plants and, in its north-east reaches, a decidedly unlinks-like, but thoroughly charming, grove of cottonwood trees. The man-made, on the other hand, comes in the form of the Maxwells' skilled, highly authentic contouring, not just on the ever-undulating greens but also across the fairways, where a good deal of hand-shaped pitch-and-roll results in very few level lies. Throw in one final natural feature, the constant Kansas winds, and Prairie Dunes is a healthy challenge for any golfer.

### THE FAMOUS 2ND

After a long but fairly nondescript opener, the golfer faces a sterner test at the 161-yard 2nd, a visually striking, slightly uphill par three. The problems here are many: the green, which angles towards ten o'clock, is particularly ill-suited to the prevailing left-to-right cross-wind. Further, it is backed by a large, thicket-covered dune and otherwise surrounded by five bunkers, the largest, which sits front and centre, being some 10 feet (3 metres) deep. A back-left pin is particularly difficult, but three is a solid score no matter where the hole is cut.

Following the 168-yard 4th played to a similarly elevated green, three of Press Maxwell's 1957 additions – all solid, none overwhelming – set the scene for the challenge that is the club's most recognized hole, the 430-yard 8th.

### ONE OF AMERICA'S BEST

Selected by *Sports Illustrated* as one of America's 18 best in 1966, the 8th is a long dogleg right favouring a drive carved into the prevailing left-to-right cross-wind – the green being completely visible only from

# PRAIRIE DUNES COUNTRY CLUB – Hutchinson, Kansas

Perry Maxwell, 1937 and J. Press Maxwell, 1957
Major events: US Women's Open 2002; US Women's Amateur 1964, 1980, 1991;
US Senior Open 2006; Curtis Cup 1986

## CARD OF THE COURSE

| HOLE | NAME | YARDS | PAR | HOLE | NAME | YARDS | PAR |
|---|---|---|---|---|---|---|---|
| 1. | Carey Lane | 432 | 4 | 10. | Yucca | 185 | 3 |
| 2. | Willow | 161 | 3 | 11. | Honey Locust | 452 | 4 |
| 3. | Wild Plum | 355 | 4 | 12. | Briar Patch | 390 | 4 |
| 4. | Hilltop | 168 | 3 | 13. | Sumac | 395 | 4 |
| 5. | Quail Ridge | 438 | 4 | 14. | Cottonwood | 370 | 4 |
| 6. | Cedar | 387 | 4 | 15. | The Chute | 200 | 3 |
| 7. | Southwind | 512 | 5 | 16. | Blue Stem | 415 | 4 |
| 8. | The Dunes | 430 | 4 | 17. | Pheasant Hollow | 500 | 5 |
| 9. | Meadowlark | 426 | 4 | 18. | Evening Shadows | 382 | 4 |
| **OUT** | | **3,309** | **35** | **IN** | | **3,289** | **35** |
| | | | | **TOTAL** | | **6,598** | **70** |

*Played on an elevated green surrounded by bunkers, dunes and thicket, there is little room for error at the 161-yard, par-three 2nd.*

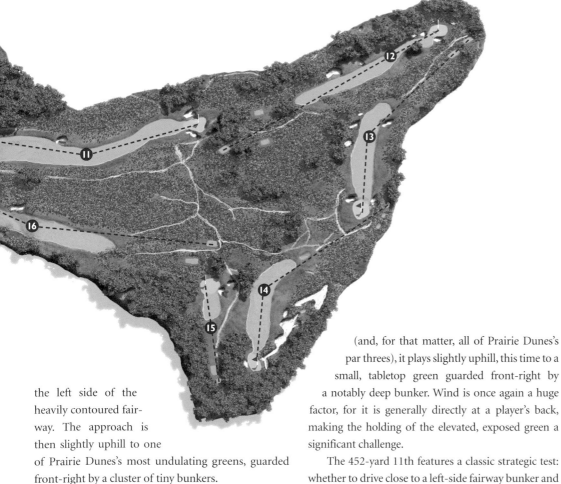

the left side of the heavily contoured fairway. The approach is then slightly uphill to one of Prairie Dunes's most undulating greens, guarded front-right by a cluster of tiny bunkers.

Widely considered to be of comparable merit is the 426-yard 9th, yet it is the 185-yard 10th that is recorded as Perry Maxwell's personal favourite. Like the 2nd (and, for that matter, all of Prairie Dunes's par threes), it plays slightly uphill, this time to a small, tabletop green guarded front-right by a notably deep bunker. Wind is once again a huge factor, for it is generally directly at a player's back, making the holding of the elevated, exposed green a significant challenge.

The 452-yard 11th features a classic strategic test: whether to drive close to a left-side fairway bunker and thicket or to face a long approach to a shallow green angled behind sand and in front of a prominent mound that deflects most run-up shots.

## COTTONWOODS AND NATIVE GRASSES

Then comes a stretch of four holes in which the cottonwoods can affect play, most obviously at the 390-yard 12th, where the approach must avoid several of the tallest trees, and the 370-yard 14th, whose green is recessed within an ancient grove. Although hardly typical of true links golf, the trees do provide welcome shade from the intense summer sun, which is of more importance in Hutchinson than at St Andrews (see page 40).

The modern player may feel the need to reach the straight 500-yard 17th in two, but finding this green – a tiny, elevated, hump-backed affair – is especially difficult with the prevailing wind blowing against, a large, yucca-dotted bunker left and a steep bank right. Though only 382 yards long, the 18th is similarly appealing, drifting between walls of native grass to an angled, heavily bunkered green. Little altered by contemporary hands, Prairie Dunes remains a timeless classic.

# SAND HILLS
## Mullen, Nebraska

When it opened for play in June 1995 Sand Hills Golf Club was appreciated for being one of the most natural courses built in the United States since the First World War.

Given the origins of the game along the North Sea, golf has always enjoyed an element of escapism, a sense of getting away from it all. In an ever-crowded world, this sensation becomes more cherished. Fortunately, ease in modern travel allows golfers access to out-of-the-way places. As a result, golf clubs and resorts from the Oregon coastline in the United States to Bali to Tasmania in Australia have been developed in recent times whereas, before, they would not have been economically viable. One such club is Sand Hills Golf Club, located in the expansive sand-hills range in north central Nebraska.

### SUPERB TERRAIN FOR GOLF

The credit for finding and providing this primal reunion of golfer with nature belongs to Dick Youngscap and his partners. Long aware of the great sand-hills range and of the Ogallala aquifer, Youngscap searched this unique area for several years looking for property with landforms that might yield holes of high golfing quality. As Youngscap noted: 'Not all sand hills are created equally.' An option on 8,000 acres (3,237 hectares) was secured in August 1990, and Ben Crenshaw and Bill Coore made their first visit to the site the following month.

Numerous visits followed over the next two years and by spring 1993 they had discovered more than 130 holes, from which 18 were selected and a routing plan finalized. During that year, most of the work was concentrated on the irrigation system, which comprised 85 per cent of the total golf-course construction cost. Fairways, greens and tees were created by mowing existing vegetation to ground level, then tilling all areas to a depth of 6 inches (15 centimetres). After minor finish grading on the greens, all that was needed was to apply seed, fertilizer and water.

Such a straightforward process highlights how little of the land was disturbed during the course construction. Furthermore, due to the excellent sand

particles, the cost per Sand Hills green was less than one per cent of that of a USGA specification green because neither drain tile/gravel under the greens nor special greens mix was required.

### USING THE NATURAL ELEMENTS

Consistent with the huge scale of the place, the course enjoys massive fairways 50–90 yards (45–80 metres) wide, which weave in and out and over and around the sand hills in every possible manner. This is a consequence of Bill Coore and Ben Crenshaw's marvellous routing, where they were more interested in following

nature's lead and in finding the best holes than they were in having a formulaically balanced course of five par fours, two par threes and two par fives per nine holes. Thus, the final sequencing of the holes that they settled on was certainly not conventional. The 1st is a three-shotter, and there is not another par five until the 14th. The 7th and 8th are short two-shotters but, as they lie in opposite directions, they rarely play the same in the windy environment.

Nonetheless, the challenge to route 18 consecutive holes that played well together in all wind conditions was a monumental one. Shaped by the elements over

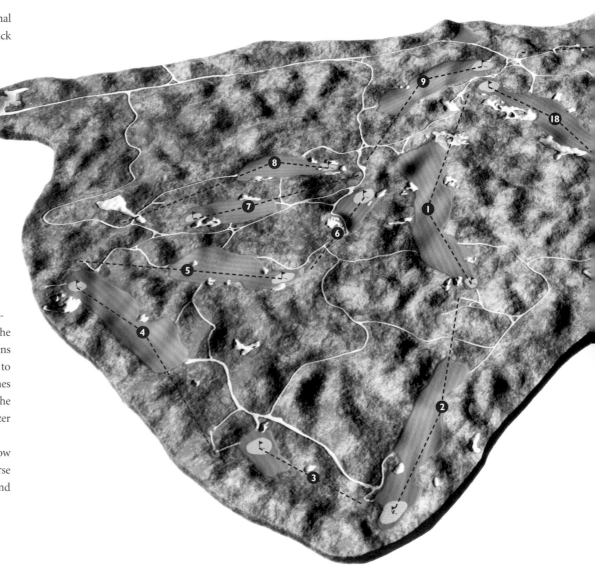

thousands of years, the unique natural landforms were of great beauty and all parties concerned agreed that as many of them as possible needed to be included in the final course. In addition, the game of golf is a walking one, and the green-to-tee walks needed to be short. Patience was required to find such a layout, and Bill Coore and Ben Crenshaw walked the property for 30 months before settling on the routing that yielded the best 18-hole sequence.

Another crucial task was the detail work on and around the greens, which is the heart and soul of any course. Here, Coore and Crenshaw reintroduced the all-important (and all-but-dead) art form of tying the entrances of the greens to the greens themselves. The majority of the greens are open in front, allowing the course to play well in all winds.

## A LINKS COURSE FAR FROM THE SEA

In all respects other than its physical proximity to water, Sand Hills plays like a links course. And, like the great links in the United Kingdom, the wind comes from all directions and so to discuss the holes at Sand Hills in terms of par is meaningless. One day, a 3-wood reaches the 283-yard 7th, while the next day the golfers need to punch a 7-iron low and under the wind for the second shot. The 16th hole at more than 600 yards (549 metres) can be reached in two downwind or requires a wood for the third shot if played into the wind. Typical inland courses do not possess this day-to-day variety.

Also, like the great links, a walk around Sand Hills is a study in hazards, both in bunker placement and bunker construction. Coore's favourite quote on bunkers comes from Robert Hunter who wrote in *The Links* that bunkers 'should have the appearance of being made with carelessness and abandon with which a brook tears down the banks which confine it, or the wind tosses about the sand of the dunes…forming depressions or elevations broken into irregular lines. Here the bank overhangs, where there it has crumbled away.' Coore must have been pleased by his design team's handiwork as that is exactly the effect that they achieved at Sand Hills. Indeed, as man's hand feels very light in the construction of the entire course, all golfers feel a strong reconnection with nature when playing here.

## INTRIGUING GOLF HOLES

For all the sensitivity displayed towards nature throughout the construction process, the quality of the individual golf holes remains what matters most. After all, in order for its members to want to travel great distances to get here, the prospect of playing the holes must be an enticing one. Starting with the false front at the 1st green, which can send balls 20 yards (18 metres) back off the elevated green, the course is rich with vexing features. How best to use the slope left of the 3rd green to feed the tee ball onto the large green is a shot that a golfer never tires of playing.

Though plenty of big hitting is required across the rolling topography, as highlighted by the 472-yard 10th and 467-yard 18th, the holes that require the most finesse are often cited as among the game's finest. Examples include the eminently drivable 283-yard 7th, the 508-yard 14th with its small green angled against a dune and the one-shot 150-yard 17th. This wide variety of challenge makes the course such a delight to play, year after year.

Coore, characteristically modest, stated: 'The Sand Hills site was ideal. The challenge there was to create a course equal to the potential of the land. To have constructed anything less than an extraordinary golf course on that site would have been a failure.'

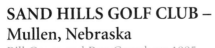

## SAND HILLS GOLF CLUB –
## Mullen, Nebraska
Bill Coore and Ben Crenshaw, 1995

CARD OF THE COURSE

| HOLE | YARDS | PAR | HOLE | YARDS | PAR |
|------|-------|-----|------|-------|-----|
| 1. | 549 | 5 | 10. | 472 | 4 |
| 2. | 458 | 4 | 11. | 408 | 4 |
| 3. | 216 | 3 | 12. | 417 | 4 |
| 4. | 485 | 4 | 13. | 216 | 3 |
| 5. | 412 | 4 | 14. | 508 | 5 |
| 6. | 198 | 3 | 15. | 469 | 4 |
| 7. | 283 | 4 | 16. | 612 | 5 |
| 8. | 367 | 4 | 17. | 150 | 3 |
| 9. | 402 | 4 | 18. | 467 | 4 |
| **OUT** | **3,370** | **35** | **IN** | **3,719** | **36** |
| | | | **TOTAL** | **7,089** | **71** |

*Though the shortest par three on the course, the 17th with its tiny green is an elusive target in the wind. The ability to control one's ball flight is a must.*

# WEST COAST STATES

According to rumour, the game of golf first appeared in Riverside, California in 1891, and on Catalina Island and at several sites in the northern half of the state a year later. As a matter of generally accepted fact, it began in both the San Francisco Bay area town of Burlingame and in Riverside in 1893.

I n the Bay area, golf caught on quickly, with several more documented facilities in existence prior to the dawn of the 20th century, and a fine list of additions opening during the Golden Age. The Olympic Club's Lake Course (see page 242) remains one of the perennial landmarks, while other less celebrated layouts include Dr Alister MacKenzie's Meadow Club[1], secreted away in the hills north of Mt Tamalpais, Willie Watson's Orinda CC[2], which features such fascinatingly named holes as Inspiration, Mouse Trap, Despair and Gibraltar, and George Thomas and Billy Bell's now-altered layout at Stanford University[3] on which both Tom Watson and Tiger Woods played college golf.

## SAN FRANCISCO GOLF CLUB

No account of the finest golf courses in and around San Francisco would be complete without mention of the San Francisco Golf Club[4], one of the oldest clubs in the west, having been founded in 1895. It began within the confines of the former Presidio military base, adjacent to the Golden Gate Bridge, the club moving twice before settling into its present site along the city's southern boundary, just south-east of Lake Merced. This was an area destined to become a competitive golfing centre: by the mid-1920s The Olympic Club had built 36 holes just across the lake; Harding Park's[5] fine municipal 18 occupied the northern shore; and the Lake Merced Country Club[6] was completed less than half a mile (1 kilometre) to the south. This gave San Francisco a cluster of first-class courses – and professional championship venues – to be envied by almost any city in America.

Within this closely situated group, only the San Francisco Golf Club has elected not to embrace major tournament play, the sum total of its national events being the PGA Tour's San Francisco Match Play title in 1938 (Jimmy Demaret winning by 4-and-3 against Sam Snead) and a 13–5 American victory in the 1974 Curtis Cup. Such assiduous avoidance of the spotlight

has allowed the club to maintain a degree of reclusive anonymity nearly unsurpassed in American golf. This in turn has made its splendid course one of the least seen among the nation's elite. The damp Bay area climate encourages the growth of trees and shrubs, which allied with the undulating topography, produces picture-perfect playing corridors, truly uplifting to those members and the few visitors fortunate enough to play here.

It seems entirely in keeping then that for course design aficionados the architectural history of the present San Francisco layout has long been a source of some puzzlement. Its creation has been officially attributed to A.W. Tillinghast – that stalwart of eastern Golden Age design – though in reality his 1920 work represented alterations to a course already in place, and of unknown origin. How or why the club chose Tillinghast is also unknown. He was not particularly well established in the late 1910s and, so far as is recorded, had never ventured west of San Antonio before being hired.

Making matters even more curious is San Francisco's trademark bunkering, which is of a scale and style visibly at odds with virtually all of the Tillinghast portfolio. Where Tillinghast tended to focus mostly on intimidating greenside hazards, San

Francisco also features scores of fairway bunkers placed at varied angles and distances, and their considerable scale and flowery shaping is in stark contrast to his more restrained norm. Very likely, they were rebuilt before the Second World War by the California architect Billy Bell (whose style they suggest), but whoever was responsible it is apparent that multiple hands built today's San Francisco design.

Like many Golden Age courses, this once wide-open, wind-exposed layout is today largely tree lined, perhaps a detriment architecturally but surely not in terms of ambience, for San Francisco's rolling, cypress-bordered fairways must rank among the most attractive in American golf. Considerable charm also lies in the fact that 15 of its 18 holes are virtually unaltered strategically since before the war, except for the addition of some longer tees and the unnoticeable removal of a few extraneous bunkers. The three exceptions – the 13th, 14th and 15th – were replaced in 1950 in anticipation of an adjacent freeway expansion that, in the end, actually encroached little on the property. Thus after more than a half century of using three postwar mongrels, in 2005 the club hired Tom Doak to restore, as faithfully as possible, Tillinghast's originals.

The 134-yard 13th is the most welcomed revised hole, for this was a widely photographed one-shotter in the early years, its tiny, bunker-surrounded putting surface earning it the nickname 'Little Tilly'. Doak's 423-yard 15th is also impressive, especially its imposing right-side fairway bunker whose original edges were unearthed, in true archeological style, during the restoration.

## FURTHER CALIFORNIAN ABUNDANCE

Moving down the coast from San Francisco, in Santa Cruz lies MacKenzie's Pasatiempo[7] (where he lived in a house beside the 6th fairway for his final years), while on the Monterey Peninsula Pebble Beach (see page 244) and Cypress Point (see page 248) have forever remained household names to golfers everywhere. The Bay area lacked land for widespread postwar course development, but Monterey's golfing growth has continued well into the modern era, with Spyglass Hill (see page 252) opening in 1966 and the Links at Spanish Bay[8] (built by Robert Trent Jones Jnr, Sandy Tatum and Tom Watson) following in 1987.

In southern California, Santa Barbara features another Alister MacKenzie gem, the Valley Club of Montecito[9], while the state's southernmost regions – Los Angeles, San Diego and Palm Springs – all have extensive golfing histories. In Los Angeles, where

nearly as many fine courses have been lost as still exist, George Thomas's famous 'triumvirate' excel: Riviera (see page 254), the North Course at the Los Angeles CC[10] and his uniquely routed canyon course Bel-Air[11]. Sherwood[12] – a Jack Nicklaus design in suburban Thousand Oaks – is notoriously upmarket, while Moorpark's Rustic Canyon[13] (built by Gil Hanse and Geoff Shackelford) is one of the west coast's most thought-provoking public courses. San Diego has long been known for Dick Wilson's quintessential 1960s design at La Costa[14], as well as for 36 public holes at scenic and exceptionally tough Torrey Pines[15], host to the 2008 US Open, although Max Behr's Rancho Santa Fe CC[16] (built in 1929) and several nearby newcomers cannot be overlooked.

And then there is Palm Springs, which is virtually a golfing universe of its own with well over a hundred courses laid out across the Coachella Valley's vast desert floor. Unfortunately, the general sameness of terrain has inevitably led to a rather uniform standard of design, with distinctly man-made water hazards frequently providing the lion's share of the test. It is not surprising, then, that most of the area's best courses also rank among its least stereotypical, with Pete Dye's Mountain Course[17] at La Quinta utilizing a bit of higher terrain, Tom Doak's Stone Eagle[18] taking this concept to even greater heights and Tom Fazio's Quarry at La Quinta[19] offering all manner of interesting (if entirely man-made) features. Pete Dye's Stadium Course at PGA West[20] ranks among the very hardest courses ever built.

## MODERN DESERT COURSES

Few states have seen greater modern golf development than Arizona, much of it taking place around Scottsdale and in more temperate getaways (for example, Flagstaff and Prescott) to the north. Arizona is also responsible for spawning the modern conception of American desert golf: a forced-carry, target-oriented game necessitated by water-conscious state laws limiting new courses to a maximum of 90 acres (36 hectares) of maintained turf. The result, once again, is a certain sameness of style, yet northern layouts such as Pine Canyon[21], The Rim[22] and both the Canyon and Meadow courses at Forest Highlands[23] certainly provide a different feel. Like Palm Springs, Scottsdale's best courses often gain their edge by utilizing some attractive mountain terrain, most notably Tom Fazio's Estancia Club[24], Jack Nicklaus's Desert Highlands[25] and his six-course megacomplex at Desert Mountains[26]. On the older side, Carefree's Desert Forest[27], an ultra-natural 1962 Red Lawrence design, is a perennial regional favourite.

The last of the West's desert states, Nevada, was a true latecomer to the game, with nearly all of its top courses being modern tests in the vicinity of Las Vegas. Casino mogul Steve Wynn's Shadow Creek (see page 236) is by far the state's highest-rated course, with Rees Jones's Cascata[28] and the Nicklaus-designed complex at suburban Lake Las Vegas[29] demonstrating innovative ways of creating interesting golf in inhospitable landscapes. Beyond Las Vegas, Mesquite's spectacular Wolf Creek[30] is blasted through a rocky moonscape only metres from the Utah border, while Jack Nicklaus's Montreux GandCC[31] – a regular stop on the PGA Tour – is the highest-rated course in the Reno area.

## NEW BOOM AREAS

The Pacific north-west was, for many decades, somewhat quiet golfing country, but recent resort/real-estate development in Oregon has lifted the region's profile immeasurably. The Bend/Sunriver area has gained a prominent foothold in this regard, but the region's superstar, without question, lies along the coast, where the Bandon Dunes[32] golf resort offers some first-rate courses including Tom Doak's Pacific Dunes (see page 238), David McLay Kidd's Bandon Dunes and Bill Coore and Ben Crenshaw's Bandon Trails[33].

Outside the contiguous 48 states, Alaska is predictably disinterested in the game of golf, but the resort capital of Hawaii is the polar opposite. A 1926 visit by Seth Raynor – who planned much-altered layouts at PGA Tour stop Waialae[34] and Mid-Pacific[35] – gave the islands a solid start, but it has been primarily through modern resort development that the game has boomed. On the Big Island, Robert Trent Jones Snr's Mauna Kea[36] and the newer Mauna Lani[37] lead the way, while Maui offers Kapalua[38], where Bill Coore and Ben Crenshaw's spectacular Plantation Course annually entertains the Tour professionals. Kauai, for its part, features notable Robert Trent Jones Jnr designs at the Princeville Resort[39] (45 holes) and at Poipu Bay[40] – annual site of the PGA's Grand Slam of Golf.

*The 206-yard par-three 6th hole on the North Course at Torrey Pines may play up to 40 yards shorter when the wind is in the golfer's favour. The penalties for missing the green are plainly obvious!*

# SHADOW CREEK
## North Las Vegas, Nevada

The veritable mantra of architect Tom Fazio, 'total site manipulation' was more than a design theory at Shadow Creek; it was an absolute necessity. But Shadow Creek was funded by casino mogul Steve Wynn, who could well afford such extravagance.

I n a modern era in which the majority of potentially great golf-course sites are either exhausted or too environmentally encumbered for profitable development, Tom Fazio has established himself as a designer unfazed by starting with less. Moving massive amounts of earth and engaging in 'total site manipulation', he has successfully created well-known courses in barren deserts, abandoned quarries and hilly mountain sites, all neatly framed to look as aesthetically appealing as possible. Although such large-scale projects often lack the subtle, more intricate contouring associated with courses laid more gently into the land, they have certainly served Fazio well, for there has been no bigger name in the design business since the 1980s.

### GOLFING OASIS

Such qualifications surely made Tom Fazio an ideal candidate when, during the mid-1980s, Las Vegas magnate Steve Wynn decided to build a golf course. With his then-trademark property perhaps fittingly called The Mirage, Wynn was experienced in creating something from nothing in the middle of the Nevada desert. Furthermore, as an avid golfer, he had clear ideas as to just what type of facility he desired – so much so, in fact, that Fazio himself willingly acknowledged Wynn as a co-designer when the project ultimately came to fruition.

In many ways Shadow Creek represents the modern equivalent of Charles Blair Macdonald and Seth Raynor's long-lost Lido Golf Club, a 1917 New York creation in which more than 2 million cubic yards (1.5 million cubic metres) of landfill were utilized to reclaim a previously underwater site, effectively allowing the designers to shape the landscape to their every whim. In suburban Las Vegas, reclaiming land was hardly an issue; finding more than the

faintest amount of natural contour within it was. The result was an excavation of earth massive enough not only to create the desired playing surface (plus numerous water hazards) but also to build what amounted to a giant berm around the perimeter, nicely secluding the course and also limiting the player's external view to the tops of the surrounding mountains rather than the less-attractive desert below.

### STEVE WYNN'S IDEAS

Given this blank canvas, Wynn could have patterned the course's aesthetic after any inland region or style, and he chose the sand-hills region of North Carolina. To this end, more than 21,000 mature trees were imported and their environs surrounded by pine needles, as well as pampas and other non-native grasses. Wynn also copied Augusta National (see page

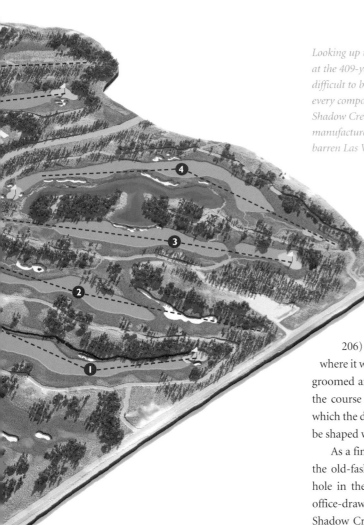

*Looking up the fairway at the 409-yard 9th, it is difficult to believe that every component of the Shadow Creek layout was manufactured out of a barren Las Vegas desert.*

# SHADOW CREEK –
## North Las Vegas, Nevada
Tom Fazio and Steve Wynn, 1989

### CARD OF THE COURSE

| HOLE | YARDS | PAR | HOLE | YARDS | PAR |
|------|-------|-----|------|-------|-----|
| 1. | 404 | 4 | 10. | 426 | 4 |
| 2. | 401 | 4 | 11. | 327 | 4 |
| 3. | 443 | 4 | 12. | 395 | 4 |
| 4. | 553 | 5 | 13. | 232 | 3 |
| 5. | 206 | 3 | 14. | 460 | 4 |
| 6. | 476 | 4 | 15. | 438 | 4 |
| 7. | 567 | 5 | 16. | 581 | 5 |
| 8. | 166 | 3 | 17. | 164 | 3 |
| 9. | 409 | 4 | 18. | 527 | 5 |
| **OUT** | **3,625** | **36** | **IN** | **3,550** | **36** |
| | | | **TOTAL** | **7,175** | **72** |

206) by minimizing rough and dictating that, where it was absolutely necessary, it should be closely groomed and minimally punishing. He also required the course to be walkable, and that its vistas – over which the designers obviously held complete control – be shaped with the perspective of the walker in mind.

As a final unique point, Wynn and Fazio followed the old-fashioned method of designing nearly every hole in the field rather than working from a set of office-drawn plans. This perhaps explains why Shadow Creek offers a bit more panache than many more office-born projects.

## MAN-MADE SPLENDOUR
Following a fine 404-yard opener, where the startlingly natural-looking Shadow Creek flanks the entire left side, and the 401-yard 2nd, things come alive at the 443-yard 3rd. This is a long two-shotter with an approach played uphill to large green that, though unbunkered, falls away at its front and right edges. The 553-yard 4th sweeps leftwards around a lake before players cross the entrance road to challenge the 'abyss' at the exciting 206-yard 5th. A solid enough par three based solely on its length, this hole features the one hazard specifically demanded by Wynn: a 60-foot (18-metre) deep, tree-filled chasm, which must be carried (with only a small left-side safety area) if the putting surface is to be reached.

The front nine's second par three, the 166-yard 8th, also relies heavily on oversized contouring. It is built into its own secluded valley accessed by a pair of tunnels: one by the tee, the other by the green. Then the outward half closes with the 409-yard 9th, a straight par four on which the creek returns, flanking the left side of the driving area before angling short and left of the green.

The back nine is best known for its big finish, although that stretch could be said to start at the 13th, a downhill 232-yarder played to a suitably large green slanting rightwards, beyond sand and a water-filled ravine. Both the 14th and 15th are long par fours with greens flanked by a lake and creek respectively, while the 581-yard 16th, comfortably the Shadow Creek's longest hole, doglegs right, then crosses tumbling terrain before climbing to a narrow, elevated green.

## ENLIGHTENED EXTRAVAGANCE
The 17th is the club's shortest and most-photographed hole, measuring a mere 164 yards – but it is nearly all-carry to a tiny, pond-fronted green set before a high, forested ridge and a large waterfall. The entire setting, though functional enough, is patently over-the-top in the middle of a desert. But first-class showman that he is, Wynn understood the delicate balance, writing of the 17th that: 'Had we delivered this kind of treatment too often, it might have been excessive. But it was irresistible to do it once.' Though a touch less fancy, the 527-yard finishing hole is comparably exciting; it is lined by a series of ponds and is eminently reachable in two provided the golfer is prepared for long water carries on each swing.

## NOW OPEN TO THE PUBLIC
During Shadow Creek's early years, Wynn lived in a mansion off the 18th fairway and reserved the course for his friends and select clients, but in 2000 he lost the property to Kirk Kirkorian's MGM Grand Resorts in a hostile takeover. Today the golf course can be accessed, for a hefty fee, by guests of Kirkorian's properties. Tom Fazio's finest work, then, has become the world's most expensive public golf course, but the sheer magnitude of its creation remains plainly apparent for all to see.

# PACIFIC DUNES
## Bandon Resort, Oregon

Mike Keiser, owner of Bandon Resort, gave Tom Doak instructions for
Pacific Dunes that every architect longs for: 'Find the best course you can
and without allowances for houses or golf-cart paths as there will be neither.
This will be a walking-only course, free of outside disturbances.'

Following the immediate success of Bandon
Dunes (see page 240) – the first course at
Bandon Resort – Tom Doak was commissioned to build Pacific Dunes on the
remaining land to the north of Bandon
Dunes. The terrain was quite diverse, highlighted by the spectacular cliff line with the
Pacific Ocean pounding below. To the east,
there was an enormous valley where the
17th and 18th holes now are. In between
the cliff and the valley, there was a gorse
plain and a large sandy bowl area.

### FUN GOLF

Having travelled together in the United
Kingdom, Mike Keiser and Doak learned
to admire the rugged naturalness of Royal
County Down (see page 116) as well as the routing
at Royal Portrush (see page 114), where each nine
reaches to the edges of the cliffs. Armed with this
knowledge and free of the restrictions that hamper
most modern courses, Doak created a course that
Keiser most cherished – one that catered for fun golf.

Notionally, it might be assumed that fun golf is
what every owner likes. After all, golf is a game meant
to be enjoyed. However, after the Second World War
and the Vietnam War, numerous courses built in the
United States were long, arduous tests, reflecting in
some ways the mood of the nation. Even through the
1980s and into the 1990s, there were only occasional
glimpses of golf-course architecture that recaptured
the joy of the game represented during the Golden Age
of golf-course design, some 80 years before the opening of Pacific Dunes, in 2001.

The pressure was now on Doak to build a great
course. He had already produced several fine ones but
had never had an opportunity of this magnitude.
Fortunately, relying on his encyclopedic knowledge
from having studied more than 900 courses worldwide, Doak was able to employ features possessed by
some world-class courses.

# BANDON DUNES GOLF RESORT
## (PACIFIC DUNES) —
## Bandon Resort, Oregon

Tom Doak, 2001
Major events: Curtis Cup 2006

### CARD OF THE COURSE

| HOLE | YARDS | PAR | HOLE | YARDS | PAR |
|------|-------|-----|------|-------|-----|
| 1. | 370 | 4 | 10. | 206 | 3 |
| 2. | 368 | 4 | 11. | 148 | 3 |
| 3. | 499 | 5 | 12. | 529 | 5 |
| 4. | 463 | 4 | 13. | 444 | 4 |
| 5. | 199 | 3 | 14. | 145 | 3 |
| 6. | 316 | 4 | 15. | 539 | 5 |
| 7. | 464 | 4 | 16. | 338 | 4 |
| 8. | 400 | 4 | 17. | 208 | 3 |
| 9. | 406 | 4 | 18. | 591 | 5 |
| **OUT** | **3,485** | **36** | **IN** | **3,148** | **35** |
| | | | **TOTAL** | **6,633** | **71** |

## NATURAL CONTOURS

On the 370-yard 1st, the crumpled fairway, complete with its humps and bumps, stands in stark contrast to the fairways of most modern courses where heavy machinery flattens the natural contours. The 368-yard 2nd hole is multiroute due to a central bunker in the fairway. Into the prevailing northerly, the golfer has to think long and hard about carrying it and reaching the lower level of the fairway from where the green opens up. Such a central hazard had all but vanished from American golf architecture during the period 1960–1995.

As highlighted for over a century by the Old Course at St Andrews (see page 40), central bunkers create multiple playing routes within holes. Golfers must decide which option is best for them, based on their own swing that day as well as the wind and the day's hole location. Most modern golf-course architects had sadly ignored this design tenet, frequently pushing bunkers to the sides of holes where they only punish a wayward shot. However, Doak's designs differ from his peers in that he featured classic design elements such as central bunkering throughout his courses. The golfer appreciates this fact again when standing on the 3rd tee, where he has a clear view of two massive central bunkers in the fairway.

Ever sensitive to the desires of the retail golfer (as he calls recreational golfers), Keiser was delighted when Doak's routing ran the 463-yard 4th along the edge of the 100-foot (30-metre) tall cliff. Most golfers travel great distances to reach the Bandon Resort, and it is spectacular, one-of-a-kind moments such as this one that make them glad they did so.

Though it moves inland for the rest of the front nine, the course continues without let-up. The 199-yard 5th green nestled in the dunes accepts balls that kick in from its high left side. This is but one example of the course's short-game interest and it is also a prime example of the superb turf conditions that the greenkeeping staff presents. With its cool evenings, rainfall, sandy soil and fescue grasses, Pacific Dunes and the two other Bandon courses (Bandon Dunes and Bandon Trails) play akin to the links in the United Kingdom. Players with the talent to play the ball low and under the wind relish the opportunity to use their full shot-making repertoire.

## A PAR FOUR TO TREASURE

Tom Doak's favourite courses, including St Andrews, Royal Melbourne (see page 286) and Crystal Downs, share a common trait of great, short two-shotters. At the 316-yard 6th, Doak created one that any course would proudly call its own. Its wide fairway is not the comfort it appears because approach shots played from left of centre come into the elevated narrow green at a progressively worse angle. The course's deepest greenside bunker is front left and is a deterrent for big hitters having a go at the green from the tee.

The 7th green complex is a prime example of the architect following nature's lead. According to Doak, the 'bunkers to the left of the green are formalized versions of natural blowouts and the dips and mounds short of the green have never been touched by equipment'. All told, it makes for a demanding green complex for a hole of 464 yards.

In beautiful contrast to the table-top 7th green is the green at the 400-yard 8th, with its punchbowl right half inspired by Doak's affection for the 3rd hole at Woking. When the hole location is right, approach shots that skirt around the high side of the central front bunker can be gathered close to the hole. The 8th becomes more demanding when the hole is set left where the green is domed and tends to shrug approach shots long into the back bunker. The front nine concludes with a par four with alternate greens whereby the high right green sets up for a fade from the tee while the lower left green calls for a hook.

# BANDON DUNES
## The start of something big

When it came to building Pacific Dunes, the questions surrounding the risk in creating a resort course along the remote coast of Oregon had been largely answered by Bandon Dunes. Indeed, the phenomenal success of Bandon Dunes had necessitated the need for additional golf. As Doak commented: 'Without Bandon Dunes, there would be no Pacific Dunes.'

The Bandon Dunes dream had taken shape in 1991. Despite strong doubts expressed by his friends and business colleagues, Mike Keiser had persisted in purchasing 1,215 acres (492 hectares) of Oregon coastal property. Intuitively, Keiser felt the terrain lent itself to good golf, given the gorse, wind and several thousand feet of ocean frontage. However, the land-use laws were such in Oregon that there was no guarantee he would be allowed to build a golf course. Even if he could gain the permits, would the public come? At this stage, many felt Keiser's dream was folly.

Once permission was obtained through the help of his partner Howard McKee, the next step was to hire a golf-course architect. Keiser's choice of David Kidd surprised everyone as Kidd had yet to build his first course. Kidd though came from a strong golf lineage – his father, Jimmy Kidd, was the long-serving director of agronomy at Gleneagles (see page 66) in Scotland. Indeed, Jimmy Kidd played a crucial role at Bandon because he selected the mix of grass seed there. The direct consequence of his getting it right is that Bandon Dunes plays firm and fast like a true links. Being young, Keiser felt David Kidd would not have any predetermined design style that he would stamp on the property, a trait that excluded many 'name' architects from consideration. This hunch proved right, because the course has a number of unique holes such as the 5th and 16th, both cliffside par fours the likes of which had never been built before.

As Kidd's routing evolved, only the 17th hole from his initial routing survived into the final 18. Like George Crump at Pine Valley (see page 186), Keiser solicited feedback from his friends whom he flew out to Oregon. When Kidd was struggling to create interesting holes on a flat section of property away from the cliff, Keiser purchased a further 400 acres (162 hectares) north of the existing parcel of land. He was adamant that golfers should not face a boring stretch of holes. One of Bandon Dunes's best stretches – the 5th to the 8th – is on this later acquired land.

The course was seeded in 1998 and opened for play in 1999. Everyone, including the media, quickly embraced this return to golf as a simpler pursuit – walking only, no carts and the concept of man battling nature free from outside disturbances.

## FOLLOWING NATURE'S LEAD

Over the next six holes, the golfer faces only one par-four hole and that is at the 13th. This unconventional sequencing of holes was not lightly settled on. Yes, the 206-yard 10th and 148-yard 11th are back-to-back par threes. However, the downhill 10th is bunkerless to a large green with subtle rolls level with its surroundings, while the 11th is the opposite: its elevated green set into the dunescape is surrounded by bunkers, making it the smallest target on the course. Ultimately, the compelling nature of each of these holes convinced Doak and Keiser that they were the best sequence for that course. Both men believed in following the natural contours and knew it was nonsensical to think that all terrain should yield nines with two par threes, two par fives and five par fours. They appreciated the unconventional aspects of some of the world's great courses. For example, Alister MacKenzie featured back-to-back par threes, par fives and short par fours at Cypress Point (see page 248).

The fall-away green at the 529-yard 12th befuddles golfers trying to get their pitch close. Routed along the top of the ridge, the 145-yard 14th appears simple, yet recovery shots are demanding because an offline tee shot puts the golfer well below the putting surface. Doak's 15th green complex with its plateau green offers the golfer the same approach options as the famed Foxy hole at Royal Dornoch (see page 54), one of Keiser's very favourite holes. A classic drive-and-pitch hole follows, this time with the general playing angles of the famous 10th at Riviera (see page 254).

Against a stunning, gorse-covered dune as a backdrop, traditionalists embrace the Redan-playing characteristics of the 208-yard 17th as they feed the ball in from high right. Typical of the rest of the holes, the golfer is given plenty of room to work the ball. Indeed, Pacific Dunes's diversity of challenge combined with its freedom to create shots are at the heart of what makes it so enjoyable to play. The round concludes with the longest hole, a twisting par five with one of the course's most fearsome hazards being the blow-out bunker that dominates the second shot area.

## INFLUENCE OF PACIFIC DUNES

Considerable impact has been made by the design at Pacific Dunes. It helped Doak gain projects on other exhilarating sites around the world including Australia, New Zealand and several in the United

*Doak considers the 13th to be the most natural hole at Pacific Dunes with its board fairway hemmed in by the cliff line on the left and a massive sand blow-out on the right.*

States. By building world-class courses on those sites as well, Doak further demonstrated the merits of this brand of architecture whereby the randomness of nature is highlighted, not hidden, in the design. Mike Keiser in turn continues to scour the world looking for, as he puts it, 'sandy sites on large bodies of water to build golf courses for the public to enjoy'. Ultimately, Keiser promotes the development of great courses in remote seaside locations, whether by contributing to them financially or just by inspiring others to pursue their dreams with the success of Pacific Dunes.

# THE OLYMPIC CLUB
## San Francisco, California

When a newly formed club chooses to call itself Knollwood, Silver Oaks or even the TPC Death Valley, the flatly generic ring does little to suggest that any sort of special experience lies in the offing. But when an organization christens itself The Olympic Club, surely that must suggest greater prospects altogether.

S an Francisco's Olympic Club, founded by a group of fitness-oriented men in 1860, has long upheld this high standard, both with its downtown athletic club and its coastal golfing facility. The latter is situated on high ground above the Pacific, just across Lake Merced from Harding Park.

### BEGINNINGS
Golf actually began on this site in 1917, when an organization known as the Lakeside Golf and Country Club opened a short-lived 6,410-yard Wilfrid Reid-designed course. The expanding Olympians purchased the Lakeside Club shortly after the First World War and quickly hired Scottish émigré Willie Watson to redesign it. Enlisting the club's future greenkeeper, Sam Whiting, as his assistant, Watson proceeded to create a pair of 18-hole courses, the 6,606-yard Ocean Course (which included several spectacular holes on the coastal side of Skyline Boulevard) and the 6,589-yard Lake Course. Not surprisingly, it was the flashier Ocean that was the club's initial attraction – that is, until a series of early landslides claimed several of its showpiece holes, leading to a complete Whiting redesign in 1927.

Even with the Ocean Course relegated to a shorter, awkwardly configured status, it took a good 20 years for the Lake Course to reach a position of golfing prominence. It initially occupied a semibarren hillside, was devoid of water hazards and out-of-bounds, and included only a single fairway bunker. Whiting addressed these issues by undertaking one of golf's grandest-ever tree planting projects, a comprehensive endeavour that added more than 30,000 pine, cypress, eucalyptus and palms to the mix. As a result, by the end of the Second World War, the Lake Course became one of the game's most demanding tests, the gnarled limbs that tightly frame its every fairway requiring an unceasing level of accuracy rarely matched in championship golf.

But if trees have succeeded in turning a relatively basic design into a test difficult enough to host US Opens, so too have they given it a distinctively beautiful atmosphere. For a game at the Lake Course is an aesthetically enriching experience, its massive walls of green secluding every fairway, standing tall amid San Francisco's frequent fog, and occasionally opening to marvellous views of the adjacent Lake Merced and the distant Golden Gate

Bridge. What the Lake Course lacks in strategic design, then, it certainly compensates for in difficulty and character.

### NEGOTIATING THE TREES
Many of the Lake's more interesting holes fall on the outward half, with few capturing the layout's challenge and ambience as well as the 247-yard 3rd. Playing from a substantially elevated tee, it is a downhill one-shotter aimed at a narrow green pinched, both at its edges and in its approach, by four prominent bunkers. The target itself is daunting, while the view above the treeline – across much of the city's western expanse towards the Golden Gate and the Marin Headlands – is nothing short of inspiring.

## THE OLYMPIC CLUB
### (LAKE COURSE) –
## San Francisco, California
Willie Watson and Sam Whiting, 1924
Major events: US Open 1955, 1966, 1987, 1998; US Amateur 1958, 1981, 2007

CARD OF THE COURSE

| HOLE | YARDS | PAR | HOLE | YARDS | PAR |
|---|---|---|---|---|---|
| 1. | 533 | 5 | 10. | 422 | 4 |
| 2. | 425 | 4 | 11. | 430 | 4 |
| 3. | 247 | 3 | 12. | 455 | 4 |
| 4. | 438 | 4 | 13. | 186 | 3 |
| 5. | 498 | 4 | 14. | 417 | 4 |
| 6. | 439 | 4 | 15. | 157 | 3 |
| 7. | 286 | 4 | 16. | 607 | 5 |
| 8. | 137 | 3 | 17. | 491 | 4 |
| 9. | 433 | 4 | 18. | 347 | 4 |
| OUT | 3,436 | 35 | IN | 3,512 | 35 |
| | | | TOTAL | 6,948 | 70 |

*A near-ground-level view of the downhill 247-yard 3rd. Few holes anywhere in the world better balance a championship-calibre test with great scenery.*

Should a golfer still not grasp the true difficulty, the course sets a sterner test at the 4th and 5th – a pair of longer par fours (438 and 498 yards) frequently rated among the toughest back-to-back holes in golf. Here a player faces the classic Olympic Club challenge, for neither hole has a fairway bunker nor, strictly speaking, bunkering that closely guards its putting surface. Both are extremely difficult driving holes, with fairways curving awkwardly against sloping terrain and tree limbs reaching out to snare even marginally wayward shots. The temptation to use a fairway metal is huge, but if accomplished safely such a tactic results in much longer-than-desired approaches.

The Lake is the odd course comprised of a front eight and back 10, for it is indeed the 137-yard 8th, with its small, bunker-ringed green, that returns to the base of the huge hill-top clubhouse. From here a run of mid-length par fours, plus a pair of shortish par threes, carry play first to the property's northern tip, then back, alongside John Muir Drive, to a somewhat offbeat set of finishers.

## CLOSERS

The 607-yard 16th is an obvious bruiser, making what seems an endless left turn to a very small, tightly bunkered green. Amazingly, it was actually reached in two by the legendary Bobby Jones in 1929, though the forest that blockades the inside of the dogleg today did not yet exist at the time.

For US Open play, the 522-yard 17th is converted to a bruising par four, though with its sharply sidehill fairway and conspicuously undersized green, it is seldom confused with the fairest of two-shotters. The 18th, on the other hand, seems a perfect closer for so quirky a course. It is a tricky 347-yard (317-metre) drive-and-pitch played downhill to a narrow fairway, then up to a dangerously pitched green built into the slopes below the clubhouse.

## THE LONGEST 6,948 YARDS IN GOLF

Olympic has hosted US Opens since the 1950s, though the men who lost those events – Ben Hogan, Arnold Palmer and Tom Watson – are better remembered than their winners, Jack Fleck, Billy Casper and Scott Simpson. Still, with its heavy seaside air, lush, sloping fairways and enough narrowness to make even the best players favour fairway metals off many tees, Olympic is likely to remain the longest-playing 6,948 yards in golf. It is also that rare Golden Age course, which, despite few design changes of consequence, actually poses more of a challenge to the world's best today than it did in its infancy. Such a recipe is likely to keep it tournament prominent for decades to come.

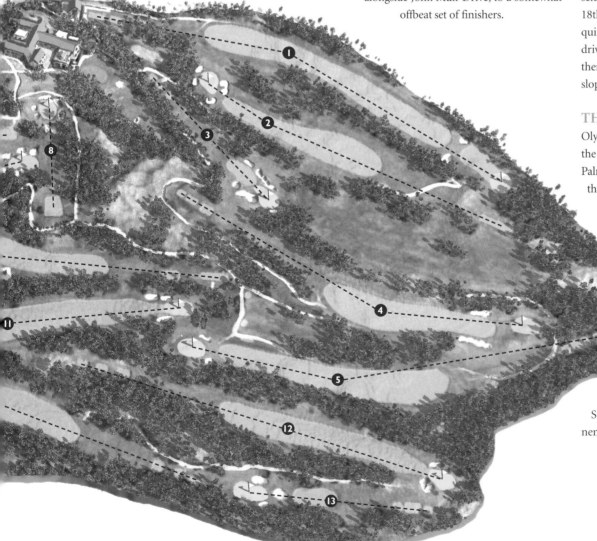

WEST COAST STATES | **243**

# PEBBLE BEACH
## Pebble Beach, California

The 19th-century novelist Robert Louis Stevenson once wrote that California's Monterey Peninsula was 'the finest meeting of land and sea in the world'. But for golfers his words have long been narrowed to describe the area's centrepiece, the Pebble Beach Golf Links, which occupies one of the most spectacular golfing shorelines of any course on earth.

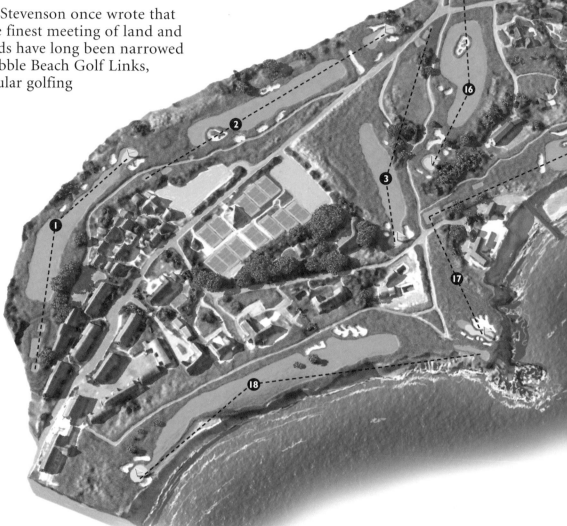

Pebble Beach was built primarily as a promotional device by Samuel Morse, president of the then-fledgling Del Monte Properties Company, and in this light much has been made of Morse's selection of golf-course architects, a pair of 'unknowns' named Jack Neville and Douglas Grant. Seldom recalled is the fact that Morse's first choice was the iconic Charles Blair Macdonald (who reportedly turned down all entreaties to make the long journey west) and that Morse was apparently of the erroneous belief that Donald Ross had returned to the United Kingdom to serve in the First World War. Names such as A.W. Tillinghast, Dr Alister Mackenzie and William Flynn were still largely unknown west of the Mississippi, and Morse was under considerable financial pressure at the time of the course's construction, so the notion of hiring a pair of amateurs – who, under period USGA rules, could not be compensated financially for their works – actually made perfect sense.

### TALENTED AMATEURS
The eventual choices, Jack Neville and Douglas Grant, had impressive golfing credentials. Neville, who was already on Morse's payroll as a real-estate salesman, was twice California champion at the time of his selection, and would ultimately go on to claim the state title an impressive five times. Grant, the heir to a large California development fortune, was a Pacific Coast and California champion and one of the elite amateurs of his day – a fact better known in the UK, where he lived for most of his life and claimed numerous prestigious medals, than in the United States.

Neville and Grant's original design might well be described as the skeleton around which the modern Pebble Beach layout has filled out, for it followed virtually the same routing but featured far less sand, smaller greens and a back-tee yardage of only 6,107. It also suffered a plethora of maintenance issues in those early years, with rocks cluttering the fairways and the

herd of sheep brought in to maintain the turf doing far more harm than good.

### A MAJOR RENOVATION
Thus when the US Amateur was awarded to Pebble Beach in 1929, a two-time winner of the event, H. Chandler Egan, was hired to bring the scenic-but-diminutive course up to national championship standard. Aside from stretching the total yardage to 6,661, Egan strengthened the great majority of holes by rebuilding greens, adding bunkers and, at the 4th, 6th, 7th, 10th and 17th – aesthetically fine creations, which sadly could not survive the economic

rigours of the Depression. Egan, it will be noted, was not alone in performing 1920s alterations at Pebble Beach, for the extension of the then-325-yard 18th to world-renowned par-five status was done by British architect Herbert Fowler in 1921, while the rebuilding of the 8th and 13th greens was directed by Dr Alister Mackenzie during his 1928 construction of nearby Cypress Point (see page 248).

### UNIQUELY SPECTACULAR GOLF
Though some of its inland holes may not be quite as thrilling as those along the water, Pebble Beach today stands as one of golf's singularly great playing experi-

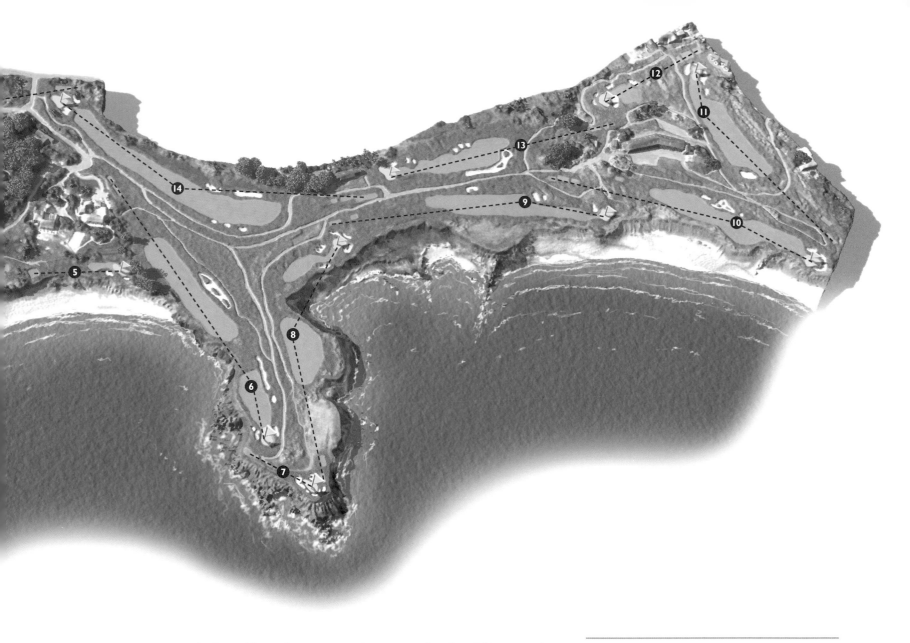

ences, its figure-of-eight routing leading golfers to the cliff tops from the 4th tee through the 10th green, then back again at the 17th and 18th. Multimillion dollar homes line most of the inland holes (though generally set back at an appropriate distance) and the resort's racquet and beach clubs also occupy choice land within the course's boundaries. Indeed, few first-class layouts are bisected by as many roads and additional facilities as Pebble Beach, but given the setting, the sound and scent of the crashing surf, and the thrill of playing so many world-famous holes, such incursions into the golfing landscape hardly seem to matter.

The skilled player knows that he or she must come out firing, for the greatest opportunities to score are found over the first six holes. Following a fairly tame 376-yard opener, the 502-yard 2nd provides just such a chance. Despite a deep cross-bunker 75 yards (68 metres) shy of the putting surface and more sand recently added on the left side of the driving area, it is often reachable in two and thus a real birdie

opportunity – except when the USGA converts it to a 484-yard par four, as they now do during once-a-decade US Open visits.

The 374-yard 3rd, a dogleg left that dares the golfer to cut off a large chunk of a shallow barranca, runs southwards, leading to the first encounter with the ocean at the 327-yard 4th. In truth, though the hole's right side does flank Stillwater Cove, the width of the fairway, combined with the tendency of better players to lay up with a fairway metal off the tee, often renders the water irrelevant. Regardless, the approach is delicate, because the green – which once sat among Egan's dunes – is tiny, nearly surrounded by bunkers and sloped substantially from back to front.

## A NEW 5TH

For the better part of eight decades, the 5th was a 166-yard inland par three, unavoidably routed through the trees because Samuel Morse had sold the adjacent oceanfront land shortly before selecting the site for his

## PEBBLE BEACH GOLF LINKS –
## Pebble Beach, California

Douglas Grant and Jack Neville, 1919 and
H. Chandler Egan, 1928
Major events: US Open 1972, 1982, 1992,
2000; USPGA 1977; US Amateur 1929, 1947,
1961, 1999; US Women's Amateur 1940, 1948

CARD OF THE COURSE

| HOLE | YARDS | PAR | HOLE | YARDS | PAR |
|------|-------|-----|------|-------|-----|
| 1. | 376 | 4 | 10. | 430 | 4 |
| 2. | 484 | 4 | 11. | 373 | 4 |
| 3. | 374 | 4 | 12. | 201 | 3 |
| 4. | 327 | 4 | 13. | 393 | 4 |
| 5. | 187 | 3 | 14. | 572 | 5 |
| 6. | 500 | 5 | 15. | 396 | 4 |
| 7. | 106 | 3 | 16. | 401 | 4 |
| 8. | 416 | 4 | 17. | 208 | 3 |
| 9. | 462 | 4 | 18. | 543 | 5 |
| OUT | 3,232 | 35 | IN | 3,517 | 36 |
| | | | TOTAL | 6,749 | 71 |

golf course. Generally viewed as the layout's least engaging hole, it was replaced by the present Jack Nicklaus-designed 187-yarder in 1998 after the Pebble Beach Company finally found an owner willing to sell – for the tidy sum of US$8.75 million. Nicklaus's hole, which played quite tough during its maiden US Open in 2000, hugs the cliff top tightly.

The last of the early scoring holes, the 500-yard 6th runs downhill to a fairway guarded left by a huge bunker and right by Stillwater Cove. Its small green is usually reachable in two by better players, but the second shot must be carried across a corner of the cove to a steeply elevated headland, with the putting surface guarded by sand on both sides and, more dangerously, a rocky plunge to the sea on the right.

## RENOWNED CLIFF-TOP HOLES

The 106-yard 7th is among the most photographed holes in golf, and with good reason. Set at the tip of the headland, exposed to the Pacific elements, its downhill tee shot can range from half a pitch to a full mid-iron, depending entirely on the wind. The green itself has undergone numerous changes, from Jack Neville and Douglas Grant's large, squared-edge configuration, to H. Chandler Egan's smaller dunes-enclosed version, to the present mid-sized putting surface ringed by six bunkers. As scenic a test as the game can offer, it is, quite simply, one of golf's defining holes.

The golfer now reaches what is widely considered Pebble Beach's hardest stretch, for the 8th, 9th and 10th are all cliff-top par fours of major challenge and worldwide distinction. The 416-yard 8th is the shortest of the three, but the forced lay-up required on its tee shot (lest one's driver plummet off a cliff) results in a disproportionately long second. This approach highlights yet another of Pebble Beach's legendary images, for it is played across a deep, ocean-filled chasm to Dr Alister Mackenzie's sharply sloping green, which sits just above the cliff top, menaced by bunkers long and short.

Probably the most difficult hole on the course, the 462-yard 9th follows the coastline but not too tightly. The fairway slopes heavily from left to right, frequently resulting in hanging lies for what amounts to one of golf's toughest long-iron approaches. The green seems a bit too small for its purpose, and is guarded front-left by a particularly deep bunker and right by a rugged, iceplant-filled slope to the beach. A four has seldom left anyone disappointed here.

The last of this dangerous trio, and arguably Pebble Beach's toughest driving hole, the 430-yard 10th offers little room for error – its sloping fairway being pinched by sand left and the ocean right. The approach comes from another hanging lie, this time to a green tucked behind a cliffside crevice and nearly ringed by sand, with the wide crescent of Carmel Beach serving as an attractive backdrop.

## INLAND STRETCH

From here the routing moves inland to a stretch of holes that are solid, but a touch less exciting. The 373-yard 11th plays uphill to a tiny, left-to-right angled green, while the 201-yard 12th turns westward, back into the prevailing wind. This green was described by H. Chandler Egan as being 'of the Redan type' and indeed a gaping front-left bunker is the hole's primary hazard.

The 393-yard 13th offers the second green complex to bear the handiwork of Dr MacKenzie, though perhaps more memorable is the huge left-side fairway bunker or, to a lesser degree, the three smaller right-side bunkers added prior to the 2000 US Open. More sand has recently been added at the 14th and 15th as well, the former receiving three new bunkers in its driving area, the latter a rather incongruous cluster of five (with one positioned awkwardly within the fairway) down its left side.

# TRIUMPH AND HEARTBREAK FOR NICKLAUS
## Pebble Beach's Famous 17th

*Jack Nicklaus has called Pebble Beach his favourite golf course, hardly surprising given that he has won both a US Amateur (1961) and a US Open (1972) there. But rarely has a single hole represented such high and low points of a single man's career as has Pebble Beach's 17th for Nicklaus. In 1972, he stood on the 71st tee with the wind blowing and the outcome still very much in doubt. From 218 yards (199 metres) away, he laced one of history's great 1-irons, a low, wind-cheating bullet that hit the base of the flagstick and stopped only centimetres away, thus clinching the title.*

*Ten years later, however, it would be an altogether different story. Already in the clubhouse with a four-under-par total of 284, Nicklaus looked a likely US Open winner when Tom Watson arrived at the 71st tied for the lead, then hooked a 2-iron into some nasty greenside rough. Confident that Watson would now do well just to force a Monday play-off, Nicklaus looked on as his arch-rival proceeded to hole one of the game's most memorable chips, then calmly birdie the par-five 18th, ending Nicklaus's last great chance to capture a record fifth Open title.*

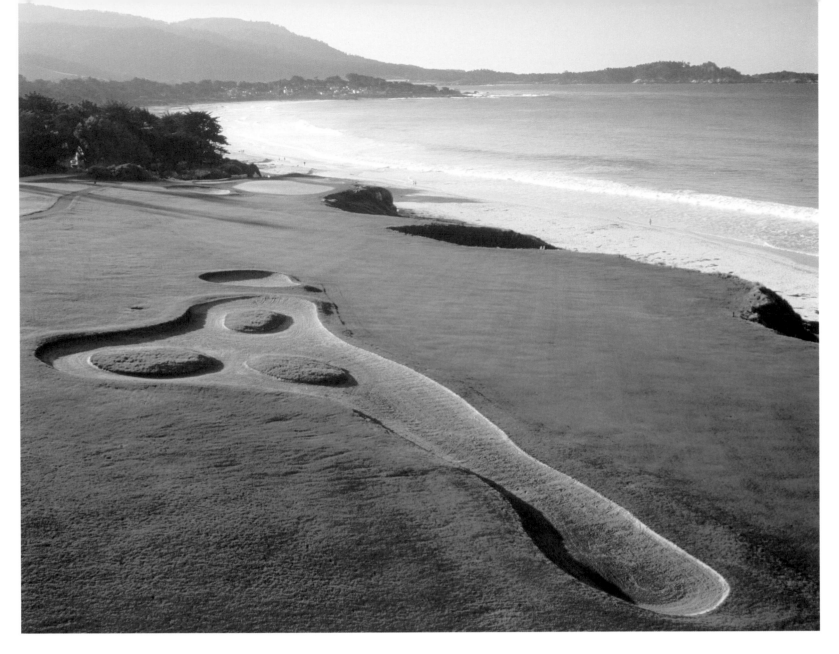

*The 430-yard 10th, where a drive played close to this fairway bunker leaves the ideal approach. This small green is nearly ringed by sand and perched above Carmel Beach.*

Turning for home, the 401-yard 16th is best played with a laid-up tee shot as balls driven too far face the twin perils of a downhill lie and an approach angle significantly obscured by overhanging trees. A long iron or fairway metal placed close to a pair of right-side fairway bunkers leaves a short-iron approach over a bunker-filled ravine to a green that falls steeply from right to left.

## WORLD'S MOST FAMOUS FINISHER

With the possible exception of St Andrews (see page 40), it is doubtful that any golf course has a more illustrious pair of finishers than Pebble Beach, beginning with the treacherous par-three 17th. Measuring 178 yards (a longer 208-yard tee across the beach club access road is reserved strictly for championship play), this unique one-shotter features a terribly narrow green in the shape of a tilted hourglass, its two halves clearly divided by a prominent ridge. The entire front of the putting surface is protected by a single huge bunker while seven smaller hazards flank the back. Given the often strong Pacific breezes, the ocean itself – which lies just a few metres off the left fringe – can also creep into play.

And then there is the 543-yard 18th, perhaps not the game's finest finisher in architectural terms but very likely its most scenic, and absolutely its most famous. Played from a promontory tee, the drive dares a golfer to shorten things by skirting the rocky coastline, while bailout options have been lessened in recent years with the addition of a second right-side fairway bunker some 30 yards (27 metres) past the original. With the prevailing wind blowing against, most second shots will be placed safely right of the long bunker and sea wall – not too far right, lest the remaining pitch be affected by a 21-metre (70-foot) Monterey cypress tree that stands guard short of the putting surface. Since even the game's longest hitters will seldom be capable of reaching this green in two, the 18th may not rate among golf's most purely strategic holes, yet its grandeur and ambience are, without a doubt, second to none.

Even at the 6,749 yards used for US Opens, Pebble Beach is hardly a long golf course. But with its small, heavily pitched greens, strong coastal winds and plethora of thrilling holes, it remains rigorous enough to challenge the world's best, and more than exciting enough to rank near the very top of every golfer's list of 'must plays'. It remains, in its tenth decade, one of the game's genuine and perennial icons.

# CYPRESS POINT
## Pebble Beach, California

Residing at the top of any list of golf's most magical spots, the Cypress Point Club has stood synonymous with both superior design and sublime, almost other-worldly beauty since its opening in August 1928.

The task of assessing the attractiveness of a golf course is largely a subjective one, not so different, really, from judging a painting, a starlet or a new model of automobile. Just as a Rembrandt may be difficult to compare with a Willem de Kooning, how does the coastal magnificence of Pebble Beach (see page 244) compared with, say, the lush azalea-and-pine parkland of Augusta National (see page 206), the gentle rolls of St Andrews (see page 40) or North Berwick (see page 46) with the hillier dunescapes of Shinnecock Hills (see page 178) or the National Golf Links of America (see page 166)?

### DEFINING PERFECTION

To such rhetorical questions there are, of course, no definitive answers. Taste is taste, and the very fact it is possible to debate such aspects of golf goes a long way towards explaining the almost religious spell it has cast over its followers for several hundred years. But what if a golf course could be built on terrain so beautifully varied as to include all of the types mentioned above? An area incorporating rocky, beach-strewn coastline, massive silver-white sand dunes and lush forests as lovely as any national park? This question is not rhetorical, because the game has been blessed with a single exemplary answer – Cypress Point.

The club's inimitable site, which the renowned golf writer Herbert Warren Wind once observed 'possesses a diversity of terrain possibly unmatched', certainly provided a magnificent foundation. Also noteworthy was the then highly uncommon role of a woman – 1921 US Women's Amateur champion Marion Hollins – in the club's founding. A New Yorker by birth, Hollins had already created Long Island's novel Women's National Golf and Tennis Club (today's Glen Head Country Club) before moving west in 1923. There she soon carved a successful niche for herself in the real-estate division of Samuel Morse's Del Monte Properties Company. Given that Cypress Point's initial raison d'être was the sale of expensive properties, Hollins's golfing background made her an ideal choice to lead the syndicate that financed the club's development. Part and parcel of this role, apparently, was the hiring of a golf-course architect.

### HIRING DR MACKENZIE

Cypress Point is widely viewed as the defining point of the great Dr Alister MacKenzie's design career, yet he was not, in fact, Hollins's first choice. That honour went to Seth Raynor, who was a disciple of the renowned Charles Blair Macdonald, consultant on the Women's National design and builder of gems such as Fishers Island (see page 170), Shoreacres and Yale. Raynor's mandate was to build not just Cypress Point but also two more courses at the nearby Monterey Peninsula Country Club as part of Morse's grand scheme to cater for multiple levels of retirement-home buyers. Unfortunately, Raynor died in 1926 having only partially completed one of the two Monterey layouts – today's Dunes course – leaving construction of its sister Shore Course to be postponed some 35 years. But at Cypress Point, the matchless property and the involvement of some big-name founders necessitated the project continuing and quickly, so Hollins turned to Alister MacKenzie.

In considering the universal acclaim heaped on Cypress Point for its powerful run at aesthetic perfection, it must be remembered that MacKenzie – a Boer War veteran – was a noted expert in the art of camouflage. Such might suggest a particular ability to make a golf course's artificial features appear considerably less fabricated, and at Cypress Point MacKenzie's talent manifested itself in the course's 125 original bunkers. Whereas most period MacKenzie hazards bore spirited, cape-and-bay-filled shaping, at Cypress Point, where the windswept cypress trees bear an unmistakeable jaggedness, MacKenzie gave his bunkers a sharper, rough-edged look, creating a subtle artistic cohesiveness with the stunning forest background.

### MACKENZIE'S OBJECTIVES

On taking over the Cypress Point project, MacKenzie opted to discard all previous plans and instead devised on his own a routing that had to accomplish three key objectives. Firstly, the finishers were to be placed near to, or directly alongside, the ocean, creating a closing run universally ranked among the world's most dramatic. Secondly, holes were to be woven in and out of the dunes and forest throughout the round, giving the layout an adventurous, ever-changing feel. And

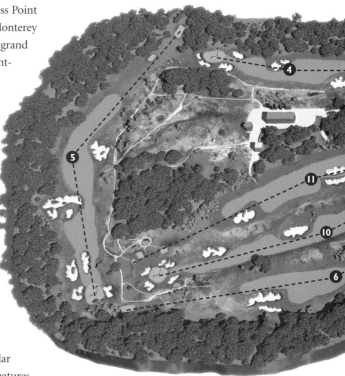

finally, MacKenzie's routing succeeded in utilizing a single huge sand dune as an attractive backdrop for no fewer than four holes (the 3rd, 6th, 9th and 11th), a splendidly efficient adaptation of form to function.

The peripatetic Alister MacKenzie left Cypress Point's construction under the watchful eye of his western partner, the noted Socialist, Robert Hunter. It

# CYPRESS POINT CLUB –
## Pebble Beach, California

Dr Alister MacKenzie and Robert Hunter, 1928
Major events: Walker Cup 1981

CARD OF THE COURSE

| HOLE | YARDS | PAR | HOLE | YARDS | PAR |
|------|-------|-----|------|-------|-----|
| 1. | 421 | 4 | 10. | 480 | 5 |
| 2. | 548 | 5 | 11. | 437 | 4 |
| 3. | 162 | 3 | 12. | 404 | 4 |
| 4. | 384 | 4 | 13. | 365 | 4 |
| 5. | 493 | 5 | 14. | 388 | 4 |
| 6. | 518 | 5 | 15. | 143 | 3 |
| 7. | 168 | 3 | 16. | 231 | 3 |
| 8. | 363 | 4 | 17. | 393 | 4 |
| 9. | 292 | 4 | 18. | 346 | 4 |
| **OUT** | **3,349** | **37** | **IN** | **3,187** | **35** |
| | | | **TOTAL** | **6,536** | **72** |

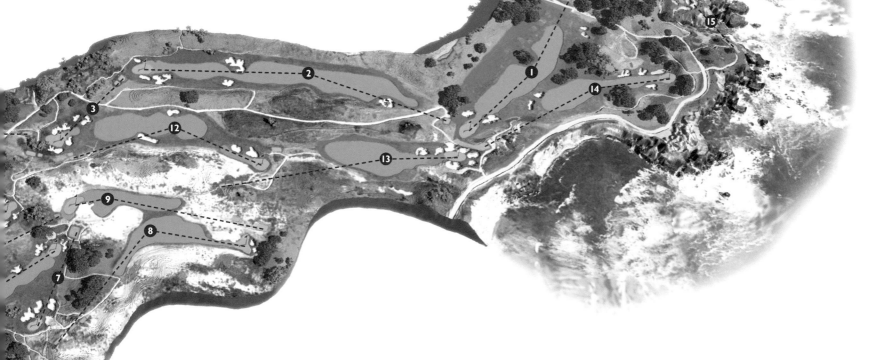

is difficult to say what role, if any, the affluent, crusading Hunter played in the actual design process, but, whatever the creative balance of power, MacKenzie was pleased enough with the results to draw pre-opening comparisons with St Andrews. 'For years I have been contending that in our generation no other golf course could possibly compete with the strategic problems, the thrills, excitement, variety and lasting and increasing interest of the Old course', MacKenzie wrote, 'but the completion of Cypress Point has made me change my mind.'

## THE OPENERS

Cypress Point's 421-yard 1st opens with a tee shot across Seventeen Mile Drive, and right away MacKenzie has the golfer thinking: is it possible to carry the cypresses that cluster on the right side some 230 yards (210 metres) down the fairway (thus shortening things noticeably) or would it be safer to play away to the longer left side? Regardless of choice, with the ocean tumbling into nearby Fan Shell Beach and the slightly elevated green framed by a massive backdrop of silvery dunes, golfers know immediately that they are indeed entering hallowed golfing ground.

The 548-yard 2nd is the number one stroke hole and moves south-eastwards across the top of a long ridge, its right side flanked by out-of-bounds (and the course's only immediately adjacent private houses), its left by a hillside falling into deep, wild grass. The 3rd, an attractive 162-yard par three, plays to the base of the large central sand dune, and then it is off into the forest at the 384-yard 4th, a hole whose once largely decorative right-side fairway bunkers (which begin at 275 yards/250 metres) are today the central strategic consideration by threatening a less-than-perfect tee ball.

Always something of an iconoclast, MacKenzie demonstrated his willingness to buck architectural convention by building back-to-back par fives at the 5th and 6th. The former, at only 493 yards, is an eminently reachable dogleg left, with longer hitters making the 265-yard (242-metre) carry of a large corner bunker, then having to clear a sand-filled rise if the green is to be reached in two. The 518-yard 6th is of particular driving interest, because the golfer must flirt with a pair of large right-side bunkers in order to gain both an ideal second-shot angle and a favourable slope. Like the 4th, the 6th has also held up well in the face of ever more powerful equipment, partly because a once-ornamental bunker some 315 yards (288 metres) down the left side now serves as a fine hedge against modern bombers slinging drives fearlessly around the corner.

Following the slightly uphill 168-yard 7th come a pair of distinctive shorter par fours, beginning with the semiblind, 363-yard 8th. This sharp dogleg right bends early, demanding the carry of an enormous sand dune with a high cut if the golfer is to be left with the anticipated pitch to an elevated, multitiered green. The 292-yard 9th then returns south-eastwards and remains one of the world's elite sub-300-yard par

fours. Its narrow fairway is surrounded by sand, and its long, terrifically sloping green is set spectacularly into the northern face of MacKenzie's ever-present central dune.

## AESTHETIC PERFECTION

Beginning a run of four wonderful par fours is the 437-yard 11th. Here a pair of narrow, centre-line bunkers invade the fairway beginning at the 275-yard (250-metre) mark, typically calling for a laid-up tee shot, and thus a fairly long approach to the last of the greens positioned beneath the ever-present dune. The 404-yard 12th, on the other hand, requires a long left-to-right drive to skirt some dangerous ground in order to find the optimum approach angle to a small, elevated green bunkered front-left.

Most famous among this quartet is surely the 365-yard 13th, a highly photogenic hole with its impressive backdrop of the Pacific and Fan Shell Beach. Its narrow green, sited within a natural semicircle of dunes, is more accessible from the right side of the fairway – the side, naturally, that requires the longer diagonal carry over a sandy wasteland from the tee. Finally, the 388-yard 14th features clumps of mature cypress trees,

which narrow the fairway severely beginning at 265 yards (242 metres), often impeding approaches played up a long slope to a small skyline green.

## THE CRÈME DE LA CRÈME

Ranking among the game's best-known short par threes, the 143-yard 15th is played across a rocky Pacific inlet from a tee balanced on an exposed headland. The green is a wildly shaped affair, with narrow extensions at both its front and far right inviting numerous fascinating pin placements, and six magnificently sculpted bunkers providing danger and some wonderful artistic definition. The ocean itself can swallow a badly topped shot, and length is hardly a factor, but playing the necessarily precise approach in what is, quite inevitably, a stiff ocean breeze is a very real measure of any golfer's talent.

A 100-yard (90-metre) oceanside walk through the cypresses brings the golfer to one of the greatest and most spectacular golf holes ever built – the breathtaking 231-yard 16th. Interestingly, MacKenzie initially planned this legendary one-shotter to be a short par four, later crediting Marion Hollins with convincing him otherwise. Played across a broad,

# A ROUTING OF UNMATCHED QUALITY
## A variety of beautiful landscapes

*Dr Alister MacKenzie's course at Cypress Point has long drawn attention because of its unorthodoxy, notably the inclusion of back-to-back par fives (the 5th and 6th) and par threes (the 15th and 16th), as well as for its colossal finish, which sees the 15th, 16th and 17th all hanging thrillingly above the Pacific.*

*Yet the true beauty of MacKenzie's plan lies in its ability to take the golfer in and out of the several splendid landscapes that inhabit the site, never dwelling in any one for too long. Whereas at neighbouring Spyglass Hill (see page 252), Robert Trent Jones Snr built his first five holes in the dunes, then inexplicably ignored them thereafter, MacKenzie shows the ocean at the opening, then again – with a vengeance – at the finish. In between, holes march back and forth between lush cypress forest and glistening sand dunes, with occasional glimpses of the Pacific interspersed. The cumulative effect is remarkable – all told, as fine an aesthetic experience as exists anywhere in the golfing world.*

*The 143-yard 15th, which requires little more than a pitch to this tightly bunkered, cliff-top green. Though less famous than the epic 16th, this is one of golf's most beautiful holes.*

rocky bay, it requires a direct carry of nearly 220 windswept yards (200 metres) to reach the putting surface. However, it also offers the faint of heart a wide stretch of left-side fairway on which to play safe. With its bunker-ringed green occupying the beginning of a huge, rocky headland, the 16th probably represents the finest blend of challenge, beauty, strategy and simple, jaw-dropping awe in the history of the game.

Remarkably, the 393-yard 17th measures up almost equally in this regard, except for its slightly smaller scale. Its drive must rate among the most thrilling anywhere, played across another vast bay to an angled fairway nestled above a daunting bulwark of rock. A large clump of cypress trees springs up in the right-centre of the fairway at 275 yards (250 metres). This is rather an awkward obstacle by modern standards, but is easier to understand when it is remembered that before decades of coastal erosion a dangerous-but-rewarding corridor of drivable fairway once existed to the right of the trees. Today, these cypresses serve mostly to threaten longer tee shots and impede the view of the approach, which, played to a

green angling out onto one final promontory, is not easy, especially in a high wind.

## A LETDOWN AT THE CLOSE?

Long maligned as an interloper in this otherwise perfect collection of golf holes, the 346-yard 18th is short and strategically limited, and it is because of this out-of-character closer that Cypress Point has often been called 'the greatest seventeen-hole course in the world'. But the 18th is hardly a pushover. Its doglegged fairway is narrowed precipitously by cypress trees just at the bend, and its second shot is played uphill and through the glade to a narrow putting surface.

More than 80 years after its opening, Cypress Point is still universally hailed for the grandness of its hazards, its remarkable variety of holes, its almost supernatural beauty and for the fact that, some minor changes notwithstanding, its 6,536-yard layout manages to retain its fundamental shot values better than the vast majority of great Golden Age designs.

For American golfers born after the First World War, no name is more synonymous with the field of golf course architecture than Robert Trent Jones Snr. A native of Ince, in Lancashire, England, Trent Jones emigrated to the United States as a youth before pursuing a self-designed college curriculum whose focus on agronomy, engineering and landscape architecture specifically prepared him for his chosen work. It was this expertise – combined with a dearth of postwar competition – that would eventually lead to an unmatched degree of worldwide industry dominance.

## AN ARCHITECTURAL PIONEER

Perhaps more importantly, Trent Jones single-handedly changed the architectural medium, leading it away from the strategic approach of the Golden Age towards what he called the 'Heroic' school of design: big, power-oriented layouts with copious bunkering, large, undulating greens and an overall degree of difficulty that he aptly summed up as 'a hard par or an easy bogey'. Trent Jones ultimately completed more than 450 global projects, performed redesign work on numerous Major championship sites and generally dominated his profession so extensively that half a generation of American architects began prominently using their own middle names in desperate attempts at keeping up.

What Trent Jones's work frequently lacked, however, was a polished aesthetic and a real degree of variety, with all too many holes amounting to long, nearly symmetrically bunkered tests largely interchangeable from site to site.

## A REMARKABLE SETTING

Much of Spyglass Hill's lingering appeal lies in its great beauty. This is a golf course laid out amid a rare mix of glorious golfing backdrops: 13 of its holes cut through the Del Monte Forest – a stunningly green wonderland of gnarled cypress trees and tall California pines – while the remaining five tumble westwards towards the Pacific, breaching a splendid expanse of high, windblown sand dunes. In addition, Spyglass Hill bears the distinction of being, in many ways, rather an atypical Trent Jones design. It is not, for example, excessively long by contemporary standards (though its original 6,972 yards was certainly imposing enough in 1966); it features a number of interesting shorter holes; and its largely unbunkered driving areas offer the golfer a bit more room to manoeuvre than is found at courses such as Oakland Hills (see page 220) or Firestone. Yet despite such relative anomalies, Trent Jones still provided a considerable dose of his architectural stock-in-trade: sheer, unmitigated toughness.

Tales of Spyglass Hill's terrors abound, particularly during its infancy when its putting surfaces (since remodelled) were exceedingly contoured and lightning quick. Teamed with timeless stalwarts Pebble Beach (see page 244) and Cypress Point (see page 248) as a tri-host of the then Bing Crosby Pro-Am, it was easily rated the toughest of the three courses by the professionals (who seldom even saw the back tees), particularly on the windiest of days when its northwestward exposure could occasionally make the dunes holes borderline unplayable.

Spyglass Hill was also, in those early years, the rare course to maintain a USGA rating above 76, leading Pulitzer Prize-winning sportswriter Jim Murray to call it 'a privateer plundering the golfing man' and 'a 300-acre unplayable lie'.

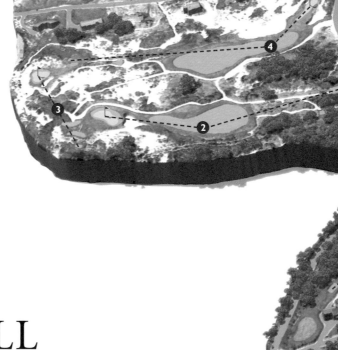

# SPYGLASS HILL
## Pebble Beach, California

From a portfolio that once regularly boasted at least a dozen courses widely rated among America's top 100, Robert Trent Jones Snr's course at Spyglass Hill today remains the best of only a handful still regularly considered for such honours.

# SPYGLASS HILL GOLF COURSE – Pebble Beach, California
Robert Trent Jones Snr, 1966

CARD OF THE COURSE

| HOLE | NAME | YARDS | PAR | | HOLE | NAME | YARDS | PAR |
|---|---|---|---|---|---|---|---|---|
| 1. | Treasure Island | 595 | 5 | | 10. | Captain Flint | 407 | 4 |
| 2. | Billy Bones | 349 | 4 | | 11. | Admiral Benbow | 528 | 5 |
| 3. | The Black Spot | 165 | 3 | | 12. | Skeleton Island | 178 | 3 |
| 4. | Blind Pew | 370 | 4 | | 13. | Tom Morgan | 460 | 4 |
| 5. | Bird Rock | 197 | 3 | | 14. | Long John Silver | 560 | 5 |
| 6. | Israel Hands | 446 | 4 | | 15. | Jim Hawkins | 130 | 3 |
| 7. | Indian Village | 529 | 5 | | 16. | Black Dog | 476 | 4 |
| 8. | Signal Hill | 399 | 4 | | 17. | Ben Gunn | 325 | 4 |
| 9. | Captain Smollett | 431 | 4 | | 18. | Spyglass | 408 | 4 |
| **OUT** | | **3,481** | **36** | | **IN** | | **3,472** | **36** |
| | | | | | **TOTAL** | | **6,953** | **72** |

## WHY THE DUNES?

From a design standpoint, students of golf architecture have long puzzled over why Trent Jones elected to begin, rather than end, his layout amid the dunes. The 1st is a colossal 595-yard par five that, though somewhat downhill, is no simple three-shotter. Its fairway is initially tree lined (demanding a straight first drive) before opening gently leftwards, towards the Pacific.

What follows is an exciting stretch of four shortish holes played at the complete mercy of the wind, beginning with the 349-yard 2nd, a drive-and-pitch whose approach climbs to a narrow, left-to-right sloping green nestled high amid the sand hills. The 165-yard 3rd then tumbles downhill with the Pacific as a scenic backdrop, while the 370-yard 4th is one of Trent Jones's more creative holes, a dogleg left played to an extremely narrow putting surface, which curls semi-blind behind a low-lying dune. Then the 197-yard 5th runs slightly uphill to a green guarded by a line of bunkers and a patch of the area's dreaded ice plant, before the tough, two-shot, 446-yard 6th climbs back into the forest.

## INTO THE FOREST

It might be argued that the remainder of the layout is more 'typical' Trent Jones, with the par fours growing in stature, and the practice of excavating a pond in front of an otherwise nondescript green complex occurring on four occasions (it was five before a new-millennium renovation of the par-five 11th). But despite at least partially fitting these stereotypes, most of the inland holes are still quite appealing, in many cases simply because they achieve their difficulty without being saddled with overbearing length. Prime examples are a pair of shortish par threes considerably more engaging than any brutish 240-yard (220-metre) hole: the 178-yard 12th, played downhill to a green angled right-to-left beyond a narrow pond; and the 130-yard 15th, a challenging, fascinating test, which between water, sand, cypress trees and some uneven terrain offers numerous ways to a disproportionally high score.

Despite modern equipment softening up even the hardest of courses, Spyglass still poses plenty of challenge to the world's best, with the aforementioned 446-yard 6th, the uphill 399-yard 8th and the 476-yard, dogleg-right 16th annually ranking among the toughest holes on the PGA Tour. Much of this continuing toughness comes from the one component equipment cannot substantially mitigate – the wind – but more than 40 years after its opening, the overall quality of Trent Jones's design should not be minimized. There are many who wish that more of his courses held this sort of flavour – but then how many sites offered these sorts of possibilities?

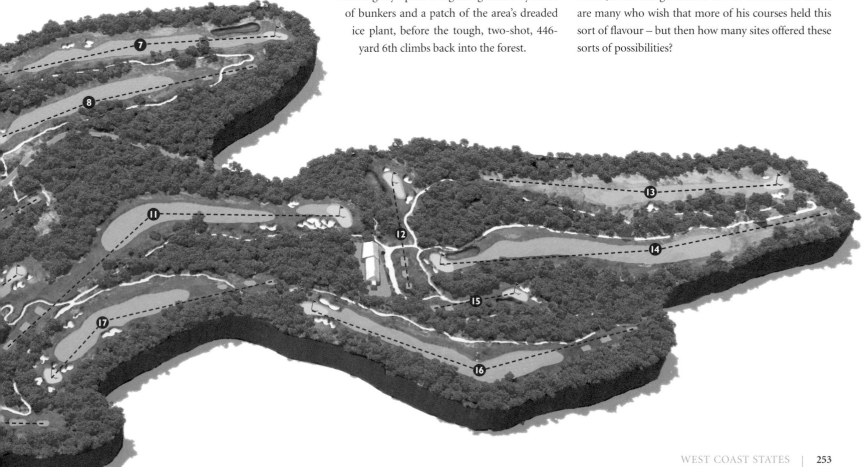

# RIVIERA
## Pacific Palisades, California

Set along the floor of Santa Monica canyon, in the once-sleepy Los Angeles suburb of Pacific Palisades, the Riviera Country Club has, since its 1926 inception, stood tall as southern California's most glamorous golfing address.

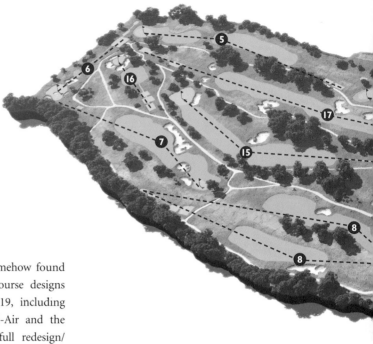

The Riviera Country Club has had a long and close association with Hollywood: since the early days of Douglas Fairbanks and Charlie Chaplin, actors and celebrities have held court at the club en masse. To the public, however, its eminence derives from its being far and away the region's most prominent tournament venue. Riviera remains the only southern California course ever to host the US Open, in addition to two PGA championships, a US Senior Open and, on an annual basis, the PGA Tour's Los Angeles Open. However, the biggest reason for Riviera's enduring fame is a much more fundamental one: it is, quite simply, one of the best-designed golf courses in the world.

### GEORGE THOMAS'S MASTERPIECE
Riviera was built by Philadelphia-native George Thomas, an affluent Golden Age Renaissance man who never accepted payment for his work. Equally well known as a hybridizer of roses, a dog trainer,

a fisherman and a writer, Thomas somehow found time to complete ten original golf-course designs after moving to Beverly Hills in 1919, including such additional area stalwarts as Bel-Air and the Los Angeles Country Club, and a full redesign/ expansion of the 36-hole municipal facility at Griffith Park.

It was at Riviera that his skills were best displayed, for here was a compact, largely barren site that, except for a single narrow barranca, was nearly devoid of significant natural features. Yet on such unpromising land Thomas, with help from his construction man Billy Bell, created a strong, yet beautifully varied layout – a golf course that has few peers in its number of architecturally significant holes. In addition, he managed to create a generously proportioned routing that still left more than enough room for modern lengthening – no small accomplishment on a tract measuring only 127 acres (51 hectares).

### A CLASSIC START
Though primarily a flattish course, Riviera's 503-yard opener plays from a starkly elevated tee squeezed tightly against the grand Spanish-style clubhouse. It is a classic thinking-man's test: with a boomerang putting surface offering a wide variety of pin placements, players must effectively plan their shots from the green backwards. For a dead-straight hole with only two bunkers, it has few strategic equals.

After two stiff par fours running towards the property's lower reaches, the player encounters the 236-yard 4th, a hole once described by Ben Hogan as 'the greatest par three in America'. Generally played directly into the prevailing wind, the 4th offers two options: an all-carry route across a spectacular bunker,

*This view is from the 1st tee. From 70 feet (21 metres) above the fairway, left-side out-of-bounds and right-side trees come ever more into play on this 503-yard par five.*

### RIVIERA COUNTRY CLUB –
### Pacific Palisades, California
George Thomas and Billy Bell, 1926
Major events: US Open 1948;
USPGA 1983, 1995; US Senior Open 1998

CARD OF THE COURSE

| HOLE | YARDS | PAR | HOLE | YARDS | PAR |
|------|-------|-----|------|-------|-----|
| 1. | 503 | 5 | 10. | 315 | 4 |
| 2. | 463 | 4 | 11. | 564 | 5 |
| 3. | 434 | 4 | 12. | 479 | 4 |
| 4. | 236 | 3 | 13. | 459 | 4 |
| 5. | 444 | 4 | 14. | 176 | 3 |
| 6. | 200 | 3 | 15. | 487 | 4 |
| 7. | 408 | 4 | 16. | 166 | 3 |
| 8. | 462 | 4 | 17. | 590 | 5 |
| 9. | 496 | 4 | 18. | 475 | 4 |
| OUT | 3,646 | 35 | IN | 3,711 | 36 |
| | | | TOTAL | 7,357 | 71 |

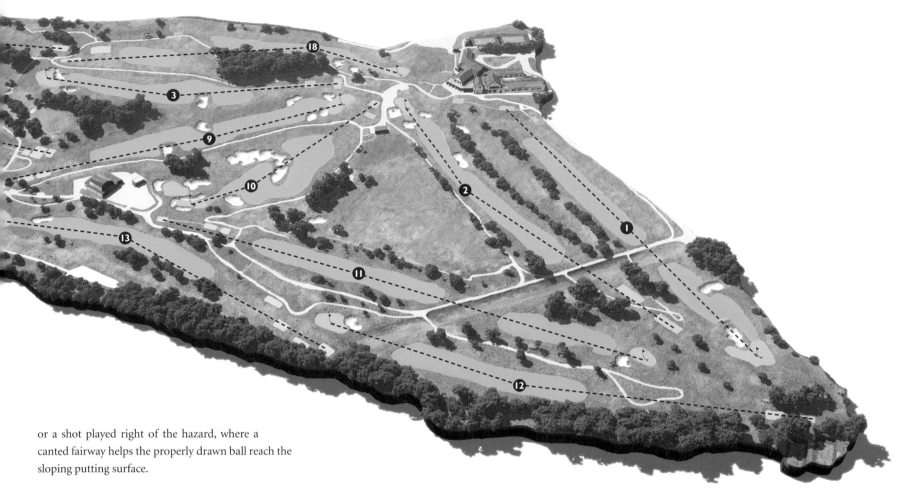

or a shot played right of the hazard, where a canted fairway helps the properly drawn ball reach the sloping putting surface.

## PLAYING THE COURSE

The front nine's second par three is of perhaps even greater note, for the doughnut-like 6th features a large, two-tiered green famously perforated by a small bunker within the boundaries of the putting surface. The net effect is a green with four distinct quadrants – two high, two low – and all manner of fascinating pin positions, the most difficult of which is back-left. Long played at 165 yards (151 metres), the modern addition of a 200-yard tournament tee makes for a particularly steep challenge indeed.

Often overlooked among Riviera's run of memorable holes is the 496-yard 9th, a par four with fairway bunkering perfectly positioned to test both the shorter and longer hitter. The approach is one of the club's most demanding, running slightly uphill to a narrow, steeply sloped green guarded front and left by particularly deep bunkers. Perhaps the 9th is so underrated simply because it is followed by the 315-yard 10th, as strategically engrossing a short par four as exists in golf. Facing perhaps the most featureless expanse on the entire property – and a short one at that – George Thomas created a diminutive two-shotter played to a sloping, terribly narrow green, the rear two-thirds of

which is tightly ringed by bunkers. From the tee the longer hitter is tempted to drive the green, but for most this is a sucker play because any ball coming up short or right leaves a nearly impossible pitch over sand, to a green falling steeply away. For most players, the smarter move is to lay up down the fairway's far-left side, leaving a much simpler pitch straight up the body of the putting surface. While equipment evolution has recently led most PGA Tour professionals to pull out the driver, for mere mortals this remains one of the game's grandest strategic tests.

The remainder of Riviera's back-nine par fours are far longer, with the 12th, 13th and 15th providing tournament tees measuring 479, 459 and 487 yards respectively – all played into the prevailing breeze. The 12th in particular does not require such length (the PGA Tour generally ignores its back tee), being a fine two-shotter played across the barranca to a green fronted right by a deep bunker and left by a grand sycamore tree. The 15th, on the other hand, doglegs around an imposing bunker, then requires a deft long-iron to a huge, deeply contoured green.

Riviera's compelling originality may not always translate well to television, for its finishers, though both varied and challenging, lack some of the visual flair apparent in many earlier holes. This does not prevent them from taking on a certain epic quality, however, particularly at the short, downhill 16th (its tiny, steep green surrounded by several splendid bunkers) and the memorable 475-yard 18th. This difficult two-shotter requires a pinpoint drive favouring the left side of a steeply elevated fairway, then a mid-iron to a green tucked into a large natural amphitheatre beneath the clubhouse.

## DREADED KIKUYU

A further component in the Riviera equation is its sticky kikuyu grass – an ultra-hearty African strain originally brought in to stabilize the surrounding canyon walls against landslides. Today covering most of the layout, it makes for lush, carpet-like fairways but nightmarish rough, particularly affecting the delicate shots around the putting surface. It is, however, a seasonally sensitive grass, making Riviera, for the most part, a perceptibly tougher course in summer than during the cooler winter months.

# CANADA

Scottish fur traders are believed to have played golf in various Canadian localities during the early years of the 19th century, and other Scottish expatriates are known to have teed up in Montreal in 1826 and in Quebec City during the 1850s.

The first club formed to play the modern game in North America was the Royal Montreal Golf Club[1], whose 1873 founding predates the earliest modern American golf club by 11 years. Unlike in America, however, the game did not expand with great rapidity; by the close of the 1870s only two additional clubs – in Quebec City and Brantford, Ontario – had come into existence, and Royal Montreal remained, for several years, the game's de facto governing body.

There are now well over 1,700 courses in Canada. Though many thousands fewer than exist in the United States, this is really rather a sizeable number for a population of fewer than 30 million and for a country with vast northern lands that are scarcely welcoming even to human population, never mind golf courses. Indeed, golf is today little seen in the Yukon and North-west Territories which, by themselves, are considerably larger than the great majority of the world's countries. Between them, they muster up only 72 holes of golf!

## EARLY COURSES

Canada's lower provinces offered plenty of available people and land, however, and by the early 20th century course construction finally began to take off. One early designer of note was George Cumming, the 1905 Canadian Open champion and long-time professional at the Toronto[2]. Another – rather more famous – designer was Willie Park Jnr, two-time Open champion and between 1905 and 1929 the builder of more than 20 Canadian courses including Quebec's Mount Bruno Golf and Country Club[3]. With its relative strategic sophistication, Park's work was in many ways ground-breaking, but in terms of a lasting legacy it was widely exceeded by that of his countryman Harry Colt,

whose two brief visits to Canada yielded a pair of perennial favourites: Hamilton (see page 260) and the Toronto. Also leaving a mark on the landscape was the legendary Donald Ross, who ventured up from America often enough to complete nearly a dozen projects, the most enduring of which are Ontario's Essex GandCC[4] and Rosedale[5], and Manitoba's St Charles Country Club[6], where Donald Ross and Dr Alister MacKenzie each built nine holes. And then there was A. Vernon Macan, a native of Dublin, Ireland who emigrated to Canada in 1910 and practised architecture both there and in the American north-west. His list of Canadian courses numbers more than 20 and includes the very popular Royal

Colwood[7], Shaughnessy[8] and Victoria[9], all located in British Columbia.

## THE LEGACY
## OF STANLEY THOMPSON

The chief architect of Canada's prewar years was Stanley Thompson, the larger-than-life product of a fine golfing family. Over a 35-year design career, Thompson completed more than 145 projects, well over a hundred of these being in Canada, and nearly half in his home province of Ontario. He began building courses in earnest in 1921, but his star would not fully rise until the opening of his 1926 design at Jasper National Park[10], a scenic and strategic wonder once cited as 'the best [course] I have ever seen' by the sometimes effusive Dr Alister MacKenzie. Additional Thompson masterpieces included the spectacular Banff Springs (see page 258), Cape Breton Highlands (see page 264) in Nova Scotia, St George's GandCC (see page 262) and Capilano[11], another splendidly scenic test situated in the foothills of West Vancouver, British Columbia. A second tier of fine courses – although little known internationally – includes Westmount[12], Cataraqui[13], Oakdale[14] and Brantford[15], leaving Thompson, by a comfortable margin, as the major figure in Canadian golf design.

Stanley Thompson's influence did not end with his own courses, however. He also served as a mentor to several younger architects, among them Robert Trent Jones Snr, Geoffrey Cornish, Clinton 'Robbie' Robinson and Howard Watson. Robert Trent Jones built only four courses in Canada, highlighted by the Mount Kidd course at Alberta's Kananaskis Country GC[16], while Geoffrey Cornish, a native of Winnipeg, lived in Massachusetts and added only five. But Robbie Robinson and Howard Watson contributed considerably to the nation's growing inventory of courses, designing more than 60 and 80 new layouts respectively, the vast majority in Ontario and, in Watson's case, Quebec.

## POSTWAR ERA

Mirroring the United States, the immediate postwar years were a quiet time, leading into a period when several big-name American designers made brief, but important, northern appearances. In addition to Robert Trent Jones's cameos, Dick Wilson built an entirely new 27 holes for historic Royal Montreal[17] in 1959, while 1976 saw George and Tom Fazio add Ontario's National GC[18], and Jack Nicklaus design the frequent Canadian Open host Glen Abbey[19]. Nicklaus also returned in 1996 to build the best of four courses associated with the Chateau Whistler Resort[20], and has

since added four more designs, three in British Columbia. Another foreign visitor, England's Donald Steel, followed in Harry Colt's footsteps by building one of the nation's best layouts during a brief 1990 visit – the minimalist Red Tail[21] in Ontario.

The modern era has also seen the rise of several important native designers, the first since Stanley Thompson to regularly build courses worthy of national – and even the occasional international – acclaim. High on this list is Rod Whitman, a former Pete Dye and Bill Coore associate whose skills are in evidence at Alberta's Blackhawk GC[22] and Wolf Creek Resort[23]. Past Robbie Robinson associate Doug Carrick has made a similar contemporary mark with nationally prominent courses such as the dune-covered Eagle's Nest[24], the Heathlands[25] course at Osprey Valley and Bigwin Island[26], all located in Ontario. Tom McBroom has also become popular, with Prince Edward Island's Links[27] at Crowbush Cove standing out among his more than 35 domestic works – a roster that includes a complete rebuild of Donald Ross's Algonquin Resort[28] course in New Brunswick, and the brand-new Tobiano[29] in Kamloops, British Columbia. Finally, Les Furber – a long-serving Trent Jones construction man – has completed more than 50 Canadian projects, the best received being the Predator Ridge[30] and Radium Resorts[31] both in British Columbia.

*Fifty teams of horses and 200 men were required to clear boulders, rocks and trees to build Stanley Thompson's Jasper Park course during 1924–25, opening to great acclaim the following year.*

Set in a spectacular corner of the Canadian Rockies, flanked by the Bow and Spray rivers and surrounded by towering peaks and thick pine forests, the Banff Springs layout surely has to qualify as one of the world's prettiest places, golf-related or otherwise. To such a spot tourists flowed early and often, with the Rocky Mountain National Park established in 1887, the first Banff Springs Hotel opening a year later and the present hotel – a massive limestone edifice and one of the world's most recognizable hostelries – taking in its first visitors in 1914.

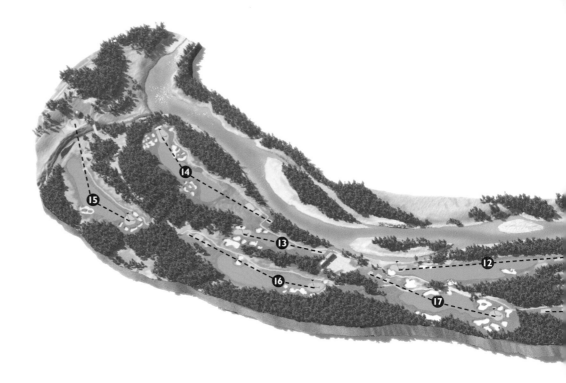

## EARLY HISTORY

Golf at Banff Springs dates to a rudimentary nine holes built in 1911, followed by a short-lived Donald Ross 18-hole course begun in 1917 but not completed until the early 1920s. Little-recorded today, the Ross layout met its demise when, in 1926, up-and-coming Canadian architect Stanley Thompson opened a highly praised course at nearby Jasper National Park. This prompted Banff Springs's owners, the Canadian Pacific Railway, quickly to hire Thompson to build them something comparable.

A large, flamboyant man with a similarly colourful design style, Thompson was a highly strategic architect with a knack for integrating his flashy bunkering into the natural flow of the landscape. This particular landscape, however, proved a difficult one on which to work, and after felling thousands of trees and dynamiting countless tons of rock, the man who would ultimately be viewed as Canada's greatest-ever designer found himself making history with the world's first $1 million golf course. The results, happily, were hardly out of line with the hefty price.

## A MODERN RESEQUENCING

It is worth noting that while nearly all of Thompson's design – though lengthened – remains either intact or restored, the 1989 addition of nine new holes (with an associated clubhouse situated more than a mile from the hotel) led to a complete resequencing of the

original 18. Lost in this process was the opportunity to walk just a few feet from the main house to the putting green and practice area, and, more importantly, to start play at what is now the 15th hole. There an elevated tee shot across the rushing waters of the Spray, aimed directly towards the slopes of Mount Rundle, was certainly among the most dazzling openings in all of golf.

If nothing else, the present configuration of the course introduces one of the game's most famous holes earlier – the 199-yard Devil's Cauldron 4th (formerly the 8th) – which is as scenically beautiful a test as any golfer might ever hope to encounter. Playing from an elevated tee, it requires a mid-iron carried across a glacial pond to a green built against the base of Mount Rundle, whose rock and pine-covered face towers almost dizzyingly above it. The green itself is fairly small and flanked by six bunkers, but it is also somewhat concave and surrounded by punchbowl-like terrain that draws marginal shots towards the centre. The challenge, really, is to summon forth even that marginal shot in the face of this once-in-a-lifetime setting.

## RIVERSIDE HOLES

Having played along the base of Mount Rundle for the first five holes, play soon progresses northwards across the valley floor, with the shortish 6th and very long 7th (a genuine three-shotter for all but the longest of hitters) leading to the banks of the Bow, and a stretch of seven attractive waterside holes. In some cases the river is merely a scenic distraction, loosely paralleling play, while in others it or one of its smaller spurs is brought directly into the action. An example of the latter is the gorgeous 158-yard 8th, little more than a pitch in the 1-mile (1.6-kilometre) high altitude, but one played to a sloping green fronted by water and backed by sand. Following the majestic 510-yard 9th, the 225-yard 10th also requires a water carry and, the Devil's Cauldron not withstanding, is surely the most testing of Banff's par threes.

Following the heavily bunkered 11th, the 449-yard 12th is a stunning two-shotter whose wide fairway progressively narrows to a triangular-shaped green guarded left by sand and right by the immediately adjacent river. The 232-yard 13th and 447-yard 14th

# BANFF SPRINGS
## Banff, Alberta

When a course is singled out from among its more than 30,000 worldwide competitors as being perhaps the most scenically beautiful, that is one very grand – and alluring – statement indeed. Such accolades have long been attached to the links at Canada's Banff Springs Hotel, and with little wonder.

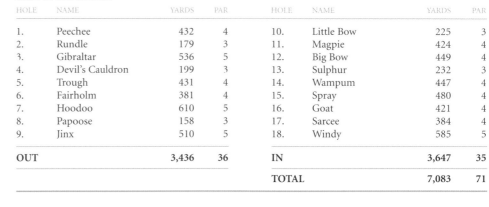

# BANFF SPRINGS GOLF COURSE (THOMPSON COURSE) –
## Banff, Alberta
Stanley Thompson, 1929

### CARD OF THE COURSE

| HOLE | NAME | YARDS | PAR | HOLE | NAME | YARDS | PAR |
|---|---|---|---|---|---|---|---|
| 1. | Peechee | 432 | 4 | 10. | Little Bow | 225 | 3 |
| 2. | Rundle | 179 | 3 | 11. | Magpie | 424 | 4 |
| 3. | Gibraltar | 536 | 5 | 12. | Big Bow | 449 | 4 |
| 4. | Devil's Cauldron | 199 | 3 | 13. | Sulphur | 232 | 3 |
| 5. | Trough | 431 | 4 | 14. | Wampum | 447 | 4 |
| 6. | Fairholm | 381 | 4 | 15. | Spray | 480 | 4 |
| 7. | Hoodoo | 610 | 5 | 16. | Goat | 421 | 4 |
| 8. | Papoose | 158 | 3 | 17. | Sarcee | 384 | 4 |
| 9. | Jinx | 510 | 5 | 18. | Windy | 585 | 5 |
| **OUT** | | **3,436** | **36** | **IN** | | **3,647** | **35** |
| | | | | **TOTAL** | | **7,083** | **71** |

are of similar (if slightly dryer) stuff. It is well worth reflecting at this stage that these were Thompson's final holes before the 1989 resequencing, with the 14th in particular – highlighted by its inspiring view across the treetops to the soaring frontage of the hotel – seeming oddly out of place at this juncture.

From here the golfer plays the 480-yard 15th (from the former 1st tee), then returns to the slopes of Mount Rundle for a three-hole dash, which concludes at the 585-yard 18th. This is a solid downwind par five made interesting by a deep dead-centre bunker some 125 yards (114 metres) in front of the green.

## GETTING ADJUSTED

Though filled with challenging, beautifully conceived holes, the biggest test at Banff Springs is probably a mental one, because the massive scale of Thompson's bunkering can be deceiving to the inexperienced eye – and that is before considering the roughly 10 per cent greater carry created by the high mountain altitude. Furthermore, it takes a remarkable degree of focus not to be distracted by the jaw-dropping surroundings, and visitors must surely be forgiven for missing many of the course's subtleties during their first or second go-rounds.

It is difficult to conceive of a layout of greater all-round beauty. If somehow Banff Springs is *not* the world's most scenic, it surely must be its prettiest genuinely great golf course, which in itself is not a bad platform to occupy.

# HAMILTON
## Ancaster, Ontario

Harry Colt's visit to the greater Toronto area in 1914 had a profound effect – directly and indirectly – on Canada's golf scene. Having designed the charming Toronto GC, he then laid out the brawny Hamilton Golf and Country Club at Ancaster. Although the styles may have been similar, Hamilton's scale is larger than Toronto GC, both in terms of the raw property and the architectural features that would match it.

Colt's indirect influence on Canadian golf-course architecture was rather fortuitous. Hamilton's long-time professional Nichol Thompson (who retired in 1945 after 37 years of service) played a key role in not only shaping Hamilton but also Canadian golf in general. In association with Toronto GC's professional George Cumming, the two would both as a duo and in consultation with Nichol's younger brother, Stanley, design courses throughout the greater Toronto area. These served as a launch pad for young Stanley Thompson, who went on to become a full-time designer – and Canada's most revered. Although their styles differed, it is clear that Colt's early architecture at Toronto and Hamilton proved the foundation and inspiration for many of the clubs the trio later created.

### COURSE CHANGES

Ancaster as the course is called (named after the town that borders the industrial centre of Hamilton) opened in 1916 in its third location since the club's founding in 1894. Colt's work was carried out by the club's John Sutherland, and he never returned to the course, although his design partner Charles Alison visited in 1920. Alison's suggestions centred on the desire to make the bunkers more penal. The most drastic change was the rebuilding of the par-three 13th, which Alison felt was too severe. These adaptations formed the final touches of the Colt–Alison team at Ancaster and stood until 1974, when the addition of the third nine caused further alterations to the course. With the expansion nine claiming the 15th green and reorienting the 16th tee, the course found its current incarnation.

Ancaster's transformations through the years have also included changes from bunkering – some deserted, others altered – to tree planting (followed by removal) and lastly amendments to several greens. Despite these, the unifying theme at Ancaster is Colt's exemplar routing through this property with its great terrain and massive scale. He placed tees and greens at the high points and required the golfer to play down and back out of the valleys. Thankfully, the stream that trickled through the property provided a wide ground for golf. Given the stress Colt placed on one-shotters, it is not surprising that he created par threes when some of the most dramatic (but also difficult) land came to be used. A sense of this can be found at the 8th. Renowned for his heathland designs, Colt must have marvelled at the drama that the rolling land allowed.

### COLT'S LEGACY

Nowhere are Colt's traits more evident than on the 408-yard 3rd, which plays dramatically downhill to a fairway bisected by the stream that he routed cleverly around and over on numerous holes. When planning the tee shot, the player must try to leave a comfortable distance to approach the uphill green, which is one of the toughest on the course. Shallow and quick, the front-left pin is not to be tussled with, but rather a well-played shot to the centre of the green is always prudent.

Once again taking advantage of the wonderful natural terrain at the 318-yard 5th, Colt created a masterful, short par four. Arguably the most difficult hole to design to this high level, it is as delightful today as it was on opening day. With the green perched on a hillock and the fairway flowing left to right, the approach is difficult, whether with a daring driver or a delicate short-iron. Colt did leave room in front to run the ball into the green, but with the slope of the fronting fairway it does require an exacting drive. Perhaps two of the most difficult recoveries faced at Ancaster are revealed to golfers who miss either right or long and have to contend with the steep slope of the hill and small putting surface as a target.

### DRAMATIC PAR THREES

After the strong set of opening holes, Colt's prowess with par threes is amply displayed at the 6th and the

8th. The former plays to a brutish 224 yards, and although only slightly uphill the hole manages to seem longer. Colt cleverly placed two bunkers into the hillside short of the green, to create the illusion that they were flush against the front of the green. However, this was simply an optical trick, because the bunkers are well short and rarely come into play. Colt further used some of the most dramatic terrain for the 8th, on which the player is faced with a do-or-die par three, measuring 210 yards. Playing from ridge to ridge, bisected by the river valley, it manages to produce one of Ancaster's prettiest, yet most difficult shots.

*The 3rd playing from peak to peak through one valley illustrates the broad canvas provided to Harry Colt for his design.*

On making the turn, Colt created a nifty three-hole loop to begin the back nine. Each of the trio holes crosses the stream and plays within the broader loop of the front nine, before the 12th turns east and begins to open up the rest of the back nine. This hole is one of the highlights. Playing to a modest 383 yards, the gentle hole plays back uphill into a benched green, set into the hillside. With trees flanking both sides of the fairway, the player must stay alert and accurate to prevent a stroke slipping away.

Alison's redesigned 13th blends seamlessly into the overall design, although the 415-yard 15th and 185 yard 16th bore the greatest brunt of the changes to Colt's routing, and sadly the course is not better for them.

### A MEMORABLE ENDING

Hamilton features a strong finish with the 548-yard 17th followed by the 442-yard 18th – one of the great closers in Canada, where the meandering stream's central role at Ancaster reaches its peak. Quite literally snaking across the fairway at the 300-yard mark, only the longest hitters can

reach it from the tee. However, its presence causes many golfers to ease off, which can lead to a ball that fails to funnel to the ideal spot and forces a long and arduous uphill second shot.

Hamilton's stately clubhouse (which was built 13 years after the golf course opened) looms large as the backdrop of the closing green complex, and the uphill nature results in many shots left short. It was here at the 2003 Canadian Open that Bob Tway defeated Brad Faxon, with a bogey from the greenside bunker.

High drama at the last has cemented Ancaster's role in professional golf's history, but it was Harry Colt's brilliant routing over wonderful terrain that makes the course worthy of study to this day.

## HAMILTON GOLF AND COUNTRY CLUB –
### Ancaster, Ontario
Harry Colt, 1916
Major events: Canadian Open 1919, 1930, 2003, 2006

CARD OF THE COURSE

| HOLE | YARDS | PAR | HOLE | YARDS | PAR |
|------|-------|-----|------|-------|-----|
| 1. | 404 | 4 | 10. | 412 | 4 |
| 2. | 431 | 4 | 11. | 481 | 4 |
| 3. | 408 | 4 | 12. | 383 | 4 |
| 4. | 532 | 5 | 13. | 234 | 3 |
| 5. | 318 | 4 | 14. | 443 | 4 |
| 6. | 224 | 3 | 15. | 415 | 4 |
| 7. | 411 | 4 | 16. | 185 | 3 |
| 8. | 210 | 3 | 17. | 548 | 5 |
| 9. | 438 | 4 | 18. | 442 | 4 |
| OUT | 3,376 | 35 | IN | 3,543 | 35 |
| | | | TOTAL | 6,919 | 70 |

Stanley Thompson's flamboyant style in life mimicked the grandiose designs that made him famous. What St George's lacked in natural beauty Thompson made up for with a wonderful layout. Saving the most severe points for dramatic par threes, he would both attack and retreat within the routing, providing enormous diversity. Using his trademark bunkering – which rivalled only Alister MacKenzie's in its artistry – he seamlessly fitted St George's hazards within the big scale of the property.

## LATER COURSE ALTERATIONS

Although St George's played host to its first of three Canadian Opens in 1949, the course was lengthened only for the final tournament, held in 1968. Thompson died in 1953 and so his right-hand man Robbie Robinson handled the changes, which ranged from slight modifications to rather significant alterations such as a complete rebuilding of the par-three 3rd, which remains bemusing to this day.

In 2002 architect Ian Andrew, of Carrick Design, was employed to restore the bunker style of Thompson, which had been lost through many years

of maintenance and change, and he remarked: 'St George's is a testament to Thompson's ability to create bold enough bunkering to draw your attention, yet artistic enough to still blend seamlessly into the surrounding landscape.'

## CLUBHOUSE POSITION DILEMMA

Beginning its journey on the east side of Islington Avenue, the course opens gently with a nearly perfect welcome to the round. From the elevated 1st tee play is down to a slender fairway, before climbing again to the well-protected green site. Thompson, however, did not generally subscribe to such a 'gentle handshake' to open the round. He always believed that the current 1st would be the closing par four and that golf would begin on the current, difficult, 466-yard 2nd, which is situated beside an ideal area for a clubhouse. In the end the clubhouse was not built there but over the road, away from the course.

The actual reason for the unorthodox separation of the clubhouse and course is

## ST GEORGE'S GOLF AND COUNTRY CLUB – Etobicoke, Ontario

Stanley Thompson, 1929 and Robbie Robinson, 1966
Major events: Canadian Open 1949, 1960, 1968

CARD OF THE COURSE

| HOLE | YARDS | PAR | HOLE | YARDS | PAR |
|---|---|---|---|---|---|
| 1. | 370 | 4 | 10. | 377 | 4 |
| 2. | 466 | 4 | 11. | 528 | 5 |
| 3. | 198 | 3 | 12. | 399 | 4 |
| 4. | 474 | 5 | 13. | 213 | 3 |
| 5. | 432 | 4 | 14. | 466 | 4 |
| 6. | 201 | 3 | 15. | 570 | 5 |
| 7. | 446 | 4 | 16. | 203 | 3 |
| 8. | 223 | 3 | 17. | 470 | 4 |
| 9. | 538 | 5 | 18. | 451 | 4 |
| OUT | 3,348 | 35 | IN | 3,677 | 36 |
| | | | TOTAL | 7,025 | 71 |

# ST GEORGE'S
## Etobicoke, Ontario

Laid out by Stanley Thompson in 1929, St George's original charge was to provide golf facilities for the Royal York – the stately downtown hotel whose name it bore. By 1946, the arrangement with the hotel had come to an end and henceforth the club became St George's Golf and Country Club.

not known for certain, but the theory advanced by the club is that bar facilities could be included if the club-house was positioned on the west side of Islington Avenue, and not if it were to be set amid the course itself on the east side of the road, where the drinking laws were different.

Although the 1966 changes to the 198-yard 3rd are out of character with the rest of the course, Robinson's relocation of the 4th green into the hillside added length to both the 474-yard 4th and 432-yard 5th. Here, though, Thompson's routing of the course through the valleys is what really stands out, and where they were most severe he crossed them, as on the delicious par-three 6th.

The 446-yard 7th seemingly plays longer than the 466-yard 2nd, because of its steady rise from tee to green. Thompson swings golfers left with a large bunker that dominates the right side of the fairway, then forces them back-right with a large bunker short-left. This clever approach gives the feeling of a double-dogleg in what is a straight corridor. Favouring the more aggressive line on both the drive and approach can shorten the hole significantly, while allowing the golfer to approach from the preferred angle. Though Thompson created ample fairway on the left side of the 7th, the approach shot is then over a difficult bunker complex to a green that slopes to the front and right. Contours of the green demand special attention, and many golfers have surely wished to have been 10 yards (9 metres) shorter with their chipping club than face a long putt on this beguiling green.

*With its idyllic parkland setting, it is easy to forget that St George's is located in a sprawling metropolis.*

Using 'nature as his guide' as Thompson was prone to say, the golfer can smile at the 223-yard 8th. With the green nestled behind a hillside, the majority of the putting surface is hidden, yet Thompson was smart in his use of the natural landform. A large bunker on the left side, which appears to the eye as flush against the green, is actually well short and a ball that manages to carry it continues down the hill and onto the receptive green. In following the flows of the land, Thompson managed to inject some controversy, while allowing for a surprisingly playable hole.

## HANDSOME, UNDULATING COURSE

Thompson's stretch of golf from the 10th to the 12th provides a striking example of his use of the topography. Although at 377 yards the 10th is a relatively short par four that looks fairly flat from the tee, this visual trick is revealed by a valley that collects most drives, leaving a blind, short-iron approach. Finding a level stance can only be secured by laying well back of the valley, but few take this longer route. From the 11th tee, the golfer plunges back down into the valley, and the elevation allows the stronger golfer a chance at birdie if the well-staggered bunkers can be avoided. Climbing out of the valley at the 399-yard 12th, the golfer faces the most dramatic bunker complex on the course, which lures tee shots just left of this fairway. An abrupt 12-foot (3.6-metre) rise to the table-top green, which sits on a hillock, leaves ticklish approaches to a front hole location.

Playing steadily downhill, the 466-yard 14th requires a strong drive to catch the sloping fairway and gain advantage of the topography. Level lies can be a great reward, because the approach is what garners this hole's fame. Hugging the right side of the area and bisecting the hole is a stream, which then meanders in front and guards the left greenside. With three bunkers guarding the hillside green, disaster looms for a weaker shot. Relatively subdued, the putting surface is a welcome respite.

Stern back to-back par fours – the 470-yard 17th and 451-yard 18th – make nursing a good score down the final stretch a tall order. Indeed, St George's as it stands today may be Thompson's toughest test, but with great land and restored bunkers it also reflects his great style. Interestingly, on its opening, the course was not considered among Thompson's more picturesque ones – these being Banff Springs (see page 258), Capilano, Highlands Links (see page 264) and Jasper Park. Perhaps the greatest testament to Thompson as a designer is that as St George's has matured it has come to be considered an equal to his other famous designs.

# HIGHLANDS LINKS
## Ingonish Beach, Nova Scotia

During the Great Depression in the early 1930s, Canada suffered economic hardship. Therefore the federal government, wanting to capitalize on the success of Banff Springs (see page 258) and Jasper Park in attracting visitors, sought to establish a great golf course on the eastern tip of Canada. Thus Highlands Links was born.

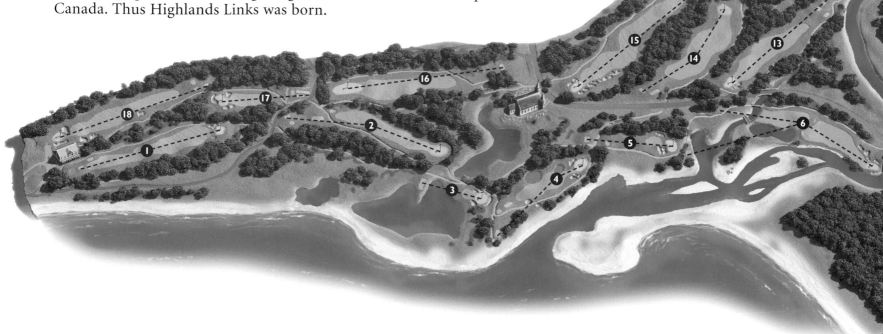

Cape Breton Highlands Links (the name has since been shortened to Highlands Links) was created on a spit of land called Middle Head Peninsula. This is barely wide enough to accommodate the parallel opening and closing holes, because it juts into the Atlantic. Famous Canadian architect Stanley Thompson first came to the site on Cape Breton Island, Nova Scotia, in 1937. Even though he had already designed courses on several outstanding sites, such as at Banff and Jasper, Thompson still found the setting of Cape Breton to be spectacular.

Originally, the government's commission was to create a nine-hole course. However, as he walked the land and studied the aerial photographs, Thompson became keen to do an 18-hole routing. When the nine holes then cost $12,500 below the $70,000 budget, Thompson convinced the authorities to extend the golf course. Of the original nine, it would use holes 1 to 4 and 14 to 18. His new routing was both on a coastal stretch, which dominate holes 1 to 6, and on some 'mountainous' terrain, which begins at the 7th. Although pressure was put on Thompson to extend the holes farther up the coast, beyond the 6th, he remained certain that the best golf was offered by turning west into the hills and up the Clyburn Valley. Having won over his patrons, it is little surprise that the 7th, named Killiecrankie, is arguably Canada's best par five. To access the extra land up the valley, several local residents had their land expropriated, something Thompson paid tribute to in his naming of the 13th hole Laird after these displaced residents.

### MANUAL LABOUR

Because the government undertook the Highlands Links project not only to create a future draw for tourism but also to generate work for the locals, it took measures to ensure the latter requirement was met. Only two pieces of excavation equipment were permitted on site, and their use was restricted to one day a week. Thus the construction crew swelled to as many as 180 at a given time and provided 300–400 jobs for local labourers. Given the severity of the terrain and the presence of rocks, a great deal of work was done by hand.

Such attention to detail resulted in a golf course with some fine architectural points, including great fairway contours and a marvellous set of greens. These are an undulating set that (with the exception of a repair to the 13th) mercifully have not been tampered with through the years. Thompson achieved many of the unruly contours at Highlands Links by burying piles of rocks in the fairway, to create humps and bumps reminiscent of the Scottish courses he loved.

### PLAYING THE CONTOURS

Such uneven terrain is very much in evidence on the stern uphill 1st, with its lumpy fairway. However, the task facing the golfer gets harder at the 447-yard 2nd. Widely hailed as one of the finest bunkerless par fours in golf, the hole doglegs right, with the heaving fairway lying down the hillside. From the tee the golfer is challenged to take the direct line along the trees to attain both a level lie and a reasonable distance. However, players who take the conservative line left may have to cope with a downhill lie from well in excess of 200 yards (183 metres). Regardless of the route, as the corner is rounded the dramatic vista of the Atlantic as the backdrop to the tremendous 2nd green is revealed.

From here the golfer plays north along the coast for the next four holes. Diversity is the key – the 3rd

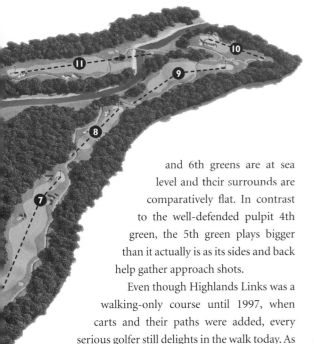

## HIGHLANDS LINKS – Ingonish Beach, Nova Scotia
Stanley Thompson, 1941

CARD OF THE COURSE

| HOLE | NAME | YARDS | PAR | HOLE | NAME | YARDS | PAR |
|---|---|---|---|---|---|---|---|
| 1. | Ben Franey | 405 | 4 | 10. | Cuddy's Lugs | 145 | 3 |
| 2. | Tam O'Shanter | 447 | 4 | 11. | Bonnie Burn | 512 | 5 |
| 3. | Lochan | 160 | 3 | 12. | Cleugh | 240 | 3 |
| 4. | Heich O'Fash | 324 | 4 | 13. | Laird | 435 | 4 |
| 5. | Canny Slap | 164 | 3 | 14. | Haugh | 398 | 4 |
| 6. | Mucklemouth Meg | 537 | 5 | 15. | Tattie Bogle | 540 | 5 |
| 7. | Killiecrankie | 570 | 5 | 16. | Sair Fecht | 460 | 5 |
| 8. | Caber's Toss | 319 | 4 | 17. | Dowie Den | 190 | 3 |
| 9. | Corbie's Nest | 336 | 4 | 18. | Hame Noo | 410 | 4 |
| **OUT** | | **3,262** | **36** | **IN** | | **3,330** | **36** |
| | | | | **TOTAL** | | **6,592** | **72** |

and 6th greens are at sea level and their surrounds are comparatively flat. In contrast to the well-defended pulpit 4th green, the 5th green plays bigger than it actually is as its sides and back help gather approach shots.

Even though Highlands Links was a walking-only course until 1997, when carts and their paths were added, every serious golfer still delights in the walk today. As they cross the bridge over the Clyburn river – often complete with fishermen below – they can sense the unique connection with nature that Thompson felt some 80 years earlier. On crossing the bridge, the oceanside is left for the mountains and the 7th tee. With its wonderfully undulating ground, this 570-yard par five feels a worthy foil to the ocean. Its land formations flow from the left, then the right, so the player must thread a drive into the narrow chute. From the landing area, the hole rises steadily to the wild green that caps this hole. The out-and-back nature of the course's routing is revealed at the turn when the golfer descends back into the river valley on the 145-yard 10th hole.

On finishing the 12th, the golfer experiences something rarely found on a golf course – something that Thompson believed to be a key component to the course. A walking path of nearly 500 yards (457 metres) hugs tightly to the river bank and is barely wide enough for playing partners to walk side by side. The walk's serenity appropriately embodies the entire golf experience.

A strong drive is required at the 435-yard 13th to find the fairway, which cants heavily from right to left and allows two distinct levels of play. The higher, right side affords more short grass and the clearer angle, while the lower left allows the use of slope as a springboard and shortens the hole significantly. Thompson carefully shaped the fairway leading into the green with

*The 15th hole combines majestic vistas with the wonderful land that makes the course so unique. Despite playing steeply downhill, the sidehill undulations create the strategy that helps create this world-class set of par fives.*

a generous slope to feed the ball in. Watching the shot play out along the ground is thrilling and aids appreciation of the ground game options tied to this 'links'.

### THE CLOSING HOLES
Marking the turn for home is another set of back-to-back par fives – a rare feature among world-class courses. Again, Thompson uses the natural slope to dare the stronger player to hug the tree line left and carry the hillock to be rewarded with a level lie and a chance to get home in two on the 540-yard 15th. Nevertheless, most drives find the fairway right and are forced to lay up over the hill to a heavily bunkered landing area. On coming up over the rise, the vista is once again extraordinary, with the aptly named Whale Island in the background and the church steeple in the foreground. This culmination at the 15th makes it easy to see why Thompson labelled Highlands his 'mountains and oceans course'. The 460-yard 16th's name of 'Sair Fecht' (hard work) is deceiving because plenty of golfers have hopes of reaching this green in two.

One of Highlands Links's great attributes relative to Thompson's other works is highlighted at the last two holes, namely that the greens are still largely as he designed them. The undulations found in these 17th and 18th putting surfaces display Thompson's flair for green construction, and they make for a fitting finish to the course.

### END OF AN ERA
Highlands Links marked the end of Thompson's illustrious designs. Although he worked for a further 12 years after the opening, it was never on a world-class canvas. At the course's 75th anniversary, golf historian and architect Geoffrey Cornish recounted that Thompson's big five (Banff Springs, Capilano, Jasper Park, Royal St George's and Highlands Links) were viewed in Europe as being not merely Canada's best courses but also five of the world's. This is a testament to the huge country's natural beauty, which Thompson maximized whenever he was given the opportunity.

# CENTRAL AMERICA AND THE ATLANTIC ISLANDS

Apart from Mexico and Costa Rica, most of Central America remains on a colonial-era golf footing, with the game enjoying only small pockets of popularity, usually in areas populated by foreign nationals or the odd affluent native. In the islands the golfing emphasis is on resort golf.

Cabo San Lucas

G olf's first recorded appearance in Mexico came in 1897. The game's initial popularity there, however, was limited to a handful of courses frequented by British or American business-men, and the occasional local. This changed only after the Second World War when Percy Clifford, a Briton born and raised in Mexico, enlisted the help of both the government and American designer Lawrence Hughes in building the Club de Golf Mexico[1] (twice a World Cup host). This was easily the nation's first truly prominent facility. Clifford and Hughes went on to enjoy prolific design careers in Mexico, with Clifford actually building nearly half of the roughly 80 layouts that dotted the country *c.*1980.

A handful of courses (notably Clifford's Vallescondido[2]) vied with the Club de Golf Mexico for period superiority, but even these are today largely overshadowed by a resort boom that began in the long-established Acapulco, Mazatlán and Cancun, before spreading to a variety of locations, mostly along the Pacific coast. With frequent pushes from a tourism-friendly government, Puerto Vallarta, Manzanillo, Ixtapa and even the less-glamorous Tijuana/Ensenada region near the American border now offer golfing destinations on par with many of the finest resorts in the hemisphere, often featuring courses built by American designers such as Robert Trent Jones Jnr, Jack Nicklaus and Robert von Hagge. The unques-tioned centre of Mexican resort golf, however, is the Los Cabos/Cabo San Lucas area at the southern tip of Baja California, where the Nicklaus name is king, and seaside/desert golf of a very high calibre abounds.

Costa Rica is a growing American tourism/retire-ment destination, and a country in which Jack Nicklaus, Robert von Hagge and Arnold Palmer have all designed golf courses for the mass market. Palmer's resort course at Papagayo explores a dense tropical forest yet enjoys great ocean views.

## TYPICAL ISLANDS COURSES

Golf in the Atlantic Islands has, for the most part, always been resort-based, initially on a small scale in British-controlled Bermuda and the Bahamas, then, during the 1960s and '70s, in Puerto Rico, Jamaica and the Dominican Republic. Today the game has grabbed a strong foothold – usually in association with one luxury resort or another – on almost every island large enough to hold it, from New Providence to Aruba.

Bermuda was home to the region's first great lay-out, Mid Ocean (see page 272) and today mixes the old with the new. Robert Trent Jones Snr's Port Royal[3] (1970) and Roger Rulewich's Tucker's Point[4] – a 2003 rebuild of the old Castle Harbour Golf Course – are among the island's best.

In the Bahamas, early golf was played primarily by British expatriates around Nassau, but today the game has reached most of the country's major islands. On Great Abaco there is Dick Wilson's Treasure Cay GC[5], while Grand Bahama is highlighted by 36 holes at the Lucaya resort in the form of Dick Wilson's Lucayan course[6] (which dates from 1962) and by Robert Trent Jones Jnr's Reef course[7], an addition in 2000. Great Exuma offers Greg Norman's spectacular design at the Four Seasons Emerald Bay[8], where six holes occupy a narrow oceanfront peninsula, while New Providence golf includes the Bahamas' oldest course – the much-altered Cable Beach GC[9] – as well as Dick Wilson's once-prominent 1960 design at Lyford Cay and Tom Weiskopf's remodel of an early Wilson work on Paradise Island.

*Cabo del Sol on the tip of Baja California in Mexico is a Jack Nicklaus design which marries the desert landscape with ocean backdrops impressively.*

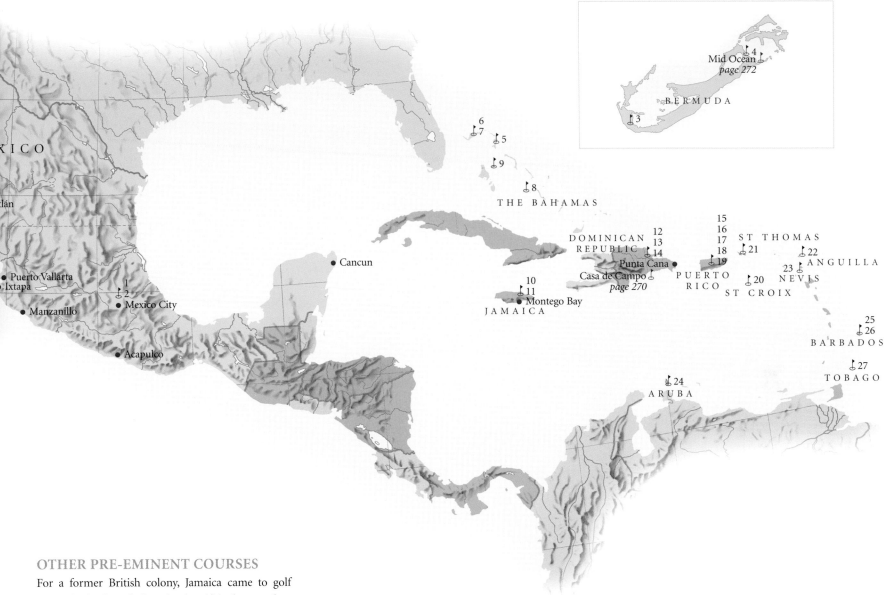

## OTHER PRE-EMINENT COURSES

For a former British colony, Jamaica came to golf relatively slowly and, though a handful of prewar layouts still exist, its best courses are of a decidedly newer vintage, particularly those clustered along the north shore, around Montego Bay. The oldest of the bunch, the Tryall GC[10], is from 1958 and, although altered a bit in recent years, remains among the elite of the Caribbean. Close on its heels came Robert Trent Jones Snr's 1961 design at Half-Moon Bay, which today is part of a 54-hole Rose Hall[11] resort facility that includes a pair of newer Robert von Hagge designs – Cinnamon Hill and the spectacular White Witch.

The Dominican Republic became a sudden fashionable golfing destination in 1971 with the debut of Pete Dye's spectacular Casa de Campo (see page 270), and this La Romana resort has since added two more Dye courses to go with yet another of his highly rated creations, the nearby La Romana Country Club[12]. The Dye name carries considerable weight in these parts still, because Pete's son P.B. has built several Dominican courses, including an exciting coastal course at the Punta Cana resort, a popular destination at the island's eastern tip. An earlier Robert Trent Jones presence can still be felt here as well, with his work at Playa Grande[13] and the Santo Domingo CC[14] generally rating among the island's best.

The American territory of Puerto Rico was an early player in regional golf development and today features four 36-hole resorts of distinction: Dorado Beach[15] (East and West Courses by Robert Trent Jones), Cerromar[16] (North and South Courses also by Robert Trent Jones), Rio Mar[17] (Ocean Course by George Fazio, River by Greg Norman) and Palmas del Mar[18] (Palm Course by Gary Player, Flamboyan by Rees Jones). Also noteworthy is the El Conquistador resort[19], once a wildly distinctive Robert von Hagge creation since entirely renovated by Arthur Hills.

## SMALLER ISLAND ATTRACTIONS

Several courses of merit dot smaller islands, led by Robert Trent Jones Snr's well-known Carambola GC[20] (née Fountain Valley) on St Croix and George and Tom Fazio's Mahogany Run GC[21] on St Thomas, a shortish layout featuring some spectacular cliff-top terrain. Anguilla offers Greg Norman's Temenos GC[22], while Robert Trent Jones Jnr left his mark at three noteworthy facilities: the Four Seasons resort in Nevis[23], Aruba's windswept Tierra del Sol[24] and Barbados's stylish Royal Westmoreland[25]. Also in Barbados is a pair of Tom Fazio designs at the Sandy Lane resort[26] – the Country Club and Green Monkey Courses. And finally, the southern island of Tobago features the Mount Irvine Bay Hotel GC[27], a 1969 design by John Harris, the former Royal Navy commander who built a number of distinctive 1960s and '70s courses in the tropics.

# CASA DE CAMPO
## La Romana, Dominican Republic

Widely rated among the world's finest courses immediately upon its opening in 1971, Pete Dye's Casa de Campo certainly succeeded in making the Dominican Republic an international golfing destination of note in the Caribbean.

Probably more than any high-profile designer of the postwar era, Pete Dye has long had a reputation for, to borrow from Ben Hogan, finding his golf courses 'in the dirt'. He has always created courses the old-fashioned way by walking his properties, selecting his routing, then working out his design concepts on the ground, shaping them as he goes.

### WORKING WITH THE LAND

Such a painstaking, traditional approach has served Dye well over the course of his five-decade career, but surely nowhere more so than at Casa de Campo, on the south-east coast of the Dominican Republic. Known alternatively as 'Cajuiles' (the name of a local cashew tree) or 'Teeth of the Dog' (after the jagged-edged coral that inhabits the property), Casa de Campo began life as a way for the Gulf and Western Corporation to invest its local sugar production profits into Dominican tourist development. As such, the decision was made to build the sort of golf course that would attract attention in the faraway American markets so vital to the Caribbean winter trade. With the company owning

400,000 acres (161,870 hectares), Dye had a marvellous selection of coastal sites to choose from, though in the end he still managed to exceed the property boundaries, necessitating the last-minute purchase of several adjoining tracts.

Because state-of-the-art earthmoving equipment was scarce in the Dominican Republic in 1971, Dye had to put together a workforce of locals to reshape the property by hand. Initially this involved clearing dense underbrush with machetes, though more challenging tasks included carting away hundreds of boulders and blasting – with hand tools, not dynamite – the countless coral patches that dotted the coastal expanse. The disintegrated coral was often laid, piece by piece, into the small walls that line select bunkers and, in perhaps the most labour-intensive construction move on record, several fairways were actually hand planted, blade by painstaking blade. As Dye later rather understatedly wrote: 'The opportunity to carve out Teeth of the Dog was a once-in-a-lifetime experience.'

### SEVEN OCEANFRONT HOLES

Casa de Campo includes nearly 3 miles (5 kilometres) of ocean frontage, which allowed a total of seven holes (four on the front, three on the back) to be built directly on the water. The clubhouse, however, lies inland, necessitating an opening run of four dry holes of varied lengths, a quartet brought to life by several vast waste bunkers, a touch of replication – the 4th, for example, is loosely based on the 3rd at Pinehurst No 2 (see page 202) – and their routing into the prevailing east wind.

The course takes on an epic quality, however, immediately on reaching the water, with the 155-yard 5th setting the tone. Here a narrow, almost crescent-shaped green sits on a rocky outcropping, its bulk-headed front and left side guarded by a

narrow bunker and the splashing waters of the Caribbean. The 449-yard 6th is the most forgiving of the seaside holes – its immense fairway allowing plenty of room for safe shots, and even a preferred angle of approach from the drier right side.

The respite is only temporary. The 225-yard 7th is an all-carry proposition, requiring a long-iron across a wide curvature of water to a right-to-left angled green. In its early years – when it was selected to be among the first *World Atlas of Golf*'s best 18 holes worldwide – nearly all of this coastal area was covered by open sand, giving the 7th a slightly more rustic appearance than it enjoys today.

Finally, the 417-yard 8th follows the shoreline to a distinctive L-shaped green backed by a dangerous grass bunker. Hoping to inject a meaningful water carry into the drive, Dye created a peninsula tee by piling so many rocks in the surf that 'the natives thought I was building a causeway to Puerto Rico'.

### THE BACK NINE

Though largely unheralded, the back nine's inland holes feature several appealing tests, beginning with the 377-yard 10th, a dogleg left around a huge waste bunker that, particularly downwind, might well

### CASA DE CAMPO (TEETH OF THE DOG) – La Romana, Dominican Republic

Pete Dye, 1971

CARD OF THE COURSE

| HOLE | YARDS | PAR | HOLE | YARDS | PAR |
|------|-------|-----|------|-------|-----|
| 1. | 401 | 4 | 10. | 377 | 4 |
| 2. | 378 | 4 | 11. | 540 | 5 |
| 3. | 545 | 5 | 12. | 445 | 4 |
| 4. | 327 | 4 | 13. | 175 | 3 |
| 5. | 155 | 3 | 14. | 505 | 5 |
| 6. | 449 | 4 | 15. | 384 | 4 |
| 7. | 225 | 3 | 16. | 185 | 3 |
| 8. | 417 | 4 | 17. | 435 | 4 |
| 9. | 505 | 5 | 18. | 440 | 4 |
| OUT | 3,402 | 36 | IN | 3,486 | 36 |
| | | | TOTAL | 6,888 | 72 |

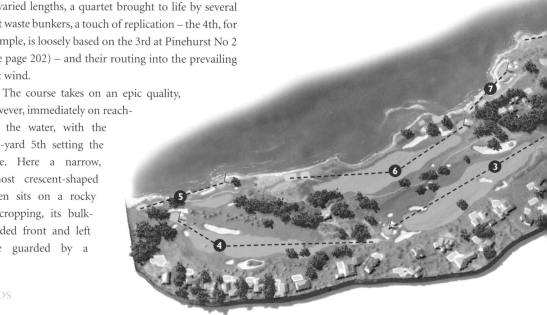

*A ground-level view of the 225-yard 7th, a difficult oceanside par three played to a narrow green wedged between rock, water and sand. There is little room to miss here.*

185-yard 16th features more of the same – its left-to-right putting surface curving around a large bunker to a back corner again lined just above the waterline by coral.

The last of the coastal holes is the 435-yard 17th, a strong two-shotter made even tougher by both the prevailing breezes and the tendency to hit the tee shot out to the left side of a wide fairway, leaving a straight-on – but dangerously long – approach to the final waterside green. Generally overlooked after this spectacular oceanfront run is the 440-yard 18th, a snake-like double-dogleg with sand guarding the optimum right side of the fairway and a narrow green tucked away behind a wooded pond.

## INTERNATIONAL GOLFING DESTINATION

Within four years of its opening in 1971, Teeth of the Dog had succeeded in making La Romana an international golfing destination of note. Its success spawned a second Dye layout known as the Links Course and, more recently, a 7,770-yard Dye-designed monster opened in 2004, giving the resort easily the largest and widest-ranging golf facilities in the Caribbean.

be carried. The 175-yard doughnut 13th is also memorable, for its green is an island set amid coral-lined sand and several overhanging trees.

The 505-yard lagoon-protected 14th runs close to the ocean, but play then returns to the coastline for real at the 384-yard 15th, a gentle dogleg right whose green is situated on a promontory, backed by sand and bulkheaded with coral. Playing into the prevailing wind, with its fairway flanked right by the sea and left by a surfeit of bunkers, this is certainly one of the game's most dangerous sub-400-yard par fours. The

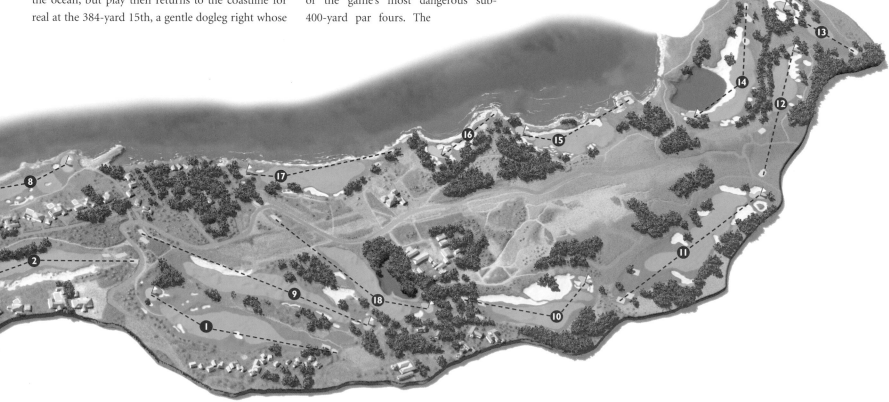

# MID OCEAN
## Tuckers Town, Bermuda

Britain's oldest overseas territory, the 135 tiny islands that constitute Bermuda sit in scenic Atlantic Ocean splendour, some 650 miles (1,046 kilometres) south-east of Cape Hatteras, North Carolina. Blessed with a consistent sub-tropical climate, no fewer than eight golf courses fill its landmass of 22 square miles (57 square kilometres), led by the sublime Mid Ocean Golf Club.

One man who in the years before commercial air travel recognized the tourist potential of Bermuda was the legendary Charles Blair Macdonald, a driving force behind golf's early American growth and designer of the seminal National Golf Links of America (see page 166) in 1911. Seeking a sunny retreat from the cold of the New York winter (not to mention a place where alcohol was legal in the brand-new era of Prohibition), Macdonald piggy-backed onto the development interests of the Furness, Withy Steamship Company when he purchased the 600 Tuckers Town acres (250 hectares) that would eventually become the Mid Ocean Golf Club. The location, Macdonald believed, was perfect. Years later, he would observe that: 'One leaving New York about noon Saturday in the dead of winter can by ten o'clock Monday morning be teeing off in a summer climate and play over this wonderful, unexcelled course.'

### THE MACDONALD/RAYNOR PARTNERSHIP

Thus motivated, the semiretired Macdonald became actively involved in Mid Ocean's design, walking the site with his talented partner Seth Raynor, and bringing in future architects Charles Banks (who would later build the well-known Castle Harbour Golf Club immediately next door) and Ralph Barton to aid in construction. With agronomic prospects vastly better in the property's lush valleys than on its coral-based hills, a routing was developed that stuck primarily to the lowlands. His plans so drawn, Macdonald left their construction to Raynor, Banks and Barton. On the course's 1921 completion, Macdonald proclaimed Mid Ocean to be 'an achievement in a semitropical

## MID OCEAN GOLF CLUB – Tuckers Town, Bermuda
Charles Blair Macdonald and Seth Raynor, 1921

CARD OF THE COURSE

| HOLE | NAME | YARDS | PAR | HOLE | NAME | YARDS | PAR |
|------|------|-------|-----|------|------|-------|-----|
| 1. | Atlantic | 418 | 4 | 10. | Mercer Hill | 404 | 4 |
| 2. | Long | 471 | 5 | 11. | Trotts | 487 | 5 |
| 3. | Eden | 190 | 3 | 12. | Hillside | 437 | 4 |
| 4. | Mangrove | 330 | 4 | 13. | Biarritz | 238 | 3 |
| 5. | Cape | 433 | 4 | 14. | Leven | 357 | 4 |
| 6. | Brow | 360 | 4 | 15. | Punch Bowl | 504 | 5 |
| 7. | Short | 164 | 3 | 16. | Lookout | 376 | 4 |
| 8. | Valley | 349 | 4 | 17. | Redan | 203 | 3 |
| 9. | Sound | 406 | 4 | 18. | Home | 421 | 4 |
| OUT | | 3,121 | 35 | IN | | 3,427 | 36 |
| | | | | | TOTAL | 6,548 | 71 |

green perched on an oceanside cliff. This is also one's initial encounter with rows of tiny fairway bunkers, which are the residue of a 1953 Robert Trent Jones Snr visit during which nearly all of Raynor's larger hazards were inexplicably divided up.

A lost stroke might well be reclaimed at the short par-five 2nd before the golfer faces the first of the replica holes, the 190-yard Eden 3rd. Unlike the original 11th at St Andrews (see page 40), Mid Ocean's 3rd features a rocky left-side plunge to the ocean rather than the eponymous estuary behind the green. The 330-yard 4th, while not a replica, is decidedly Old World in style, crossing a quiet local road before requiring a blind pitch to a squarish, two-tiered green.

## THE FAMED FIFTH

What follows, the 433-yard 5th, is not only Mid Ocean's best-known hole, but also one of the most recognized in all of golf. Conceptually modelled after Macdonald's original Cape hole – the 14th at the National Golf Links of America – the 5th wraps itself around the shoreline of Mangrove Lake, its angled fairway and steeply elevated tee providing both a remarkable view and an opportunity to bite off as much of the water carry as possible. Assuming that some part of the fairway is safely found, what remains is a fairly long approach to a platform green angled right-to-left above the shoreline, and flanked (particularly front-left) by deep, grassed-face bunkers.

Though less talked about, the 164-yard 7th is a charming one-shotter at least somewhat based on another Macdonald original at the National Golf Links – the bunker-ringed Short. Here a nice variation is provided by a small pond that replaces sand in front and to the sides of the green, an enhanced difficulty at least partially offset by both the absence of the traditional horseshoe-shaped ridge within the putting surface and the fact that the hole plays noticeably downhill.

While the blind approach on the 406-yard 9th represents something of an Alps rendition (see page 45), the strongest remaining par four is the 437-yard 12th. This is the longest of the two-shotters and one requiring a demanding uphill second shot to a pitched green whose entrance is narrowed by seven small bunkers.

## REPLICAS OF NOTE

Both of the back-nine par threes are replicas, one following its template exactly while the other adds something of a new wrinkle. The more predictable is the 238-yard 13th, a rendition of a perennial Macdonald/Raynor favourite, the Biarritz. This requires a long approach to a squarish green flanked on either side by geometric bunkering and with a narrow, deep swale in front. Except for its elevated tee, Mid Ocean's version is indistinguishable from numerous others, but with a long-iron or wooden club in hand par is always a good score.

Following the return of the uphill par-four 16th to the clubhouse, the 203-yard 17th differs somewhat from a traditional Redan, plunging substantially downhill in direct contrast to North Berwick's flattish, semiblind original (see page 49). Like so many Macdonald/Raynor Redans, however, its challenge lies in choosing the proper line of approach to a fall-away green angled right-to-left behind a cluster of bunkers – the Trent Jones-divided remains of a larger, more frightening hazard that originally existed here. This high ground is also Mid Ocean's windiest spot, with the incumbent breezes making the golfer's long-iron approach particularly difficult to judge.

The 421-yard 18th begins with a tee placed seductively above a secluded beach and, though routed parallel to the ocean, is actually situated far enough from the cliff that only a prodigious slice will bring the water into play. Though a strong par four since its inception, the hole today features an alternate bluff-top tee measuring 521 yards, from which it becomes an excitingly reachable par five.

## SOURCE OF PROSPERITY

While Macdonald's observation that prior to his arrival 'there was no golf course in Bermuda worthy of the name' may have been true, the construction of Mid Ocean quickly sparked a golfing boom on the island. Indeed, courses soon popped up at Riddell's Bay, the Belmont Hotel and Castle Harbour, and today this tiny territory with its six regulation and two short courses is among the most dense golfing destinations on Earth.

climate as great as the National Golf Links of America has been in the temperate zone'.

Macdonald's characteristic immodesty notwithstanding, Mid Ocean certainly was a unique proposition for the tropics. Its rolling, highly scenic design easily exceeded anything in Britain's various warm-weather territories or, for that matter, any course yet built in Florida. Like all Macdonald/Raynor projects, it included several template holes borrowed from the great links of the Old World, though on this occasion these replicas were confined mostly to the par threes.

## A CHALLENGING START

From a clubhouse situated on high ground, Mid Ocean begins with a difficult 418-yard two-shotter played to a

# SOUTH AMERICA

Golf gained a foothold in South America when the British came to this continent toward the end of the 19th century to assist with infrastructure requirements, especially the construction of railway lines. Mar del Plata Golf Club[1], for example, in Argentina was formed in 1896 by British executives of the Southern Railway.

S ituated nearly 250 miles (400 kilometres) south of Buenos Aires, Mar del Plata Golf Club (GC) captures the best of links golf, with fast-running playing conditions over broken land. Though not long, its small greens are difficult to locate in the ever-present wind. Just as golf luminaries Henry Cotton and Seve Ballesteros have delighted in this course's charms, so too have lesser golfers, who appreciate how well the game has travelled from the United Kingdom to here in the southern hemisphere. This point is reinforced at the 18th, when the golfer drives over a deep sleepered bunker and heads towards the green at the base of the imposing, Tudor-style clubhouse.

## MACKENZIE COURSES

While much of the rest of the world was mired in economic depression in the late 1920s and 1930s, Argentina being rich in natural resources was enjoying a boom, so Dr Alister MacKenzie was delighted to make the journey down from California to build two courses for The Jockey Club (see page 278) outside Buenos Aires. Though his impact was not as great as in Australia (see page 282), he nonetheless crafted what many still consider to be the finest course in South America – the Red Course. Despite The Jockey Club's inland setting, numerous of the most time-heralded design features from the United Kingdom – such as Redan; Punchbowl; and the Eden, Road hole and Valley of Sin (see St Andrews, page 40) – were captured within this design. The Blue Course with its shared 9th and 18th greens is further evidence that the Old Course at St Andrews was not far from MacKenzie's mind as he built these two courses. Assisting MacKenzie at The Jockey Club was Luther Koontz who went on to construct the equally admired Olivos GC[2] 9 miles (15 kilometres) away.

Because the North American economy was still in the doldrums, MacKenzie had no reason to rush home. Therefore, after the completion of The Jockey Club, he accepted an offer to advise at Club de Golf[3] Uruguay. Situated across the broad Rio de la Plata from Buenos Aires, this course at Punta Carretas

offers views of the coastline and across to Uruguay's capital of Montevideo itself. MacKenzie's routing made the most of the gently sloping hillside, and the most notable feature was his original bold interior green contours. Sadly, they have been softened with time, leaving the course with little of MacKenzie's characteristic flair.

## POSTWAR GOLF

For some time after the Second World War, economic instability in South America highlighted by hyper-inflation tended to make golf an afterthought. Several American architects including Robert Trent Jones Snr at El Rincon GC[4] in Bogotá, Colombia and Dick Wilson at Lagunita CC[5] outside Caracas in Venezuela brought long, hard tournament-style designs to this continent in the 1950s and 60s. However, the real bright spot was the play during these times of its greatest champion, Roberto de Vicenzo. Beloved around the world, this consummate Argentinian won scores of worldwide tournaments, for ever highlighted by his Open win at Royal Liverpool (see page 82) in 1967, when he held off a fast-closing Jack Nicklaus. Perhaps no country is more closely tied to the golfing exploits of one man than Argentina enjoys with Vicenzo. His easy manner and effortless grace let everyone know what a fine reception they would receive whenever they ventured there. And venture golfers did, because in 2000 Buenos Aires GC[6] hosted the World Cup, and spectators were treated to a great duel between the Argentines Eduardo Romero and Angel Cabrera against the Americans David Duval and Tiger Woods. The tight contest featured numerous clutch shots by both teams, although the US team pulled out a narrow win over the final few holes. Enthusiasm generated from the event served to increase local interest and growth in the game.

Economic devaluation of the peso in 2002 further helped to make Argentina a sought-after tourist destination for the United States and European market. Thanks to its famous wine and beef, world-class hunting and fishing, tourism continues to increase year after year.

## GOLF IN THE 21ST CENTURY

Argentina still has the preponderance of golf courses in South America with more than 200 courses, which is nearly the number of courses in the other South American countries combined. A basis for the game's growth there has been its numerous driving ranges, something the other countries lacked until recently, and one result is that there are now more than 100,000 golfers registered with handicaps in Argentina.

Boasting a strong economy, Brazil is the next golfing hotspot, which is no surprise given its size and the fact that it boasts the world's longest Atlantic coastline along which are to be found some of the most exciting golf projects. West of Brazil landlocked in the interior of South America is Bolivia, home of La Paz GC[7]. Opened in 1912, it is 13,000 feet (4,000 metres) above sea level, making it the highest grass-covered course in the world.

Positioned along the west side of South America, Chile has seen several beachside resorts and second-home communities with fine courses built in recent years including the world-class La Serena GC[8] in 2001, which is 300 miles (480 kilometres) north of Santiago. Located along the Pacific, in an arid desert terrain, this links weaves through dunes 5–15 feet (1.5–4.5-metres) high. Several other modern Chilean golf courses, combined with high-class residential developments, have been built since 2000 in the country's interior,

with the courses in the foothills of the mighty Andes enjoying the most spectacular scenery.

The concept of secure residential communities coupled with the desire of people to escape big cities in favour of a more suburban lifestyle is fuelling further golf-course construction throughout South America. Also, the new generation of players are taking up where Roberto de Vincenzo, Eduardo Romero and Vicente Fernandez left off and are making their mark on the worldwide tours. Angel Cabrera gained the 2007 US Open title at Oakmont (see page 194), while his young exciting fellow Argentinian Andres Romero won on the European Tour. As their heroics are broadcast back home, golf's popularity continues to climb.

From the gorgeous area of Frutillar well to the south in Chile to along the Venezuelan coastline in the north, the golfing possibilities are endless for a continent of such diverse beauty. It is to be hoped that developers steer clear of the rainforest.

*The Lagunita Country Club outside Caracas was one of Dick Wilson's last designs and was mostly constructed by his assistant Joe Lee.*

Argentina enjoys a rich golf history. Before the turn of the 19th century, the British helped the Argentines to develop the country's infrastructure, especially the railways. With the British came golf and, as far away as 300 miles (483 kilometres) from Buenos Aires, golf courses such Mar del Plata were built pre-1900. To this day golfers at Mar del Plata contend with canted, non-irrigated fairways and deep, sleeper-lined bunkers. The spirit of golf has indeed been alive and well in Argentina for more than a century.

## MACKENZIE IS COMMISSIONED

It was in 1925 that The Jockey Club acquired more than 785 acres (318 hectares) on which to build some golf courses in what was then the outskirts of Buenos Aires (today's sprawling city of 12 million engulfs the perimeter of the property). Then in the late 1920s Dr Alister MacKenzie was commissioned to create two 18-hole courses of equal merit.

MacKenzie at the time was living in California and had already designed three of his masterpieces, namely Cypress Point (see page 248), Crystal Downs and the West Course at Royal Melbourne (see page 286). With North America in the grip of the Great Depression and business slow, MacKenzie delightedly made his way by boat to Buenos Aires. Once there, there was no rush to return and, consequently, both courses at The Jockey Club were the beneficiaries of his full attention.

MacKenzie's primary challenge was that the property with which he had to work at San Isidro was flat. Giving character to feature-rich sites such as Lahinch and Pasatiempo never proved difficult to Mackenzie. However, what would he do in this case where no natural features existed to lend the holes good golfing qualities?

## ECHOES OF SCOTLAND

Along with the legendary golfer Bobby Jones, MacKenzie may be considered the greatest admirer of the Old Course at St Andrews (see page 40). Early on,

MacKenzie made a connection between the wide expanse of short grass at St Andrews and the potential for a wide expanse of short grass at San Isidro. In regards to the construction of the Cancha Colorada (Red Course) and the Cancha Azul (Blue Course), Mackenzie in his book *The Spirit of St Andrews* wrote: 'We made the ground extremely undulating by constructing a series of irregular swales radiating to the lowest point, and these swales gave us the following advantages: they cheapened and facilitated the drainage. They gave us plenty of soil for making greens and creating undulating ground, and above all they gave the place a natural appearance that the undulations appear to have been created by the effects of wind and water thousands of years ago. The course has a greater resemblance – not only in appearance but in the character of its golf – to the Old Course at St Andrews than any inland course I know.'

From a golfing perspective, the random humps and bumps mean that one day the ball may be slightly above the feet; the next day, slightly below. Thus, the golfer must make minor tweaks to the stance and set-up from round to round. In doing so, both courses at The Jockey Club remain fresh for generations of rich Argentines.

Assisting MacKenzie during construction was Luther H. Koontz, an engineer specializing in drainage and irrigation. Koontz stayed behind in South America and went on to build the nearby Olivos Golf Club, another Argentine course famous for hosting big events. Part of the highlight of the work of MacKenzie and Koontz is the astonishingly

## THE JOCKEY CLUB (RED COURSE) – San Isidro, Argentina

Dr Alister Mackenzie, 1931
Major events: Argentine Open 1931, 1935, 1946, 1953, 1954, 1954, 1976, 1978, 1980, 1981, 1993, 1995, 1997, 1998, 2000, 2001, 2005

### CARD OF THE COURSE

| HOLE | YARDS | PAR | HOLE | YARDS | PAR |
|------|-------|-----|------|-------|-----|
| 1. | 425 | 4 | 10. | 470 | 4 |
| 2. | 350 | 4 | 11. | 506 | 5 |
| 3. | 148 | 3 | 12. | 175 | 3 |
| 4. | 490 | 5 | 13. | 444 | 4 |
| 5. | 340 | 4 | 14. | 390 | 4 |
| 6. | 355 | 4 | 15. | 511 | 5 |
| 7. | 425 | 4 | 16. | 401 | 4 |
| 8. | 208 | 3 | 17. | 170 | 3 |
| 9. | 415 | 4 | 18. | 354 | 4 |
| **OUT** | **3,156** | **35** | **IN** | **3,421** | **36** |
| | | | **TOTAL** | **6,577** | **71** |

# THE JOCKEY CLUB
## San Isidro, Argentina

The Jockey Club itself was founded in 1882. At the time, golf was not included in the club's prospectus but horses were, and the club set the tone for equestrian activities across Argentina and beyond. Some 40 years later, this social centre for high society in Argentina decided to add golf to its offering.

diverse green complexes, which range from ones featuring pronounced mounds (such as the 13th and 16th) to ones that seamlessly rise up from the fairway with fall-offs behind (6th and 14th), to others that hug the ground and appear as mere extensions of the fairway (8th and 9th). This variety allows the golfer to play all sorts of approach shots – a most desirable attribute.

## A CHANGE IN CHARACTER

While still expansive, the links-like feel that the Red Course once enjoyed has been altered, because many hardwood trees and softwood pines have been planted since MacKenzie's day. Fortunately, they are generally out of play and provide a handsome backdrop for the game. Nonetheless, they do define the broad playing corridors, something not found on the Old Course.

*As seen from behind, MacKenzie ringed the 16th green with three huge mounds, which serve to kick balls of slightly offline approach shots in all sorts of interesting directions.*

## THE CHALLENGE STIFFENS

A round on the Red Course is one of pure delight. To lose a ball is practically unheard of with plenty of room greeting the golfer off most tees. Rest assured though that the challenge toughens as a golfer approaches the greens, many of which are pushed up with the surrounding short grass feeding slightly missed approach shots well away from the putting surfaces.

These playing characteristics are seen in the first three holes. The rippling landscape that MacKenzie and Koontz created is particularly noteworthy at the 425-yard 1st, which requires two good shots. The 2nd calls for a precise pitch to a green that is built upwards of 3 feet (1 metre) or so from its surrounds, sloping away on all sides. A long but narrow green greets the golfer standing on the tee of the one-shot 3rd. Like all the par threes here, it is an exacting target causing a golfer to marvel how MacKenzie made it so, while seemingly moving very little dirt. So the front nine continues, alternating between demands for finesse and distance.

## THE BACK NINE

Outstanding holes on the back nine continue to highlight the influence that the Old Course in particular and links golf in general had on MacKenzie when he designed the Red Course. Famous the world over, the green complex at the 10th is the mirror image of the one on the Road hole at St Andrews. Fronting left and right bunkers separated by the green's false front at the 12th have similarities with St Andrews's Eden hole. At the 444-yard 13th, hitting a running approach into MacKenzie's bold two-tiered green and wondering if it will climb onto the back tier perfectly replicates the feeling of suspense that MacKenzie often praised in links golf.

Additional playing features are borrowed from the United Kingdom on the final three holes. Set in a field, three enormous mounds emerge to ring the long 16th green, provoking the sensation of playing into a punchbowl. With the 7-foot (2.1-metre) tall mounds tightly mown, all sorts of interesting recovery shots are possible, limited only by the imagination. Elusive to find in regulation, the green at the one-shot 17th enjoys Redan playing characteristics.

Straight from St Andrews, the 18th hole is bunker-less, with its own version of the Valley of Sin. This hole perfectly captures the essence of the Red Course: not overly long and within reach of everyone yet it requires care and thought to play it well.

Walking off the green, the golfer enjoys seeing the double green from the 9th and 18th holes on the 6,350-yard Blue Course to the right and the stately Tudor-style clubhouse straight ahead. They serve to reinforce the point that The Jockey Club is one of the world's great sporting clubs.

# AUSTRALIA AND NEW ZEALAND

# AUSTRALIA AND NEW ZEALAND

Golf in Australia and New Zealand is a popular game, cheap and accessible. While there might be disagreement from golfers braving a cold winter's day in Dunedin or Hobart, both countries enjoy ideal climates for year-round play.

Because the Australian countryside is a harsh environment for golf, there are few notable inland courses away from the main cities along the coastline. Scarcity of water is an increasingly important issue. Evidence suggests rainfall patterns are altering, and, for the world's driest continent, that is a significant problem for golf clubs to address in the future. Clubs in the outback survive, often with fewer than a hundred members, because everybody pitches in to maintain the playing surfaces. Sand greens are commonly employed in places where growing and managing fine turf grass are impractical, and they are testament to the passion of intrepid golfers.

## MACKENZIE'S INFLUENCE

Arguably the most significant period in Australian golf history came at the end of 1926, when Royal Melbourne Golf Club (see page 286) commissioned Dr Alister MacKenzie to redesign its course. To offset his charges, the club arranged for MacKenzie to consult at neighbouring and interstate clubs. MacKenzie worked with Alex Russell, a good player, and they engaged the skills of Royal Melbourne greenkeeper Mick Morcom, who proved adept at making man-made features appear indistinguishable from natural ones. MacKenzie's greatest legacy was to convince many that the game should be organized strategically, to give the greatest pleasure to the greatest number. For its time, this was a revolutionary concept. Russell and Morcom embraced MacKenzie's principles, and the trio together built some of the most dramatic and beautiful bunkers in all golf.

Many of the finest Australian courses are concentrated on the Melbourne sandbelt, in the southern suburbs of the city. Royal Melbourne, Kingston Heath (see page 292), Victoria[1], Metropolitan[2], Woodlands[3], Yarra Yarra[4], Commonwealth[5], Huntingdale[6], Spring Valley[7] and both courses at Peninsula GC[8] are in this sandbelt, which boasts one of the finest collections of golf courses in the world. Many of the new breed of Australian professionals including Geoff Ogilvy, Robert Allenby, Stuart Appleby, Aaron Baddeley, Steve Allan and Richard Green grew up as members of the sandbelt clubs. These are wonderful courses on which to learn golf. They are difficult, and the combination

• Darwin

NORTHERN TERRITORY

QUEENSLAND

AUSTRALIA

WESTERN AUSTRALIA

SOUTH AUSTRALIA

NEW SOUTH WALES   22

25
Brisbane •  24

20
• Sydney
19
21
23

14
15
Royal Adelaide  16
page 290  • Adelaide

1
2
3
4   9
5   10
6   11
7   12
8  13

Perth •  17
18

Royal Melbourne  • Melbourne
page 286

Kingston Heath
page 292

Barnbougle Dunes
page 294

TASMANIA

26  • Hobart
27

of wind and firm ground demands players do more than simply smash the ball off the tee and fly high irons to soft targets. Sandbelt bunker shots are some of the most demanding in the world.

A second concentration of terrific courses in Victoria is found just over an hour's drive south from Melbourne on the Mornington Peninsula. The National Club[9] has three courses: The Old (designed by Robert Trent Jones Jnr in 1988) and the more recent Moonah (Greg Norman and Bob Harrison) and Ocean (Peter Thomson and Mike Wolveridge)

### NEW ZEALAND

NORTH ISLAND

● Auckland
↳28
↳29

Cape Kidnappers ↳
*page 298*

Paraparaumu ↳
*page 296*
● Wellington

*SOUTH ISLAND*

*A timeless classic, the 14th hole at New South Wales is only 353 yards long. Modern equipment has not lessened the challenge of finding the correct part of the distant fairway from which to approach the tiny, exposed green.*

courses. Close by is Moonah Links[10], a public Peter Thomson-designed course created specifically for the Australian Open. It is not universally loved but is difficult and the best work of the five-time Open champion. Just around the corner from it is St Andrews Beach[11], a fine Tom Doak test when the wind blows with any strength. The two best traditional clubs on the peninsula are Portsea[12] and Sorrento[13].

On the sand close to the Adelaide beaches in South Australia are five good courses: Royal Adelaide (see page 290), Kooyonga[14], Glenelg[15] and the 36 holes at The Grange[16]. Meanwhile Lake Karrinyup[17], an Alex Russell course, is the premier club in Perth, Western Australia. Kennedy Bay[18], a public course opened in 1997, is an excellent design and one of the best courses built in Australia since the 1930s.

Sydney, the biggest city in Australia, boasts relatively few courses to match the quality of those in Melbourne or Adelaide. Sadly, the influence of Alister MacKenzie is long gone from The Australian[19], given a complete makeover by Jack Nicklaus when Kerry Packer was turning the world of professional cricket on its head. Royal Sydney[20] has been significantly altered in the intervening 80 years since MacKenzie's consulting visit, and a freeway was cut through The Lakes[21] in the late 1960s. The second best course in New South Wales is in Newcastle, a steel town 100 miles (160 kilometres) north of Sydney. Its rolling, tree-lined, sand-based hills make Newcastle[22] and Woodlands in Melbourne the two most underrated courses in the country. So, which is the best course in New South Wales? It is, appropriately, that of the New South Wales Golf Club[23], dramatic and great fun.

### NEW SOUTH WALES

If exhilaration is what is wanted then there is no better course in Australia to satisfy a yearning for golfing thrills than at the New South Wales GC perched high up on the cliffs above Sydney's Botany Bay. It is one of the severest tests of golf in a high wind.

Credit for the course at New South Wales goes as much to Australian Eric Apperley as to the more widely acknowledged Alister MacKenzie. Apperley made alterations to MacKenzie's routing and added the famed, across-the-water 6th.

In an age before large-scale moving of land with big machines, designers when saddled with difficult pieces of ground expected golfers to hit over a big dune in order to open up a fine second shot. The 3rd at New South Wales is such a hole. It is a sharp dogleg to the left with a high dune standing just to the left of the tee. For first-timers the line appears to be down the fairway, but for the better player it is far to the left, straight over the dune covered with low-growing vegetation. The shot is completely blind and the player is never quite sure where the ball is until they get to the top of the hill.

The 512-yard 5th is the most spectacular hole in Australia, and the extraordinary view from the top of

the hill out across Botany Bay is really special. There are seminal moments in all golfers' lives, and one of these is the first time they reach the top of the hill here. This is also one of the genuinely unusual holes in golf. Short hitters who cannot drive far enough to reach the plateau more than 220 yards (201 metres) from the tee are confronted with a blind second straight up and over the steep hill, and it is no easy task to guess the right line for the second shot. Played downwind, drives that reach the far edge of the plateau topple over and roll an additional 100 yards (90 metres) down the hill, leaving only a pitching club to the green.

Following that, the 194-yard 6th is a stunningly beautiful hole. The tee is out on a rocky promontory and a mid-iron shot is fired across the ocean to a small green favouring a shot moving from right to left. It is a hole that a golfer could never tire of playing.

Yet another blind shot occurs on the 8th, a 552-yarder with a long, blind second over a steep dune. Again, in an age of big machines some might have been tempted to obliterate the sand hill to open the view, but the golfer here, in contrast to the confusing 3rd, instinctively knows to play right through the middle of the saddle and there are no surprises or blind hazards over the hill.

The finest run of holes comes in a four-hole stretch of brilliant two-shotters from the 13th, a dogleg left with an approach played down then up to the elevated skyline green, dramatically suggesting that going over the green is an over-clubbing crime of the severest proportions. Following that, the 14th is a brilliant 353-yarder with a huge tumbling fairway shared with the next hole. There is a diagonal ridge to carry with the tee shot and the farther left the drive flies the longer the carry. However, there is the additional reward of a shorter approach and a better angle into the small green perched up on the 14th's highest and most dangerous point.

The tee shot, up to and over the saddle at the 407-yard 15th, particularly when it is into the wind, must be one of the half-dozen most difficult tee shots in world golf. There is simply no place to escape from trouble – even fearsome tee shots such as the final hole at TPC Sawgrass (see page 210) or the Road hole at St Andrews (see page 40) give players a place to miss. The first half of the 15th at New South Wales plays uphill, the fairway being uncommonly narrow, and both sides of the driving area are lined with unplayable lies in the indigenous scrub.

Much like the 15th, the 441-yard 16th has unplayable lies. The closer the golfer drives to the toe of the dune the shorter and significantly easier becomes the approach. Playing through this great four-hole stretch in even fours is no mean feat and thoughtful and brave shots will suffice.

In the early 1980s the course was in terrible condition and its unfashionable location far from the centre of the city saw the club advertising for members in the local newspapers. That it recovered its reputation was a matter of importance to golf in Australia because it is such a significant course. As conditions improved, New South Wales became the most sought-after membership in Sydney. It is the closest Australia has to the brand of golf made famous by the cliffside links at Pebble Beach (see page 244) and for those who love raw golf, where the chances of fighting a battering wind are high, it is the greatest thrill in Australia.

## QUEENSLAND

Queensland, a huge state, is a place with similar physical and climatic characteristics to Florida and, not surprisingly, the golf is similar – except there is nothing close to matching the wonders of Seminole (see page 212). The best of the newer resort courses was created by Peter Thomson at Hope Island GC[24]. Developers with more interest in property sales and profit than golf have commissioned big-name overseas architects, and the resulting courses have conspicuously failed to match the quality of courses Alister MacKenzie and Alex Russell left generations earlier. Royal Queensland[25] was the one Brisbane club to avail itself of MacKenzie's services, but it was altered beyond recognition in the intervening years and has now been entirely relocated. Unlike the resort-style courses that dominate golf in Queensland, the new Royal Queensland has an understated, old-fashioned type of layout celebrating wide fairways that give golfers the freedom to decide for themselves where best to hit.

Tasmania, the island state south of the mainland, has two main private clubs – Tasmania GC[26] and Royal Hobart[27] – but in 2001 they were far surpassed by Barnbougle Dunes GC (see page 294), a public course on the north coast. Not only did Barnbougle Dunes elevate beyond recognition the reputation of Tasmanian golf but it was also recognized as one of the best five courses in Australia.

## UNSURPASSED GOLFING POTENTIAL

New Zealand is one of the world's most beautiful countries, and only the commercial reality of a small population precludes it from boasting as many fine courses as the United States or Britain. There is brilliant land for inland and coastal golf but, in the modern era, only the American Julian Robertson

has been prepared to invest in great golf architecture. Before Tom Doak's Cape Kidnappers GC (see page 298), the one first-class course in New Zealand was Alex Russell's links at Paraparaumu Beach (see page 296).

There is much usable land for golf in New Zealand, but with fewer than four million inhabitants there are many small clubs where golfers play a fairly rudimentary form of the game if the measure is the architectural quality of the courses. While on a visit to Auckland in 1926, Alister MacKenzie designed the route for Titirangi[28], a typically interesting course, highlighted by a notable set of short holes; it is the best course in the country's biggest city.

MacKenzie later said that: 'Golf in New Zealand, unlike Australia, is dead. In fact it has never been alive. Green committees there do not seem to realize that the game is played for pleasure; they use long grass as a penal hazard, and the consequence is that golfers will not put up with the annoyance of losing balls.' Traditional New Zealand courses are narrow and tree lined, and in many instances MacKenzie's criticism is as relevant today as it was in 1930. Newer courses have been built on good sites but they have been muddled by forces more intent on selling houses than providing stimulating, strategically interesting golf.

Kauri Cliffs[29] and, to an even more significant extent, Cape Kidnappers have demonstrated that world-class golf is possible. However, green fees at both courses are the equivalent of four, eight or even 12 months' subscription at regular clubs and they are far from New Zealand's biggest cities.

## MACKENZIE'S LEGACY

The future of golf architecture in Australia and New Zealand is dependent on golfers demanding not just better-conditioned courses but better-designed ones. In the meantime golfers in these countries continue to marvel at Alister MacKenzie's genius, and they owe him and Alex Russell a great debt.

*Designed by Florida-based golf-course architect, David Harman, Kauri Cliffs is an impressive layout in a contemporary style, as evidenced by the dramatic bunkering on the 472-yard 17th hole.*

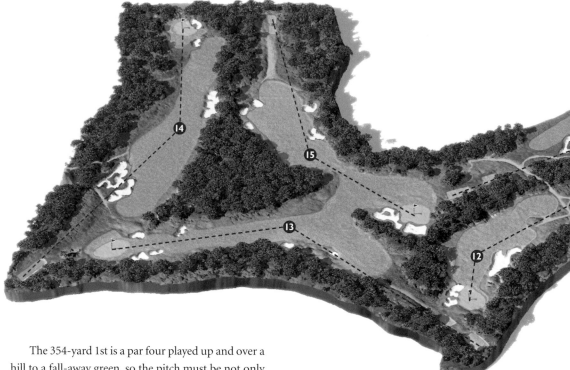

The first course at Royal Melbourne was surrounded by houses and played over ground ill-suited to golf. A band of members therefore secured a perfect stretch of sand-based terrain covered in the beautiful natural heath that abounded in the bayside suburb of Black Rock, much farther from the city centre. They had identified a tract of land not dissimilar to that of the outer London heathlands, and with links-like playing characteristics featuring seaside winds and firm ground.

A little less than a century later the club's two courses are once again surrounded by houses, local schools, sports ovals and two other golf clubs, Victoria GC and Sandringham GC. What was then a long trip by train to the course is now a short drive for most members. Well-known Melbourne author and sociologist, John Carroll, has called Royal Melbourne 'one of only two man-made things in Australia of any worldwide architectural significance'. The other is, of course, the Sydney Opera House.

### TWO COURSES IN ONE

At Royal Melbourne there are two regular courses (MacKenzie's West and the less-fashionable East) and a composite one (the President's Cup Course). The East Course was created by Alex Russell and is good enough in its own right to rank among the top six or seven courses in the country. The President's Cup Course comprises a dozen holes from the West Course and six from the East. This combination, with all the holes inside the boundaries of the club's main 'paddock', was conceived in 1959 for the World Cup. Such an arrangement meant that no roads need be crossed by spectators or players. The order of holes was altered for the 1998 President's Cup, and the course now finishes with a string of long par fours. However, the change has never been favoured by the players or the members, and perhaps the next big championship at the club will revert to the original 1959 routing. This description, however, refers to the holes as they are numbered on the current President's Cup Course.

The 354-yard 1st is a par four played up and over a hill to a fall-away green, so the pitch must be not only perfectly struck but also played from the correct angle to have a reasonable putt for a birdie. A diagonal swale cutting across the front of the green makes a simple hole difficult, because any pitch to a pin in the front half of the green must confront the reality that the brave shot must just carry the front edge and anything short is swept away from the green. On the 1959 Composite Course the opening hole on the West had served as the 1st, but it became the President's Cup's 17th; while it is a brilliant starter in the spirit of the 1st at the Old Course at St Andrews (see page 40), it has proved to be an anticlimatic 17th. The fairway is wide, not easily missed, and the large green is essentially undefended by the course's famed and fearsome bunkers. This is not a hole liable to extract a big mistake early in the day, as MacKenzie understood that there would be plenty of opportunity to do that later in the journey.

On the 499-yard 2nd, the blind drive flies over deep bunkers embedded into the facing dune and, while rated a par five, it is easily reached in two by the championship player unless the wind is against. Played across a valley to a green set in the opposite hill, the 176-yard 3rd is a marvellous, short hole. The front is protected by a steep, closely mown bank that feeds the under-hit shot well away from the green and leaves one of the most difficult, short shots coming back up the hill. What is so wonderful about the construction of this man-made hole is that it appears as if a few sand hazards were scraped out and a little seed thrown down on what became the green.

A great dogleg follows, the 451-yard 4th turning at right angles around the bunkers and heath that

# ROYAL MELBOURNE
## Black Rock, Victoria, Australia

Royal Melbourne is the crowning achievement of Dr Alister MacKenzie's 12-week visit to Australia in 1926, but the course he laid out is more than 12 miles (19 kilometres) from the original home of the club in inner-suburban Caulfield.

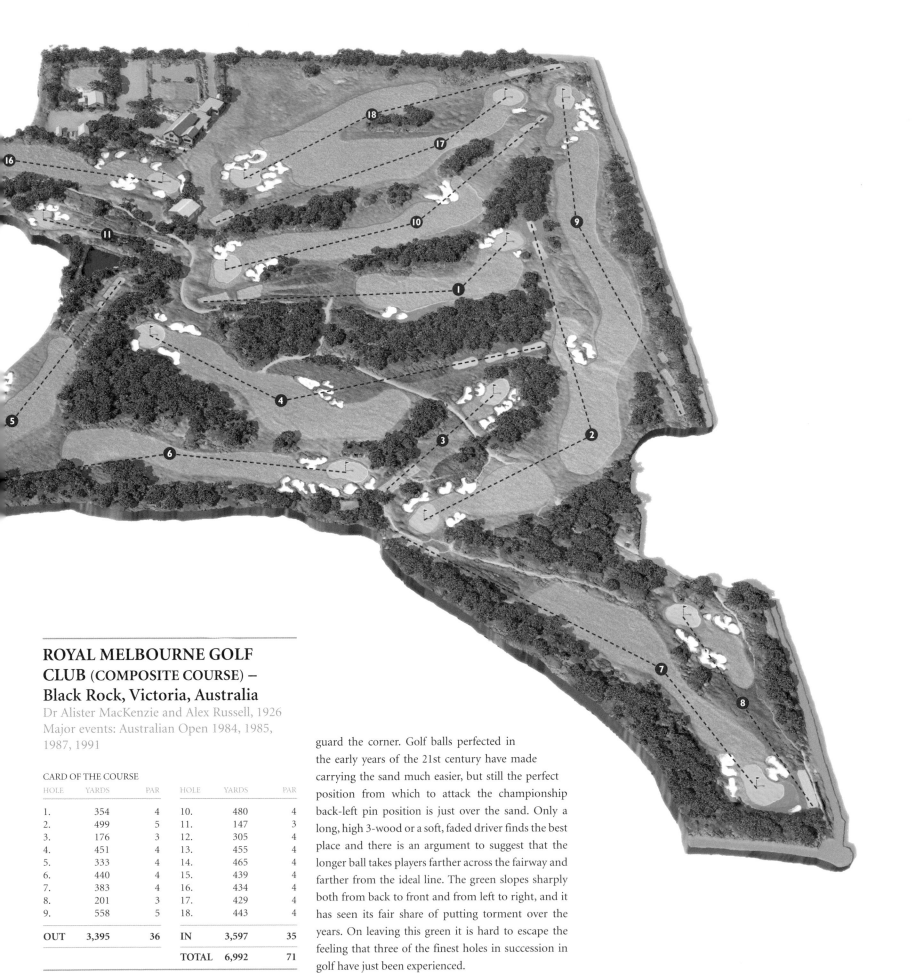

# ROYAL MELBOURNE GOLF CLUB (COMPOSITE COURSE) – Black Rock, Victoria, Australia

Dr Alister MacKenzie and Alex Russell, 1926
Major events: Australian Open 1984, 1985, 1987, 1991

CARD OF THE COURSE

| HOLE | YARDS | PAR | HOLE | YARDS | PAR |
|------|-------|-----|------|-------|-----|
| 1. | 354 | 4 | 10. | 480 | 4 |
| 2. | 499 | 5 | 11. | 147 | 3 |
| 3. | 176 | 3 | 12. | 305 | 4 |
| 4. | 451 | 4 | 13. | 455 | 4 |
| 5. | 333 | 4 | 14. | 465 | 4 |
| 6. | 440 | 4 | 15. | 439 | 4 |
| 7. | 383 | 4 | 16. | 434 | 4 |
| 8. | 201 | 3 | 17. | 429 | 4 |
| 9. | 558 | 5 | 18. | 443 | 4 |
| OUT | 3,395 | 36 | IN | 3,597 | 35 |
| | | | TOTAL | 6,992 | 71 |

guard the corner. Golf balls perfected in the early years of the 21st century have made carrying the sand much easier, but still the perfect position from which to attack the championship back-left pin position is just over the sand. Only a long, high 3-wood or a soft, faded driver finds the best place and there is an argument to suggest that the longer ball takes players farther across the fairway and farther from the ideal line. The green slopes sharply both from back to front and from left to right, and it has seen its fair share of putting torment over the years. On leaving this green it is hard to escape the feeling that three of the finest holes in succession in golf have just been experienced.

Players then walk up the hill to the 333-yard 5th, which is the 1st on the East Course. On this par four, the driving line to a fairway that is perhaps 80 yards (73 metres) wide is determined by the position of the pin. When the pin is cut high up in the front-right corner, just over the deep bunker, the line is far to the left of the fairway, but when it is in the back-left corner the ideal drive is played to the right third of the fairway.

That 5th is an Alex Russell hole, as are the next four: a difficult two-shotter with a downhill tee shot and a second played up to a green well above the golfer; a short, downhill par four; a difficult, long, uphill par three; and the 558-yard 9th that used to be a three-shotter for all with cross-bunkers well in play about 60 yards (55 metres) short of the green.

## MORE MACKENZIE HOLES

Members play the 480-yard 10th as a par five, although it is now considered a par four for big events. It is followed by a difficult, short, uphill par three – a relatively simple play to the unguarded, left-front quarter of the green. However, that leaves a long, sloping putt across the hill to the flag, which usually sits behind the deep, guarding, front-left bunker. With a 4-iron there is no shame in playing away from a guarding pin, but who cannot be tempted with only an 8- or 9-iron in hand?

Another world-class hole is the 305-yard 12th, very likely the finest par four of that length in golf. Drivable from the tee, it is probably even more dangerous now that more players can drive the green with their ever more powerful clubs. The penalties for missing in any place except in front and short are severe, and a good pitcher can play a long-iron from the tee and expect to be close enough from 80 yards (73 metres) or so to have a reasonable putt for a three. A huge bunker guards the inside of the dogleg and missing a drive in the sand leaves one of the most difficult 50-yard (45-metre) bunker shots in golf. It is, however, a punishment worthy of the crime, and most still shy away to the right with the tee shot.

## THE FAR TURN

From here the course gets to its difficult run home as it turns around the holes at the far corner of the course. The 455-yard 13th plays down from the tee then turns left up the hill to the green. A tee shot turned from right to left earns the perfect line into the flag. Most, however, fly right away from the left corner of the hole and find a much longer shot from a poor angle. The fairway is wide, befitting MacKenzie's principle of making the course playable for all, but it takes a fine, brave drive to find the ideal spot.

Like the 10th, the 14th is a members' par five, but at 465 yards it is hardly that for a good player, yet it is another fine hole. Once again a right-to-left tee shot is ideal to pick up the extra run on the ground that slopes in that direction. If a golfer plays for the green in two, the second shot must carry the bracken and heath that run across the left half of the fairway. Those playing it as a three-shotter aim along the fairway to the right of the bracken and then pitch to the green. In the summer, when the ball is running and the tempera-

# THE 12TH HOLE ON THE COMPOSITE COURSE
## An extraordinary shot

*The 12th hole on the Composite Course is a short par four that turns left around a massive fairway bunker and in 1978 at the Australian PGA Championship all the sensible players, lead by Graham Marsh and Hale Irwin, played safely, as they always did, to the corner at the top of the hill and pitched the remaining 80 yards (73 metres) or so from there. Not Severiano Ballesteros. A man who promised those who watched that he would leave them with at least one shot so extraordinary that it would live forever in their minds. Every day he took his longest club and flew the most perfect of drives straight at the distant green. Every day he carried the bunker but he never could manage to reach the green. Instead he found the sandy, scrubby wasteland a few yards from the edge of the green and from there he blew perfectly blasted shots with his sand wedge onto the green. His reward for the week was three birdies and a par.*

*Here was a great MacKenzie hole challenging the most exciting player in the world and no one would have appreciated the Spaniard's audacity more than the master architect. MacKenzie would have adored Ballesteros's approach to the game and it is hardly surprising his greatest days came at St Andrews and Augusta and two years after his first visit to Royal Melbourne he won there as well.*

*The flag of the 10th hole sits temptingly at the top of the far dune. For the modern professional it is within reach, but the cost of failure is obvious.*

tures are high, the hole is little more than a drive and a mid- or short-iron, but in the winter, when the fairway run is at a minimum, if the wind is against the hole can still play as a couple of long woods for even the strongest players. One of the problems with tournament golf at established clubs is that big tournaments usually happen in the middle of summer when the courses are at their shortest. One wonders if critics would think Royal Melbourne so short if they confronted it in the middle of winter.

## CLOSING HOLES

The 439-yard 15th is a model dogleg to the left, with a perfectly placed bunker in the top-left corner of the hole guarding the ideal driving line. There are 50 yards (45 metres) of fairway to the right to play into, but every yard away from the bunker makes the second shot correspondingly more difficult. The green is flanked by a huge MacKenzie bunker on the right and it is all but impossible to get close from the right quarter of the fairway.

At the 434-yard 16th the tee shot is played over a nest of bunkers in the facing hill and the fairway falls from right to left, but a draw from the tee runs the risk of sliding all the way across the fairway into the tea tree. A copse of tea trees also guards the corner of the dogleg 18th, turning left around it, and, as always at Royal Melbourne, those driving close to the hazard are rewarded with both a shorter shot and a better angle into the flag. Naturally, many fly right away from the unplayable lies on the left and make the hole more difficult than it need be. Once again, it was a more fearsome test with a persimmon driver and balata ball, which not only flew shorter than the modern ball but was also significantly more difficult to control in the wind.

## A WORTHY MEMORIAL

Many of the game's greats have triumphed at Royal Melbourne, but one of the finest pars made here was by the wonderful, little Australian professional, Billy Dunk. In the 1975 Chrysler Classic his long-iron second found the island of heath inside the front-right bunker, but from the desperate spot he pitched close enough to save par, and David Graham, coming behind, could not match Dunk's target. The island has been known thereafter as 'Dunk's Island', a fitting memory of what was a fabulous shot.

Great is a much-overused word, and it surely should be introduced sparingly to describe only things that are genuinely so. It can be said with confidence, however, that Royal Melbourne is one of the world's truly great golf courses.

# ROYAL ADELAIDE
## Seaton, South Australia

For a course so highly rated, the first impression of Royal Adelaide is often one of bemusement. How could such a seemingly flat piece of ground with a railway line running right past the clubhouse and through the middle of the course accommodate a course of such high reputation?

D r Alister MacKenzie had an influence here, and some of his suggestions were adopted but many were ignored. MacKenzie, for example, had planned a hole from the current 10th tee to the 11th green, and he wished to reorganize the finish by adding a hole after the current 15th and reversing the direction of the short 16th. His most notable contribution, however, was the extraordinary 3rd, a short par four that matches the brilliance of his short 15th at Kingston Heath (see page 292).

Local legend Cargie Rymill laid out the original course at Royal Adelaide 20 years before MacKenzie's 1926 visit, and the combination of the work of these brilliant men left golf holes of the highest class.

### PLAYING THE FRONT NINE

The initial impression of a dull piece of land is soon dispelled when the golfer gets to the fine 2nd after playing the somewhat pedestrian 381-yard 1st, which swings around the mounds on the corner of the dogleg left. This 547-yard 2nd is bunkered strategically to punish those taking an unwise gamble with a long second shot, and those who lay up must pitch to a large but well-guarded green. To reach the tee, set left of the original on the other side of the railway line, requires a shot ever so slightly across the line of the fairway.

One of the great, short par fours is the aforementioned 3rd. At 291 yards the green is reachable with a perfect tee shot, but the whole of the right side of the fairway is protected by a fearsome sand dune. The sensible shot is to punch a long-iron through the saddle at the top of the hill and then pitch to the long, narrow green with a ridge running all the way along its left side. Nick Price won a South Australian Open at Adelaide in the late 1980s when he holed a wedge for a two on the final afternoon, but 40 years earlier in an Australian Open Norman von Nida made a ten here, taking a risk in a vain attempt to catch Ossie

# ROYAL ADELAIDE GOLF CLUB –
## Seaton, South Australia

Cargie Rymill, 1906 and Dr Alister MacKenzie, 1926

Major events: Australian Open 1910, 1923, 1926, 1929, 1932, 1938, 1962, 1998

CARD OF THE COURSE

| HOLE | YARDS | PAR | HOLE | YARDS | PAR |
|------|-------|-----|------|-------|-----|
| 1. | 381 | 4 | 10. | 377 | 4 |
| 2. | 547 | 5 | 11. | 386 | 4 |
| 3. | 291 | 4 | 12. | 224 | 3 |
| 4. | 449 | 4 | 13. | 432 | 4 |
| 5. | 459 | 4 | 14. | 487 | 4 |
| 6. | 459 | 4 | 15. | 498 | 5 |
| 7. | 191 | 3 | 16. | 181 | 3 |
| 8. | 392 | 4 | 17. | 517 | 5 |
| 9. | 542 | 5 | 18. | 419 | 4 |
| **OUT** | **3,711** | **37** | **IN** | **3,521** | **36** |
| | | | **TOTAL** | **7,232** | **73** |

*The pitch from the top of the hill at Royal Adelaide's 3rd hole. Some drive at the long, narrow green but that is a reckless or desperate option on a brilliant and dangerous short four.*

Pickworth. 'That week was unquestionably the best golf Ossie ever played', von Nida remarked many years later.

Played blind, the drive at the 449-yard 4th completes a run of spectacular shots early in the round, and is fired out over a wild, sandy waste sure to intimidate the high markers, but it makes for a wonderful-looking shot. Over the hill the hole doglegs to the left, and the tumbling fairway ensures there is the possibility of an odd stance to add to the puzzle of the approach.

## MORE MARVELLOUS HOLES

Three other fine holes on the front nine are the 459-yard 6th – a two-shot hole playing up to a green at the top of the dune around which the best holes on the front nine play – the short 7th and the par-five 9th. The 191-yard 7th, with its tee just to the left of the previous green, plays slightly uphill and into the sea breeze; even strong players will be hitting fours and fives. A string of bunkers surrounds the front of the green, which itself has more than a hint of slope from back to front. Winding its way to the far boundary is the 542-yard 9th, where the long, uphill second must avoid sand that flanks both sides of the fairway. The threat for the errant shot is the prospect of a horribly difficult, 60-yard (55-metre) bunker shot.

One of the least satisfactory holes at Royal Adelaide is the 377-yard 10th, and the suspicion has to be that Dr Alister MacKenzie could have done something spectacular here if he had been able to make the hole from the 10th tee into the green site of the Crater hole 11th. On this 386-yard par four, long shots are confined from the tee because of the sandy wasteland

that crosses the fairway at the 250-yard (230-metre) mark. From the top of the hill the second shot is fired down to the green in the crater at the base of a huge dune that for many years was covered in pine trees. Happily they have been removed to restore the look of the original hole, and the surface of the green is immeasurably better. It is followed by the challenging, 224-yard, downhill 12th.

The best hole on the back nine, on the other hand, is the 487-yard 14th, turning to the right around a number of fairway bunkers guarding the inside corner of the dogleg. It has undulation, strategy and a wonderful green site, and it demands two of the golfer's absolute best shots. Irishman Eamonn Darcy won a big event here in 1981 in a play-off with Sam Torrance. Darcy had made a horrible mess of the 18th, carding a six from the middle of the fairway, but at the first hole of the play-off he ripped an 8-iron second into this 14th green and tapped in from 4 feet (1.2 metres) for a winning three.

## BEST SHORT HOLES IN AUSTRALIA?

With a tiny, exposed, upturned green that accepts only the finest of iron shots, the final hole of real class is the 181-yard 16th. It takes one good swing to find the target, yet its look intimidates many into making a poor one. Because of the hole, as well as the 7th and 12th, Royal Adelaide has a strong claim to possessing the most difficult group of short holes in Australia. Certainly they are the most awkward collection of holes to hit the greens in regulation. All in all, Royal Adelaide is a course of unmistakable quality, and it has hosted some of the country's biggest tournaments for many years.

# KINGSTON HEATH
## Cheltenham, Victoria, Australia

The two Australian courses over which Dr Alister MacKenzie had the most influence were Kingston Heath and Royal Melbourne (see page 286). While the latter is on a grand scale befitting the available land, Kingston Heath is an intricate golf course on an unimpressive piece of sandy land and much of the brilliance of the golf course is due to the original 1923 routing of a Sydney professional, Dan Soutar.

### KINGSTON HEATH GOLF CLUB
**Cheltenham, Victoria, Australia**
Dan Soutar, 1923 and Dr Alister MacKenzie, 1926
Major events: Australian Open 1948, 1957, 1970, 1983, 1989, 1995, 2000

CARD OF THE COURSE

| HOLE | YARDS | PAR | HOLE | YARDS | PAR |
|------|-------|-----|------|-------|-----|
| 1. | 456 | 4 | 10. | 140 | 3 |
| 2. | 385 | 4 | 11. | 416 | 4 |
| 3. | 294 | 4 | 12. | 556 | 5 |
| 4. | 391 | 4 | 13. | 353 | 4 |
| 5. | 189 | 3 | 14. | 566 | 5 |
| 6. | 430 | 4 | 15. | 154 | 3 |
| 7. | 505 | 5 | 16. | 428 | 4 |
| 8. | 435 | 4 | 17. | 461 | 4 |
| 9. | 362 | 4 | 18. | 428 | 4 |
| **OUT** | **3,447** | **36** | **IN** | **3,502** | **36** |
| | | | **TOTAL** | **6,949** | **72** |

All the best Melbourne-based clubs such as Kingston Heath reinvented themselves within a couple of decades of their formation by heading away from the poor ground their founders had originally chosen and settling to the south of the city on sandy land that was perfect for golf. The Kingston Heath members found their plot only a few kilometres from their first course in Elsternwick and Dan Soutar was employed to lay out the new course.

## MACKENZIE'S IMPROVEMENTS

While it is Dan Soutar's routing that largely remains, it was the bunkering scheme of MacKenzie that transformed 'The Heath' into something special. The biggest change MacKenzie made to Soutar's routing was to build an entirely new 15th hole, replacing Soutar's short, blind par four. He constructed a hole of 154 yards to a green on top of the highest dune on the course and the result was a stupendous hole that many think is the best one-shotter in Australia.

The original course measured just over 6,800 yards (6,220 metres), an astounding length for a golf course in that age, and little has been added subsequently. Yet this is not a course that can be conquered by power alone. Firm, fast greens and the almost ever-present winds off the nearby bay ensure Kingston Heath is a course to be treated with respect.

## A RUN OF PAR FOURS

Originally a par five, the opener heads to the east and at 456 yards it is an uncommonly stern beginning. The fairway rises up from the tee to a high point 220 yards (201 metres) away, and from there it tips down to a green guarded by

bunkers on the right. Long running shots are encouraged by a green that is open at the front. When the pin is tucked into the right corner of the green a drive down the left half of the fairway is better placed.

Among the wonderful sub-300 yard par fours in the Melbourne vicinity is the 3rd at Kingston Heath. This masterful 294-yarder on flat ground gave the designers very little in the way of natural undulation to

work with. Its tiny green, set on a diagonal from left to right, rewards those playing from the left corner of the fairway which is protected by a fairway bunker a couple of hundred metres from the tee. Finding that bunker leaves the golfer with one of those horrid-length bunker shots that no one in the game can play with any certainty. A tee shot flared away from the left bunker leaves a difficult pitch across sand, and in a championship when the greens are firm it is one of the more difficult pitches in Australia. Some, including champion golfers Greg Norman and Robert Allenby, take their longest club, even though it is all but impossible to stay on the green; they head for the bunkers surrounding the green and hope to get up and down for their birdies. Five is almost certain for a misplayed stroke, an unwise gamble or a simple failure to understand how the hole needs to be played.

The 430-yard 6th plays alongside the opening fairway back towards the clubhouse and features a tee shot that is up and over a hill so the final resting place of the ball is blind from the tee. A bunker lying across the left half of the fairway on the 505-yard 7th forces big

*Alister MacKenzie described the original short, blind par four as a blot on the course and during his 1926 visit to Australia he transformed it into the finest short hole in the country.*

hitters to be accurate if they hope to reach the green with a mid-iron. Likewise at the 435-yard 8th, a bunker crosses half of the fairway, this time on the right. On the 362-yard 9th, the tee shot over a small ridge makes the fairway blind from the tee, adding to the challenge.

Following the 140-yard 10th is the first of two holes where central fairway bunkers determine the strategy – the 416-yard 11th. Much like the short 3rd, the 556-yard 12th lies over an almost dead flat tract of land but it is, strategically, one of the more interesting par fives in Australian golf. The tee-shot strategy is dominated by bunkers that sit right in the middle of the fairway, requiring a carry of almost 280 yards (255 metres). Most elect to play to the left or right of the sand, but it is a decision to be made on the day, depending on the wind. From there bunkers farther along on the left need to be avoided, while the green is set to

reward the golfer who plays close to the sand. Woe awaits the long hitter who misplays either of the first two shots.

## THE CLOSING HOLES

Another excellent par five is the 566-yard 14th. From here begins the long and difficult finish that has decided many a tournament at Kingston Heath. The famed 15th is one of the world's best examples of an uphill par three and this sand-surrounded beauty is highlighted by a brilliant green. At 154 yards, it takes a perfectly flighted iron to get close and when the hole is into a strong wind it is the most difficult shot on the course.

Although often criticized for its blindness, the tee shot of the 428-yard 16th is a fine examination of nerve at the end of a round. The course ends with what once was a strong par four, but the longest hitters now play a wedge to the green. That does not make it any less of a hole – it is just a shorter and therefore easier one.

## A SUBTLE TREASURE

Kingston Heath is not a spectacular golf course to entrance those looking for quick and obvious thrills. It is a course with multiple layers of complexity that take more than a few rounds to uncover, and its wonder is that the more a golfer plays it the greater the appreciation of its sophistication, its class and its understated beauty.

# BARNBOUGLE DUNES
## Bridport, Tasmania, Australia

Among the first great, modern, remote golf courses were Sand Hills (see page 230) in Nebraska and Pacific Dunes (see page 238) on the edge of the Pacific Ocean. The most unlikely course to be a part of this new phenomenon is Barnbougle Dunes on the northern coast of Tasmania, the island state south of the Australian mainland.

Unlike the founders of Sand Hills and Pacific Dunes, who were golf lovers, Barnbougle's owner Richard Sattler knew nothing of the game. 'I don't play it and I don't even really like it' was one of Sattler's early quips. 'I hated those dunes. It was just land where I couldn't grow potatoes,' commented the owner of this 11,000-acre (4,450-hectare) potato farm bordered by 5 miles (8 kilometres) of beachfront sand dunes.

In 2000 a young man phoned asking to view the land with the idea of building a golf course. Sattler thought Greg Ramsay a 'complete nutter' yet agreed he could take a look. What Ramsay found was a perfect piece of ground for golf with stunning views over the ocean: it was windy, like all golf by the sea, and it was remote. Undeterred by the problems, Ramsay called architects Mike Clayton and Tom Doak and suggested they visit the site.

Doak sent his trusted lieutenant Bruce Hepner, who with Clayton understood the potential of the land, but questioned whether Greg Ramsay could raise the money for such a development. After Ramsay's early financial model failed, Doak himself visited Barnbougle, as did Pacific Dunes owner Mike Keiser. Together they convinced the owner that his land had

the potential for a world-class golf course and that the financial risk was worth taking. Keiser took Sattler to Pacific Dunes to show him how the golf worked there, and Sattler found some investors willing to contribute.

## A LINKS COURSE

The site itself is a narrow strip of dunes in the fashion of the out-and-in links made famous by the Old Course at St Andrews (see page 40) and Royal Troon (see page 58). Unlike those courses, however, the clubhouse at Barnbougle is at the mid-point of the course, and each set of nine holes heads in opposite directions to distant points at the 4th and 14th greens.

The opening four holes play into the prevailing easterly wind with the 554-yard 1st having a wide opening fairway and a pair of bunkers 80 yards (73 metres) short of the green that determine the strategy of the second shot. Uniquely, the 417-yard 2nd is not bordered by dunes or sea on both sides, and that alone has singled it out for criticism as 'boring'. In no way is it a poor hole or even a boring one and it brings to mind a quote of A.W. Tillinghast: 'When I speak of a hole being inspiring it is not intended to infer that the visitor is to be subject to attacks of hysteria on every

tee.' The left side of the 2nd adjoins farmland, and while there are dunes to the right it is a relatively flat hole. Fairway bunkers protect the perfect line to the flag and the right edge of the green is on a left-to-right diagonal, which makes approaches from the wide right side of the fairway more difficult.

At 296 yards the 4th poses the 'What on earth do I do here today?' question, and the answer varies from day to day, depending on the wind and the pin position. The massive, natural, blow-out bunker on the direct line to the flag is 235 yards (215 metres) to carry and from there the ball kicks down towards the green, but into the wind only the strongest players attempt the carry. Although the fairway is almost 90 yards (80 metres) wide in front of the bunker, when the pin is in the right half of the green the only way the player earns a view of the flag is by driving to the left quarter of the fairway. When the pin is tucked right behind the small dune, the best line to the flag is from the far right side of the fairway.

## AT THE FAR POINT

The 5th is a 220-yard par three that mostly plays downwind but the 120-yard 7th makes for a much

*Played into the prevailing wind, the 17th hole demands two perfectly flighted long shots and only with the wind behind can the longest hitters carry the sand.*

more difficult shot. It interrupts the run of holes back to the clubhouse with the wind behind, and on many days it is a 5- or 6-iron shot to the small, upturned and exposed green protected by a deep bunker left and slopes taking the ball away at the right and back of the green.

Most difficult of all the holes is the 8th, a 489-yarder with a fairway split by a dune in the middle and a green sitting high above a deep hollow that finishes about 60 yards (55 metres) short of the target. Those going for the green in two have to carry the steep dune at the end of the hollow and those laying back face a blind pitch up the hill. Another short par four, of only 278 yards, is the 12th, and again it poses classic club-and-line question of holes of this genre. Drivable with no wind, it nevertheless plays as a drive and a running pitch for most of the time.

The most controversial hole at Barnbougle is the 13th, a 206-yard par three with its green paying homage to the sadly lost, wildly sloping MacKenzie green at Sitwell Park in England. The green refuses to be attacked with a high, long, stopping iron. Instead the player must produce a shot of perfect trajectory and shape that lands in the right place and feeds to the cup, whether it be in the back-left shelf, the back-right hollow or in the undulating surface at the front. Some hate the 13th and some love it, but it is hard not to have fun here.

## INTO THE PREVAILING EASTERLIES

Turning back into the wind, the 15th is a 351-yarder with a bunker in the middle of the fairway. The bravest line is right of the sand and over the dune on the right to a piece of fairway that is blind from the tee. It is as dangerous a shot as playing close to the boundary at St Andrews's 16th and those playing left have room to spare, but the approach is more difficult from the safe side.

The final two holes are big, strong par fours playing right back along the beach. A bunker-embedded dune protects the right side of the 17th fairway and, while it cannot be carried from the tee, those driving right are blind to the flag. At the 440-yard 18th the drive is up and over a dune and from there the play is down to a green almost literally on the edge of the beach. It suits a long, running approach, and it is a thrilling place to end a game of golf.

## BARNBOUGLE DUNES –
# Bridport, Tasmania, Australia
Tom Doak and Mike Clayton, 2004

CARD OF THE COURSE

| HOLE | YARDS | PAR | HOLE | YARDS | PAR |
|------|-------|-----|------|-------|-----|
| 1. | 554 | 5 | 10. | 447 | 4 |
| 2. | 417 | 4 | 11. | 520 | 5 |
| 3. | 371 | 4 | 12. | 278 | 4 |
| 4. | 296 | 4 | 13. | 206 | 3 |
| 5. | 220 | 3 | 14. | 556 | 5 |
| 6. | 417 | 4 | 15. | 351 | 4 |
| 7. | 120 | 3 | 16. | 167 | 3 |
| 8. | 489 | 4 | 17. | 438 | 4 |
| 9. | 438 | 4 | 18. | 440 | 4 |
| OUT | 3,322 | 35 | IN | 3,403 | 36 |
|  |  |  | TOTAL | 6,725 | 71 |

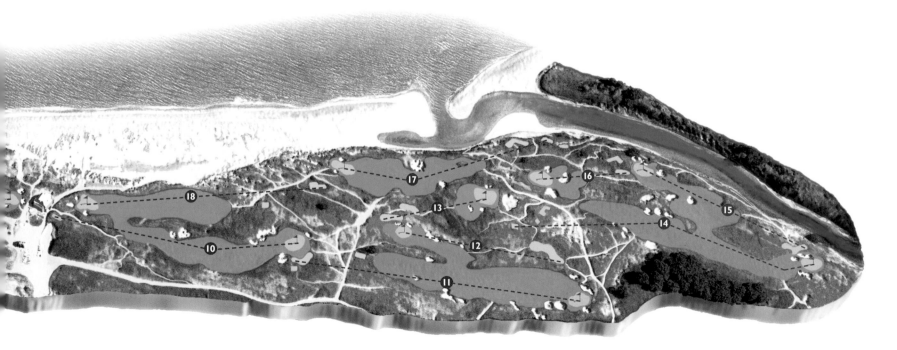

# PARAPARAUMU BEACH
## Paraparaumu Beach, New Zealand

While the quality of New Zealand's courses has never matched the potential of the land, the course at Paraparaumu Beach proves that some of the finest golf courses in the world could be built there in the future.

Yearning for the type of golf found in Britain, the founders of Paraparaumu Beach GC located a perfect, albeit small, site for their ideal course. It was on the Kapiti coast, a 35-mile (56-kilometre) drive north of Wellington. Alex Russell then designed a course that added to his already established reputation as a first-class architect.

### A RUSSELL TREAT

Russell was a wealthy man and golf architecture was not his full-time profession, but he formed an alliance with Alister MacKenzie when the Scot visited Australia in 1926. While the hallmark of Russell's Australian courses was big, sand-faced bunkers, at Paraparaumu Beach he created much smaller, pot bunkers perfectly suited to the restricted windy site.

All well-designed links are routed with the winds in mind, and they are by necessity not difficult if the air is still. As soon as the breeze comes up, however, the golf is harder, and on the windiest days links are the most extreme tests in the game. Although Paraparaumu Beach is far from the being most difficult links course in the world, Russell did design a wonderful test, full of fun. It is perfectly balanced between being a fine test for championship players and a course members can enjoy without being discouraged by the sorts of scores they might manage at places as difficult and intimidating as Royal County Down (see page 116) or Carnoustie (see page 50).

### FABULOUS LINKS GOLF

Heading towards the distant mountains, the 403-yard 1st turns left to a green big enough to get play underway without requiring an approach of great accuracy. The following four holes do, however, demand a stream of quality shots. The 197-yard 2nd is played over broken ground with a short bunker to carry, and much of the putting surface is blind from the tee. Into the wind a straight-faced iron is the perfect club, but holes like this are simpler now that the modern ball is infinitely easier to control in the wind. Tiger Woods was no fan of this green where four putts on his final

day of the 2000 Open finished his chances of catching Craig Parry and Michael Campbell.

Into the wind, the 464-yard 3rd is a difficult hole with a wildly undulating fairway, guaranteeing odd stances, and a small green protected by bunkers on the left. Switching direction, playing back towards the 2nd green, is the 446-yard 4th. Its left-to-right, diagonally angled green, protected by bunkers on the right, rewards drives fired along the left third of the fairway. These two holes work perfectly in combination if the wind is up with the 3rd playing as a long par four and the other as a much easier proposition.

Another brilliant short hole is the 162-yard 5th. Russell must have delighted in its construction. Its green sits high above the surrounding ground and he found no need for protecting bunkers because anyone missing the green faces a pitch so difficult that saving par here is something requiring great skill.

The other fine hole on the front nine is the 371-yard 8th, doglegged to the right, with a drive played along a narrow ridge forming the fairway that falls off on both sides. A perfect drive is rewarded with a pitch down the line of the green, but those dropping off the fairway to the right are forced to play across the right bunker to – what is from the wrong angle – a very small target.

After the 310-yard par four to begin the run home, the 427-yard 11th is the most difficult driving hole at Paraparaumu Beach. Houses all the way along the left warn of the out-of-bounds line just off the edge of the fairway, and Russell set the green perfectly among small dunes to reward those who had driven close to the boundary.

The most spectacular and the most difficult hole is the 446-yard 13th. About 240 yards (220 metres) from the tee the fairway drops to a much lower level and,

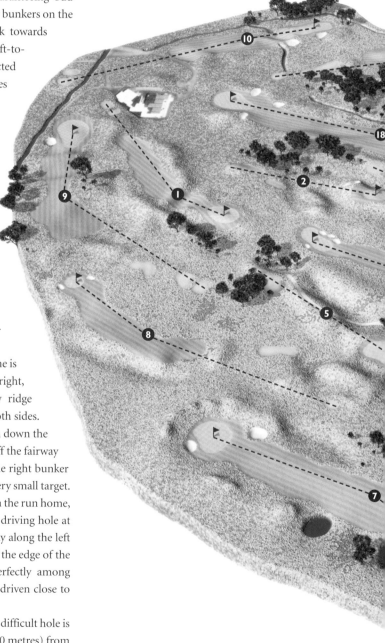

from the top of the hill, players face a long approach across the valley to a green set high in the opposite hill. Those driving long have a shorter iron – perhaps a 7 or an 8 – but the long, narrow green sits high above and it is no easy task to hit it with even a short-iron. Sadly the 146-yard 14th is not a Russell-original par three, having been altered to alleviate a problem with neighbouring houses.

## HIGHPOINT OF THE COURSE

Coming home, the 15th is a wonderful 372-yard par four, but it is the next two holes that really stamp this course as one of excellence. The 16th is a 138-yarder and, as at the 5th, Russell found a green site so narrow and difficult that there was no need for bunkers. A steep bank off the right edge of the green is a constant concern, and here is a wonderful example of a world-class hole significantly less than 150 yards (137 metres) long.

Russell's 442-yard 17th at Paraparaumu Beach is an alternate fairway hole with the easier shot to the lower fairway leaving a long second to a green that sits across the player, making it effectively wide and shallow. Those who take the more difficult route to the higher fairway face a long, narrow green with another steep bank to the left that sweeps errant shots far from the green. The diagonal ridge separating the fairways makes the carry longer for those hoping to get within a short-iron of the green. Intriguing, alternative strategic decisions, each with its own reward, mark this as one of the finest half-dozen holes in Australian and New Zealand golf.

*The long par-four 13th plays across the most tumbling piece of ground at Paraparaumu. Difficult holes are not necessarily good holes, but the 13th is a perfect example of a great hole.*

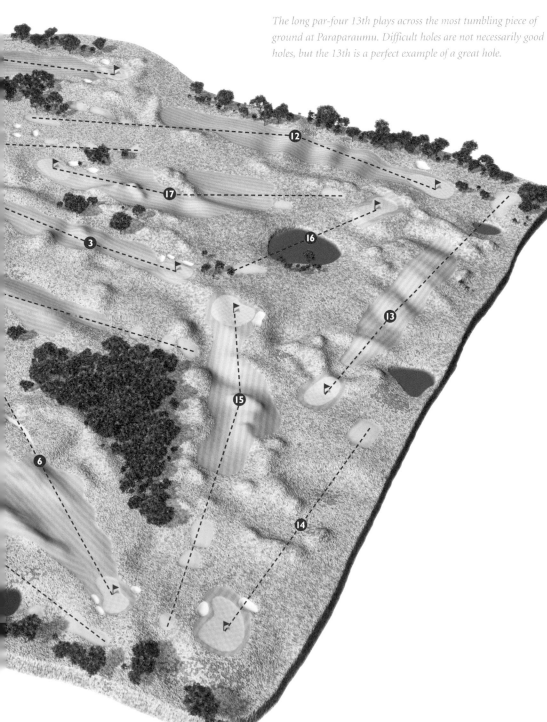

## PARAPARAUMU BEACH GOLF CLUB – Paraparaumu Beach, New Zealand

Alex Russell, 1949
Major events: New Zealand Open 1959, 1966, 1972, 1984, 1988, 1989, 1991, 1992, 1993, 1996, 2000, 2002

CARD OF THE COURSE

| HOLE | YARDS | PAR | HOLE | YARDS | PAR |
|------|-------|-----|------|-------|-----|
| 1. | 403 | 4 | 10. | 310 | 4 |
| 2. | 197 | 3 | 11. | 427 | 4 |
| 3. | 464 | 4 | 12. | 545 | 5 |
| 4. | 446 | 4 | 13. | 446 | 4 |
| 5. | 162 | 3 | 14. | 146 | 3 |
| 6. | 325 | 4 | 15. | 372 | 4 |
| 7. | 500 | 5 | 16. | 138 | 3 |
| 8. | 371 | 4 | 17. | 442 | 4 |
| 9. | 393 | 4 | 18. | 550 | 5 |
| OUT | 3,261 | 35 | IN | 3,376 | 36 |
| | | | TOTAL | 6,637 | 71 |

# CAPE KIDNAPPERS
## Hawke's Bay, New Zealand

Situated on the east coast of the North Island, Cape Kidnappers is an exciting course showing what is possible in New Zealand if a first-class architect is given a wonderful site.

Driven by a desire to expand New Zealand tourism, New Yorker Julian Robinson chose Tom Doak to design a layout on a huge piece of land that by any definition is breathtaking. 'The sheer openness of the site was the first thing that struck me,' said Doak. Matching the site is a course with wide holes luring players close to the edges of destruction if they are to earn the easier approach shots. The most spectacular landforms are on the back nine, where fingers of land, each one wide enough to fit a golf hole, spread out into the ocean and players feel missing the target is akin to missing the world.

## A COURSE WORTHY OF ITS SITE

Tom Doak's key was to uncover a routing that used the spectacular land while ensuring that the rest of the holes fitted together into a coherent and easily walkable golf course. Some of the most dramatic moments are not necessarily the ones right on the cliff tops.

Cape Kidnappers has perhaps the longest entrance road in golf – it takes 15 minutes to reach the clubhouse from the front gate. Once there, the 440-yard 1st poses a far from easy opener, with its green sitting on the diagonal from right to left and guarded by bunkers on the left, clearly rewarding the drive to the right side of the hole. In the fashion of logical, strategic architecture the player is offered a wide expanse of fairway to the left but a likely bogey for edging too far to the right.

A fine, 540-yard par five follows, bunkered well enough to make for interesting shots all the way along the hole. Fairway bunkers sit on the right side of the drive and cross-bunkers farther along are influential if the wind is against. The green is open on the left and bunkers sit into the front-right corner, while golfers hitting leftwards face a difficult pitch down the slope of the green. Fine hole that it is, the 2nd seems almost pedestrian in comparison with the remaining three long holes – the 4th, 15th and 16th.

## MEMORABLE GOLFING MOMENTS

The blind tee shot at the 544-yard 4th is best aimed down the left side of the wide expanse of fairway and a ravine full of unplayable lies runs along the side of the second half of the hole. Anyone hoping to reach in two must play the most adventurous of long second shots. From a tee almost literally hanging off the side of the ravine at the 420-yard 5th, the golfer hoping to avoid a bunker just right of the centre of the driving area needs to hit a long shot into the slot that opens up the green, with bunkers protecting the front right. The longer drive left makes for a shorter iron but one played by necessity across the greenside bunkers.

## CAPE KIDNAPPERS – Hawke's Bay, New Zealand
Tom Doak, 2003

CARD OF THE COURSE

| HOLE | YARDS | PAR | HOLE | YARDS | PAR |
|------|-------|-----|------|-------|-----|
| 1. | 440 | 4 | 10. | 470 | 4 |
| 2. | 540 | 5 | 11. | 224 | 3 |
| 3. | 215 | 3 | 12. | 460 | 4 |
| 4. | 544 | 5 | 13. | 130 | 3 |
| 5. | 420 | 4 | 14. | 348 | 4 |
| 6. | 225 | 3 | 15. | 650 | 5 |
| 7. | 453 | 4 | 16. | 500 | 5 |
| 8. | 182 | 3 | 17. | 463 | 4 |
| 9. | 403 | 4 | 18. | 480 | 4 |
| OUT | 3,422 | 35 | IN | 3,725 | 36 |
| | | | TOTAL | 7,147 | 71 |

What makes the 5th so intriguing is that the golfer is faced with an entirely different-looking shot from one side of the fairway to the other. Imaginative thought and holes like this demonstrate the possibilities of wide expanses of short grass, well-placed hazards and strategically orientated greens.

The 225-yard 6th, an epic hole across a deep ravine, is followed by a 453-yarder where a good drive earns extra run-off down the slope in the middle of the fairway. A short-iron approach to the upturned green is one of the more difficult to hit at Cape Kidnappers. Into the wind it takes a drive beyond most players' capability to get down the slope, so a player adopts a long-iron approach to the most difficult of targets. On the 453-yard 7th, the second shot down the hill to the green is a fabulous shot to play.

## MENTAL CHALLENGES

Very good though the next three holes are, it is from the 12th tee that players are left with the most spectacular holes and memories. In keeping with the nature of this most strategic of courses, the 460-yard 12th has a hugely wide fairway. From the fairway, the green sitting right on the skyline gives the

impression that anyone going over might never be seen again.

After the 130-yard 13th, set on the edge of the cliffs, comes the 348-yard 14th, a terrific, drive-and-pitch hole. The green is positioned so it is extremely difficult for those driving long and left, and the most influential hazard is a tiny pot bunker right into the face of the green. It has significant gravitational pull, attracting anything coming close to its edges. Much like the Road hole bunker at St Andrews (see page 40), a tiny sand hazard here determines the entire strategy, and while it can be avoided it cannot be disregarded.

The 650-yard 15th is quite possibly the most difficult, intimidating and dangerous long hole in golf. Seemingly stretching out interminably it runs all the way along the cliff edge on the left with the attendant 500-foot (150-metre) drop to the surf below and an unplayable ravine to the right. Downwind it is possible to reach the green in two if the ground is firm, but few if any would attempt that in anything other than a practice round. With the wind against a player, the hole is capable of frightening everyone from legendary champion Tiger Woods downwards. Nothing other than three straight, low, piercing shots will find the green in regulation, and no round is safe until this hole has been passed.

## THE CLOSING HOLES

The run home towards the clubhouse from the far point of the 15th green begins with the short but dangerous par-five 16th where picking up a stroke is feasible. Both finishing holes are long two-shotters. Stretching 463 yards, the 17th is divided into two by a diagonal ridge stacked with bunkers that must be carried with the long second, and those out of position from the tee can play farther along the lower fairway and pitch up over the far edge of the bunkers.

Highlight of the 480-yard 18th is its punchbowl green lying far below the level of the fairway to the left. Most architects would have built the green on the high ground, but Tom Doak chose the low point, which allows players to run the long second shot in from the left. However, there is no certainty that shots will fall down the slope, and those flying just too far left stay up on the top leaving a difficult pitch down. The trick is not to take the easy way but to aim at the flag and fire off one last great shot.

*These dramatic fingers of land stretching out into the ocean were used by Tom Doak to create some of the most visually intimidating holes in golf.*

ASIA

# ASIA

The game of golf has developed in fits and starts on the continent of Asia, although it can boast the oldest golf club outside the British Isles, Royal Calcutta , which brought the game to India in 1829. Under Imperial British rule, golf in the sub-continent was very much a thing for the expatriates.

JAPAN

9
11
Tokyo
8
10
12
Hirono
*page 306*

6
7
Seoul
Beijing
SOUTH
KOREA
5
15
16

CHINA

Delhi

4
Mission Hills
3

INDIA

1
Hanoi
Calcutta

THAILAND
13
Bangkok
VIETNAM
2

14
BRUNEI
21
NEW
GUINEA
Jayapura
20

17
19
INDONESIA

Jakarta
BALI
JAVA
18
Nirwana Bali
*page 308*

Following independence in 1947 all that changed and golf there soon became an Indian sport, with top-level professionals and amateurs competing on the international circuits that now visit Indian courses on a regular basis. Elsewhere in Asia they were largely colonial outposts where golf became established, from Dalat Palace in Vietnam to Hong Kong Golf Club (formerly of 'Royal' moniker) and, as usual, it was merely an activity for expatriates.

The lone exception to the colonial legacy of Asian golf is Japan, where the game took hold and expanded to the point in the 1980s that that country had became a golf superpower in terms of courses per population density, equipment and certainly passion. Driving ranges were filled with golfers content to hit balls into far-off nets, while never playing real courses, which were prohibitively priced. Once golf in Japan hit fever pitch, golfing facilities for both locals and tourists took off in the rest of Asia. Countries, such as Thailand and South Korea, became hotbeds of development activity.

## GOLF IN CHINA

With about 60 per cent of the world's population residing in Asia, the future of golf is inexorably linked with this continent. China got into golf development with a flurry in the late 1980s, and it soon surpassed all but Japan in having the most courses per country. Since 2004, however, there has been a Chinese moratorium on further golf-course construction. Although affection for the game itself within China is uncertain, the burgeoning middle class within its immense population will ensure that many more courses will be built there in the years to come.

Current luminaries within China include the 36-hole resort Spring City , which is located in the historic region of Kunming. Robert Trent Jones Jnr

*The 8th hole at the Jack Nicklaus-designed Pine Valley outside Beijing. There is a further*
*27-hole course designed by Nicklaus's son, Jack II.*

and Jack Nicklaus, respectively, laid out the Lakes and Mountain courses there. While these two courses may be considered among the finest in the country, for sheer quantity Mission Hills in the southern Shenzhen province lays claim to the world's largest golf resort. With an astounding 12 courses, the resort is literally a destination in itself. Tiger Beach on the Huang Hai Sea is another modern marvel, crafted under the supervision of Chinese businessman Sung Kuang Man. The course benefits from 1 mile (2.2 kilometres) of beach frontage, which creates a rare find – a links-style course in Asia.

Even Beijing boasts great golfing opportunities. Jack Nicklaus's Pine Valley course is a good test and hosts the Pine Valley Beijing Open. Although not perhaps in the same league as the esteemed eponymous course in Clementon, New Jersey (see page 186), Pine Valley is not the only club to borrow intellectual property: Golden Pebble Beach – Peter Thomson's design – in Dalian also draws on a world-famous golfing name (see page 244). If imitation is the sincerest form of flattery, China is on the right track to expand the game in the centuries ahead.

## ASIA'S GOLF EPICENTRE

Japan's love of the game began when the British expatriate Arthur Groom built the Kobe Golf Club in 1903. Set in the cool mountains above Kobe, the course helped create a love affair with the game that few golfing regions can rival. In fact, only the United States boasts more ground for golf than this small island nation. A century later Japan's greatest golf courses are not only the best group of courses in Asia but also among the world's best.

A similar effect to Dr Alister MacKenzie's short visit to Australia in 1926 was felt in Japan after British architect Charles Alison arrived in 1930 and went on to have a profound impact on Japanese golf-course architecture. His first course – Tokyo GC – opened in 1932 and was widely hailed as the country's first outstanding one. From there Alison tacked south to the seaside estate of Baron Kishichiro Okura, named Kawana . The rocky coastline perched high above the sea offered Alison one of the most diverse and spectacular sites he was ever afforded. Given the lack of

natural soil on site, Alison worked hard to route a golf course at Kawana that today features dramatic elevation changes and some truly world-class holes.

Further travels through Japan led Charles Alison to his *pièce de résistance* – Hirono (see page 306), outside Kobe. Hirono today has been softened from its rugged beginnings, but it remains without a doubt the best course in Asia and is also Alison's lasting legacy. Other notable courses, including Kasumigaseki County Club  and Naruo GC , benefited from Alison's visit. The esteem in which Charles Alison is held in Japan is reflected in the Japanese term for a deep bunker, which is simply an 'Alison'.

Although golf in Japan is very respectful of its British roots – down to featuring English characters in their logos – its golfers have made a culture surrounding the game all their own. Peculiarities to the Western golfer start with the distinct break between nines, with a full lunch served in the clubhouse. Of course this leads to long rounds, which are synonymous with the culture, where full-day rounds and nary a sense of urgency exist. Following the final putts, golfers retire to a ritualistic experience, which is highlighted first by

showering on a stool. Once the cleaning has been concluded, the golfer retires to a deep soaking pool, where the water at a seemingly inhumane heat offers a remarkable reprieve to sore muscles. Although these events remain unique to the Japanese golf culture, one trait has found its way to most other Asian golf courses – female caddies. Charming women, dressed in subdued garb, guide trolleys (some electric, many still manual) around the courses with upbeat attitudes and wide-brimmed sun hats. Minus bag carrying, these women provide all the same services with a bounce in their step.

## GOLF EXPANSION

Fuelled by the Japanese passion for the game, now more than ever golf has developed at a rapid pace throughout Asia, especially in such countries as Thailand, India, Indonesia, Malaysia and South Korea. A combination of high humidity and a preference for ornate landscaping means that golf there has been less about strategic principles in recent years.

Because of its close links with Japan, golf then developed in Thailand, where there are now more than

*The Canyon Course at Blue Canyon in Thailand was designed by the Japanese architect Yoshikazu Kato. This is the final hole.*

200 courses. Thus this country has truly established itself as a golfing destination. Both Thai CC  in Bangkok and Blue Canyon CC  in Phuket, with their emphasis on conditioning, are highly ranked throughout Asia. In this, the latter was helped by hosting the Johnnie Walker Classic, which boasts such champions as Greg Norman and Tiger Woods. Woods made a great impression in 1998, with his booming drive on the 390-yard, par-four 13th, which found the green. A plaque remains to mark the spot of this key shot in a tournament in which Woods came from nine shots behind to tie Ernie Els, before defeating him on the second play-off hole.

Initially, South Korea squeezed courses into often harsh landscapes. The development of golf on Jeju Island has shifted this trend, as seen with the creation of such modern gems as the Club at Nine Bridges

*The 4th hole of the Majlis Course at Emirates is a tricky par three with water protecting the front and right of the green.*

and Pinx CC . Both courses lie on an island to the south of the mainland and are the work of American golf architects.

Indonesia may fairly lay claim to the highest-quality golf in the region. This quality can generally be attributed to the fine land that some architects have had to create courses in the archipelago. Given the country's 17,508 islands, it is not surprising that many courses boast seaside land. As well as Nirwana Bali (see page 308), there are several other courses worth noting, including Jack Nicklaus's work at the Bintan Lagoon Resort and at the Taman Dayu Club , and Gary Player's coastal work at Ria Bintan GC . Perhaps no more intriguing course exists than the work of Bill Coore, Ben Crenshaw and Rod Whitman at Klub Golf Rimba Irian in Papua New Guinea. Designed to withstand the frequent torrential rain that batters its rainforest location, Klub Golf Rimba Irian has been described as the 'world's most remote championship golf course'.

## HIDDEN GEM

Perhaps the most surprising course in Asia rests in the tiny sultanate of Brunei, which has only five courses. Among these is one of that continent's best golf resorts and certainly its most opulent – the Empire CC , a Jack Nicklaus design, laid out on the South China Sea. With the nines looping in opposite directions from the grand hotel, the course takes full advantage of its coastal terrain. The front nine is routed over the high ground, while the back nine drops down to the sea at the 549-yard, par-five 15th. The closing hole follows the coastline and has dramatic cliffs flanking the left side, leaving little margin for error. In the background of this challenging finisher is the five-star Empire Hotel. Fit for a sultan, the Empire certainly ranks among Asia's must-play courses.

Malaysia and India are also among the leading golfing nations of Asia, yet they have still to produce anything on a par with the other continental greats. Recent course openings in Cambodia and Vietnam highlight the fact that golf is also thriving in other parts of Asia.

## GOLF IN THE MIDDLE EAST

Golf's humble beginnings in the Middle East lay in desert courses on which there were oiled greens. These rudimentary layouts were meant simply to appease expatriate workers, and in Dubai for example they are now the style of the past. Resembling Palm Springs or Scottsdale from the air, the number of shimmering green fairways seems to be expanding as fast as the city's skyline.

Emirates GC remains the face of golf in the United Arab Emirates, with its dramatic clubhouse fashioned after Bedouin tents. The Majlis Course was designed by the American Karl Litten and was the first all-grass course in the Middle East. It hosts the annual Dubai Desert Classic, which continues to draw the world's top players. With courses opening regularly, its reign atop the regional golf scene may be challenged in the years to come by such nations as Bahrain, Oman and Qatar, where golf is still in its infancy. The desire to create things to rival the best of the world gives hope that something spectacular may be yet to come.

# HIRONO
## Shijimi, Hyōgo, Japan

In 1930, Charles Alison aboard the steamer *Asama Maru* arrived in Tokyo harbour. An Englishman, Alison was the first golf architect invited to Japan and his three-month visit transformed Japanese golf.

Collaborator and partner of Harry Colt and Alister MacKenzie, Charles Alison was also a journalist and experienced golfer. Following the lead MacKenzie blazed on his Australian tour of 1926, Alison began work on a portfolio that remains the core of Japan's finest courses. Indeed, his work may have lit the fire for a country known for its golfing soul.

### ENGLISH ORIGINS OF JAPANESE GOLF

Beginning with Tokyo GC, Charles Alison went on to design Kawana, Naruo and Kasumigaseki golf clubs. Eventually, he became acquainted with a unique opportunity on property owned by an ex-feudal warlord named Viscount Kuki. The terrain bore similarities to England's Surrey heathlands – Alison found vales, rivulets, hillocks, woodlands and natural water features.

After walking the land, Alison ensconced himself in a local hotel with his notes and contour maps. After a week, he emerged with precise and detailed drawings for Hirono. Yet, he would be absent for construction. Relying on these plans were locals Seiichi Takahata and Chozo Ito (Japan's top golf journalist), who brought Hirono to life with astounding attention to detail. Most notable was the fierce, flashed bunker faces, which today are still known as 'Alisons'.

Playing near-championship length from its creation, Hirono always offered tremendous scale and fearsome hazards to surmount. A premium was placed on tee-shot accuracy due to the angles necessary to attack greens sloped deviously to repel approach shots. Few golf courses in the world utilized the land for such a variety of the golfing experience, and Alison gave his holes distinctive names, thus heightening the drama.

## HIRONO GOLF CLUB – Shijimi, Hyōgo, Japan

Charles Alison, 1930
Major events: Japanese Open 2005

### CARD OF THE COURSE

| HOLE | NAME | YARDS | PAR | HOLE | NAME | YARDS | PAR |
|------|------|-------|-----|------|------|-------|-----|
| 1. | Okko | 502 | 5 | 10. | Mekko | 351 | 4 |
| 2. | Twin Barrows | 453 | 4 | 11. | Akashi Shore | 458 | 4 |
| 3. | Nanten Isle | 461 | 4 | 12. | Pine Beach | 596 | 5 |
| 4. | Lake Point | 451 | 4 | 13. | Loch Lomond | 167 | 3 |
| 5. | Fiord | 152 | 3 | 14. | Quo Vadis | 388 | 4 |
| 6. | Alps | 425 | 4 | 15. | Ichino Tani (One Valley) | 568 | 5 |
| 7. | Devil's Divot | 211 | 3 | 16. | Harima Fuji | 401 | 4 |
| 8. | Cedar Grove | 353 | 4 | 17. | Lake Side | 231 | 3 |
| 9. | Boulevard | 542 | 5 | 18. | Home Cliff | 459 | 4 |
| **OUT** | | **3,550** | **36** | **IN** | | **3,619** | **36** |
| | | | | **TOTAL** | | **7,169** | **72** |

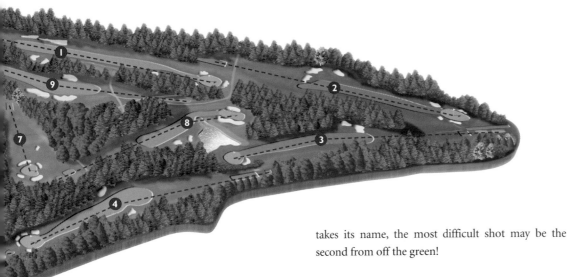

Sadly, the ravages of the Second World War greatly affected the course. Used as a runway for the Imperial Air Force, Hirono was then the victim of intensive tree planting, which still hinders the course. Restored in 1948–49 by Osamu Ueda and Toyohiko Inui based on Charles Alison's original plans, the current course is parkland in feel and features tighter corridors and grassed face bunkering.

## PAR THREES TO REMEMBER

Hirono's 502-yard 1st is a straight, par five surrounded by pine trees and parallel bunkering. Because it is spacious, the golfer is free to hit any kind of tee shot. Such a gentle introduction to the course quickly ends at the 453-yard 2nd, where an imposing, 40-yard (36-metre) wide cross-bunker requires a 210 yard (192-metre) carry in order to reach the fairway. Even though Hirono is not about sheer length, the 461-yard 3rd builds on the 2nd. Often holes of this length can be a long slog, yet Alison ingeniously placed the green site in an area where it is pinched by a bunker left and pond right.

The player's first introduction to Alison's fabulous quartet of par threes is the 152-yard 5th, where a simple short-iron surmounts a small inlet to a bunker-laden island plateau green. A high dropper with a hint of fade works best. Finding the sand will immediately require top-notch bunker play to avoid a lost shot. Because of their steep sides, a wide-open clubface is required from the bunkers and ideally the ability to spin the ball.

A marriage between heaven and hell is evident at the 211-yard 7th known as Devil's Divot. Surrounded by sand and a gouged-out gully from which the hole

*Hirono's journey culminates with a par four requiring the golfer to shape shots off the tee and then contend with a green protected by sand and a pond on the port side.*

takes its name, the most difficult shot may be the second from off the green!

## AROUND THE TURN

Trees stand as the primary obstacle on the 353-yard 8th, where a small pond pinches in by the green to capture tepid approaches. Here Alison employed a classic strategic ploy – an ideal tee shot is a draw followed by a faded approach. Meanwhile remembrances of Pebble Beach's 18th (see page 244) will stimulate the golfer at the 596-yard 12th, where the tee is on a lake peninsula and the hole bends left around the water. Trees guarding the shoreline render the lake out of play. Expect three solid shots to reach the green.

Using a peninsula green again for intimidation, the 167-yard 13th is a fine, mid-iron test. Due to lengthening of the 12th in 2000, the 13th tee is perpendicular to where it once stood. For the club golfer the water remains a hazard, but the low handicapper will not feel any twinge of fear.

Alison's creativity is on display at the crafty 388-yard 14th, where a severe sidehill slope demands a tee shot to the right side of the fairway. Alison protected this area originally with sandy waste, but it has gradually disappeared, making a hook lie the primary obstacle.

## OUTSTANDING CHALLENGES

Strategically speaking, the 568-yard 15th is Hirono's best hole. A true three-shotter, the hole bends left and any attempt to cut the dogleg off and shorten the hole is blocked by a tall Japanese black pine tree standing sole sentinel 330 yards (300 metres) from the tee. With the tree central to any strategy, most drives fall to the outside of the dogleg bringing into play two natural gullies. The first gully is 175 yards (160 metres) from the green and has an attractive array of cross-bunkers cut into the depression; the second ravine is near the green and forms part of the putting surface. In 1963, during an exhibition and playing with traditional persimmon drivers, Jack Nicklaus became the first ever to reach this hole in two shots. Mere mortals will find this near-impossible to replicate.

A high plateau green surrounded by mounds at the wings is the 401-yard 16th's main defence, while the 231-yard 17th hole completes the compendium of short holes. Again, from a lakeside tee, a corner of the water must be carried. Two options are available: a low draw can run up an approach fairway and hold the elevated green; or a graceful fade wedged in between flanking sand also can find the putting surface.

Cross-bunkers cut diagonally into a gully and requiring a 250-yard (230-metre) carry are the final test at the 459-yard 18th. Bending sharply left, a right-to-left shot is the best play off the tee in order to get a shorter approach into a low-profile, elevated green protected by sand and a pond left. Although this is the end of play, an epilogue remains. The bones of Charles Alison's design remain but the course's scale and driving avenues have tightened considerably. Invariably, maintaining a balance between Hirono's former treeless grandeur and the Japanese cultural love of arboreal splendour is difficult. When struck correctly, the result only serves to polish this unique gem.

As its backdrop, the west-facing cliff-top property at Nirwana Bali boasts not only dramatic landscapes and sunsets but also one of Bali's most famous monuments – the Tanah Lot temple, located on a promontory in the ocean. Strangely, it was this temple that assured that the most dramatic land would be retained for golf, something rarely seen in Asia because of the high demand for real-estate development. The Indonesian client was reluctant to integrate the sea with its sea snakes and steep cliffs into the adjacent temple resort, so the shoreline was handed to Bob Harrison, Greg Norman Design's vice-president of design. The sea snakes have long been rumoured to provide protection for the Tanah Lot.

## HEAVY VEGETATION

With the excellent opportunity posed, it is easy to see why this is the firm's best course. Bob Harrison's portfolio of 30 courses in Australasia makes his declaration that Nirwana Bali was 'a once-in-a-lifetime opportunity' even more meaningful.

The course routing weaves through verdant jungle, along the cliffside, through dense forest and over working rice fields. A tribute to the design and construction is that so many golfers marvel over the rice terraces' timeless attributes as an essential part of the golf course. Harrison's creation becomes more impressive when you appreciate that the original raw property was rolling land that had been totally cleared. Crucial to its overall balance was the decision to split the oceanside land between both the front and the back nine.

Despite the lush environment at Nirwana Bali, the course plays well year round. To cope with the heavy rains that frequent the winter months in Indonesia, there are canted fairways to drain the course; they also provide a number of delicious hanging lies.

## INITIAL IMPRESSIONS

Thankfully the relatively tame, but pretty, 383-yard 1st allows the player to get into their round unscathed, unless the front-to-back green proves problematic. Following that, rice terraces separate the player from the green on the 188-yard 2nd. As the approach is made to the green with its right-to-left slope, it is clear that its strategic merit is equal to its beauty. A clever play uses the short grass front and right to feed the ball into the centre of the green, avoiding any flirtation with the bunkers and jungle left.

After transitioning through rice fields at the 400-yard 3rd, the player then reaches a brutish par four befitting of a closing hole. Indeed, the 439-yard 4th originally was the closing hole, explaining why its green is located in close proximity to the clubhouse.

On reaching the 6th, the tumbling land leads to the first glimpse of the Indian Ocean. Coming around the corner on this 501-yard par five, the sea is evident behind the green, which is flanked by bunkers; these are all that stand in the way of the best birdie opportunity.

# NIRWANA BALI
## Tabanan, Bali, Indonesia

Given that so many of the world's greatest courses occupy oceanfront real estate, architects covet the opportunity for unspoiled land on the sea, but these are now very rare. One site of such beauty was bestowed on Greg Norman Design, in the form of Nirwana Bali GC, on the Indian Ocean.

## STUNNING GOLF HOLES

The high point at Nirwana Bali is the 214-yard 7th. The hole plays north along the coast with both the tee and green jutting into the ocean. Bob Harrison was torn between directions to route the hole, but the temple's location persuaded him of its current setting, which is to the course's benefit

After the jaw-dropping 7th, the course heads back towards the clubhouse, before returning to the oceanside on the 381-yard 12th, where the drama lies in the approach. Guarded short with a Balinese stone wall, the green is wide and shallow. As the tide comes in, the stream in front of the green rises up to 1 foot (30 centimetres) and makes the delicate, downhill wedge shot all the more trying.

On making the turn south on the 13th tee, the dramatic seashore presents a distinctly different challenge. Although the hole is a modest 337 yards in length, the waves crashing on the beach to the right cause few golfers to take the direct line to the green. When the course originally opened, only those with champion golfer Greg Norman's prodigious length could attempt to drive the green. With improvements in club technology, more players are now drawn towards the direct line, which proves to be a poor decision. While there is ample fairway for the weaker golfer, the preferred angle of approach is from the left – one of the most heavily bunkered on the course.

Whereas the 186-yard 14th would surely be considered one of Asia's most dramatic par threes, it does tend to get overshadowed by the 7th. Not only does the 14th offer a change in wind direction but also it is flanked on the right side by the ocean. Pins set in the right-hand location, devilishly tucked behind the deep bunker, require the golfer to tackle a nervy shot. Played out over a long stretch of black sand beach, it is not surprising that many balls come to rest left of the green. A guarding bunker or the abundant rough awaits the cautious play.

## CLOSING HOLES

Turning inland again on the 447-yard 15th, it is difficult to maintain the high drama that playing alongside the ocean affords. With a pair of challenging par fours – the 447-yard 15th and 431-yard 16th – and a risk-reward closing hole, it is easy for a good score to unravel as the player is caught soaking in the memories of the crashing surf.

The 520-yard 18th is fronted by a ravine that requires the player to decide whether to risk the carry for a chance of an eagle or to lay up into the sliver of fairway that is protected on the right by a large fairway bunker. This hole does afford a good range of scores and is a testy finisher to any match, which can often yield birdie as the winning score.

When architects are presented with an opportunity such as Bob Harrison was afforded at Nirwana Bali, they understand the pressure to deliver. In his self-effacing Australian way, Harrison noted: 'If you get a site like this, you don't want to muck it up, and you want to squeeze the absolute best out of it.' With the great Tanah Lot temple standing alongside, he did just that.

*The blue waters of the Indian Ocean lap arond the base of the Taneh Lot temple to distract the golfer from the stern task of hitting and holding the 7th green at Nirwana Bali.*

## NIRWANA BALI GOLF CLUB –
## Tabanan, Bali, Indonesia
Greg Norman and Bob Harrison, 1997

### CARD OF THE COURSE

| HOLE | YARDS | PAR | HOLE | YARDS | PAR |
|---|---|---|---|---|---|
| 1. | 383 | 4 | 10. | 445 | 5 |
| 2. | 188 | 3 | 11. | 211 | 3 |
| 3. | 400 | 4 | 12. | 381 | 4 |
| 4. | 439 | 4 | 13. | 337 | 4 |
| 5. | 441 | 4 | 14. | 186 | 3 |
| 6. | 501 | 5 | 15. | 447 | 4 |
| 7. | 214 | 3 | 16. | 431 | 4 |
| 8. | 544 | 5 | 17. | 349 | 4 |
| 9. | 388 | 4 | 18. | 520 | 5 |
| OUT | 3,498 | 36 | IN | 3,307 | 36 |
| | | | TOTAL | 6,805 | 72 |

# AFRICA

# AFRICA

The golfing exploits of South Africans Sid Brews, Bobby Locke, Harold Henning, Gary Player, Ernie Els and Retief Goosen and Zimbabwean Nick Price have ensured that the African continent has been well represented on golf's highest honours boards for more than 80 years. And it was to South Africa that golf was introduced well over a century ago.

Following a meeting in November 1885, a rough-and-ready course, the first in Africa, was laid out at the Wynberg Military Camp by Scottish soldiers campaigning in the Boer War. Thus was born the Cape Golf Club[1] and, importantly, competitive golf in Africa. Other clubs followed, but it was by no means a continent-wide golf explosion. The climate and the fact that golf was a white man's sport saw to that.

Africa's weather and its terrain of desert or jungle were incompatible with the grasses suitable for golf. An early solution to the problem of providing adequate greens was to roll oiled sand until suitably compacted (a method used also for many years in the southern United States), while a mat carried by the golfer (more likely a caddie) served as a mobile fairway. At all but the wealthiest clubs, which could afford the provision of expensively obtained water to maintain the greens, this was the norm in much of Africa and still is in the more rural parts throughout the continent.

## CHEQUERED HISTORY

As the white man's influence spread in Africa, so did golf. Courses of one kind or another came to be laid out in most African countries. Political upheaval has seen the demise of many of them. However, some of the oldest survivors are in Kenya where farmers and landowners established a number of clubs that thrive today, the oldest being Royal Nairobi[2] of 1906. Nor were the clubs limited to the capital and its surroundings, as courses followed in Nyeri[3] in 1910, Mombasa[4] in 1911, Nakuru[5] (begun in 1923) and Kitale[6] (founded in 1924). Altogether, there are now 44 golf clubs in four separate areas of Kenya.

Perhaps the best-known of the Kenyan golf clubs is Karen GC[7], where the first nine holes were laid out in 1933 on a former coffee farm owned by Baroness Karen von Blixen (remembered for her memoir *Out of Africa*). It is now a course of almost 7,000 yards in length and a genuine championship test – a regular stop on the European Challenge Tour.

Surely the saddest of the African golfing casualties is Foulpointe[8] in Madagascar. In 1939 *The National Golf Review* (a short-lived, but respected American golf magazine) published a list of the 100 top courses in the world. Its selection panel was impressive (including Bobby Jones, Walter Hagen, Bernard Darwin, Glenna Vare, Percy Alliss and the Duke of Windsor) and Foulpointe was ranked tenth in the world, with Royal Melbourne (see page 286) ninth and Augusta National (see page 206) eleventh! A course exists there today, but it is not the same, being a nine-holer dating from 1967.

## NORTH AFRICA

Robert Trent Jones Snr's assessment of King Hassan II of Morocco was that: 'The king, to put it kindly, is a golf nut.' In fairness to the late king, he caused to be constructed a number of fine courses among which the two 18-hole Trent Jones courses at Royal Golf Dar Es Salam[9] (built between 1970 and 1974) are both testing and beautiful. Trent Jones also built the Palmeraie[10] course at Marrakech, while Cabell Robinson has contributed the visually arresting Amelkis[11] at Marrakech and El Jadida[12], overlooking the Atlantic. Frank Pennink's Royal Country Club[13] outside Tangier dates from the early 1950s.

Tunisia boasts a number of attractive courses, such as Flamingo[14] and Palm Links[15] at Monastir and Citrus[16] at Hammamet. It also has the 36-hole Kantaoui GC[17], which is a popular host to European Seniors Tour events.

At the eastern edge of north Africa lies Egypt, where improvised desert golf has been played by Europeans living in Cairo for many years. Yet it is on the Red Sea coast at Soma Bay that in 1999 Gary Player designed the Cascades Course[18] as part of a luxury resort complex that was formerly a military base. Land mines had to be cleared before construction could begin. The course enjoys fine Red Sea views.

## SOUTH AFRICA

Although Gary Player is at the forefront of golf course development in South Africa today, it is first necessary to note some of South Africa's older classics, such as the Durban Country Club (see page 314) and Humewood[19] at Port Elizabeth, one of the rare links

*With only nine holes and desert-sand fairways, Henties Bay golf course[27] in Namibia is very much in the spirit of pioneering golf in the continent.*

courses outside the British Isles. The latter was designed in 1929 by Colonel Stafford Vere Hotchkin, he of Woodhall Spa fame (see page 98). Hotchkin also worked on several South African courses. From this period, too, came a number of courses designed by the gifted South African golfer Bob Grimsdell, not least the East and West courses at Royal Johannesburg[20], dating from 1933. (The club, however, has a history back to 1890.)

South Africa today is promoting its resort golf in a major way and Gary Player has been involved in much of it, such as the Links[21] at Fancourt, Leopard Creek[22], Erinvale[23] and the Gary Player[24]. Interestingly, it was his old adversary Jack Nicklaus who won the contract to redesign the famous old Houghton course in Johannesburg – the scene of many an important professional tournament.

## IMPORTANCE OF TOURISM

And there is other design talent emerging, such as the team of Peter Matkovich (originally from Zimbabwe)

and Dale Hayes (former Tour professional). To date their highest profile course is the highly acclaimed and very scenic Leopard Rock[25] in Zimbabwe, while their bushveld course, Zebula[26], in South Africa's Limpopo province, gained the *Golf Digest* Best New Course award in 2004.

Inevitably, the volatile political climate prevailing in many African countries dissuades tourists from visiting. Tourism, however, is at the root of most new golf-course development in the continent. Outstanding golf courses in prime condition must be provided in order to encourage tourists to travel many thousands of kilometres from another continent to play resort golf, so it is only at the high end of this particular market that new developments are likely. With that, there are certain stylistic obligations, so plenty more 18th holes playing to island greens with resident crocodiles to add spice can be expected.

# DURBAN
## Durban, South Africa

Unlike many of the world's venerated golf institutions, Durban Country Club was not conceived with such a lofty status in mind. Instead, it was created in a hurry after the 1919 South African Open nearly drowned on the low-lying links of the nearby Royal Durban Golf Club.

The continent of Africa is the world's second largest. It occupies more than 11 million square miles (28.5 million square kilometres) – more than 20 per cent of the Earth's landmass – and contains 61 countries or political territories. Heavily impoverished, it includes vast interior regions where the game of golf has probably never even been heard of, never mind played. Yet even in such non-golfing territory, it is no small accomplishment for a single course to remain so large a continent's highest rated for more than eight decades. But such is indeed the status of South Africa's Durban Country Club – Africa's golfing standard since 1922.

### CARVED OUT OF THE BUSH
Afraid of their city losing its place in the rota hosting the South African Open – the world's second oldest national open championship – because of flooding at the 1919 championship, the founders of Durban Country Club leased a patch of coastal land and set about building a course that featured, among other things, reliable drainage as a central commodity. The architects, little-known George Waterman and four-time South African Open champion (and St Andrews native) Laurie Waters, had a difficult task, because in those early days of course construction virtually all clearing and shaping had to be done by hand. Given the thickness of the site's native bush, as well as Waterman's lack of design experience, the resulting layout was, by any measure, quite remarkable.

To understand Durban is to appreciate the uniqueness of its property, a large triangular expanse that is extremely narrow at its southern end and considerably wider to the north. Though separated from the beach by the M4 Freeway, the club is flanked to the east by the Indian Ocean, whose high coastal dunes define the terrain of more than half the holes. These dunes are not of the sandy, Scottish variety, however. They are often covered by thick trees and bushes, and, after 85 years of maintenance as a golf course, lush fairway grasses. The result is rather a distinctive appearance, with the wildly pitched terrain resembling a sort of velvet moonscape and individual holes separated by walls of equally green bush. Furthermore, a number of tees and greens are situated on (rather than below) the dunes – a fundamentally different approach from traditional British links and one that maximizes exposure to the often stiff coastal breezes.

### FAMOUS DUNELAND HOLES
Not surprisingly, virtually all of Durban's best holes are situated along its eastern flank, amid the dunes, with the opening five carrying a well-earned measure of international fame. The 1st, a 387-yarder, runs directly northwards, with out-of-bounds down the right side, clumps of bush to the left and an elevated, bunkerless putting surface. Then the 188-yard 2nd plays from a high tee across a valley to another elevated green, this one surrounded by four bunkers, considerable native flora and a fall-away short-left.

A par five of international repute, the 512-yard 3rd was cited among the original *World Atlas of Golf*'s best 18 holes worldwide. Running parallel to the freeway (but well buffered by dense vegetation), it begins from another lofty tee before tumbling downhill, through a narrow gauntlet of dunes and bush, to a slightly elevated, unbunkered green. At a glance the hole may not seem overwhelming: there is no spectacular hazarding nor the go-for-it-or-not decision-making demanded by water or sand closely guarding the putting surface. But the relative narrowness of the green allows it to shrug off all but the most precise run-up approaches, a large right-side bunker creeps in uncomfortably some 40 yards (36 metres) short, and both the mounding and thick vegetation are constantly nipping at the fairway's edges, making for a distinctive challenge indeed. Another fine one-shotter is the 181-yard 4th, playing to a sunken, tightly bunkered green that, once upon a time, was hidden entirely from the tee by a now-removed hill top.

### A LONG, TOUGH MID-SECTION
The narrow 460-yard 5th, probably Durban's toughest par four, is hemmed in entirely by the bush, before play moves inland to the first of several holes situated

*The 402-yard 17th. The approach to this mid-length par four offers a fine sense of Durban's tumbling terrain, where grass-covered dunes are flanked by thick, native bush.*

# DURBAN COUNTRY CLUB – Durban, South Africa

George Waterman and Laurie Waters, 1922
Major events: South African Open 1924, 1928, 1939, 1950, 1956, 1963, 1969, 1973, 1976, 1980, 1988, 1991, 1993, 1998, 2001, 2004

## CARD OF THE COURSE

| HOLE | YARDS | PAR | HOLE | YARDS | PAR |
|------|-------|-----|------|-------|-----|
| 1. | 387 | 4 | 10. | 560 | 5 |
| 2. | 188 | 3 | 11. | 480 | 4 |
| 3. | 512 | 5 | 12. | 156 | 3 |
| 4. | 181 | 3 | 13. | 339 | 4 |
| 5. | 460 | 4 | 14. | 527 | 5 |
| 6. | 352 | 4 | 15. | 194 | 3 |
| 7. | 372 | 4 | 16. | 417 | 4 |
| 8. | 501 | 5 | 17. | 402 | 4 |
| 9. | 434 | 4 | 18. | 274 | 4 |
| OUT | 3,387 | 36 | IN | 3,349 | 36 |
| | | | TOTAL | 6,736 | 72 |

holes to follow: the tree-lined 560-yard 10th and the 480-yard, par-four 11th, the latter requiring the carry of a small lake off the tee, then a long second shot to one of Durban's more tightly bunkered greens. More memorable, however, is the 156-yard 12th, a tricky one-shotter played uphill to a narrow, volcano-like green perched on a particularly high dune. There are single bunkers long and short, but the real danger lies in missing left or right, because the ground falls away as much as 30 feet (9 metres) on either side, offering the potential for tragedies akin to the infamous 17 scored by the Prince of Wales during a visit in 1925.

Play turns for home with the 527-yard 14th and 194-yard 15th – both solid if unspectacular tests – while the 417-yard 16th is one of the few holes to have been substantially altered in the postwar era, now bending gently rightwards along a curve of the adjacent M12 motorway instead of following its original straight path.

Fittingly, Durban returns to the dunes for its closers, with the 402-yard 17th favouring a drive along the fairway's right side, lest one face a blind second shot from a large depression down the left.

## THE GLORIOUS 18TH

It is the par-four 18th, however, that stands tallest among closers, for this is one of golf's most memorable finishers despite measuring a minuscule 274 yards. With modern equipment the prospects for driving the green are obvious – today's touring professional occasionally encounters par threes this long – but pulled tee shots can easily skip onto the adjacent bowling green (out-of-bounds), the clubhouse closely flanks the back of the putting surface, and anything missed right tumbles down a steep slope towards the club's practice ground. Part of the hole's allure is that it is not a victim of modern technology, having tempted capable ball-strikers to go for the green since its inception. Indeed, in the 1928 South African Open, Jock Brews needed a birdie-three to tie his more famous brother Sid at the 72nd – then proceeded to drive his ball to 15 feet (4.5 metres) and hole the putt to win, most dramatically, by one.

Brews's triumph set the stage for what has been a remarkable run as South Africa's most visited championship venue, with The Open visiting the club an unequalled 16 times. Predictably, the nation's two greatest players have shined there, with Bobby Locke capturing the crown in 1939 and 1950, and Gary Player prevailing three times, in 1956, 1969 and 1976. More recently, contemporary superstar Ernie Els claimed the title in 1998, highlighting Durban's continuing ability to identify the very best.

on distinctly flatter terrain. This stretch is a bit less inspiring – sound parkland golf certainly, but little different from countless other courses around the world. There are exceptions, however, when the course briefly returns to the edge of the dunes, the most notable coming at the 501-yard 8th, whose fairway traverses a bit of rolling terrain before climbing to a small, elevated green.

The 434-yard 9th tees off from adjacent high ground and sets the stage for two particularly long

# INDEX

McEvoy, Peter 81, 96
McKee, Howard 240
MacKenzie, C.A. 150
MacKenzie, Dr Alister 14, 16, 25, 73,
	126, 144, 156, 216, 227, 232, 234,
	244
	Alwoodley 92–3
	Augusta National 206–8
	Australian courses 282–3, 286–9,
		290–1, 292–3
	in California 234, 244, 246, 248–50
	Canadian courses 256
	Irish courses 111, 113
	Jockey Club, Argentina 278–9
	New Zealand courses 284
	Prairie Dunes 228
Mackenzie Ross, Philip 39, 68
McLay, David 234
Madagascar 313
Madeira 35
Madrid 141
Maiden, Stewart 53
Maidstone 158
Maidstone, New York 182–3
Malaysia 305
Man, Isle of 35
Mangrum, Lloyd 191, 227
Mannelli, Massimo 139
Marr, Dave 174
Marsh, Graham 288
Massachusetts 161–2, 164
	Country Club 161, 184–5
Massey, Arnaud 198
Matkovich, Peter 313
Maule, Sir Robert 36, 50
Maxwell, Perry 186, 216, 226, 227,
	228
Melbourne 25, 239, 282–3, 286–9
Merion 190–3, 220
Mexico 19, 27, 268–9
Michigan 215–16, 220–1
Mickelson, Phil 71, 119
Mid Ocean, Bermuda 272–3
Middle East 305
Miller, Johnny 195
minimalist design 162
Minnesota 216
Mitchell, William 157
Monterey Peninsula Pebble Beach 234
Montreal 256, 257
Moore, Jonathan 117
Morfontaine 134–5
Morocco 313
Morris, George 50, 82
Morris, Old Tom 13, 40, 44, 45, 46, 50,
	54, 65, 88, 166
	Irish courses 113, 116, 117
Morris, Young Tom 46
Morrison, John 146

Morse, Samuel 244, 245–6, 248
Moses, Robert 176
mountain courses 147
Muirfield 23, 36, 46, 60–3, 118
Muirfield Village, Ohio 216, 218–19
Muirhead, Desmond 218
Mulcahy, John 122
Murray, Jim 252
Musselburgh Old Links 12, 39
Myrtle Beach 157, 199


Nairn 37, 39
Namibia 315
National Golf Links of America 49,
	156, 158, 166–9
Nebraska 227, 230–1
Nelson, Byron 188, 227
Nelson, Larry 195
Netherlands 124, 125–9
Neville, Jack 190, 244, 246
New England 160–4
New Jersey 159–60
	Pine Valley 76, 160, 176, 186–9
New Mexico 227
New South Wales 283–4
New York 158–9, 164
	Bethpage Black 158, 176–7
	Fishers Island 170–1, 199
	Maidstone 182–3
	the National 49, 156, 158, 166–9
	Shinnecock Hills 23, 158, 167,
		178–81, 182
	Winged Foot 172–5
New Zealand 284, 296–9
Newmarket 75
Nicklaus, Gary 226
Nicklaus, Jack 18, 27, 34, 63, 91
	American courses 157, 164, 193, 195,
		203, 204, 209, 210, 216, 227
	Asian courses 305
	Canadian courses 257
	Chinese courses 302, 303
	Johannesburg course 313
	Mexican courses 268
	Muirfield Village 218–19
	Pebble Beach 246
Nirwana Bali 308–9
Nordwall, Peter 152
Norman, Greg 18, 104–5, 157, 219,
	268, 269, 308
North Africa 313
North Berwick 12, 36, 46–9, 60
North Carolina 144, 198–9, 199,
	202–3
Norway 151
Notts Golf Club 73–4
Nova Scotia 264–5
Nugent, Dick 215

Oakland Hills 220–1
Oakmont 194–7, 220
O'Connor, Christie 34
O'Connor, Christie Jnr 111
Ogilvy, Geoff 282
Ohio 218–19
Oklahoma 227
Olazábal, José Maria 141
Olympia Fields 214
Olympic Club 232, 242–3
O'Malley, Peter 67
Oman 305
Ontario 256, 257, 260–3
Oregon 238–41
Ouimet, Francis 184


Pacific Dunes 234, 238–41
Packard, Larry 215
Palm Springs 157, 234
Palmer, Arnold 35, 59, 157, 195, 203,
	243, 268
Papua New Guinea 305
Paraparaumu Beach 284, 296–7
Park, Mungo 118
Park, Willie Jnr 15, 37, 74, 118, 124,
	147
	American courses 156, 164, 182–3,
		214
	Canadian courses 256
	Sunningdale 100–1
Park, Willie Snr 118
Parks, Sam 195, 220
Pate, Jerry 211
Patino, Jaime 141
Pau Golf Club 132
Pavin, Corey 181
Pebble Beach 144, 244–7
	Cypress Point 248–51
	Spyglass Hill 252–3
Pennink, Frank 104, 125, 150
Pennsylvania 160, 190–7
Pern, Jeremy 34
Peskin, Hy 193
Philadelphia 160
Pickeman, W.C. 118
Pickworth, Ossie 290–1
Pine Valley, Beijing 303
Pine Valley, New Jersey 76, 160, 176,
	186–9
Pinehurst 144, 198–9, 202–3
Plant, Henry 199
Platt, Woody 189
Player, Gary 34, 63, 157, 269, 312, 313,
	315
Poland 34
Portmarnock 111, 118–19
Portugal 34, 140–1, 144–5
Prairie Dunes 226, 228–9

Prestwick 13, 44–5, 58, 60
Price, Nick 290, 312
Puerto Rico 268, 269
Purdy, Hal 164
Purves, Laidlaw 104, 106
putting greens 24


Qatar 305
Quebec 256
Queensland 284


Ramsay, Greg 294
Ray, Ted 63, 94, 184
Raynor, Seth 161, 167, 176, 200, 205,
	223, 248
Reid, John Jnr 160
Reid, Wilfrid 242
resort courses 157
Rhode Island 164
Rhodes 35
Riviera 26, 241, 254–5
Roberts, Clifford 206
Robertson, Alan 50
Robertson, Julian 284
Robinson, Cabell 140, 146
Robinson, Clinton `Robbie' 157, 257
Robinson, Julian 298
Romero, Andreas 53
Romero, Eduardo 277
Roquemore, Rocky 140
Ross, Alex 159
Ross, Donald 14, 16, 156, 160, 162,
	164, 198, 215
	Canadian courses 256, 257, 258
	Oakland Hills 220–1
	Pinehurst 202–3
	Seminole 212–13
Ross, George 118
routing the course 22–3
Royal Adelaide 283, 290–1
Royal Antwerp 124
Royal Belfast 110
Royal Birkdale 86–7
Royal Calcutta 302
Royal Cinque Ports 79
Royal County Down 110, 111, 116–17
Royal Dornoch 36, 46, 54–7, 241
Royal Hague 128–9
Royal Liverpool Golf Club 73, 82–3
Royal Lytham 88–91
Royal Melbourne 25, 239, 282, 286–9
Royal Montreal 256, 257
Royal North Devon (Westward Ho!)
	12, 72–3
Royal Ostend 125
Royal Porthcawl 81, 108–9
Royal Portrush 110, 111, 114–15

# ACKNOWLEDGEMENTS

## AUTHOR ACKNOWLEDGEMENTS

**Iain Carter** 82–85, 88–91, 94–99, 108–109; **Mike Clayton** 282–299; **Ben Cowan-Dewar** 260–265, 302–305, 308–309; **Tom Doak** 12–31; **Eric Franzén** 150–153; **Noel Freeman** 306–307; **Richard Goodale** 36–71, 110–123; **Martin Hawtree** 86–87, 92–93, 100–103; **Ulrich Mayring** 138–139, 146–147; **Ran Morrissett** 104–107, 126–131, 134–137, 202–203, 230–231, 238–241, 276–279; **Mark Rowlinson** 8–9, 34–35, 72–81, 124–125, 132–133, 140–145, 148–149, 312–313; **Daniel Wexler** 156–201, 204–229, 232–237, 242–259, 268–273, 314–315.

## ILLUSTRATOR ACKNOWLEDGEMENTS

**Industrial Art Studio (www.ind-art.co.uk)** 46–47, 58–59, 60–61, 66–67, 70–71, 82–83, 88–89, 92–93, 98–99, 104–105, 126–127, 136–137; **Brindeau Mexter** 13, 20, 23, 26, 29, 42, 49, 56, 63, 85, 90, 102, 106, 159, 169, 188, 192, 196, 208, 246, 269, 288; **Arthur Phillips** 68–69, 122–123, 262–263, 306–307; **Sebastian Quigley (Linden Artists)** 44–45, 94–95, 128–129, 152–153, 170–171, 178–179, 190–191, 202–203, 212–213, 220–221, 222–223, 230–231, 290–291, 296–297; **Steve Weston and Sam Weston (Linden Artists)** 40–41, 50–51, 54–55, 64–65, 86–87, 100–101, 108–109, 114–115, 116–117, 118–119, 120–121, 130–131, 134–135, 138–139, 142–143, 144–145, 148–149, 166–167, 172–173, 176–177, 182–183, 184–185, 186–187, 194–195, 200–201, 204–205, 206–207, 210–211, 218–219, 224–225, 228–229, 236–237, 238–239, 242–243, 244–245, 249–249, 252–253, 254–255, 258–259, 260–261, 264–265, 270–271, 272–273, 278–279, 286–287, 292–293, 294–295, 298–299, 308–309, 314–315.

## PICTURE ACKNOWLEDGEMENTS

**Alamy** Alan Dawson Photography 34; Author's Image 266; Brian Morgan 227; David R Frazier Photolibrary Inc 274; isogood 147; Mark J Barrett 30; Martin Westlake 4; Michael Diggin 112; Peter Titmuss 313; Renee Iijima/Photo Resource Hawaii 10; Scott Kemper 2. **Chris Gallow Photography** 265. **Circolo del Golf di Roma Acquasanta** 139. **Clive Barber** 28, 154, 261. **Corbis** Alan Schein Photography 22; Bettmann 17, 180; Catherine Karnow 35; Richard Hamilton Smith 217; Roger de la Harpe 310; Tony Roberts 156, 157, 160, 189, 233, 237, 243, 247, 250, 251, 268, 273. **David Scaletti Sportscapes** 289, 291. **Eric Hepworth Golf Course Photography** 12 above and below, 24 above, 25 left, 37, 48, 57, 59, 69, 73, 74, 91, 93, 99, 107, 109. **Forrest Richardson & Associates** 24 below. **Getty Images** Brian Morgan 19, 71; David Alexander 18, 41, 203, 223, 307; David Cannon 1, 6, 8, 21, 52, 65, 76, 79, 97, 103, 121, 153, 193, 225, 231, 279, 297, 299; Jonathan Daniel 215; Ross Kinnaird 84; Stephen Munday 96; Warren Little 141. **GolfArchitecturePictures.com** Frank Pont 125, 149. **GolfClubAtlas.com** 134. **GolfPhotos.com** John R Johnson 229. **Hobbs Golf Collection** 14, 15, 16. **Kevin Murray** 31, 32, 43, 80, 81, 87, 115, 119. **Neil Regan** 29 above and below, 171, 175. **PA Photos** Matthew Ashton/Empics Sport 305; Rob Carr/AP 209. **Phil Sheldon Golf Picture Library** Larry Petrillo 277; Liz Anthony 25 below right, 197; Nic Brook 78; Phil Sheldon 38, 67, 77, 123, 131, 177, 181, 199, 219; Richard Castka 285. **St George's Hill Golf Club** 27. **The Golf Picture Library** Aiden Bradley 257, 271; Evan Schiller 161, 163, 192, 201, 211, 235; Larry Lambrecht 168, 174, 213; Matthew Harris 26, 62, 75, 111, 117, 145, 185, 240, 241, 254, 293. **Visions in Golf/Mark Newcombe** Christer Hoglund 151, 221; Claudio Scaccini 133; Clive Barber 263; Darren Kirk 53; Gary Lisbon 280, 283, 295; Gary Lisbon/Golf Select 25 above right; Michael Hobbs 45; Richard Castka 300, 303, 304, 309, 315; Robert Walker 127, 162, 165.

## PUBLISHER'S ACKNOWLEDGEMENTS

The publisher would like to thank the following people and organizations for their help with the book: Martin Bond (Royal Porthcawl Golf Club), Tuck Clagett (St Enodoc Golf Club), Amy Crampton (Hawtree Design), Philip Gawith, Chris Hunt, Robert Klinesteker, Lahinch Golf Club, Adam Lawrence, Jason McNamara, Wayne Morrison, Frank Pont, Tony Ristola, Royal Lytham & St Annes, Christopher Spencer (The North Berwick Golf Club), Russell Talley (Hawtree Design), Chris Veldkamp, Robert Walker (Friar's Head), Paul Ware, The Westin Turnberry Resort, Michael Williams, www.golfarchitecturepictures.com.

**Executive Editor** Trevor Davies
**Managing Editors** Clare Churly and Camilla Davis
**Editorial Artwork Consultant** Charles Hallam
**Editor** Joanna Chisholm
**Proofreader** Jo Murray
**Indexer** Isobel McLean
**Design Manager** Tokiko Morishima
**Picture Research Manager** Giulia Hetherington
**Picture Reseacher** Zoe Spilberg
**Designer** 'OME Design
**Retouching and digital imagery of maps** Ian Atkinson
**Production Manager** David Hearn
**Additional assistance** Joseph Espiner, Mike Faith, Fiona Robertson, Karen Sawyer, Mark Stevens and Kate Verghese